KEYNESIANISM
Retrospect and Prospect

KEYNESIANISM–

RETROSPECT and PROSPECT

A Critical Restatement of Basic Economic Principles

by

W. H. HUTT

*Professor of Commerce and
Dean of the Faculty of Commerce*

UNIVERSITY OF CAPE TOWN

Chicago • HENRY REGNERY COMPANY • 1963

The assistance of the
Institute for Economic Inquiry, Chicago, Illinois,
in the publication of this book
is gratefully acknowledged.

"There is no doubt that Keynes . . . thought that all was fair in argument, and that a man should not have a grievance if he was refuted without mercy. . . . If sensitiveness was not in place in a game, still less was it so in discussion of public affairs or economic problems."

Harrod, *The Life of John Maynard Keynes*, pp. 329-330.

PREFACE

This work is put forward as a positive contribution to economics. It sets out to re-state some of the essentials of "orthodox" or "classical" economic teachings in a form which is intended to be more appropriate for contemporary controversies.

To do this effectively, it is necessary simultaneously to expose the erroneous foundations on which Keynesian economics has been based. Such a task cannot be lightly attempted. The economic theory which has been founded on Keynes' speculations may be said, not unfairly, to constitute the economics which is expounded in most modern textbooks.

I have been concerned professionally mainly with the *application* of economic theory and particularly as it is relevant to the functions of the business decision-maker. It is, perhaps, largely because I have seen the problems at issue from the standpoint of those whose predictions and actions make the economic system work that I have become dissatisfied with Keynesian and post-Keynesian economics. But I admit to writing with the disadvantage of one whom Keynes would have described (I use his words) as having been somewhat "perverted by having read too much of the orthodox stuff."* I might be accused of never having thrown off my prejudices against the Keynesian teachings. And yet I regard myself as one who has not succumbed to the pressure to follow the current mode. In this contribution I shall be explaining why I find myself out of fashion.

In common with many others, I spent much time between 1936 and the outbreak of the war trying to understand Keynes' message. One of the first results of this was the writing of my *Theory of Idle Resources,* published in 1939. Side by side with this contribution, there was another typescript which never reached the stage of publication. Some parts of this were read by London friends during the winter of 1938-9. Had the war not intervened, the developing typescript (which soon

---

*Keynes suggested that Newcomb had not been so "perverted."[1]

vii

began to take on a much more satisfactory form, due to the light which Keynes's disciples were throwing upon his ideas) would have been submitted for further discussion with, and criticism by, my friends in London.

What helped me very much was an abortive effort which I made at writing a very elementary account of what Keynes was saying. I started this by trying to summarize the argument of *The General Theory*. It has usually been my experience that well-conceived contributions in all fields of thought summarize easily; and I have always used the test of summarization upon my own contributions. But I found it impossible to summarize what Keynes had written. Samuelson's later description of it as "random notes" was exactly my own impression. Nevertheless, my attempt to summarize and my endeavors at stating very simply what others were saying (I thought) more or less obscurely, was of some assistance in getting my own ideas clear.

Unfortunately, increasing clarity was not very comforting. It caused me to grow skeptical of and generally dissatisfied, not only with Keynes' understanding but with my own. So I continued the effort of thinking through the complexities of the subject by setting down (at frightening length, but purely for my own use) what I understood about, and my criticisms of, the various Keynesian notions which were rapidly coming into circulation. These studies overlapped the outbreak of the war. But early in 1940 the whole attempt suddenly seemed fruitless and unimportant. I tied up my voluminous typescripts, put them in a cupboard and dismissed them from my mind.

I did not, of course, dismiss the topic from my mind. Indeed, towards the end of the war, I entered into a not very important controversy about Keynesian public works policy in the *South African Journal of Economics,* and also contributed a more or less "popular" article on "full employment" in which, whilst making it plain where I stood, I avoided the difficult issues.

A major problem was that of deciding what part of the growing flood of Keynesian literature was most worthy of study. Nothing satisfied me. I disagreed persistently. In all the lengthy controversies in the journals, either no-one was putting the particular points which I thought should be made or else no-one was replying to them. My objections were to basic concepts whereas most of the Keynesian literature tacitly accepted the concepts to which I objected.

In 1946, Boulding's *Economics of Peace* and Polyani's *Freedom and Full Employment*—both convincingly and beautifully written—made me realize how attractive Keynesian teachings had proved. I was, however, still rather diffident about my opinions at that time. How

could I help wondering whether I was not just slow to understand or
subconsciously obstinate in refusing to accept revolutionary ideas? But
in 1949 I put some memoranda embodying my tentative skepticisms
to friends at the London School of Economics. I asked for criticisms
in the form of frank penciled comments on the typescript, to indicate
where I seemed to be misunderstanding current teachings, or where my
premises or reasoning appeared to be at fault. The absence of any
disturbing comment was almost the only encouragement I got.* There
was no warm support. I returned to South Africa with the feeling
(right or wrong) that I was thought to be out of fashion, not dealing
with the issues which had come to be regarded as important, and not
talking the modern language. I again got the impression that I might
be thinking on quite the wrong lines. I postponed all thoughts of
early publication. But I began to see that *there are some kinds of
language the habitual use of which hinders the perception of certain
things as well as the saying of them.* I recognized that this could apply
to my own thinking as well as to those who spoke in Keynesian terms.
But I came to see that the *weaknesses of the system which Keynes had
built rest in its conceptual foundations.* I accordingly gave attention
to devising a method of exposition which would be firstly, so simple and
direct that errors of premises or logic could be pin-pointed, and secondly
in a form which would make the issues appear as important to others
as they seemed to me.

For a while, I thought that a new approach to the theory of money
would assist. I think now that my attempt in that direction complicated
rather than simplified the issues, and I have already discarded the new
terminology which I thought would help.† But two of the contributions
I made, namely, *The Yield from Money Held*,[2] and *The Significance
of Price Flexibility*,[3] I regard as satisfactory indications of the lines
along which I have been thinking. I build on the former and incorporate some passages from the latter (in Chap. IX) in the present book.

In 1955, I was asked by the *Foundation for Economic Education*

*Friedrich Hayek was encouraging in that he asked me to contribute a paper putting
forward my ideas on wage-rate flexibility to the Mont Pelerin Conference at Seelisberg
that year.

†In my treatment of money at that time, I went wrong in two ways. Firstly, I was
trying to develop the notion of "neutral money" which Hayek and others had introduced; and I had the idea that monetary policy would be aiming at true neutrality
when it sought to maintain a constant relationship between MV and T, except when
changes in V were due to factors which, in the judgment of the monetary authority,
were abnormal or speculative. Secondly, I had accepted the quite wrong notion that
the scale of prices, and hence the value of the money unit, are determined by expenditure, instead of expenditure being made essential by the prices which happen to be
ruling, prices being determined by the whole valuing process. My present views on
these issues are presented in Chapters V and VIII.

to give some lectures to a group of American economists. I dealt with
the multiplier and accelerator fallacies. Leland Yeager and Clark
Warburton were acute and very useful critics. These lectures were
mimeographed for the benefit of those who attended, and the substance is included in Chapters X-XIV. In 1956, Paish, Ozga, A. W.
Phillips and A. D. Knox of the London School of Economics were
kind enough to read these lectures and give me the benefit of their
weighty criticisms. Their failure to shake my confidence on any point
has gradually caused me to feel that it is now my duty to publish,
however unpopular or unfashionable my contribution may appear to be.

Whilst my ideas have been developing, occasional discussions with
L. M. Lachmann have been most valuable; and since 1956, I have
submitted parts of the developing typescript of this work for the
criticism of my colleagues, H. M. Robertson, C. S. Soper (now at the
University of New South Wales), J. D. Hampton and Z. S. Gurzynski. Their comments have greatly assisted both thought and
exposition. But it would be unfair to attribute to these critics any
responsibility for my opinions. I am, of course, indebted to many
others, far too numerous to mention.

I must acknowledge my special indebtedness to the courageous and
independent work (in vastly different fields and forms) of Marget,
Mises and the late H. C. Simons. Among the economists of the last
generation, it is the contributions of Cannan and B. M. Anderson
which have most inspired the general attitude of the present work.

Hazlitt's brilliantly written, *The Failure of the "New Economics,"*
appeared just as my work was nearing completion. Although my
method is very different from Hazlitt's, his contribution has greatly
assisted me in cutting down the length of my own. I have deleted from
my script several passages in which we seem to have covered somewhat
similar ground. Some overlapping has, however, been inevitable.

Patinkin's *Money, Interest and Prices* has hardly influenced my exposition. This important contribution appears to me to have shown, by
means of a careful refinement of the methods which Keynes popularized,
that the chief "classical" or "orthodox" teachings, including the Say
Law, remain undamaged in spite of the criticism to which they have
been subjected. But because of the methods he has used, Patinkin has
been forced to follow a very tortuous route to his conclusions, and the
implications for policy of his findings are obscure. I propose to show
that, even after the sharpening which Patinkin has given them, the
Keynesian tools remain clumsy. His use of them has not, for instance,
caused him to abandon the view which he first expressed in 1948, that
Keynesian teaching has at least this validity, that even when account is

taken of the "real-balance affect," the "automatic adjustment process of the market . . . is too unreliable as a practical basis of a full-employment policy."[4] The analysis which I put forward in Chapters V to IX should make clearer the argument (which I originally advanced against Patinkin in 1954) that this contention is equally untenable.*

My task would have been easier if McCord Wright's, *The Keynesian System* (to which I have been able to devote a short appendix to Chapter XIX) had been published earlier. This scholarly essay, which appeared whilst the type of the present book was being set, seems to me to record *the gradual tacit retreat from pre-1948 Keynesian teaching* which I shall be stressing.

Wright has been, I judge, one of the most influential critics of Keynesianism, yet he avoids any clear admission of a retreat which he himself has helped to force.† Thus, he exposes the obscure, unrealistic and loosely handled assumptions on which *The General Theory* is based, but he is incomparably more lenient towards Keynes than towards pre-Keynesian economists and critics of the "new economics". I feel that Wright fails, in particular, to give due recognition to those few courageous sceptics who, despite their bewilderment at the very inconsistencies and slipshod handling of concepts which he castigates, were prepared to defend orthodox economics from unjust belittlement. The non-Keynesians have had to criticise a prolific literature which they could not always claim fully to understand; and in doing so they have had to resist an almost tyrannical fashion and a spuriously won authority.

I wish to express my gratitude to the Relm Foundation of Ann Arbor for generous assistance in the publication of this book.

W. H. Hutt
University of Capetown
1962.

---

*I do not think that Patinkin could have noticed, before he had completed his *magnum opus*, the two articles (mentioned on p. ix) in which I stressed the great importance of the aggregate value of money in real terms and the nature of price flexibility. These articles, which were published in 1954 and 1956, would have appeared several years earlier had my confidence not been shaken by the vehemence of the opposition they aroused from some eminent economists to whom I submitted them.

†In 1945 Wright published (in the *Q.J.E.*) not dissimilar conclusions to those he now presents. He received, we learned a few years ago, *private* written approval from Keynes, who was already *hinting* publicly at a wish to retreat. (See below, pp. 429-430).

REFERENCES

(1) KEYNES, *Treatise*, Vol. I, p.233n. (2) HUTT, *The Yield from Money Held*, in *Freedom and Free Enterprise*, ed. Sennholz. (3) HUTT, *The Significance of Price Flexibility*, S.A.J.E., March, 1954. (4) PATINKIN, *Keynesian Economics Rehabilitated; a Rejoinder to Professor Hicks*, E.J., 1959, p.586.

CONTENTS

PREFACE — vii

I. ACADEMIC APPEAL OF KEYNESIAN DOCTRINE — 1

II. THE NATURE OF THE KEYNESIAN THESIS — 17

III. CONSEQUENCES OF THE KEYNESIAN REMEDY — 37

IV. THE NATURE OF CO-ORDINATION THROUGH THE PRICE SYSTEM — 51

V. THE NATURE OF MONEY — 85

VI. CONCEPTS OF INFLATION AND DEFLATION — 109

VII. KEYNES' NOTION OF TRUE INFLATION — 117

VIII. INCOME AND ITS "GENERATION" — 131

IX. ARE PRICE ADJUSTMENTS SELF-FRUSTRATING? — 157

X. THE NATURE OF CONSUMPTION AND SAVING — 181

XI. THE CONSUMPTION FALLACY — 209

XII. THE MARGINAL PROPENSITY TO CONSUME — 247

XIII. THE MULTIPLIER — 263

XIV. THE ACCELERATION FALLACY — 289

XV. DEPRESSION AND BOOM — 341

XVI. CAPITAL SATURATION — 357

XVII. THE SAY LAW — 387

XVIII. ANTICIPATED INFLATION — 407

XIX. THE RETREAT — 421

INDEX — 439

Chapter I

THE ACADEMIC APPEAL
OF KEYNESIAN DOCTRINE

SUMMARY

1.—The Keynesians claim to have invented a new economics which can answer important questions that the older economics was unable to answer. This, I do not admit. 2.—The appeal of Keynesian doctrine in the universities appears to be due partly to a spurious air of science derived from its chief concepts being amenable to precise mathematical statement and manipulation (but involving the substitution of constants for preferences, judgments and decisions); 3.—partly to its apparent achievements in policy applications having been concrete and obvious; 4.—and partly because of fashion. 5.—Appendix on The Limitations of Mathematical Method in Economics.

1.—Social institutions have not developed through the medium of rational planning. They have evolved largely out of the chance events of social history. This is a precarious basis for the benefits which the peoples of Western Europe and the America's have happened to secure—especially the connected freedoms of the mind, the spirit and enterprise. We tend to treat the virtues of the system which we know as though they had fallen like the gentle rain from heaven. We are seldom reminded that the rights we take for granted were fought for by a long line of martyrs; and we have not consciously studied the course of history in order to perceive exactly how the accumulation of technical knowledge and the expansion of occupied area have proved conducive to the winning of liberty of thought, discussion and decision—that security from central or sectional force which is conferred by the institution of property.

In particular, we have failed as peoples (or our teachers and elected representatives have failed) to perceive the origin of that security which emerges from the right to enter into and rely upon contract, a right which permits co-operation without coercion—co-operation under conditions of freedom. Even less do we perceive the true source of two subsidiary yet fundamental rights, (a) *the right to work* (in the sense of the right to acquire valuable skills, and to contract with those who want our skills or with those who can organize our skills to satisfy demand), and (b) *the right to use the accumulation of valuable resources* in the manner which is expected to be most acceptable to society in its consumer rôle.

It is ultimately through the failure to understand these things that mankind has not yet learned to diagnose the causes of, and to devise means of eradicating, *the evils which are expressed either as inflation or as unemployment (depression)*.

Generalizing boldly, it can be said that there have been two kinds of diagnosis: the orthodox and the Keynesian. The orthodox diagnosis places the blame on a disco-ordination expressed through prices being fixed at levels which are inconsistent with full employment under un-inflated money income;* and it prescribes the adjustment of prices in

---

*Uninflated money income is the money valuation of income when the scale of prices is constant.

3

order to achieve full employment and stability. The Keynesian diagnosis blames lack of purchasing power or lack of "effective demand" and it prescribes (in formulae which often obscure the true nature of the prescription) the creation of additional purchasing power which will raise final prices and thereby reduce real costs. I shall argue that this second diagnosis diverts attention from the crucial issues and that the remedy associated with it is harmful.

To me, the course of the great depression of the 'thirties had provided an empirical demonstration of the soundness of the classical analysis and synthesis (not of its all-sufficiency or infallibility!) At the same time *it had demonstrated equally clearly how unacceptable, for a variety of socio-psychological reasons, disinterested teachings had become.* I was prompted by these circumstances to write my *Economists and the Public.* In that book, I dealt with the problem of authority in economic science, and the reasons for the current unacceptability of teaching in the classical tradition. It seems to me that, at the same time, others were unconsciously groping for some *more acceptable* substitute for the old economic teachings. Naturally, the Keynesians will not be easy to convince that the mere palatability of their theories had any influence upon them. They interpreted the great depression in the opposite way. To them it was the great practical refutation of the classical system of thought or fundamental parts of it. I make this point simply to show how diametrically my own reactions to the economic experience of the inter-war period have differed. Keynes' *General Theory* appeared whilst my *Economists and the Public* was in the press. Since then, rightly or wrongly, I have not moved with the tide; although Keynes' confidence, eloquence and reputation—not his reasoning, which at first left me bewildered—dealt the hardest blow to my own intellectual confidence which it has ever received.

The controversy can be well defined by the contrasted passages below. I quote first from M. Polyani's delightful, lucid, yet independent popularization of Keynesianism, and next from K. E. Boulding's most able and beautifully written *Economics of Peace.* I follow with a statement of how I see the same issues. The quoted passages represent quite fairly, I believe, the post-war attitude of the great bulk of economists—critical and uncritical—toward Keynes' teachings.* I maintain exactly the opposite.

Polyani says:

"The Keynesian discovery in 1936 of the mechanism by which the level of employment is determined revealed that conditions of over-production are actually quite common. . . . . It is difficult to see any reason why the Keynesian

---

*Polyani is a physicist by profession. But he has a very thorough grasp of economics as it was being taught when he wrote.

mechanism should not have been recognized, say, in the year 1800—or at any time between that date and the year 1936—except for the fact that men were not clever enough to see through the puzzle which was facing them. Thinking takes time. . . . . The course of past history thus appears to have been determined to a fateful degree by the slowness of human thought. . . . . The Keynesian theory is really quite simple—perhaps difficult to grasp at first, but once understood quite easy to handle. . . . . The blunders of Governments . . . . were often emphatically supported by authoritative representatives of economic science. But since the early 1930's a new and more enlightened opinion has begun to dawn upon economic science, and through the publication in 1936 of *The General Theory of Employment, Interest and Money,* by J. M. Keynes, the light finally broke through, ... and the general public is also rapidly modernizing its attitude to monetary affairs."[1]

Boulding says:

"One of the most important things that has happened in the past twenty years . . . . has been the development of a body of thought on the subject of depressions which is at last commanding general acceptance among economists. . . . . This is the theory that has grown up around the name of Lord Keynes. . . . . There has been accomplished a revolution in economic thought . . . . that transcends in importance anything that has happened in economics since Adam Smith." (The revolution consists in the recognition of) "a fragment of truth that had been unrecognized by the orthodox economists, ... that under certain circumstances there may be a deficiency of purchasing power or of consuming power, in the sense that the public is not willing to buy, at existing prices, the total volume of goods that are offered for sale. . . . . My income is always somebody else's expenditure, and my expenditure is somebody else's income. . . . . Every *transfer* of money is at the same time income to the person who receives it and expenditure to the person who gives it. This truth is so obvious, once it is stated, that it seems almost impossible that it could be misunderstood; nevertheless, the Keynesian revolution in economic thought consists essentially in the explicit recognition of this truth."[2]

I maintain:

Orthodox economists had long understood the factors which determine the rate of flow of *valuable* output (i.e., the extent to which resources are *employed* in a measurable sense).

The Keynesian kind of thinking has existed almost from time immemorial, but until well after World War I, it got little support among critical thinkers in the universities. It emerged, as a powerful academic movement, owing to a growing unwillingness of economists to face *the implications* of orthodox theory. This led, I believe, to a groping towards ways of thinking which divert attention from the fundamental issues. Economists came to regard income as created by transfer of money instead of as the flow of productive services measured in money. To such an extent did the new methods succeed in obscuring the causes of unemployment, that absurd notions like that of general over-production came to be seriously discussed. The degeneration of economic teaching appears to have been accelerated because the politicians were seeking justifications for policies which broke with tradition but which they had decided that it was expedient anyhow to pursue. If economic doctrines which support some line of action are likely to be politically useful, then undoubtedly some economists will find sincere encouragement in supplying what is wanted.

For more than a century, however, what we can now recognize as the Keynesian fallacies were relatively uninfluential. This does not mean that orthodox economics could ever have been described as having determined policy. Indeed, the teachings of the orthodox economists had nowhere led to the State adopting policies which were wholly based on their tenets. The reputation of orthodox economics had, however, *restrained* certain major irrationalities, such as recourse to schemes based on the notion that spending (as distinct from pricing) creates employment.

Since the death of Keynes, economists who before that time were inclined to accept Keynes' teachings, have been gradually discarding the ancient fallacies which he had rehabilitated. They have been slowly and clumsily feeling their way back to a scientific attitude towards monetary affairs. This has come about, I suggest, not mainly through any new theoretical insight, but chiefly through the march of world events which have obviously belied the Keynesian thesis. The retreat has taken the form not of frank admissions of earlier error—perhaps too much to expect—but rather of attempts to re-state the old orthodox truths in Keynesian terminology.

Unfortunately, the old and unrefuted truths cannot be *well* stated in Keynesian jargon and concepts. This is because the concepts themselves have sometimes been designed (as I shall show) in such a way that nearly every vital issue is obscured. For that reason, it will be necessary for me to devote some time to re-establishing conceptual clarity, and then to treat some of the basic propositions in terms of more satisfactory concepts.

2.—It is sometimes said that mankind has more to learn from experience than from theory. That may be true of a body of doctrine *labelled* "theory"; but if so, then it is very poor theory. Properly conceived, economic theory is simply the process of handling economic experience, reducing the enormous, diversified and heterogeneous actuality of existence in a changing world into intelligible categories. The supposed *abstractness* of theory is the abstractness of a spanner or a slide-rule. It is independent of the things which it handles. Hence I need hardly stress the truth that the use of unreal, abstractly conceived *premises* may be wholly legitimate and highly fruitful, provided the concepts manipulated are self-consistent and are capable of being replaced by realistic premises before conclusions are drawn. I do not therefore decry the use of highly simplified mental isolates or models; for such devices may help us to reason our way through the complex actualities of the economic system.

Now the notions on which the Keynesian exposition has been constructed, although unsatisfactory from other standpoints (as I shall show), have the virtue of being capable of precise mathematical statement (e.g., the multiplier, the accelerator, and macro-economic concepts generally); and once the disconnected ideas of *The General Theory* had been systematized by Keynes' disciples, they could be very easily grasped by the beginner (the more uncritical the student, the more easily). And provided the student possesses some facility in mathematics, he is able to progress rapidly to what has come to be regarded as advanced economics, with mere mathematical difficulties to overcome. In fact, his thoughts may well be diverted from the difficulties of economics to the ingenuities of mathematical manipulation. For the difficulties lie, not in the *manipulation* of concepts but in the constant testing, by reference to experience (including the recorded experience of history), of the premises on which models are constructed and the conclusions which have been drawn. When this is not understood—and many of the modern Keynesians fail to understand it—economists are capable of erecting impressive mathematical models upon conceptually confused foundations. Consider, for instance, a phrase like the following: "If investment is below its boom-time level, the level of national income generated will not be high enough to give full employment."[3] "Full employment" *means* "full national income" (whether that income is measured in actual money units or in "real" terms). Hence the phrase quoted states that the level of income generated will not be high enough to generate full income! I shall show that it can be given an intelligible meaning only in the light of the Say Law, a suggestion which must shock any Keynesian. The release of withheld capacity in any field—the "generation" of additional services in that field—is likely to induce the release of capacity (the generation of additional services) in noncompeting fields.

But partly because it has become the fashion to state the Keynesian ideas in mathematical form, the ideas of *The General Theory* have served as the foundation of a multitude of studies in applied mathematics. This has created—quite unjustifiably—the impression that such studies are *scientific;* for has not mathematics been called "the language of science"?* And if mathematics has produced such formidable results in physics, say, why should not the same methods prove equally successful in the understanding and ordering of the economic system? Feelings of this kind have, I feel, been a not unimportant explanation of the hold which Keynesian *methods* have acquired in many universities.

Recourse to inappropriate simplifications has led also to the recognition of what is usually a quite illusory similarity between the problems of economics and those of the natural sciences. Attempts have been made to solve questions which involve the adjustment of scarce means to competing ends through methods appropriate to the sphere of physics and engineering. I do not suggest that all such attempts have been fruitless or fallacious; for it is often possible to make use of analogies and relation-

---

*Keynes' own expressed attitude towards mathematical economics was by no means uncritical. But I am dealing with developments which have followed his own contributions.[4]

ships so discerned in a parallel but independent study of the complex world of choice and decision. But my criticisms remain valid, I believe, of a large part of the "new economics," and they are, in particular, relevant to the so-called macro-economics which consists, as Röpke has put it, "of a tendency to regard the whole economic process as something purely objective and mechanical. Hence purely mathematical and statistical methods, it seems, can be applied and the whole economic process can therefore be quantitatively determined and even predetermined. Under those circumstances an economic system readily takes on the appearance of a sort of huge waterworks, and the science which treats of that economic system quite logically assumes the appearance of a kind of engineering science, which teems with equations in ever-increasing profusion. And so oblivion threatens to engulf what, as I see it, is the actual fruit of a century and a half of intellectual effort in the field of economics, namely, the doctrine of the movement of individual prices."[5]

Economics, continues Röpke, "requires the constant application of a supreme attentiveness . . . . that intuitive power which enables us to keep our eyes on all the complicated threads at once, and to emulate the juggler who never loses sight of a single one of the balls he is keeping aloft."[6] It is the vice of the concepts and models which Keynes and his disciples have chosen to use, that they have precisely the opposite effects. They turn attention away from the most vital aspects of the rational allocation of scarce means in response to competing ends. It is because the range of attention demanded is so vast that economics is a difficult science. Its complexity often baffles scientists trained in other fields when they first turn their attention to it. Attempts to confine attention to a few relevant issues only, through the use of summarizing concepts like averages, and the creation of abstract, highly simplified models, in which *constants* are substituted for *preferences, judgments and decisions*, may greatly facilitate exposition and the mechanical part of thinking. But unless they are always accompanied by an independent consideration of the problem at issue in relation to the whole system of adapting means to ends, such concepts or the models into which they are built can be disastrously misleading. And if economists are subconsciously trying to find justifications for preconceived views—and such a possibility cannot be ignored—there must obviously be a temptation to leave analysis just when simplified models have brought it to a point at which the conclusions favor the preconceptions.*

"The model" is a set of simplified assumptions, particularly concern-

---

*In case what I have said should have left a wrong impression, I must stress that I am not attacking the use of mathematics in economics. (I return to the topic on pp. 11-14)

ing the interdependence of different factors. But the paramount reality of the economic relationship is that, in expressing preferences for ends, and in judging the productiveness or profitableness of means, every single choice or judgment affects all others. Model-making is not illegitimate in economics but it is extremely dangerous. "The model" assumes that human action is subject to mechanical rules and hence capable of being more or less mechanically predicted from assumed autonomous stimuli. Hence its function must be that of a mere step in reasoning.

So far has the fashion of abstract model-making gone, however, that Ichimura can claim that "the standard procedure of economic theory is to consider an economic system as isolated from other factors of a non-economic nature and ignoring the secondary effects of these factors on the economic system."[7] But such a procedure is incredibly superficial and misleading. Until three decades ago, the *standard* procedure—at least since Walras—was always to bring all factors into the reckoning in so far as they have any effects (direct or indirect) upon values, and to regard all such factors as "economic." One has necessarily to resort to the use of mental isolates—imagining certain factors as remaining unchanged in order to consider the implications of one or more other factors. But before any *significant* inferences can be drawn (i.e., results significant for policy) any conclusions tentatively reached have to be considered in relation to the whole complex of factors observed to be operative in the changing world.

3.—But I believe that the most important cause of the remarkable flood of Keynesian contributions from the universities has been due to a misinterpretation of the great achievements of inflation. Of course, neither Keynes nor his disciples have thought of themselves as inflationists (see Chap. VII) and I certainly do not suggest that they have been blind to the tragedies of inflation.* Yet creeping inflation does appear always to have accompanied periods in which the kind of policies their doctrines imply have been attempted. In the era which followed Keynes' *Treatise on Money*, the Keynesian-minded economists saw the recovery of the United States, and the methods adopted seemed to them to be on the right lines, in spite of the depreciation of the dollar; they saw the almost staggering recovery of Germany under Hitler which followed rearmament expendi-

---

*The inflationary nature of Keynes' thesis was never *explicit*, and the majority of modern students, if asked whether the Keynesian system is inherently inflationary, would probably answer, No. But many passages in *The General Theory*, with which I shall in due course be dealing, *imply* recourse to inflation as the remedy for unemployment. For example, on p. 10, Keynes states that "when money-wages are rising.... real wages are falling." Such an assertion, together with the implication that falling real wage-rates will restore employment, can mean one thing only, a fall in the real value of the money unit.

tures, but tended to view the accompanying inflation as incidental; they saw the more gradual recovery of Britain which slowly followed her departure from gold, but did not attribute this to the mild inflation which occurred; they saw also the enormous assistance which the abandonment of orthodox monetary policy apparently rendered to the Soviet economy during the Stalinist epoch, and the rapid recovery of all nations following the monetary policies which accompanied the vicissitudes of war, yet without adequate consideration of the rôle of inflation in the prosperity observed. Moreover, they compared these almost miraculous achievements with the black years of depression when governments had tried to keep faith with those who had trusted the contract to redeem currencies in gold. The Keynesians seemed unable, originally, to bring themselves to believe that the benefits of rectifying spending whenever activity had tended to slow down, were incapable of being won side by side with the maintenance of the value of currencies;* whilst later on they were gradually led, I shall suggest, to recommend repression of the inflation which would otherwise have resulted. They came to advocate, that is, a proliferation of imposed restrictions on the price mechanism, without perceiving the full implications—economic, sociological or political. It is, I think, largely because they have not seen the consequences of thus seeking an easy immediate solution to declining activity, that their doctrines have obtained so remarkable a hold.

4.—A further factor may have been the unwillingness of the majority to be nonconformist or out of fashion. There was an eager claim, shortly after Keynes' death, that his doctrines were "at last . . . . commanding general acceptance among economists."[8]

Such claims have now ceased. Not only does there appear to be a growing number of Keynesian-trained economists who are uneasy about the traditions he has left,† and a clearly marked retreat (which I propose later to discuss,‡ there has always been a group of eminent economists who have made it clear that they are more or less in the opposite camp.

There is a tendency today among quite a number of economists, some of whom were once regarded as among Keynes' most eminent disciples, to describe themselves as neutral. The disinclination to recant is under-

---

*A post-war shift from this viewpoint—on the part of some at least—will be considered in a later chapter.

†It is too early yet to speak with confidence on this point, although McC. Wright and Seymour Harris had reported a growing reaction against Keynesian teaching in 1945 and 1947 respectively.[9][10] See Chap. XIX. In 1956, I asked one of Keynes' disciples who had been closest to him to be so kind as to read and criticize some memoranda which, I said, disputed the very essence of Keynesian teaching. Very courteously, he regretted his inability to assist me, but emphasized that I must not think of him as a Keynesian.

‡See Chap. XIX.

standable; but it is only confusing to suggest that Keynes was partly right and partly wrong. I shall maintain that where he was right, he was not original, and that where he was original he was wrong.*

5.—APPENDIX

The Limitations of Mathematical Method in Economics

I have referred in section 2 to the limitations of mathematical method in the study of economics. In this note, I wish briefly to develop this thesis.

It is, I believe, as a result of serious conceptual confusion that some economists appear to be bewildered by the complexities of the economic interrelationships which they perceive in the actual world. The great simplifying perception which they miss lies, I suggest, in the recognition that all expressions of human preference which are relevant to the phenomenon of scarcity have an identical status and significance in praxeological studies. Man does not always choose, and make sacrifices to get, those things which are provided in the form of measurable outputs. Sometimes he prefers consumption in the distant future rather than in the immediate future. Sometimes he demands leisure. Sometimes he demands the pleasures of gambling. Sometimes he demands the feeling of security which he can achieve through risk-avoidance. Sometimes he demands all the advantages and conveniences of holding money. Through the failure to grasp the truth that each of these objectives concerns a preference which is of the very same nature as that expressed between, say, bread and cake, or shoes and shirts, or cricket bats and tennis rackets, the illusion emerges that it is essential for the "scientific" study of society to separate different kinds of human ends, or the response to these ends, into measurable categories. And this illusion has caused some economists to try to imagine *a simplified* reality in the form of ridiculously unreal "models." Instead of searching for appropriate concepts, which they could have found through a careful study of the nature of human preference and the phenomenon of scarcity, they have had recourse (especially since Keynes) to logically unacceptable constructions and abstractions which have been chosen mainly by reason of their convenience for mathematical treatment.† This is above all true of the field

---

*I wrote this sentence long before I had seen Hazlitt's comment on *The General Theory:* "I could not find in it a single important dectrine that was both true and original."(11)

†As Stigler has pointed out, it is all too easy to confuse clarity with "familiarity or susceptibility to logical manipulation."(12) Moreover, the enthusiasm of the mathematicians may induce them to "make certain basic assumptions because they are easily treated mathematically."(13) They are apt to create what Champernowne has called "mere toys" because "the assumptions which are most convenient for model building are seldom those which are most appropriate to the real world."(14)

of economic fluctuations, as exemplified in the works of Hicks, Harrod, Sweezy and others, and in respect of reliance on macro-economic concepts generally. If simplified models and notions are to be legitimately used, an explicit replacement of unrealistic simplifications by empirically determined and realistic postulates is essential; and this means in practice that allowances must be made for (i) change in the institutional set-up and (ii) change in any impinging external factors. Moreover, changes in ends and changes in means must be distinguished with the utmost clarity; when they have been distinguished they must be allowed for; and when changes in expectations are factors, allowance must be made for the fact that the working of cause and effect is profoundly complicated through the expression of free will. Events become determined not merely by what *has happened* but by *purpose,* i.e., expressed preferences. For these reasons, all attempts to understand the economic world by analogies with the world of nature are highly dangerous, a truth which both Röpke[15] and Ballvé[16] have pointed out.

Some writers have suggested that the application of mathematical methods to economics has been wholly barren. Thus D. Novick, in a trenchant, challenging and courageous article (which has been belittled rather than dispassionately answered by those who have felt themselves criticized) has roundly described the use of mathematics in the social sciences as "an addition to the *esoterica* of the sciences."[17] "There is," he says, "nothing substantively different in the use of Greek letters arrayed in algebraic form than in the use of words combined into sentence and paragraph form."[18] Now I should be the last one to suggest that the great economies of thought which mathematics permits have been fruitless in the social sciences.* But I do think that *mathematicians writing on economics* have seriously harmed economic thought of recent years. It seems unfortunately to be true that, until recently, few economists of note have been mathematicians. Even more unfortunately, many mathematicians have discussed economics, and proficiency in mathematics has tended to be regarded as proficiency in economics. Yet "the ability to judge the relevance of an economic theory and its conclusions to the real world," says Champernowne, "is but rarely associated with the ability to understand advanced mathematics."[20] Obviously, it cannot be contended that training in mathematics, or an inborn gift for the subject, is *necessarily* a barrier to an understanding of the more difficult aspects of economics! But mathematicians appear remarkably inclined to confuse mathematical clarity with valid inference; at any rate, this seems to

---

*On this matter I agree with I. M. Kirzner who quotes effectively Croce's remark that "the dignity of abstract analysis" rendered a great service to an economics which had been "darkened . . . . by the mass of anecdotes of the Historical School."[19]

be the position when they are considering the relations of economic preferences to the means for the satisfaction of those preferences.

There is no traditional or orthodox economic theory which, provided
the sort of simplifying assumptions which have become fashionable in
contemporary "model-making" are made, cannot be expressed in terms
of equations which satisfy the criterion that the number of unknowns
does not exceed the number of equations. But the possibility of stating
economic propositions in such a form is irrelevant to the truth of these
propositions. It shows that, as they are enunciated, they have self-consistency, nothing more.

Hence Novick is right beyond question when he objects to the tendency to assume that the mere expression of "theories in mathematical
form creates absolute knowledge. . . . ."[21] This truth can never be too
strongly stressed. There is a propensity to assume that, once a proposition has been expressed in the brevity and elegance which mathematics
make possible, it has been established as true. For instance, L. R. Klein
has recently referred to "the beauty and elegance" of Frisch's well-known
article on *Propagation Problems and Impulse Problems in Dynamic Economics.*[22] Yet, if my criticism on pp. 317-319, can be accepted, this
contribution has been responsible for an appalling intellectual muddle
which has led may economists into whole realms of barren speculation.

Such an example illustrates the danger to which Tinbergen has referred that, when people are "too enthusiastic for the mathematics
involved they may . . . . somewhat neglect" what he has called the "quali-
tative part of research, characterized by distinguishing different categories
of economic concepts and by their exact definition."[23] Mathematics
is merely "shorthand logic," whilst the sin of many mathematical economists has been "a regrettable failure to apprehend the significance and
importance of definition," as E. C. Harwood has pointed out.[24] And
mathematics does not, says Tinbergen, participate in "the enumeration
of the phenomena to be included in the analysis";[25] nor can it assist in
the formulation of theories and hypotheses. In particular, the models
which I have found defective fail to assist us in understanding the
motives which lead to the remoulding of the production and marketing
framework, e.g., the factors which eventually lead to a single managerial
or entrepreneurial act or several independent or connected managerial
or entrepreneurial acts which cause the setting up or the breakdown of a
cartel, or of a system of re-sale price maintenance, or of a set of trade
union demarcations.

To insist upon these limitations of purely abstract analysis is not to
argue for what has been called "institutional economics." Nor does it

---

*Frisch's article appeared in *Economic Essays in Honour of Gustav Cassel.*

suggest that special economic theories are appropriate for different institutional assumptions (e.g., that we need different economic theories for, say, a hypothetical *laissez-faire* economy, for existing capitalism and for the existing Soviet system). The economic theory which has assisted my own empirical studies has always seemed equally relevant to all kinds of societies, indeed, to have universal applicability. My present argument simply insists that the nature of economic analysis must be determined in the light of its practical limitations.

I do not think it is unfair to say that many economists have become fascinated with the *manipulation* of concepts but impatient and bored with the really difficult part of the economist's task, namely, that of achieving perfect conceptual clarity. Indeed, they have, I feel, tended sometimes to regard careful concern with the fundamentals as mere verbiage. Having recognized that certain ideas common to all thinking about economics are capable of being expressed in mathematical form, they have come to regard form as content. I have been driven to the conclusion that the extraordinary way in which the errors of Keynes have been accepted for so long by so many economists, and uselessly elaborated, has been due very largely to the fact that they have found its mathematical statement capable of elegant development and refinement.

It is always possible to state the axioms, assumptions and conclusions relevant to any practical economic problem in nonmathematical form, however complex the mathematics needed for the actual handling of the problem.* I know of no *important* case where, axioms and assumptions having been clear and acceptable, the conclusions so stated have been false as a result of *mathematical* error. It is therefore not in the manipulations that fallacy creeps in. It is in the course of distinguishing and defining categories and concepts that we can trace the confusions of this age. And it is at that stage in thought, I shall maintain, that Keynesian economics can be seen to have misled the students of a full generation.†

─────────

*Compare Champernowne(26) and Stigler(27) on this point.

†Need I repeat that this note is in no way an attack on the use of mathematics, either as an aid to thought or as a tool of exposition? There are economists who use and do not abuse the method. Thus, Machlup's important contributions, although often employing mathematical reasoning, have consisted largely of attempts to restore conceptual clarity in fields in which a structure of mathematical and abstract thinking has been erected on unsatisfactory economic notions. Referring to his long continued activities in this field, Machlup significantly remarks: "Serious terminological ambiguities and conceptual obscurites have been found to exist, some of them curable, others beyond hope of clarification."(26)

REFERENCES

(1) POLYANI, *Full Employment and Free Trade*, pp. xi-xii. (2) BOULDING, *The Economics of Peace*, pp. 126 and 132. (3) MATTHEWS, *Capital Stock Adjustment Theories*, in Kurihara, *Post-Keynesian Economics*, p. 173. (4) KEYNES, *The General*

Theory. pp. 297-8. (5) ROPKE, *The Place of Economics Among the Social Sciences,* in Sennholz (Ed.), *Freedom and Free Enterprise,* p. 121. (6) *Ibid.,* p. 117. (7) ICHIMURA, *Toward a General Non-linear Macrodynamic Theory of Economic Fluctuations,* in Kurihara, *op. cit.,* p. 194. (8) BOULDING, *op. cit.,* p. 126. (9) McC. WRIGHT, *The Future of Keynesian Economics,* A.E.R., 1945, p. 284. (10) HARRIS, *The New Economics,* p. 3. (11) HAZLITT, in *The Critics of Keynesian Economics,* p. 3. (12) STIGLER, *Five Lectures on Economic Problems,* p. 40. (13) TINBERGEN in *Review of Economics and Statistics,* 1954, pp. 366-367. (14) CHAMPERNOWNE, in *ibid.,* p. 369. (15) ROPKE, *op. cit.,* pp. 121-2. (16) BALLVÉ, *On Methodology in Economics,* in Sennholz, *op. cit.,* p. 129. (17) NOVICK, *Mathematics: Logic, Quantity and Method,* in *Review of Economics and Statistics,* November, 1954. p. 358. (18) *Ibid.,* p. 358. (19) KIRZNER, *The Economic Point of View,* pp. 67-70. (20) CHAMPERNOWNE, *op. cit.,* p. 369. (21) NOVICK, *op. cit.,* p. 358. (22) KLEIN, in *ibid.,* p. 360. (23) TINBERGEN, *op. cit.,* pp. 366-7. (24) HARWOOD, *Current Economic Delusions,* p. 9. (25) TINBERGEN, *op. cit.,* p. 367. (26) CHAMPERNOWNE, *op. cit.,* pp. 370-1. (27) STIGLER, *op. cit.,* pp. 44-5. (28) MACHLUP, *Statics and Dynamics: Kaleidoscopic Words, Southern Economic Journal,* October, 1959, p. 91.

Chapter II

THE NATURE OF THE
KEYNESIAN THESIS

SUMMARY

1.—Keynes maintained, quite wrongly, that Classical theory offers no explanation of the volume of employment or output; 2.—but before The General Theory, *orthodox economic thought was tending to the conclusion that the chief causes of fluctuations in employment and activity are to be found in price rigidity, 3.—round which issue Keynes placed a screen of obscurity. Yet it can be seen that, unless price rigidity is assumed, the principal Keynesian theses are insupportable. 4.—Thus, when Keynes blamed time preference or liquidity preference for a deficiency of effective demand, he failed to consider the* general *question of why particular changes of ends or of means—thrift and the demand for liquidity—should give rise to chronic, spasmodic or cyclical unemployment; and he failed to perceive that he was indirectly blaming disco-ordinations due to the failure to adjust relative prices. 6.—His own attempts to explain the magnitude of employment or output relied upon crude, macro-economic concepts (like that of the price of labor), 7.—which seems to have prevented him from recognizing the co-ordinative role of price, 8.—and from realizing that unemployment is caused through costs and prices—and not interest—being set too high. 9.—His macro-economic method seems responsible also for the fallacy (obscured in a monetary theory of output) that the volume of employment is determined by expenditure (or the optimum rate of interest) instead of by the extent to which valuable resources are permitted (through relative prices or the direct withholding or release of capacity) to be utilized. 10.—Whereas orthodox theory envisages the satisfaction of consumer demand as the purpose of productive effort, the Keynesians tend towards 11.—the Mercantilist fallacy that the acquisition of money is the objective of economic activity. 12.—The argument that only the stimulation of expenditure can restore employment, because price adjustment is self-defeating, is to be examined separately. 13.—The idea that the "wish" to consume or accumulate may be insufficient to absorb the full flow of valuable productive services can be simply shown to be self-contradictory. 14.—Far from monetary factors being overlooked in orthodox economics—as Keynes suggested—they are woven into its whole texture. 15.—The fashion of subtle equivocation in monetary discussion established by Keynes seems to have become a convention.*

1.—Chapter 2 of *The General Theory* begins, in the first paragraph, with a complete mis-statement of what I, at any rate, have always understood orthodox theory to be. Keynes said that most economic treatises were *"primarily concerned* with the distribution of a *given* body of employed resources between different uses. . . . ."[1] The words "primarily concerned" (which I have italicized) are not justified; but Keynes' disciples tend to go further and to omit the qualification contained in this phrase. Even the late J. H. Williams (by no means a Keynesian) referred to Keynes' great contribution in challenging "the assumption, implicit in classical economics, of a full employment level of income automatically sustained."[2] That assumption has never been implicit in *my* mind nor have I ever read it into classical or orthodox teaching. I say unequivocally that orthodox or classical economics* does not deal simply with the distribution of a given body of *employed* resources between different uses. It is concerned with (a) the causes of resources *having value*, which is the capacity to be "employed" as well as the capacity to contribute to income; (b) with the factors determining the extent to which valuable resources *are* "employed," i.e., *allowed* to produce;† and (c) with the causes leading to savings, i.e., growth in the stock of resources and hence in the flow of income. There is no assumption, explicit or implicit, about any "given volume" of employment, nor any assumption of conditions of "full employment."‡ This is surely true even of Ricardo (the only economist to whom Keynes referred for support of his assertion), who admittedly argued that "No law can be laid down respecting quantity" of "wealth" (i.e., productivity) . For Ricardo's point seems to have been

---

*Keynes referred to modern writers in the classical or orthodox tradition as "classical."

†E.g., consider Mill, *Political Economy*, chap. vii, headed "On what depends the degree of productiveness of productive agents," which he described as "the second great question in political economy."

‡"Full employment" as a *conceptual isolate* is employed as a methodological device in abstract analysis. See my *Theory of Idle Resources*, p. 34.

simply that there were no laws of growth of productivity in general, as there *were* laws of distribution of the results of productivity.*

2.—During the decade which preceded *The General Theory*, orthodox economists had been largely concerned with discovering the laws governing the relations between institutional developments and the phenomenon of scarcity. Thus, they were devoting increasing attention to the special phenomena due to structural maladjustments, monopolies, price rigidities, etc., institutional forms which were increasingly regarded as the cause of waste, idle capacity, curtailments of and fluctuations in possible income. The student learned that, in the current institutional set-up, the economist had to study a world of restrained competition in the shape of sectionalist restraints on productive power, or collective restraints in the sectional interest, and that the rational study of contemporary society had to give attention to the nature of the force restrained, namely, competition.†

In the light of that approach, the general rate of growth of utilized productive power, and the degree of utilization of that power in the modern world, were held to result from a struggle between two sets of opposed forces:

(a) On the one side was population growth; successful prospecting; the opening up of new areas; inventions; the accumulation of technical knowledge generally and skills; the application of the inventions, technical knowledge and skills accumulated; managerial ingenuities; and the accumulation of man-made resources. It was understood that population growth tends, *ceteris paribus,* and statically considered, to cheapen labor in terms of other services‡ (although every cheapening of one kind of labor implies an increased uninflated demand for all noncompeting labor); that every individual application of new technical knowledge (discoveries, inventions, managerial ingenuities, etc.) also tends, *ceteris paribus,* either to cheapen labor and other physical resources or, in the

---

*In the same paragraph Keynes alleged also that "the pure theory of what determines the actual employment of the available resources" had "seldom been examined in great detail." This last charge seems to have more substance. Indeed, my *Theory of Idle Resources* (1939) , which was intended to be a direct answer to the assertion (i.e., an answer in the form of a detailed statement of the causes of actual employment), is a tacit admission of the gap which formerly existed. *Yet, I expressly put forward that book not as anything essentially original, but simply as an ordered statement of "pure orthodoxy."* Certainly no critic has ever suggested that it is anything else. I wrote, ". . . . The types of idleness analyzed in the pages which follow are all of a kind which are implicit—if not expressed in sufficiently clear terms—in orthodox teaching. This essay is felt to be original only in the sense that, through more careful definition, it seeks to clarify what is already known and understood. It is pure orthodoxy. . . . ."(3)

†See my article, *Economic Method and the Concept of Competition*, S.A.J.E., 1934.

‡It tends to cheapen labor *in terms of money* only if M is assumed constant.

absence of wage-rate and price adjustment, to cause unemployment; that all economic progress is either labor-economizing or capital-economizing (and hence *unemployment-creating) in its immediate impact;* that each individual act of accumulation of productive capacity tends, *ceteris paribus,* to cheapen capital resources and (in the absence of price adjustment) to cause unemployment of some of those resources; yet that each economy or growth thus effected (although tending to cause unemployment) constitutes an increased and uninflated demand for the services of all noncompeting resources.

(b) Opposed to such economizing (and demand-creating) innovations and growth, were seen various kinds of output restrictions and scarcity-creating procedures—privately contrived or State imposed—practices which must be viewed as *the withholding of productive capacity and the diverting of resources from relatively more demanded to relatively less demanded uses.** It was understood that such practices restrain growth because, in preventing the full or most productive use of existing resources, they may—through reactions upon the propensity to save—render additions to that capacity unprofitable; that they cause, in particular, rigidity of prices downwards; and that they lead, therefore, to the anomaly that the growth of output in a trade due to an economy is unable to make its full potential contribution to real demand for the products of noncompeting industries.

Hence it seemed (in pre-Keynesian days) that, in studying the causes of the irregularity of economic expansion, we were concerned on the one hand mainly with the irregularity of savings, in the sense of provision for the future† (which it was understood would be influenced by irregularity of movements in the rate of interest), and on the other hand with irregularity of the withholding and release of capacity. Monetary policy was thought to be relevant only in so far as it could be shown to influence these two factors.

The most important conclusion to which orthodox economic thought was leading in this connection was that the great defect in contemporary economic organization, the ultimate source of nearly all disco-ordination, unemployment, fluctuations in activity, uncertainties and lack of security, was the absence (due mainly to such sectionalist restraints) of price

---

*By *withheld capacity* or *withheld resources,* I mean unemployed resources which would be employed if their services were appropriately priced in relation to consumers' preferences and entrepreneurial forecasts of profitability. By *diverted capacity* (or *resources*), I mean resources which would be employed in more productive ways if they were similarly priced. These notions are more fully explained in my *Theory of Idle Resources.*

†In using the phrase "provision for the future" here, I am postponing consideration of the extent to which saving in some other possible sense may *not* imply net accumulation of productive capacity.

flexibility downwards. Both theoretical analysis and economic history appeared to point to this as the chief source of the economic ills of each generation.* It is the conclusion which I have already stated and which I am about to explain further.

Keynesian thinking, on the other hand, has been responsible for a conception of the monetary system as an instrument for State use as distinct from an instrument for the use of the people; as a means of controlling "effective demand" with a view to ensuring employment instead of as a means of maintaining a money unit of defined value in terms of which contracts involving credit (State as well as private) may be concluded. I hope to show that it is utterly misleading to regard monetary or fiscal policy as determining "the level of aggregate demand." It determines the value of the money unit, and if this value *is changing,* it can influence the release of capacity which sectionalist pricing has withheld, and hence the flow of income. In this way only can what is clumsily called "the level of aggregate demand" be influenced. I hope to show, indeed, that *expenditure,* engineered through fiscal policy, is in no sense a generator of income.†

3.—But the Keynesian student is often taught that the orthodox economists believed that the world consisted of a perfectly competitive system with full employment! He seems to be taught at the same time that it is unnecessary to worry about what would happen if institutions were deliberately re-fashioned to break down the key rigidities.‡ When he is considering problems such as the achievement of full employment or the elimination of the trade cycle he is not led to consider the promotion of *competition, in the sense of the substitution of the least-cost method of achieving economic ends,* as an objective worthy of study. Prices *are* rigid, he is told. Things just happen to be like that, and realists will not waste time in arguing about what might happen if things were different.

When the co-ordinative rôle of price adjustment is understood, however, all the principal Keynesian theses seem to dissolve. I propose to demonstrate in later chapters, for instance, that *under price flexibility,* it is virtually impossible to sacrifice current consumption except for net accumulation; that, if the flow of productive services is not used in one way, it must be used in another; that the relative values placed on consumption now and in the future may, *in the extreme case,* change without actual provision for the future changing and so without any *actual* sacrifice of the present; and that there are no theoretical limits to the extent

---

*That this represents the direction of my own teaching before 1936 can be seen from my *Economists and the Public,* written before and published immediately after the appearance of *The General Theory.*

†See Chap. VIII.

‡For the argument that it would be self-defeating, see Chap. IX.

to which the *value* of the flow of services entering into final products may fall without their ceasing to be fully consumed (when consumption in the future is strongly preferred to consumption in the present), although we can conceive of realistic limits, namely, the extent to which we can imagine people *wishing* to sacrifice the present for the future and the degree of versatility of resources.

I shall show also that this conclusion is unaffected even when it is assumed that the value of the money unit is rising. For all prices and all values are, under the assumption of price flexibility, assumed to be immediately and continuously adjusted to expectations of the changing value of the unit. In other words, the general scale of prices is taken always to be perfectly adjusted to all its anticipated levels at each point of time in the future. Hence the falling prices of services and of the products into which services are embodied will not prevent their consumption.

If this argument is substantiated, it follows that the whole Keynesian case rests upon the assumption of price rigidity and the withholding of capacity which it implies.

The basic assumptions on which Keynes' rigorous analysis is based are, I think, stated for the first time in Chapter 18 of *The General Theory,* which he intended to be recapitulatory. But these assumptions are curiously unrealistic, in that the sort of things which nearly all economists are led by their empirical studies to accept as changeable, are regarded as given. Speaking of some of his assumptions, he said: "This does not mean that we assume these factors to be constant; but merely that in this place and context, we are not considering or taking into account the effects and consequences of changes in them."[4] But "in this place or context" turns out to mean the whole of *The General Theory.* Keynes' models are, indeed, almost wholly static and blatantly mechanical. Only occasionally do dynamic insights and realistic assumptions intrude and then nebulously and inconsistently. This fact will complicate exposition in every chapter of the present book.

4.—Both the *Treatise* and *The General Theory* found in thrift, and in the demand for liquidity, the principal causes of the idleness which policy is expected to rectify. It is curious that there has been no attempt (at least, I know of none) to explain the most general apparent anomaly in Keynesian thinking which is so expressed. Why should two particular expressions of preference concerning ends, namely, that between the present and the future (thrift), and that between the services of money (liquidity) and all other services, or the response to those preferences in the form of certain ways of using the scarce means available, give rise to unemployment—either as a chronic, or spasmodic, or cyclical phenomenon? Admittedly, (i) changes in the rate of savings (in either direction) and (ii) changes in demand for money (hoarding or dishoarding)* can cause a parallel contraction of real income in the absence of price and monetary flexibility; but if net accumulation declines, it is because savings decline as income declines. I shall suggest that to blame saving preference, or the savings which result, is to reverse the true position.

Keynes contended that changed expectations can not only influence the *form* of output but the *amount* of output and employment.† No-one would deny that expectations of prices provide an inducement (among all other inducements) to withhold or release productive power; but that does not justify the Keynesian thesis that only an increase in "investment" expenditure or an increase in the "propensity to consume" can counter the expectations which create that inducement. It is like saying that only (a) *a particular way of using resources,* namely, in making producers' goods (the sort of goods which are typically produced when the rate of decumulation falls short of output) or (b) *a particular change in preference about the way in which resources shall be used,* can bring resources into utilization. I can find no rigorous explanation of why (i) the particular ends for which resources *are* actually used, or (ii) the particular preferences expressed through saving preference (i.e., time preference), can affect the extent to which demanded capacity is withheld or released. Of course, if the alternative to "investing" or "consuming" is "hoarding," there will be a deflationary effect. But even this postulates (a) that monetary policy is aiming at a lower scale of prices and so does not offset the hoarding, and (b) that the deflationary policy is incomplete and lacking self-consistency because the necessary co-ordinative steps to bring prices into relation to money income are not being taken. (See pp. 42-43). But such considerations are never noticed by the Keynesians.

I shall argue that the pursuit of no economic end need result in either unemployment or depression, but that *all changes in ends* (i.e., all changes in individually or collectively expressed preferences, or entrepreneurial judgments) must, unless they are accompanied by co-ordinative action with the appropriate price changes, cause the withholding or diversion of capacity. Time preference and so-called "liquidity preference,"‡ are no different in principle or in practice from all other economic preferences.

---

*The disco-ordinative effects of dishoarding are seen when it is not offset by credit policy *and* there is price rigidity upwards. "Shortages" will develop, with queues or rationing.

†I.e., "changing views about the future are capable of influencing the quantity of employment and not merely its direction."(5)

‡The term "preference" here is not very appropriate because we are concerned rather with a choice of means than a choice of ends. But obviously, if M is constant, an increased demand for monetary services must have deflationary results.

5.—When relative demand for final products falls (owing to a rise in saving preference), *the full employment of the resources which make them is consistent with the fall in demand but not consistent with the maintenance of the prices, either of the products themselves or of the services embodied in them.* Does it not follow that the decline in real income and the consequences upon realized growth are due to disco-ordination? I shall argue, therefore, that when the Keynesians blame thrift, they are turning attention away from the failure to adjust prices to changing preferences; and when they blame hoarding (liquidity preference), they are turning attention away from the failure of governments to tackle the problem of *unstable price rigidities,* i.e., the unwillingness of governments to take the steps needed to permit prices continuously to reach a level at which further *general* price changes will be unexpected.

6.—In his attempt to remedy the supposed failure of classical economics to explain the volume of employment, Keynes set out to write economics from an entirely new angle; and it was the defects of his new approach which, I believe, were largely responsible for his misconceptions. He asked us to consider the relations and reactions upon one another of great aggregate magnitudes, like income, employment, consumption, output, savings and demand. If it is possible to conceive of units in terms in which such magnitudes can be *legitimately* expressed, there is no objection to such a method except that it is an extraordinarily clumsy way of reaching results. But I propose to show later on that the "macro-economic" method, as it is called, has not in fact been applied with the use of logically defensible units, and that it has led to a host of subtle fallacies. At this stage it will suffice to deal with two aspects:

(a) *as measurable quantities,* income, output, employment (of all resources), consumption *plus* savings (or consumption *plus* investment) are identical notions and magnitudes—merely different ways of looking at the same phenomenon. For the employment of resources can be *measured,* in any intelligible sense of the term, only by some value measurement of the flow of services rendered by them; and the magnitude of the "real" value of the flow of services not only constitutes the aggregate "quantity" of output but is ultimately what we all mean when we talk of income.* Of course all these things may be *arbitrarily defined* so as to be different magnitudes. But in the controversies with which we are concerned that has not been the position.

Moreover, aggregate demand is also identical with these magnitudes if it is carefully defined to cover the offer of productive services for the

*See Chap. VIII.

flow of productive services, i.e., so as to exclude from it demand for assets from the offer of services or demand for services from the offer of assets—the factors which, as I shall show, determine the rate of interest.

(b) The concept of "effective demand" is defective. In conformity with their macro-economic approach the Keynesians hold that economic activity declines when "effective demand" is deficient.

The term itself is as old as Adam Smith (he used the word "effectual") and was used by several of his successors to distinguish between mere wants,* i.e., what we *would* demand if we had greater means, and effectual demand, i.e., what we do demand with the limited means at our disposal. But for over a century the term "demand," unqualified, has been used to mean the offer of services or things in return for other services or things. In these circumstances, it is fatuous now to use the adjective "effective" at all; although the writers of textbooks during the last two decades have mostly followed Keynes in this usage. The term is usually employed in the sense of "aggregate demand" *measured in terms of money*. I.e., inflation (even if unaccompanied by an increase in real income) is supposed to cause an increase in "effective demand."

Keynes described effective demand as determined by the intersection of his aggregate supply function with his aggregate demand function;[8] and thirty pages later he explained the notion further as "simply the aggregate income (or proceeds) which the entrepreneurs expect to receive, inclusive of the incomes which they hand on to the other factors of production. . . . ."[9] In this typically tortuous explanation, he was clearly assuming that what entrepreneurs *expect to* receive from output determines their *current* demands for the flow of productive services which create output. But in this explanation he seems to have forgotten the aggregate supply schedule, for what he says envisages only the entrepreneurs' offer. Equally appropriately, he could have called the magnitude determined by the intersection "effective supply," meaning "aggregate supply." But if he and his disciples had always substituted the words "effective supply" where they have used the term in this sense, they would have seen all the issues in a quite different light.

It is to be my case that entrepreneurs are intermediaries and merely interpreters (as distinct from creators) of the demands they express. I shall argue that their offer† is a demand determinant of neither the real nor the money value of output as a whole; that it merely determines

---

*Adam Smith called this, very badly, "absolute demand."[6] Keynes probably inherited *the term*, although not the connotation he gave to it, from Marshall's *Principles*.[7]

†The entrepreneurs' offer is variously described as "prospective yields," "predicted return over cost," "the marginal efficiency of capital," "anticipated profits," "investment demand."

(a) the relative values of different parts of output, and (b) the rate of interest; that it is irrelevant to the magnitude or value of output (apart from its possible repercussions upon the rate of realized savings); and that only the determinants of the number of money units and the demand for monetary services can influence the *money valuation* of a given flow of productive services.

Certainly entrepreneurs demand the productive services which are embodied into assets to replace or add to inventories of products being sold, or agents of production being used or used up. But as I shall be explaining, *in their entrepreneurial rôle,* the extent of their bidding against one another for such services does not determine the "quantity" or value of output; it determines only *the form* taken by income (output in general) ; whilst (i) the particular products they demand, and (ii) the proportions in which they cause output to be appropriate for mere replacement of, or net accumulation of productive power, are a response to demands expressed by income receivers in their capacity as consumers and savers. In Chapter X, I shall suggest that the origin of the fallacy expressed in Keynes' effective demand notion is exposed as soon as we have obtained conceptual clarity (a) on the nature of the entrepreneurial function, and (b) on the distinction between the offer of assets for services (and *vice versa)* and the offer of services for services.

Without realizing it Keynes was, I suggest, actually trying, in his aggregate supply and demand functions, to represent the Say law! But such an aim is impossible under any macro-economic construction; and his fallacious method led him to think of demand in general (his aggregate demand function) as somehow originating, not in supply in general, but in entrepreneurial expectations.

But let us return to the concept of "demand in general." It is a difficult one to grasp. Carelessly or mechanically handled it can lead to quite untenable conclusions. When I use the term "demand" in contexts in which it obviously means "demand in general," I shall really mean *"demands* in general" and *not a measurable aggregate.* Because the supply of one thing is the demand for another (some noncompeting thing) and because services may be offered for other services or for assets (or assets offered for services or other assets*), all that can be meant when we talk of "an increase of demand in general" is that *services* are being priced so as to permit their exchange to a greater extent, up to the point at which they are fully absorbed, or that the flow of services is increasing because productive capacity is increasing and is being utilized. The exchange of *assets* for one another is a quite different matter. But when services are priced for full consumption or full absorption into the next stage of pro-

---

*The offer of services for assets and *vice versa* does not, I repeat, affect the scale of prices. It determines the rate of interest.

duction, there is always an "effective" demand for all raw materials, work in progress, intermediate products and final products as additional services are embodied into them. Reserves—inventories performing the productive service of availability*—constitute only an apparent exception. Demand in general becomes "effective" therefore according to the degree in which services are appropriately priced; and this implies the appropriate pricing also of the products into which they are embodied.

I shall sometimes use the term "uninflated demand" when I discuss demand in this sense; I shall then mean that the "demands" I am describing have not been accompanied by any contraction of the measuring rod of value;† and I shall show that the Keynesian "effective demand" is simply the sum of money demands, inflated in the measure necessary to bring relative prices into better co-ordination, *in the circumstances in which inflation can have that effect.*‡

It was partly through the clumsiness of the macro-economic approach that Keynes came to believe that the idleness of valuable productive resources (he stressed labor) is caused by factors other than the mispricing of the flow of services and products. For instance, the clumsy concept of *the* price of labor, conceived of as *the* hourly money wage (a sort of average wage-rate of labor of all kinds)** is, in a large part of the argument, taken as constant. And when Keynes did think in terms of this "price" having a crucial task, he seemed to assume that the adjustment required to induce full employment is an equal percentage reduction in all wages-rates (see pp. 165-9), and secondly to assume that rises or falls in the general level of wage-rates correspond to rises or falls in the general flow of wage receipts. Neither assumption is acceptable.

7.—The macro-economic approach makes abstraction of the vital and continuous process of *substitution of the least-cost method of achieving ends*, i.e., of the process of competition. Classical theory, on the other hand, has always focused attention on just this aspect, the price consequences of substitution being recognized as effecting co-ordination in a constantly changing world. Whilst economists in the classical tradition do not ignore the importance of aggregates for certain purposes, they stress rather the importance of increments and margins as the determinants which operate the system; and these are the ultimate determinants

---

*This includes inventories in the shops and in the home. Such inventories are productive assets and the services of these assets are being demanded.

†When I use the term "money demand," this will imply that the money unit *may* have changed in value.

‡I.e., when the inflation or the actual rate of inflation is unexpected by a sufficient number of people, and the money illusion is a material factor.

**Different actual units of labor are supposed to be weighted in proportion to their skill, which can only be measured in terms of value. See my *Theory of Idle Resources*, pp. 32-34.

of the magnitudes "employment" and "output," even when cheap money has facilitated the required changes in relative values.*

8.—It was out of his speculations about the demands which express time and liquidity preference that Keynes was led to his revolutionary idea of interest. He claimed that the determinants of the rate of interest are the supply of and demand for money ("liquidity"). Now, the intelligent tyro in economics jumps quite naturally to this kind of conclusion, which Keynes obviously thought he could make the keystone of his system. For instance, Boswell records how Samuel Johnson, referring to a question which had always puzzled him as a young man, remarked: "Why is it that the interest of money is lower when money is plentiful; for five pounds has the same proportion of value to a hundred pounds when money is plentiful as when it is scarce? A lady explained to me, 'It is (said she) because when money is plentiful there are so many more who have money to lend that they bid down one another.' "[10]

It is not surprising that an idea which has so immediate a plausibility should have had a powerful attraction when enunciated with all the authority of a prominent pundit. Yet as I shall demonstrate, it is wholly wrong. What is true is that *an increasing* number of money units (as distinct from *an increased* number) in relation to the aggregate real value of money will be accompanied by a market rate of interest below the natural level and, time preference being given, a reduced market rate. (See Chapter V.) But this is the pure orthodoxy with Keynes belittled.

Today, I believe, nearly all economists recognize that in dealing with this topic, Keynes was dismissing the basic and ultimate determinants of interest altogether and concentrating attention upon factors which previous economists had rightly recognized as merely short-term influences.† But because Keynes' concepts and methods had inhibited consideration of the possibility of *costs and prices* moving at levels which are chronically too high (absolutely, or in relation to expectations) to permit full employment, he was led to the conclusion that it is the rate of interest which might "fluctuate for decades about a level which is chronically too high for full employment."[11] That the value of the rate of interest which is consistent with "full employment" is simply a rate sufficiently below the natural to bring about the inflationary increase in "expenditure" needed to induce the release of withheld capacity was subtly (I do not say purposely) hidden.‡

Keynes' belief that he had found a single, universal solvent for price disharmonies dominated all his thinking. In throwing over not only the

*The actual working of this process is discussed in Chap. IV.
†I refer to his theory of interest again below, pp.102-4.
‡It is doubtful, however, whether Keynes was indeed envisaging such a divergence. (See below p. 33, third footnote).

classical theory of interest, but the whole of the Wicksellian refinement
of it, he contended that, if we must talk about the ideal rate of interest,
we should conceive of it as the rate which guarantees full employment.[12] He called it "the optimum rate." But how could any *single*
value-relationship, even so crucial a value-ratio as the rate of interest,
guarantee or ensure full employment? If the right to price services
above the point which enables their full absorption is permitted, how
can any rate of interest put things right? For instance, if the maintenance
of interest at a rate below the natural for a while is used to raise final
prices relative to costs, what is to prevent costs being raised again? This
is, of course, what has almost universally happened when such policies
have been followed. If the answer is, "But we ought not to have allowed
that to have happened," my point has been admitted. Keynes and his
disciples often appear to be expecting one value (the rate of interest)
to rectify all the disharmonies, due to sectionalist pricing, which result
in general underemployment; although at other times it is the *expenditure* engendered by "the optimum rate" which is stressed.

9.—Again, it was the sheer cumbersomeness of macro-economics which
led to the cardinal error that the "volumes" of "real income," or "employment," or "output" are determined by monetary or fiscal policy or the
rate of interest *via* the magnitude "effective demand." The truth is (and
this is orthodox teaching) that the "volume of employment" is determined, in any given state of knowledge and accumulated resources, by
the extent to which valuable resources are permitted—by relative prices
and direct withholdings—to be fully utilized. Changes in the value of the
money unit (caused by changes in the relations of market interest to
natural interest) have an influence only in so far as they affect the relations of prices (at each stage of production)* to money income.

The mere fact that the reduction of the value of the money unit happens to be one way of inducing an expansion of output or inducing increased savings (and hence increased future output) when productive
capacity has been withheld from use, does not justify the formulation
of a *monetary theory of output or employment*. There are conditions in
which monetary policy and output are not unconnected; but even in
those conditions monetary policy is but one factor in output determination. The virtue of the orthodox theory is that it takes all such factors
into account, and is therefore a general theory. The vice of the Keynesian
theory is that it is a special theory. It has often been said that the orthodox economists overlooked the connection between monetary policy and
income.† That is false. There never have been any doubts about the

---

*See below, Chap. IV.
†E.g., by Dillard in Kurihara, *Post-Keynesian Economics*, p. 3.

possibility of inducing the release of capacity through an inflationary increase in M or V; but it has been recognized that the co-ordination is achieved in exactly the same way as when it is brought about by price and cost adjustment.* It is Keynesianism which draws attention away from the crucial determinants in which monetary policy is merely one factor.

Hence, the stress in *The General Theory* on the monetary or expenditure determinants of income and demand, misdirects attention from the relevant truths (a) that monetary factors are an influence upon the *size* of real income (as distinct from its *measurement* in money units) solely through their influence upon prices at different stages of production, and (b) that those changes in prices are equally *possible* (I do not say *"equally easy"*) if the money unit (in which income and other economic magnitudes are measured) is of constant or defined value. The result of this misdirection is that it is hardly possible for the typical Keynesian to envisage the basic relationship between ends and means, expressed in the phenomenon of scarcity or utility; and it is in the light of these relationships alone that a satisfactory view of the functioning of economic society is possible.

10.—If the distinction between ends and means is clearly perceived, we can think of the people expressing preferences respecting ends for which the means are scarce (by buying or refraining from buying different quantities of different things in the market) as exercising "consumers' sovereignty." But in his justification of Keynesian doctrine, Dillard says that "it is pure euphemism to say that consumption is the ultimate purpose of production." It is, he says, "the expectation of being able to convert real goods into money at a profit" which "is the significant motivation."†(12) Yet the entrepreneur who (i) predicts successfully the nature and scale of the demands of those who exercise consumer preference, and (ii) achieves the least-cost method of responding to those preferences, is aways in the last resort an interpreter of consumers' preference. And he is rewarded by profits when his interpretation is wise or lucky (just as he is penalized by losses when he is unwise or unlucky). Is it not obvious that, merely because entrepreneurial predictions and calculations are made in terms of money values, we are not forced to a monetary theory of output?

Curiously enough, Dillard's use of the words "at a profit" ought to have led him to see that conversion into money has nothing to do with the matter. It is almost always possible to convert any product into

---

*E.g., see Cannan, *An Economist's Protest*, p. 397.

†It would of course be unrealistic to ignore "the money illusion." But it is even more unrealistic to dismiss concern with the "real."

money *at some price*; but the ability to do so does not mean that the type of good produced has been a profitable choice. It is the profit, not the acquisition of money, which is the proof of successful prediction. In other words, profit-seeking (or loss-avoidance) provides the motivation, not the fact that economic calculation usually takes places in money terms and transactions normally require the transfer of money.

11.—However, Dillard is led to the conclusion that, because firms think and calculate in terms of money, "money is genuine wealth and real goods are an artificial and transitory embodiment of hoped-for values to be realized by their conversion into money." [14] Money is, he contends, "the socially recognized *form* of wealth." Hence Mercantilism, "based on the realistic view that money is wealth (to the individual merchant)," is correct. [15] Of course, what he should have said is, "money is the socially recognized *measure* of wealth (value)." The liquid assets of firms are not "wealth" in a greater degree than any other of their assets. They are productive in the same sort of way.* And when I say this, I am not in the least blind to the fact that in practice the functioning of every business entity demands the continuous replacement of the bank balance and the cash in the till, in the same manner that it requires the replacement of all other inventories and equipment. I have stated, stressed and persistently reiterated this elementary truth to a generation of students of business administration (in discussing the "finance budgets" which must accompany a firm's "sales budgets," "purchasing budgets" and "operations budgets"). But this does not mean, in Dillard's words, that I can teach students that "money is . . . . the universal objective of business activity." [16] That is the very idea that students usually have when they come to me, before they have thought much about the subject. To give them a realistic insight into the nature of the business world it is essential to eradicate this misconception. And yet, on the same sort of elementary fallacy, the Keynesians have been attempting to build a system of thought!

It may be objected that not all Keynesians hold views as extreme as Dillard's. But I know of no renunciation of his interpretation of Keynes by any Keynesian of eminence, and Dillard obviously regards himself as a faithful disciple and expositor.

12.—Not only have the Keynesians succeeded in diverting attention from the possibility of achieving full employment through price adjustment, but on the rare occasions on which they feel obliged to refer to the issue, they seem to argue (a) that it is a politically impracticable remedy (meaning politically *unacceptable*) and (b) that in any case it would be a self-defeating remedy. They have made (b) a convenient

---

*See pp. 91, 106.

second line of defense. It was first erected with any pretense to rigorous argument* in *The General Theory*. It is based not only on the assumption that politics or other institutional factors make *difficult* or impossible the adjustments necessary for full employment, but on an argument which has had several quite different—but all wholly fallacious attempted justifications. "It cannot be done," they seem to say, "and in any case it is a waste of time trying to show that it can be done, because we can produce even more fundamental arguments to show that it must necessarily be self-defeating." The most plausible of such arguments are to the effect that the reduction of those wage-rates or prices which have resulted from, or have themselves caused wasteful idleness, is a futile method of bringing back resources into use because it must inevitably result in a shrinkage of income. The chief *originality* in Keynesian teaching rests in this thesis. What is new is the argument that price and cost adjustments must *aggravate* the situation. Harrod has stated the Keynesian position as follows: "If a certain level of interest is established, which is inconsistent with full activity, *no flexibility or mobility in other parts of the system will get the system to move to full activity*."[17]†
(My italics). It is obvious that, in this passage, Harrod is thinking, as was Keynes himself, of the absolute level of market interest and not of its relation to the natural level.‡

13.—In one of the approaches which has proved to be most influential, the Keynesian doctrine is based on the notion that the community may wish to consume *plus* accumulate net ("invest") an "amount" which is less than the full flow of valuable (i.e., scarce) productive services. But this notion has always seemed to me to be self-contradictory. Productive services have value (i.e., they are scarce) solely (i) because people *want* to consume them, or the products into which they can be embodied (or the products which such products can in turn provide), either in the

---

*See Chap. IX
†The tiny element of truth in Harrod's rather subtle statement rests in the power of deviations of interest from the natural level to co-ordinate. But the rate of interest proper is simply a ratio. It is something which *results from* economic choice and activity, not something which can be said to influence the volume (as distinct from the form) of activity. It is determined, like all other manifestations of value, by preferences on the one side and scarcities on the other. And the action needed to cause the money or market rate of interest to diverge from the non-inflationary or non-deflationary level (the natural level) can be regarded as a determinant of the volume of activity, only in so far as it indirectly brings about co-ordinative adjustments in relative values. That is the tiny element of truth.
‡This is equally obvious in Keynes' reference (quoted above, p.29) to a rate of interest which might "fluctuate for decades about a level which is chronically too high for full employment;"[18] for had he meant the noncoincidence of market and natural levels, he would certainly have said, "with the scale of prices falling for several decades," or "with the value of the money unit rising," or words to the same effect.

immediate future or the more distant future, and (ii) because people not only *want* these services but have something valuable to offer for them. It seems to follow that demands in general can be deficient only in the sense that supply is withheld. In the course of this book I shall be trying to show that there are no exceptions to this simple thesis.

14.—It is appropriate to conclude this brief statement of the nature of Keynesianism by insisting that because orthodox theory rejects the mercantilist view of money, it does not overlook or segregate the monetary factor, as the Keynesians like to assert. On the contrary, monetary theory is more of an integral part of economic theory as a whole in the orthodox analysis than it is in the Keynesian. Indeed, in the orthodox treatment, monetary theory is so intimately woven into the general texture of theory that superficial economists have failed to perceive the implications of money in every line, paragraph, page and chapter, and explicitly in every reference to price or value. It would be less unfair to say that the Keynesians (and some of the post-Wicksellian Swedish economists) have tended to think of—or at any rate to treat— monetary theory as something quite apart from economic theory as a whole. Then, having fallen into all the logical traps to which so indefensible a procedure has led them, they try to marry the creature of their misunderstandings—monetary theory—to "real theory" in order to explain income or employment, and to decry orthodox theory for attempting to be fruitful without such a marriage.* And this seems to have led the new Keynesians, like the old, to the belief that monetary or fiscal policy, through the control of spending, can act as a universal solvent of all price disharmonies and, like an invisible hand, make unnecessary, or less necessary, the difficult task of overhauling the institutions which make up the price system.

15.—I find it quite impossible to judge exactly how much of Keynes' basic teachings are still held by those who originally accepted them; for many of those who seem unprepared to defend reasoning of the kind to which I have been referring continue to use the defective concepts which emerged out of it. *Keynes established, I suggest, a fashion of subtle equivocation in monetary discussion, a fashion which, through habit and domination, has become almost a convention. This comes out in countless different forms to which I shall have to be constantly referring.* An example is found in the modern tendency to attribute inflation to "excess demand" instead of to monetary policy (i.e., instead of to a policy which causes or permits MV to increase relatively to T). It is all very well to answer, "But we all know that is what is meant!" The fact is that this manner of expression and a host of others (a recently published

---

*I return to this topic on pp. 88-90.

British report—the Radcliffe Report—teems with examples) , diverts attention from the deliberateness or weakness of action which results in every depreciation or loss of parity of a currency.

Consider, for instance, the Radcliffe Committee's reference to what they call "the pre-war dilemma of choosing between an absolute contraction of money incomes or changing the terms of access to foreign currencies and commerce."[19] Such a remark typically presents the real "prewar dilemma" in a false light. The alternative which then created the statesman's quandary was that of choosing between direct co-ordination to permit an expansion of real and money incomes without changing the terms of "access to foreign currencies", and cheap money which did change those terms. Of course, direct co-ordination was politically difficult; whilst, because in those days the inflationary consequences were not perceived by the community, cheap money was politically less difficult. But that was the true dilemma; and, if the argument of my Chapter XVIII is accepted, that same dilemma is likely once again to confront those who fashion the economic policies of governments.

It is because of an approach which tacitly suppresses these issues that the Radcliffe Committee are led to the untenable conclusion that "the immediate pursuit" either of "the ideal of monetary stability," or that of "full employment"—*regarded as alternatives*—will "disrupt" the economy. But the *current dilemma*, which they believe they thus describe exists only because of a failure to recognize that full employment is obtainable without the sacrifice of monetary stability, through the elimination of those activities which cause the source of uninflated income to contract.

So firm a hold has Keynesianism obtained, however, that it is now common to talk of checking expansion when what is meant is curbing inflation. Everything is looked at in terms of the State, through the monetary authority, controlling the rate of activity by determining the rate of expenditure. But if governments are to be regarded as responsible for *economic progress*, they can play their part in two ways: (a) by providing and administering a framework conducive to (i) security of contract (and a defined value of the money unit is crucial here) and (ii) flexibility (and this includes price flexibility); and (b) by encouraging or compelling thrift. And if they are expected to control the "level of economic activity," then as I shall show, they can do no more than influence or regulate the release of productive capacity which has been withheld from use by sectionalist pricing or control of output (perhaps imposed by the State itself). And this they may do through inflation, or by means of policies designed to induce direct co-ordination.

In the assumption that monetary control of activity is the means to economic health, hesitant lip service is quite often paid to the ideal of stability of prices—usually with a casual reference to the supposed orthodox attitude towards monetary stability. It is implied, as a rule, that such stability was not an objective under the gold standard. The student is not told that the objective of a stable real value of the money unit was implied by the choice of the standard; that, under wise administration of the system (in which the ability to convert was never subjected to strain), the real value of the money unit was expected to vary very little from year to year; and that although monetary policy was not regarded as in any way concerned with the objectives of full employment and steady growth, the monetary authority was recognized as having its part to play in a stable and progressive economy (namely in the scrupulous avoidance of cheap money, so as to eliminate the necessity for deflationary rectification and the fluctuations in the scale of prices so caused).

Admittedly, the notion that any defensible monetary or fiscal policy could ensure the pricing of goods and services so that people are always able and willing to buy them, would have been generally regarded as absurd by the orthodox economists. But it *is* absurd! The Keynesians have merely introduced involved ways of saying things which have made such a notion appear plausible.

Yet so attractive has the Keynesian teaching proved that most modern governments seem to be actuated by the conviction that a co-ordinated economy requires collective action to ensure a "balance" between (a) "savings" and "investment," (b) government revenues and expenditures, and (c) imports and exports. In subsequent chapters, I shall pursue more deeply the origins of these notions, which I shall trace in part to the fallacy that expenditure generates money income and "effective demand" (discussed in Chap. VIII), a fallacy which is aggravated by conceptual confusion concerning the magnitudes "savings" and "investment" (discussed in Chap. X).

REFERENCES

(1) KEYNES, *The General Theory*, p.4. (2) WILLIAMS, *An Appraisal of Keynesian Economics*, A.E.R., Proceedings, 1948, p.279. (3) HUTT, *Theory of Idle Resources*, p.34. (4) KEYNES, *op. cit.*, p.245. (5) *Ibid.*, p.vii. (6) ADAM SMITH, *Wealth of Nations*, chap. VII. (7) MARSHALL, *Principles*, 8th ed., pp.511, 699. (8) KEYNES, *op. cit.*, p.25. (9) *Ibid.*, p.55. (10) BOSWELL, *The Life of Samuel Johnson*, Newnes ed., Vol. II, p.295. (11) KEYNES, *op. cit.*, p.204. (12) *Ibid.*, p.243. (13) DILLARD, *Theory of a Monetary Economy*, in Kurihara, *Post-Keynesian Economics*, p.27. (14) *Ibid.*, p.28. (15) *Ibid.*, pp.28-29. (16) *Ibid.*, p.30. (17) HARROD, *Keynes, The Economist*, in Harris, *The New Economics*, p.69. (18) KEYNES, *op. cit.*, p.204. (19) Report of Radcliffe Committee (Committee on the Working of the Monetary System), par. 42.

Chapter III

CONSEQUENCES OF THE KEYNESIAN REMEDY

SUMMARY

1.—As a method of bringing relative prices into co-ordination, the inflation which Keynesianism implies has the following defects. 2.—It can have no co-ordinative or stabilizing tendency if a stable scale of prices is to be maintained, and it demands the continuous deception of the public. 3.—It leaves intact the basic causes of disco-ordination, 4—and indeed discourages truly effective remedial action. 5.—Its effects are arbitrary, 6.—and because of uncertainty about the speed and duration of inflation, it necessitates recourse to all the paraphernalia of exchange controls and other authoritarian measures. 7.—It transfers power from society to the politicians. 8.—Its sociological consequences are deplorable. 9.—It buys off antisocial pricing at an appalling cost, a cost which technological progress has hidden of recent years. 10.—Bronfenbrenner seems to welcome Keynesian policy because it is, he says, succeeding (through secular inflation) in achieving the ends for which Marx was striving. 11.—But this trend may be reversed through current, bitter experience; and through the rise of "defense groups" demanding (i) resistance to the pressure groups and (ii) the permanent cessation of inflation.

1.—To consider the *consequences* of Keynesian policies, one can hardly avoid discussing the phenomenon of creeping inflation. But as I have already conceded, not all Keynesians will agree that the tacit approval of inflation is implied by their teachings. I must therefore ask those readers who may feel that I am here misrepresenting Keynesian thought to withhold their judgment at this stage. They will readily admit that, wherever Keynesian ideas have been influential in policy, inflation has in fact been experienced; and in this chapter I am concerned with the apparent results of that policy. They may well object that Keynesian maxims must not be held to be responsible for the inflationary experiences to which I shall be referring. But I shall try to convince them that, if they take that line, they are assuming that imposed restrictions or controls can effectively repress forces which would otherwise be expressed in open inflation, whilst I hope to make it clear in due course that the repression of inflation merely destroys its crude co-ordinative power. Hence the reasonableness of *my assumption* in this chapter that the full employment which the world has witnessed since the 'thirties is attributable to inflation and not to other virtues of Keynesian policy must be judged from arguments which will be developed in later chapters.

The issue can be summarized as follows: The Keynesians have centered attention upon the possibility that, in the equation $PT = MV$, an increase in MV (i.e., in M or in V) may cause an increase, not in P but in T (output) owing to the release of withheld capacity. Economists have always known that an increase in MV *could* result not only in an increase in P but subsequently in an increase in T; and this has been explicitly recognized at least since the days of Hume. But since Hume and before Keynes, it was almost always tacitly accepted that that was a very bad way of increasing T (as compared with co-ordination through price adjustment).

In Keynes' earlier writings, the possibility of a rise in prices was ignored and stability of the scale of prices was accepted as the ideal. Subsequently, however, the argument *seems* to have developed that, whilst prices will rise as increased expenditure stimulates output, the inflation is nevertheless defensible. (See Chap. VII). I.e., it is assumed that, up to the point of full employment, output will increase in sufficient measure to make inflation a lesser evil than withheld capacity.* Had the assumption been unambiguously enunciated in these terms, subsequent controversies would have been more fruitful. The main issue would have boiled down to the effectiveness and justice of inflation as a means of releasing capacity, in comparison with other means available.

2.—The Keynesians seem often to be claiming that their remedy in some way creates stability. Yet if a tolerable scale of prices (or any form of convertibility) is to be maintained, the "maintenance of effective demand" seems inevitably to lead to a boom; and hence either to the necessity for a period of drastic general price adjustments or to a period of depression. For just as cost rigidity downwards is the main cause of the persistence of depression (in the absence of inflation), so is the very much less marked cost rigidity upwards, which is experienced during an inflation, the main cause which prolongs a boom. The lag of cost-increases below revenue-increases explains why inflation succeeds in stimulating outputs—the *real boom;* and the fact that the flow of residual incomes (generally speaking, entrepreneurial incomes) increases relatively to the flow of wage and other contractual incomes and contains an illusory element (due to capital gains—caused by interest below the natural—tending to be treated as income), explains in part why inflation can so easily induce a *speculative boom* (through causing exaggerated predictions of yields).

Obviously, then, we are unable to draw a common (and politically very popular) Keynesian conclusion, namely, that if wage receipts rise as rapidly as residual receipts, the boom can be prolonged. What *is* true, and this is the truth which is often missed, is that if wage-rates and other costs were perfectly flexible upwards, it would not pay to indulge in inflation. Inflation would then be purposeless, ceasing to have any co-ordinative tendency (although it might certainly continue through mere habit, like continuance with a drug which has been known to give relief in the past). For as I shall be reiterating in this work, the public's expectations tend to force the scale of prices towards the level to which it is believed that policy is aiming (drift being regarded as one policy). Anticipated inflation becomes pointless; and the use of the monetary system as an instrument of "national policy" is practicable only as long as the public do not understand or can be deceived about objectives.

Indeed, the degree of inflation needed (in any given situation with unemployment) to bring relative prices into co-ordination, increases in proportion to the extent to which the inflation can be forecast. In the absence of "controls" which, if politically tolerable, would make the inflationary remedy redundant, the so-called "maintenance of effective de-

---

*See p.21, first footnote.

mand" can succeed only when the majority of people can be misled into thinking that the expansion of credit is about to cease or that it will be much more moderate than it is destined to be. Unless this deception is possible, those who are in a position to raise prices and wage-rates will do so in advance of the declining value of the money unit so that the original degree of withheld capacity will tend to be perpetuated. To this important question, Chapter XVIII is devoted.

Inflation once commenced appears, indeed, to be self-perpetuating and, in the Keynesian atmosphere, inevitable. Theoretically there is no limit to the extent to which V can rise for this reason. But if M does not increase, and the monetary authority does not in fact intend to increase it, it seems likely that wrong expectations will soon be corrected; for as prices rise (through the *increasing* V) more money units will be required for the same real volume of transactions and more demanded therefore. In the present age, however, monetary authorities nearly always remove this deflationary barrier to the private reinforcement of their policy. For by this time they have all forgotten the simple lessons which economists learned in the days of the pre-1844 currency controversies, and it appears to be their unmistakable duty to respond to the "obviously legitimate" demand for money so expressed. Moreover, it has been noticed that, in so far as any inflation is initiated or enforced *via* budget deficits, each deficit tends to generate an inflation of government expenditure in anticipation of revenue, and hence to cause a succession of further deficits.

3.—In practice, it is seldom possible to resort to inflation merely as a transition from an era of dislocating rigidity to an era of price flexibility. Raising the general scale of prices can hardly serve as a stepping stone to a regime in which it will be possible to establish a defined measuring rod of value as well as maintain full employment. *For the institutional setup which permits the rigidities evaded by the inflation will remain unreformed.* Withheld capacity will return and further inflation will be demanded on the same old grounds.

It is, I think, for this reason that, even during the practice of inflation itself, some concrete recognition of the true remedy seems often to be discernible; for whilst the depreciation of the money unit is in progress, it is almost universally accompanied by measures to prevent, or at least to discourage direct disco-ordination of the price system. It is recognized that antisocial sectionalist action to force up wage-rates and prices, unless checked, would cause *runaway* inflations. But the required checks are usually imposed, not in the form of strict antimonopoly control or action to prevent trade-unions from reducing aggregate uninflated wages, but by the crude expedients of price control, moral exhortations to industry, commerce and organized labor, and very occasionally wage-ceilings.

4.—Perhaps the strongest objection to the attempt to maintain co-ordination by "maintaining effective demand" is, then, that it removes (a) pressures to co-ordinating adjustments within the existing framework of institutions and (b) the incentive to fundamental reform of the frame-work. The politicians may feel that far-reaching reforms are needed. But cheap money eases things for the time being and enables them to procrastinate. For this reason it permits the survival of distortions in the price structure or concomitant distortions in the form taken by produc-tion functions. This is partly because it *obscures* the inherent contradic-tions and inconsistencies in the functioning of economic institutions due to sectionalist pricing, but partly because it *destroys the collective incen-tive* to refashion institutions. Perpetual recourse to the line of least re-sistance results in unplanned institutional modifications which stand as powerful, semipermanent obstacles to a more efficient, just and stable social order.

I have already referred to the easy solution which inflation offers to the problems created by disco-ordination. It is because the method is so easy that the great nations have been able superficially to eradicate vir-tually all signs of the "trade cycle"—beyond minor recessions and up-swings—since the 1930's, without any attempts at major institutional re-form. What "sound finance" *did* do in the pre-Keynesian era was to create every incentive to reprice services and products the sale of which was being held up, as well as to create a strong social motive to eradicate practices which reduced the flow of uninflated income. In the private sphere, the pressures were fairly successful, and had it not been for con-trary action by the State, they could, I believe, have rescued the economy —without inflation—from the great depression. But the reaction of gov-ernments was, typically enough, to impose further disco-ordination. For instance, the multitude of relatively small-scale withholdings of capacity throughout the world which had developed during the 1920's had caused so serious a contraction in uninflated demand that large-scale State-imposed output and trade restrictions were resorted to (at that time mainly valorization schemes and tariffs). The repercussions of the situ-ation caused by these measures aggravated the decline in uninflated world demand. There was then an enhanced incentive for cheap money. But the degree of inflation which was possible before the general aban-donment of convertibility in the 'thirties could not, as B. H. Beckhart has pointed out, "bring about that readjustment of retail and wholesale prices and costs, on the basis of which any substantial improvement in business must be founded."[1] It is precisely because there could have been no other way out if there had been perseverance with "sound finance," that the demand for direct co-ordination and institutional re-form may well have become irresistible (especially if the bulk of the economists had recognized the necessity and pressed for the reforms required).

The actual working of the mechanism of value determination certainly needed re-designing. Difficult institutional changes were called for —not simple monetary panaceas, but carefully planned structural adjustments based on patient, painstaking studies of the psychological, sociological and political resistances likely to be encountered. No attempts whatsoever have been made at such replanning.

It is possible to achieve a money unit of stable value without the general problem of economic co-ordination having been successfully solved. But if so, it must be at the expense of *more conspicuous forms* of waste, including unemployment. Only if the problems of inflation and disco-ordination are tackled simultaneously is it possible for "sound money" to accompany "full employment." *Hence, seriously to advocate the cessation of inflation is to recommend far-reaching but perfectly obvious reforms of a nonmonetary kind.* Wise monetary policy *demands* non-monetary co-ordination; and that means in practice reforms to achieve such flexibility of values and prices as permits the free allocation of means to ends (whether those ends are expressed individually or collectively).

5.—The arbitrariness of the inflationary remedy should be obvious; for is not the extent of the withholding of capacity in different sections of the economy (which it is intended to offset) wholly arbitrary? We are often told by those Keynesians who admit the inflationary nature of their proposals, that only a "moderate" measure of inflation is needed,* just sufficient to reduce real wage-rates by the required amount. But are we to judge the moderateness of inflation by the measure in which the withholding of capacity is raising costs relatively to the flow of output? That is, can we say that inflation is "moderate" if it no more than keeps pace with the rate of withholding—in the sense that the rate of release of the flow of productive services is equated with the rate of withholding? The notion is preposterous.

Moreover, recourse to the maintenance of "effective demand" as a means of countering withheld capacity discourages mobility of resources in response to change and leads to misdirection of resources and effort in many forms. For instance (especially when devaluation is needed in order to permit its continuance), it assists export industries at the expense of (i) a burden (*not necessarily an unfair burden*) on the sheltered industries, and (ii) a burden (an unfair burden) upon industries using imported materials and upon consumers of imported goods. And the relief obtained by devaluation is due to a particularly short-sighted

*See pp.126-7.

type of adjustment. Prices are adjusted for foreign purchasers but not for the benefit of domestic purchasers. Is it not a stupidly crude way, in a civilized society, of bringing resources in the export industries into full utilization and international values into equilibrium?

6.—I referred earlier to the claim that Keynesian policy creates stability in some sense. The truth is that the inflationary policy implied gives rise to a relatively painless, yet for that reason a more insidious form of uncertainty. One of the weaknesses of *deliberate deflations* (such as that by means of which Britain returned to gold, from 1920 to 1925, and then maintained parity until 1931) is the difficulty of estimating the extent to which prices will ultimately fall (a weakness due to the existence of price and wage-rate rigidities believed to be unstable. See pp. 64, 170-4). But with *inflation,* where convertibility obligations no longer exist, or where for other reasons such obligations are accepted on an insufficiently wide scale,* it is never possible to forecast its duration, or the rate at which it is to occur, or the currency value which will ultimately be established; and if it were possible to predict its future course with certainty, the inflation would, for the reasons to which I have just referred (sections 2 and 3, and see Chap XVIII), lose its ability to release withheld capacity.

Hence, in the absence of convertibility (and I include an obligation to maintain the scale of prices constant as a form of convertibility) or fixed exchanges (which imply some kind of convertibility), an inflationary policy will prove to be far too disco-ordinating to be tolerated without exchange equalization or exchange control. Unless resort is had to such controls, exchange rates will be left subject to the changing balance of speculative predictions, and fluctuations of a wide amplitude tend to destroy all sense of entrepreneurial security. Ah!, my Keynesian friends will say, "you are admitting the deficiencies of the price mechanism." But it is folly to suggest that exchange control is called for during inflation *because of the deficiencies of the "unassisted market mechanism."* When a market is dealing in packets of commodities, the amount of the contents of which is constantly changing in an unpredictable manner, we can hardly expect the market to do more than reflect current guesses of speculators about what the packets will prove to contain at different future times. And when monetary authorities everywhere are trying to "create confidence" by statements, gestures and procedures which are intended to mislead or at least to mask the true situation,† it is small wonder that the forecasts of speculators lead to disconcerting fluc-

---

*E.g., as under the convertibility of the dollar into gold since 1934 and the maintenance for long periods (buttressed by exchange and trade controls) of many other currencies at parity with the dollar.

†See Chapter XVIII.

tuations. In such circumstances, exchange equalization or control is inevitable. But it can provide security only against short-run fluctuations. It can, of itself, create no certainty of long-term stability; it is no substitute for the security of convertibility; and from the standpoint of international dealings it is wholly disco-ordinative machinery.*

7.—Not only does the Keynesian system require arbitrary State controls, but the particular form of inflation which Keynes recommended—the "socialization" of investment, which he thought would facilitate the spending of income—means, in practice, the transfer of power to determine ends from the market to the State, from the people to the politicians, from society to a group, from the many to the few. Some will welcome such a transfer: others will deplore it. The tragedy is that many of those whose ethical convictions cause them to abhor the totalitarian system, have failed to perceive that the transfer of power from society to the politician is a step towards the destruction of the good society which is their ideal.

8.—Not the least serious of the consequences of having abandoned the policy of "sound money" has been adverse sociological reactions. Almost all inflations have some of the features of *repressed* inflation. And where "controls" intended to curb the effects of an increase in deposits and currency in circulation exist, enterprise tends to be diverted into black-market operations, and to lobbying for licenses or dealing in them, etc. We all know that, as the necessary "controls" increase, opportunities for corruption multiply and the temptations to corruption are fostered. For this reason also, the incentives to the investment of time, effort and money in skill acquisition are dampened through the resultant narrowing of the gap between the remuneration of skilled and unskilled work. But most important of all, cheap money tends to weaken the process of what Turroni has called "the natural selection of firms."[2] The cessation of bankruptcies, which is so often and so easily hailed as evidence

---

*Once obligations to redeem currencies have again been undertaken, and once the willingness and ability of the authorities to maintain those obligations have been accepted, the money markets of the world will be fully capable of re-creating the pre-1914 measure of orderliness in monetary relations. True, the I.M.F. creates some order in the relations between currencies today; but that is not because it has provided a superior mechanism to the gold standard: it is because it acts as *some* limitation or brake on the autonomy of individual monetary authorities (although it is not effective against inflation of the dollar). But many countries still need to rely on exchange controls in order to carry out their agreements. And other contracts between nations have had to be concluded in order to curb monetary nationalism. Is it not significant that the virtues of all these agreements are those which are found in the fullest measure when currencies are based on clear-cut, iron-clad contracts to convert, as they were in the gold standard days?

of "prosperity" is properly seen, wrote Turroni, "a symptom of the ma-laise of the economic system."[3] It means that the incentives of both rewards for efficiency or success and penalties for inefficiency or failure of entrepreneurial activity are weakened.* Nor can we be blind to the distributive injustices associated with inflation; its merciless treatment of the politically weak;† its tendency to reward those responsible for the disco-ordinations which it so crudely rectifies; its penalization of those whose actions have in no sense been responsible (those classes which loathe the idea of striking or threatening to strike—the salaried middle classes, the thrifty *rentiers*, the learned and charitable institutions which have relied upon interest on endowments, the pensioners, and so forth) ; its encouragement of a sordid scramble on the part of each organized group to get more for itself out of the common pool; its destruction of the motive to give of one's best in the common social task, particularly at the entrepreneurial level; its weakening of the rewards for ingenuity, enterprise and effort; its sapping of the incentive to thrift and growth; its discouragement of individual responsibility towards one's own future and that of one's dependants; its creation of resignation towards a tax-ation system which robs the community of capital for the financing of innovations; its encouragement of acquiescence in the squandering of the community's capital; its need, in practice, for a multitude of officials and controllers with delegated judicial and legislative powers, able to make or destroy fortunes and subject to the temptations of corruption; and the tendency it serves towards the degeneration of representative gov-ernment into a system of vote-buying.

9.—I want my Keynesian friends to consider whether it is not fair to claim that, as it has in fact worked out, the policy of maintaining "effec-tive demand" has amounted to the buying off of antisocial pricing. Thus, when credit expansion is accompanied by an expansion of output *plus* some measure of inflation, then the inflationary part of the expansion of money income can be defined as that part of the increase in MV which is not accompanied by an equivalent increase in T. This inflationary part of money income may be regarded as *the cost incurred by the com-munity of persuading those who are withholding capacity to release it*;

---

*I have not included among these consequences the tendency of cheap money to bring about reduced real earnings. This has often been the consequence of inflations, but the effect need not follow. When authoritarian redistribution is resorted to, and when the future progress of a community is sacrificed for the purpose, the artisan and laboring classes may gain, at least in the short run.

†Keynes' cynical reference to the *"euthanasia of the rentier"* is hardly appropriate. In many countries, his policies have borne *cruelly* upon the rentiers in the middle classes, who, deserted by the politicians in whom they had put their trust, have had largely to suffer in silence.

and in general, the withholding to be bought off is not that due to the money illusion or to those price rigidities which are caused by mere inertia. It is *that withholding which is attributable to the attempt by certain sections to draw more for themselves out of the common pool, by collusive action, which the Keynesian remedy seeks to rectify.* Is it now a satisfactory solution that society should be forced to pay ransom, so to speak, to those who would otherwise throw the whole economic system out of co-ordination?

That since the widespread adoption of Keynesian policies the Western world has progressed in productive capacity and standards of living for the masses is obvious. But this advance has been mainly the outcome of great developments in technology and management, whilst monetary policy and the inevitable "controls" which accompany creeping inflation have braked the process. The political support of labor generally, and agriculture in many parts, has been purchased by means which are parasitic on technological progress. Although "full employment" has been enjoyed in Western Europe, it has been achieved at the expense of a serious divergence from ideal resource allocation, and it has caused the gravest injustices. In particular, the clumsy ways in which labor scarcity has been perpetuated have undoubtedly caused distortion in capital structure and production arrangements. The tragic irony of the situation is that there are virtually no ultimate beneficiaries.

Since the war, Keynesian policies in the Western world have not explicitly aimed at maintaining full employment, simply because prices have been forced up as rapidly as, or ahead of, wage-rates and costs.* The burden of the maintenance of peace (which, in face of the Soviet threat, has involved an enormous cost in armaments and armies) has appeared to make the chief problem that of confining demands for normal consumption and development in the degree dictated by defense needs. But instead of this objective being rationally sought, through the price mechanism, it has seemed expedient not only for governments to finance the necessary measures through inflation instead of through overt taxation, but to employ much of the funds so easily raised for the purchase of political popularity. And it has been made very easy for governments to pursue such policies because the attempt to establish stable international monetary arrangements (through the I.M.F.) has been vitiated by Keynesian escape clauses. Each country has been able to blame world inflation for its own contribution to that inflation; and provided it has no more than kept pace with the general rate of currency depreciation, it has had the implied unqualified blessing of the I.M.F. and the E.P.U.

---

*Since 1958, the phenomenon of anticipated inflation has forced action to protect the gold value of the dollar, and this seems to have induced price restraint and (to a markedly lesser extent) wage-rate restraint in the U.S.A.

10.—Mises' contention that "inflation is the fiscal complement of stat-ism and arbitrary government . . . a cog in the complex of policies and institutions which gradually lead towards totalitarianism"[4] has been recently confirmed by one who obviously welcomes this result. In what is probably the most effective recent defense of Keynesianism, Bronfen-brenner has argued that the great virtue of the doctrine has been that, through its influence upon policy—through the consequent secular infla-tion—the "peaceful acceptance" of Marxian aims has been secured. Where the drastic measures which Marx himself contemplated would have failed, Keynesian methods have quietly succeeded.[5] "Secular infla-tion" has, in fact, proved to be the "principal weapon for extortion of surplus value,"[6] and has had "the net effect of permitting all 'active' pressure groups to gain at the expense of the 'dead hands' of the salariat, the *rentier*, and the pensioner."[7] Bronfenbrenner describes inflation as a "social mollifier" which permits the politically dominant groups, like the trade-union movement and organized agriculture, to increase their share of the real national income "without decreasing the money income of anyone else, and therefore without arousing the volume and vehe-mence of opposition which might be expected."[8]* This triumph of Marxian aims by more subtle methods than Marx's own, this gradual process which we are currently witnessing of the euthanasia of the politically weak classes is, according to Bronfenbrenner, to be preferred to what he apparently regards as the inevitable alternative, expro-priation on orthodox Marxian lines. When totalitarianism in one form or another has triumphed, he thinks, inflation will probably "grind grad-usually to a halt!"[10]† Although he claims that Keynesian policy "may with little exaggeration be credited with having saved capitalism in the 1930's,"[11] it was presumably saved from a sudden death in order to experience the only conceivable alternative, slow death by strangulation. "Inflation was always a terrible instrument for the redistribution of wealth," wrote Turroni, discussing the great German inflation which followed the first world war.[12] But the great British inflation which followed the second world war redistributed income just as "terribly" and cruelly, although in a quite different way. The intensity of cruelty is not to be judged by the intensity of squeals.

11.—I am not questioning Bronfenbrenner's realism. It is true, as he

---

*Bronfenbrenner talks of the "ethical convictions" of the agricultural and labor sections, and the fact that they have the "normal voting strength necessary to backing up these convictions."[9] The words "ethical convictions" are an interesting description of the realistic avarice of organized agriculture and organized labor. The sole ethical principle is that of might is right.

†I think Bronfenbrenner is wrong here. Inflation has certainly helped to rectify the disco-ordinations of the totalitarian regime in Soviet Russia.

says, that Keynesianism "has been tried and found good by those potent bodies, the farm and the labor votes."[13] It is true also that it is likely to be politically disastrous if politicians "use their monetary authority deliberately to chastise inflationists with unemployment."[14] And one can agree also that, for this reason, economic conflicts have had to be resolved "by giving higher money incomes to all the combatants at the consumers' expense."[15] But this means at everybody's expense and to nobody's advantage except those who, through political influence, are permitted to exploit the rest.

Bronfenbrenner talks of all the combatants demanding gains "at the consumers' expense." He does not consider the possibility of new combatants. May not "defense groups" arise to fight the pressure groups? Is it beyond the bounds of the conceivable that schoolteachers and the "white collared" groups generally, should get together and threaten to strike for exorbitantly higher salaries, or *alternatively for a solemn pledge on the part of the government* (a) *to take effective action against the pressure groups—if necessary by declaring strikes illegal,** and (b) to issue index bonds (securities bearing interest, at the current rate, but with a guarantee that their real value shall be maintained)? A nation-wide organization which would lead to bank clerks, office employees, professional engineers and others withdrawing their labor *en bloc* could have the effect of a war to end war—the eradication of a type of economic warfare in which one side has been aggressive whilst the other has so far been passively submitting to gradual dispossession.

But what of the role of academic teaching? Is the situation which Bronfenbrenner apparently so shrewdly welcomes and realistically describes one which the economist as teacher should represent to his students as unchangeable? Is not this situation itself largely due to the fact that, for many years, in hardly any university have the students been taught that it was the possibility of this very political situation developing which motivated the economists' protests against Keynesian nationalism in the 1920's. Is not the use of monetary policy as "an instrument of national policy" (i.e., political policy) at least in part due to academic acquiescence? How many students have their attention drawn to the pertinent debate with F. D. Graham in the *Economic Journal,* where Keynes tacitly but strikingly refrained from facing the surrender to "rackets" (as Graham described the chief vested interests) which the approach in *The General Theory* implies? If university teaching had been explaining the nature of the nauseating fight for higher money incomes which Keynesian policy renders inevitable, an incalculable impetus would have been given to the reactions I have been describing.

*I mention the banning of strikes particularly, simply because they have been the chief coercive weapon responsible for restricting the flow of uninflated wages and income.

REFERENCES

(1) BECKHART, quoted in Brown, *The International Gold Standard Interpreted*, Vol. II, p.977. (2) TURRONI, *Economics of Inflation*, p.219. (3) *Ibid.*, p.219. (4) MISES, *Theory of Money and Credit*, 1953 ed., p.428. (5) BRONFENBRENNER, *Some Neglected Implications of Secular Inflation*, in Kurihara, *Post-Keynesian Economics*, p.54. (6) *Ibid.*, p.50. (7) *Ibid.*, p.36. (8) *Ibid.*, pp.35-6. (9) *Ibid.*, p.52. (10) *Ibid.*, p.53 (11) *Ibid.*, p.49. (12) TURRONI, *op. cit.*, p.286. (13) BRONFENBRENNER, *op. cit.*, p.38 (14) *Ibid.*, p.38. (15) *Ibid.*, p.39.

Chapter IV

THE NATURE OF CO-ORDINATION THROUGH THE PRICE SYSTEM

SUMMARY

1.—Co-ordination is achieved when the rates of flow of services, inter-mediate products and final products through the various stages of production and into consumption are synchronized at the least-cost, the rates of flow being determined by prices. 2.—Perfect synchronization is achieved when the price at each stage is so fixed (in relation to income and expectations) as to create the ability and willingness to maintain the full flow of output. 3.—The incentive to such price fixing is that of entrepreneurial loss-avoidance and profit-seeking in the presence of competition. 4.—"Competition" is defined as "the substitution of the least-cost method of achieving any economic end," whatever the machinery which secures the substitution. 5.—Contrived scarcity (which may be the result of mere price inertia) implies either "withheld capacity" or "diverted capacity." 6.—The role of the State in the achievement of a co-ordinated system lies in the fashioning and operating of the appropriate institutions (a) in order to protect the right of substitution—7.—rather than in direct price fixing—8.—and (b) in order to cause prices to be as flexible downwards as they are upwards (a difficult but not a visionary aim; for the "effective price flexibility" sought can be observed to be attainable). 9.—Sociological problems created by rigid wage-rates appear to constitute the chief obstacle. 10.—But when price rigidities are dissolved, an expansion of uninflated money income tends to follow the improved access to markets which is thereby ensured. 11.—Price changes are, thus, socially purposive. 12.—Errors of entrepreneurial interpretation of individual price trends are not subject to infectious or cumulative error, except when the money unit has no defined and trusted value. 13.—The Keynesians wrongly diagnose inability to sell and unwillingness to buy (as opposed to unwillingness to sell at appropriately adjusted prices and inability to purchase at actual prices) as the cause of depression, 14.—an error which breeds confusion in the discernment of co-ordinative and disco-ordinative reactions to depression. 15.—Properly understood, the "successes" of inflation expose the extent to which the tolerance of institutions which prevent co-ordination frustrate the most effective use and growth of productive power. 16.—The dynamic consequences of the achievement of price flexibility upon the development tempo would be far-reaching, 17.—and

51

would imply the abandonment of no ideals or objectives—such as those of time and liquidity—whether expressed collectively or through the market. 18.—Theoretically, moratoria to permit cheap money can be used to assist co-ordination by the State; but they weaken market pressures to co-ordination. 19.—Appendix: The Attitude of the Cohen Council.

1.—It has been said that the early economists were prepared to leave the fate of the economy to the price mechanism—that they placed full reliance on mythical "automatic" stabilizers. Those who make such assertions do not understand that the price mechanism* was regarded as a vast system of disciplined decision-making which, because it relates every individual decision to every other economic decision, acts as the supreme co-ordinator of the economic system. The older economists believed that, *properly administered,* with the State performing *its* appropriate rôle in that administration, the price system could maintain values and prices in harmonious relationship with one another. And they believed also that, if resources became unemployed, so that the flow of uninflated income contracted, it was due to a remediable defect in the administration of the system. They regarded scarcities (i.e., values) expressed in prices as essential data for self-consistent, rational action, whether of the normal co-ordinative action guided by the entrepreneur or of any remedial co-ordinative action taken collectively when the whole economy has got seriously out of gear and depression has descended.

In this respect, the older economists saw much deeper than those of the Keynesian generation. Keynes diagnosed wrongly the source of the disease of fluctuations in employment. He thought he could find it in monetary, banking and fiscal institutions, and in propensities to consume or spend, and not in the price mechanism as a whole. From the very first of his contributions he was brushing aside with the most scant references the purpose of changes in *relative* values, their consequences upon income, and the task of facilitating the movement of versatile resources in response to such changes, as well as to changes in the money valuation of income.†

---

*By the "price mechanism" or the "price system" is meant the framework of institutions through which the value of services and assets are expressed in terms of the value of a unit known as *the money unit.*

†In his earlier writings he had recognized that what matters is the relationship between various subsidiary price levels, prosperity depending upon these price levels being adjusted to one another. But he failed to see or to stress the *general* problem of co-ordination to a changed situation, through the diversion of marginal capital and labour to new employments in response to changing values expressed as changing prices.

Yet I have maintained above that the apparent success of Keynesian policy is attributable to its serving as a crude (although cruel and unjust) method of bringing the economic system into co-ordination; that it can merely *offset* co-ordination failures; and that it cannot remedy the ultimate causes of disco-ordination.* What is usually needed is *not a blanket change in price-cost relationships, but a mass of individual adjustments*.† An understanding of this point throws light, I think, on the phenomenon that inflationary credit has often failed for some time to bring much conspicuous idle capacity into operation, even when it has led to an intensification of activity in certain parts of the economy.

This chapter is concerned with the nature of the co-ordination of the economic system and the possibility of achieving the required co-ordination *directly*, i.e., by means of price adjustments and without recourse to Keynesian expedients (inflation—through banking or fiscal policy—with or without centralized control of investment or expenditure).

An economic system is well co-ordinated when (a) *the rates of flow* of all productive services, materials (and other semifinished goods) and final products through the different stages of production and into consumption are such that, whilst there are reserves (inventories) at different points, there are no gluts or bottlenecks, and (b) the needed synchronization is achieved in such a way that each good flowing into consumption is produced at least cost‡ (i.e., with the minimum sacrifice of other goods). Because we are here interested in the conditions which secure the continuous utilization of productive capacity ("full employment"), our concern will be centered principally on this question of synchronization.

The rates of flow of final products into consumption are determined by the prices charged. "Prices have work to do," wrote B. M. Anderson. "Prices are to guide and direct the economic activities of the people. . . . . Prices must be free to tell the truth."[1] But the Keynesians have enormous difficulty in recognizing the essential function of prices which Anderson so effectively stated.**

In so far as Keynes himself recognized price and wage-rate adjustment as a means to the restoration of activity, he seems to have thought of it

---

*In my judgment, it is most unlikely that a situation can ever exist, in practice, in which the release of unemployed capacity can be *induced* by *noninflationary* credit expansion. Theoretically this *could* happen, however, if the unemployed capacity has been induced by an inadvertent or purposeless deflation. See pp.125-6, 150-1.

†See pp.166-9.

‡The term "cost" here covers *inter alia* the cost of remunerating the entrepreneur. "Least-cost" is achieved in this respect when there is no "contrived scarcity" element (See below pp.59-60).

**Polyani, for instance, appears to approve of the frequently heard view that "while unemployment prevails it is not far from the truth to call pounds, shillings and pence 'meaningless symbols'."[2] Yet unemployment itself may be regarded as a consequence of the meaning of these "symbols" not having been perceived.

almost entirely in terms of its effects upon profit expectations—changes in the marginal efficiency of capital which make "investment" profitable. Admittedly, the pricing of services to permit the employment of the assets which provide them can be said to make their employment "profitable." But the *proportion* of the aggregate flow of income which accrues or its expected to accrue as remuneration of entrepreneurial effort (profits) does not determine *the "volume" of activity* (although— as we shall see—it may certainly influence *the form of activity*). The decisions of entrepreneurs are as much motivated by the wish to avoid further losses as they are by the wish to achieve profits on the *original* value of services invested.

2.—If the production* of any particular commodity is perfectly co-ordinated with the system as a whole, the price fixed for sale to consumers will be such that consumers are (a) *able to* buy and (b) *willing to* buy the full flow coming forward. *Ability* to buy is determined (i) by what people can afford, i.e., their income and (ii) by the extent to which they prefer the product in question (at its current price) to all other valuable things. *Willingness* to buy (i.e., willingness to part with money for things in general) is determined by people's expectations about future prices† and the current necessity for the services provided by commodities in general. If, at any stage, the price of a material or intermediate product is reduced, the rate of flow at that stage will, *ceteris paribus,* tend to increase because, demand remaining the same, *final output is likely to increase;* and if the price is raised, the rate of flow will tend to decline. (Here also, of course, expectations must be brought into the picture). It follows that the rate of flow of directly consumed services and work in progress, through all the stages of production, and into consumption as final products, is determined by the prices asked.‡ Keynesian teaching is really a challenge to this sort of assertion. But if every particular price is adjusted to all other current and expected prices, and provided services offered are not for any reason *valueless,* the rate of flow of any one needed thing *can* be synchronized, through pricing, with the rates of flow of all complementary things. The exceptions which it is possible to imagine are only apparent exceptions. For unless services *are* valueless there must be a demand for them and, in the absence of

---

*The term production here is used in its *general economic* sense, i.e., it includes the marketing function.

†Abstraction is made here (for simplicity) of the services rendered by money itself.

‡Strictly speaking, I should say *by the values* asked. Services are acquired for direct consumption, or for embodiment into resources at the next stage of production, when the owner of the resources values the services so as to permit this. I explain the by no means simple concept of the rate of flow of productive services as a whole on pp.

restraint, the products into which they are embodied will move through the stages of production towards and into consumption.

If prices are co-ordinatively determined, then, not only are final prices fixed in relation to money income and consumer preference but the prices of services and intermediate products at all stages of production are fixed in relation to expectations of demand at the next stage;* and prospective prices at the next stage of demand are in turn derived from predictions of demand at subsequent stages, including the ultimate demand for the final product.

In a state of barter there is never any reason why any commodity which one individual produces should not be exchanged if the producer wishes to exchange it (i.e., if he does not require it himself, and does not think he will improve the terms of barter in his favour by destroying or withholding it), whilst others regard it as valuable. The Keynesian objection will be shown to resolve itself into the idea that people may cease demanding nonmoney services and goods because they demand (with what they are producing) the services of money. I shall in due course deal with this objection (in Chaps. V to XIII). At the present stage, I make abstraction of the issue. But provided this objection can be met, real income, or employment as a magnitude is determined *by pricing*.

The *wasteful* form of idleness in resources arises when their services are so priced that people are unable or (in the light of expectations) unwilling to purchase the full flow. It then becomes unprofitable for entrepreneurs to direct the full flow of services into the replacement or net accumulation of inventories or agents of production. By the word "unprofitable," I mean that the prospective yield from the utilization of such services falls below interest.

The prices which are too high to permit full utilization may occur at any stage in the productive process. But the *critical* price is that of the final product, for that price is, in a sense, the sum of the prices of all the services (including the marketing and entrepreneurial services) which have been embodied into it.

It is unnecessary to discuss all the circumstances in which a price change at one stage of production will not immediately affect prices (and hence rates of flow) at other stages. It is merely essential to show the relationship and to show that price changes tend to influence rates of flow. Hence unless some subtle fallacy vitiates the above reasoning, the system can be brought into synchronization if the right prices are fixed at the appropriate stages. How can such pricing be achieved?

---

*If "work in progress" moves to the next stage (i.e., if further services are embodied into the product) within a firm, it will be because the present discounted value of the prospective sale value makes that profitable.

3.—The answer is that there is an incentive to effect the co-ordination needed, an incentive which is *dependent upon* the power of substitution which we all possess to some extent when we act in the economic sphere, whether we are acting as consumers or entrepreneurs. The *entrepreneurs' incentive** is what I think it is best to call *the loss-avoidance, profit-seeking incentive* or, in the less appropriate phrase which is usually used, the profit motive. When both the power of substitution and this incentive are present, the synchronization tends to be "automatic" (in a sense which I shall shortly explain). For entrepreneurs, who *direct* the rendering of productive services (labor and skill or the services of capital resources), will endeavor so to utilize these services that their prospective return on the value of services or resources devoted to any use will not fall below the rate of interest, and in the expectation that it will exceed the rate of interest. I define "loss" as a realized yield on any increment of investment which falls short of interest, and "profit" as a realized yield on any increment of investment which exceeds interest.

It is important that what I call "the profit motive" (the loss-avoidance, profit-seeking incentive) shall not be confused with *acquisitiveness* (that is, private thrift, the motive of the individual to replace and accumulate). The urge to use resources "profitably" or rationally has nothing to do with acquisitiveness. Yet these two conceptually distinct motives are nearly always confused. The profit incentive we are discussing is merely to the rational use of productive power in response to ends—ends being expressed by consumers. For if the power of substitution to which I have referred is effective, there is an inducement for people as entrepreneurs to treat as paramount the preferences of consumers, i.e., of those people in the community who make the effective decisions about the form and amount of consumption. (The "consumers" in this sense may be income receivers in general—as in democratic societies, or commissars—as in totalitarianism communities. I.e., by "consumers" *in this context* I mean those individuals who are permitted what I have called "consumers' sovereignty").† The essential condition is that this power of substitution, or "competition," shall be effective. If the argument which follows is accepted, this will be seen to be another way of saying that *the market mechanism shall be allowed to function freely.*

4.—For many years now, I have defined "competition" in lectures as "the substitution of the least-cost method of achieving any economic

---

*The parallel consumers' incentive is for the achievement of consumers' surplus.
†All who express economic ends (whether or not those ends are influenced by advertising, or propaganda) are expressing "consumers' sovereignty." See my *Economists and the Public,* Chap. xvi and my article *The Concept of Consumers' Sovereignty,* E.J., 1940.

end," a definition which corresponds, I think, to what economists have always *ultimately* meant by the term. As all economic ends are expressed by people in their consumer aspect, this always means substitution for the consumers' benefit. Such a definition may appear at first not to conform to the notion of "perfect competition" which has become conventional in the last three decades. But the term "perfect competition" (which I have always maintained is an inappropriate one)* merely refers to a condition which is brought about when each producer can provide only a very small part of the aggregate supply of any commodity. It is a static description of a particular situation, whereas competition realistically envisaged is of a dynamic nature and demands a dynamic definition.

I call the achievement of the least-cost method 'competition" no matter what machinery may be used to bring about the required substitutions. Thus, in pure theory we can imagine circumstances in which price rigidities will not *further* disco-ordinate the economy in face of changing preferences so that there is no contraction of income. We can think of (i) a decline in activity in industry A being offset by increased activity in industry B to which demand is transferred, the additional idleness in the resources devoted to A being offset by a decrease in the idleness of resources devoted to B (assuming of course some initial idleness in B); or (ii) a decline in industry A being accompanied by a transfer of labor, through State direction, from industry A to industry B. The true case of co-ordination is that falling under (ii), and it can qualify as "competition" under my definition. In a very crude way the same result can be achieved under socialist planning. The difference is that, in a private enterprise economy, this result is achieved, not by the whip (direction) but by the carrot (incentives). The command is not that of the State but that of society, which induces the transfer by making it "profitable."

Just how effective can this process of substitution be when reliance is placed upon the carrot—"the fundamental incentives"? Even in the most flexible economic system imaginable, there would be hardly any producer or dealer who had no *short-term* monopoly power. But this does not mean that, in respect of the price which it will pay him to charge—taking into account the long-term repercussions he can predict—he may not be as helpless as the hypothetical producer who is confronted with a horizontal demand schedule (the case of so-called "perfect competition"). It can be shown, I think, that when the economic framework of society has been appropriately planned to secure flexibility and the State is performing its rôle, that will be the approximate position.

---

*See my review article of Mrs. Robinson's *Economics of Imperfect Competition*, S.A.J.E., 1933. We do not talk of "perfect" or "imperfect" gravity because there are such things as balloons.

5.—Keynes' terminology, concepts and models appear to draw a veil over what I have called the *withholding of capacity*, especially when this occurs in the field of labor. His only use of the term *withholding* that I can recall in *The General Theory* concerns leisure preference, which he seems to assume covers all motives for the withholding of *effort*. "Every kind of reason which might lead a man, or a body of men, to withhold their labor", he classes under "disutility.*(3) That the purpose of a body of men in withholding labor (or the services of other resources) may not be "disutility" in any sense but the enhancement of claims on the consumer or intermediaries is ignored.

The point which the Keynesian models and concepts persistently obscure, I have felt it to be desirable persistently to reiterate—almost *ad nauseam,* some readers may feel. I shall be constantly reminding the reader that downward price adjustments in fields in which scarcities have been contrived, can restore (and, indeed, are the only means of restoring) *uninflated* income; and uninflated income is uninflated power to purchase the full flow of productive services without net decumulation of productive power.

The practices which result in contrived scarcity occur with varying degrees of deliberateness. They range from organized restriction of output at one extreme to a mere failure to reduce prices in response to a fall in demand at the other extreme.† They occur whenever resources which (through the loss-avoidance, profit-seeking incentive) would otherwise be devoted to the production of a particular commodity, are prevented from being so utilized. *The effect of such a contrivance may be that certain resources become unemployed* (through collusive action or natural monopoly) *but the more usual result is that the resources excluded from the most productive uses are gradually diverted to less productive uses.* The consequence in practice of restraint of the market mechanism is, indeed, less frequently what I have called "withheld capacity" than the much less conspicuous form of waste which I have called "diverted capacity" or "diverted resources,"‡ in which the *composition* of replacement and net accumulation is adversely affected.

---

*His phrase continues, "rather than accept a wage which had to them a utility below a certain minimum." Having mentioned "disutility," this is a mere tautology.

†This concerns the case which has been much discussed of recent years under the term "administered prices".

‡See definitions on p.21 (footnote) and my *Theory of Idle Resources,* pp.139-142. For various reasons (connected I sometimes think with the desire to stress the politically fruitful slogan of "full employment") the Keynesians have stressed "unemployment," particularly of labor. But in so far as there is any content in their analysis at all, it is not merely "withheld capacity" (idle resources) which they want to be released for employment, through the forms of expenditure which they recommend, but diverted capacity—that is, *employed resources* which become more productively used.

The Keynesians could say that they do bring "diverted capacity" into the reckoning,

The relative burden on the community of "withheld capacity" (unemployed resources) and "diverted resources" (resources employed to satisfy relatively less urgently preferred ends) is difficult to judge. Diverted capacity is probably responsible for far more *waste* than unemployed or underemployed resources. Idleness of resources is, in other words, by no means the only or the most important aspect of waste. But in practice idleness —"unemployment"—is the most obvious objective expression of *the first stage* in the continuous fight against expanding productive power and expanding income. When resources are excluded from employment in a particular field, in the long run they are either scrapped or they seek other employments, whilst further services are not embodied into forms which are specialized for that field. Hence actual unemployment may ultimately disappear although the waste persists.

For simplicity of exposition, *I propose usually to refer simply to the withholding and release of capacity, when strictly speaking one should take into consideration the full consequences of "diverted resources,"* i.e., those productive factors which have been diverted from more profitable to less profitable employments.

The contrivance of scarcity is not necessarily deliberate. It may be the result of sheer inertia. If the demand for a particular product falls, the price may be maintained. Some part of the *specific* resources employed must then either fall idle or be diverted to still less profitable uses. It is my considered opinion that withholdings or diversions due to *mere inertia* are not of great practical importance, although I do not propose to assume this. (I shall deal with some possibilities of this kind later).*

Of the causes of contrived scarcity which I have specified above, the most difficult to explain, although in my opinion the least important, is what may be called "irrational reaction to costs incurred." I have in mind here producers' behaviour in relation to (i) what are called (very misleadingly) "fixed costs" or "overhead costs," and (ii) to contractually fixed prices.

In the first place it must be made quite clear that "fixed costs," "overheads" and contractually fixed prices (or contractually fixed rates of in-

as unemployment of the kind that Mrs. Robinson has termed "disguised unemployment." But I do not think that they have made much use of that concept since she gave that name to it.

*Atwood and Henry Thornton had drawn the attention of the classical economists to the rigidities (particularly in respect of the price of labor) which existed at the end of 18th and early 19th centuries, referring to the same kind of phenomena as we are faced with today. In the judgment of their contemporaries, however, these phenomena were not important. But we now know that trade union organization in Britain at the time was powerful (the Combination Acts were leniently enforced) and that monopolistic organization in other forms was more effective than the contemporary economists believed it to be.

terest) are, in themselves, in no sense price rigidities.* They concern the division of the value of output. True prices are market prices which, in any case, may exceed or fall short of contractual prices being paid, the difference being made up of an element of speculative gain to the one party and speculative loss to the other. Only if producers can be assumed, in the presence of such gains or losses, (a) to act irrationally or (b) to be subject to a *special* inducement to act collusively in respect of output and prices, can the existence of so-called "fixed" or "overhead" costs and contractually fixed prices be held to influence the pricing of final products, and hence to affect the co-ordination process.

The irrationality to which I have referred may, however, *conceivably* be highly important as a cause of price rigidity. It resembles "the money illusion" which is believed by some economists to be so important in the pricing of labor. It has probably been aggravated by conventional cost accounting practice. But unless it influences collusive action (as it definitely does today in many countries), I do not think it can have more than a negligible force, just as "the money illusion" would probably have an inappreciable effect if it were not for collusive labor organization.

6.—The condition which I call "price flexibility" must be thought of as being achieved more or less perfectly according to the wisdom with which economic institutions have been planned and are being operated. *As an abstractly conceived ideal*, it envisages a system in which as a result of all the different initiatives required—those of the State as well as those of entrepreneurs and consumers—prices are adjusted in a manner which is consistent with the achievement at least-cost of *all* economic objectives and ideals,† with no valuable productive services being allowed to run to waste. And the price adjustments needed in response to change must always be fully adapted to the relevant expected prices.

How different is the world of reality! The institutional pattern of contemporary society is ultimately responsible for myriad price rigidities. Cartels, output restrictions, price rings, divisions of territory, aggressive selling through price discrimination, resale price maintenance, trade-union standard rates, demarcations, restriction of entry, etc., sometimes cause the virtual freezing of the sort of adjustments which I have been discussing. These practices are, I suggest, made-made obstacles to a co-ordinated and stable society; and they are responible for the *dilemma of inflation or wasteful idleness (or diverted capacity);* yet they are in no sense inherent in the nature of a free economic system. In saying this, I

---

*For an example of a recent discussion which is vitiated by a failure to face this point, see Schultze, *Recent Inflation in the United States*, p.2.

†This includes all "nonmaterial" objectives which involve a sacrifice or cost to *those seeking them.*

do not imply that "perfect price flexibility" is attainable. (See below p. 63).

7.—The attempt to bring prices into co-ordination directly, by fixing maximum prices, may be merely correcting a symptom rather than the disease. Thus, unless the reduction of wage-rates (in a trade in which they have been fixed at a level which causes labor to be unemployed), is accompanied by the unemployed workers being *permitted* to return to employment, there is no reason why the price of the product should fall to a level consistent with full employment of the resources which can make it; and an effective step towards reco-ordination of the economy may not have been achieved. The aim must be (a) that of restoring the right to accept employment (for men and other resources) at full employment wage-rates or prices, so that all resources make their greatest possible contribution to real income and demand *in their existing employments*; and (b) that of restoring the right of men and other resources to move to *new occupations* when they judge their contribution to income will be thereby increased. Price fixing by edict can be successful only when it is a device for setting such reactions going.* Thus, during the course of *a transition* to a noninflationary full employment situation, prices and wage-rates generally might have to be reduced with the same frequency and severity as they had previously been raised during the inflation. The appropriate method of achieving this result with the minimum of friction could conceivably be through the medium of *temporary enactments* of maximum price and maximum wage-rate controls in certain fields. The success of such a policy would be judged, however, by the speed at which the controls could be removed (through the consequent recovery or expansion of the flow of uninflated wages and income).

8.—To achieve a less imperfect co-ordination of economic activity (and in particular to eliminate the succession of boom and slump), we shall need an institutional reorganization to cause costs and prices to be as flexible downwards as they are upwards. *The obvious sociological difficulty of such a task must not cause economists to inhibit consideration of it.* Admittedly, the reforms needed demand a reversal of the tendency of the last century. We now have a long tradition of the State acting in the sectional interest, and refraining from acting in the collective interest, for fear of offending powerful groups.

But even under the existing economic order, and over a wide range of

---

*Exactly the same considerations apply to all attempts to set the economy going by deliberately fixing any particular variables. Thus, attempts to work through influencing expenditure in such categories as "investment" or "consumption" are equally examples of attempting to put things right by tackling symptoms. Such attempts are, as we have seen, futile unless accompanied by inflation.

activities, the co-ordinating machinery can be seen to be operating; for *the fundamental incentive* still exists, and adjustments are brought about, spasmodically but continuously, first at one point and then at another, in the form of competition. Co-ordination is much more clumsy, sporadic and inefficient than it need be, but it does occur, even although considerable withheld or diverted capacity exists. If the synchronizing functions of the price system were clearly understood, it would be possible so to plan institutions that the prices of products and services in all fields could be adjusted in an orderly way, not only in response to changes of preference (including time preference) but also to meet moderate changes in the value of the money unit (such as occasionally occurred in the gold standard era), or even to meet large changes in the scale of prices (which might have to be brought about after inflation in order to honor obligations). Changes in preference and changes in technology (economizing innovations) demand also changes in those established routines and habits which enable the so-called "automatic" working of an exchange economy. But when prices are flexible, society is in a position to adapt its routines with ease to both sets of changes. There is then no greater problem in discarding set usages and conventions than there is in discarding obsolete equipment.

It is important, however, to distinguish between the theoretical notion of perfect price flexibility and the notion of "effective price flexibility." "Perfect price flexibility" implies not only the existence of incentives to price for the full absorption of particular outputs but for the full absorption of outputs in general *when the value of the money unit* (the scale of prices) *changes*. This means, in other words, the absence of the money illusion. When I think of *perfect* price flexibility I suppose (i) that people regard the money unit as a measuring rod which expands or contracts without affecting the size of the things measured, and (ii) that they are indifferent to appreciations or depreciations of the money unit which have taken place, or are taking place, or which are expected to take place. If, for any reason, MV has changed, is changing, or is expected to change in relation to T, people will always adjust the prices of everything in such a way that (a) the full flow of productive services is absorbed; (b) that no "shortages" (queues, rationing or black markets) emerge; and (c) that no speculative hoarding or dishoarding is induced, because all prices are immediately adjusted to expectations. (I deal more rigorously with this question at a later stage).*

In practice, admittedly, nothing which closely resembles *perfect price flexibility* has ever existed or may be expected to exist. Indeed, in order to understand certain aspects of monetary theory, it is important to accept

---

*See Chap. IX.

as a realistic assumption the existence *of unstable price rigidities* (which give rise to a speculative influence in the demand for money).

Hence, when I talk of price flexibility, unqualified, I shall mean "effective price flexibility"—the sort of flexibility which is empirically observable under appropriate conditions; *i.e., under suitable economic policies*—given the sort of institutions with which the student of business administration and business practices is familiar.

In depression, of course, much more drastic adjustments are demanded in order to bring the system into co-ordination. And if the depression is due to resistance to a policy of restoring the value of a depreciated currency, a sudden and acute deflation may well be more conducive to the orderly co-ordination of prices than a gradual one. Indeed, I think it could be maintained that the deflationary burden is greatest when the adjustment attempted is mildest!

9.—Turning now to wage-rate flexibility we find that labor and skill are, on the whole, naturally highly versatile and can (in the absence of trade-union restrictions such as demarcations) be transferred from the production of one commodity to another as preferences or supply conditions change. There are, however, special institutional and sociological causes of rigidity in this field, and the history of adjustment in the modern world has usually been that of powerful opposition to the required revaluations. Strikes, bitterness and lasting resentments have normally accompanied action by means of which the flow of uninflated wages and income has been restored or increased. Perhaps the major economic problem of this age (or should I perhaps not have said, *political* problem?) is how society can overcome the trade-union fight against the means to an increased flow of real wages and the wage-rate stability which flexibility in the price of labor would achieve.

Keynes himself placed chief emphasis on the *inflexibility of wage-rates* when he did refer to prices as a cause of disco-ordination. I prefer myself to discuss *price rigidity*—regarding wage-rate rigidity as a special case—because the problem is a quite general one and because I do not wish to place all the blame for policies which force down the flow of wages and income on the trade-unions. Yet on empirical grounds, Keynes' emphasis does appear to be justified.

In Bronfenbrenner's opinion, the so-called "Austrian" remedy for industrial depressions "will no longer be permitted to work for any length of time in a democratic society, despite such spectacular instances of success as the depression and recovery of 1920-22 in the United States."[4] But the orthodox or "Austrian" policy was more one of *avoiding* depressions than curing them. Had that policy been adopted, quite different reforms would have been encouraged. It is impossible to be dogmatic about what the results would have been. *Certainly the benefits would not have been spectacular. For social institutions which work well are taken for granted, seldom discerned or recognized, and hardly ever accorded the credit they deserve.*

At a later stage (Chap. IX), I shall examine the contention that policies of wage and price adjustment are self-frustrating. But it must be remembered that the Keynesian attack is on a policy which has never been experimentally tested. For whilst there is a great deal of evidence of wage-rate adjustments *forced by depression* being followed by recovery, no deliberate attempt to increase uninflated income (including the flow of wages) by reducing all prices which appear to be above the natural scarcity level (including wage-rates) so that all prices and wage-rates below the natural scarcity level may rise, has ever been purposely pursued. Actual policies have, for decades, been based precisely upon the politically attractive rule, justified by Keynesian teaching, that disharmony in the wage-rate structure must not be tackled but offset; whilst the current tendency is to assume dogmatically, with no adequate examination of the institutional and sociological factors involved, that to advocate wage and price adjustments is to recommend the conquest of the moon.*

10.—The orthodox remedy for a disco-ordinated economy is, then, the improvement of price flexibility directly, by dealing with the causes of contrived scarcity. In such a solution, an increase of uninflated money income is the accompaniment of and a facilitating condition for, and not in any other respect a cause of, improved synchronization. In the Keynesian solution, the increase of money income is regarded as the cause of the reco-ordination.

It can be said that effective price flexibility is secured when free access to markets has been guaranteed. Curiously enough, the Keynesian thesis sometimes takes the form of an argument which seems to be to this effect. We are told that it should be the object of economic policy to "assure markets" which are not assured "automatically."† But the policy im-

---

*See, for instance, Schultze, *op. cit.*, p.68. Schultze abandons rigorous analysis and resorts to sheer irony when he refers to the policy of achieving price co-ordination without the assistance of creeping inflation. He mocks as "pulverisers" those "who would attempt to solve the problem by strengthening the various antitrust laws, applying them, in modified form perhaps, to labour as well as business" (*Ibid.*, p.41). One cannot help wondering how far his attitude is due to his apparent acceptance as an inexorable law of nature, to be treated with due reverence, the fact that "wage increases do, and price cuts do not win union elections" (*Ibid.*, p.68) .

†The word "automatic" has been used of the continuous and conscious entrepreneurial decision-making needed for this purpose. But that term can be justified only in the sense that *discretion* in the vital predictions and decisions is limited by rule and not by whim, the ultimate controlling forces being social in origin (expressed in

plied by orthodox teaching is exactly this, although the word "automatically" is usually vague and ambiguous. What is essential in a co-ordinated economy is the *right of access* to markets for all resources and services; and in a money economy, this requires *pricing* to permit exchange, i.e., to satisfy both buyer and seller. "Markets" can be "assured" *for producers as a whole* in no other way. All other methods are essentially either protectionist—assuring markets for some by excluding others from them—or inflationary. And the inflationary method itself operates by bringing relative prices into co-ordination. Lavington perceives the true principle when, asking why entrepreneurs operate resources at low pressure during depression, he answers that the absence of reasonable expectation of being able to sell additional output is due to consumers failing to purchase *"because they themselves are not producing."* The consumers' proper name is, he says, "other producers."[5] He continues: In depression, "the individual firm is working at low pressure because other firms are working at low pressure. Each is inactive because the general power to consume has fallen; and the general power to consume has fallen because of and in proportion to the general decline in the activity of production. The inactivity of all is the cause of the inactivity of each. No entrepreneur can fully expand his output until other entrepreneurs expand their output."[6]

I suggest, therefore, that rational policy must pursue, consciously and deliberately, the objective of "full employment" at uninflated prices; for that means full output and full demand. The aim must be *to keep the flow of output going* (whether for replacement of consumption or for net accumulation) (i) by pricing for this end, and (ii) by tackling rationally—in the light of current misunderstandings of the situation—the rigidities which have to be dissolved. At the same time, policy should endeavor *to minimize the likelihood of drastic downward price adjustments becoming necessary.* But this does not enable us to jump to the conclusion that price adjustment to changes can ever be *avoided.* Whilst statesmanship demands compromise—wisdom in the recognition of the contemporaneous—it never requires the abandonment of principle.

It has not been recognized, I think, that successful strategy to bring formerly rigid prices into co-ordination (or to effect the elimination of contrived scarcities generally) may be viewed as *an act of innovation.** In particular, the constant search by managers for the least-cost methods

---

markets) and not political in origin. But the Keynesians are accustomed to use the term "automatic" in a manner which ridicules and misrepresents their critics. They suggest, indeed, the kind of system in which the co-ordinative functions of the State are blindly neglected.

*Innovation is only a stimulus to "prosperity" and growth when it is of an economizing nature and hence increases (a) income *and* (b) savings. Otherwise, it merely changes the form of replacement and net accumulation.

of achieving ends should be regarded as the most important kind of inno-vation activity which can lead to a rise in the marginal efficiency of cap-ital. Indeed, every act of competition, every substitution of an econom-izing method for the consumers' benefit, and *every breach of a price rigidity, is an act of expansive innovation*; for it is bringing about a more productive use of scarce resources.* Far from the cutting of rigid prices bringing about a fall in the marginal efficiency of capital, it is conducive to its rise. *But—and this is the point on which the Keynesians appear to be most undiscerning—such innovations do not mean that prospective yields are bound to rise in any industry in which an economy is intro-duced. Yields will tend to rise for all noncompeting industries.* The in-novator—including the price-cutter—will usually find that it pays him to increase the stock of resources which he is using; but unless the demand for the product is highly elastic, or unless general expansion elsewhere in the economy happens to be raising the demand schedule, the expan-sion which his decisions effect will cause loss of profits to his competitors or even make it profitable for some of them to disinvest.

11.—The apparent Keynesian failure to appreciate the process (a) through which the myriad economic aims which people are seeking are brought into consistency, and (b) through which a synchronized co-oper-ation in response to those aims is achieved, can be traced, I think, to an unawareness of the social purpose of price changes.

Price changes (both *individual* changes and changes in the *scale of prices*)† are socially purposive. The more "violent" the changes, the more serious the disco-ordinations which have to be rectified, or the greater the magnitude of the changes (i) in the availability of resources or (ii) in preferences to which adjustments must be made. The general tendency on the part of the Keynesians to regard price fluctuations as an evil in themselves, to be rectified directly, is the source of a big dis-tortion of thought. It causes pressure to co-ordination to be diagnosed as the origin of disorder. The distortion in question is typical not only of Keynesian thinking but of "Leftist" thinking as a whole. The essen-tially stabilizing nature of the pressures which are expressed through the price mechanism, and which form a major part of its co-ordinative task, tends to be ignored or overlooked.

12.—Admittedly, the price mechanism will perform its co-ordinative task defectively if the data tend, either at particular crucial times, or gen-

---

*It was, perhaps, Schumpeter's most serious blind spot that, in his perception of the enormous importance of innovation, he failed to perceive—or at least to *stress*—this reality.

†The full meaning of this assertion will become clear later. Fluctuations in the scale of prices may be evidence that monetary co-ordination is needed.

erally, to be misinterpreted by entrepreneurs. If the environment created by current prices and current price trends induces the wrong reactions, disco-ordination will ensue. But entrepreneurial decision-making is continuous and subject to perpetual adjustment, whilst individual errors of interpretation incur increasingly heavy penalties the longer the period before they are rectified. Only if there are, so to speak, *infectious* errors of prediction can it be argued that reliance upon the mechanism of price adjustment has inherent defects.

In my judgment, entrepreneurs are not *unwisely* optimistic or pessimistic when they observe the growth or decline in economic activity and judge the profitableness of expanding or curtailing their own activity accordingly. Where apparently contagious errors in forecasting, with cumulative results, can be observed, it seems to me that this is due to general uncertainty about future governmental policy as a whole (and the results of that policy). The situations envisaged by those who fear infectious misinterpretation of prices and price trends nearly all arise— as I shall show—because the objectives of monetary policy are vague. That is why I place such great stress on the desirability of the monetary authority being committed to *the maintenance of a money unit of defined value.* If the majority of entrepreneurs have faith in the willingness and ability of treasuries and central banks to achieve the objective of a *defined* money unit, most of the self-perpetuating cumulative movements of prices will be eliminated. (See below, pp. 100-101).

It is the basic function of money in an advanced society to permit a sensitive, detailed and well co-ordinated response to the competing ends for the fulfilment of which the individual must distribute his income.* Is it not almost self-evident, then, that this function can be *most efficiently* carried out when monetary institutions are so planned that *some defined value* is conferred on the monetary unit? The required stability is one which is relevant to a co-operating community, and especially relevant to a community which co-operates largely through the medium of contracts and loans.

13.—To the Keynesian mind, however, depressions occur as a result of the *unwillingness of people to buy goods,* or the *inability to sell goods,*†

---

*This aspect of the subject has often been excellently treated. Money is an essential part of the mechanism which enables the efficient realization of individual preferences.
†This "inability to sell" is often assumed also to lead to an increased demand for money. But there is no reason why the accumulation of inventories should not be accompanied by a *fall* in cash and bank balances; for inventories are gradually self-liquidating and small turnovers need smaller investment in money. As we shall see, money assets only become preferred investments as a result of growth in the prospective yield they offer. Of course, a speculative demand for money may arise in these circumstances. That is a separate point. I deal later with this issue, in Chap. v.

both of which may be brought under the idea of *absence of markets.* The truth is the contrary. Depressions occur as a result of an increasing *unwillingness to sell* things at prices consistent with the maintenance of noninflated money income and a consequent increasing *inability to buy* at the prices fixed. For the failure to buy all the *valuable productive services* available (including goods into which they are embodied) cannot be due not to the failure to demand them but to the *failure to release them.* The fact that they have value is proof that they are demanded; and they have value if they would be purchased at some price above zero. Failure to sell is frustration of the buyer, not of the seller. If consumption declines, whilst no services normally devoted to making final products fall *valueless,** it is impossible to attribute any idleness of resources to some inherent propensity of consumers. The factors responsible for the slowing down of activity cannot be expressed in any "consumption function" derived from some "psychological law." *The responsibility lies wholly in a sectionalist ignoring of the social purpose of prices.*

What is essentially the same issue can be expressed from another aspect. When investments generally have proved to be less remunerative than had been predicted, there has in no sense been either "over-investment" or "over-production" *in general.* For there is always complete absorptive capacity for all *productive services which have value,* and for many which have not. Price rigidity due to monopoly or inertia may prevent absorption, so that the final stage in production, namely, sale for consumption, is not completed. But such a situation ought to be described as *underproduction* through disco-ordinative pricing.

When it is said that "the income and spending power of consumers should be sufficient to clear the market of goods," etc. I should put it exactly the other way round. I should say, "Prices should be fixed so that, in the light of expectations, the money income and spending power of consumers can always clear the market. . . ." Depression develops when the failure of one set of interests to price in the collective interest, motivates or reinforces the unwillingness of another. This sets up a chain reaction which can lead to panic repercussions which aggravate the cumulative withholding and lead to privately disastrous declines in the values of certain kinds of inventories.

A more radical cleavage of opinion could hardly exist. Is it "unwillingness to buy" or "unwillingness to sell" at co-ordinated prices (i.e., at prices which bring the flow of production within the range of people's incomes) which leads to valuable resources falling into disuse? The Keynesians fail to see that *the cutting of prices in any field is simply the creation of additional demand for noncompeting goods*—because power

---

*See my *Theory of Idle Resources,* pp. 41-56.

to purchase is released for other purposes. Indeed, they tend to regard such price adjustments as the cause, not the cure of crises and depression. (See Chap. IX). The adjustment of prices early in the process, as prices have been getting out of the range of consumer income, appears to them as a likely initiating cause of a cumulative decline. Thus, Dillard contends that "slight provocation may set up a cumulative wave of liquidation. . . . Every business transaction on the selling side involves an embryo crisis."[7] How hopelessly wrong it all is!

Dillard sums up Keynes' position on the issue as follows: "Elasticity in the supply of output and in the size of inactive balances provides the basis of flexibility whereby the economic system adapts itself to the shocks which orthodox theory assumed *could and would* be absorbed by flexibility of prices."[8] (My italics). The orthodox position is misrepresented of course. Had Dillard expressed the case he was attacking fairly and accurately, he would have used the words "could and *should*" instead of "could and *would*." In so far as the orthodox writers whom Keynes criticized believed that the economic system *could* adjust itself, through price adjustment, to the shocks of demand changes, their belief was founded upon observation. And when they assumed that institutions were such that the condition of full employment, once departed from, would tend to be restored, this was *on the assumption that policy would aim at the required adjustments.*

It must be emphasized again that the Keynesian remedy itself relies tacitly upon the price mechanism and the same fundamental incentive. The restraints imposed in practice upon the substitution of the least-cost method (competition), and serious errors of judgment or prediction, may upset the reactions upon which the Keynesian remedy relies, just as they may frustrate attempts to co-ordinate in the orthodox manner. But very broadly, Keynesian policy seeks to restore co-ordination by making it possible for people to *afford to buy*, not by enabling them directly to increase their contribution to real income, but by increasing their money income in the expectation that this will cause an increase in the contribution of others to real income. The Keynesians admit that price rigidity perverts the market mechanism, but they seldom explain clearly that the increase of money income they recommend merely *circumvents* the disco-ordinating rigidities by inflating income to meet inflated prices. Moreover, their admissions on this point are obscured by the assumption that, even in the absence of price rigidities, it is essential to preserve the flow of services and products by maintaining expenditure (or certain categories of expenditure) by means other than that of adjusting prices in harmony with current income and expectations. (See Chap. IX).

14.—The confused thinking which arises through the use of such unsatisfactory notions as "lack of markets" (see above, p. 66.) has, I think, had most seriously adverse results upon the co-ordination of international trade relations. The history of the great depression of the 'thirties' records two kinds of pricing reactions to the situation created: (a) disco-ordinative, those which tended to aggravate the chaos, (b) co-ordinative, those which tended to mitigate the depression. Now, *by no means the least cause of the persistence of the depression was the tendency in influential circles to class these opposites together*, as though they were of the same nature. For instance, in a discussion of international trade, Loveday (by no means a Keynesian in later years!) wrote (in 1937): "Prices on world markets were forced down by import restrictions imposed by this or that country to improve its balance of payments. Each country tried to obtain a larger share in the melting snowball of international trade by reducing costs; each undercut the other. This competitive attempt to obtain a common objective failed. The universal attempt by each country to arrest the depression on its frontiers by stopping *the germ carriers, the low priced foreign goods*, failed no less inevitably".[9] (My italics). Like so many of his contemporaries and subsequent economists, *Loveday did not perceive that cost-reduction and price-cutting were merely an expression of the increase of uninflated demand for which the world was languishing*, whilst import restrictions were an expression of the eradication of that demand. The producers of the goods which were offered at cut prices were demanding goods in exchange, whereas the exclusion of goods by import restrictions was exterminating demand. Had the arrival of cheap foreign goods in any country been followed by similar price adjustments internally, or had the nations of the world been successfully encouraged by their international advisers to cut tariffs and mitigate restrictions, a rapid world recovery *with a great expansion of real and money demands would have eventuated*. It is dodging the whole issue to object that the price-cutters were demanding not goods but money. *The pricing of services so as to keep inventories cleared and the full flow of services absorbed is the very condition which calls forth a noninflationary expansion of credit and expenditure, and hence the revival of money demands*. The economic tragedy of the world during the period 1929 to 1931 arose less out of any defects in the monetary mechanism in use, than in the failure to employ the co-ordinating mechanism as a whole. The various countries adjusted to the shrinking world demands by restricting output instead of adjusting prices, thereby causing a further shrinkage.* Instead of each country adapting its prices and costs so that there was a new balance between internal and external demand for its products,

---

*See M. Gilbert, *Currency Depreciation*[10], where Britain's reaction is described. It is just as applicable to other countries.

the tendency was for each of them to seek a way out through a further insulation of its economy. Both exports and home consumed products should have been sold at prices which fully reflected the cheaper materials which were being incorporated in them. As things were, the employed sections of labor and capital tried, with disastrous results, to retain the benefit for themselves. Naturally, the world flow of money income which was compatible with convertibility into gold was bound to contract. Governments everywhere acted in complete unawareness of the social purpose of pricing, creating new rigidities rather than breaking down those which had already developed. In so far as recovery resulted from direct (as distinct from inflationary) adjustments it was—with few exceptions—in spite of State policy.

15.—One of the most serious consequences for which the Keynesian doctrine and influence must accept blame is that it has helped to prevent a clear insight into the inherent contradictions and consequent inefficiencies of the economic institutions of the contemporary "capitalist" world. In the stress it has laid on the notion of *lack of purchasing power* or of "effective demand," instead of the less easily grasped, but realistic, notion of *defective co-ordination,* it has hindered the emergence of a fuller understanding of exactly why inflation has so often drawn idle resources into activity. The apparent successes of inflation could have assisted us in diagnosing the defects of the co-ordinative mechanism in its absence. Inflation has been successful in stimulating production in peace and war solely because it has brought prices into better relations with one another. *Its "successes" are, in effect, proof of what noninflationary co-ordination is capable of achieving* with incomparably greater efficiency and lower cost, if *political institutions rendered that possible.*

Inflation has co-ordinated also (in the same indirect and crude manner) in reducing entrepreneurial fears of exploitation by organized labor following investment in specific, capital intensive forms.* For instance, in Britain during the inter-war period, the danger of strikes subsequent to such investment discouraged modernization in many vital industries, probably most seriously in coal mining. During the post-1945 period, however, the expectation that aggressive union action to force increases in wage-rates could be met out of continuously inflating demands for output, seems to have provided the required inducement for investment in labor-economizing and capital-economizing equipment. Yet how much more beneficial would have been legislation to prohibit the private use of coercive power! If trade-union action calculated to destroy

---

*In general, entrepreneurs avoid specific forms of investment which they anticipate are likely to be exploited by trade-union action subsequent to the investment. (See my *Theory of Collective Bargaining,* 1954 ed., pp.120-6) .

entrepreneurial incentives (and hence to hold back a growing flow of wages and income) could be outlawed, productive power would expand in the most economic forms.*

Once the lesson has been clearly learnt and taught by economists, it will appear to be intolerable that society should allow disco-ordination to be rectified only through inflation—*a remedy which leaves the genesis of the disease undisturbed,* or even aggravates the disease. And most economists have so far not learned the lesson because, at the moment when world events were proclaiming the true answer, Keynes shouted an answer which the wishful thinking of politicians and business men made far more acceptable—that the idleness of valuable resources was due to insufficient spending.

I deny that money has any function or power to "promote" or "stimulate" economic life, or production, or the "development" of the economic system, except (a) in the sense that any efficient technical mechanism plays its part in the productive process (e.g., the transport system), or (b) in the sense that the multiplication of money units may (when expectations are not adjusted to such a policy) be used as an alternative to the direct co-ordination of prices.† There is no other manner in which money can be said to "lubricate" or "stimulate" the economic system.‡

I have used the phrase "crude co-ordination" of policies which aim at achieving full employment through the maintenance of expenditure (effective demand). Not only do such policies remove pressures to co-ordination, they create inducements to disco-ordinate. For instance, if organized labor knows that full employment of labor is guaranteed, demands for wage-rate increases will be relatively uninhibited. And if "employers" know that inflation will follow in order to enable them to pay the higher rates, they will tend to lose sight of their social duty to resist the fixing of wage-rates by the threat of private force. Indeed, for such reasons, when inflation is generally anticipated, its co-ordinative effects are completely destroyed. (See Chap. XVIII.)

Keynesian doctrine sometimes rests on the assumption of wage-rate rigidity (and sometimes on price rigidity generally). And the Keynesians

---

*Productive power *in all forms* would then be likely to expand through the stimulus to savings via the interest offer. (See Chaps. x-xi).

†Similarly, the multiplication of money units may be used as a means of temporarily restricting consumption and forcing "real saving." It is equally true that deflation (resorted to in order to honor agreements) is not disco-ordinative, except in the sense that other factors cause it to be so.

‡The term "stimulation" applied to economic activity can be rightly applied, I suggest, only to output (the source of real demand) or anticipated output. Economizing inventions "stimulate" because they permit greater output. *All* additional output, priced for absorption at home or abroad, has an expansive effect on the whole economy. It makes no difference whether that output is to be sold for home use or in the form of exports. What is essential is its pricing for sale, so that it adds to uninflated income.

might claim that their doctrine does allow for unemployment caused by
wage-rates and prices being fixed too high. But they show an obvious
reluctance to explain actual depression phenomena in terms of rigidity
or in terms of costs or prices having been forced too high. They might
contend of course that the advocacy of a return to noninflationary co-
ordination under current political conditions is mere nostalgia, a visionary's dream. But that is to argue that it is hopeless to expect mankind
to profit from past blunders. And if that is really the Keynesians' conviction, they should say so in explicit, unequivocal language, and face the
controversy which will follow.

In discussing the current retreat from Keynesian teaching (discussed
in Chap. XIX), Fellner contends that Keynesianism "by-passes the question of the consequences of money-wage and price adjustment with an
answer that is *evasive.*" Nevertheless, he maintains that the answer is
not *"meaningless"* because "we frequently wish to proceed as if a self-
adjustment mechanism . . . did not exist." For even in a free market, he
says, it is "a very sluggish mechanism, operating with lags and detours
and impeded by institutional obstacles."[11] (My italics). He continues,
"Keynesianism favors policies that work towards the restoration of the
balance without reliance on significant changes in the general level of
money wages and prices. These policies include counter-cyclical regula-
tion of the relationship between fiscal revenues and fiscal expenditures
as well as central banking techniques."[12] But orthodox policy does
not rely on changes in "the general level" of money wage-rates and
prices, except as a rectification of a previous divergence from orthodox
policy which has already disturbed that level. Fellner's treatment actually
amounts to a virtually unqualified admission of orthodox criticisms of
the Keynesian case, with the suggestion that, for the reasons stated, the
Keynesians still adhere to the policy of co-ordination otherwise than
through price adjustment. But that must mean through some measure of
inflation. As a just representation of Keynesianism, the passage *seems to
imply* that stability of the scale of prices is envisaged. In fact the word
"significant" is the loophole which leaves the way open to creeping
inflation.

Controversy is thus brought to the following position. The orthodox
advocate the deliberate planning of the institutional framework to
eliminate lags and general sluggishness so as to permit the more effective
co-ordination of the economic system without changes in the general
level of prices. The Keynesians, on the other hand, believe that institutional defects cannot be effectively tackled, and that the crude co-ordination achievable through the *gradual* depreciation of the money unit
(not sufficiently rapid to cause "significant" changes in the level of
prices) must therefore be adopted. Thus they commit themselves to the

persistent deception of the public or the totalitarianism which (as I shall show—see Chap. XVIII) are the inevitable alternatives under continuous inflation.

16.—The recognition that, when unemployment exists, the recovery in real income and employment can come about only as a direct result of (a) the release of withheld capacity through direct price adjustment or inflation (which releases demands) or (b) net accumulation of productive capacity* through thrift, (which adds to the capacity to demand), does not guarantee a parallel recognition of the effects of flexibility upon the *dynamics* of expansion. Realism demands that we always keep in mind also the *indirect or time* results of the release of capacity. *Complementarity* (in the broad sense of the principle that the demand for any commodity is a function of the supply of noncompeting commodities) allied to thrift, constitutes the most potent dynamic element in the determination of the development *tempo*. In a world of co-ordinated prices, it would not be the mere current absence of withheld capacity which would stimulate the simultaneous growth of productive capacity and consumption power. The stimulus would come from the knowledge that capacity would not be withheld in future (through the collusive fixing of prices and wage-rates, etc.), with the result that there would be a generous *inducement* to thrift and growth.† The enormous importance of the elimination of the arbitrariness of sectionalist pricing and output control can hardly be exaggerated. And the resulting stimulus to inventiveness in techniques and management due to the consequent elevation of risk-taking to a new level has also to be brought into the reckoning.

In particular, the reactions of wages upon wages seem to me to have been seriously neglected. Under conditions of unemployment due to union-enforced wage-rates, it is certainly not essential, as Keynes assumed, for average real wage-rates to fall in order that recovery may occur (still less, of course, that average real earnings on the part of all, including the presently unemployed, shall fall). It is downward adjustments of some *nominal* wage-rates which are called for;‡ and while for short periods that *may* involve sacrifices of real earnings per head in formerly favored fields, experience suggests that real wage-rates and real earnings per head recover rapidly as reductions in exploitative nominal wage-rates are made. For instance, during the wage-rate and price adjustments

---

*Net accumulation of productive capacity is intended to include the capital value of discoveries and inventions. (See Chap. x).

†See Chaps. x and xi.

‡And, except in severe deflations such as those of the early 'twenties, and in the 'thirties, probably in a minority of occupations.

which occurred in the United States over the period 1920-1922, there was a substantial rise in real wage-rates.

The dynamics of contraction are no less important. When the mechanism of price adjustment is defective, a wave of self-perpetuating and self-aggravating withholding of capacity may be set up by any factors which lead to an initial decline in real income. We have, for example, disturbances such as bad harvests, or external changes which reduce the volume of imports which a given volume of exports is able to earn. The phenomenon can be illustrated by the latter case, i.e., that of a reduction in the real profitableness of foreign trade. A clear instance is to be found in the United States in the early 'thirties. It was the cessation of demand for American agricultural products due to the cessation of her lending to Europe, and the fact that the Fordney and Hawley-Smoot tariffs made it impossible for Europe to buy American products with earned income, which depressed firstly the earnings of United States agriculture and, in turn, the earnings of industry. Then, in reaction to the situation so created, both sectors of the economy attempted in vain to preserve money earnings by trying to curb the fall of prices rather than by adjusting prices to the new situation. In this attempt, they reduced still further their mutual demands for one another's products. The general depression was inevitably intensified.*

But the *initiating* cause of cumulative withholding may arise not from natural or external events but through internal action which results in disco-ordination. Thus, a wave of union-enforced increases in wage-rates may be responsible. Moreover, in the modern age, business men are confronted with large "overheads"; and the widespread existence of withheld capacity causes them to become aware that they are producing under decreasing average cost.† They perceive that, in the existing state of demand, and because they are collaborating on an industry-wide basis, it will not pay them to cut prices, although price cutting would be to the advantage of any individual firm, if it could rely upon the others in the industry failing to follow suit. The situation develops because non-competing industries, also organized to maintain prices, find themselves in the same position. Price maintenance has a cumulatively depressing effect.

When capacity begins to be generally withheld, complete price adjustment at any one stage of production in a particular industry may still not prevent *some part of the capacity* from becoming *temporarily value-*

---

*In this case, price and cost adjustment in both fields ultimately reversed the cumulative withholding into a cumulative release of capacity from about the middle of 1932. This recovery would, I believe, have persisted had a policy of encouraging further adjustment been adopted. But N.R.A. policy intervened to prolong the depression.

†I have suggested above that there *may* also be an element of irrationality present owing to the psychological consequences of overhead costs.

less (especially if the resources employed lack versatility). This condition implies that it will be unprofitable for any entrepreneur to utilize that capacity *even if it is offered for use at a hire value sufficient only to cover depreciation through use.* Such a condition is, I think, less frequent than is usually assumed, even in the most disastrous depression. What in fact happens most often when business men become apprehensive is that the normal intensity of utilization of productive capacity appears to be dis-advantageous, in the sense that the reduction of former revenues is be-lieved to be minimized when capacity is withheld. The withholding in such a case is socially *unjustifiable,* for it contributes to the perpetuation of depression. Yet it is hardly *unjust.* The failure to take advantage of the power to act in collusion (or of any other monopoly power enjoyed) will mean the temporary penalization of those producers who initiate recovery. That is precisely why the State ought not to be allowed to neglect its co-ordinative rôle.

In the development of a depression, the cumulative effects of one such withholding upon others seems often to have given rise to a situation in which there is a sudden catastrophic general fall in the prospective profit-ableness of replacement and growth. This is the origin of what Keynes regarded as the collapse of the marginal efficiency of capital and the disappearance of "investment opportunities." It was this which led him to believe that we must "set investment going" again. But he did not perceive that to do this without inflation, it would be necessary to restore the prospective demand for the product of each industry through cost and price adjustments *in the industries which had not been competing with that industry.* (See pp. 166-8).

In this background, we can consider the belief of many Keynesians that we can find in the condition of specificity and durability of resources in the constructional industries the origin of a situation in which (to use my own terminology) an initial withholding of capacity is induced by a change in time preference, which sets going a chain reaction of further withholdings. The resulting decline in real income is believed, in turn, to dry up part of the source of savings, which in turn dries up also the prospective profitableness of net accumulation, which in turn further reduces the incentive to save, and so on. The crucial initial withholdings are supposed to occur in the consumers' goods industries (although this is not always made clear) or in the marketing stage (the failure to replace inventories) because, owing to an increase in savings, demand for con-sumers' goods declines. This argument is discussed at length in Chaps. X and XI.

Our discussion above suggests, however, an explanation along the fol-lowing lines. When productive services and products in the consumers' industries have been generally priced too high in relation to (a) current preferences, (b) the size of current incomes and (c) anticipated prices, it will undoubtedly appear unprofitable to add to or even to replace full productive capacity. The inability of entrepreneurs in one field of activity to acquire productive services at prices which are consistent with *a prospective yield in excess of interest* on the inventories or other assets acquired, tends to be aggravated through further cumulative withholding in noncompeting fields, and a general running down of the economic system. Because labor, manufacturers and merchants are unwilling to sell at prices which can keep inventories turning over and other assets employed, it *looks* as though people are unwilling to buy. In such circumstances, the deflationary action necessary to preserve the convertibility or parity of a currency, can well *appear* as an aggravation of a depression initiated by a burst of thrift; and the deflation might well, as some Keynesians suggest, affect the constructional industries differentially at first, causing the withdrawal of part of their contribution to aggregate real demands (through the withholding of capacity or through some capacity falling temporarily valueless). This might in turn call forth further withholdings in many fields, thus making still further deflationary action essential in order to maintain convertibility or parity of the currency.

Such an analysis is sometimes not without plausibility as an explanation of what I have called the chain reaction in withholding capacity. But time preference merely expresses *ends,* and *credit contraction is not a cause but an effect of unrectified discoordination and consequent idleness.* Admittedly, changes in saving preference—in either direction—may cause disturbing value changes, just like all other major changes in preference or changes in supply conditions; and as we have seen, in a badly co-ordinated economy, withheld capacity may result. But the reactions described are not attributable to defects in noninflationary *monetary* policy.

17.—Thus, in recommending recourse to monetary policy in order to restore the "effective demand" needed to employ idle resources, the Keynesians tend to blame for the idleness, not errors in pricing, but changes in freely expressed preferences—including time and liquidity preference —and changes in entrepreneurial predictions.* It is all too easy to assume, when policy has *permitted* major inconsistencies to arise in the economic system (or when it has itself *created* such inconsistencies) that the cause lies in "collective behavior"—the choice of certain ends (such as provision for the future) or the choice of certain means (such as money, when prices are regarded as *unstably* rigid in a downward direction).†

*See Keynes' reference to expectations affecting "the quantity of employment and not merely its direction."(13)
†See Chaps. V and XI.

The origin of such "economic disturbances" must be attributed, I suggest, solely to the factors which prevent the value system from performing its co-ordinative task. For *there are no economic ends, and no entrepreneurially chosen means which are incompatible with "full employment."** Entrepreneurs will never fail to utilize the full flow of productive services if the price mechanism is allowed to work or made to work. *The only "collective behavior" to be set right is that of the propensity to resist price adjustment.* The weakness of the Keynesian nostrum is, as we have seen, that it tries, not *to correct* that behavior, but *to offset it.* The Keynesians never discuss the *general* problem of why *particular* shifts in social preferences, propensities and predictions should cause disco-ordination, they do not plead for the organization of a more flexible and more sensitive adjustment to the particular shifts of demand which are alleged to be responsible; and they do not suggest, as far as I know, any system of overt taxation of or discouragement of demand for those services to which "too much" demand is supposed to be transferred in order to force people to continue to demand as before. Instead, they recommend, as we know, the inflation of money demand for those services of which the community want less, but without reducing demand for those services of which the community want more.

The supposed effect of changes in liquidity preference upon the market rate of interest plays an important rôle in Keynes' system. But he completely missed, I suggest, the *co-ordinative* rôle of interest. That is, he failed to recognize that the market rate is the most vital value-ratio in the whole economic system, bringing consistency of values between the immediate and distant future; that when the monetary authority functions efficiently, the market rate set (determined in the same way as other market prices) permits the measuring rod of value—the money unit—to be almost as satisfactory over time as it is over space; and that because entrepreneurial decision-making is dominated by perpetual forecasting—the cautious extrapolation of present trends into the future—market interest (in relation to the natural level) becomes the one value to which all other values are adjusted *via* the value of the money unit which it determines.

The fact that, under the *unrealistic* assumption that the number of money units is constant, changes in liquidity preference will affect the relation of market interest to the natural level, does not cause changes in this preference to upset the coordinative functions of interest. But owing to the common confusion of time preference with liquidity preference it is difficult for the Keynesians to perceive this. They usually confuse the issue by tacitly attributing to saving preference the disturbances which accompany "hoarding" (the exercise of liquidity preference).† But it is

---

*See above, Chap. II, sec. 4.
†This point is developed below, particularly in Chaps. XI and XIII.

wrong to blame "speculative hoarding" (still less "autonomous hoard-ing") for the strains which major value changes create in the economy; for to do so is to confuse *a response to a disturbing condition* with the disturbing condition itself. As we shall see, people hoard, not because they become miserly, nor in my opinion (in the absence of *repressed* inflation) because they demand money through sheer inertia when the volume of money units happens to be increasing, but because economic policy has brought about serious anomalies in the value system which cause the prospective yield from money (a non-pecuniary yield) to in-crease relatively to that from other assets.*

18.—There has been some discussion about whether the great depression was or was not a monetary phenomenon. The answer is simple: the fall of prices obviously was; the unemployment and the fall in real income was not appropriately so described. The Macmillan Report said that the British depression of the 'thirties *could* be regarded as a monetary phe-nomenon because monetary policy had failed to solve the problems caused by "a conjunction of highly intractable nonmonetary phenom-ena." *But why should monetary policy be expected to solve such prob-lems?* We are abusing any monetary system if we try to use it to rectify nonmonetary disco-ordination. There was, I maintain, no conceivable response on the part of individual *monetary* systems (or by a world *monetary* institution had one then existed) to the depression situation of 1931, which could have eliminated unemployment and waste without inflation; but it is just that which the critics of the pre-1932 world were expecting monetary policy to achieve. Admittedly, in the disorder which five years of attempting to persevere with both cheap money and con-vertibility had produced in Britain, in 1931, it could have been seriously argued that the situation was remediable with least resistance by a re-sponse to the panic demand for liquidity which had arisen—through credit expansion in whatever form seemed most expedient from the political angle. The case for such a policy (which in the climate of expectations then ruling would have meant the temporary abandon-ment of convertibility) supposed, however, the enforcement of a drastic reduction of wage-rates in the sheltered industries in order to restore the flow of wages. I am not concerned at this stage with the case for (or against) that view. But if Keynes had enunciated a *special theory* based

---

*The hoarding which is sometimes experienced during an inflation (especially when it is accompanied by rationing and other "controls") is not, I think, attributable to inertia. In the situation caused, which I call *latent inflation*, present opportunities for consumption or investment in nonmoney assets are less promising than predicted opportunities. Thus, in this case also, it is anomalies caused by policy which induce hoarding as an accompaniment of saving. The hoarding does not itself create the anomalies.

on special assumptions of this kind, it would not have been necessary to write this book. As things are, he turned what *might* have been accepted as the wisdom of expediency in a difficult situation into an article of faith.

The justification for such a "special theory" would have been that it was part and parcel of a complete or general theory touching the fundamental reco-ordination of the economic system. That is, it would have had to cover the whole sphere of economic institutions and not merely the provinces of money, interest and credit. It would have had to envisage, as a concomitant of the relief to be afforded by cheap money, efforts being made to design a society in which it was no longer possible, through collusive action or otherwise, to price a large part of the flow of goods and services so that they were outside the reach of uninflated income or out of harmony with expectations.

It is a *dangerous* policy that I am here contemplating. For although moratoria to permit cheap money *might* assist State action to force real exploitative wage-rates down and the flow of wages up, they must, in themselves, tend to weaken market pressures to basic adjustment. Only if the State proposes to act powerfully in breaking down permanently the economic anarchy which the appeasement of sectional protectionist pressures has created, can a case be made out for any temporary abandonment of convertibility, on the principle of *reculer pour mieux sauter*. But *The General Theory* was virtually blind to this aspect of reform; and until recent years, it was seldom, if ever, to be discovered in the writings of the Keynesians.

19.—APPENDIX

The Attitude of the Cohen Council

In spite of the great wisdom reflected in the Reports of the Cohen Council *(The British Council on Prices, Productivity and Income)*, they have failed, I think, sufficiently to focus attention on the fundamental rôle of price adjustment. Thus they say that "it is important to be candid about the fact that" a check to the growth of production "is to be expected and tolerated" if inflation is to be brought to an end. [14] "Excessive demand" (meaning inflation) "cannot be restrained if at the same time it is sought to wring the last ounce of output out of a given constellation of human and material resources." [15] "In our opinion," they say later, "it is impossible that a free and flexible economic system can work efficiently without a perceptible (although emphatically not catastrophic) margin of unemployment." [16] They feel that it is essential to reduce prospective yields so that employers will offer stiffened resistance to wage demands. [17] But this *assumes* that deliberate accompanying action to maintain or increase the flow of wages and income has to be ruled out. Such a reliance upon the pressure of unemployed or under-employed resources can be defended only on grounds of expediency.*

The Council recognizes the importance of the State taking the required action in the sectors of the economy to which the *Monopolies and Restrictive Practices Act* applies, especially in their recommendation that consideration should be given to the suppression of resale price maintenance, even when enforced by individual manufacturers.(18)   If they could assume not only that the State would not shirk its duty in this field but that it would act with similar disinterestedness in the fields of labor and agriculture, they could avoid the dismal conclusion that only the pressure of idle resources is capable of bringing the economy into co-ordination. Their phrase, "wring the last ounce of output out of the system," merely means using resources with the maximum economy; and I fail to see how *this* process can ever be "over-extended," as they fear.

The cessation of inflation need have no tendency to "dampen demand," which is the Council's phrase.† Private reactions to such a policy may perhaps do so. But if the State is allowed to perform its planning and co-ordinative functions, private interests will not be permitted to cause any contraction of the source of demand. Far from leading to a situation in which competition for labor is likely to decline, we should then be more likely to witness an increase in the so-called "poaching" by managements, higher overtime offers and the offer of employment to pensioners (i.e., increased bidding against the demand for leisure), as well as increased inducements as a form of bidding against less well remunerated occupations, like those of housewives.

Of course, it would be perfectly legitimate for the Council to say that, *given the existing institutional set up,* any tendency for the rate of inflation to slow down must mean some decline in prospective yields, realized profits and employment; and that this may be expected in the long-run to lead to reasonableness in the fixing of wage-rates and prices. My criticism is that they place insufficient stress on their vital assumption of a defective framework of institutions. They fail to emphasize *the source* of the dampening effect. I have the feeling that they *perceive* the source, but see no way of effectively describing it.

---

*To ask "employers" to act as the defenders of the flow of wages and full employment against trade-union attacks, is to call upon private people to fight coercive action because the politicians wish to avoid the unpopularity of doing so. But only expediency can justify any failure to proclaim and enforce the principles that all private use of coercive power should be outlawed and all deliberate contrivance of scarcity should be forbidden.

†The Council's approach is weakened by their failure throughout to make explicit the distinction between inflated and uninflated income and "demand." See p.136.

A far more deplorable example is to be found in the last Report of the President's Council of Economic Advisers. In an apparently frank support of the principle of private enterprise, the Council recommend that there shall be no interference with union-negotiated wage bargains. At the same time they refer with approval to the discipline of antitrust in the business and industrial sectors of the pricing system. Why, then, do they not advise a similar discipline in *all* sectors of the pricing system? The need for an explanation is glaring. Well-known economists serve on the Council. It is a pity if they think it their duty to write on such issues with the casuistry typical of politicians.

REFERENCES

(1) ANDERSON, *Economics and the Public Welfare*, p.550. (2) POLYANI, *Full Employment and Free Trade*, p.123. (3) KEYNES, *The General Theory*, p.6. (4) BRONFENBRENNER, *Some Neglected Implications of Secular Inflation*, in Kurihara, *Post-Keynesian Economics*, p.48. (5) LAVINGTON, *The Trade Cycle*, p.23. (6) *Ibid.*, p.24. (7) DILLARD, *Theory of a Monetary Economy*, in Kurihara, *op. cit.*, p.29. (8) *Ibid.*, p.12. (9) LOVEDAY, *Collective Behaviour and Monetary Policy*, in *Lessons of Monetary Experience*, ed., Gayer., p.428. (10) M. GILBERT, *Currency Depreciation*, pp.12 et seq. (11) FELLNER, *What is Surviving?* A.E.R., P and P., May, 1957, p.68. (12) *Ibid.*, pp.68-9. (13) KEYNES, *op. cit.*, p.vii. (14) Cohen Report *(First Report of the Council on Prices, Productivity and Incomes)*, par. 117. (15) *Ibid.*, par. 117. (16) *Ibid.*, par. 135. (17) *Ibid.*, par. 137. (18) *Ibid.*, par. 155.

Chapter V

THE NATURE OF MONEY

SUMMARY

1.—The most impressive branch of classical economics was that of monetary theory, which was treated as part of the general theory of value. 2.—The Keynesian contribution, far from assisting a much needed development of monetary theory, profoundly disturbed it. 3.—I distinguish between "pure" and "hybrid" money. 4.—In my use of the conventional quantity theory identity, V covers all factors other than T (the flow of services) which influence demand for money. 5.—The term "money" is defined so as to cover every commodity, token or document which can serve the purpose of a medium of exchange and is demanded for that purpose. 6.—The quantity of money may be measured in actual money units, M, or in abstract money units of constant real value—"real terms," M_r. 7.—The value, M_r, is determined by the prospective wantedness or productivity of monetary services 8.—whilst the value, M, is determined by the banks and other credit issuing institutions, which can influence the market rate of interest. 9.—When restrained by effective convertibility obligations, the credit system is neutral. 10.—All changes in $\frac{M_r}{M}$ may be ascribed to "monetary policy" 11.—and it is misleading to think of monetary action being somehow ineffective in determining this ratio. 12.—But the wise administration of monetary policy not only ensures the settlement of debts in units of the same defined value as those in which they were contracted, it avoids recourse to exchange controls and other restraints on the price system, and achieves stability. 13.—Misled by a defective theory of interest, Keynes failed to perceive the determinants of M in a credit economy, 14—and confused time preference with liquidity preference. 15.—Appendix A, on The Use of the Term "Neutral." 16.—Appendix B, on The Irrelevance of the Absolute Level of Interest to the Demand for Money. 17.—Appendix C, on The Concept of the Aggregate Real Value of Money.

1.—It has been claimed that in one respect at least Keynes brought about a notable advance, namely, in the principles of money. Before the great new insight brought to us by his *Tract*, his *Treatise* and his *General Theory*, it is suggested, monetary theory had been in an unsatisfactory state.

Of course, every branch of a science is always capable of progress. Yet in my judgment, ever since the remarkable contributions of Locke and Hume, monetary theory has been one of the least unsatisfactory branches of economics. "On what subject do modern specialists find the classical economics most impressive and instructive?," asks Stigler. He answers, "Without question it is money and banking. A whole series of modern scholars—Angell, Gregory, Viner, Wood and Mints, to name only five extensive explorers of the last twenty-five years—have concurred in the high quality of this discussion."[1] And the major contributions subsequent to Hume in this field (I think first of Adam Smith, Say, Henry Thornton, James Mill, Ricardo, Torrens and J. S. Mill) evolved out of the insight recorded in those earlier expositions. Although subjected to far-reaching developments by such economists as Wicksell, Walras, Marshall, von Wieser, Mises, Cannan, Robertson, Pigou and Fisher, the core of classical teaching about money had not been seriously challenged before Keynes' attempt at "debunking."

But after about 1925, there does seem to have been a great deal of intellectual groping. It began about the time when Keynes started contributing. The uneasiness which it reflected was due less to dissatisfaction with what had been already established, than to a feeling that, whilst the general substance of previous teaching was beyond challenge, it did not permit a complete explanation of all the phenomena of the time. The situation did not seem to be one which called for a *revolution* but suggested rather that careful development was needed. Quite a number of speculations of promise were made in this spirit. They mostly ran into difficulties; and there was undoubtedly scope for and need for a major work of refinement and synthesis.

Keynes did not help in supplying what was needed, nor did he hasten the time when such a contribution could have been expected.

For all its defects, pre-Keynesian monetary theory had certain clear-cut virtues. It was conceived of as an essential, integral and vital part of the theory of value (price) and production. The study of monetary phenomena was woven realistically into the study of economic theory as a whole.* Economists were trained to think simultaneously in terms of money prices and in real terms—to be continuously aware of the reality under the veil (the very real veil) of money. The monetary system and monetary policy were viewed in their relation to the expression of preferences, entrepreneurial responses and their effects upon values and the money expression of values.

As incipient praxeologists, the early economists had perceived the inherent unity of all economic relationships.† In one respect only did the classical economists and their orthodox successors fail, it seems to me, to bring monetary policy sufficiently closely into relation with the general body of their science. They did not understand *clearly* enough that money assets are productive, that they provide services in exactly the same manner as other assets, and that they are invested in for the same reasons. Economists tended to speak, wholly unjustifiably, of money having *a yield of nil*. It has been in this respect that the orthodox treatment of money has been most defective—its inadequate generality, its assumption (often inconsistently held) that pecuniary yields are the only yields, and therefore that money is "barren," "dead stock."‡ It is, however, the Keynesians and not the orthodox economists who have built heavily on this error.**

I regard it as a misrepresentation for the Keynesians to say, of pre-Keynesian teaching (I quote Harrod), that "those who discussed general economic theory, namely, the supply of and demand for commodities and factors of production . . . were living in a different world from those who discussed banking policy and the general level of prices."(3) Occasionally, of course, economists made abstraction of money as a means of simplifying *one stage* in analysis. And admittedly, *because of its importance,* money tended to be treated not merely in the course of an analysis of the prices and quantities of "real" factors, but in a separate literature of its own. This literature was mainly in pamphlet form during the nineteenth century, and in the form of separate volumes—great treatises—in the twentieth century.††

---

*Marget, in particular, has demonstrated this.(2)

†This was clearly implicit in the remarkable insight, probably inspired by James Mill, of J. B. Say. It was ultimately clearly *explicit* in the developments for which Wicksteed was responsible.

‡I have dealt with this issue in my article, *The Yield from Money Held.*(4)

**The Keynesians seem never to realize the implications of the fact that money performs continuous services for the owner whilst he owns it, and that its services cease for him when it is spent.

††The works of Wicksell, Irving Fisher, Mises, Cannan, Marshall and Dennis Robertson.

2.—But Keynes, both in the *Treatise* and *The General Theory*, tried to find in the factors determining the value of the money unit the genesis of output and income (although *he* would not have described his aim in such words). He linked monetary theory to the economic world only through unsatisfactory concepts like employment, income and effective demand.*

In macro-economic models and formulae, he drew attention away from the crucial phenomena of price adjustment, the revisions of entrepreneurial plans which are implied in every price change, and the nature of resistances to co-ordinating adjustments. Moreover, this approach replaced the formerly realistic treatment of the functioning of the credit system with an analysis developed on the assumption, for ease of model construction, of a constant number of money units.†

Hence Keynes did not, as some have supposed, *assimilate* monetary theory to the general theory of value and production. Rather he attributed to monetary policy, co-ordinative functions which are normally performed in a quite different way. In this manner, it was he himself who *segregated* the monetary factor from other factors, and in doing so, he showed that he misunderstood the classical tradition. He stated that, before he began writing *The Treatise*, he was still "moving along the traditional lines of regarding the influence of money as something so to speak quite separate from the general theory of supply and demand."[5] But this was not "traditional." It was merely *the form* which Marshallian exposition had taken; and it seems to have encouraged Keynes to jump to the opposite standpoint, to try to invent a monetary theory which would provide a full explanation of "income" or "employment." That monetary and interest policy were *relevant to* the use of resources (employment and output) was never denied by the economists whom Keynes belittled; nor was the denial ever implicit. Consider, for instance, Part III, Chapter V of Mises' *Theory of Money and Credit*. Section 4 of this chapter is headed, "The Influence of the Interest Policy of the Credit-Issuing Banks on Production." That is, however, a quite different thing from alleging a monetary explanation of production.

Keynes' treatment was in no sense progress. Even in matters of detail, it is difficult to find valid originalities. The erudite Marget's *Theory of Prices* abounds with examples of how supposed originalities in the *Treatise* and *The General Theory* were part of the common heritage of economics. The truth is, rather, that Keynes' chief originality lay in his ironic attack on orthodox thinking about money and other things. His attack created, I believe, so much confusion in the minds of the young

---

*See pp.25 et seq., 205-6. See also my *Theory of Idle Resources*, pp.31-5.

†The failure of subsequent Keynesians to recognise the vital importance of changes in M (except *via* interest, through "investment") may be due to this assumption.

economists of the subsequent generation, that it has set back progress by
at least a couple of decades. Such development as has occurred since the
'twenties has been mainly in the contributions of the Swedish School
(spoilt by the Keynesian influence), in those of the Chicago School,* in
the works of that robust and independent thinker, Dennis Robertson and
in those "refinements" of Keynesian theory (largely by supposed Keynesians) which have in fact, if not in form, amounted to a recantation.†

3.—I do not propose in this contribution to attempt a new treatment of
the fundamentals of money and credit. But I think it will help exposition
if I make use of a few unfamiliar although quite simple concepts which
have assisted my own thinking. I shall distinguish between "pure money"
and what I find it convenient to call "hybrid money," meaning by the
latter assets which have "moneyness" ("money substitutes," "near
money," "secondary liquidities," etc.), i.e., assets which provide not only
monetary services but other satisfactions or output as well.

4.--I shall use the conventional quantity theory identity, $MV \equiv PT$,
as follows: M stands for the number of money units; V for all the factors
other than T which influence demand for money‡; P for the scale of
prices (an index number of the prices of productive services) and T for
that demand for money which tends to vary with output (i.e., with the
flow of productive services). The identity shows necessary relationships,
not causes. It is a useful tautology, that is all. Thus, if MV is constant
and capacity is withheld and this is not offset by growth, or if net
decumulation is in progress (i.e., if productive capacity is declining) so
that T declines, the scale of prices, P, must rise. Similarly, P must fall if
capacity is released, or added to as a result of growth, unless MV expands.

I intend T and $\frac{1}{V}$ to represent the expression of demand for monetary
services derived from (a) preferences concerning ends (subjective valuations of monetary services) and (b) choice of means to ends. It seems to
be convenient to distinguish between those elements in the demand
expressed which are a function of the output of services (income), which
I call T, and *all the other elements in this demand,* which I call $\frac{1}{V}$. These
"other elements" make up what Keynes called "liquidity prefer-

---

*Particularly Milton Friedman.
†See chap. xix.
‡I use this term V because, if so defined, it causes the identity $MV \equiv PT$ to be
very useful. The *term* "velocity" has, however, proved to be not only inappropriate
but misleading. The more rigorous economists have, in fact, used the term "income
velocity" where the use of the term V, as I have defined it, would make no difference
to their reasoning.

ence," a decline in V meaning a rise in liquidity preference, and *vice versa*. But both equally represent demand for monetary services (through the offer of nonmoney).

In the conventional *equation*, P is regarded as a dependent variable. But in a society in which prices can be influenced by collusive or State action (whether through control of outputs, or through nonmarket price-fixing with outputs adjusting themselves), it cannot be regarded as a dependent variable. In these circumstances, both V and T would have to be dependent variables (for quite different reasons) if one intended to treat the identity as an equation. But M would have to be an independent variable. For in the presence of convertibility, the magnitude M is always a question of policy in the short run and the value of the commodities or currencies into which the money unit is convertible in the long run; and in the absence of convertibility, it is a question of policy in both the short run and the long run.

But because the quantity theory which I believe to be both valid and useful is a simple tautology (and my subsequent argument tries to justify this point of view), a change in any factor, whilst it implies an offsetting change in one or more of the other factors, does not itself record any causal connection. Thus, if an increase in M is not accompanied by an increase in P, there must be a decline in V or an increase in T.* But in facilitating conceptual clarity, the identity does not permit mere mechanical thinking. For example, the factors which may cause an increase in P otherwise than through an increase in M or V *must* cause a reduction in T; whilst (in a society in which withheld capacity exists) if the increase in P *is* caused by an increase in M or V, it is likely to exert a co-ordinative effect and cause a rise in T.

5.—"Money" may be defined as that which produces monetary services, It cannot be usefully restricted, as is commonly done, to "deposits *plus* currency in circulation" (the chief forms of "pure money"). It covers every commodity, token, document or claim which *can* serve the purposes of a medium of exchange, etc., and which *is* demanded for those purposes, irrespective of whether these commodities, tokens, documents or claims are performing other economic functions also. The test is whether the value of such assets is influenced by reason of their being demanded for the monetary services they provide. If they *are* so demanded I call them "money" or "money assets."

To *measure* the quantity of money we must have a unit. The pound,

---

*This does not imply an instantaneous reaction to the change in any term of the identity. For instance, if there is a successful forgery and we include the forged units under M, the necessity for the forgers to off-load the results of their crime slowly must be shown as a V below the normal, because the extent of the forgery will become known only gradually and P will not immediately rise therefore. (See pp.140-1).

the dollar, the florin and the franc are money units—what I shall call "actual" money units. We can, however, conceive of an *abstract money unit of constant real value* in terms of the flow of productive services which constitute income. Actual money units may have a defined value (e.g., in terms of a price index number—a "real value"— or in terms of a metal or a combination of metals, or in terms of some foreign currency, etc.), or they may have no defined value. If the money unit has no defined value, there must be some legal tender provision or some custom which causes certain documents or tokens to be accepted as the measuring rod of value.

When I refer to the number of money units, M, *I shall mean the aggregate value of money assets* (pure *plus* the pure money equivalent of hybrid*) *in terms of some actual money unit,* e.g., in terms of pounds, dollars, etc.

6.—A very useful concept is that of the "aggregate value of money in real terms."† There is no *physical* measurement of the "amount" of money, as there is for individual commodities. It is no more measurable in physical terms than is output in general. It is a value measurement of the quantity of abstract units of constant "real value." Its only relation to physical measurement is through the physical quantity factors in the weights of the index numbers which are chosen to define real values. I shall represent it by the symbol M_r.

The term "constant real value" has meaning, of course, only in relation to a price index which is regarded as appropriate; and it is quite impossible to conceive of a practical method of compiling an index of prices which will have an unchanging significance for all members of society. The metaphysical speculations which have taken place on this issue have led to some interesting explorations up blind alleys; but the explorers have found nothing which can help the economists to advise wisely those who are engaged in the urgent practical task of improving the economic organization of the world. If, however, the democratic ideal is accepted, no insuperable difficulties arise out of the problem of

---

*The hybrid money *unit* is an amount equal to the value of a pure money unit out of that proportion of the value of assets which has moneyness (i.e., out of hybrid money). Thus, if the long term rate of interest is 5 per cent, and the rate of interest on a short-term security is 2½ per cent, a security worth £1 will represent 10/— in pure money equivalent. And if the long-term rate of interest is 6 per cent, and the interest on a short-term security is 2 per cent, then 13/4d. out of each £1 security will be money, i.e., two thirds. The marginal return from this type of hybrid money will be, pecuniary interest 2 per cent, monetary services 4 per cent. Because the moneyness increases, and the pecuniary yields of securities decline as maturity approaches, *ceteris paribus* the magnitude M increases as the average life of a given volume of debt in the community is diminished, and declines as the average life is lengthened.

†The notion has had surprisingly little influence in economics. See Appendix C to this chapter.

the constitution of the ideal index.* The ideal index is simply one which covers most successfully those items which are observed to be typical of the community's demands. Theoretically, it should give equal weight to every component of the flow of productive services (into direct consumption or into replacement and net accumulation of assets) which constitutes real income.†

7.—Attacking what he called "the fetish of liquidity" as one of the maxims of the "economics of orthodox finance," Keynes insisted that there is "no such thing as liquidity of investment for the community as a whole."[6] How wrong he was! Society can become more liquid just as an individual may, simply by using its resources in a different manner and bidding up the value of money assets in the aggregate‡ (by offering more nonmoney for money).

The magnitude, M_r, increases when monetary services come to be more highly valued in terms of nonmoney services; and this can occur (a) owing to an increase in T (T varying with the flow of services as a whole, i.e., "output," in which the aggregate value of monetary services forms a very small proportion) or (b) owing to a decline in V (V varying with all the factors apart from output which affect the demand for monetary services). This demand will tend to vary with changes in (i) business institutions and procedures,** (ii) habits, and (iii) expectations about the future value of the money unit and about changes in the market rate of interest.

Given the part of the demand for monetary services which (in the conventional quantity theory identity) is represented by $\frac{1}{V}$, it is the productive system which "creates" the money contained in money units (i.e., M_r) and not the credit system. And T (a function of output, or the flow of services) being given, it is the demand for money represented by $\frac{1}{V}$ which determines the magnitude, M_r. The expansion of credit

---

*This is not to suggest that the *practical problem* of constructing such an index is not a big one. But the difficulties are technical rather than theoretical.

†The value contained in money units consists of rights to obtain either capital goods or services; but the value of which I conceive in the notion of "constant value" is uninfluenced by *relative* scarcities of capital goods on the one side and the services of such goods on the other. Such valuations influence (as I shall later show) only the rate of interest.

‡Keynes was of course curiously blind to the essential productiveness of the liquidity condition, especially when its origin is what he called the "speculative motive." He regarded liquidity-preference in times of general uncertainty as peculiarly deleterious. But in a world of unstable price rigidities, no-one is able to avoid speculation. Indeed, to remain passive in respect of the liquidity-composition of one's assets is merely one form of speculation, a stupid form!

**Monetary institutions (e.g., clearing machinery) are included under this heading.

merely reduces the content of each money unit just as forgery does, unless society is (i) currently producing additional productive services (an increase of income) out of which additional monetary services are demanded, or (ii) for other reasons placing a greater value on money in relation to nonmoney assets.

An increase in T and a decrease in V both cause an increase in M_r but for different reasons. In the case of an increase in T, the additional content of M_r is supplied by an increased flow of services into the products of which money units are exchangeable. In the case of a decline in V, the value of M_r rises because money and monetary services are valued more highly for other reasons, i.e., in spite of real income not having changed.

8.—The number of money units, M, is determined by the issue or withdrawal of credit;* and this process has no influence on M_r unless it happens to influence the wantedness or prospective productiveness of money. That is, whilst changes in M or in V or in T influence P, changes in V and T do so through influencing M_r whilst, statically considered, changes in M do not. Only if changes in M influence expectations or encounter the "money illusion" will they influence V and hence M_r; and only if changes in M induce the release or withholding of capacity, will they influence T and hence M_r. If the Keynesians had merely placed great stress on this last possibility, they would have precipitated much less controversy in the theoretical field.

I have always had the strongest objection to the idea of banks "manu-facturing money,"† or even of the State doing so. When the credit expansion is inflationary they can "manufacture" it only in the sense that forgers manufacture it; and when the expansion is noninflationary they respond to an increasing M_r. Banks dilute money, so to speak, when they "advance credit" to an extent or in a manner which must involve (a) depreciation of the money unit in terms of a convertibility obliga-tion, or (b) depreciation in terms of scarce things in general. Banks may increase the real value of the money *unit* (and cause appreciation, again in either of the two senses) when they "withdraw credit". But when they "expand credit" in circumstances which do *not* spell depreciation (in either sense), their action is merely a response to something which has happened in the economic system as a whole. The aggregate real value of money assets is not "created" or "destroyed" by the banking or credit system. It expands or contracts, as we have seen, with the community's decision to hold (i.e., to use) assets for the monetary services they can

---

*See pp.95-7.

†Cf. Sayers: "Banks are not merely *purveyors* of money but also in an important sense manufacturers of money."[7] Hartley Withers was, I think, responsible for intro-ducing this seriously fallacious notion, in his *Meaning of Money*.

perform; and *ceteris paribus* the community's demand for this purpose will vary with the flow of productive services in general (i.e., the flow of products).

The number of money units may change as a result of the deliberate expansion or contraction of credit by some monetary authority with an unfettered or limited discretion, or as a result of the "automatic" working* of economic institutions *under given convertibility obligations.* Thus, the factors which determine the demand for or supply of any monetary metal, or any commodity or commodities forming the standard, are *among* the determinants of the number of money units.† But monetary authorities like central banks and treasuries are merely intermediaries in the exchange of debts. The ultimate issuers of bank credit are those holders of deposits and notes who are not themselves indebted to the banking system, and they can, in the absence of restraint, withdraw credit at any time. When credit is withdrawn by those who have advanced it from abroad, the loss of gold and foreign exchange is experienced; the contraction in M so caused is induced by factors which can be seen to determine a contraction in M_r; and if the monetary authority then fails to bring about a parallel contraction in M, inflation (expressed at first in balance of payments difficulties) must follow.

It should be noticed that I do not regard the expansion or curtailment of credit as accelerating or retarding the "virtual" velocity of circulation of money units (as some important writers, notably Wicksell,[8] have suggested), but as changing their quantity. The difference is important. Whilst an increase in M and an increase in V imply the same effects upon P, a change in V means a change in M_r, whilst a change in M does not. And one of the factors which may influence V is anticipation of changes in the content of money units.

The credit system is operated through all actions which, the natural level of interest being given, influence the equilibrium market rate of interest. Such actions cover not only re-discount operations, open market operations, the issue of notes, the sale of treasury bills and fiscal policy, but various other actions.‡ If they influence the value of the money unit,

---

*By "automatic" working is meant responsible entrepreneurial decision-making within the framework of a contract-limited discretion.

†The commodity or commodities may of course be chosen in the first place, or accepted over the years, because, working together with the credit system and other factors, the effects of this demand and supply can be expected to result in a stable scale of prices. In practice, it seems to me, a high degree of price stability was so achieved through the gold standard system when it was judiciously administered; and this was, I think, responsible for its long survival, under the relatively more effectively planned and co-ordinated economies which existed before 1914.

‡Successful forgeries have the same effect as credit expansion, except that when M contracts through the eventual refusal to honor the forged note or coin, an innocent holder is penalized. In the case of true credit, no-one suffers when the volume of deposits and notes in circulation contracts.

they are credit or monetary measures, whether they are in the form of "free banking" with convertibility, conventional central back action, treasury action or so-called "direct controls." The tendency to confine the notion of monetary operations to central bank activity has caused much confusion. Thus, reserve ratios; credit rationing (restriction of bank advances otherwise than by a common, nondiscriminatory market rate of interest); restriction of hire purchase and building society operations; the limitation of private capital issues; these and all similar controls are crude—and usually discriminatory—efforts at credit contraction. They may have some deflationary effect, but all too often they tend to act rather like shutting one door and leaving another open. In so far as they are effective, they raise *the equilibrium rate of market interest* (as distinct from the nominal rate) or lower the natural level. Obviously, then, they are monetary measures and are intended to be such.

9.—When the money unit has a defined value (and that implies convertibility in some sense) the market rate of interest is set by the judgment of the monetary authority reacting to the demand for monetary services. The market rate coincides with the natural rate when M is caused to vary in direct proportion to M_r; but the market rate may always be set with a view to maintaining any defined value of the money unit, *even a changing one.*

For when M is determined by the issue or withdrawal of credit, an increase in the number of money units does not mean a permanent addition to an "existing stock." It means that the number of units, M, *may* expand or contract flexibly according to all the other factors which influence M_r. Whenever there is any use made of the credit device, there is *some* flexibility of this kind. The measure in which it in fact works this way depends upon monetary policy. But *when this policy embraces the convertibility of a currency, it provides incentives which, to the extent to which the defined value or standard is noninflationary, tend to prevent the credit system from causing the depreciation or appreciation of money units.* The policy may then be said to be neutral.

10.—By "monetary policy," I mean the policy adopted by "the monetary authority." And by "monetary authority" I mean (a) the central bank or other note-issuing authority,* *plus* (b) any institution which issues such loans as serve as hybrid money (without an accompanying withdrawal of credit equal in value to the pure money element in the hybrid assets),† *plus* (c) all institutions which are influenced by govern-

---

*Even if there is no "central" or "reserve" bank so-called, treasuries may issue notes.
†E.g., treasuries which issue treasury bills. On the notion of the value of the pure money element, see p.92 above (footnote) .

mental pressure or exhortation in credit policy.* It is a convenient simplification to think of the monetary authority as consisting of the central
bank and the treasury.

The "monetary authority" *so defined* is solely responsible for the magnitude M. I am afraid, however, that this simple assertion is likely to
provoke resistance. For instance, the typical discussion of monetary policy seems *to assume* that the failure to balance budgets is inflationary or
deflationary, according to whether there is a deficit or surplus. But fiscal
policy as such is neutral. It is only when governments incur or settle
debts on such terms that they influence the relation of market interest
to the natural level that policy can be said to cause MV to change in
relation to T; and that *is* monetary policy, whatever we may like to call
it! The fact that deficits create an incentive for governments to call upon
monetary authorities to inflate by lending at rates below the natural,
whilst surplusses facilitate monetary policies which lead to the cessation
of inflation (or conceivably even to a rectifying deflation) must not be
allowed to confuse the issue.

Similarly, it is nearly always taken for granted that "hoarding" (an
abnormal demand for monetary services) is deflationary and "dishoarding" inflationary. But hoarding is deflationary only in the sense that
economizing inventions or the release of capacity are deflationary! We
must beware of assuming away monetary policy. Because the value of
the money unit is either (a) laid down by convertibility obligations or
(b) a matter of government or treasury expediency (acquiesced in by a
central bank), we have to recognize that hoarding does not create deflation nor dishoarding inflation. Hoarding creates a condition in which
the avoidance of open deflation causes latent inflation, or in which latent
inflation is prevented from becoming open (because hoarding happens
to accompany an increase in M). *Latent inflation* means a condition
in which the withdrawal of credit will become necessary, in order to
avoid open inflation, at some future date, when dishoarding ultimately
ensues.†

I do not suggest that it must necessarily be misleading to treat increases
in T and decreases in V as *deflationary tendencies,* and decreases in T
and increases in V as *inflationary tendencies,* to be *offset* by the monetary authority in a degree determined by the nature of the defined
money unit value. It is indeed natural that the officials of a central bank
should regard their task as that of *rectifying such tendencies as do not
accord with the objectives to which they are committed by treasuries or*

---

*Commercial banks subject to differing reserve requirements imposed by the treas-
ury or the central bank are, so to speak, agents of the monetary authority.

†The failure to withdraw credit in these circumstances is deliberate if reluctant. The
maintenance of security prices has been one motive.

governments. Hence, the term "monetary policy" as I shall use it refers
solely to the function of so operating the credit system that *a defined or
a desired value of the money unit* shall be achieved. (The word "desired" here has reference to the desires of the State).

If banking were conducted by pure private enterprise, it would be difficult to conceive of a monetary *authority*. There would simply be the
contractual or legal obligations accepted by the banks to pay out deposits
on demand and to redeem notes on demand (supported, possibly, by
reserve ratio requirements).

I am not suggesting of course that, under central banking, the policies of the private banks have no effect upon the value of the money
unit. But the commercial banks themselves are not then called upon to
maintain or change that value. This obligation is taken off their shoul-
ders. They act only *within the limits* set by discount policy, or open
market policy, or reserve requirements, or other action taken by the
central bank, or the treasury, etc., to influence M in relation to M_r. But
if my interpretation of the situation is correct, although the commercial
banks play an important part in *operating* the system which causes
changes in M (relatively to M_r), they may only be said to *determine*
that policy to the extent to which they submit to pressure or exhortation
to exercise credit restraint or the reverse. And when they do so act,
they virtually become part of the central banking system. (I.e., their
position then resembles in some measure that of the Bank of England
when, for a long time before it was nationalized, it submitted to Treasury hints or pressure).

*It is difficult to discuss monetary policy unless we assume that the
authority has some clear-cut objective.* Thus, if we are concerned with
the situation in which the treasury is prepared to take the risk of being
faced with the subsequent dilemma of the alternatives of deflation or
devaluation, we can realistically assume that it wants to postpone the
necessity to face this dilemma for as long as possible. Such a postponement must then be regarded as the objective. Ought not the treasury,
therefore, to make clear from time to time the rate at which it regards
it as expedient that the inflation shall proceed? But if there is no ultimate defined goal of this sort, there is a frustrating void in any policy
discussion. I shall accordingly use the term "inflationary policy" or "deflationary policy" to mean monetary policy with an inflationary or deflationary objective, even when the treasury tolerates or dictates mere drift,
week to week pragmatism, hoping that inflation will not occur but not
being prepared to authorize or require the only steps which can effectively prevent it.

As it is within the power of the monetary authority to maintain or
change any long-term value of the money unit, *I shall regard all such*

changes as due to policy, i.e., as ascribable either to the aims pursued or to the degree of success in achieving those aims. For instance, if V increases and M does not contract, that is due to policy.

It is always a matter of discretion, or of judgment, about exactly how an obligation to maintain a particular value of the money unit may best be achieved. Thus, if M_r changes (owing to the growth or decline of output, or institutional changes, or through various speculative reactions) and M does not change, market interest, i, will diverge from the natural level, r. Whenever $i \neq r$ the divergence must be regarded as caused wholly by the failure of the monetary authority (whether by aim or erroneous judgment) to adjust M in accordance with changes in M_r. Presumably any passivity of the monetary authority is deliberate. If so, the resulting depreciation on appreciation of the money unit must express policy; and in particular there seems to be no reason why M should not be allowed fully to respond to that determinant of M_r which Keynes termed "speculative" (caused by predictions of capital loss from a rise in interest rates), provided that the monetary authority remains willing and able to compensate any subsequent decline in M_r (as the rate of interest rises) by an immediate contraction of M.

11.—Nothing could be more confusing than to imagine depreciations or appreciations of currencies as phenomena which may be beyond the full control of the monetary authority. The notion of treasuries "fighting inflation" without success, for instance, is absurd (unless all that is meant is that they are—necessarily unavailingly—trying to keep internal prices stable, whilst another currency to which their money unit is tied by fixed exchange rates is depreciating). But if there are convertibility obligations (or if fixed exchange rates have to be maintained, or if a rising scale of prices is regarded as politically inexpedient) and latent inflation is inadvertently allowed to emerge, it is certainly beyond the control of the monetary authority to fulfil its obligations without recourse to rectifying action. The post-war inflations of Western Europe and the United States have been due to policy weaknesses, weaknesses which, in my judgment, have been dictated by treasuries actuated by political considerations—supposedly validated by Keynesian teachings—rather than by the technical requirements of a stable monetary system.

It is because governments are so often trying to use the administration of money and credit in order to achieve other ends than the simple one of providing an efficient mechanism of exchange that we so often hear it argued that mere monetary action is ineffective. But there is never any obstacle to the effective use of measures which determine the volume of bank deposits *plus* currency in circulation (in the light of hybrid money and the factors which determine the demand for monetary services), so as to maintain a money unit at any enacted or desired (constant or changing) value.

In modern controversies, for instance, we often meet the contention that bank rate action is ineffectual. The truth is that, used with sufficient boldness, it can never fail,* however clumsily it operates in relation to, say, open market operations. Of course, when latent inflation is verging to open inflation, far more drastic action of this kind may be needed than in a more normal situation. But obviously, if monetary stability is to be achieved whilst the government's power to borrow from the central bank on their own terms remains unchecked, the restriction of credit offered *to the private sector* may have to be severe.

12.—Although the task of a monetary authority is a professional, technical matter of great difficulty, the nature of that task is simply enough *defined*. When orthodox objectives are accepted, the aim is that of seeing that the operation of the credit system permits debts to be settled in units of the same *defined value* (ideally in units of the same real value) *as those in which they were contracted*. But a wise aim, sincerely pursued, may not necessarily be wisely administered. The test of the soundness of the *administration* of a credit system lies in two things.

Firstly, its ability to maintain the defined value not only without recourse to any control of capital issues, credit squeezing (or other rationing), or exchange control, but without any other limitations being placed on speculation, flight capital, and so forth. For if monetary institutions have been wisely designed and their administration is being wisely executed, any speculation which does not *assist* policy objectives will subject the speculator to the penalty of severe pecuniary losses. All "controls" ("exchange," "import," etc.) other than those imposed entrepreneurially in order to fulfil *contractual* obligations, frustrate the co-ordinative mechanism of the price system.

Secondly, administration is sound when it maintains the defined value of the money unit in the short run as well as in the long run, i.e., *together with stability*.† This aim may be said to be achieved when any deviation from the defined value (i) encounters, or (ii) itself brings into operation, forces (including "automatic" or routine policy reactions)

*In my opinion, this is amply demonstrated by British experience in 1957. But bank rate merely determines broad limits, within which there is a wide range for discretion in credit policy, e.g., open-market operations.

†Short term variations in the productivity of money (and hence in the value M_r) due to the periodic concentration of tax payments, large transactions in government securities, etc., may be responded to by various methods of changing the normal ratio (dictated by prudence, convention or rule) of liquid assets to liabilities in the banking system as a whole. In this way M can be maintained in that relation to M_r at which monetary policy is aiming *in the short run as well as the long run*.

which *tend* to press the value of the unit in the direction of the defined value. In the best imaginable economic system, the process of recovery from an initially uncompensated disturbance is bound to be affected by innumerable chance influences, some assisting, others hindering the achievement of equilibrium. All sorts of unstable rigidities, resistances of unpredictable duration, rebounds, elasticities and inelasticities are to be expected. But the essential stability will have been accomplished (a) if the pressures towards the defined value build up continuously and cumulatively, and (b) the *milieu* in which they operate tends to iron out the inevitable fluctuating tendency. And the *milieu* will exert this stabilizing effect when there is faith in the intentions and ability of the monetary authority. It will, of course, be impossible to eliminate the "too much—too little" reaction; but fluctuating divergences from the defined scale set up by any single disturbance will tend always towards a narrowing amplitude.

Wicksell realized that credit *could* act simply "as a corrective to an occasional shortage of the medium of exchange," so that there would be an automatic and self-regulating canceling out of "fluctuations in the amount of money."* "But," he said, "as everybody knows, this does not happen."[9] If my interpretation of the situation is correct the reason why it does not happen is that, in practice, policy in respect of convertibility (or the maintenance of the value of the money unit), and the expectations created by that policy, are inconsistent with the objective of convertibility. And they are inconsistent, I believe, partly because the problem has not been perceived with sufficient clarity, but mainly because monetary stability has conflicted with the desire to avoid the consequences of price disco-ordination in the easy way—through cheap money.

Given a stable measure of value, depression is the penalty of cheap money, in the sense that it is the inevitable outcome of the rectification of the inflationary consequences, and perhaps even of the mere cessation or braking of an open inflation. Only in the absence of a stable money unit can cheap money persist for any length of time without a deflationary reaction. Serious depression has been avoided in most countries since the 1930's, simply because cheap money has been accompanied by a money unit of no defined value, with creeping inflation. *Indeed, chronic or creeping inflation is nothing else than an alternative form of the disease we call "depression"*—a far more serious and debilitating form, because (as we have seen) it permits continuous procrastination and postponement of efforts to rehabilitate the machinery of economic co-ordination.

---

*Wicksell regarded credit as affecting velocity of circulation and not as influencing the number of money units. (See above, p.95) .

13.—I can turn now to the Keynesian objection to a money unit of defined value. In general terms the Keynesians feel that mankind should be free from the "tyranny" of a rigid measuring rod, and the "balanced budgets" which that "tyranny" in general makes expedient. Their attitude on this point seems to derive from their conviction (which we have already noticed)* that certain economic preferences, judgments or values can throw the economy out of co-ordination, causing "effective demand" to contract; and hence that the results of such preferences, judgments and values need rectifying, by State edict, in the field of monetary action.†

Keynes himself never understood that these preferences and judgments, when concerned with the time factor, are *the sole cause* of that market rate of interest which is neither reduced by inflation nor raised by deflation. Hence he failed to perceive the true determinants of M in a credit system.

In the classical tradition, the theory of interest, *paraphrased in a manner which relates to my own exposition,* has been to the effect that, on the one side the desire to provide for the future, and on the other side the search by entrepreneurs for the most productive and profitable ways of combining and changing the form of the assets acquired by savers, are brought into equilibrium by market interest. In order to show that this is not so, and that interest somehow influences *expenditure* and effective demand, Keynes appealed to liquidity preference and maintained that interest is "the price which equilibrates the desire to hold wealth in the form of cash with the variable quantity of cash."‡(10 This tantalizing confusing definition** turns out to mean that it is the demand for and supply of money (liquidity) which determines interest, i.e., that judgments concerning the relative profitableness of holding money and nonmoney assets (liquidity preference) are a determinant. Keynes was, in fact, thinking solely of market interest, and pushing aside the determinants of the natural level. He explicitly denied that saving was relevant although, curiously enough, he regarded it as important in determining what he called "investment," and although he continued, in discussing interest, quite inconsistently, to bring in the notions of dis-

---

*See pp.23-4, 79.

†Keynes never explicitly considered in this context the general truth which Wicksteed had helped to clarify, that in a rational, self-consistent order the organization of economic activity must be viewed as *subordinate to preferences,* i.e., that the productive system must *accept commands from expressed preferences* about how the community's resources are to be utilized (whether the government, politicians and officials, or the people—i.e., the "free" market—have the right to express those preferences).

‡The theory has been riddled with criticism; but Keynesians who no longer defend it have not always abandoned the doctrines in which it is an essential link.

**Had he said something like the following, it would have been *clear* enough: "The rate of interest equilibrates the utility of money, held as an end or as a means to ends, with the utility of nonmoney assets in general."

counting and the propensity to consume. In reality, liquidity preference can affect the relation of market interest to the natural only under the unrealistic assumption of monetary rigidity (a constant M, which Keynes did not always realize he was postulating).*

Not only did he hold that *changes in* the volume of money (meaning *changes in* M, but not clearly distinguished from a *changing* M or a *changing* MV in relation to T) can affect interest, he went further and claimed that it is a weakness of private enterprise that, whereas it can produce everything else, it cannot produce money.† Accordingly, he thought, private enterprise is prevented from bringing the marginal efficiency of money into relation with the marginal efficiencies of other assets; the production of nonmoney things is slowed down; and the marginal efficiencies of the two categories of assets are thus brought into equilibrium.[11] This is one of the chief grounds for his contention that unemployment is a monetary phenomenon, a phenomenon which is inevitable under *laissez-faire*.

He was implying here, of course, that "private enterprise" cannot cause a change in M. But if by "private enterprise" we mean institutions which include note-issuing, credit-issuing commercial banks, bound by obligations to maintain a defined value of the money unit (i.e., bound to convertibility in some sense), "private enterprise" certainly *is* in a position to cause M to change and it has in fact always done so.‡

14.—The natural level (or the noninflationary level**) of the rate of interest is unaffected by monetary policy. But monetary policy must

---

*Such monetary rigidity is, however, the general assumption of *The General Theory* in rigorous exposition. It is justified only as a mental isolate for a stage in reasoning. More generally defined, "monetary rigidity" means the condition in which M remains constant or varies less than proportionally to changes in M_r (see above, p.96). It could be regarded as a particular form of monetary policy.

†Keynes attributed to orthodox economists the view that the marginal efficiency of money differs fundamentally from that of other assets, in that changes in its volume affect merely prices and not interest. What orthodox economists do believe is that a *changing* M in relation to T, V being constant, affects both market interest and the scale of prices, but that a *changed* M having eventuated, the change will not have affected interest (V being unchanged). Similarly, they believe that a *changing* V in relation to T (M being constant) must influence market interest. I should remind the reader that by V, I mean all factors other than those represented by T which influence the demand for monetary services.

‡Thus, if privately owned central banks, or other privately owned banks, issue notes convertible into gold, and the value of gold happens to be more or less constant in real terms under that system, they will obviously have to operate credit so as to cause M to vary in direct proportion to M_r (whether the latter changes through changes in T or V).

**These are not the same things. I use the phrase, "noninflationary level" here *in relation to any monetary standard,* and the phrase "natural level" *in relation to any standard which maintains the real value of the money unit constant.*

react to changes in the natural level according to the nature of the obligations undertaken by the monetary authority. Keynes diverted attention from these vital issues. Both he and his successors have written as though the value-ratio established by time preference and prospective yields (the noninflationary rate of interest) *needs correction*. They have treated interest as a value which *should be determined by authority* or, as S. E. Harris has put it, "according to the requirements of the domestic economy"—as a value which should be regarded as "the handmaid of industry."[12] Such phrases are found ultimately to mean nothing more than a market rate set sufficiently below the natural level to be consistent with full employment under price rigidity and withheld capacity.*

I shall argue later that Keynes confused time preference and liquidity preference. It was this confusion, I think, which led him to the conclusion that intended saving can exceed planned investment. He thought that liquidity preference could drive the rate of interest up to a level at which it is unprofitable to employ resources to the full. He was, I suggest, misinterpreting a hypothetical situation envisaged by those pre-Keynesian economists who had read Wicksell. They understood that, in the course of *a declining* magnitude of MV in relation to T, there will be a rise in market interest above the natural; that if we make the unrealistic assumption that M is constant, the value of the money unit will be rising or falling as the demand for monetary services (through a changing T or V) is rising or falling; that this will cause the market rate of interest to be above or below the natural level respectively; and that if we are thinking of the market level, then we are tacitly taking the natural level as given.

If Keynes had merely been objecting to a *purposeless* deflation,† we should have known where we stood. But he was (in *The General Theory*, at least, and in his controversy with Graham)[13] clearly opposed to *any* monetary policy which aims at maintaining a money unit of *any* defined value, whether the gold standard, a commodity reserve standard, or any other. Possibly because of his obsession on this point, he thought he perceived the origin of the alleged fallacy in traditional teaching that money as such is irrelevant to employment and output. Yet as we have seen, traditional economics does not regard monetary policy as *irrelevant* to output and employment. It has a different view of its relevance. It simply makes it clear that, if cheap money is to be accepted as a method of restoring employment, its implications shall be faced unequivocally.

The popularity of Keynesianism has been due to its having focussed

---

*As a corollary, it follows that contractual relations between national currencies (fixed exchanges) should be abandoned in the interest of the inflationary method of bringing each individual national economy into co-ordination.

†E.g., as some would allege occurred in the United States from 1930 to 1933.

attention on the stimulus of an increase in MV (brought about by interest or fiscal policy) in relation to T, whilst diverting attention from the
essentially temporary nature of the stimulus. The Keynesians have spread
the alluring notion that monetary and fiscal policy can somehow make
nations prosperous or wealthy, not by providing an efficient but otherwise
neutral mechanism of exchange, but by creating "effective demand." The
cost is either ignored or unseen. Believing originally that their recommendations were noninflationary and compatible with a money unit of
stable value, they later came to recognize that a depreciation of the money
unit *was* implied, whilst insisting that it should not be called "true inflation" if the release of any withheld capacity was induced by it. (See chap.
VII). But I suggest that monetary policy is inherently unsuitable as a
means of adjustment to (a) changes of preference (including time preference) other than changes in liquidity preference, or (b) changes in the
conditions of supply which make profitable the devotion of services to
new kinds of uses, or (c) changes in entrepreneurial optimism or pessimism, unless these things are judged to be causing a change in M_r and so,
M remaining unchanged, tending to cause the value of the money unit
to diverge from its contractual value.

15.—APPENDIX A

The Use of the Term "Neutral"

When monetary policy maintains a money unit of defined value, it
seems to me to be the most appropriate use of terms to call that policy
"neutral," and if the defined value is constant in real terms to call the
monetary standard "neutral." Thus, *policy* could be neutral although
the *standard* itself might not be. The neutrality rests merely in the fact
that the measuring rod of value can be relied upon in the formulation
of entrepreneurial plans, in the sense that other weights and measures
may be relied upon. The money unit is neutral as yards, ounces, pints
and ampères are neutral.

The actual standard defined is solely a matter of convenience. It *could*
be, theoretically, a unit which depreciated in terms of a price index by
an announced and fixed percentage per annum. What is fundamental
is that the meaning of contracts made in terms of money shall be explicit. When this is the position, the monetary implications of contracts do
not change.

The term "neutral" in connection with money has often been used in
quite different connotations. But in its everyday meaning, the word does
aptly describe (a) monetary policy which attempts merely to create certainty about the values in which debts are to be settled and future out-

puts in general are to be priced, or (b) monetary standards in which the defined value of the money unit is constant in real terms.

16.—APPENDIX B

The Irrelevance of the Absolute Level of Interest to the Demand for Money

It is important to insist that the demand for money is not, as the Keynesians teach, a function of the absolute level of the rate of interest. It may be held to be a function of the relation of current market interest to expected market interest (or a function of the relation between the current and expected scales of prices*, or between current and expected prospective yields); for these relations may induce a speculative demand (positive or negative). And a speculative demand, unless offset by a change in M, will cause a divergence between the market rate and the natural rate. But this has nothing to do with the *absolute* market level of interest. The extent to which people will sacrifice *pecuniary* interest in order to hold money is completely uninfluenced by the absolute level; for a similar sacrifice has to be made in order to acquire or retain all other assets. Obviously, we shall not acquire or retain them unless we expect the yield (in some sense) on their current value to exceed interest!

Keynes' treatment of interest is, indeed, hopelessly wrong and muddled (although to many economists it seemed at first to be the keystone of the Keynesian arch). The confusions for which it was responsible have obscured both the crucial rôle of interest and the true task of monetary policy in the co-ordination of the economy. (See pp. 79-80).

17.—APPENDIX C

The Concept of the Aggregate Real Value of Money

Hume seems to have had the germ of the idea of the real *content* of money. He said, "Money is nothing but the representation of labor and commodities, and serves only as a method of rating or estimating them."[14] Greidanus†[15] and Patinkin[16] are among the few economists who have perceived that the concept of the *real value of money assets* is useful and used the notion explicitly. (It is largely because of his perception of the relevance of the concept that the latter's view of latent infla-

---

*Such a speculative demand will emerge when prices are in some measure *unstably inflexible,* and it will last until the scale of prices has become adjusted to the new situation. This is another way of saying that speculative demand will cease when the money unit has reached its expected value. The market rate of interest will exceed or fall short of the natural level whilst this equilibrium is being attained—whilst the scale of prices *is falling or rising.*

†Greidanus talks of "the quantity of money in terms of goods."

tion is similar to that which I myself have formed). There was some suggestion of the notion in Wicksell's reference to the possibility of money
being regarded as "an abstract symbol, a mere quantity of value."[17]
But somehow Wicksell failed to use the distinction I have made between money assets as a whole measured in real terms and actual money
units. He was therefore led to the conclusion that "the laws governing
the general level of concrete commodity prices and its changes, are quite
different from the laws determining the exchange value of the commodities themselves . . . . simply because money is not a commodity like
other commodities."[18] This view is clearly due to a confusion between
money measured in real terms, which is not a commodity, and *money
units*, which act like commodities, and the value of which is determined
in a manner which is identical with that of the determination of the
value of all commodities.

Many economists have, of course, made good use of the concept of the
real value of cash balances.

REFERENCES

(1) STIGLER, *Five Lectures on Economic Problems*, p.35. (2) MARGET, *The Theory
of Prices*. (3) HARROD, *The Life of J. M. Keynes*, p.460. (4) HUTT, *The Yield from
Money Held*, in *Freedom and Free Enterprise*, Ed. *Sennholz*, p.460. (5) KEYNES, *The
General Theory*, p.vi. (6) KEYNES, *op. cit.*, p.155. (7) SAYERS, *Modern Banking*, p.1.
(8) WICKSELL, *Lectures*, Vol. II, pp.65-67. (9) WICKSELL, *op. cit.*, Vol. II, pp.65-66.
(10) KEYNES, *op. cit.*, p.167. (11) KEYNES, *The Theory of the Rate of Interest*, in Gayer
(ed.) *Lessons of Monetary Experience*, p.147. (12) HARRIS, *Keynes' Influence on Public
Policy*, in *The New Economics*, p.13. (13) KEYNES, *The Objective of International Price
Stability*, E.J., 1943, pp.185-7, and *A Rejoinder*, E.J., 1944, pp.429-430. (14) HUME,
Essays, chap. xxv. (15) GREIDANUS, *The Development of Keynes' Economic Theories*,
p.36. (16) PATINKIN, *Keynesian Economics and The Quantity Theory*, in Kurihara,
Post-Keynesian Economics, p.136. (17) WICKSELL, *op. cit.*, Vol. II, p.19. (18) *Ibid.*, p.20.

Chapter VI

THE CONCEPTS OF INFLATION AND DEFLATION

SUMMARY

1.—"Inflation" and "deflation" are defined to mean a rise or fall in the value of the money unit in terms of some defined standard, which may be an abstract unit of constant real value. 2.—"Latent inflation" of which "repressed inflation" is a particular case, exists when V is abnormally low. 3.—The term "inflation" has sometimes been used to describe any disequilibrating growth in a particular set of incomes, although this need not be accompanied by "inflation" as defined above. 4.—The terms "imported inflation," and 5.—"price-induced," "cost-induced", "wage-induced", "cost-push" and "demand-pull" inflation are seriously misleading.

1.—By the terms "inflation" and "deflation," unqualified, I mean one thing only, namely, a fall or rise respectively in the value of the money unit in relation to some defined or understood standard. It does not matter whether changes in MV or in T are responsible.

Under the international gold standard, in which a large proportion of the world adopts currencies based on gold, there may be advantages *in normal times* in accepting gold as the criterion for inflation. So conceived, inflation will occur only when inconvertibility leads to loss of parity. When there is no money unit of defined value, it is possible to use these terms only in relation to some abstractly conceived money unit of constant value. But as in practice any *defined* value (monetary standard) fixed is likely to have been chosen by reason of its long-term stability of value, when I talk of "inflation," I shall be implying, for most practical purposes, that MV has increased in relation to T (M in relation to M_r).

Moreover, it is important for some periods or some purposes to consider the significance of rising or falling prices in terms of gold itself; for there may be a fall or a rise in the exchange value of gold in terms of goods and services in general.* This is particularly likely if only one or only a few countries adhere to a gold standard. It will then be possible for their money units to decline very greatly in terms of goods as a whole without the gold value of the currency being influenced or convertibility threatened. Thus, the great United States inflation since 1934 has occurred without any change in the gold value of the dollar.

The notion of a money unit of "constant real value" is a purely abstract conception, based on the notion of an index number. When I use the term, I envisage (as I have explained) an index which is devised so as to give equal weight to all the elements which make up the flow of productive services in the country concerned. This notion will become clearer, I think, when the reader has considered the concepts of

---

*There have been occasions when adherence to the gold standard would have meant serious inflation in terms of money units of constant *real* value (e.g., as in Sweden during the first world war when, in order to prevent inflation *in this sense*, they allowed gold to rise to a premium).

income, consumption and savings, which I discuss in chapters VIII and X. Used as the criterion of "inflation," such an abstract unit of value is not the same thing as a measure conceived in terms of the value of *final goods and services*. That is, my definition does not think of the value of the money unit as accurately reflected in the value of consumers' goods and services or the "cost of living." For instance, in the early stages of an "inflation" as I conceive of it, a "cost of living" index may be expected to exaggerate the extent of the depreciation (i.e., in terms of the value of *all* services currently flowing into direct replacement and net accumulation). Moreover, the money unit may retain its value in terms of the internal prices of a country but lose value in terms of external prices.

But apparently intractable problems of this kind merely serve to remind us of the inherent limitations of concepts which are based on measurement through averages, such as index numbers. When I talk of a unit of "constant real value," however, *I am thinking of the internal prices of a country*.

It is both purposeless and misleading to confine the term "inflation" to large, exceptional, inordinate or catastrophic rises in the scale of prices, as some writers have done. There may be small as well as big inflations. My usage does not exclude the use of special terms to describe the extent or speed of inflations. Thus, we may perhaps talk of "hyper-inflation" or "creeping inflation" to describe, say, the depreciation of British and other currencies achieved since 1945 according to whether we are thinking of the scale or the tactics employed; or use the term "run-away inflation" to describe the policies resorted to in Germany, Russia, Hungary, etc., after the first world war; or refer to "secondary inflation" to describe a typical phase in many inflations, namely, the stage at which an increasing M induces (through expectations) an increase in V.

2.—We sometimes talk of "repressed inflation" to mean an inflationary condition in which, owing to various kinds of rationing, price controls, etc., the actual scale of prices as indicated in some official price index does not rise (although if these controls were removed a fall in the value of the money unit—as defined by such an index—would occur without material changes in M); or we may talk of "latent inflation" (a broader, more general term which covers "repressed inflation") to mean a situation in which V is abnormally low for a wider variety of reasons. Hence, conditions or situations in which it is probable that open inflation in the unqualified sense will sooner or later occur, or for conditions or situations which make it essential to reduce M in order to prevent the emergence of expressed or open inflation, may be termed "latent inflation." When Paish says that a rise in prices is not "the essential characteristic of an inflation, although it is normally a sympton of it,"[1] he is defining as "inflation" what I call "latent inflation."* This condition does not necessarily spell inflation as I have defined it. Just as a substance may be explosive without an explosion actually occurring, so may a situation threaten inflation without inflation actually resulting. In general terms, if an increase in M is accompanied by a decline in V so that the value of the money unit remains unchanged, inflation is likely to be latent, simply because it can be assumed that V will probably regain some "normal" value. In the meantime, the money valuation of income may not have risen. But under the "controls" which are essential for repressed inflation, the meaning of such an assertion is by no means simple. What is important in the present context, however, is that the possibility and probability of subsequent open inflation may well be there.

Similarly, MV may have increased in relation to T, whilst conditions which must be regarded as essentially short-run in character (such as the consumption of normal reserve stocks, or the release of a larger flow of imports—when the value of a currency has been maintained by import or exchange controls) may prevent the value of the money unit, *as defined in a conventional price index*, from falling immediately. In this case, inflation is "latent" in a slightly different sense, but an actual rise in the index might still be avoided. For reasons of this sort, an increase in M or in MV which has not led (a) to the suspension of convertibility (an act which *would* cause the money unit to lose value in terms of the standard), or (b) even to the fear that convertibility will be suspended, may nevertheless produce a situation in which a reduction in M (credit contraction) becomes essential for the preservation of convertibility. But if it is expected that appropriate action will be taken sooner or later, there may be no probability of open inflation following.

Nothing could be more misleading than the description of latent inflation (by the modern Keynesians) as "excessive liquidity;" for when M is increasing relatively to T, it is only the abnormal demand for liquidity—the fact that for some reason people want to be more liquid than normally—which prevents open inflation. If the term "excessive" is to be used at all in this connection, it ought to refer to the continued issue of credit on an undiminished scale as hoarded money tends to be offloaded. For when V increases, M can be reduced as fast as debts are settled, thus allowing dishoarding to substitute for credit. The Keynesians tend to write of the condition in which latent inflation is breaking into open inflation as though it is something for which current credit policy can renounce responsibility. There is no foundation for such a view.

---

*Paish's definition is due to his thinking of money income as a certain kind of money receipts, instead of the money valuation of the flow of services. He talks of "a rise in money incomes rather than in prices," whilst real income is not increasing as rapidly.(2) This notion of money income, which at one time I also thought was serviceable, I can now see to be defective. (See Chap. viii).

3.—Again, it is possible to talk without ambiguity of "wage-inflation," or "cost-inflation;" and, indeed, any disproportionate and disequilibrating growth *of one set of incomes* could be similarly described by an appropriate adjective.* It is important, however, that if such terms as "cost-inflation" or "wage-inflation" are used to describe portions of the community's income which may be held to have risen "unduly" in some defined sense, thus causing strains or distortions of the economy as a whole, we are not led to confuse the problem of the general loss of value of the money unit with the disco-ordinations which bring about such distortions. As I have constantly stressed, it is frequently because relative values and sectional incomes are permitted to get out of harmony with one another (in the sense that the price mechanism would have disclosed a different social valuation) that resort is had to inflation (although the reverse may sometimes be true, inflation itself appearing as the cause of such distortions). But it is all too easy to use these terms in a manner which leads us to confuse the causes of inflation with the inflations caused.

4.—We often hear of "imported" inflation or deflation, or of inflationary and deflationary "impulses" from abroad. Such influences may be regarded as affecting the situation in two ways. They may tend to change the magnitudes of M_r or of M.

Let us first consider the situation in which M_r is caused to change. This will be brought about according to the extent to which the profitableness of foreign trade causes T to change. If T increases because of increasingly profitable trading of domestic goods and services for foreign goods and services, M_r will increase and there will be an imported deflationary influence unless M increases. Similarly, an "imported" inflationary influence will arise when there is a contraction in that part of aggregate output which is due to trade with those abroad. But whether inflation or deflation will actually occur, is purely a matter of the monetary standard or monetary policy.

Turning to the situation in which M is influenced by external conditions, we see that when a currency is tied to a foreign currency by fixed exchange rates, and the foreign currency depreciates, the currency in question will be subject to what is usually *called* "imported inflation." But actually a type of deflationary pressure is exerted, in the sense that an increase in M or V relatively to T will become essential to prevent the domestic currency from appreciating *relatively to the foreign currency*. The modern tendency to call any inflation which thereby results

*Although such conditions are usually *likely* to be "inflationary," they need not be. The increase of one set of incomes may be accompanied by the decrease of another; and unless there is a change in the relations of MV and T, this result *must* follow.

"imported inflation" is a loose and—I sometimes think—a reprehensible use of terms. Revaluation is always possible.

5.—Equally misleading are the terms "price-induced," "cost-induced" and "wage-induced" inflation. For although the fixing of certain prices, costs and wage-rates at levels which must cause the cumulative withholding of capacity, *in the absence of countervailing reductions elsewhere in the economy*, may be said to "induce" governments to resort to the inflationary remedy, this use of words inevitably leaves the false impression that in some sort of automatic way the process of fixing the prices of certain products *causes* MV to increase relatively to T. The value of the money unit is either a matter of contract or of discretion—policy. For the same reasons we ought, I suggest, to reject the common distinction between what have been called "cost-push" and "demand-pull" inflations. All such "wage-price spiral" theories, as Morton has put it, mistake "the instrumentality by which inflation occurs for its causes"[3] and lead to the fallacy that wage-rates and profit margins determine the scale of prices. Of course, governments find comfort in this fallacy because, as Morton points out, they prefer to exhort or threaten labour and business rather than take straightforward monetary action. He does not deny that action to discourage monopolistic price enforcement may render non-inflationary monetary aims more acceptable politically. But he holds that anti-monopoly action to meet a threat of unemployment should be undertaken "for its own sake; it need not be done in order to control the general price level."[4]

REFERENCES

(1) PAISH, *Open and Repressed Inflation*, E.J., 1953, p.528. (2) *Ibid.*, pp. 528. (3) W. A. Morton, *Trade Unionism, Full Employment and Inflation*, A.E.R., May, 1950, p.15. (4) *Ibid.*, p.38.

Chapter VII

KEYNES' NOTION OF
TRUE INFLATION

SUMMARY

1.—In his earlier writings Keynes appears to have believed that cheap money is compatible with price stability. 2.—By 1936 he had quietly changed his position, implying that rising prices, however rapid, do not constitute "true inflation" if employment is increasing. 3.—Some Keynesians attempt to distinguish between good and bad forms of inflation, but they have no clear criteria for the distinction, 4.—whilst in theoretical analysis they tend to assume, unrealistically, that elasticity of supply will permit price stability as expenditure restores full employment. 5.—But only if unemployment is deflation-induced has such an assumption any plausibility. 6.—In unequivocal language, the Keynesian thesis seems to be that an inflationary element in credit expansion should be endured for the sake of the noninflationary element. 7.—But if the inflationary element envisaged as necessary is small, it implies that a small measure of reasonableness in respect of wage-rates and prices would eliminate the need for any inflation; 8.—and the Keynesians do not consider what the repercussions would be if a "gentle" rise of prices became a declared objective. 9.—At root the Keynesian thesis does not differ from that of the "monetary cranks."

1.—It is sometimes claimed that Keynes was not an inflationist. The well-known passage in his *Economic Consequences of the Peace,* in which he attacked the process of secret and arbitrary confiscation which is the essence of inflation, has been quoted in support of this claim. Debauching the currency, he said, was a subtle and sure means of "overturning the existing basis of society."*

Moreover, his argument in his *Tract on Monetary Reform* had been for *stability* of prices. Indeed, before 1925, although his idea that State spending could always put things right seemed already to be in process of formation, he was suggesting that convertibility obligations could be safely abandoned and the internal value of a currency left under the control of a monetary authority responsible to the State. He apparently believed that governments would not abuse the powers entrusted to them.† The monetary authority would, he suggested, allow only such an expansion of credit or of the note issue as would not allow a rise in the scale of prices (for in 1924, a stable internal value of the money unit was still his expressed ideal).‡ But this plea for stability seems to have

---

*The putting into practice of Keynes' doctrines has, in fact, been performing the sinister rôle which Lenin is supposed to have attributed to inflation—and with greater subtlety by reason of the very gradualness with which it has spread, and the succession of emergencies to which appeal has been made to discourage or stifle criticism. The consequences were quite clearly perceived, I believe, by some of the shrewd and influential Leftists among Keynes' supporters; but they have been totally unobserved by the majority of those who have acquiesced. (See pp.48-9).

†Harrod assures us that this was his conviction, and describes as a "bogy" the fears of Keynes' critics in 1923-4 that under such conditions an inflation would be likely.[1] But continuous inflation *has* actually followed the entrusting of such powers to governments.

‡This notion of using monetary and fiscal policy to achieve "full employment at a stable price level," involves an inherent contradiction, unless all that is meant is that a money unit of constant value assists the process of pricing for full employment. The bogus results obtained under repressed inflation are in practice short-lived achievements.

The power of a sound, stable and *trusted* currency to bring about recovery, provided there is some collective attempt to reco-ordinate an economy through price adjustment, is very great. But Keynes was the last person to see or stress the importance of that point. In 1923, Cannan declared that the "introduction of trustworthy currency" was more important for the salvation of Germany than any "abatement or settlement of reparations or even the evacuation of the Ruhr."[2] It was Cannan who forecast correctly, as early as 1923, that the Germans would in fact return to gold before the British.[3]

been used as a casuistic strategy in his campaign for the abandonment of the gold standard. He found it expedient to stress, in his *Monetary Reform*, not the danger of depression, but the danger of the gold standard forcing a period of rapidly *rising prices* which, he argued, was being prevented only by the current deflationary action of the Federal Reserve Board in gold buying. In *The Treatise*, he contended that "inflation is unjust, deflation is inexpedient." And when, previously, it had been regarded as a matter of honor (as well as a question of creating long-term monetary confidence), to restore the contractually agreed gold value of the pound sterling—when he *should* have said, "to avoid deflation is unjust"—he had argued (on grounds of expediency) for stability of the price level.

In his early writings, however, he appeared to be denying that cheap money would mean inflation either in the sense of a straining of the ability to convert or in the sense of causing an actual loss of parity or a decline in the real value of the money unit. He seemed to have had a deep, though never explicitly expressed conviction that cheap money was not the cause of rising prices. Although they had opposed the return to gold, Keynes and his disciples still *seemed* to believe, between 1925 and 1931,* that cheap money (without rectifying deflation later) and convertibility were compatible. They advocated what they called a "managed gold standard." But if that had meant cheap money, it would have demanded not only the management of the standard but permanent reliance on trade and exchange restrictions, indeed, the sort of system which has, in fact, been built up since that time.

2.—Now when (a few years later) Keynes wrote *The General Theory*, when he spoke of the euthanasia of the *rentier*, he seemed to have forgotten about the advantages of a stable scale of prices. At any rate, he made no attempt to reconcile his change of front. Already, when the American President had inaugurated the long inflation which grew upon the devaluation of the dollar, not only had Keynes declared Roosevelt to have been "magnificently right," but had described this action as a challenge to the world.[4] Clearly, he was then pressing for the *abandonment* of the ideal of stability of real value. But he always avoided stating this in unequivocal terms. Whereas in the *Treatise* he had made use of Wicksell's indispensable concept of the natural rate of interest, in *The General Theory* he dismissed it with the comment that it is "merely the rate of interest which will preserve the *status quo*; and, in general, we have no predominant interest in the *status quo* as such."[5] But a money unit of constant or defined value has no more tendency to pre-

---

*Keynes' position on this point seems, however, to have been changing *during* 1931.

serve the *status quo* than a constant pint, ounce, yard or ampère.*
Keynes was, in fact, inhibiting explicit thought about the value of the
money unit, and at the crucial point at which the issue of the compat-
ibility of cheap money with the maintenance of a defined value, real or
metallic, for the money unit ought to have been faced, it is evaded. The
obscure implication is that any rate of depreciation of the money unit,
however rapid, is not to be termed "true inflation" provided it brings
any idle resources, however insignificant in amount, into activity.[7] He
rejected the view (his words) that "any increase in the quantity of money
is inflationary (unless we mean by *inflationary* merely that prices are
rising)."[8] These vital phrases are almost casually expressed, as though
they were referring to some minor side issue. It has been alleged that he
was here defending "reflation" not inflation. But this could only have
been justly contended if he had specifically and unequivocally argued
(in 1936) for the restoration of some previously existing scale of prices,
and demanded other means of maintaining employment when that scale
had been attained. This, he conspicuously failed to do. Others have
asserted that he did not advocate inflation but merely removed inhibi-
tions against its use. But if you conduct propaganda to remove inhibi-
tions about using heroin, are you not in fact *advocating* its use? That
some measure of inflation is always tacitly implied in the Keynesian proposals is clear from the fact that the admitted purpose is that of reducing
real wage-rates (to be accomplished not through direct co-ordination of
values but through the depreciation of the money unit). There is, however, usually a lack of frankness on the issue.†

"In his later days," admits Harrod, Keynes came "to be regarded as
something of an inflationist—whether truly so depends on the definition
of that term."[9] It is a pity that on this point Harrod refrains from
giving a definition of "inflation" under which Keynes could *not* be regarded as an inflationist. Keynes himself defined "true inflation" as a
condition in which "a further increase in the quantity of effective demand . . . . entirely spends itself on an increase in the cost-unit fully proportionate to the increase in effective demand."[10]‡ In the light of the
context in which this definition appears, it can be paraphrased, quite
fairly, as follows: "Rising prices do not constitute inflation. Only a rising scale of prices which is more than sufficient to bring into operation
productive capacity the services of which have been priced too high to

---

*Hazlitt remarks that "it is hard to call" the passage I have quoted "anything else
than a deliberate misrepresentation."

†Meade, Polyani and Lerner are among the exceptions who are quite frank on the
point.

‡Rather typically, Keynes did not adhere rigidly to this definition in subsequent
writing, and already, in 1937, he was talking of "inflation," in spite of the existence of
much unemployment of labor. (See *The Times*, March 11, 1937).

permit their employment can be properly called *inflation*. Thus, inflation has nothing to do with the rapidity at which prices are forced up. What *is* relevant is the degree to which that process fails to bring into utilization resources which society could not previously afford to employ." The popular appeal of Keynes' teachings has rested largely upon his failure to state this proposition in frank and clear language of this kind.

It has been claimed also, in defense of these passages, that he was opposed both to inflation and deflation, but that he regarded the latter as the greater evil. Yet I know of no economist who has ever *advocated* deflation except as a correction for inflation, and even then only on grounds of distributive justice and the moral necessity for honoring contractual obligations. Orthodox teachings may be said to have defended deflation only in the sense that a surgeon may defend the amputation of a gangrenous limb.

Keynes was obsessed by his conviction that monetary and fiscal policy, freed from any obligation to maintain convertibility or a defined value of the money unit, can always maintain full employment. (He did not consider what the effect would be if the depreciation of the money unit could be forecast). *Paraphrased in the terms which I prefer to use,* he contended that monetary policy can achieve this by increasing the number of money units in relation to the demand for monetary services and the flow of real income, through maintaining an interest rate below the natural; or, *as he would have preferred to put it,* through maintaining such an interest rate as will stimulate sufficient "investment" to absorb "savings"—that being the rate consistent with full activity. His convictions on this point led him to the idea that this result could be achieved more directly than through overt monetary policy, namely, through governmental action *via* the budget (a) "to maintain investment" by expenditure on public works, in which case the inflation needed to permit the expenditure was regarded rather as a subsidiary policy of a neutral nature; or (b) to maintain expenditure on consumption, a remedy which had the great political advantage of implying the desirability of income redistribution from the thrifty to the less thrifty or from the more productive to the less productive members of the community. These ideas were expounded without any emphasis on the effects upon the scale of prices (the value of the money unit).

It was, then, subsequent to the *Treatise,* that he appears to have realised that the benefits of cheap money can be won solely through a rise in final prices with lagging costs (or through depreciated exchanges which cause prices in foreign currencies to fall, without a fall in domestic prices). He appears accordingly to have quietly changed his conception of inflation as his convictions gained in realism. After Britain's departure from gold, he treated it as something which it was best not to mention, or as something which at any rate ought not to be *called* "inflation" as long as it was performing the beneficent rôle he attributed to it. The tradition persists. For instance, there are to-day Keynesians, headed by Harrod, who are contending that, in spite of creeping price increases in terms of almost all currencies, there is a shortage of international liquidity which is having a deflationary influence. Because they expect a world-wide increase in M to stimulate economic growth and international trade, they think it appropriate to regard the current rate of inflation as deflationary!*

And other Keynesians have tended to follow their master in thus fogging the issue. Quite often they have argued that expenditure (or certain kinds of expenditure, or money income, or the circulation of money, etc.) ought to be sufficient to prevent the emergence of unemployment and to secure the fullest utilization of resources, but not high enough to "endanger the currency," or to "threaten financial stability," or some other equally inexplicit notion. They have never asked unequivocally, *Are these aims compatible? Is cheap money in any form compatible with any kind of contractual or defined value of the money unit?* The truth is that these objectives are absolutely incompatible.†

The attempt of the "moderate" Keynesians to follow their master's tactic of refusing to call a rise of prices "inflation," has led them into a dilemma of recent years. Alarmed at the results, they have been referring to the mounting cost of living as "inflation." But there is no consistency in their so describing the rise in prices since 1946, especially as they are inclined to talk of "wage-induced inflation." For, costs *in certain fields* having been forced up by the action of trade unions and rings, *every rise of prices has been an essential concomitant of the maintenance of full employment through the maintenance of "effective demand," and so ought not, in terms of Keynes' definition, to be regarded as "inflationary."*

3.—When typical Keynesians do deign to consider the evils of inflation they are infuriatingly vague. For instance, Harrod, in his *Trade Cycle,* tries to distinguish between good and bad depreciation of a currency. He approves of it if it "occurs as the natural and inevitable result of strenuous internal measures undertaken by a country to secure higher activity and greater employment at home. . . ."; but his approval is withheld if it is "artificially engineered as a means of stimulating economic activ-

---

*See Machlup's reference to Harrod and others on the point in his *Plans for Reform of the International Monetary System* (pp. 8-10). This penetrating essay was published whilst the type of the present book was being set.

†Under price flexibility (which would deprive the Keynesian case for inflation of all of its content) cheap money could create latent inflation, which could persist for some time without convertibility being threatened. But it would have to be followed by a credit contraction.

ity."[11] It is "impossible to lay too much emphasis" on this distinction, he says. But where is the distinction? Under "full employment" the Keynesians admit that there can be no stimulation of activity. At what point, then, do "strenuous measures" to cause depreciation (as a means of inducing the release of capacity) become "artificial"? And in what sense is depreciation up to that point "natural"?

The Keynesians have no criteria at all. They feel that they cannot defend run-away inflations, but they have enunciated no standards to tell us just what rate of inflation is beneficial and how much harmful. The term "artificial" is meaningless.

4.—This unwillingness to face frankly and unequivocally the issue of inflation and re-employment is, I believe, common to almost all the Keynesians. They tend usually to dodge the issue in theoretical analysis by *assuming* (tacitly or explicitly) perfect elasticity in the flow of output up to the point of "full employment." In the words of *The General Theory*, "so long as there is unemployment, *employment* will change in the same proportion as the quantity of money."[12] The qualification of the principle by the explanation that, for various reasons, "we have in fact a condition of prices rising gradually as employment increases,"[13] is treated as though it was a minor qualification!

A host of factors can prevent the price stability which the Keynesians assume, *in theoretical discussions,* will be maintained (up to full employment) as expenditure increases. The most important, as I see things, is that whilst there are some fields in which (given price rigidities) a more intensive utilization of resources will mean the sale of larger outputs at constant prices, there will be others in which it will be judged that the greatest short-run gains will be obtained if prices are raised. That is, in different sectors of the economy, price rigidity will have caused the withholding of capacity in varying degrees. As expenditure in any field increases, release of this capacity without prices being forced up is more likely, the greater the amount of withheld capacity which exists. That appears to me to be the most plausible assumption which we can make.[14] The notion that the supply of productive services is elastic up to the point of full employment, and inelastic beyond that, has therefore this measure of validity, that the greater the extent of withheld capacity, the more elastic will the release of capacity tend to be. But the cumulative effects of the release must necessarily *slow down* as any remaining withheld capacity is coaxed into operation. Hence credit expansion is likely to be less inflationary during the earlier part of an inflation-engineered recovery from depression than it is as the point of full utilization of resources begins to be approached or after it has been achieved.

5.—Perhaps the chief blind spot on this question lies in a failure to see that the withholding of capacity is itself inflationary unless, in reaction to the decline in the flow of services, there is a countervailing contraction of credit. If capacity has been priced out of employment in the absence of realized deflation, i.e., if any credit contraction has merely been that required to prevent inflation, it will be impossible to bring about the release of capacity by any form of noninflationary credit expansion.

The Keynesians seem always to distract attention from this consideration. In my judgment, the most important issue in practice is the fact that *it is no more true to say that all unemployment (withheld capacity) is induced by deflation than it is to say that inflation must always restore employment.*

6.—In order to consider the restoration of employment through the "stimulus" of "increased expenditure" we should bear in mind the origin of the unemployment which is to be rectified. Thus, wage-rates may remain stationary *in a certain trade* whilst demand is directed to other things, with resulting unemployment. It may then happen that an increase to the former level of money demand for *the product of that trade* will result in the full restoration of employment. There may be a very high elasticity of supply of labor (and co-operant services) in this sense. But it is impossible, I suggest, for this to be the position *in general.* For in the absence of deflation, why should there have been a decline in money demands for most things? Only because the prices of certain services have been pushed to, or maintained, above the level consistent with their full employment (whether or not through the encouragement of latent inflation).* *A nondeflationary decline in demands in general* (measured in money) can only be a reaction to the withholding of capacity (or to some other cause of a decline in the flow of services) and not its cause. Hence, *the idle capacity which Keynes seemed to think would be released under maintained monetary demands must in fact require inflated monetary demands to induce its release.* It is solely in the case of a purposeless deflation (i.e., one which is not rectifying a previous inflation) that Keynes' argument could hold. In that case, but in that case only, is the term "reflation" admissible.

Admittedly, then, in the purely imaginary case in which an expansion of MV merely reverses a former *purposeless deflation,* it may *restore prices* in the industries which did not withhold capacity and *restore outputs* in the industries which did withhold capacity. But it is a matter of some doubt whether a *purposeless* deflation (i.e., a deflation which is not a

---

Ceteris paribus the level consistent with full employment will be higher in any trade the more rapidly prices are falling to the full employment level in noncompeting trades.

deliberately chosen means to an end, such as rectifying injustices in the distribution of income, or a determination to fulfil contractual convertibility obligations) has, in fact, ever occurred except inadvertently.* At the same time, I do not think that any orthodox economist would deny the possibility that there have been times in which deflations have been misconceived or ill-advised.†

In my judgment it is in those rare circumstances in which deflation has been unintended, that credit expansion may be justified solely by the release of capacity which it itself may be expected to induce. And only in so far as it fails to call forth a proportionate increase in output is credit expansion "inflationary" in my sense.‡ What the Keynesians must contend is that the only way to achieve the noninflationary element in credit expansion—given what they regard as inevitable rigidities—is to endure the inflationary element. But few Keynesians would like their case to be put as clearly as this!

7.—Now *if, owing to a high elasticity of release of withheld capacity, a small measure of inflation will result in a rapid transition to full employment, the chief objection to the achievement of this result through direct co-ordination falls away.* For in the light of such assumptions, it can be cogently argued that a relatively small measure of reasonableness in respect of the adjustment of wage-rates and prices may be expected to call forth the output reactions which justify a large expansion in non-inflationary credit and a rapid recovery of demands in terms of money.

This argument appears never to occur to the Keynesians. Polyani, for instance, is explicit that the benefits which a "moderate" rise in prices brings about are due to the effect it has of reducing real wage-rates. "Expansion," he says, "will cause (real) wage-rates to decline and contraction will cause them to rise." [16] Obviously, he believes that moderate reductions of real wage-rates will be sufficient to bring about full employment. Then why does he not ask, "If moderate adjustments of

---

*The world has witnessed a purposeful deflation which has not been a *rectifying* deflation. For instance, during the two years preceding World War I, the French, Germans and Russians were deliberately pursuing austere deflationary policies with a view to building up strength for war. Their abnormal attraction of gold at this time seems to have forced some deflationary action and mild recession in other parts of the world.

†There are several non-Keynesian economists (notably Milton Friedman and Clark Warburton) who interpret the United States deflation of 1930 to 1933 in this light. Even so staunch an anti-inflationist as B.M. Anderson recognised the defects of Germany's policy a year after her return to gold. In 1925 she was maintaining plentiful funds in the short-term money market but starving her industries and the business world of working capital.

‡Beyond the point of full employment, the speed of noninflationary credit expansion will obviously be dependent upon the extent to which the community prefers to sacrifice the present for the future.

real wage-rates can cause a material increase in activity and prosperity, why should we not seek these moderate adjustments directly, and so avoid all the difficulties and restrictions which are the inevitable concomitant of inflation in practice? Because just a *little* reasonableness and public spirit on the part of the trade unions could produce a great increase in the flow of wages, and in employment, surely it is better for us to plead for that public spirit and, if our plea fails, to enforce it." It is strange that he is not led to any such suggestion; for a solution of that kind would be much more conducive to the avoidance of the disaster which, he warns us, must inevitably result from "any serious attempt to raise the level of wage-rates and salaries to compensate for rising prices."[17]

8.—Today the distinction between "true inflation" and "inflation" is seldom made; but the securing of a rise in the scale of prices is still not regarded as inflationary when it is a method of bringing withheld capacity into utilization. But Polyani is, I think, the most explicit of the Keynesians in admitting that an expansion of the circulation may be expected always to affect the price level[18] if it is to have any employment-restoring effects. And he brings in a criterion which is not to be found in *The General Theory*. He advocates (without defining) "a moderate increase of prices."[19] He adds that governments should "clearly recognize the implications of an expansion policy for the price level" and refrain from "anti-inflationary regulations."[20] But what does he mean by these words, "clearly recognize the implications"? Is he trying to tell governments that they must rid themselves of the idea which earlier Keynesian propaganda had spread, and *The General Theory* had not clearly renounced, that cheap money is consistent with stability of the money unit?* Or is he suggesting that governments should proclaim their position as follows: "We stand for a policy of inflation—*moderate* inflation. We are striving to achieve an increase, a *gradual increase*, in the cost of living." If that *is* Polyani's suggestion, he should ask, What would be the repercussions of an honestly adopted and confessed policy of inflation in a free society?† But he does not ask this question. This is curious; for he seems to come very near to asking it. "Wage adjustments will follow on

---

*According to Harrod, Keynes himself had earlier favored a "gentle upward trend of prices" but, "in view of the difficulty of getting any good policy adopted and of the need for having definite rules of action for the various authorities concerned, he deemed it better to keep to the clear objective of a stable price level."[21] But an objective of a gentle upward trend of say 1 percent per month, or 12 percent per annum is an equally clear objective, and equally prescribes a "definite rule of action." Should not Harrod have said that people would have been too shocked if Keynes had advocated such gentle inflation? Or was it that Keynes feared that if a "gentle inflation" became the declared objective, people would be so misguided as to discount the gentle rise in prices and defeat its purpose?

†I discuss this question in Chap. xviii.

rising or falling prices," he says, "but will never quite catch up with these changes. . . ." But "the power of the workers to exercise pressure for an advance in wages increases rapidly with the approach of full employment."[22] What sort of reaction, then, can be expect from the trade unions when they come to understand the policy he is recommending?

It is only since the last war, however, that *some* of the Keynesians* have been openly recommending continuous depreciation of the money unit. Because of the inherent weakness of the Keynesian method of bringing relative prices into co-ordination—because that method leaves the causes of economic disco-ordination unremedied—Keynesians of this school feel that they are forced to argue that whenever activity declines (i.e., whenever trade-unions, agricultural organizations, price rings, and so forth, have caused a contraction of the flow of uninflated income, by maintaining prices and costs too high in relation to any current money valuation of output) inflationary action must be resorted to as a matter of policy. For instance, E. Nevin complains of the failure of the British banking system "to create the extra money supply needed" in 1937. This was at a time when the index of wholesale prices (which increased by 34 per cent in the period 1933 to 1937 was rising at an accelerating pace. He describes the hesitation on the part of the Treasury as "a curious development . . . in the light of the repeated official affirmations of adherence to a cheap money policy. . . . Credit was not," he says, "subsequently expanded *pari passu* with the rise in demand for active balances so as to maintain the level of interest rates which had been achieved by the conversion operation of 1932."[23] The attitude may be not unfairly summed up as: "Maintain gilt-edged interest low and don't worry about prices." But those who try to take this line are now gradually finding themselves confronted with the dilemma—to which I have already referred—that confessed inflation is anticipated inflation; whilst anticipated inflation can bring none of the beneficial effects which have accompanied inflation in the past—not at least unless it is accompanied by controls to maintain a continuous lag in wage-rates and costs in relation to final product prices.† And "controls" to keep wage-rates and costs in a co-ordinated relationship to final prices are so obviously possible in the absence of inflation that, when resort to such measures has to be advocated, it seems that the every essence of theoretical Keynesianism is being abandoned.

9.—The Keynesians like to praise the "cranks" such as Hobson, Gesell,

*E.g., Slichter, H.G. Johnson, Vickery, Nevin, Schultze.

†For when the classes who suffer grow too conscious of what is happening, they demand compensation, or start a scramble for higher incomes, or become disinclined to lend at current interest rates. (See Chap. xviii.)

Townsend, Douglas, Foster and Catchings, on the grounds that they at least recognized the defects of the system which (it is alleged) orthodox theory had created. At the same time the Keynesians insist upon differentiating themselves from the naive reasoning and naive panaceas of the "cranks." They would be ashamed to hold, as the latter in effect did, that merely to dole out additional money is the cure for unemployment. And yet the Keynesian remedies amount to nothing more than this. The identical ideas in all their naiveté are at the root of Keynes' teachings, but obscured in a mass of conceptually unsatisfactory theoretical paraphernalia. And when it is suggested that it is expenditure on "investment" which essentially creates the employment (because the propensity to save would otherwise cause expenditure on "investment" to contract, income to shrink, and savings to fall in a like manner), the Keynesians are merely expressing their faith in the beneficence of an increase in MV in relation to T, through a formula which, by reason of the tortuous route through which it leads the student's mind, hides the fact that (as with the "cranks") it is on expenditure as such that they have placed their trust.

Polyani has referred to the absence of principle in schemes such as Meade once advocated for doling out money to consumers.[24] But the State could distribute the additions to M with at least as much principle as it distributes income or property acquired by overt taxation. Thus, if one has agreed criteria for the ideal redistribution of property or income, one can presumably advocate the doling out of money to those whom the State has decided to favor. In this way the ends of full employment and distributive objectives may be served at one and the same time. On such grounds an attempt might be made to defend Beveridge's recommendations for the doling out of the inflated money in the first place in the form of various kinds of social security benefits. Polyani objects to the Beveridge proposals because they entail "enlargements of the public sphere of responsibilities . . . which the public would otherwise not wish to adopt," and because they generally confuse the issue by linking full employment policy with things like governmental control of investment and consumption, greater equality of incomes, etc.[25] But political control of investment, subsidization of consumption and redistribution of income in favor of the unthrifty *are* implied in the Keynesian thesis, even if they are regarded as, or intended primarily to serve as its selling points. And from the standpoint of "creating employment" in the Keynesian manner, it does not matter a tinker's cuss *how* M or MV happens to be increased in relation to T (current output) if the aim is merely to bring what I have called "withheld capacity" into operation, or "diverted capacity" into more productive uses. Polyani himself appears to recognize this when he asks, quite logically, "If you require a budget deficit . . . why spend only on 'constructional' and not on 'current' items?"[26] The answer is that, when it comes to inflation, the sole question is whether the disguised taxation is used for acceptable purposes.

There is no doubt, however, as I have continuously insisted, that provided inflation is not generally anticipated (i.e., provided costs lag), it can bring about not only the release of capacity which is being withheld by being priced out of utilization, but the release also of *diverted capacity* for more productive uses. The "cranks" perceived this. They failed, as the Keynesians fail, to perceive the implications.

REFERENCES

(1) HARROD, *Life of J.M. Keynes*, p.345. (2) CANNAN, *An Economist's Protest*, p.349. (3) *Ibid.*, pp. 347-8 and 359-62. (4) HARROD, *op. cit.*, p.445. (5) KEYNES, *The General Theory*, p.243. (6) HAZLITT, *The Failure of the "New Economics,"* p.248. (7) KEYNES, *op. cit.*, pp.119 and 303. (8) *Ibid.*, p.304. (9) HARROD, *op. cit.*, p.272. (10) KEYNES, *op. cit.*, p.303. (11) HARROD, *The Trade Cycle*, p.188. (12) Keynes, *op. cit.*, p.296. (13) *Ibid.*, p.296. (14) See *Ibid.*, pp.296 *et. seq.* (15) ANDERSON, *Economics and the Public Welfare*, pp.149-50. (16) POLYANI, *Full Employment and Free Trade*, p.88. (17) *Ibid.*, p.88. (18) *Ibid.*, pp.87-8. (19) *Ibid.*, p.89. (20) *Ibid.*, p.89. (21) HARROD, *Life of J.M. Keynes*, p.410. (22) POLYANI, *op. cit.*, p.88. (23) NEVIN, *The Mechanism of Cheap Money*, p.118. (24) MEADE, *Consumers' Credit and Unemployment.* (25) POLYANI, *op. cit.*, p.134. (26) *Ibid.*, p.126.

Chapter VIII

INCOME AND ITS "GENERATION"

SUMMARY

1.—The value of the flow of productive services, measured in money, is money income. 2.—It is generated by whatever results in the release or maintenance or growth of productive capacity. 3.—It must not be thought of as receipts from or expenditure upon the flow of products, and it must be regarded as including services consumed without exchange and those embodied into all valuable products, whether or not they are exchanged for money. 4.—Most discussions of the generation of income confuse the factors which determine the size of the measuring unit with those which determine the size of the income measured. 5.—Expenditure does not determine prices or the money valuation of income; but prices or the money valuation of income determine the expenditure which is necessary to acquire a given flow of services. 6.—The value of the money unit (and hence the money valuation of income) is determined by the factors which lead to acceptable bids to buy and offers to sell, which bids and offers precede transactions. 7.—But observed acts of expenditure constitute data on which valuations of the money unit are based, 8.—the scale of prices emerging as the value of the money unit is brought into consistency with other values. 9.—Hence, T being given, the money valuation of income is determined by the determinants of M and V. 10.—But V is purely a question of judgment of the productivity of money, 11.—the term "velocity of circulation" being seriously misleading. 12.—There are no definable money receipts which constitute money income, 13.—for although the flow of services which make up income is normally sold, the flow precedes the sale. 14.—Strictly speaking, we cannot be said to spend income. We spend assets, in the form of money; for even in the complete absence of any barter transactions, income usually accrues before there are any payments or receipts of wages, dividends or interest; 15.—and income does not "circulate." Money circulates from hand to hand, but does not generate income in so doing. 16.—It is the flow of services (products) and not the circulation of money which is the origin of demand. 17.—This was demonstrated by Say, 18—who warned against "confounding the money into which revenue may be converted with the revenue itself." 19.—But of course in a prosperous economy "money circulates" briskly. 20.—Even Patinkin tends to confuse spending and demanding. When we sell goods we are not contributing to the demand for money unless we retain the money proceeds. 21.—The aggregate flow of nonmoney services is not demand for monetary services but merely the source out of which they (like all other services)

*are demanded. 22.—An initial increase in V or M has no "multiplier"
effects unless it induces an increase in V (for speculative reasons or owing
to the money illusion) or an increase in M (which may be noninflationary
credit expansion due to the release of capacity). 23.—The confusion of
an increased money valuation of income with an increase in its valuation
in real terms, obscures the fact that income may be generated by co-ordinative
pricing. 24.—The idea that monetary policy can generate real income without inflation is based on the tacit assumption that a purposeless deflation
is being rectified. 25.—The harm wrought by the Keynesian notion that
expenditure generates income may be illustrated from the recent (non-
Keynesian) works of Paish, 26.—the Cohen Council and 27.—Hawtrey.*

1.—It has been contended by M. W. Reder that, "prior to *The General Theory,* there was no coherent theory of the level of (national) income and employment in existence," in the sense that it was "regarded as an unknown to be determined by the equilibrium of the system."[1] Pre-Keynesian economists are said to have held that the magnitude of income is determined by factors irrelevant to the equilibrium conditions of the system, namely, (i) technical progress, (ii) population and (iii) the stock of capital.

That is, I think, only a fair statement of pre-Keynesian orthodoxy if it is qualified by two further conditions, namely, (iv) saving-preference—the ultimate determinant of capital formation, i.e., of changes in the "stock of capital" and (v) the extent to which productive services are withheld from the process of exchange, or diverted to less productive uses. The Keynesian theory of income or employment is simply an attempt to *substitute,* through a theory in which price rigidity is not an essential assumption, something else for condition (v). In this attempt, the Keynesians are led to the view that there can be equilibrium without the "full employment" condition. But if, as I maintain in Chapter IX, this theory must be rejected, there can be no alternative *equilibrium* theory to explain income, unless it accounts for the factors which determine the extent of the withholding or release of capacity which occurs. And that is entirely a question *of policy*—of institutional and administrative planning, upon which no imaginable equation can throw the slightest light.

But the most seriously fallacious notion on which the typical theory of income generation rests is the rôle given to spending. For spending *generates* neither the *money valuation* of income nor the *size* of income, although the whole Keynesian analysis is couched in terms which assumes that it does. And the error is magnified when the relations of broad categories of expenditure (on "investment" or on "consumption," for instance) are also supposed to be influences. The acceptance of these infectious ideas is, of course, not confined to the Keynesian camp. I shall contend, however, that the income analysis approach which has become conventional is basically defective.

The present chapter is devoted to an attempt at rigorous examination of the theory that income is generated through expenditure; and I propose to show, by means of a careful consideration of concepts, that neither money income nor real income can be said to be generated by spending.

By "money income" I mean "real income" measured in a particular way, namely, the value of the aggregate flow of our services and the services of the resources we own, measured in terms of actual money units. "Real income" *is* "money income," but we call it the one thing or the other according to whether we measure its changes in *abstract money units* of constant real value or in *actual money units*.

2.—Income is "generated" by whatever results in a flow of services. Services flow from resources (a) automatically or (b) through effort, and that effort may be either (1) simple effort, as when a person supplies his own services without the use of non-human resources, or (2) effort combined with the services of assets. Now we have seen that resources (which supply services) may be withheld, so that their services or potential services run to waste, thus causing a contraction of income. Hence, the forces which "generate" income are those (i) which prevent, or remove the incentive for, the withholding of resources from use or (ii) which take the form of a certain use of income, resulting in the realized replacement or realized net accumulation of resources. In other words, *income is generated by whatever results in the release, or maintenance, or growth of productive power.*

3.—"Money income," as I have defined it, is neither the same thing as the rate of receipt of money units from the sale of the flow of nonmoney products (which has often been the definition accepted as appropriate) nor the rate of expenditure of money units on that flow. In my definition, the value of the whole of the flow of services, *including* those embodied into any unsold portion of the resulting products, is measured in money units, and not merely that part of the flow which happens to be exchanged for them.

In adopting this definition, I am breaking with a convention which I have always found confusing and rejecting an assumption which is quite unacceptable.* "By convention," said Pigou, economists "do not reckon as real income the whole of this net flow" (the stream of goods and services), "but only a part of it—only that part which is paid for with money or is *easily represented in money terms*."†(3) (My italics). That

---

*The fallacy that aggregate receipts (described as "money income") are the same thing as the value of real income (or output as a whole) measured in money units, has been exposed by Haberler.(2)

†We can trace back this usage on the part of Pigou to his *Theory of Unemployment* (Part IV, Chap II), where he defined "real output," quite arbitrarily, as the "net fruit . . . . of services for which money payments are made." He did not regard services as "economic" unless money is paid for them.

may be justified, for convenience, in empirical statistical studies. But for logical purposes, the value of *all* net products can be *equally easily envisaged and represented in money,* and I can see no justification for excluding any part of the stream from the notion of "real income" and hence from the notion of "money income." The ultimate purpose of the convention I am criticising appears to have been the desire to think of money income as a certain flow of money receipts. But I propose to argue that, when we are concerned with income, there is only one relevant "flow," and that is of services. The movement or transfer of whatever assets happen to be used as the measuring rod of value is in no sense income but something which accompanies it. A thing does not need to be exchanged for money in order to have money value. Thus, gratuitous services, which the conventional definition excludes, have a money value like all gifts. Indeed, whether a commodity has been exchanged for money once, or several times, or not at all does not, in itself, influence its money value.

Some part of real income is, then, always unsold. It is consumed directly without entering into exchange *via* money or barter. Thus, we have the income of "gratifications" received from consumers' capital goods, as well as all the services and goods which we produce for ourselves and families, like the flowers and vegetables we grow in our gardens, the repairs we make to the house, etc.* But apart from these, a portion of the flow of products *intended for ultimate sale* is, at times, accumulated.† In these circumstances, the entrepreneurs—the residual claimants—who are accumulating assets, will not have been *paid for* their contribution to the money value of the net products in their ownership.‡ The money value of such assets (which may be stock in trade, materials or parts, or instrumental capital) will exceed what has been paid out or incurred as a debt, in order to acquire them. But money income, as I conceive of it, values the unsold and accumulated portion of the flow of outputs (the part which has at no time been exchanged for money) at the present discounted value of the anticipated receipts from future sales of the accumulated portion. In other words, the valuation (in money units) is the entrepreneur's reserve price in each case.

The logical difficulties encountered in a conception of income which includes home produced and unsold products** merely bring out the

---

*We bid against others for our own services or the products of our services (or the services of our assets and their products). Hence all "real income" represents "real demand," so that "money income" (the same thing measured differently) must represent "money demand." (But see pp.205-7).

†If, for any reason, the accumulated stocks are valueless, there will obviously be no contribution to income.

‡Goods which have not been "paid for" because ownership has not changed must be distinguished from goods sold on credit. Credit has "paid for" the latter.

**Kuznets has dealt exhaustively with these difficulties.(4)

enormous and inevitable arbitrariness in any notion of income *as a measurable quantity,* and hence the limited usefulness of any such concept. My approach seems at any rate to *minimize* these difficulties, although not of course for the statistician. But to the praxeologist (e.g., the economist who has grasped the principal lesson of Mises' *Human Action)* the logical difficulties are unimportant. What we are trying to measure (in the notion of income as the flow of services) is *the degree of success* in the achievement of *the most preferred uses* of scarce resources which are in process of decumulation, replacement and net accumulation.

4.—There are two important questions to be considered: (a) What determines the money valuation of the flow of services? and (b) What determines the valuation of this flow in "real terms" (i.e., its "size" measured in money units of constant value)? The second question is the really important one, the first having to do merely with the size of the measuring rod. But because in this case a *changing* measuring rod can affect the absolute size of the thing measured, the two are related.

These questions are usually discussed in these days under the title of "the generation of income." I do not think the word "generation" is a very apt term, but it need not mislead and I have persevered with it. Yet discussions of the topic frequently confuse the two logically separate questions covered by (a) and (b). We ought always to distinguish explicitly between any inflation of money income (a mere change in the unit of measurement) and any "generation" of income which it induces through the release of capacity. Thus, if MV increases in relation to an unchanged T, it means that the flow of income measured in money units of constant value has not increased. On the other hand, measured in depreciating units, it has increased in proportion to MV. But if by "money income" we mean real income measured in money units of changing value, we can hardly usefully say that *the thing measured* is changing. Indeed, one cannot properly talk of "measuring" with a changing measuring rod. And yet the sort of income propagation theories which have become popular of recent decades have confused reactions upon the size of the thing measured (the flow of productive services) and reactions on the size of the measuring unit.

I propose to deal first with the issues which arise under (a), the money valuation of income.

5.—Can we say that the money valuation of income (real income being given) is determined by expenditure? It is usually held that a decline in the rate of expenditure must mean a decline in money income. Thus, the postponement of expenditure (or "hoarding," or a decline in V, or a rise in liquidity preference—however we like to put it) is regarded as taking the form of (i) receipts (from nonmoney products sold) exceeding expenditure; or (ii) an increasing average interval between purchases from the flow of nonmoney, (i) and (ii) being regarded as different ways of looking at the same phenomenon.

A few years ago, I still regarded what I prefer to call "hoarding" and "dishoarding" as influencing the rate of expenditure, *and hence* as influencing the scale of prices. I still thought that we could distinguish between those movements of money which do not affect the general scale of prices and those movements of money (expenditure) which influence the money value of the flow of services, or income.

I have since come to see that the general rate of expenditure (the movement of money) is a *consequence* of the value of the money unit and not its cause. I.e., it is the size of the measuring rod of value which *determines* the expenditure necessary to obtain goods in general. *Expenditures do not determine prices. Prices determine expenditures.**

Under conditions of barter, the rate of exchange of one commodity for another will alter as people's subjective valuations of the things they hold, or are acquiring from output, happen to change. This being so, exchanges of products are the results and not the causes of values, values being established by the acceptance of *bids or offers* to exchange. Consider the barter of nuts for apples and suppose something makes people believe that there is going to be an abnormally plentiful harvest of apples. The value of nuts in terms of apples will immediately rise. *Subsequent* transactions will be at a different ratio. We can, indeed, imagine the change in values (prices in terms of nuts) occurring during a public holiday whilst no transactions are taking place. Obviously, then, transactions do not *cause* the values in exchange which emerge, they are *a consequence* of changes in values; and the number of transactions is unrelated to the ratios established.

Similarly, transactions involving money are a consequence and not a cause of the prices which scales of preference, expressed in demand and supply, have brought about. It is *demand and supply expressed in terms of money* and not the *spending* of money which determine prices. Buying and selling involve pricing in that they imply the acceptance of a bid to buy or of an offer to sell. But it is the value of the money unit determined in the course of *the total bidding for monetary services and nonmoney products,* and neither the number of exchanges between money and nonmoney (the actual passage of currency or cheques), nor

---

*The Radcliffe Committee appear to be getting near to this notion when they say: "Spending is not limited by the amount of money in existence; but it is related to the amount of money people think they can get hold of.[5] Had they substituted for the phrase "spending is not limited," the words "the value of the money unit is not determined," they would have come still nearer to hitting the nail on the head.

the terms of individual transactions,* which brings about individual prices, and so the scale of prices, at any time.

When I buy a commodity from a shop, part of what I pay may be held to remunerate the shopkeeper. But it is my prospective demand, of which my actual purchase is the fulfilment, which has generated the services which are embodied in the product I acquire (i.e., the element of income generated). And the source of my demand is not money but my income— that is, the output of my personal services and the assets I own.

The fact that, say, a camera is one of my purchases is because its acquisition appears to me to be the best way of using the rights I possess (a) in my stock of capital and (b) in the contribution I am making (or the contribution my property is making) to the flow of productive services, i.e., to income. My capital and income are the *source* of that demand. The capital value which I wish to hold as money (which is determined by the value I place on monetary services) is one of countless influences on the price of the camera and upon the amount I bid for all other services or assets. The complexities arise because, if people want to hold a greater real aggregate value in the form of money, and M is constant, the value of the money unit rises and prices fall. But this is not *because* spending falls (in the sense that the average interval between purchases falls). If spending falls, it is *because* the value of the money unit rises and less has to be spent to get a given quantity of nonmoney, just as the seller can obtain less money for any given quantity of things in general.

It is sometimes said that it is *expectations* of expenditure which influence prices. But even that statement is inaccurately expressed. Expectations that greater or less expenditure *will be necessary* to purchase given products later on will influence their current prices. But that is only a clumsy way of saying that expected prices influence current prices..

6.—If the passing of money could be regarded as a determinant of prices then selling would have to be held to have the same effect as buying! Economists could equally logically (and equally wrongly) conceive of the money valuation of income having its origin in selling, which draws money into circulation. Admittedly, when I refrain from acquiring the nonmoney product of others, I *may* reduce my *expenditure.*† Yet it is equally correct to say that other people then reduce their selling (their money receipts). Both aspects have the same relevance. The actual rate of buying (and hence selling) which emerges is clearly *the result* of the

---

*For individual transactions represent *relative* values in money terms and only reflect the real value of the money unit in the sense that the price of each commodity reflects in part the value of all other commodities.

†I stress the word "may" because I may have been acquiring those products *without expenditure,* i.e., by some barter transaction with another person or firm. Indeed, to increase my money stocks I may have to sell the goods I have previously bartered'

valuations which influence *the desire* to buy *or* sell more or less rapidly and *not its cause.* Hence selling no more influences the money valuation of income than does spending. It is the making of such bids to buy or such offers to sell as are accepted which has this influence. Money income (output measured in money terms) is determined by the value of the money unit, which is determined in turn by the total consequences of *acceptable* bids and offers. Of course, the *terms* of transactions *reveal* or *record* values and prices, and current values (and trends in values) are data which are considered in the process of valuation. But if one refrains from spending at the former rate because one believes that the value of the money unit is rising or is going to rise, that is *because* the present value one puts on it *has risen.**

The Keynesians are not the only economists to see the origin of the money valuation of income in buying, expenditure, the passing of money. Indeed, in an earlier treatment which I have now discarded, I myself tried to distinguish between those transfers of money (which can be viewed either as receipts or as expenditures) which affect the valuation of income and those which do not. I had not then seen how misleading and question-begging is the concept of the *income velocity* of circulation of money. I held that "mere sales of capital goods (which do not affect demand for the flow of nonmoney products)" and transfers such as when "a father pays pocket money to his child, or when a government pays an unemployment dole" have no influence on the money valuation of income.† But I still thought that an increase in spending on the flow of services must *cause* an increase in money income because people will be receiving more money as income. Like most economists, I failed to see that this was like saying, "increased *selling* must cause an increase in money income (through drawing more money into circulation)." It now seems to me that those notions of money income which regard it as receipts of money or as caused by expenditure are subtly fallacious. (See below pp. 143-154).

When purchasers in general openly bid up or bid down the money value of nonmoney goods (by bidding higher prices than were previously paid for a limited supply, or by offering to pay less than the ruling price

---

*It is not "the expectation or intention to buy more than is available" (Lerner, *The Inflation-Process*, R of E and S, August, 1949, pp.194-5) which causes people to reduce their valuation of the money unit, it is the discovery that they have *wrongly forecast* the future amount of nonmoney available (e.g., as reflected in the depletion of inventories) and/or the future magnitude of MV.

†The controversies (largely in discussions of "income velocity") which have taken place concerning exactly what receipts or payments do, and what do not, enter into "income" appear to have been influenced also by the fallacy that money units perform their services by circulating. I.e., the services are regarded as occurring at particular points of time separated by periods of idleness. But when A pays or gives a dollar to B, it ceases to perform services for A and begins to perform them for B.

in the case of a supply of which inventories are accumulating, or even through passively causing inventories to accumulate), the value of the money unit is determined *by bids and offers which precede transactions.* And when sellers in general think that it will be profitable to raise or reduce prices, their changing judgment covers one of the two sets of factors which cause the scale of prices and the value of the money unit to change.

Consider a given flow of services (real income), the whole of which is purchased, and suppose that the average size of purchase is doubled. If M remains constant, the expenditure of a period will be the same. But if it is found that, with larger average purchases, the marginal value of monetary services falls in terms of nonmoney services, acceptable bids and offers in terms of money will rise and the real value of the money unit will fall. *Ceteris paribus,* greater expenditure will then be *required* for the flow of services. But the increased expenditure required will no more *cause* the higher prices than will the reduced supply of nonmoney services which will be parted with for a given sum of money.

7.—Expenditure can increase in the short run, broadly speaking, in two ways: (i) through dishoarding (ii) through credit expansion.

(i) In the case of dishoarding (T and M being constant) people are placing a lower value on the money unit. M_r contracts. There is an *increased willingness* to exchange a money unit for nonmoney at existing prices. This eventually causes changed relative valuations of money and nonmoney. New prices emerge as consistency is established.

(ii) In the case of *inflationary* credit expansion (T being constant), M_r remains constant and M increases, but the same principle applies. Prices do not change (and hence expenditure does not change) until sellers and buyers perceive the new data,* and different offers and bids become acceptable. The inflation remains latent until lower subjective valuations begin to be placed on the money unit; and this is usually some time after the rate of buying and selling has changed. Only then do values reach consistency and new prices begin to rule. That is, the change in M does not work mechanically. For example, the actual spending of the results of a large successful forgery (e.g., as in the great Portuguese bank-notes forgery) will have no effect upon prices until (a) the forgery gets known, in which case the value of the money unit is likely to be adjusted *before* any further expenditure follows, or (b) until a more

---

*This case cannot be represented in the identity, $MV \equiv PT$ *under my definitions,* when what is happening is that inventories are being decumulated at an abnormal rate. To use the identity, T must be defined to mean, not "the flow of services which make up output," but "output *plus* the net disembodiment of services through the net decumulation of inventories (including consumers' inventories)."

rapid depletion of inventories than is normally experienced, *being recognized,* causes the value of the money unit to be reduced (i.e., prices to be raised). It is not the more rapid passing of money which brings about that result; for that may have occurred for some time previously. And when prices in general have risen (T being assumed constant), it is not our continuing to pay more for things which maintains their prices. Exactly the opposite. As I have just insisted, we must part with more money units *because* their prices have risen. But our ability to pay more* for things and the fact that we continue to do so (thus depleting inventories) *is* proof that we have more money units to spend and so a factor which influences the price charged.

What answer, then, can we give to the question: Output being given, does expenditure determine the scale of prices or does the scale of prices determine expenditure? The answer is, I suggest: *The scale of prices determines expenditure, but acts of expenditure constitute part of the data which lead to changed bids and offers becoming acceptable, thereby changing the value of the money unit.* The *number* of such expenditures —"*velocity*"—is not an influence but a consequence.

8.—If people in general think that it will be profitable to demand higher prices for what they and their assets produce, T and M remaining constant, yet the position of monetary services on people's scales of preference does not change, the value of the money unit as I have defined it, will fall. But there will be inconsistencies in the situation. Assuming the absence of the money illusion, people will refrain from acquiring as much as before of the nonmoney product of others, in an attempt to retain *additional* money units (i.e., to replace *the same* real value in money assets). And if they act consistently, they will be *under an incentive to change the price situation,* i.e., to reduce the price of the goods they produce and sell, in order to acquire the additional money units they need, thus restoring the original scale of prices. It is through the equilibrium or self-consistency between values so established that the scale of prices (which determines the real value of the money unit) and hence the money valuation of income is determined. If people *do not* act consistently and they maintain the higher prices (whilst trying to hold the same real value as money assets) they will force a contraction in T and, M being constant, the value of the money unit will fall, thus bringing this value into equilibrium.

9.—Let us consider the question of credit expansion. The issue of credit, when it has merely reached the form of an advance which the borrower has not yet used to buy anything, already influences his bidding, or

---

*I mention ability to pay more (and not willingness) in this paragraph, simply because I am illustrating the case of a large forgery.

his acceptance of offers, and hence influences prices in the field in which he purchases. Even the *belief* that credit will in fact be available will influence money valuations. A few years ago, I could still write (in an unpublished draft): "Credit can only be regarded as actually issued when it is spent and enters into current circulation." I now realize that this is most misleading.

Hence, T *being given,* the money valuation of income is determined *firstly* by the value which people put on money—the determinants of V— and *secondly* by the determinants of *M*. But this is a mere truism, for $\frac{M_r}{M}$ is the value of the money unit. Obviously, V, the so-called "income velocity," is no *velocity* at all. It covers all the results of people's judgments and preferences as an influence upon the magnitude M_r. The statement that inflation occurs when MV increases more than in proportion to T simply means that when, through such a change, there is a fall in the value of the money unit, income measured in money increases by more than income measured in real terms. We cannot say that expenditure in excess of money income *causes* inflation. It is a consequence of it.

10.—I am afraid my suggestion that an increase of expenditure in relation to the flow of output is a consequence and not a cause of the depreciation of the money unit (the rise of prices) may appear to many readers to be hair splitting. It is not. It is fundamental. The value of the money unit is wholly a question of judgment of the productivity of money, and the number of money units. If the length of the yard is reduced by legal enactment from 3 feet to 2 feet, so that a field which was formerly reckoned to be 100 yards long is now reckoned to be 150 yards long, it would be absurd to say that the increased size of the field has caused a fall in the length of the yard or that measuring with a smaller yard has caused the field to grow. We must similarly regard changes in the money valuation of things, including the money valuation of income, as caused by changes in the value of the money unit and not the other way round. Money affects money income because the value attached to its services by those who want to hold it affects the capital value of each unit (M being constant).*

11.—But the rate at which the money is exchanged *may* vary considerably without the value placed upon it changing at all. At times, some people will be reducing their stocks of money rapidly whilst others will be accumulating money equally rapidly; and a little later the process

---

*Expected changes in the value of the money unit are of course among the factors which affect the productivity of the unit, and hence (unless they are offset by changes in M) they are a determinant of its value.

may be reversed. In such circumstances, the more rapid *circulation* (increase in money transactions) results because a greater demand for monetary services by some is accompanied by a smaller demand by others. The aggregate demand for these services may well remain constant. The transfers of money are dependent upon the rate at which the *relative* productiveness of money assets to different individuals fluctuates; and because there is in general no greater demand for the services of money, if M is constant, the value of the money unit will not change and money income will be unaffected.

This has been recognized of course in discussions of the concept of *"income velocity* of circulation," the latter term being introduced in order to meet the point at issue. Nevertheless, "income velocity" is a clumsy and seriously misleading concept.

To sum up. What affects the value of the money unit and hence income measured in money terms is the value people attach to its services (its marginal productivity) and not the number of exchanges of money for nonmoney. *The ratio of exchange* of the money unit for other things in general is no more influenced by *the number of exchanges* (the rate of circulation) than the capital value of goods which are available for hire is determined by the average of the lengths of time for which they are hired.

12.—If we cannot regard expenditure as a *determinant* of money income, still less can we regard money-receipts as *constituting* money income. For it is not only the services which form income which are sold for money but assets. When I buy something from a shop, part of the money I pay remunerates services performed by the owner of the shop and by his assets. But he has already settled, or has contracted to settle, with those from whom he has acquired his inventories. Hence the rest of my payment is a mere exchange of *my* assets (money) for *his* assets (nonmoney). It is solely my purchase of retailing services which may be held *to record* (not cause) the money valuation of income.

To say that the whole of the sum I pay forms, or enters into, somebody's income is wrong. Income will already have been received by somebody for the whole of that part of my payment which does not remunerate the storekeeper. For it is the prospective value of products which induces the purchase of valuable services, at various stages of production, for embodiment into the developing final product (including, of course, marketing and entrepreneurial services).

Admittedly, in a money economy we normally *sell* our own services and those of our assets, receiving wages, dividends and interest. But as a rule this use of the monetary mechanism comes *after* the flow of income has occurred. Thus, the weekly wage earner's income is contributed, and accrues—as the right to wages—while his product is being received during the week by his employer. Similarly, those who enjoy income from property usually receive interest and dividends for the services which their assets have contributed to income, only once or twice in the course of a year.

Even in a complete money economy (i.e., in which there are no transactions which resemble barter), one's income is normally saved at first, accumulating as nonmoney assets, according to contract until the date at which wages, dividends or interest are due; and then, in time for the due date, the assets into which income has been embodied are converted into money. At that stage money begins to perform a service for the wage-earner or investor, whoever has produced the income (as it has previously been performing—for a short time—a service for *the employer* of the worker or of the assets remunerated). Obviously, money receipts for services rendered (usually rendered some time previously) must equal *what income was at the moment when the contract to provide services was fulfilled.* But money is utilized merely for an instant *as a medium of exchange.* The passage of money does not imply a negative demand for money. It represents the cessation of demand for money by one and the beginning of such a demand by another. Hence although receipts of money *in payment for services* may be regarded as *roughly* corresponding to the money valuation of income in what I have called a "complete money economy," it is quite wrong to regard them as *representing* money income.

If there are many changes of ownership during the period in which services are being embodied into a product, more money will be needed than if all the processes are carried out within one firm. This *will* influence the demand for monetary services, and *ceteris paribus* it will have an influence upon the value of the money unit (and hence on the magnitude of the money valuation of income). But that does not justify our regarding money income as receipts.

14.—Strictly speaking, we do not *spend* income although we can *consume* services or assets up to or exceeding its value. We *spend* assets—money, our stock of which is replenished by the sale of those services which constitute income, or by the realization of nonmoney assets.

There is, thus, no reason why money income as I have defined it should vary *in proportion* to aggregate money receipts from expenditure on the flow of nonmoney products. It will do so only when, in a complete money economy, and on balance, *no unsold and accumulated portion* of the flow of net products, *intended for ultimate sale,* is being accumulated or decumulated. And the statement is then truistical. If every part of a money income of given value is being sold for money, obviously the receipts from such sales will be equal in value to money income.

15.—Thinking of income *as money received* leads us to such absurdities as the notion of the "circular flow of income." *Income does not circulate.* Income *flows* as output (the flow of services for (i) direct consumption or (ii) utilization in maintenance, replacement or net accumulation of inventories and producers' goods). It is money units which *circulate.* There is no *flow* of economic significance except the flow of monetary services; and this flow, which is always used by the holder, ceases when he parts with money held! The confusion arises from the belief that money *renders services* (and affects money income) through its *circulation* (i.e., its movement, or change of ownership). In reality, it renders services through being held.* Hence there is a subtle fallacy concealed in the simple statement that increased expenditure or an increase in money receipts either *causes* or *is* increased money income.

16.—The attempt to think of the money valuation of this flow of services as corresponding more or less to some measurable passage of money units from hand to hand has also been responsible for the idea that expenditure in different forms "generates" income because it "puts money into circulation"! That income is output, and that demand is the offer of part of this output (or part of the accumulated product) the Keynesians, in particular, do not fully understand. The limits to a person's power to demand are fixed by his income and capital, not by his bank balance. Yet Heilbroner says: "The economy does not operate to satisfy human *wants*—wants are always as large as dreams. It turns out goods to satisfy *demand*—and demand is as small as a person's pocket book."[7] This passage summarizes beautifully the weakness of the Keynesians' thinking. They think of pocket books and purses, not of assets and incomes (outputs). Demand to them is the spending of money, not the flow of products. In reality, a *person's* demands in the aggregate are as small as the value of his output (his own services and the output of his property) *plus* the value of that part of his property which he offers in exchange. His demands are completely unrelated to that small part of his total assets which consists of money.

"The central characteristic of an economy," says Heilbroner, "is the flow of incomes from hand to hand. With every purchase that we make, we transfer a part of our incomes into someone else's pocket. Similarly, every penny of our incomes . . . . derives from money someone else has spent. . . . . . Consider any portion of the income you enjoy and it will be clear that it has originated in someone else's pocket."[8] The notion is hopelessly wrong. When one purchases, one does not transfer *income* (the flow of services): one transfers capital—assets. And neither income nor assets originate in pockets: they originate in output.

---

*I have shown elsewhere how, when we part with money, its services for us cease.[6]

17.—I maintain that the circulation of money, i.e., mere payments and receipts of money, have no income generating effects at all. The tendency to believe that expenditures must have this effect was simply but very effectively answered by Say, who wrote: "It has been a matter of some doubt, whether the same value, which has already been received by one individual as the profit or revenue of his land, capital, or industry, can constitute the revenue of a second. For instance, a man receives 100 crowns in part of his personal revenue and lays it out into books; can this item of revenue, thus converted into books, and in that shape destined to his consumption, further contribute to form the revenue of the printer, the bookseller, and all the other concurring agents in the production of the books, and be by them consumed a second time? The difficulty may be solved thus. The value forming the revenue of the first individual, derived from his land, capital, or industry, and by him consumed in the shape of books, was not originally produced in that form. There has been a double production: (1) of corn perhaps by the land and the industry of the farmer, which has been converted into crown pieces, and paid as rent to the proprietor; (2) of books by the capital and industry of the bookseller. The two products have been subsequently exchanged one for the other, and consumed each by the producer of the others."[9] In short, it is the production and not the expenditure which creates income.

18.—Thus, whilst income may be, and usually is *measured* in terms of money units, it does not *consist* in the receipt of money units. To quote Say once more, "although the greater part of revenue, that is to say, of value produced, is momentarily resolved into money, the money . . . . is not what constitutes revenue. . . . . Indeed, some portions of revenue never assume the form of money at all. . . . ."[10] He specifically warned his readers against "confounding the money, into which revenue may be converted, with the revenue itself. . . . ." "Property passing from one hand to another" forms, he said, no portion of annual revenue; and money he recognized as one form of property passing from hand to hand. The annual revenue consists solely of products (or as I would put it, services, usually embodied into assets), whether or not that revenue is originally received in the shape of money.[11]

19.—To argue thus, is not to miss the importance of transfers of money *as a link* in the causation of prosperity. It is to see the functioning of money in its correct relationship to the other phenomena of exchange. The heading of Chap. XVI in the 4th ed. of Say's *Political Economy* reads as follows: "Of the benefits resulting from the brisk circulation of money and commodities." The benefits of rapid turnover are, he believed, of the same nature whether it is money or other assets which move. In a prosperous economy, goods (and hence money) are turning over continuously and rapidly. The process sometimes flags, Say suggested, through various "obstacles."

20.—The confusion between *demanding*, i.e., exercising preference between different ends and hence causing values to change, and the mere use of the money apparatus, *i.e., spending*, has led even so rigorous an economist as Patinkin into quite unnecessary difficulties. He begins his book with the proposition that "money buys goods, and goods do not buy money,"[12] but he says that there is nothing logically wrong with procedures which regard goods as buying money, thus shifting "the center of emphasis from the markets for goods to the market for money. . . . . The semantic liberty of saying that goods buy money and of describing, accordingly, a demand function for money" (which he thinks characterizes Keynesian and neo-classical economics) merely makes the demand function for money "the obverse of the demand function for goods."[13] I am criticising what Patinkin *says*, not what I believe him to *mean*.

His jump from "spending" (in both senses) to "demand" is unjustified. It is not merely a question of clumsiness. Both approaches are *wrong. Spending* on goods is not demanding them with money but demanding them with *income* or *capital* as a whole. Of course, if we *retain* smaller stocks of money (measured in real terms) we are regarding nonmoney as more profitable than money, and we may be said to be demanding additional nonmoney with money. Hence, an increased demand for goods (assets) from the offer of money (assets) occurs only when the aggregate real value of money is bid down (and M being constant, the value of the money unit). Similarly *selling goods is not demanding money*. But selling goods and *retaining* the money proceeds to add to one's existing stock of money *is* demanding additional money.

21.—In short, the aggregate flow of nonmonetary services is not a *demand* for monetary services—it is simply the source out of which monetary services are demanded,* just as it is the *source* also out of which the demand for all other productive services is derived. Nor is the aggregate stock of nonmoney assets a *demand* for money. The proportion of the aggregate flow of nonmoney services (which together with monetary services constitutes income) which will be exchanged for monetary services is determined by preferences and entrepreneurial judgment, just as is the

---

*This does not of course prevent us from assuming, as I have indeed myself assumed (pp.90-1), that an important element in the demand for monetary services tends to vary in proportion to T.

proportion of the aggregate flow which will be exchanged for the services which go into producing, say, wheat, or plows. Moreover, as far as the stock of assets is concerned, through changing ends or changing judgments about the profitability of different means, the relative values of money and nonmoney assets may alter. A fall in the money value of peanuts is certainly a *contribution* to the source of demand for all *assets* which are not peanuts (including money), and a fall in the value of the services devoted to making peanuts is similarly a *contribution* to the source of demand for all *services* which are not devoted to producing peanuts (including monetary services in general). We cannot say more than this.

Patinkin is misled by his method. In order to make the simplified assumptions necessary for mathematical analysis, he asks us to assume that the only nonmoney goods which exist are provided miraculously and free, like manna from heaven,[14] with a fixed amount of money in the system of which each individual has a certain sum carried over from the previous period.[15] Assuming then that the individual will find it convenient and agreeable to hold a certain average real value of money, Patinkin argues that, "if the individual's initial balances are for some reason increased above the level which he considers necessary, he will seek to remedy this situation by increasing his amounts demanded of the various commodities, thereby increasing his planned expenditures, and thereby drawing down his balances." The increase in the real value of money balances, he believes, in general causes an increase in demand, i.e., dishoarding. Under his assumptions there is certainly an increased money demand for nonmoney in the sense of a fall in the value of the money unit; and this is the only sense in which we can then talk of an increase in demand for nonmoney as a whole (if we assume also that the flow of the miraculously provided supplies of commodities remains constant).

If M is constant, the *desire* to disinvest from money *does* imply an increase in demand for nonmoney assets in money terms. But theoretically that can happen simply by a change in prices without any money actually passing, i.e., *without any spending*.

22.—The notion that spending is a determinant of the money valuation of income or the actual origin of income lies at the root of one of the most subtle and serious fallacies in the Keynesian system, namely, *the Multiplier*. The effects of an increase in M upon the money valuation of income are in no way *multiplied* simply as a result of the *passing on* of the increased units in successive purchases. Only if (a) *the relative demand* for monetary services falls (which is what is really meant by the phrase "an increase in the income velocity of circulation") or (b) if a secondary increase in M is induced, will there be any "multiplication."

All the factors which the Keynesians are trying to understand or explain when they discuss the "multiplier," I include under V or M in the identity $MV \equiv PT$. If an initial increase in V or in M results in a further increase in V or M (whether or not it is accompanied by an increase in T—which will mitigate any tendency for the value of the money unit to depreciate), that is the multiplier. And any increase in V is simply an expression of the fact that money is being regarded as less productive or that monetary services are falling lower on people's scales of preference. The sole reason for such changed valuations (as far as I can imagine) must be either (i) predictions about the intentions or consequences of monetary policy, which the initial increase in expenditure may have influenced or (ii) the money illusion. Any increase in "velocity of circulation" in the conventional sense of the actual passage of notes or deposits from the ownership from one person to another, is a mere reaction to the changed value of the unit. If capacity is released by the initiating increase in V or M, an induced increase in M may occur in the form of a non-inflationary credit expansion.* (I return in Chapter XIII to possible repercussions upon M).

The initial increase in expenditure, which the theory of the multiplier assumes, is the consequence of one of two circumstances which must be brought about: (a) a reduced valuation is placed on the money unit [(i) through reaction to an increase in M, or (ii) autonomously, or (iii) speculatively], MV increasing therefore in relation to T; or (b) the valuation of the money unit does not change because, although MV increases, so does M_r (through an increase in T).

In case (a) (i), when the reduced value placed on the money unit is a reaction to an increase in M, the new valuation will emerge in the same way that, in the barter of apples for nuts, *either the fact or the prospect* of an exceptionally good harvest of apples will cause the value of apples to fall in terms of nuts; but it is *theoretically* possible that the money illusion will strongly influence the new valuation (i.e., that people will desire to hold the same nominal value instead of the same real value in the form of money), forcing the value of the unit still lower. Most probably, however, as we have seen (pp. 140-1, above), the reaction to an increase in M, T being constant, will be a temporary contraction of inventories or a decline in V. The changed real value of the money unit will only gradually become apparent, as people begin to reduce to the normal the real value of the money they wish to hold. As Hume put it in the eighteenth century (in discussing an increase in the quantity of specie), "at first, no alteration is perceived; by degrees the price rises, first

---

*If this is what Keynes meant, he failed to make it clear.

of one commodity, then of another; till the whole at last reaches a just proportion with the new quantity of specie."[16] I shall develop this argument in Chapter XIII, on *The Multiplier*.

23.—The rather subtle fallacy that expenditure generates money income would have done little harm if it had not been for the fact that, in the Keynesian treatment, it is merged into the theory that expenditure also generates *real income*, i.e., output or employment (through inducing the release of capacity). Such an approach effectively hides the fact that real income is generated—in the case assumed—not by spending (buying and selling) but by (a) co-ordination through pricing or (b) the net accumulation of productive power.

Even if it can be argued that circumstances are such that any tendency for the value of the money unit to fall will result in a release of capacity which has multiplied effects, it will still be misleading to say that increased *spending* multiplies income. An increase in uninflated demand is then occurring because the release of capacity in one field is inducing a similar release in some noncompeting field. If capacity is being released, each rectifying expansion of credit implies an increase in both real and money income; for the additional services purchased had previously been allowed to run to waste.

In every case the generation of income has its origin in production. For instance, if the value of my services increases owing to a rise in the real demand for them, that permits me to generate the same income (measured in terms of what my services can command) with less effort or a greater income with the same effort. But the "generation" of income originates in each case in the production of output.* The increased real demand for my services will, of course, have had its origin either in a transfer of demand from the services of others, in which case no increase in *society's* real income will have been "generated," or in an increase of aggregate output in noncompeting fields, in which case the increased aggregate income will have been "generated" by the expansion of output.

24.—The argument remains that monetary factors *can* generate income without inflation because they can bring withheld capacity (due to price rigidity) into utilization without a rise in the prices of services (i.e., of products). But as we have already noticed, if *all prices* are imagined as being absolutely rigid—upwards as well as downwards—then an increase

---

*The rise in the real value of certain assets in such circumstances, the rate of interest being constant, I treat as a contribution to the flow of services, i.e., as production. See p.190.

in MV will, up to the point of full employment,* seem to determine the rate of flow of services, which will vary in proportion to the rate of expenditure. Expenditure will apparently "generate" real income *through releasing withheld capacity* as it "generates" money income. This is the situation which I discussed earlier (in connection with the Keynesian concept of "true inflation"), in which an initial deficiency in MV is tacitly assumed to be caused by a purposeless deflation. But except as a rectification for purposeless deflation, noninflationary credit expansion cannot *induce* the release of capacity. It can merely *respond* to it.

25.—We can perceive the effects of the bad Keynesian tradition upon non-Keynesian thinking in an attempt by Paish, a decade ago, to persevere with the notion of money income as money receipts and yet to bring his concepts into consistency. In using this attempt as an illustration, I want to repeat that, until fairly recently, I was trying to think along virtually the same lines myself. In July, 1953, I discussed verbally some of the difficulties with Paish, and he showed me the script of his forthcoming article on *Open and Repressed Inflation*. I thought then that his efforts to resolve the anomalies, and the efforts which I was making did not substantially diverge. I had already discerned at that time the great importance of recognizing the productiveness of money held; yet although in our discussion I criticized the concept of "idle balances," I had not seen how completely untenable are the notions of "income velocity" and income envisaged as a certain category of money receipts. I accordingly thought that his endeavor to trace through the history of a money unit *via* its various expenditures from its "creation" to its "cancellation" would provide a sort of clarification which was urgently needed. I believed that an analysis of that kind could show how the unit performed, in turn, valuable services for all who held it for different periods. I can now see that it ought to have led me to challenge the idea that any part of *expenditure* (as distinct from demand) generates income, either its money valuation or its "real" content.

In order to take account of *all* expenditures, which Paish realistically regards as essential in any study of the value of the money unit, he defines the cause of inflation as "an excess of total money payments over total money receipts."[17] Then, recognizing that receipts and payments must always be equal, he says: "I think, however, we can overcome this conceptual difficulty if we think of receipts occurring, not quite simultaneously with payments but an instant later. We then get a lack of identity between payments and *previous* receipts."[18] But that assumption is invalid and dodges rather than solves the difficulty.

---

*Beyond the point of full employment, of course, an increase in MV must involve rationing or shortages (under the assumption of price rigidity upwards).

What he is really saying is that, having received money, we may (for instance) value its services more than we did the moment previously, so that we are then prepared to part with it (for nonmoney) only at lower prices. Yet this would mean a decline in both payments *and* receipts in the future. Thus, whilst *individuals* may spend more money units than they are receiving (i.e., whilst *individuals* may dishoard in that sense) society cannot do this. Society can merely change its judgment about the productivity of money, and hence *increase or decrease together* its rate of *receiving and paying* money for given quanta of other things in general. Of course, Paish understands this as well as I do. His difficulties arise solely because he is trying to make sense of a wholly fallacious concept of income. And this fallacy prevents him, I think, from perceiving the important truth that when, M being constant, society receives and spends money more rapidly, that it is the consequence of and not the cause of the fall in the "commodity value" people place on the money unit.

Throughout, whilst Paish believes that he is discussing the movement of money in the purchase of services (which is what I also originally thought could be termed the "income velocity of circulation"), he is in fact discussing (a) the value of services measured in terms of money (the magnitude of real income being what it is and the value of the money unit being what it is), and (b) the factors which determine the measuring-rod, the value of the money unit.

There is no logical way of distinguishing, in transactions which involve the use of money, those which affect the money valuation of income and those which do not. All transactions, *in the expectation of having to make which* we acquire money, influence the value M_r in the same sort of way, whether these prospective transactions are the purchase of services (income) or the purchase of assets (capital). And, T and M being given, the determinants of M_r are the determinants of money income. No fallacy can send our thinking astray more than the idea that it is possible to make a distinction between income-creating expenditure and other expenditure.

26.—The very real harm to clarity of thought which can be traced to the conception of income as receipts, and its generation as in some way due to decisions to spend, may be further illustrated by a consideration of the First Report of the British *Council on Prices, Productivity and Incomes.* The wisdom of Sir Dennis Robertson shines through this Report, which I regard as strongly anti-Keynesian. Yet the thinking on which it is based, as well as the exposition have, I suggest, been vitiated by Keynesian notions. The Council say that "if prices rise in a country, *it must mean* that money paid out for all goods produced and imported has risen faster than the actual quantities of home-produced goods and services and imports."[19] (My italics). This is quite correct and yet quite misleading! What they would have said, I suggest, in pre-Keynesian days is: "If prices rise in a country, so that people *are obliged to pay* more for the flow of goods and services, including those obtained in exchange from abroad. . . . ." This would have removed the notion that the *payment* of money is one of the factors determining the value of the money unit. The Council say further that "it is clear that the relationship between the rise in real production and the rise in money incomes . . . . is central to the problem of rising prices."[20] But the rise in the money valuation of income (real production being given) *is* the problem of rising prices. I must repeat that, in making this point, I run the risk of appearing hypercritical. But I am not hair-splitting. I believe that the Council's way of stating this proposition would never have been used by economists forty years ago; and it illustrates to me the manner in which *the modes of thinking* of nearly all modern economists, even those who are far removed from the Keynesian camp, have been handicapped by the Keynesian trend. Of course, during an inflation, people's income measured in actual money will increase more than in proportion to output measured in money units of constant value (or in "physical terms"). But that *is* inflation. It is not its *cause*.

Through their wrong approach to the question, the Council are led to the conclusion that the cause of inflation is to be found in the pursuit of "a number of objectives arising naturally from the circumstances of the time, and in themselves desirable, but making in the aggregate a greater demand on the industry and thrift of its citizens than they have had the power or the will fully to satisfy."[21] But the pursuit of objectives—whatever the enthusiasms which may accompany it—is merely the choice of ends. It can never have any inflationary effect unless inflation is chosen as the means.

It is only fair to state that the passage just quoted is immediately followed by references to what I have called post-war dishoarding, and the official policy of cheap money. But the Council still refer to the "full employment" policy as inflationary through *encouraging* business men "to maintain a high level of capital expenditure,"[22] which suggests to me that they are confusing the form taken by purchases—"expenditure"—under inflation with the causes of inflation itself. The fact that, during successful inflations, wage-rates and prices tend to be below their equilibrium values, so that there are a large number of vacancies for employment, is not, as the Council claim, support for the view that "the level of demand" is an important factor in inflation.[23] Similarly, because their approach stresses "excessive demand" rather than the determinants of the value of the money unit as the cause of inflation, they are lured into the fallacy that a rise in the prices of imported goods and materials can be regarded as *the cause* of a rise in the general scale of prices. But if certain materials and products (those imported) increase in price and hence absorb a larger proportion of uninflated income and demand, other materials and products will be able to command correspondingly less, *in the absence of inflation.** If they had meant that, in the situation they envisage, a further measure of inflation is likely to be regarded as politically expedient, they ought to have expressed it that way. They argue as though a "sharp rise" in the prices of imports of food and raw materials justifies an exception to their general advocacy of a stable general scale of prices.[24] Yet the only case which can be made out for such an exception is on the grounds that it is politically difficult to permit or enforce co-ordination through the price mechanism, so that resort must be had to the inflationary alternative. Curiously enough, the corollary of their suggestion, namely, that the scale of prices should be allowed to fall in the case of a sharp fall in the world prices of food and materials, is not mentioned. Moreover, the same fallacy leads also to the notion that the removal of rent control could, in itself, cause a rise in the scale of prices.[25] But if rents rise on decontrol, and monetary policy is noninflationary, the prices of other constituents of the flow of services must decline or a cumulative withholding of capacity elsewhere must eventuate. The Council can certainly claim that influences in the United States were a factor in the British inflation; yet only on the grounds that, like most other currencies (apart, of course, from the devaluations of 1949), sterling was being kept, partly by controls but partly by market forces, at a fixed rate of exchange with a dollar which was depreciating in real terms.

Finally, the same fallacious notion is responsible for the way in which they state the argument of a certain "school of thought" to which they refer. They do so in the following confusing phrase: "If wages and other incomes are pushed up, the level of money expenditure will tend naturally to rise with them."[26] But if *certain* wage-rates and prices are pushed up, in the absence of inflation other wage-rates and prices will *fall*, or a cumulative withholding of capacity elsewhere must follow. If "wages and other incomes are pushed up," that is *because* inflation occurs. It is not a cause of it.

27.—When the notion that spending creates or determines income is combined with the confusion of saving with hoarding (i.e., when "saving" is defined as failing to spend all money income received) confusion becomes confounded. A good example of the extraordinary reversal of cause and effect which can result is to be found in Hawtrey's statement

---

*And, of course, in the absence of cumulative withholding of capacity.

a few years ago of a main thesis in his *Towards the Rescue of Sterling*. He says: "Inflation and an adverse balance of payments, are both attributable to *excessive spending*"[27] (my italics), by which he means "spending in excess of income"; and he believes that this is a phenomenon which can be rectified by thrift. But spending in excess of *money* income is not *dissaving*, and attempts to curb inflation by appealing to the people *not to spend but to save* are hopelessly confusing to those to whom the appeals are made. *Spending and consuming are unrelated.* What *can* be legitimately contended is that an increased rate of saving will permit the maintenance of relatively low rates of interest and plentiful credit without inflation. For the individual, "spending in excess of money income" is simply substituting nonmoney assets for money; this act *need* not be accompanied by dissaving; and even if dissaving does accompany it, neither the spending nor the dissaving can be blamed for inflation. The dissaving *can* be blamed for raising noninflationary interest; for the situation means that a higher market rate of interest (i.e., a contraction of credit) is essential in order to *avoid* inflation).

Admittedly, the phrase, "spending in excess of money income," may be intended to mean that today's money income is larger than yesterday's although real income is constant, whilst the excess is spent and not hoarded. If so, what is implied is that inflation is caused by people not hoarding as M increases! *Is it not remarkable how the phrases I am criticising divert attention from the monetary and credit policy which is solely responsible for inflation?*

Of course, Hawtrey would not *wish* to do this. I am criticising the tools he is using rather than the use to which he has put these tools or the product which has emerged. He has in fact reached conclusions in respect of *policy* similar to those which I myself am urging. He recognizes that "excess spending" (in his sense) is "only possible if people have the *money* to spend, or facilities to procure it."[28] "Spending in excess of income presupposes a supply of money in excess of that received by way of income. If the supply of money is cut short, the spending becomes impossible."*[29] That is the crucial reality which makes the spending itself merely incidental and robs the term "excess spending" of meaning. Hawtrey ends by recommending a severe contraction of credit and government borrowing, and the imposition of heavy taxation to *curtail private expenditure.*

Even so, his view of inflation caused by over-spending disturbs his view of the responsibility for it; for he wants *government* spending to continue unchecked, and it seems to him that if this is to be achieved

---

*The point is not rigorously expressed. The rate of spending is influenced by changes in M only in so far as they affect the value of the money unit. (See above sections 8-10).

without inflation private expenditure must be cut.[30] Hence, he appears to imply, private expenditure has to bear the blame for inflation. Of course the argument could be put, with equally challengeable logic, exactly the other way round. It could be said that State expenditure is responsible for inflation, which would be just as wrong.* What Hawtrey could have said is that the desire of the State to spend may be *an incentive to inflation*; but so equally may be the desire not to withhold from the people the *cheap money* which they have been encouraged to expect. The source of his error lies, I suggest, in the belief that "underlying the rise of prices, and preceding it, is the excess spending,"[31] as distinct from an excessive M (in relation to M_r).

If monetary policy ceased making inflated credit available, overt taxation and unprivileged government borrowing would be the only source of State expenditure.† Once monetary policy is neutral, the State and private people may spend to their hearts content, possibly not without disaster *if the spending is incidental to decumulation*, but certainly without inflation.

Income is generated by the factors which determine output—the flow of services. And the money valuation of income is, in turn, determined by the factors which are responsible for the value of the money unit, in short, by monetary policy.

---

*Of course, the way in which the State obtains funds for expenditure *is* often responsible for inflation!

†Apart from the revenues of nationalized industries.

REFERENCES

(1) REDER, *The Theories of J.M. Keynes—Discussion*, A.E.R., P. & P., May 1948, p.295. (2) HABERLER, *Prosperity and Depression*, pp. 178-9. (3) PIGOU, *Income*, p.7. (4) KUZNETS, *National Income and its Composition*, pp. 22-4. (5) Report of the Radcliffe Committee (Committee on the Working of the Monetary System), par. 390 (6) HUTT, *The Yield from Money Held*, in *Freedom and Free Enterprise*, Ed. Sennholtz. (7) HEILBRONER, *The Great Economists*, p.222. (8) *Ibid.*, p.217. (9) SAY, *Political Economy*, Vol. II, pp. 82-3. (10) *Ibid.*, p.81. (11) *Ibid.*, p.82. (12) PATINKIN, *Money, Interest and Prices*, p.1. (13) *Ibid.*, p.1. (14) *Ibid.*, p.8. (15) *Ibid.*, p.16. (16) HUME, quo. Becker and Baumol, *The Classical Monetary Theory*, Economica, 1952, p.369. (17) PAISH, *Open and Repressed Inflation*, E.J., 1953, p.530. (18) *Ibid.*, p.530. (19) *Cohen Council (Council on Prices, Productivity and Incomes)*, Report I, par. 24. (20) *Ibid.*, par. 33. (21) *Ibid.*, par. 78. (22) *Ibid.*, par. 80. (23) *Ibid.*, par. 81. (24) *Ibid.*, par. 105. (25) *Ibid.*, par. 107. (26) *Ibid.*, par. 88. (27) HAWTREY, *Towards the Rescue of Sterling*, p.vi. (28) *Ibid.*, p.vi. (29) *Ibid.*, p.40. (30) *Ibid.*, p.vii. (31) *Ibid.*, p.13.

Chapter IX

ARE PRICE ADJUSTMENTS
SELF-FRUSTRATING?*

SUMMARY

*1.—Before 1936 there was growing agreement among economists about aims (although not about methods) of institutional reform. 2.—*The General Theory *ended this trend to unanimity through the politically attractive theory that the maintenance of wage-rates and costs is a means of maintaining effective demand. 3.—Keynes argued not only that the price of labor has to be regarded as inevitably rigid but that wage-rate cuts are self-defeating in depression, even under price flexibility. 4.—At first, he treated this notion as self-evident, 5.—but before the Macmillan Committee he argued that attempting to adjust wage-rates would lead to a "vicious circle" of international competition. 6.—He did not perceive that what he was fearing was a means to a general recovery of world demand, and that the true "vicious circle" is the cumulative withdrawal of output. 7.—Roosevelt's application of such theories in 1933 proved to be a fiasco. 8.—In the* General Theory, *Keynes argued that real wage-rates could not be reduced by reduction of money wage-rates because this implied reduced prices and hence reduced effective demand, 9.—an argument which implies that costs do not limit but call forth output. The cost adjustments needed are, however, simply those which increase real income. 10.—Uncritical thinking about aggregates, with the clumsy concept of "the wage level" appear to have been responsible for Keynes' fallacy. 11.—It is not blanket or uniform wage-rate adjustments which are required but selective adjustments. 12.—The repercussions of price adjustments upon MV do not need discussion because that is purely a question of monetary policy. 13.—Keynes' assumption (in rigorous analysis) that M is constant would have seemed absurd to pre-Keynesian economists. 14.—Imposed rigidities of costs and prices reduce speculative hoarding; but that does not upset the case for price adjustment. 15.—An attempt has been made to rehabilitate the notion of unemployment equilibrium by assuming that at low interest rates there will be an infinitely elastic demand for money. 16.—But if we make so far-fetched an assumption we can equally validly assume that prices will fall as rapidly as demand*

*I must thank the Economic Society of South Africa and the D. von Nostrand Company Inc. (Princeton) for permission to incorporate in this Chapter many passages from my article *The Significance of Price Flexibility*, which appeared in the S.A.J.E., March 1954, and was reprinted in Hazlitt's *The Critics of Keynesian Economics*.

for money increases. 17.—The notion that unemployment disequilibrium can exist, with the practical consequences with which Keynes was concerned, 18.—is equally untenable under any price flexibility which permits adjustment to expectations, 19.—and the notion does, in fact, tacitly assume price rigidity. 20.—If price inconsistences are never in process of cumulative worsening but always in process of rectification at the same rate as they arise, unemployment need never exist. 21.—The Keynesians were led to a false diagnosis of the causes of chronic unemployment.

1.—In chapter IV, I placed great stress on B. M. Anderson's phrase, "Prices have work to do. Prices should be free to tell the truth." It is curious that I should have thought this to be necessary, or that there could be any object in my explaining the social purpose of price changes. For there has been no controversy among serious economists about the desirability of a system which tends to ensure that different kinds of prices shall stand in a certain optimum relation to one another, or about the desirability, in a changing world, of continuous *relative* price adjustment in order to bring about some conformance to the ideal relation. From the so-called "socialist economists" of the Lange-Lerner type to the so-called "individualist economists" of the Mises-Röpke type, there has been agreement that the price system has important equilibrating and co-ordinative functions. Yet the reality that changes, and especially those changes effected by rational planning (i.e., economizing), normally entail the unemployment of certain marginal resources *in their existing uses*, is seldom fully recognized by modern economists. There would have been a gap in my exposition for many readers if I had not dealt explicitly with the need for co-ordination to dissolve, by price changes, the continuously caused unemployment which is the inevitable attribute of any society in which demands and income are growing (See pp. 20-1). Nevertheless, until the appearance of Keynes' *General Theory*, in 1936, the measure of agreement about the *aims* of institutional reform for the better working of the price system seemed to be slowly but definitely growing. There was not the same marked tendency towards agreement about *methods*. Some thought that improved pricing could be achieved through a greater centralization or sectionalization of economic power, with the final voice to decide both preferences (choice of ends) and productive policy (choice of means) entrusted to elected representatives or syndicates. Others thought that the required reforms involved exactly the reverse—the breaking up and diffusion of economic authority so that the final voice about ends rested with the people as consumers, whilst the final voice about the choice of means rested with those who stood to gain or lose according to the success with which they allocated scarce resources in accordance with consumer-determined ends. But in spite of this apparently basic clash, as soon as explicit plans for the devising of a workable economic system were attempted, even the divergence of opinion about methods appeared to be narrowing. The so-called "socialist economists" were clearly attempting to restore *the market* and the *power of substitution*. So much was this so, that I believed the result of their labors would ultimately be the re-building of *laissez-faire* institutions, in elaborate disguises of name and superficial form, the result being regarded as the perfect socialist pricing system.*

2.—This interesting trend towards unanimity of opinion in several fields was overlapped by and rudely broken by Keynes' *General Theory*. Since 1936, the economists have become sharply divided about the nature of the price changes which ought, in the interests of "full employment," to take place in any given situation.† Consider trade union or State-enforced wage-rates. At one extreme, we have the Keynesians who argue that, in maintaining wage-rates, we are maintaining consumer demand, creating a justification for new investment, and so preventing the emergence of depression. At the other extreme, we have those who argue that each successive increase of wage-rates so brought about renders essential a further element of inflation in order to maintain "full employment"—a development which tends permanently to dilute the money unit.

The Keynesian theory on this point proved enormously attractive. The idea as such was not novel; but before *The General Theory* it had enjoyed a negligible following in respectable economic circles. After 1936, it gave many economists what they seemed to have been waiting for, a non-casuistic argument for the tolerance of the collusive enforcement or State fixation of minimum wage-rates.

Curiously enough, Keynes' challenge was based on a sort of admission of the evils of collective bargaining and a further admission (by no means explicit, but an inevitable inference)‡ that labor in general was unable to benefit in real terms, at the expense of other parties to production, by forcing a rise in the price of labor. Gains achieved by individual groups of organized workers were paid out of the pockets of other work-

---

*In a discussion with A. P. Lerner about 1933, I pointed out to him that, however opposed our approaches might seem superficially to be, the institutions which we were seeking would, in the end, turn out to be exactly the same things. He refers to this conversation in the Preface to his *Economics of Control*.(1)

†Today, says Viner, different groups of economists "give diametrically opposite advice as to policy when unemployment prevails or is anticipated."(2)

‡Compare A. Smithies' statement of the implications of *The General Theory*. " . . . .Concerted action by the whole labor movement to increase money wages will leave real wages unchanged. Real wage gains by a single union are won at the expense of real wages elsewhere."(3)

ers.* At the same time, Keynes's new teachings seemed to support strongly those who cried, "Hands off the unions!" Although his thesis was accompanied by the charge—not wholly without foundation—that orthodox economists had closed their eyes to the consequences of the wage rigidity caused by trade union action, he always seemed to range himself on the side of the unions in their resistance to wage-rate adjustments. The reasons for his views on this question were two-fold.

3.—*Firstly*, he argued that the price of labor had to be regarded as *inevitably* rigid.† This empirical judgment about economic reality is, of course, not confined to the Keynesians. Where Keynes was original was in *the weight* he placed on the subsidiary and supporting assumption that what other economists have called "the money illusion" is a basic cause of the rigidity.‡

Secondly, he argued that, in any case, wage-rate flexibility downwards, even if other prices are flexible, will aggravate and not alleviate depression. For even under perfect wage-rate flexibility and perfect price flexibility generally, the equilibrium achieved would not be inconsistent with unemployment. He would have preferred to rely wholly upon the second argument. But he kept the first, as Schumpeter has put it, "on reserve."

These two propositions are very much confused in his exposition and it is usually difficult to know, at any point, on which proposition he was relying. The exceptions are in passages which are rather puzzling when related to the rest of his argument, as on pages 191 and 267 of *The General Theory*. One is never quite certain when wage-rate rigidity or price rigidity is assumed and when it is not. Even before *The General Theory*, he often wrote as though his propositions would apply under the most perfect price adjustment (although he made no explicit attempt to justify such a position), whereas at other times he was clearly relying upon the failure of the price co-ordinating mechanism. The same applies to his disciples.

---

*This theory is a counterpart of the theory that organized labor is unable to *reduce* real wages. I return to this topic shortly (p.164).

†A subsidiary argument seems to imply that such rigidity is justifiable on *ethical* grounds. "A *relative* reduction in real wages" on the part of a group, said Keynes, "is a sufficient justification for them to resist it."(4) Because of the absurdity of the implications, we should perhaps assume that Keynes meant, "the unions in fact regard it as a sufficient justification."

‡Earlier economists were certainly aware of the illusion. Cannan once put it this way: "The ordinary person's feelings are outraged by any change in prices which tells against him more than they are gratified by a change in his favor. If his wages are doubled at the same time as the prices of the things he has been accustomed to buy rise by one-half, he will not be thankful for the actual rise in his real wages, but will be infuriated by the belief that somebody has cheated him out of part of his rights."(5)

Now it is one thing to argue that wage-rate flexibility does not exist. It is another thing to argue that we should not tackle the problem of creating it. On this point the Keynesians seem often to be either silent or dogmatic. When they touch on the subject, they usually do so briefly, or in passages of great obscurity.*

4.—Keynes himself had expressed the idea—almost as though it were self-evident—for some time before he provided the sophisticated theoretical justification to be found in *The General Theory*. Thus, in 1931, in a report to the British Prime Minister on the United States slump, Keynes reported (according to Harrod) that "wage-rates had not been much reduced—this was a satisfactory point."[6] (Harrod's words). Satisfactory to whom? To the British, whose fear of United States competition would be mitigated and who would be under a reduced compulsion therefore to tackle the problem of labor costs? Or satisfactory to the people of the United States? Orthodox teaching would have answered without hesitation:

> It is against the advantage of both. Readjustment of labor costs in the U.S. economy will restore the real contribution of American demand to world demand which is so much needed today. In the current resistance to wage-rate adjustment in the U.S., we have the principal reason for the failure of the flow of uninflated dollar income rapidly to recover.

Keynes' influence (whether great or small at that time) was, I suggest, thrown in on the side of the continuance of depression in the United States itself and indirectly in the world.

5.—The lines along which he was thinking emerge a little more clearly in the argument which he put before the Macmillan Committee to the effect that wage-rate adjustment in one country might force similar adjustments in other countries and lead to a "vicious circle of competitive wage-rate reductions."[7] Such a policy would, he contended, enable the country making the wage-cut to capture a larger proportion of world trade, but that country would simply gain at the expense of the rest. In fact, his fear of the "disastrous process of competitive international wage-cutting" was not accompanied by any clear explanation of why openly obtained reductions of money wage-rates should have any worse inter-

---

*The *policy implications* have never been obscure. Thus, Leon Keyserling (then a member of the Council of Economic Advisers) actually urged labour unions in the United States, during 1949, to press for increased wage-rates in order to boost effective demand and prevent unemployment.

national effects than the disguised undercutting brought about by inflation, or by protection with dumping.

6.—Was he not expressing here fears of *a vicious circle of increasing world demand*, i.e., of world output? And is it not typical of the underlying idea in so much of Keynes' teachings—his *fear of plenty?** In the passage just quoted, it is in the form of the notion that there is only a fixed lump of international trade in the world, so that if one country gets more, some other country will have to be content with less. The fallacy rests on the failure (to which I refer again in Chapter XVII below), to recognize that every individual output is adding to the demand for all noncompeting output. The truly vicious circle is that produced through the attempt to adjust to change by the withdrawal of output and therefore of real demand. And in the international sphere this is seen in the pushing up of tariff protection, or the enactment of quotas or exchange controls in response to or in retaliation against tariff protection, import quotas, exchange controls, etc., imposed by other countries.†

7.—I cannot help feeling that these ideas of Keynes in some way had a considerable influence in the United States at the time. Indeed, the N.R.A. epoch appears almost as though it was an attempt to test in practice what Keynes had been teaching on this specific point. It was the most deliberate and clear-cut experiment at increasing business activity by the raising of labor costs. This policy was adopted by Roosevelt in the middle of 1933. What was the result? The Federal Reserve Index of Industrial Production dropped from 100 in July to 72 in November![8] N.R.A. had, in fact, reversed the rapid credit-fed recovery which had lasted from March until July of that year; and the resumption of recovery had to wait until the Supreme Court had ruled N.R.A. unconstitutional, in May 1935. It seems probable that, had the N.R.A. codes been strictly enforced, the adverse effects upon business activity would have been even worse.‡ And far from the constructional industries having benefited, as Keynesian theory would have supposed, they were exceptionally heavily hit.[9]

---

*I discuss this fear of Keynes in Chaps. xi and xvii.

†These are all developments which Keynes failed to foresee in advising the Macmillan Committee,—developments the importance of which he subsequently tended to minimize or actually to defend.

‡In fighting for survival, large numbers of small firms completely disregarded the codes. This took place on so wide a scale in many districts that it was impossible to take effective action against them. The result was that those firms and districts which showed an old-fashioned respect for the law often suffered huge losses and insolvencies; whereas those firms and districts which treated the law with contempt managed to survive and even prosper.

Of course it will be argued that Roosevelt went much *too far* with perfectly sound policies. But if a policy is sound it ought to be possible to define just how far it should go. If costs can constitute demand in any sense, there ought to be a clear answer to the question: To exactly what extent, or under what conditions, ought labor costs to be raised in order to create additional demand when resources are not being fully utilized? One seeks in vain for an answer to this question in the Keynesian literature; and it is truly astonishing that Keynes learned nothing from the bitter experience of N.R.A.

8.—Keynes does seem, however, to have recognized that his earlier explanations were unsatisfactory; yet he could not get rid of his hunch; and in *The General Theory*—in difficult and obscure passages—he enunciated a number of subtle objections to attempts to secure co-ordination with price adjustment.

The chief argument to this effect is that wage-rate cuts must in any case be ineffective, as a means of restoring employment in labor, because it is possible to cut money rates only and not real wage-rates. Reduced money wage-rates, he argued, bring reduced prices, reduced money income, reduced wages in the aggregate and reduced effective demand. Hence the wage-rate rigidity which former economists had been inclined to criticize ought, in his opinion, to be regarded as a virtue in times of depression. Cuts in wage-rates, through causing prices to fall, reduce prospective profits and cause the profitability of offering employment to decline. Exposition on the point is far from clear. Burrows interpreted Keynes' position—quite fairly, I think—as follows: "Since lower money wages would reduce marginal costs, competing producers would reduce prices. Thus real wages and profits would not be changed and employers would not be encouraged to offer any additional employment."[10]

At three points, Keynes appeared to have some misgivings about this thesis. He admitted firstly that if the real price of labor *could* be flexible, things would be different, i.e., if it were "always open to labor to reduce its real wage by accepting a reduction in its money wage. . . . ." This condition assumed, he said, ". . . . free competition amongst employers and *no restrictive combinations amongst workers.*"[11] (My italics). And he explicitly admitted later that, if there were competition between unemployed workers, "there might be no position of stable equilibrium except in conditions consistent with full employment. . . . ."[12]. But he did not attempt to reconcile these passages with apparently contradictory passages. Here it looks almost as though, after all, he was admitting that restrictions on price adjustment must be held responsible. Finally (but this he meant as a special case), he thought that in some circumstances wage-rate cuts could create a psychological boost favorable for recovery.[13]

9.—We are left, then, with the principal contention, namely, that changes in wage-rates are "double-edged," affecting both individual outputs and general demand.* As this infectious doctrine has been developed by Keynes' disciples, costs as a whole are no longer regarded as merely *limiting* output, but as *calling forth* output through demand. But it is fallacious to regard the *prices* of services (as distinct from the aggregate money value of services) as the source of demands in general. *It is the flow of services (output) priced (a) for absorption into direct consumption, (b) for embodiment in assets to replace current consumption and (c) for embodiment in additional assets, which is the source of all demands for noncompeting output.*†

Moreover, there is no reason why *prices in general* should fall, through downward price adjustment toward values consistent with optimum employment (of those prices which exceed such values). This will happen only if T increases in relation to MV.‡ Price adjustment cannot cause a decline in the scale of prices for any other reason. And in the absence of a purposeful deflation, there is no reason why M should not respond to changes in T or V. It must be remembered that the only cost adjustments which defenders of price flexibility advocate are those which must always increase real income, and hence always increase money income under any system in which the value of the money unit is maintained constant.

Because the Keynesians have failed to perceive the meaning of *coordination* through price adjustment, which I have treated in chapter IV, they think of price-cutting as income-cutting.** *But far from this price-cutting defeating the process of restoring the flow of income, it is*

---

*What seems to be a variant of this proposition is a wholly contradictory assumption in *The General Theory*, namely, that reductions of wage-rates will not restore employment because marginal costs *will rise* with increasing outputs. But if real wage-rates have been fixed too high for full employment (which is ultimately Keynes' assumption), then presumably the co-operant resources which the unemployed labor previously used must also have been left idle. Keynes was assuming a relatively full employment of other resources. In fact, such an assumption can be maintained only with the support of a mass of other unrealistic assumptions. As, however, this line of reasoning in support of the proposition appears to have been finally abandoned by Keynes in his 1939 retreat in the *Economic Journal*,(14) *it is unnecessary to deal further* with it.

†In other words, the flow of services is the source of demands for output from output. Demands for services from assets or demands for assets from services (the determinants of interest) must always be explicitly distinguished.

‡Very early in my thinking about the nature of co-ordination, I realized that "every contrived scarcity involves an incidental plenitude."(15) This implies that every reduction of a contrived scarcity price (T and MV remaining constant) causes some other prices to rise.

**This must not be confused with a much more sophisticated argument, attributed to Paul Douglas, to the effect that if higher-rates are forced, employers will be able to demand inflation successfully (alleged by F.H. Knight in McC. Wright, *The Impact of the Union*).

an essential link in the required reco-ordination. If we concentrate attention upon wages, it can be said that the reductions of money wage-rates needed are such as are likely to increase the flow of uninflated wages, although *statically considered,* not necessarily (or even probably) in any industry making the adjustment. (See section 11). For, on the reasonable assumption that the growth of real income will not mean a large re-distribution against the *relative* advantage of the wage-earners, the effect of the wage-rate reductions which are advocated must always mean an *absolute* increase and not a decrease in aggregate wages received, and an increased demand for wage-goods.

10.—The attempt to handle the problem in terms of *income conceived as money receipts* (instead of as the money valuation of the flow of services), and in terms of the crude concept of *"the* price of labor" was, I judge, largely responsible for Keynes' confusions. (See above, pp. 28-9).

I have already dealt with the concept of income. Let us now consider the notion of *the* price of labor. In reality, we are concerned with the prices of different kinds of labor, whilst the index number concept of "the wage level" screens off from scrutiny all the issues which seem to me to be important.* Throughout chapter 19 of *The General Theory,* Keynes talked simply of "reduction of money wages." And he discussed the orthodox view of the desirability of price adjustments as though it was based on a "demand schedule for labor in industry as a whole relating the quantity of employment to different levels of wages."[17]

Through thus thinking rather uncritically about aggregates, Keynes appears to have *assumed* that wage-rate reductions imply reduction of aggregate earnings,† irrespective of whether the labor price which is cut is that of workers in an exclusive, well-paid trade, or that of workers doing poorly paid work because they are excluded from well-paid opportunities.‡

---

*Compare criticisms of "the wage level" concept by R.A. Gordon who refers to " . . . . the concentration of attention upon aggregates and upon distressingly broad and vaguely defined index number concepts—with insufficient attention being paid to those interrelationships among components which may throw light upon the behavior of these aggregates . . . ."[16]

†It is an interesting commentary on the uncritical nature of current assumptions that Viner has felt it necessary to remind economists that it does not necessarily follow, "and I think that many economists have taken that step without further argument," that an increase of wage-rates at a time of unemployment will increase the pay-roll. "An increase of wage-rates may quite conceivably reduce the pay-roll."[18]

‡*Average* real wage-rates may be expected to rise during a recovery brought about by downward adjustment of nominal wage-rates. Several economists have referred to empirical evidence that demand for labor is highly elastic under conditions of unemployment. Unless that evidence is for some reason misleading, average real earnings must rise through the reactions of downward wage-rate flexibility under depression conditions.

11.—When the Keynesians do think of adjustments in individual wage-rates, they think of blanket changes. At one point Keynes objected to price flexibility as a remedy for idleness in labor on the grounds that "there is, as a rule, no means of securing a simultaneous and equal reduction of money-wages in all industries.*[(19)] But it is not *uniform* reductions which are wanted, it is selective reductions, the appropriate selection of which can be entrusted to markets when nonmarket *minima* have been adjusted.†

Even if equi-proportional wage-cuts were enacted, however, in a regime in which there was much unemployment, uninflated aggregate and average earnings might still tend to increase, owing to the redistribution of workers over the different wage-rate groups. It would become profitable to employ more in the higher-paid types of work, whilst in the lower-paid types there would have to be rationing.‡ Keynes' static, short-term methods exclude consideration of these reactions.** Clarity will not be gained whilst we try to think in terms of "wage levels." We have to think in terms of changing frequency distributions. This is important enough for the consideration of employment in individual industries, but still more important in relation to employment as a whole.

The Keynesian argument is that it is no use cutting the wage-rates of say, carpenters, if there is employment among them because, even if *their* employment fully recovers, their incomes and expenditure will fall and so cause the demand for the labor of other workers to fall.†† But the case for price flexibility by no means assumes that a moderate fall in carpenters' wage-rates, together with a corresponding fall in the price of the product will, in itself, greatly increase the employment—still less the money income—of *carpenters.* Such a reaction, although *possible,* is unlikely. Moreover, whilst wage-rate and price adjustments are required to dissolve withheld capacity among carpenters, to adopt that remedy *in individual trades* and on a small scale would bring severe distributive injustices in its train. Indeed, the aggregate wage receipts of the larger number employed in any trade *might* be smaller than before the increased employment.

The correct proposition can be put this way. Under conditions of

---

*It was partly this which led Keynes to argue that wage-rate adjustment would be possible only in a Communist or Fascist State.[(18)]

†Actually, Pigou has shown that equi-proportional wage-cuts, even under Keynes' other assumptions, must mean increased employment of labor if the reaction is a reduction of the rate of interest. Pigou suggested that this reaction is "fairly likely."[(21)]

‡For simplicity, I am assuming that *maxima* are enacted.

**The possibilities of transfers of workers from low-paid to high-paid work are magnified in the long run, because it will be possible to train for the well-paid employment opportunities which are brought within reach of income.

††Boulding has used this actual example and argument.[(22)]

widespread unemployment through general price (and wage-rate) rigidity, *increased employment among carpenters can be most easily induced
as the result of wage-rate and price reductions on the part of those persons who ultimately buy the carpenters' services.* The assumption is that
the reductions result in the release of withheld capacity in the industries
which do not compete with carpenters, whilst the increasing flow of products becomes (a) real demand through being priced to permit its full
sale, and (b) money demand through credit reactions. *This* is the argument which the Keynesians should answer.

12.—In his *Prosperity and Depression*, Haberler expresses doubts about
this type of argument. He states the case for it briefly, in a footnote,[23]
but adds that it assumes MV to be constant. It seems to me, however,
that whatever the reactions of MV may be, the value adjustments needed
to secure the consumption or use of all goods and services may still be
brought about.* Haberler argues also that we cannot infer the truth
of the proposition from facts which appear to support it. During the
depression, outputs and employment were maintained in the agricultural field, in which the fall of prices *could not be* effectively resisted, but
shrank in industry, in which prices *could be* effectively maintained. It
would seem, then, that full employment and outputs could have been
maintained in industry also, had price competition been effective. That,
says Haberler, "has not yet been rigorously proven."[24] But is it not
self-evident that, given any monetary policy, *selective* reduction of the
prices of industrial goods would, in general, have made smaller reductions of agricultural prices necessary (in order to secure full employment
in that field), whilst the maintenance of outputs as a whole would have
eased the task of financing full production without depreciation of the
money unit?† And is it not equally obvious that, had the prices of
agricultural products been maintained, so that these products absorbed
a greater proportion of the total power to purchase, industrial unemployment would have been still more serious?

The argument that downward price adjustments may lead to deflationary reactions upon MV does not appear to me to be vital to my
case. For the magnitude of M (and hence of MV) is purely a matter of
monetary policy. Admittedly, the view that co-ordinative reductions or
increases of wage-rates must always tend to increase real income (and
probably real wages in the aggregate also) does not imply that money

---

*In my view, however, under orthodox monetary policy MV *would* expand in reaction to such adjustments.

†I feel that Haberler would now admit this argument, in view of his unequivocal
rejection, in 1951, of Keynesian teaching about unemployment equilibrium under price
flexibility.[25]

income (and money wages) will *also* increase, except on certain assumptions about the nature of the monetary system which exists, or the monetary policy being pursued. Perhaps the pre-Keynesian economists could be criticised for having made tacit instead of explicit assumptions on this point.

13.—But orthodox economics (as I understand it) did not overlook what is now called "the income effect." The tacit assumption* was that the monetary system was of such a nature that the increased real income due to the release of productive power in individual trades (through the acceptance of lower wage-rates) would result not in a reduction but in an increase of money income. No-one suggested that the monetary system *had* necessarily to be like that; but from the actual working of the credit system (when previous inflation had not made a rectifying deflation necessary), it seemed to be unnecessary to consider the case in which an expansion of production would not be accompanied by an increase in money income induced by this expansion. The assumption on which Keynes built his rigorous analysis, namely, that the number of money units is fixed, would have seemed absurd to most pre-Keynesian economists, unless they were considering the economics of a community so primitive that a fixed number of tokens (shells, for instance) served as the sole medium of exchange, whilst no lending or credit of any kind existed.

In a credit economy, it was believed, there could never be any difficulty, due to the mere fact that outputs had increased, about purchasing the full flow of production at ruling prices. That is, expanding real income could not, in itself, have any price-depressing tendencies. Only monetary policy was believed to be able to explain that. But given any monetary policy, they believed that unemployment of any type of labor was due to wage-rates being wrongly related to the "amount of money" existing at any time.† It followed that downward adjustments of minimum wage-rates and prices could never *aggravate*—on the contrary would always *mitigate*—the consequences of any deflationary tendency caused by monetary policy.

Hence, the wage-rate adjustments needed to restore employment (when high wage-rates are the cause of current unemployment) does not mean a continuing decline in the scale of prices, as Keynes assumed.

---

*Some economists in the pre-Keynesian era, in attempting to deal with the relations of employment and wage-rates, made *explicit,* highly simplified assumptions consistent with the assumption as I have worded it, for purposes of abstract analysis. But I do not know of any economist who has stated the fundamental assumption as I have done. Quite possibly the point was made.

†Compare F. Modigliani, *Liquidity Preference and the Theory of Interest and Money,* (Econometrica, January, 1944).

As we have seen, there is no reason to suppose that when T increases, M will not increase also. Not only do such cost and price reductions bring a larger flow of products within reach of existing money income, thus permitting noninflationary credit expansion, but every reduction in one price releases purchasing power for noncompeting purposes. And far from reduced wage-rates causing a contraction in the flow of real or money wages, the effect is to *increase* the uninflated earnings of labor.

14.—At this stage the objection can be expected that I am simply *assuming* the absence of deflation. I am not ignoring the need for a rectifying deflation following a period of cheap money. And I am certainly not denying that a *primary* deflation may not induce a *secondary* deflation. But as we have seen, speculative hoarding—"postponement of demand," with its self-perpetuating consequences—arises when current costs or prices are higher than anticipated costs or prices, whilst *the hoarding assists correctly discerned policy.*

In more general terms, expected changes in costs or prices, unaccompanied by immediate cost and price co-ordination to meet expectations, lead to "secondary" reactions. A *cut in costs* does not induce demand postponement; nor, indeed, do *falling costs* necessarily have this effect. Postponements arise because it is judged that a cut in costs (or other prices) is less than will eventually have to take place, or because the rate of fall of costs (or other prices) is insufficiently rapid. It follows that "secondary" deflations are attributable to *the unstable rigidities* which prevent the continuous adjustment of the scale of prices to the level at which policy is believed to be aiming.* If speculative hoarding accompanies the downward adjustment of wage-rates and it is not offset by credit expansion, *a rectifying deflation* must be in progress.

Now when, for any reason, a change in the value of the money unit becomes the declared object of policy, or the expected consequence of policy, *the whole price system is immediately thrown out of co-ordination.* Thus, if the value of the money unit is expected to rise, then until the necessary adjustments have all taken place, "willingness to buy" must necessarily fall off—most seriously where values of services and materials in the investment goods industries do not at once respond.†

---

*Although Keynes never got near to perceiving this broad generalization, he appeared at one point, in a passage which it is difficult to reconcile with most of his argument, to recognize it. See his reference to the restoration of a depressed economy by drastic wage-rate cuts, in *The General Theory*, pp. 265-6.

†This is no conclusive argument against policies seeking to increase the value of the money unit, as tardy rectifications of the distributive injustices of inflations. Nor is it a good argument against rectifying price disharmonies which have been allowed to develop and strain the ability to honor convertibility obligations.

Confusion arises on this issue, I think, because secondary deflation can be brought to an end, not only by true co-ordination, but at the expense of a prospective sacrifice—a more or less permanent sacrifice—of real income, i.e., through the imposition of cost and price rigidities (in the form of *minima*) which are expected to continue indefinitely.*

15.—I turn now to a variant of the theory that price adjustment induces a speculative decline in V, namely, the suggestion that, in certain circumstances, there exists an infinitely elastic demand for money. The emergence of this notion appears to reflect the realignment of Keynesian ideas on this topic following attempts of disciples like Lange, Smithies, Tobin, Samuelson, Modigliani† and Patinkin to defend or strengthen the new creed. Successive refinements which they have introduced have gradually paved the way for the ultimate abandonment, by would-be Keynesians, of the view that wage-rate and price adjustments are powerless to secure full employment. The contributions of some of these very friendly critics, said Schumpeter, "might have been turned into very serious criticisms" if they had been "less in sympathy with the spirit of Keynesian economics."[26] He added that this is particularly true of Modigliani's contribution. Schumpeter could have made the same remark about a contribution of Patinkin on the same issue, which appeared two years later. But the criticisms of these writers *were* very serious in any case. The apparent reluctance of some of them to abandon standpoints which their own logic was urging them to reject, clouded their exposition; but it did not weaken the implications of their reasoning.

Modigliani (whose 1944 article[27] quietly caused more harm to the Keynesian thesis than any other single previous contribution) seems, almost unintentionally, to reduce to the absurd the notion of the co-existence of idle resources and price flexibility. He does this by showing that its validity is limited to the position which exists when there is an *infinitely elastic* demand for money ("the Keynesian case"). Modigliani does not regard this extreme case as absurd, and, indeed, declares that

---

*Imposed cost and price rigidities *in the form of maxima* (i.e., ceilings) may similarly prevent secondary inflation, but in this case, *the effect is the opposite.* In so far as the maxima force down monopoly prices nearer to marginal cost, there is a mitigating co-ordinative and deflationary action which creates an incentive to increased outputs (i.e., increased real income). This is, however, not an adequate argument in favor of maximum price fixation as a co-ordinative instrument. (See above, p 62).

†It may be unfair to describe Modigliani as a Keynesian, and Patinkin has moved still further from Keynesian teaching since 1948. Indeed, the implications of the latter's treatment are devastating. It is difficult to pick out the other non-Keynesian economists who have been most influential on the point at issue; but Marget, Knight, Friedman, Haberler, Machlup, Viner, Simons, F. A. Lutz and Clark Warburton must take much of the credit.

interest in such a possibility is "not purely theoretical.[28] Pigou regarded the contemplation of this possibility as a mere academic exercise. He described the situation envisaged (although he was not criticising Modigliani) as extremely improbable, and he added, "Thus, the
puzzles we have been considering . . . . are academic exercises, of some
slight use perhaps for clarifying thought, but with very little chance of
ever being posed on the checker board of actual life.[29] And Keynes
himself, in dealing explicitly with this case, described it as a "possibility"
of which he knew of no example, but which "might become practically
important in future."[30] Yet there are many passages in *The General
Theory* which (as Haberler has pointed out)[31] rely tacitly upon the
assumption of an infinitely elastic demand for money. "The new
Keynesians" appear to be trying to substitute this "special theory"
(Hicks' description) for the "general theory" which they admit must be
abandoned. If an infinitely elastic demand for money *did* exist, there
would, of course, truly be a "bottomless pit for purchasing power."
Every increase in M would be accompanied by a parallel decline in V.
But it is my present view that any attempt to envisage the "special
theory" operating in the concrete realities of the world we know—even
under depression conditions—must bring out its inherent absurdity. No
condition which even distantly resembles inflnite elasticity of demand
for money assets has ever been recognized, I believe, because general
expectations have always envisaged either (a) the attainment in the not
too distant future of some definite scale of prices, or (b) so gradual a
decline of prices that no cumulative, general postponement of expenditure has seemed profitable. General expectations appear to have rejected the possibility of a scale of prices which sags without limit, because of such things as convertibility obligations, or the necessity to
maintain exchanges, or the political inexpediency of permitting prices
to continue to fall.

But let us keep the discussion to the theoretical plane. The most
plausible suggestion in explanation of the idea that there may exist an
infinitely elastic demand for money is that, at very low rates of interest,
such as will accompany thrift when prospective yields are very low, the
cost of investment (in nonmoney assets) will exceed interest. Hence, the
argument continues, there is a flight from nonmoney into money.

16.—Now if one can seriously imagine a situation in which heavy
saving persists in spite of its being judged unprofitable to acquire additional non-money assets, with the aggregate real value of money being
inflated, and prices being driven down catastrophically, then one may
equally legitimately (and equally extravagantly) imagine continuous
price co-ordination accompanying the emergence of such a position.

We can conceive, that is, of prices falling rapidly, keeping pace with expectations of price changes, but never reaching zero, with full utilization of resources persisting all the way.* We do not really need the answer which first Haberler, and then Pigou, gave on this point, namely, that the increase in the real value of cash balances is inversely related to the extent to which the individual (or for that matter the business firm) prefers to save, whilst the rate of saving is a diminishing function of the accumulation of assets which the individual holds.†

17.—I have argued above that the weakness of Keynes' case rests on his static assumptions; and that once we bring dynamic repercussions into the reckoning (via the co-ordination or disco-ordination of the economic system) his arguments for unemployment equilibrium under price flexibility fall away. Strangely enough one able critic of Keynes, Patinkin, has attempted to confer some sort of validity upon what Keynes had in mind when he spoke of unemployment equilibrium under price flexibility, by appeal to dynamic theory. He argues that, whilst Keynes' own analysis (essentially static) cannot be defended, the proposition survives if it is explained through dynamic analysis. But in this attempt to retain Keynes' conclusions, Patinkin has abandoned the very roots of his reasoning.

Of the original Keynesian arguments concerning unemployment equilibrium, Patinkin says, writing in 1948: It should now "be definitely recognized that this is an indefensible position."[35] Yet Keynes' errors on this point, and the similar errors of his manifold enthusiastic supporters over the period 1936-1946, are represented by Patinkin as quite unimportant. The truth which the early critics of *The General Theory* fought so hard to establish (against stubborn opposition at almost every point),‡ namely, that price flexibility is inconsistent with unemployment, he describes as "uninteresting, unimportant and uninformative about the real problems of economic policy."[36] In spite of the mistakes which led Keynes to his conclusions, he did stumble upon the truth.

Let us consider, then, the conclusions concerning price flexibility of what Patinkin continues to describe as "Keynesian economics" (meaning by that an economics which rejects the logic but retains the conclusions of *The General Theory*). This version of "the new Keynesianism"

*Compare Pigou [32] and Haberler [33] on this point.
†In any case, this argument is no answer to the case in which the saving is accompanied by speculative hoarding. For this reason Haberler claims only that there is a "strong probability" and no "absolute certainty" of there being a lower limit to MV so caused.[34]
‡For an example of the stubbornness, see Keynes' reply to criticisms in his *Relative Movements of Real Wages and Output*, Economic Journal, March, 1939.

contends—again in Patinkin's words—"that the economic system **may** be in a position of under-employment *dis*equilibrium (in the sense that wages, prices, and the amount of unemployment are continuously changing over time) for long or even indefinite, periods of time."[37] (Patinkin's italics). "In a dynamic world of uncertainty and adverse anticipations, even if we were to allow an infinite adjustment period, there is no certainty that full employment will be generated. That is, we may remain indefinitely in a position of underemployment disequilibrium.[38]

18.—This sounds like pure orthodoxy. Indeed, the use of the word "*dis*equilibrium" implies that some Keynesians have now completely retreated. And the reference to "uncertainty and adverse anticipations" seems to refer to hypothetical situations which, using my own terminology, can be described as follows:

> *Given price rigidities regarded as unstable,* deflation will cause the emergence of withheld capacity. Three cases arise: (a) general expectations (i.e., typical or average expectations) envisage a fall of prices towards a definite ultimate scale which is regarded as most probable; or (b) general expectations are constantly changing so that the generally expected ultimate scale of prices becomes continuously lower; or (c) general expectations envisage a certain rate of decline of the scale of prices in perpetuity.
>
> In case (a), the withholding of capacity will last over a period which will be longer the more slowly the predicted price adjustments come about. In cases (b) and (c), the withholding of capacity will last over an indefinite period, *unless downward price adjustments take place as rapidly as or more rapidly than (i) the changes in expectations, or (ii) the generally expected rate of decline,* in which case full employment will persist throughout. In short, when the scale of prices is moving or is expected to move in any direction, the notion of perfect price flexibility must envisage current prices being adjusted sufficiently rapidly in the same direction, if the full utilization of all productive capacity is sought. This means that, if my definition of price flexibility is accepted (see pp. 63-4) wasteful idleness of resources is incompatible with it.

19.—In admitting that Keynes cannot be said "to have demonstrated the co-existence of unemployment equilibrium and flexible prices," Patinkin explains that this is because "flexibility means that the money wage falls with excess supply, and rises with excess demand; and equilibrium means that the system can continue through time without change. Hence, *by definition,* a system with price flexibility cannot be in equilibrium if there is any unemployment."[39] Now if by "excess supply" is meant more than can be sold at current prices, *it remains true, equally "by definition," that price flexibility so conceived is inconsistent with wasteful idleness, even when we take into account the full dynamic reactions which are theoretically conceivable under a condition of falling or rising prices.* For price flexibility then requires that all prices shall be continuously adjusted so as to bring the spot and future values of the money unit into consistency; in other words, to establish harmony between current and expected prices. Under such adjustments, even unemployment *dis*equilibrium is ruled out.

Do not the words "adjustment period" in the passage quoted above show that Patinkin, in using the term *"dis*equilibrium," is in fact still envisaging some price rigidity? What other adjustments, apart from changes in prices and effective exchange values can he be envisaging? How else can the terms "uncertainty" and "adverse expectations" be explained, unless in relation to unstable price rigidities? And the same tacit assumption of rigidity is present in his statement of what he terms, "the Keynesian position, closest to the 'classics'." In this position, he says, although price flexibility would eventually "generate" full employment, "the length of time that might be necessary for the adjustment makes the policy impractical." He tells us that this statement (like that in the previous quotation) is *not* "dependent upon the assumption of wage rigidities."[40] But what "adjustments" other than tardy cuts in rigid wage-rates has he in mind? He must be thinking of unstable price rigidities *somewhere* in the system.*

The development of Patinkin's thinking since 1948, recorded in his *Money, Interest and Prices,* has not led him to discard the "unemployment *dis*equilibrium" fallacy.[41] In answering Hicks' attempts to defend Keynes' position in respect of unemployment equilibrium, he still maintains that, even when due consideration is given to the "real-balance effect," and price flexibility is "supplemented by monetary policy," the restoration of full employment demands more than "auto-

---

*A critic writes that this argument seems to overlook *inevitable* rigidities. In practice, he says, contracts cannot be varied constantly, so that costs tend to follow prices with some interval. Thus, copper miners' wages can hardly change every time the price of copper changes. But I do not think that this is Patinkin's case. As we have seen, contracts are not rigidities. They are distributive agreements (see pp. 60-1); and collective agreements with trade unions merely cover the price of labor and virtually never guarantee employment at the agreed rates. It is when the unions insist upon adherence to any such "contracts" that they condemn many of their members to unemployment and throw the system out of co-ordination. Thus, if the wage-rates of the miners are maintained when actual or expected copper prices have fallen to such an extent that formerly marginal seams become unworkable at current costs, the disequilibrium is clearly due to a rigidity. The most complete measure of price flexibility practically attainable involves discontinuities at both the cost and the final product ends. But periodic adjustments through recontract (as idleness threatens) can meet that situation. (Sliding scales can render the need for recontract less frequent).

matic" price adjustments.[42] But the only noninflationary steps on the part of the State to aid full employment of which I can conceive are in the form of inducements to or enforcements of price adjustments; and Keynes' argument was directed as much against such adjustments as it was against those which might be more conventionally termed "automatic." In any case, it is on "expectations" that Patinkin bases his thesis, and not on imperfect price flexibility. He has, I suggest, not perceived the truth on which I have laid so much stress, that expectations can have a disequilibrating effect solely in the presence of price rigidities which are regarded as unstable.

That he has adhered to his former views on this issue is surprising to me because of the use he makes of the concept of the "real-balance effect." For as we have seen, unjustified expectations about the aims or results of monetary policy are (under price rigidities regarded as unstable) determinants of the productivity and real value of money; whilst under the kind of monetary system to which Keynes was opposed, M would tend to vary in direct proportion to M_r.

20.—In the light of these considerations, I have been led to the conclusion that the only kind of price flexibility for which we can reasonably hope is, in practice, what I have called (p. 63. above) "effective price flexibility," a situation in which the price inconsistencies which must exist at any point of time *are never in process of material or cumulative worsening* and always in process of rectification at about the same rate that they arise. That need not mean unemployment. Contract covers the short run. And inconsistencies need not accumulate. Hence, "the dynamic approach" does not, as Patinkin maintains, obviate the necessity for the assumption of rigidities and revalidate the Keynesian fallacies. On the contrary, it was largely Keynes' neglect of the dynamic coordinative consequences of price adjustment which led him into the error that wage-rate and price adjustments are no remedy for unemployment.*

21.—The theory of unemployment equilibrium which I have been discussing has, I think, been made plausible through a misinterpretation of the phenomenon of chronic unemployment. Such a condition existed in a particularly serious form in Britain whilst Keynes' ideas were emerging. It was due mainly to the nature of the unemployment insurance system.

To discern the real causes of chronic *idleness* of productive capacity,

---

*The confusion in this field ultimately stems, I feel, from a failure to achieve conceptual clarity, and particularly owing to the absence of a sufficiently rigorous definition of price flexibility.

we must first remember that the waste of productive power in a rigid system takes the form of *actual idleness* (withheld capacity) only temporarily.* The idleness is merely an initial condition. It dissolves gradually into "diverted capacity": (i) in the case of labor, by the failure to recruit for trades in which the price of labor is kept above that which would induce the ideal investment in and utilization of human resources, and (ii) in the case of capital equipment, through the disinvestment of those resources which become redundant when scarcities are being contrived. In so far as labor is concerned, the resources excluded by disco-ordinative pricing are always sufficiently versatile, in the absence of imposed specificities, to be devoted to *some* other uses, in which they can at once be fully employed, in spite of the waste. It follows that, if withheld capacity continues to exist as *idle but valuable* resources, it must be in some way subsidized, and fall into the category "participating idleness"† or be "preferred idleness." Hence it is wrong to think of an equilibrium in respect of unemployment of the withheld capacity type; and although there could well be an equilibrium in the case of labor, in respect of what I have called "preferred idleness,"‡ this is not the sort of unemployment which the Keynesians envisage.

I conclude that the chronic unemployment in Britain which Keynes was trying to explain was due to a combination of three elements: it was subsidized through the so-called unemployment insurance benefits; the subsidy aggravated the preferred idleness element; whilst a participating idleness element (*plus* the expectation that there would be a revival of demand in the trades to which the unemployed workers had a prior right to employment) was an additional influence.

No economist who observed and contemplated the continued unemployment in Britain during the period 1925 to 1929 could have had any

---

*See p. 60.

†*Withheld capacity* in physical equipment is in *participating idleness* when its scrap value remains unrealized, not solely because of an expected revival of demand (although in some cases this may be a necessary condition), but because the physical maintenance of the idle capacity permits a contractual or prospective share in the increased revenues achieved through some collusively arranged contrived scarcity. Withheld capacity in labor is in participating idleness when it remains "attached to" the industry or occupation in which it has become unemployed and refuses other available work, because it thereby maintains a claim to be first employed in that trade (in which contrived scarcity has enhanced the earnings of those who retain employment) if demand revives or if employment is ultimately restored by a wage-rate cut. For a further explanation of this term (as well as "preferred idleness") see my *Theory of Idle Resources*, pp. 82-135.

‡The term "preferred idleness" does not imply blame. It may well be held that the pride which prevents the skilled man from accepting unskilled or menial work, or work at very much lower rates of pay than the rates to which his expectations have become adjusted, is not to be condemned; but his unemployment is not "involuntary" in any realistic sense.

doubts about the possibility of unemployment persisting even in times of boom. It seemed obvious that every market pressure which could have eliminated unemployment was being effectively frustrated. I see no justification for T. Wilson's suggestion that Keynes' teachings enlighten our understanding of such a "weak boom," as he termed it,*(43) or for his belief that the facts in some way refute the old orthodox view that depressions can be eliminated by preventing the inflationary booms which they rectify. Earlier economists had realistically assumed the existence of the institutions of the age in which they wrote; whilst the period during which Keynes' influence was growing witnessed a new and rapid degeneration of the institutions of the price system in Britain. There was nothing in orthodox teaching which implied that it was impossible more or less permanently to price resources out of full utilization and to keep the displaced labor in subsidized idleness.

Similarly, it seems to me unjustifiable to call the chronic unemployment which characterized the long drawn out depression in the United States and Europe, which followed 1929, "unemployment *dis*equilibrium" and to claim that Keynes' theories supply an acceptable explanation of the phenomenon, or even that they throw light upon it. Admittedly the position was generally regarded as unstable. During the depression, entrepreneurs felt that it was unprofitable, with the means at their disposal, to purchase the full potential flow of services at *the wage-rates and other costs* which were being demanded. In so far as liquid assets appeared to offer greater prospective yields than the replacement or net accumulation of nonmoney assets, that must have been due to the expectation of lower costs later on. It was the slowness with which policy permitted the required cost adjustments to occur which frustrated recovery.

The truth is that, during the 'twenties and 'thirties, economists were facing an entirely novel situation owing to what I have just called the degeneration of the price system. We can hardly blame them for having failed to adapt their teachings in detail to phenomena which they had never previously experienced.† But Keynes' sophisticated theory of unemployment equilibrium set the greater part of the academic world of economists on a false trail.

I have, I think, exposed the fallacy in the theory that there is an in-

---

*Wilson thinks that, on this topic, we find "the essential content" of Keynes' thought.

†Nor is it defensible to give Keynes credit for having brought these phenomena into discussion. Contemporary economists were, I know, convinced that the apparently chronic unemployment which existed in the early 'thirties was eradicable, *but for politics.* Economists like Cannan did not stress more persistently the barriers which were preventing the full employment of resources simply because they felt that it would be superfluous to reiterate the obvious to their fellow economists and futile to make any attempt directly to influence the politicians.

herent defect in the price mechanism, price adjustments being self-frustrating. Yet this fallacy was the foundation on which the "new economics" (or the "Keynesian revolution") was built.

We are now forced back to the stark truth that the elimination of wasteful idleness in productive capacity is attainable only through the continuous adjustment of prices *or* the continuous depreciation of the money unit.

REFERENCES

(1) LERNER, *Economics of Control*, p.viii. (2) VINER, *The Rôle of Costs in a System of Economic Liberalism*, in *Wage Determination and the Economics of Liberalism*, (Chamb. of Com. of the U.S.) p.31. (3) SMITHIES, *Effective Demand and Employment*, in Harris, *The New Economics*, p.561. (4) KEYNES, *The General Theory*, p.14. (5) CANNAN, *An Economist's Protest*, p.136. (6) HARROD, *Life of J. M. Keynes*, p.438. (7) Quo. in Harrod, *op. cit.*, p.425. (8) ANDERSON, *Economics and the Public Welfare*, p.334. (9) *Ibid.*, pp.338-9 (quoting C. Roos). (10) BURROWS, *J. M. Keynes, Part II—his Theory*, S.A.J.E., p.249. (11) KEYNES, *op. cit.*, p.11. (12) *Ibid.*, p.253. (13) *Ibid.*, pp. 264-5. (14) KEYNES, *Relative Movements of Real Wages and Output*, E. J., 1939. (15) HUTT, *Natural and Contrived Scarcities*, S.A.J.E., Sept., 1935. (16) GORDON, R. A., A.E.R. *Proceedings*, May, 1948, p.354. (17) KEYNES, *The General Theory*, p.259. (18) VINER, *op. cit.*, p.32. (19) KEYNES, *op. cit.*, p.264. (20) *Ibid.*, p.269. (21) PIGOU, *Money, Wages and Unemployment*, E.J., 1938, p.137. (22) BOULDING, *Economics of Peace*, pp. 141-2. (23) HABERLER, *Prosperity and Depression*, p.493. (24) *Ibid.*, p.243. (25) HABERLER, *Welfare and Freer Trade*, E.J., 1951, pp. 779-80. See also HABERLER, in Harris, *The New Economics*, pp. 167 *et. seq.* (26) SCHUMPETER, *Keynes, the Economist*, in *The New Economics*, p.92n. (27) MODIGLIANI, *Liquidity Preference and the Theory of Interest and Money*, *Econometrica*, Jan. 1944, p.74. (28) *Ibid.*, p.75. (29) PIGOU, *Economic Progress in a Stable Environment*, *Economica*, 1947, pp.187-8. (30) KEYNES, *op. cit.*, p.207. (31) HABERLER, *Prosperity and Depression*, p.221 (footnote). (32) PIGOU, *op. cit.*, pp.183-4. (33) HABERLER, *op cit.*, pp.499-500. (34) *Ibid.*, p.390. (35) PATINKIN, *Price Flexibility and Full Employment* (A.E.R., 1948). Quotations are from the revised version in the A.E.A. *Readings in Monetary Theory*, p.279. (36) *Ibid.*, p.279. (37) *Ibid.*, p.280. (38) *Ibid.*, p.281. (39) *Ibid.*, p.278. (40) *Ibid.*, p.282. (41) PATINKIN, *Money, Interest and Prices*, pp.233 *et. seq.* (42) PATINKIN, *Keynesian Economics Rehabilitated*, E.J., 1959, p.586. (43) WILSON, *Professor Robertson on Effective Demand*, E.J., 1953, p.568.

Chapter X

THE NATURE OF
CONSUMPTION AND SAVING

SUMMARY

*1.—To obtain conceptual clarity on the subject of consumption and saving
it is essential to distinguish clearly four separate economic rôles ("producer," "consumer," "saver" and "entrepreneur") which are normally
assumed simultaneously by the same individual. 2.—"Income" is the flow of
all valuable services, measured in value units ("real" or money). It is partly
consumed directly but mainly embodied into a stock of assets which is in
process of decumulation, replacement and (normally) net accumulation.
3.—One could define "consumption" broadly as the achievement of all
economic ends, 4.—but I shall here mean by "consumption" either (a) the
process of exterminating final services as they are rendered and the decumulation of the stock of assets into which services have been embodied, or
(b) the magnitude of this process—the rate at which it occurs. 5.—The consumer is he who finally exterminates services or assets. 6.—The magnitude
"consumption" may be termed "realized" or "supposed" according to
whether "replacement" is reckoned to maintain the real or the money value
of assets intact. 7.—"Consumption preference" is expressed through the
extermination of value in final srevices or in assets decumulated. 8.—"Saving"
(without a plural "s") is defined to mean the acquisition of assets in return
for services, whether or not there is incomplete or full replacement or net
accumulation. 9.—"Consumption-saving preference" concerns the time of consumption, 10.—"saving preference" meaning the offer of services for assets
(the offer of income for capital). 11.—"Savings" (with a plural "s") occur
when saving preference results in the net accumulation of assets (whether
the assets are inventories of consumers' goods or producers' goods), 12.—and
may be "supposed" or "realized." 13.—The terms "savings" and "net
accumulation" are synonyms which stress different views of the same magnitudes. 14.—In offering services for assets, savers do not demand particular
assets: 15.—entrepreneurs do that. Every choice of assets, even of money or
gilt-edged securities, is the exercise of entrepreneurship, i.e., investment;
16.—shareholders typically delegating to directors the right to make entrepreneurial (and saving) decisions on their behalf. 17.—It is useful to use*

the terms investment and disinvestment to refer to entrepreneurial choice of the form or composition *of gross accumulation and not to mean the* magnitudes, *"net accumulation"* or *"decumulation." 18.—Appendix A, on "The Concept of Aggregate Demand." 19.—Appendix B, on "The Entrepreneur and the Contrivance of Scarcity."*

1.—In this and the following chapter I seek to expose the conceptual confusions inherent in Keynesian teaching in respect of (a) the relations between "consumption" and "investment" and (b) the incentives for the net accumulation or decumulation of assets. I hope to show that the adjustment of consumption to what Keynes called "investment" (and *vice versa*) is a process which cannot be considered macro-economically because it is concerned at its very roots with the determination of the *form* of replacement and net accumulation by entrepreneurs in myriad separate yet inter-connected spheres. In arguing this thesis, I shall not be denying that it is possible to generalise validly about the value magnitudes (income components) "consumption" and "investment". Indeed, I shall be discussing the true determinants of these magnitudes. Properly seen, what are called by such terms as "capital formation," the "development *tempo,*" "net investment," etc., are wholly and solely the aggregate expression of individual saving-preferences resulting in savings achieved, i.e., of thrift—the rate of interest, the initial form and magnitude of income and population being assumed constant. If any other factors whatever are brought in to explain the phenomena so described, they must be concerned (I shall argue) merely with the form or composition of capital growth, and not with its magnitude (real or money). Autonomous factors will be shown to create no exceptions.

Provision for the future, which I am about to show is simply the acquisition of assets for replacement or net accumulation, is conceptually distinct from the choice of *particular* assets for this purpose. Equally separate notions are, *on the one hand*, (a) time preference (loosely, the supply of "savings"), and (b) predictions about the wantedness or productiveness of assets in general (loosely, the demand for "savings"), and *on the other hand*, the actual rate of net accumulation which results from these preferences and predictions, i.e., the time magnitude of growth as distinct from the resulting composition of replacement and net accumulation.

As I see things, through a faulty perception of these distinctions, the Swedish economists since Wicksell, and the great majority of British and American economists since Robertson's *Banking Policy and The Price Level*, have been led into several different attempts to show that certain conceptually identical *magnitudes*, namely, savings and investment, may be unequal.* And these attempts have received their most seriously fallacious development in Keynesian thought, in spite of Keynes having tried to show the *necessary equality* (as distinct from the *identity*) of these magnitudes.

The use of the terms "consumption" and "savings" (as magnitudes) in *The General Theory* has, indeed, created more confusion in the minds of critical readers than any other notions ever treated in economics. Keynes attempted to show, *firstly*, that savings and investment are necessarily equal; *secondly*, that savings tend constantly to exceed investment; and *thirdly*, that in some sense savings are a bad thing, causing income to contract, whilst investment is a good thing (like consumption) causing income to increase (in Keynes' words, "the decisions to consume and invest between them determine incomes").[2]

He defined "savings" as income *minus* consumption; hence we are not allowed to regard it simply as *unspent* income. Accordingly, in my own attempt to reduce Keynes' use of the term to the least absurdity, I have assumed him to mean by it "that part of income which, given expenditure on consumption, will be unspent unless it is spent on investment." But this does not get rid of the absurdity completely; for what are we then to call the parallel concept, i.e., "that part of income which, given expenditure on investment, will be unspent unless it is spent on consumption"?

Clearly, he was confusing two different fallacies, (a) that demand for the services of money, and (b) that demand for assets as a whole (which, I shall show is necessarily the form taken by the expressed desire to provide for the future), cause "effective demand" to contract.

The extent of Keynes' confusion between spending and consuming (or between not spending and saving) is revealed in his reference to the objects "which lead individuals to *refrain from spending* out of their incomes."[3] (My italics). For in spite of the reference to refraining from spending, he did not mention liquidity as an objective of such conduct, and referred simply to provision for "old age, family education or the maintenance of dependants," the desire to enjoy "a gradually improving standard of life," etc. Under the eight headings he listed, only "miserliness" has any relevance to the choice of money, and yet he used

---

*Myrdal says that the "distinction between saving and investment is the essence of the modern monetary theory which starts with Wicksell."[1]

the words "refrain from spending." He tried to find, instead, the supposedly depressing effects of saving in the fact that the saver may merely acquire existing and not new or additional assets, which "forces some other individual to transfer to him some article of wealth old or new," whilst such transfers "may be actively inimical to . . . the creation of new wealth."[4]

The failure of the attempts which have been made to *explain away* (as distinct from explaining) these confusions (e.g., the suggestion that a lag is implied, the suggestion that it is *attempted* saving which reduces income and *attempted* investment which increases it, etc.), has been shown in Hazlitt's study,[5] and I propose in this chapter simply to confine myself to an independent examination of basic concepts.

In this task, I have found the choice of terminology difficult. Economics abounds with tendentious and inappropriate terms. Current jargon has been so affected by the political exigencies which, I feel, economists have all too often been subconsciously serving that, when a writer begins to use language neutrally, solely in the interests of clarity of thought, he is apt to be accused of writing emotively.* I should have liked to avoid altogether the euphemisms and emotively toned expressions which have infiltrated into conventional theory. But that has not seemed to be practicable. If I attempted to use terms too differently, few readers would remember that I was using words in their literal sense and not in their acquired conventional sense. But when terms have been conventionally used so *loosely* as to cover categories which exclude like or identical things or actions, or are ambiguous in other respects, I have felt it to be imperative to break with current usage. Here I must ask the indulgence of the reader. He may for instance be irritated by my talking of "net accumulation" where he would have used the word "investment." But he will see that, on other occasions, I use the word "investment" where he also would have used it, but where it means something completely different. I have introduced new terms, however, only where they seem to me to be essential to bring out *vital* distinctions. And as it is one of my chief contentions that the root errors of Keynesianism are to be found in the concepts employed, the re-definition of central notions like consumption, saving, investment, the entrepreneur, etc., will form a considerable part of my contribution.

Although my treatment is independent, I regard it as original only in the sense that it tries to state more rigorously what I think economists in the orthodox tradition have, on the whole, understood. I shall be

---

*See, for instance, Lindley Fraser's objection to my use of the term "consumers' sovereignty" and my reply.[6]

attempting to establish conceptual clarity in notions which I have felt to be essential for an understanding of the process of accumulating assets (which constitutes saving), and the process of decumulation (which constitutes consumption).

Some years ago, in criticising an unpublished essay which I had sent to him, Haberler wrote:

> There has been a lot of confusion in the literature on the definition of investment, consumption, etc., and there may be still cases where people get enmeshed in contradictions; but on the whole, in my opinion, this phase of the discussion can be regarded as closed. The best discussion of these matters of definition I know of is to be found in Irving Fisher's book *The Nature of Capital and Income*. It is a pity that the Keynesian literature which abounds with confusions had no firm grounding in Irving Fisher's writings.

I agree with this appraisal of Fisher's work. But far from agreeing that the fruitful discussion of these concepts can be regarded as closed, I hold that some of the basic ideas need re-examination and refinement, and that the required refinement can throw clear light on many current controversies. The concepts and analysis which I present have obviously been indebted to Fisher's pioneer work, although they differ considerably from his. My indebtedness to Wicksteed and Mises is equally great.

My main thesis is that, in order to understand the connected notions of consumption and saving, we have to recognize that every individual has four conceptually distinct economic rôles, *which are normally exercised concurrently*. "The producer," "the consumer," "the saver" and "the entrepreneur" are normally to be regarded as the same person in what usually appears as one simple act! Whilst it is essential to keep these *functions* distinct in our minds, it is equally desirable not to think about people, in the performance of the four rôles, as belonging to four separate categories. Every person (apart from young children and the insane, who make no economic decisions of their own) ought to be seen as *continuously and simultaneously exercising* all the functions which these terms describe. Thus, when I refer to, say, "entrepreneurs," it must be remembered that I am referring to people who are exercising entrepreneurial functions, but recognizing that they are at the same time savers, consumers and producers.

We must, in particular, distinguish between the "entrepreneur" and the "producer," and between the "entrepreneur" and the "consumer-saver."

The producer as such is simply the seller of services. He sells his personal services, or those of his assets, *passively*—at a price which is determined under the pressures of the price system. He can, however, sometimes influence the price by withholding capacity. (I shall explain later why this is *not* to be regarded as an entrepreneurial act).

The consumer-saver as such exercises a preference concerning *ends*. When I give him this double-barreled name, I merely wish to stress the simultaneity of the two rôles. (See section 9, below).

The entrepreneur as such bears responsibility for the interpretation of preferences, chooses *means* accordingly, and bets on the results of his choice. In doing so, he creates production functions through combining the services of existing resources in the manner which he predicts will prove most productive (in the sense that the ultimate final product will be most wanted—and hence demanded—by consumers). *The entrepreneur is never responsible for the replacement and net accumulation (or net decumulation)* of assets, but merely for *the form* in which this is done, i.e., for the particular assets chosen for particular purposes. The demand to replace or accumulate net is the demand of those who chose between consumption now and consumption in the future,* i.e., of consumer-savers. (See pp. 202-3).

A successful (wise or lucky) bet brings him (the entrepreneur) a realized yield in excess of interest ("profit") and an unsuccessful bet a realized yield which falls short of interest ("loss"). The entrepreneur, *who is normally the residual claimant* on the value of the product,† may pay someone else (a manager) to make the choice of means on his behalf.

The State may act as entrepreneur; and so-called public investment is, if rationally undertaken, influenced by current interest rates in exactly the same way as so-called private investment.‡

2.—The diagram which follows represents an analysis of the composition of income. The magnitudes indicated are those which are influenced by people in the four rôles which I have specified.

The length of each rectangle represents income—or a part of income— the flow of productive services, either (a) during a period, or alternatively (b) the rate of flow of services, measured in money terms.

---

*Consumption of the assets accumulated or of their services.

†I say "normally" because when contractual remuneration exceeds interest on the value of the resources or services invested in a venture, the excess is entrepreneurial remuneration. (See p. 202).

‡Of course in practice the State can always assume that its purposes stand highest on the scales of preference of the people, without actually testing this assumption by bidding against private preference. Moreover, the State is nearly always allowed to borrow on privileged terms.

DIAGRAM I

(All Magnitudes in "Actual Money Units," i.e., all are "Money Values.")

		Flow of Services (Output, Production or Income)		
	Final Services	Gross Accumulation		
Supposed	Final Services	Decumulation = Replacement	Net Accumulation	
		Consumption		Savings
Realized	Final Services	Decumulation = Replacement		Net Accumulation
		Consumption		Savings

For some readers it may assist if these relations are expressed as algebraical identities.

Let Y represent the value of income, production or output;

F, the value of final services, consumed directly;

G, the value of "gross accumulation";

R, the value of "replacement" or "decumulation";

S, the value of "savings" or "net accumulation";

C, the value of "consumption";

and the subscripts s and r, the attributes "supposed" and "realized," which attributes refer to different ways of envisaging the value magnitude "replacement" or "decumulation"—*a distinction which is quite unconnected with the usual distinction between "planned" and "realized" aggregates.*

Then,

$$Y \equiv F + G$$
$$\equiv F + R_s + S_s$$
$$\equiv F + R_r + S_r$$
$$\equiv C_s + S_s$$
$$\equiv C_r + S_r$$
$$C_s \equiv F + R_s$$
$$C_r \equiv F + R_r$$

In the analysis of the flow of services or income, I have purposely given different names to the same components when they are seen in different aspects. That they are *appropriately* and *usefully* defined, so as to describe the same things in different aspects, has to be demonstrated.

I have defined "income" earlier as *the flow of valuable services,* which may be measured in actual money units, or in abstract money units of constant value ("real terms"). The former is "money income," the latter "real income." Income so defined is essentially a value concept. The notion of real income as a "quantity" appears to me to be absurd, (See my *Theory of Idle Resources*, pp. 30-36). Yet *all the difficulties but one* which have been raised by Keynes[7] and Lindahl[8] are avoided if we regard is as *the value* of the flow of services. The difficulty which is *not* avoided is that arising out of the satisfactoriness or otherwise of the measure of value (including real value) envisaged.*

We are all too apt to forget, under the simplifying influence of price index numbers (as Heilperin has insisted),[9] "the heterogeneous reality that they are supposed to represent. . . . . It is the changing *structure* of economic quantities that really matters most rather than changes in *averages*." It is not enough merely to perceive the difficulties of index number interpretation. Even Keynes did this, but his so-called "macro-economic" method in fact ignored these difficulties at the very point at which they were crucial.

Teaching in the Marshallian tradition has relied on the notion of "the national dividend," meaning by this a flow to be *divided* in a certain way. In this approach, *commodities* (not necessarily material) as well as services, are included in the magnitude. But if any particular commodities are included, then the services being embodied into certain other commodities must be excluded according to some not very clear principle. To get to a rigorously definable idea of what pre-Keynesian economists really understood by *real income* or *net produce*, we need simply value the full flow of services.

Of this flow, a very small proportion (it may be called "final services") is consumed immediately, but the larger proportion is embodied into a stock of assets which is in process of parallel contraction or growth. With income so conceived, we need not worry about what is "net" in it. Only when we are concerned with that part of gross accumulation which exceeds decumulation and causes therefore the aggregate value of assets to increase, does the notion of "net" become important.

I could have adopted a terminology closer to that of some other writers and defined "output" as what is put into the stock of resources and "income" as what is taken out of the stock ("final services" consumed directly being regarded as part of both output and income). But income so defined, would be identical with "consumption," i.e., that part of output which is consumed. It seems to be much more in keeping with everyday usage to regard output (the flow of services) as identical with income, for it all "comes in" as remuneration, satisfactions or accumulated assets. Moreover, my definition helps us to avoid such

---

*See above, p.92.

confusions as arise inevitably out of attempts to conceive of saving as an exchange between present and future *income*. As I use terms, the notion of any exchange between income now and income later has no meaning, whereas we *can* think usefully of an exchange between present and future *consumption*.

The services which form income are, then, either consumed directly ("final services") or embodied into the stock of assets (including inventories of final products in the course of trade or otherwise), which stock is in process of decumulation, full or partial replacement, and possibly net accumulation. The flow includes all services which have scarcity and hence value, *whether or not those services actually enter into the circle of exchange*. (See pp. 134-6). It embraces those provided (i) by natural resources (e.g., the services of land, valued at rent) (ii) by man-made resources (e.g., plant, equipment, houses, furniture, all stock and inventories, patents, and copyrights, etc.), (iii) by money and (iv) by people.

The owners of all these four kinds of resources (including money!) are to be described as producers, for production is regarded as the supply of valuable services. The entrepreneur is a particular producer under this definition and the value of his services is included.

All valuable resources are assets. Even people may be regarded as assets, for investment in human capital is of the greatest importance.

Because entrepreneurial services are included in the total flow of services, the definition makes no distinction between "inputs" of services and "outputs" of products. The flow of services *is* the flow of "outputs" (or products). "Inputs" are simply the value of the flow of services *minus* the aggregate value of entrepreneurial services.

Similarly (*à propos* of input-output analysis) it is common to distinguish prices (meaning the prices of final products or other assets) from wage-rates or from "costs." I propose, however, to regard the prices of final products and other assets as reflecting the prices of all services embodied into them. I include as services, not only those provided in the course of the marketing function, but I treat as *services embodied* any increase in the capital value of assets, however caused (interest being constant); and I include as consumption (disembodiment of services) any loss of capital value (interest being constant).

Services flow from assets (a) automatically or (b) through effort (effort being the services of *people*). As we have seen, effort may be either (1) simple effort, as when a person supplies his own services without the use of nonhuman resources (a virtually nonexistent case), or (2) effort combined with the services of nonhuman resources.

Only those services which have scarcity (and hence value) are included in income. The services of valueless resources are themselves valueless and hence, however important to man's existence and well-being, are excluded. Thus, the sun's light and warmth, the air that we breathe, productive forces like gravity, and the accumulation of human knowledge, although essential for the material welfare and indeed for the survival of mankind are, by reason of the fact that their use by any person does not deprive any other person of any part of their use, not economic goods. Similarly, when the services of valuable resources are temporarily valueless, then, whether they are used or not, their services are not regarded as entering into the flow of services; for that flow can be *measured* only in value terms.

Wasted services, i.e., valuable services which are withheld from consumption or embodiment into assets, are excluded. Thus, "withheld capacity" never contributes to income. On the other hand, as the subsequent explanations will make clear, the waste of services which have been earlier embodied into assets, through the waste of those assets themselves, must be treated as consumption. Unless such waste is covered by replacement it is negative real income.

The income from money which is privately held* is nonpecuniary but can, nevertheless, be measured in money terms and hence in real terms. That is, the income can be valued at interest on the capital value of the resources providing monetary services. Such services form part of society's *real* income just as the services of one's house, one's lawn mower and one's pipe form part of real income, consumed directly.† Hence they enter into money income as I have defined it and influence its magnitude.‡

A distinction is made between those services ("final services") which are *consumed directly,*** and the rest, which are embodied into assets.†† The stock of assets, or resources, is in process of constant decumulation and replacement (partial or full) or growth. The aggregate value of services embodied into assets of all kinds may be termed *gross accumulation*.

Of those services which are embodied into assets, the value of some goes to make up *replacement* of what is being decumulated (possibly

*The term "privately held" excludes those who hold money (in a till, in a banking account or in some other form) for business purposes.

†I value income from consumers' assets at interest on their capital value, regarding this as the market price of the services they render. That is, consumers' surplus is not regarded as entering into income. (See p. 203).

‡Thus, the services we obtain from television certainly compete with and influence the real and money value of the services provided by the cinema.

**What I have called "final services" corresponds to what J.B. Say called "immaterial products, or values consumed at the moment of production,"(10) giving as examples the physician, the musician, the actor, the priest, the lawyer, the servant, and the immaterial returns of a public edifice, a bridge, a highway, or public gardens.

††The services of money are *embodied into assets* when they are used in business just as are, say, the services of the site of the undertaking. They may be regarded as *consumed directly* when used privately.

with assets which are physically quite different), whilst the value of the rest (if any) makes up *net accumulation*. If replacement falls short of what is being decumulated, the deficiency may be called *net decumulation*. When we consider that case, we need also the concept of *gross decumulation*. I shall, however, use the term *decumulation*, unqualified, to mean the value of assets decumulated, in other words, that part of consumption which is not consumed directly as "final services." It may be regarded as the disembodiment of services formerly embodied into assets. Different parts of gross accumulation have different rates of *turnover* (decumulation matched by replacement), and it is this, rather than the vague conventional distinction between "consumption goods" and "production goods", which is important in economic analysis (although it is not very important in the argument which I am developing here).

3.—Broadly defined, the term consumption has reference to *the achievement of economic ends*. Consumption in *this* sense may be contrasted to production, which is *the response to the expression of economic ends*. The *form* of consumption so envisaged is, in other words, the response to "consumers' sovereignty"; and consumers' sovereignty is effective to the extent to which it determines the form of subsequent production, i.e., firstly the form of the stock of assets, and secondly the form of the subsequent flow of services.

Among the consumers' preferences so expressed are those of leisure preference, time preference, risk preference and to some extent liquidity preference.* As we have seen, the form of the stock of assets, and the form of the flow of services (production), is influenced by the expression of these preferences in exactly the same way that it is influenced by the expression of all other preferences.

4.—*In the remainder of this discussion, however, I shall use the term "consumption" in the more restricted connotation which is normally given to it,* attempting at the same time to give it greater clarity. I shall use it to mean either a *process or a magnitude*. The context will make clear what is meant.†

The *process* consists of (i) the actual current extermination of final services as they are *rendered* and (ii) the current disembodiment and

---

*When liquidity preference is pressed in the course of business, it may be regarded as choice of means and not as preference concerning ends. When a private individual, or a firm on his behalf, holds money, it may be the result of a choice of ends *or* a choice of means. It is a *choice of ends* if the purpose is private convenience, the desire for security or miserliness. It is a *choice of means* if the money assets are accumulated speculatively. We can, if we wish, distinguish the two purposes for demanding liquidity by the terms "consumption-liquidity" and "production-liquidity."

†In the parallel concepts, the process and the magnitude of "saving," I have thought it desirable (for reasons to be explained) to use a separate term "savings" (with a plural "s"), for the *magnitude* involved.

extermination of services previously embodied into assets, i.e., the de-cumulation of the stock of assets (in process of full or partial replen-ishment or growth).

The *magnitude* consists of the aggregate value of what is so extermi-nated over a period (measured in money or in real terms), or the rate of that extermination.*

When "final services" are consumed, nothing *physical* is exterminated; but the *value* of the services is exterminated. On the other hand, the valuable services of the assets used in a business, or assets used in some forms of home production (e.g., a sewing machine), are embodied in products, which means that they are not consumed; whereas the valu-able services of "consumption assets," like a gramophone or a picture *are* exterminated, i.e., consumed even though the assets themselves may not be subject to consumption (e.g., as with a picture).

One *consumes assets* through their extermination, which can be seen as the decumulation of a stock.† But the physical extermination is inci-dental. As J. B. Say pointed out, consumption is "the destruction of utility, and not of substance, or matter . . . . an extinction of that which made it an object of desire and of demand," and "being the de-struction of value, is commensurate, not with the bulk, the weight, or the number of the products consumed, but with their value. Large consumption is the destruction of large value, whatever form that value may have happened to have assumed."[11]

All services which *are not wasted* or incorporated into assets are consumed directly. I have referred to them as "final services" or as "directly consumed services." The term covers all services which need not be embodied into assets before being consumed. The proportion of the flow of services which is consumed directly, as "final services," is probably very small.‡ Most services are embodied into assets, at least for a small period of time, before they are disembodied into consump-tion.

All assets which *are wasted*, in the sense that they lose value (at con-stant interest) without rendering unwasted services, are to be consid-ered as consumed. Assets which are *"used up"* in business and industry are not to be considered as consumed but as transformed, if at least an equivalent value is embodied into other assets—products.

Consumption may be deliberate or inadvertent. Thus, a car may be

---

*Strictly speaking, the statement that such loss of value is consumption needs the assumption, "the rate of interest not having risen."

†We are accustomed to talk, loosely, of the "consumption" of fuel, materials, etc., in the course of production. Such resources are, however, not to be regarded as consumed but as embodied into other resources, just as, say, the services of the site, building, machinery, and liquid assets are embodied into the products of a firm.

‡The biggest contribution towards "final services" may well be that of the services flowing from "consumers' assets," e.g., from one's house, furniture, car, etc.

consumed through wear and tear in use or through an accident which destroys it.

When we express the results of "consumption" as a magnitude, it means the aggregate value of "final services" (consumed directly) *plus* the value of services disembodied from assets (the value of resources decumulated). In other words, "consumption" as a magnitude is the aggregate value of output *minus* "savings" ("net accumulation").

5.—He who consumes services or whose assets are consumed—exterminated—is a "consumer." Thus, the shareholder in a company of which the assets are used unwisely or unluckily, so that they lose value (through physical extermination or otherwise—but interest being assumed constant), must be regarded as a "consumer."

6.—What constitutes the magnitudes *decumulation* and *replacement* may be conceived of in real or money terms. That is, by replacement we may mean either (a) the value of that flow of services which, when embodied into assets, maintains the real value of assets intact (i.e., their value if measured in *money units of constant value*), which we can call *realized replacement*, or (b) the value of that flow of services which, when embodied into assets, maintains their money value intact (i.e., their value in terms of *actual money units*), which we can call *supposed replacement*. Corresponding to these concepts, we have *realized decumulation* and *supposed decumulation.**

Both realized and supposed replacement (or decumulation) may be measured either in real or in money terms.

The value of final services (which are consumed directly) *plus* the value of decumulation (assets decumulated) make up the magnitude, *consumption*, which I shall describe as "realized" or "supposed," according to whether it is reckoned from realized or supposed decumulation. The value of the rest of the flow of services represents *net accumulation* which, once again, may be realized or supposed.

7.—"Consumption preference" does not express demand but exterminates it; yet it is accompanied by demand for replacement, namely, the offer of (a) *existing assets* (including money) or (b) *final services* for other services of two kinds (i) other final services,† or (ii) services to be incorporated in assets of which stocks greater than current stocks cannot

---

*This distinction between "supposed" and "realized" does not correspond to the usual distinction made between "planned" and "realized" aggregates.

†In the case of *services*, the demand is normally coterminous with consumption. But when I buy theatre tickets, I am demanding assets; and when I use them, I exterminate their value.

be profitably carried through time. The value of demand (ii) must equal the value of those services which are, so to speak, disembodied out of the assets into which they have been previously incorporated.* But, except in the case of final services, any *demand* expressed is for replacement (full or partial), and that contributes to or makes up saving preference.

Consumption as such is in no sense demand for anything.† *Strictly speaking*, therefore, it is incorrect to speak of "consumption *demand*" at all (except, perhaps, when we imagine the consumer buying "final services." For in the act of consumption, the consumer is always depleting his own stocks, and making no offer of any kind except to himself; and when he is replacing or accumulating, he is saving *and* exercising entrepreneurship. (See p. 202). In demanding consumers' goods, he is *investing* in replacements with the intention of consuming these replacements. This part of demand to replace (or accumulate net) forms the greater part of *so-called* "consumption demand."‡ But the consumers' inventories being replaced must normally be consumed (wastefully or otherwise) relatively soon** (at various times, depending upon perishability, storage costs, etc.). They are "unproductive" except for short periods of time because it is unprofitable to try to carry them through time. Hence, continued re-investment in replacement of consumers' goods may, if we wish, be *loosely* termed "consumption demand," provided that it is always remembered that the origin of the ability to replace is not consumption but production—the flow of real income out of which the replacements are demanded.

The fact that consumption cannot be regarded as in any sense the source of any demand is vital to my thesis, and I return to it in the following chapter.

8.—I shall use the term "saving" (without a plural "s") to mean *the act* of an individual or *a process* of society, namely, the acquisition of assets (capital) in return for services (income). When the individual saves, he expresses a particular preference concerning the use of the flow of services, which is the same thing as the use of the stock of assets. This choice or preference is being constantly made. Hence the term "saving" describes the action taken to sacrifice consumption now for

---

*We shall see that the *offer* of *existing* assets for services to be embodied into new assets (for replacement or net accumulation) is society's demand for saving (the converse of the saver's *demand for assets*). Demand for saving is for services to make (ultimately) assets for replacement or net accumulation. This demand, which is an expression of prospective yields, is conveyed through entrepreneurs, and is competing against consumers for the flow of services. This competition contributes to the inducement for additional savings or diminished dissavings, namely, interest.

†I shall be forced to re-iterate this truth in several later contexts.

‡It must be remembered that directly consumed services ("final services") form a very small proportion of income and consumption.

**Relatively soon, that is, in comparison with producers' goods.

consumption later (of the assets acquired *or of their services*). It may be equally usefully envisaged as the result of an intention *not to decumulate* at more than a certain rate, the stock of assets which services are replacing or building up. Saving implies therefore an intention *to hold* some of the assets. This should be our *first* view of the act.

I shall, then, call the aggregate expression of all individual acts of saving, *the process of saving* or, for short, simply *saving* (without a plural "s"). It should be noticed that this term covers the general expression of time preference, *whatever its intensity*, i.e., whatever the relative values placed by society upon current and future consumption, and *irrespective of whether the process results in full or incomplete replacement, or net accumulation*. In conformity with the above definition, I shall describe people as "savers" when they are exercising time (i.e., saving) preference. They are dissaving when their decumulation of assets is not fully replaced by their saving.

9.—In order to stress the nature of the choice which has to be expressed, I have introduced the term, "consumer-saver." All "consumption-saving demand" is an expression of preference. The distinction between saving preference and consumption preference, as I shall use these terms, is solely one of time. The process of consumption consists of the *current* extermination of final services and of assets, whereas saving preference is for *future* consumption in this sense (and hence expressed as a demand for assets which can be carried through time). That is why all gross accumulation, i.e., the greater part of all output, has to be regarded as a response to saving preference although the inventories accumulated are partly or wholly in process of current decumulation.

When I use the term consumer-saver, I am thinking not only of individuals but of corporations, and even of the State. For shareholders delegate to directorates, in addition to the right to invest (or disinvest*), i.e., to make entrepreneurial decisions on their behalf, the right to save on their behalf. And it is certainly possible for the State or its agencies to save net as well as to consume (dissave). For example, the State is contributing to savings when it pays off part of the national debt, or when it taxes for capital purposes.

10.—By "saving *preference*," I mean the *offer* of services for assets, including money (whether the current rate of decumulation is leaving additions to, or only replacement of, or only partial replacement of the

---

*The right to dissave purposely is not delegated by the shareholder, but merely the right to return capital as dividends.

stock of assets). It should be noticed that an increased offer of services for assets does *not* mean that the flow of services into assets increases, but that the ratio of exchange between services and assets is altered. In the next chapter, I shall explain how if we, say, double our offer of services for assets (income for capital), we halve the rate of interest; i.e., how we must sacrifice twice as much income to get a given "amount" of capital (i.e., an "amount" which will offer a given annual yield). To be "saving preference" the demand expressed must originate in income, i.e., in the flow of services. The offer of assets for assets *cannot be* an expression of saving preference. The offer of services for assets *is*.* It is because services cannot be carried through time, whereas assets can be, that the process of saving *necessarily* involves a demand for assets through the offer of services (a demand for capital through the offer of income).

The term "assets" is intended to include such things as share certificates, securities of all kinds and even unsecured rights for the return of a loan. No double counting is thereby caused. Thus, the value of any individual's assets consists of the gross value of the assets of which he has custody, less the value of his "debts" (i.e., the assets which he may be called upon to return on demand, or on a particular date, or following some contingency).

11.—When the demand for assets expressed as saving preference causes an accumulation great enough (or, the same thing, a rate of decumulation small enough) to result in net accumulation (supposed or realized) I shall call the value of the additional resources acquired, *savings* (with a plural "s"). When that demand is insufficient to bring about full replacement (supposed or realized) I shall call the net decumulation, *dissavings*. The terms express, therefore, the measurable results of response to time preference.

It has seemed convenient to call the expression of time preference by one name (i.e., saving) whether it happens to induce partial replacement, full replacement, or net accumulation (supposed or realized); for in practice every individual has *some* preference for the future.† But it seems to be straining the ordinary meaning of words too much to call *the amount by which the act of saving induces gross accumulation,* "gross savings," and the amount by which it causes net accumulation,

---

*In one very confused passage, Keynes seemed to think that the exchange of assets for assets somehow implies *dissaving*. He wrote: "No-one can acquire an asset which he did not previously possess, unless *either* an asset of equal value is newly produced *or* someone else parts with an asset of that value which he previously had. . . . In the second alternative someone else must be dissaving an equal sum."(12)

†If he had not, he would always *immediately* consume the whole of his resources, exchanging any durable resources which he possessed for decumulable resources.

*"net savings."** For the word "savings," unqualified, and in its usual connotation, has reference to *an excess* of income over consumption. I accordingly use it in that sense when I spell it with a plural "s".

The notion of the *magnitude* of savings gives rise to difficulties simply because the value of the assets acquired by the saver is inserted in the aggregate value of a stock which is in process of partial or complete replenishment or of net accumulation. To simplify exposition, I propose to use the phrase, *"an increase in savings"* (or similar expression), to cover also the notion of *"a decrease in dissavings,"* and the phrase, "a decrease in savings" to cover also the notion of "an increase in dissavings."

It was Wicksell who originated the practice of considering the significance of the *magnitudes* "saving" and "consumption"; but clarity was vitiated through his attempt to conceive of the supply of goods which constitutes real income as falling into two categories—"consumers' goods" and "capital goods." For inventories of consumers' goods are themselves capital goods (productive capital), until they are consumed in the sense of being exterminated. And capital goods are nearly all subject to *physical* consumption; for they are liable to depreciation (through use, physical deterioration over time, and obsolescence). The clarity of complete generality is, I think, obtained in the categories that I call "consumption" (which includes replacement—matched by decumulation) and "net accumulation." There may be net accumulation of consumers' goods, and there is always *physical* consumption of capital goods in progress. And when I wish to refer to the form in which income is being received, I distinguish simply (a) final services (consumed directly), (b) services embodied in assets of which it is judged that greater quantities than existing inventories cannot be profitably carried through time, and (c) services embodied in assets intended to be added to the existing aggregate of assets. The products of category (b) *could* be called "consumer goods" and those of (c) "capital goods." But that is *not* what is normally meant by these terms; nor would a distinction based on rates of turnover (see above, p. 192) conform to the vague conventional distinction between these categories.

12.—The magnitudes, *savings* or *dissavings,* may be *measured* from two different points: (a) the point at which *supposed replacement* is complete or (b) the point at which *realized replacement* is complete. The terms describe therefore either (i) the amount by which (interest being assumed constant) the money value of the community's assets increases

---

*On the other hand, it does *not* seem misleading to describe a process which is currently adding to stocks as "accumulation," in spite of the fact that an even more rapid decumulation of those stocks may be taking place.

over a period, to be called *supposed savings,* or (ii) the amount by which the real value of those assets increases over a period, to be called *realized savings.**

Before supposed or realized savings can begin to accumulate, a preference must have been expressed for *the continuance in the future* of at least the current rate of consumption. The response to that preference covers replacement. Savings result, then, when people refrain from such decumulation as *they believe* entails a reduction or fails to provide for an increase of the real value of assets. But if such savings merely maintain the money value, and not the real value of assets, they are supposed savings only.

When the magnitude of savings in either sense is negative, they can be called *supposed* or *realized dissavings,* the cause (i.e., the act or process) being insufficient saving (which is another way of saying, too much consumption). I shall be dealing with objections to this assertion.

If realized savings fall short of supposed savings,† all that the latter will show is the extent to which savers will have the right to *spend more* (in money units) in the future, whilst the former will show the extent to which they will have the right to *acquire more* (in real terms), whether for consumption or net accumulation.

13.—The term "savings" is, of course, merely an alternative term for "net accumulation." As I define these terms, they are synonyms for *different aspects* of the same magnitude. The "supposed savings" of a period always equal the "supposed net accumulation" of that period (the amount by which the aggregate value of assets has increased when measured in terms of actual money units). Similarly, "realized savings" always equal "realized net accumulation" (the increase in the value of the sum total of assets when replacement is measured in terms of money units of constant value—interest being constant).

The notion of savings as gross accumulation *minus* decumulation coincides, I think, with what Myrdal envisages when he talks of "un-

---

*The same terms may, as we have seen, be used to describe *the rate at which* the money or real value of assets increases or decreases.

†The use of the word "supposed" depends on a simplifying assumption (a rather unrealistic assumption), namely, that people suffer from "the money illusion." It is assumed that they always regard the achievement of *supposed* savings, which has occurred when the money value of their assets has increased (interest being constant) as meaning that they have accumulated real assets. That is, they are assumed to "suppose," wrongly, that their real power to consume in the future has increased. I have felt it essential to make use of some such terms because the terms *money savings* and *real savings* (instead of supposed and realized savings) would be ambiguous. Both supposed and realized savings may be measured either in money or in "real" terms (as, indeed, all the other magnitudes which the adjectives "supposed" and "realized" describe).

consumed income." But it certainly does not correspond to Myrdal's definition of "savings," as that part of income "which is not used in the demand for consumption goods."[13] For gross accumulation includes the replenishment of inventories of consumers' goods; and it is theoretically possible for the money value of consumers' goods (conventionally defined) accumulated to increase whilst, through depreciation, the value of the aggregate stock of producers' goods (conventionally defined),* is declining.

The distinction (on which the Keynesians have attempted to build) between *expenditure* on "consumption," or what is earned in making final products, and expenditure on "investment," or what is earned in making investment goods, is ambiguous; for earnings from the maintenance, repair and replacement of equipment are equally "consumption" in the sense intended.† Thus, although I am using the term "savings" to mean the flow of services "devoted to *increasing* the future flow of income" (Stigler's words,[14] my italics), it has to be remembered that the decision to replace (i.e., to *maintain* the future flow of income, in whole or in part), is equally a decision as between consumption now and consumption later (of assets or the product of assets.)‡

We sometimes encounter the term "gross investment," but it seldom appears to mean what I have called "gross accumulation"; for it is clear that those who use the expression do not regard it as a magnitude which (by reason of the small proportion of "final services") falls very little short of income. For this reason, the term "gross investment" is, in my experience, singularly ill-defined. Obviously it must be intended to include an arbitrary part of replacement.

Consumption is mainly (i.e., apart from the relatively small magnitude, "final services") out of inventories—out of capital. Saving is refraining from the consumption of capital inventories in process of accumulation, and demand for the assets which form those inventories. Income (output, the flow of services) is *mainly* a contribution to inventories, that is, gross accumulation. Hence the identity, *income* = *con-*

---

*I am not dealing in this chapter with the notion that savings are "income" which is simply not "spent" on things intended to be decumulated, implying that it may not be "spent" on assets. If income is accompanied by decumulation of lesser value it *must* be accompanied by net accumulation. What Myrdal (and Keynes who uses the same notion) means is that *nonmoney assets* (as distinct from income) may be used to demand liquidity, i.e., offered in exchange for money.

†In any case, neither replacement nor net accumulation need involve *expenditure*. If a farmer working on his own account allows his flocks and herds to breed and does not sell the increase, he is saving and accumulating net. If he *employs* a shepherd or other labor in the process, however, and does not remunerate in kind, the remuneration (subsequent to the accumulation) *will* be effected through the medium of expenditure.

‡Stigler talks in other places of "net savings," which is obviously what he means by his definition.

sumption + *net accumulation (or savings)* could well be phrased, *income ≡ replacement + net accumulation (or savings)*, in which form it is less conducive to misunderstanding.*

The concept of saving has to do, then, with the exercise of time preference through the exchange of valuable services now (which confer the power to consume now) for assets (which confer the power to consume later). *Because saving is the acquisition of assets (for replacement or net accumulation) in exchange for services, there can be no such thing as society saving more than can be invested. The separation of saving and investment decisions* (on which so much emphasis has been placed by the Keynesians) *is valid only when the notion of "investment" is confined to the taking of responsibility for the form of accumulation.* These are vitally important points which I propose to explain further at a later stage.

14.—The consumer-saver's function is the expression of preferences (a) concerning products and (b) *concerning time.* We call him a saver when we are thinking of the latter preference. As a saver he accumulates resources—*any* resources—by refraining from using all his rights to consume (represented by his stock of capital into which his contribution to income is constantly flowing). His rôle is as *passive* as that of the producer in that, *as* a saver, he does not choose *particular* resources to hold. As a *pure* saver, he receives no entrepreneurial remuneration from his savings: he receives interest only. But as he always must choose (unless he acquires assets at random) he must always be an entrepreneur.† As a saver, his preferences influence the composition of income in one sense only, namely, the form appropriate for the amount of net accumulation (or net decumulation) to the demand for which he is contributing. But in all respects, the form of income is ultimately determined *via* entrepreneurial prediction of ultimate consumer preference.

15.—The entrepreneur's task is, as we have seen, that of *assuming responsibility for* the choice of the means needed for the response to consumer-saver preferences. In other words, his rôle is to take responsibility for *determining the form* to be taken by income and hence *the form* of gross accumulation (replacement and net accumulation). He

---

*It would be possible, of course, to regard "final services" as forming part of inventories for an *instant*, in which case the identity *income ≡ replacement +net accumulation* could be stated without qualification.

†We are forced to make an entrepreneurial choice at the stage in which our product, or our claims, are exchanged for money; for it is continuously in our power to change the form in which our assets are held. The decision to make no change is itself a decision. Hence, it might be maintained that there can hardly be such a thing *in practice* as a pure saver.

does this by contracting with and directing *producers.* Given the definitions we are using, this is another way of saying, "by causing existing
resources to be used in a particular way." In determining the form of
accumulation, he is of course influencing the current and future form
of real income itself. He relies on his forecasts of future preferences as
a whole and, in choosing means for the satisfaction of those preferences,
he relies *inter alia* upon interpretations of two sets of factors: (a) saving
preference; and (b) all the factors which determine what it is usual
today to call "the marginal efficiency of capital."* His direction of
services into different channels is itself a valuable service.† Hence the
entrepreneur may be regarded as belonging to a special class of producer.
Indeed, in backing expert judgment—his own or that of others—the
entrepreneur is vitally productive. The definitions I am using merely
isolate this important kind of productive action.

But we nearly all make entrepreneurial decisions at times. Thus, when
a person who is saving *deliberately selects* certain assets (e.g., money,
gilt-edged securities, or equities, in a certain industry or firm, or fixed
property) which he expects to bring him the highest return (pecuniary
or otherwise) compatible with the satisfaction of his risk-preference, he
is to some extent acting as an entrepreneur. Because every person who
is a saver *must* decide to keep his nonconsumed income in some form or
other, every saver must have at least *some* entrepreneurial influence. *As
a saver,* however, he is a *passive* purchaser of assets. *As a saver,* he thinks
only of acquiring or retaining assets in some form or other. *As an
entrepreneur,* he chooses particular assets to hold, the value consequences
of his choice influencing the form of replacement and net accumulation. This distinction can be clearly envisaged if it is remembered—as
has just been stated—that the pure saver can expect a yield of interest
only. Indeed, one of the best ways of envisaging interest is to think of
it as the average prospective yield from the *random* acquisition of assets.

A further clarification of the distinction between entrepreneurs and
producers may be helpful. The producer usually receives a defined
contractual remuneration; but as the contract to which he is tied and
to which he has tied others may turn out to be favorable or unfavorable
(such that if he recontracted now he would get less favorable or more

---

*The schedule of the marginal efficiency of capital represents the complex of pre-
dicted productive potentialities, from the wise or lucky perception of which, wedded
to the necessary initiative, the entrepreneur is able to win a profit or avoid losses (in
the sense of a realized return above or below interest) by directing the application of
services in accordance with predicted demand.

†Some readers may wonder why the entrepreneur is here regarded merely as dealing with services and not with assets. But as we have seen, when assets are devoted to
certain uses, it is really their services which are being utilized in a certain way, even
when the resources are acquired in the expectation of capital gain (other than gains
due to changes in interest).

favorable terms) some element of his remuneration will be, strictly speaking, profit or loss. Hence, in entering into any contract, every producer is inevitably an entrepreneur.

Moreover, strictly speaking, even the person whom we usually think of as a *consumer* is performing the entrepreneurial function. Thus, we *acquire* durable consumer goods (replaced or accumulated net) up to the point at which we prefer their prospective services to what we can get from interest on the sum we invest in them. Similarly, we *retain* consumer assets when we prefer their services to what we can get from interest on the sum we can realize from their sale. For the interest we sacrifice equals the value of what we can obtain in the form of other directly rendered services or the services of other assets. *Durable consumer goods* stand in this respect in exactly the same position as all other productive assets except that, in this case, we do not regard the prospective return exceeding interest (in "gratifications") as "profit" although Murray Rothbard has recently called it "psychic profit". We think of a return in excess of interest as "profit" when—through division of labor—we acquire assets and combine their services on behalf of other consumers, predicting what they will want in the future. We are then *more obviously entrepreneurs,* directing resources in such a manner that points are reached at which further increments invested in any particular kind of production will (so we predict) be less wanted by consumers than they will be in other employments. At those points, prospective yields from further investment will fall short of interest.*
But basically, all assets we retain, whether "privately" or in business, are held for the same reasons.

The term *investment* is commonly used to mean net accumulation. But when a firm replaces a machine, it "invests" in a new machine, just as it has been disinvesting (instead of merely consuming) the old one (if it has been making the needed arrangements to cover depreciation). I wish to avoid the potential confusions which lurk in such a terminology. Hence, when I use the word "investment" in inverted commas, I shall be using it to mean a magnitude in its Keynesian meaning, i.e., its loose or popular meaning. As such, it is usually meant to be what I call "net accumulation," although it is often impossible to know from current texts whether the word "investment" is intended to cover what I have called "supposed" or "realized" net accumulation. When I use the word without inverted commas, it will mean simply "placement" decisions—entrepreneurial decisions concerning the form to be taken by replacement and net accumulation. (See section 17, below).

---

*Our maximum profit and the optimization of "consumers' surplus" will, of course, only coincide when institutions have been fashioned so as to permit the substitution of the least-cost method of achieving consumer-determined ends, and when pricing is such that long-term marginal cost equals price.

16.—The position is complicated because, as we have seen (p. 196), the ordinary shareholder always delegates to the company in which he has invested, not only authority to make decisions for which he assumes entrepreneurial responsibility, but also at least a limited authority to make saving decisions on his behalf, namely, the right to maintain the firm's resources intact, i.e., to replace. And to the extent to which the shareholder acquiesces in undistributed profits (i.e., in company decisions to add to the firm's resources) the amount that he saves is not of his own direct choosing. But he is still the entrepreneur and still the saver. Hence directors or managers have a dual rôle, both sides of which are covered by the managerial function. They are salaried employees of entrepreneurs and of savers. They express simultaneously entrepreneurial judgment and saving preference: an entrepreneurial judgment because there is a calculation of the *most profitable* form in which to hold and use resources, and a saving preference because there is a choice concerning *the amount* of resources to be maintained or acquired (out of disinvested funds *plus* profits). Both rôles are merged, on behalf of entrepreneurs and savers, in the company. Obviously, the managerial function is of the utmost importance. But directors and managers are interpreters or agents, in spite of the fact that, in choosing means, they have the vital role of creating new production functions.

17.—I have explained that, in so far as any person's decisions affect the real or money value of net accumulation or decumulation, he is acting in his consumer-saver rôle. To avoid confusion, therefore, the concepts of investment and disinvestment have been defined so as to have reference solely to *the form or composition* of accumulation. For entrepreneurs may be said to *invest* or *disinvest* when they allocate or withdraw resources or services, in varying combinations, to or from the manufacture of *different kinds of products or different methods of production,* and to or from *particular undertakings.* When an entrepreneur invests, he must either use his own resources or resources entrusted to him by (i.e., borrowed from) others. As an entrepreneur (e.g., as a shareholder), he may disinvest from particular firms, which is what happens when he gets back capital as dividends. But whether he then decides to reinvest such dividend receipts in other assets or ventures, so as to maintain his capital intact, or to treat the receipts as though they were income and eat up the capital, the decision always is that of a consumer-saver and not of an entrepreneur. A preference is involved, not a responsibility concerning the use of services.

In each individual case, it is true, the entrepreneur invests (i) a chosen value (ii) in chosen resources and operations. *But each amount of services so invested, prevents some other entrepreneur from investing a similar amount. That is, it represents a particular way of using the services of scarce resources and is in no sense a determinant of the rate of net accumulation.*

18.—APPENDIX A on

The Concept of Aggregate Demand

In chapter II, I referred to the defectiveness of the concept of aggregate effective demand.* But even without the tendentious adjective "effective," the notion of "aggregate demand" or "demand in general" is objectionable. We can, as I have explained (pp. 25-9), envisage *"demands* in general"; but strictly speaking we cannot, I hold, describe such demands as *"demand* in general" or "aggregate demand" without the danger of misleading ourselves and others.

Demands in general can be classified into three categories:

(a) for services to be embodied into assets (to replace the same or other assets being decumulated, or to add to the aggregate stock of assets);

(b) for final services (to be consumed directly);

(c) for existing assets.

Those demands which fall under (b) *plus* those demands under (a) which are for replacement may be called "consumption demand."

The source of these demands is (i) the flow of services, i.e., income, and/or (ii) the stock of assets, i.e., capital.

Demands in general ("aggregate demand") *for assets* from *the offer of assets* are in no conceivable sense something which can be measured, because it is impossible to measure *preferences* in general! It is wholly a matter of changes in *relative values*. The number of exchanges of assets is no measure of anything. The value of particular assets or of different kinds of assets may change considerably (through changes in preference) without any exchanges actually occurring; and there is no way of *aggregating* the preferences so expressed.

But is it possible to measure that part of the demands for services which arises from the offer of services? The flow itself—the income—can be measured in value units; and in measuring in *value* units, demands are assumed; for without demands (i.e., without the ability to exchange for other things) there will be no value. But I do not think that demands in general for services from the offer of services (as distinct from income) can be *measured* in any sense, any more than the aggregate demand from the offer of assets for assets can be measured. Again, it is purely a question of relative preferences.

---

*At the same time I have at times conformed to current usage to the extent of using the term "demand" (in general) in contexts in which it is synonymous with "income."

Services which make up the flow of income are either retained (con-sumed, or embodied into assets for the owner) or exchanged. In each case they are demanded. If retained, their owners outbid others.* If exchanged, their owners are outbid by others. Now although the whole of the flow of valuable services *is demanded,* and although it is part of *the source of demands in general,* we surely cannot say that it *is* demand. But when economists have talked of "demand in general" or "aggregate demand," and they have been thinking of demand from the flow of services, then they have merely been using another term for "income." Income *is* what they have meant by "aggregate demand."

Moreover, in the category "demands in general" are demands for services from the offer of assets, and demands for assets from the offer of services. Let us assume that we are measuring the flow of services in money units of constant value (the index used weighting equally each portion of the flow of services). Demands of this nature will clearly not affect the aggregate value of the flow of services measured in terms of services ("real terms").† They will influence only *the ratio* between the values of services and the values of the assets from which services flow, which ratio constitutes, as we shall see, the rate of interest.

It is therefore imperative that we should separate quite clearly in our minds (i) demands for services from the offer of services, and (ii) demands for services from the offer of assets (and for assets from the offer of services). Lumping together "demands" in such different senses, in a blanket concept of "demands in general," can only lead to the most serious confusions, still more so if it is thought of as forming part of a measurable complex called "aggregate demand."

Clarity on this issue will assist the reader in the chapters which follow.

19.—APPENDIX B on

The Entrepreneur and the Contrivance of Scarcity

In Appendix A, I assumed that services retained by the producer are consumed by him or embodied into assets owned by him. But he may withhold services, i.e., withhold capacity, so that some potential services do not form part of income, and hence cannot be the source of any demand. In section 1, I said that I regarded the withholding of capacity as a producer's and not as an entrepreneur's action. My reasons are as follows.

I have already suggested, and I propose to reiterate this view in the

---

*Thus, when I grow cabbages in my garden, I am demanding them (preferring them to the products of the farms) ; and when I shave myself I am demanding (preferring) my own services to those of the barber.

†See above, pp. 194-5.

following chapter, that entrepreneurship is a determinant of the *composition* but not of the *magnitudes* of the various components into which I have divided income. Nor is it a determinant of the *magnitude* of income as a whole, except in the sense that it contributes to income—because entrepreneurs' services are productive. Entrepreneurship is solely concerned with the *composition* of income as a whole. The magnitude of income must be regarded as determined (a) by the output contributed by existing resources and (b) by the extent to which saving preference, facilitated by autonomous factors (such as population growth, discoveries and inventions), is resulting in the net accumulation of productive power; and (a) envisages people acting in their producers' rôle. It is in that rôle that they are regarded as releasing or withholding capacity, and hence determining the flow of productive services.

There is not the slightest reason why the general withholding of capacity should increase *profits* as a component of aggregate income. Nor, I think, is there ever any question of entrepreneurs (as particular producers) withholding *their* services.* The difficulties arise for another reason, namely, because entrepreneurship cannot be exercised independently of ownership. That is, entrepreneurs must bet on the success of the combinations of resources which they effect. They must, so to speak, stake some of the resources they combine in the hope that they will avoid losses and achieve profits on each increment invested. But this inevitable merging of the rôles in practice does not prevent their conceptual separation.†

At first sight, admittedly, this separation may seem to involve some inconsistency because there may be a prospective yield from *the withholding* of resources, just as there may be from *the combination* of resources to yield a particular output. Yet when we are trying to think macro-economically, there is a fundamental difference. The former implies a decline in demands in general, and if entrepreneurial actions are rational, that means a decline in prospective yields as a whole, (i.e., a decline in the marginal efficiency of capital), whereas the wise combination of resources, because it happens to be the most fruitful form of productive activity, implies a rise in prospective yields as a whole. If it were impossible to unravel attempts to fix such outputs as maximize

---

*It is, of course, possible to conceive of a contrived scarcity of managerial services—the services of those important producers to whom entrepreneurial discretion (and saving discretion) is often delegated. Thus, it could well be held that an educational system, or institutional and sociological barriers (such as the present color bar in South Africa), may result in the withholding of opportunities for managerial training.

†The fact that something resembling the contrivance of scarcity may be necessary to confer property upon the results of successful research, prospecting, reproducible achievements in the fields of art, music, literature and other forms of innovation (through patents, sole exploitation rights, copyrights, or reliance upon certain inertias in the working of competitive institutions) does not, I suggest, blur the distinction.

private or sectional income from those reactions to the price system which (owing to the institutional framework) result in outputs which tend to maximize *the aggregate income of society*, there would be no logical basis for any efforts in the field of monopoly dissolution and control.

REFERENCES

(1) MYRDAL, *Monetary Equilibrium*, p.90.   (2) KEYNES, *The General Theory*, p.64. (3) *Ibid.*, p.107. (4) *Ibid.*, p.212. (5) HAZLITT, *The Failure of the "New Economics"*, particularly in chaps. viii, ix and x. (6) FRASER, *The Doctrine of Consumers' Sovereignty*, E. J., 1939, and HUTT, *The Concept of Consumers' Sovereignty*, E. J., 1940. (7) KEYNES, *op. cit.*, chap. 4; *The Treatise*, Vol. I, Book II. (8) LINDAHL, *The Concept of Income*, in *Essays in Honour of Gustav Cassel*. (9) HEILPERIN, *International Monetary Economics*, p. viii.   (10) SAY, *Political Economy*, 4th ed., Vol. I, p. 136. (11) *Ibid.*, Vol. II, pp.221-222. (12) KEYNES, *The General Theory*, pp.81-2. (13) MYRDAL, *Monetary Equilibrium*, p.90. (14) STIGLER, *The Theory of Price*, p.325.

Chapter XI

THE CONSUMPTION FALLACY

SUMMARY

1.—I propose to show that the magnitude *of net accumulation (as distinct from* the form *of gross accumulation) is determined solely by the factors which (interest being given) determine consumption-saving preference,*
2.—replacement being equally a response to this preference..3.—The individual achieves savings as his products or claims to remuneration accumulate, and in doing so he always contributes to net accumulation. 4.—It is fallacious to assume that hoarding and dishoarding of money, or inflation and deflation, can upset this thesis; or to think of "savings" being absorbed into "investment"; 5.—or to think of the saver as one who "demands nothing" with income; 6.—or to think that the specialization of saving preference and entrepreneurial choice somehow influences the rate of growth; 7.—or to think that entrepreneurial optimism and pessimism are determinants of growth (except in so far as (i) savings respond to the interest inducement, or (ii) prospects influence the release or withholding of capacity).
8.—It is theoretically possible, however, that changes in consumption-saving preference may not be responded to, the sole effects being expressed in changes in interest (which may become negative) and other values. 9.—But net accumulation may occur under negative interest, if saving preference is sufficient. 10.—Diagram II represents how (if my reasoning is valid) saving preference and prospective yields determine (a) interest and (b) (real income being given) the rate of net accumulation (or decumulation).
11.—The analysis holds not only under the assumption of constant real income, but when growth is assumed. The rate of net accumulation will be influenced, however, by the form *in which real income changes through the release or withholding or growth of capacity. 12.—The fallacious notion that consumption is the origin of demand for replacement and growth is due partly to the failure to make the distinctions to which I referred in the previous chapter, and partly to the fact that* the form *of consumption is one determinant of* the form *of gross accumulation. 13.—But changes in consumption-saving preference (whether autonomous or induced) influence the proportions in which the flow of services is incorporated into producers' goods or consumers' goods. 14.—Neither investment decisions nor saving decisions can immediately influence the magnitude of employment or income, although all changes may cause variations in real income under price rigidity. 15.—The source of realized "consumption demand" is the complementarity of the services which make up replacement and net accumulation.*

16.—Recapitulation and conclusions. 17.—Our conclusions are not upset by monetary factors or by the argument that plentiful savings do not automatically provide entrepreneurs with means for expansion unless they are offered as risk capital. 18.—It is a misinterpretation of the phenomenon of unstable price rigidities which seems to be finally responsible for the consumption fallacy. 19.—Appendix A: The relevance of expenditure by the State and foreigners. 20.—Appendix B: The notion of "failure to spend" without "hoarding."

1.—In the previous chapter, I have used the term "savings" in its ordinary, everyday connotation. In such a sense its value magnitude as a constituent of income is identical with net accumulation. And I have suggested that, given the factors which determine interest, consumer-savers determine the *"amount" and value* of net accumulation, and entrepreneurs *the form* of gross accumulation. But I am not optimistic enough to suppose that I shall have convinced all readers of the futility of those approaches which make use of the notions of the availability or nonavailability of "outlets for investment," or of the "absorption (or nonabsorption) of savings in investment." I propose therefore to examine further the nature of the response to consumption-saving preference.

An increase or decrease in the demand for assets by the offer of services, i.e., an increase or decrease in saving preference, may be *induced* or *autonomous*. It is *induced* if called forth by a change in the rate of interest (brought about by a change in prospective yields). It is *autonomous* if it is brought about by all the other factors, apart from the rate of interest, which influence time preference.* By a "change in the rate of interest" I mean a change in the relative values of services and assets (income and capital), as will shortly become clear.†

I shall argue that, given the entrepreneur's offer of interest, which reflects his judgment of prospective yields, the magnitude of net accumulation (or decumulation) is determined *solely* by the factors which are expressed in saving preference. Similarly, given saving preference, this magnitude is determined by prospective yields, which are reflected in the entrepreneur's interest offer. Changes in the rate of savings (or dissavings) being the same thing as changes in the rate of net accumula-

---

*The term "autonomous" is not *ideal*, for included under it is the reaction to all value changes other than those expressed in the rate of interest.

†In Diagram II, p.227, "autonomous" changes in time preference are represented by shifts in the curve representing saving preference and "induced" changes by movements along this curve caused by shifts in the curve representing the demand for saving. (See p.195n)

tion (or decumulation), shifts in the demand schedule of entrepreneurs wishing to borrow, can influence the magnitudes in question only in so far as the rate of interest can influence the preferences which determine the rate of savings (or dissavings). Entrepreneurial optimism or pessimism can otherwise determine merely *the form* in which resources are replaced or accumulated net.

The form taken by gross accumulation (indeed, the form of income generally) is, however, in every case an entrepreneurial decision. The entrepreneur's inducement is the *relative* prospective profitableness of accumulation in different kinds of assets. This is so in spite of the fact that, to the typical entrepreneur, a fall in the rate of interest appears as a fall in costs. As the subsequent analysis will make clear, if realized savings increase, this will be due entirely to an additional flow of services having been left available for entrepreneurs to embody into the additional assets which savers are demanding.

I can at this stage anticipate an objection. It will be said that this reasoning can hardly hold if the market rate of interest is fixed below the natural (with a consequent increasing MV in relation to T). But unless people *wish* to save a larger proportion of their increasing money incomes, it will cause no increase in the rate of realized net accumulation in real terms but merely a higher money valuation of the flow of income generally. (I refer to a slightly different form of the fallacy on pp. 216-7).

2.—We must keep constantly in mind two fundamental truths: (a) that replacement is a response to the same kind of saving preference and carried out to the same limits as net accumulation (the limits being the points at which the marginal prospective yield of the assets to be acquired* has fallen to the rate of interest); and (b) that the greater part of all output is in some degree a response to this preference, i.e., a response to the demand for the *capital* represented by inventories and stocks of all commodities. The only services which are in no sense a response (through the entrepreneur, and indirectly) to saving preference are those final services which are consumed as they are rendered, and those which are embodied into immediately perishable goods.† Thus, the replacement part of output is, *by definition*, accompanied by decumulation at an equivalent rate (unless *net* decumulation is in progress). But it remains one part of the response to saving preference. That is, some part of gross accumulation is *overlapped* by consumption. Hence, the inducement to the entrepreneur is the same whether or not

---

*Expenditure on maintenance and renovation is, of course, regarded as the acquisition of assets in the form of replacement.

†Perishability means that inventories can never be more than negligible in magnitude.

net accumulation occurs.* It is a serious fallacy to imagine that pro- spective profits (in the sense of a yield in excess of interest) are essen- tial to induce net accumulation, but not essential to induce any measure of replacement.†

It is because the same kind of preference calls forth the part of gross accumulation which overlaps decumulation, as well as the part which does not, that I call the whole process by one name, "saving." If we concentrate attention on the excess of gross accumulation over de- cumulation (i.e., "savings"), or on the excess of decumulation over gross accumulation (i.e., "dissavings") we are apt to forget that gross accumu- lation and decumulation are independently determined magnitudes.‡ The former can be realized only out of income whereas the latter must be out of capital. My approach endeavors to concentrate attention upon these magnitudes themselves and not merely upon the overlap.

Nevertheless, I expect to be told that it is straining the meaning of words to describe the process of demanding assets to replace inventories consumed as "saving preference," instead of confining this term to demand for the excess above replacement (resulting in what I have called "savings"—with a plural "s"). But saving preference in my sense is perfectly homogeneous.

Saving, i.e., *the process*, is in practice always occurring even although dissavings are being realized and capital consumption is in progress! That is, *saving preference* may be effectively exercised, even if it is not currently leading to any replacement. This can be seen whenever the consumption of a decumulable stock is spread over time. For instance if Robinson Crusoe carefully conserves his pile of grain from one harvest

---

*Even if we play with the idea of zero or negative interest, the proposition is not disturbed. For if interest is zero or negative and any replacement occurs, it means that current capital consumption is nevertheless preferred less than the future consumption which is made possible by the replacement. There must therefore be a *positive prospec- tive yield in excess of interest* (profits) on all replacement which comes about, to offset the loss in capital consumption (the "disutility") which the replacement causes. (See sec. 9, below)

†Of course, one cannot consider the prospective profitableness of replacement or net accumulation of particular resources in isolation. It becomes profitable to replace or add to the stock of one kind of productive resources because it is at the same time profitable to replace or add to the stock of various co-operant resources needed. But this in no way weakens the principle stated.

Nor is the proposition disturbed in the case in which a firm decides to "run at a loss" for a temporary period in order to preserve the goodwill of staff or customers. It re- mains true that, from the long-term point of view, profits in the sense of an eventual yield above interest must be expected from the value of services embodied into assets. The fact that profits are expected from all replacements does not mean that *realized* profits (realized yields in excess of interest at the time of the investment) will *eventu- ate*. Still less does it mean that profits in the accounting sense will be made.

‡When we consume anything, we need not replace with the same thing or we need not replace at all—we may live on capital.

throughout the year in order to make it last until the next harvest, he is all the time exercising consumption-saving choice. And if he decides to consume more slowly (and his grain reserves are his only decumulable stocks), the decline in the rate of decumulation means, in effect, a rise in saving preference and decreased dissavings.

A decline in real consumption always means an increase in real savings (or a decrease in dissavings) and *vice versa,* unless there is some other *conceptually quite independent* reaction. For instance, if Crusoe's decision to consume more slowly means that some of his stocks perish, or if similar action in an exchange economy means some destruction or withholding of productive power, it might *appear* that we cannot regard saving and consumption merely as indicating two different ways of treating resources and services. But that is what they are, and to recognize this fact in no way prevents our taking into account the possibility of all sorts of predictable or unpredictable reactions upon the flow of services or the stock of assets, owing to such changes in preference.

3.—Let us now notice in greater detail the process by which the individual, in achieving savings, contributes to savings by the community.

A person acquires savings by acquiring assets with his contribution to income and refraining from the consumption of a value of assets greater than the value of his contribution to the stock of assets into which services are flowing. In practice, he either (i) accumulates the product of his own efforts or property (e.g., Crusoe building a hut), or (ii) accumulates assets in the form of *contractual claims* for remuneration, interest or dividends in return for the product of his efforts or property. This stage in saving is almost always ended through the temporary conversion of the assets accumulated (products or claims) into money.* Thus, if the saver is an employee who is paid his wages weekly, he is saving from the beginning of the week until the end of the week; for he is accumulating assets in the form of his legal claim for wages on his employer. If during that week he has decumulated a smaller value of assets (food, clothing, etc.) than the value of those he has accumulated as claims, he will have achieved savings. He neither saves further nor accumulates further in turning one form of assets into another, e.g., in exchanging rights to wages for actual wages (money), or subsequently by investing in a savings account, subscribing to equities

---

*In the case of both the earner and the receiver of interest and dividends, this stage is the completion of the contract which led to the personal services being rendered or the investment being made. Hence this particular exchange of assets may, perhaps, be regarded as "passive" or "automatic." The interest receiver then approaches nearest to the conception of the "pure saver"—one who has not yet made any decision about the form in which he will hold assets.

in a company in process of formation, or buying a television set. If he is working on his own account as a manufacturer of something durable, he will be achieving savings when he accumulates inventories at a rate which sufficiently exceeds his current consumption and accumulation of liabilities. If he is working on his own account selling services, like a doctor, he may be saving income as he renders his services and is either paid or acquires the right to be paid. In each case, whether or not a contribution to savings is being made depends upon whether or not a person's gross accumulation of assets *(including money)* is exceeding his decumulation of assets. Hence unless such contributions to *savings* have, in the aggregate, been offset by net decumulation on the parts of others, there will have been an *equivalent* addition to *savings* on the part of society. It follows that the amount of *realized* net accumulation by society must equal the sum of realized individual savings —individual additions to the value of assets owned (measured in real terms) *less* individual dissavings, whatever initial form such assets may have happened to take.

We have seen that saving preference means the offer of services for assets and not the offer of assets for assets (see pp. 196-7, 211-2). Similarly the response to this preference—replacement and net accumulation *in general*—can occur only through the incorporation of *services* into assets, i.e., out of income. When economists talk of the investment of *capital* they must mean (unless there is some subtle confusion in their thinking) the combination or recombination of capital assets. But mere combination of resources does not lead to any contribution to accumulation. If, when combined, the capital value of two assets is greater than when they are uncombined, and no other services have been involved in the combination, it means that the innovators' (the entrepreneurs') services have been embodied into the assets.

It should be noticed that, whilst from the standpoint of the individual saver assets may be accumulated in the form of *products, or claims, or money,* from the standpoint of society, assets are accumulated solely in the form of *products.** For claims and credit money are offset by liabilities.

4.—*The fact that all persons may prefer to hold more or less of their assets in the form of money* (and this may happen quite irrespective of whether they may happen to be saving or dissaving), *does not cause any divergence between savings and net accumulation.* Consider, for instance, the case in which a person acquires increased stocks of money equal to the value of his savings during a period. If those to whom he

---

*I should remind the reader that if certain assets increase in real value (interest being constant) I regard the increase as a product.

has sold assets (his original savings) have not decumulated them, *the aggregate stock of assets will have increased, in spite of the fact that the stock of money (neither M_r nor M) cannot be increased by saving preference or a response to it.* (I shall return to this point). But the form in which people wish to hold assets may (according to the monetary policy followed) influence the value of the money unit and thereby influence the withholding or release of capacity. Yet all changes in economic ends, and all changes in the choice of means to those ends, may have this effect to some extent.

To talk of "saving money," unless it is merely a loose or popular way of talking, is a serious solecism. One may save, and then invest in money; but the *saving* has occurred before the product into which services have been embodied has been exchanged for the money. If I grow potatoes, sell them and hoard the receipts, my saving occurs as I am accumulating the potatoes, i.e., as their prospective value is increasing, and not when I sell them.

The point at issue is no mere verbal quibble. Demand for the acquisition of money must be recognized as an expression of entrepreneurship; and it is an act which is wholly independent of saving preference. The entrepreneur will, as we have seen, choose to hold his assets in the form of money to the extent to which monetary services appear to be more profitable than the services of other assets, i.e., up to the point at which the marginal prospective yield in terms of monetary services has fallen to the rate of interest. Now what has to be explained is why this reaction to saving—why this particular entrepreneurial choice of productive factors—should cause the cessation of, or a falling off in, the rate at which services are embodied into assets. Any falling off or cessation in net accumulation must be due, in the circumstances being considered, to the services which are capable of use for that purpose not being offered at prices which are correctly co-ordinated with prospective demand. It is never argued that the scope for net accumulation contracts because potentially available services are wrongly thought to be more profitably employed in consumption uses. Hence the implication must be that such services are withheld through being priced higher than people *can afford* to pay, or higher than they *are willing* to pay (i.e., too high in relation to the future prices which buyers anticipate).

It follows that those economists who talk of savings being absorbed in investment, or of a lack of investment outlets for savings, or of "the thrift of the community" [being] "too great for the demands put upon it" (as the Radcliffe Committee express the fallacy[1]* cannot justify

---

*The unemployment which the Committee expect to result implies that they regard low noninflationary interest as a cause of unemployment. They do not seem to be envisaging disco-ordination due to a *change in thrift.*

their position on the grounds that they have had in mind "past savings"—"hoarded savings." For as we have seen, the exchange of money for other assets does not, in itself, bring about additions to the aggregate amount of all assets. Here also it is entirely a question of the chosen use of income (services) in the light of its increased money valuation* (due to the dishoarding implied), and so of any increased real income which the new valuation may have induced.

The same misconception in a different make-up is found in the notion that net accumulation may be "financed," not out of current savings but out of inflation, i.e., through a decline in the value of the money unit. Savings, it is thought will then be unnecessary. The answer is that inflationary credit issued, or notes forged, may be spent to buy either (a) final services or services to be embodied in replacement or (b) services to be embodied in assets of which additional stocks appear profitable. The value magnitudes of (a) and (b) still depend upon saving preference. To use the common terminology, if "new money" happens to be "injected" in the producers' goods industries, the decision to depreciate the money unit is linked with a command to save,† provided, of course, (i) that the production financed does not partake of the nature of boondoggling, which is disguised consumption,‡ and (ii) that it does not induce additional decumulation elsewhere in the economy.

A similar error sometimes arises in the opposite form. Net accumulation is assumed to occur "autonomously", the failure to achieve corresponding savings being supposed to force inflation, through which the necessary savings are induced. For instance, the Radcliffe Committee talk of "heavy investment in new capital assets" having occurred "without the corresponding rise in current savings necessary to finance their production without inflation."[3] But if the word *new* is intended to mean *additional*, savings must have been forthcoming through decisions somewhere.

It is far from certain, however, whether the Committee regard the

---

*It should be noticed that I refer here to "increased" and not "inflated" money valuation of income. To the extent to which "dishoarding" follows the release of withheld capacity, its effect will be neutral.

†It need hardly be stressed that, if the accumulation is sufficiently productive, it is financed by noninflationary credit, and not by inflation.

‡In attempting to answer Ohlin's criticisms in 1937, Keynes argued that "finance" (meaning credit expansion which may or may not be inflationary) "has nothing to do with saving," which is certainly true. But he continued, "At the 'financial' stage of the proceedings, no net saving has taken place on anyone's part, just as there has been no net investment."[2] This misses the real issue, with which I have dealt above. "The financial stage of the proceedings" can only be said to begin when the money valuation of a given flow of services has changed, and *someone* must have decided how the revalued flow is being utilized.

inflation as having been *beneficent* in permitting investment in heavy industry; for they refer also to "excessive demand," due to too little thrift. Yet any inflation arises from monetary policy, which an official desire for investment in a particular form—heavy industry—*may cause to be expedient* (when freely expressed saving preference does not itself make that objective sufficiently cheap). Abnormally low (or declining) thrift is not *inflationary,* as the words "excessive demand" imply, (a) unless it is assumed that the natural level of interest being raised by rising consumption, any formerly existing market rate will be inflationary, or that a rise in consumption happens to be accompanied by uncompensated dishoarding, or (b) unless the value of the money unit is arbitrarily reckoned in terms of final goods and services alone.* The only sense in which there can be said to be "too little" or "too much" thrift implies a moral judgment, or the assumption that people do not know their own interests in exercising consumption-saving preference. In this sense alone can a deficiency or excess of thrift be alleged.

The most important conclusion of this section is, however, that *the notion of an insufficiency of openings for investment in relation to the flow of savings is absurd.* It is impossible to save (i.e., impossible to replace or add to one's assets) without exercising the entrepreneurial decision of choosing the form of assets—replacement or net accumulation—judged to be most *productive,* i.e., of greatest prospective usefulness to oneself or others (including, of course, money assets).

5.—A rather different form of the same fallacy is that "saving as such is merely not spending," so that a person may save "without demanding anything at all." When we hoard, it is said, we postpone consumption, but there is no "current demand for accumulation," as I have contended above. As one objector put it to me verbally, "in the case in which some *individuals* postpone consumption and accumulate money, *society* accumulates nothing more of anything." There are two cases to consider here.

Firstly, we have the case in which money is *deliberately* accumulated. This may be either (a) for motives of convenience, etc. (the normal business and private demands for monetary services), or (b) for speculative reasons (e.g., when the value of the *money unit* or the rate of interest is expected to rise). But why, in either of these circumstances, should we not regard the assets so held as having been "invested in?"

Secondly, we have the case in which money assets are accumulated solely through inertia, as when we "just allow bank balances to pile up."

---

*For a change in saving preference implies (a) changed demands for assets in terms of services and (b) increased demands for certain services to offset reduced demands for other services. (See pp. 222-3.)

Let us consider a parallel example. On occasion, I have signed a bankers' order for a certain periodical in which I have later ceased to be interested, eventually throwing the unopened copies into the wastepaper basket, but in the meantime forgetting to cancel my subscription. Can it then be said that I am not demanding the periodical? My "inertia" has meant a claim on the scarce resources, paper, etc., which have gone into the journal. Similarly, when I "allow cash to pile up," my action is still tending to bid up the aggregate real value of money, just as it does when my demand to hold cash is deliberate and purposive. *Hence my contribution to savings is a contribution to society's savings, unless those from whom I obtain the money happen to dissave.*

The possibility that the individual saver *may*, through sheer inertia (and in another—i.e., an entrepreneurial, capacity) retain an abnormal value of assets in the form of currency or in his current account, and for an inordinately long period, has received much stress in Keynesian literature.* Now if people *are* inclined at times to bid up the aggregate real value of money more than in proportion to the increase in real income,† and monetary policy is inflexible, that will not prevent growth, unless this "hoarding" of money somehow causes (a) the growth of real income to cease (through the withholding of capacity) and partly for this reason, (b) real savings to cease.

In each case, however, when saving happens to be accompanied by hoarding, the aggregate value of assets held for the monetary services they can perform rises; and the individual who, having saved, holds more money assets than previously, will have more assets of all kinds than previously. And as we have seen (pp. 214-5) if those who acquire from him nonmoney goods or services (in return for the money which he accumulates) refrain from decumulating the goods, or use the services in the production of assets, they will not have fewer real assets than before. *In that case, society must have accumulated.* In other words, unless the rest of society *waste or consume* what he (the hoarder) would otherwise have withdrawn from the flow of nonmoney products (for consumption or accumulation), realized net accumulation must have been achieved. *The future flow of all wanted things will be greater by reason of his savings having occurred.* If waste *does* occur, however

---

*It is seldom considered whether a person may not be equally passive in respect of his whole portfolio of assets. The truth is, I think, that in general people are *less* passive and uncritical about money holdings than they are about any of their other resources. They realize usually that it is wasteful to hold "idle money"—money without a purpose—whilst they perceive less often that some of their *nonmoney* assets offer prospective yields below interest on their current sale value.

†The aggregate value of money (in real terms) tends to vary in proportion to real income, in the same sort of way that the aggregate real value of land *tends* to change in this way. See pp. 93-4.

(and in the contemporary sort of world we all know that it can occur—because capacity may be withheld), it may be at the expense of net accumulation. But in that case saving preference, even when it is accompanied by hoarding, cannot be held responsible for the waste. Blame must fall on the withholding of capacity, whether owing to price rigidity or other causes.*

6.—We must beware of misinterpreting the fact that the entrepeneur's demand for services seems in practice to be *financed* by the saver's demand for assets. Certainly, in the most common case, the saver buys securities, thus passing the power to demand services to other entrepreneurs; but that is just how he may escape the making of *the more difficult* entrepreneurial decisions† and remain more or less a pure saver (i.e., a demander of assets). The aggregate entrepreneurial demand for services for embodiment into assets is not increased by the passing of that power. The very useful specialization in practice of saving preference on the one hand, and entrepreneurial judgment and action on the other, in no way upsets the argument. For instance, when a "pure saver" lends to the entrepreneur (short term, long term or permanently), he acquires *assets,* in the form of *securities,* from the entrepreneur; whilst to the entrepreneur is transferred the power to decide what services to purchase for replacement or net accumulation. This is one aspect of *the constant offer, through the medium of entrepreneurs, of assets for services;* and it occurs equally when the same person is the saver and the entrepreneur, and when the saver *lends* to the entrepreneur.‡

Entrepreneurial decisions can, therefore, have no direct effect upon the rate of net accumulation of products. Entrepreneurs can merely (i) change the composition of replacements to and additions to the stock of assets and (ii) offer interest. They can only *utilize* the flow of services by arranging those combinations of assets which they forecast will be most profitable. They cannot add to the excess of that flow above consumption (except in so far as they are, at the same time, savers). Subsequent exchanges of one kind of assets for another involve

---

*Tobin's interpretation of Keynesian teaching to the effect that expenditure on the flow of services from a given income may decline without hoarding is dealt with in Appendix B.

†He still makes an entrepreneurial decision in choosing a particular security to purchase, or a particular borrower. See 186-7, 201-2, above

‡If a person uses services for embodiment into assets, through the offer of his personal services or the services of his own property (i.e., out of his own income) he is at one and the same time a saver and an entrepreneur. He is a saver in that he demands assets. He is an entrepreneur in that he demands services for embodiment in *particular* assets.

no further net accumulation.* Hence the assumption that "saving" is done by one set of persons, and "gross investment" (replacement *plus* net accumulation) by another set of persons is absolutely wrong. It is "placement" or investment decisions—decisions which determine the ultimate *form* of gross accumulation—which may be said to be made *in some degree* by a specialized class of persons. Savings or dissavings (and hence the rate of net accumulation or decumulation) are always due to the decisions of those who refrain from consuming or who consume. In short, changes in the sum total of assets are determined solely by saving preference; and they can be studied only through the factors which determine that preference.

7.—If the above argument is valid, then entrepreneurial optimism and pessimism are irrelevant to the rate of net accumulation except through their influence on *prospective* output in general (the source of prospective demands in general and hence prospective yields), which may influence (i) (through the interest offer) the expression of saving preference, and (ii) the release or withholding of capacity and hence the magnitude of real income.† But rigorously considered, the withholding and release of capacity are not entrepreneurial but producers' acts. (See pp. 206-8).

In his discussion of the "aggregate demand function," Keynes assumed wrongly that entrepreneurial expectations‡ are (in my terminology) a source of demand *for* the flow of services *out of income,* i.e., *from* the flow of services itself. But such expectations give rise only to demand for services from the offer of assets. (See pp. 196-7).

Now the optimism or pessimism of producers (often in practice those who make entrepreneurial decisions also) may influence the withholding or release of capacity (and hence the magnitude of money income under monetary flexibility) so that these psychological attitudes *are* relevant to the development *tempo.* But the important consequence of optimism in this respect is not that it causes net accumulation directly, but that it causes the growth of real income; for normally it results equally in an increase in consumption. The reaction upon income must be kept distinct in our minds, therefore, from both (a) the rise

---

*But see above, p. 215.

†That is, to the extent to which the offer of interest induces a reduction of the relative rate of consumption, it *can* cause an increase in net accumulation.

The confidence which induces people (1) as producers, to release capacity and (2) as entrepreneurs, (a) to raise their interest offer, and (b) perhaps dishoard, is justified when it is based on the correctly discerned bringing of relative prices into a co-ordinated relationship.

‡The proceeds which the outputs from "various hypothetical quantities of employment" are expected to realize.

in the entrepreneurial demand for services, i.e., the increased bidding which raises the rate of interest, and (b) the effects upon the productivity of money, i.e., any inducement to dishoarding. In many treatments all three influences* seem to me to be confused.

I am not denying—indeed I wish to stress—the enormous importance of the decisions which determine investment, i.e., the choice of *the form* in which replacement and net accumulation occur. In proportion to the extent to which entrepreneurs correctly discern the most profitable and productive forms of gross accumulation they will not only influence their own contribution to real income but *stimulate* real income and hence increase the *ability to save*. At the same time, the boost to output is likely to raise prospects, and hence the interest inducement, and so (perhaps) the *willingness to save*.

Hence entrepreneurs, in predicting and devising the least-cost production functions, can affect the rate of growth only because they can influence the composition of replacement and net accumulation in response to thrift; because their interest offer may influence the expression of thrift; and because their successful activity causes real income to expand and so facilitates the achievement of savings.

8.—If at any time the aggregate real value of productive capacity is not increasing, that means that individual savers cannot, on the whole, be adding to the real value of their assets; i.e., *the representative consumer-saver* cannot be achieving savings. At best, he can merely be replacing. Now obviously, saving preference *may* sometimes be like that. Indeed, it is the only explanation of nonexpanding societies. But I find it difficult to conceive why, in the conditions which we can observe to be ruling in all countries of the contemporary world, it should ever be assumed to be *impossible* for all would-be savers to accumulate net. Only if it can be assumed that for some reason the reaction to saving preference must be a fall in real income, whilst consumption *cannot* fall to compensate, can it be said that *savings and net accumulation* are impossible of achievement. And if it is assumed that the representative consumer-saver *cannot* curtail current consumption, as his income falls, that is an assumption about the nature of preferences. Of course, as a producer, he may withhold capacity, but that is a separate issue.

We are unable to assume, however, that in practice there is always a flow of services available not only for replacement uses, and to maintain any existing rate of net accumulation, but for an *increased* rate of net accumulation. The *additional* services needed for that purpose can

---

*I.e., upon income, the offer of interest and the productivity of money.

become available (i) through the release of withheld capacity of the required type; or (ii) through the release of some of the services of *versatile* resources at present devoted to the replacement of inventories of consumers' goods (a release made possible through a decline in the rate of consumption) for use in the manufacture of *more productive* assets; or (iii) through the form of current replacement and net accumulation favoring further net accumulation. But such reactions will not necessarily follow (e.g., if there is full employment, if the resources making consumers' goods are, in the short run, absolutely specific* and if the form of current growth is not such as facilitates continued growth). In that case, what will be the effects of changes in consumption-saving preference?

There are two aspects of such changes: (a) a change in values and (b) a consequent *gradual* change in the composition of the future flow of services, in spite of short-run specificities. Theoretically, the former can occur without the latter. For instance, the desire to save more may simply cause the values of those services which replace inventories of consumers' goods to fall whilst causing the values of those services which replace or add to relatively fixed resources to rise. Moreover, when this occurs, the values of assets in general will increase in relation to the values of the services they provide. In other words (as we shall see), the rate of interest will fall. But if there is any versatility as between these broad uses of the resources employed—if it is possible to replace any kind of worn out specific assets by another kind—the discrepancies in the relative values will induce *action* (response to demand). It is solely because such action may occur that any desire to increase the rate of provision for the future can ever be realized *by society*. Unless the composition of current income is appropriate for growth, or unless resources can be and are released from replacing inventories of consumers' goods (of which net additions to current stocks *cannot be profitably carried through time*) in order to produce additions to the stocks of those assets of which additional stocks *can be profitably carried through time* (we may call the latter "economically durable" resources), it is possible for one set of persons to acquire savings only if others are simultaneously decumulating their assets (by exchanging long-life assets for short-life assets or final services).

It is important, therefore, to distinguish changes in "consumption preference"—changes in the relative value placed on current consumption—from changes in the *actual* consumption of final services *plus* the decumulation of consumers' goods inventories and other assets. In pure

---

*I say, "in the short run," because to the extent to which there is depreciation there must always be possibilities of making large changes in the form of the stock of productive capacity at the time of replacement.

theory, at least, the *value* of consumption may decline, owing to a rise in saving preference, without any change in its physical composition (the "amounts" of different things decumulated); and this is simply another way of saying that the value of net accumulation may increase without any change in the composition of gross accumulation as a whole. Such changes in relative values will be experienced when changes in demand (expressing saving-consumption preference) induce no response or an incomplete supply response.*

For simplicity, let us imagine that there is no withheld capacity and that the resources used for replacing consumers' goods inventories are sufficiently specific to prevent their being transferred to the production of "economically durable" assets, and that no net accumulation has been occurring. In these circumstances, what will limit the acquisition of savings *by individuals?* The answer is, exactly the same factors as limit the achievement of all other economic ends, the cost of so doing.

9.—In the sort of world of which we have had experience, the acquisition of savings has always been subject to the additional inducement that savings multiply themselves through positive interest. But in an imaginary society in which aggregate net accumulation is impossible (i.e., in which it is impossible for people in general to refrain—except by obvious waste—from consuming an aggregate value which falls short of the value of their product), and in which the desire by some to provide for the future (at the current cost of so doing) is not wholly offset by the desire on the part of others to enjoy the fruits of past provision for the future (through decumulation), the rate of interest must be negative. Instead of thrift being, so to speak, subsidized by positive interest, it will be penalized by negative interest.

Let us consider the implications of such a society, assuming that all products are *perishable.†* In this case *society* would no more attempt to achieve savings than a country in the twentieth century would attempt to improve its climate by changing the angle of inclination of the earth's axis! People *in general* would not want to provide more for the future because the cost of so doing would be prohibitive.

When products are durable, however, the position is not so simple. But if it is thought to be unprofitable to carry greater stocks than the current stocks of *durable* products through time, that must be solely because it is judged that people will not sufficiently want additional quantities of such goods in the future to render the production of

---

*This is another case in which no concept of a money unit of constant real value can provide a satisfactory measure of the magnitudes "consumption" and "savings."

†We can think of Keynes' banana community example, used in his *Treatise*. The rate of interest would equate the net decumulation by some with the net accumulation of others.

"time utilities" profitable. Such a prediction of future demand is society's judgment about a *preference,* namely time preference. "Time utilities" will be regarded as too expensive and entrepreneurs who try to provide them will incur losses. It seems probable, then, that if savings were incapable of adding to fixed resources but only to inventories of physically durable final products, there would be little or no net accumulation *by society.* The absence of a yield over and above the satisfaction of time preference might cause net accumulation (which would necessarily take the form of stock-piling of final products) to become impossibly costly. The value of the yield would be unlikely to cover storage costs.

If, however, it is *physically possible* to accumulate any kind of durable assets, and if any net addition to the existing stock will have *any* future value, *however rapidly the value of the assets accumulated may decline, or however high the costs of holding may be,* the acquisition of savings (net accumulation) is possible. In other words, even under negative interest, net accumulation can result. But if interest is negative, even replacement will *include* assets the values of which are falling. The productive services which will be rendered by such inventories will include those which, consumed as they are rendered, make up the *time preference product.* Entrepreneurs will carry replacement and net accumulation in different directions up to the point at which the marginal prospective yield equals the negative interest, but solely because those from whom they borrow will pay them to borrow, or because the prospective yield from the current value of the resources employed, if lent to others, will involve the same negative yield.

Consideration of these rather fantastic possibilities does not make necessary any modification of the principle that the achievement of savings by individuals, not countervailed through decumulation by others, will always and necessarily mean net accumulation by society.

To sum up, changes in consumption-saving preference may, theoretically, influence interest only and cause no change, or a nonproportional change, in the embodiment of services into assets or their decumulation. And when I talk of such changes, I envisage them as being expressed partly or solely in value changes (including interest), as distinct from changes in the form of output.

10.—It follows that thrift — saving preference — is the source of all growth of productive capacity which does occur (net accumulation), although it may not always be strong enough to bring forth growth. Such an argument seems to imply that, in a community in which realized net accumulation is in progress, it is savers who are *ultimately* demanding the services which are being embodied into the growing volume of assets; and that, if savers are merely trying to maintain their capital intact, in that case also they are ultimately demanding the services which flow into the replacement of resources. That is true enough; but the problem is rather complex and subtle, and a seriously wrong interpretation is easy. An increase in savings certainly gives rise to an increase in demand for certain services and a decrease in the demand for others. But savers also *bid down* the value of services in terms of assets. I.e., as I have already shown, they *offer* services (income) for accumulation and *demand* assets with them, thus causing the rate of interest to fall. The demand for those services is expressed via entrepreneurs, who accept *responsibility* to society (i.e., to future consumer-savers) for the prediction of their preferences, including their saving preference.*

Interest is *determined* when entrepreneurs offer assets for services and savers offer services for assets: but interest is not affected when assets are offered for assets or services for services. *Even the exchange of money for nonmoney assets leaves interest unchanged.*† The services offered by savers are those contributed as income (for only income can be devoted to replacement or net accumulation). The assets offered are existing resources, their value being influenced by (among other things) entrepreneurial estimates of the costs of replacing or adding to them. The value in terms of assets of the services drawn into gross accumulation will be determined through the ratio thus established.

Diagram II, p. 227, illustrates (a) the determinants of interest as I see them, and (b) the difference between *induced* and *autonomous* changes in saving preference. Interest is represented on the vertical axis, whilst on the horizontal axis is represented (to the right and left of the origin) the rate at which services are embodied into assets, i.e., gross accumulation, measured in real terms.‡ It is assumed for simplicity that the flow of "final services" is unaffected by any changes in the data which are to be considered; and as a small part of the flow of all services is consumed in that manner in practice, this is a practically useful assumption. It is assumed also that real income is constant (i.e., that no withheld capacity is being released and no realized net accumulation is in progress *initially.*** In other words, it is assumed that the rate of gross accumulation is constant.

---

*Entrepreneurs interpret saving preference in that they predict the extent to which savings are adding to unwithheld productive power; and the rate of interest they offer will vary with their prediction on this point.

†But obviously, if M *is changing* in relation to M_r, there will be a divergence of market interest from the natural level.

‡The fact that this measurement (in abstractly conceived money units of constant real value) is an index number conception and hence a particular measure of *the value,* and not of *some supposed physical quantity,* of the flow of services (and parts thereof) is very important at certain stages of the argument.

**It will be seen that, when the "saving preference schedule" moves from S_1 to the position, S_2, net accumulation will occur, and real income must then increase unless additional capacity is withheld.

This assumption causes the model to be dangerously unrealistic. For in practice savings increase normally and most easily, not through a sacrifice of the former rate of consumption (in money terms or in real terms) but through income increasing (owing to past savings or the release of capacity) with some part of the additional income being added to savings. Moreover, the representation of gross accumulation in this way makes abstraction of its *composition* and the potentialities of growth in different forms. Thus withheld capacity may exist in the industries

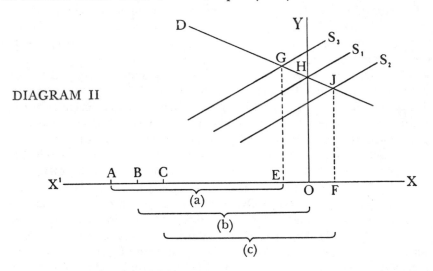

DIAGRAM II

which make those goods of which it is unprofitable to carry inventories greater than currently exist through time,* or in industries which contribute output that it is expected can be profitably added to the aggregate stock of assets. The form of any unutilized capacity will influence the form in which income is likely to increase and the manner in which it will be devoted to the different purposes indicated in Diagram I. Finally, movements in the demand schedule represent changes in circumstances which may (as we have seen) influence the withholding or release of capacity—i.e., the magnitude of real income. The model represented in Diagram II makes abstraction of these very important aspects of the topics we shall be discussing. But I use this very simplified model solely to *illustrate* my argument. *In itself it proves nothing.*

Curve D is a demand schedule representing the rates of interest which entrepreneurs (in competition with one another) estimate that it will be profitable to bid for the flow of services which enter into gross accumulation at different rates of consumption (i.e., different rates of savings or

---

*This does not mean that it will not be profitable to increase the *outputs* of these goods but only that additional *inventories* will not be a profitable form of net accumulation.

dissavings).* Alternatively, it may be said to represent the rates of interest which entrepreneurs find it profitable to offer for the hire of the capital with which they can acquire (by barter or purchase) the services made available for different kinds of uses. The height of the schedule is determined by prospective yields. From the angle of the community, the curve represents the prospective usefulness (as interpreted by entrepreneurs) of resources to replace or add to power to consume in the future.

I have explained that entrepreneurs take responsibility merely for *the form* in which the flow of services is embodied into assets and not for the rate at which this occurs. In accepting such a responsibility entrepreneurs are "demanding" the full flow of services; and the shape of the curve merely represents the extent to which their demand influences the value of the flow in terms of assets (i.e., the rate of interest). Entrepreneurs always demand the full flow of services (other than final services), for by definition all *services* have value, and if they have value someone must be choosing the assets into which they are being incorporated.

Curves S_1, S_2 and S_3 are three different positions of the supply schedule representing three different consumer-saver reactions to scales of interest rates. For brevity the supply schedule will be called the "saving preference schedule." EA, OB and OC + OF represent the same amount of gross accumulation under the three different positions of the saving preference schedule. Each curve shows how, at different rates of interest, consumption-saving preference will cause the form of gross accumulation to change in respect of the relative real values of replacement (decumulation) and net accumulation.† From the angle of the community, these curves may be interpreted as representing the cost of making provision for future consumption (i.e., replacement and net accumulation), namely, the sacrifice of current consumption.

It is possible now to re-state the above proposition about the shape of the demand schedule (determined by the marginal efficiency of capital). It shows the way in which changes in consumer-saver preference (i.e., movements of the saving preference schedule) will influence the interest it will pay entrepreneurs to offer, and hence the relative value of assets and services.

It follows that an increase in the rate of consumption (whether caused by a shift in the demand schedule *or* in the supply schedule) is represented by a shift to the left of the flow of services into gross accumulation, e.g., from OC + OF to OB (or to EA) (or from (c) to (b) [or to (a)]);

*The concept corresponds roughly to Ohlin's concept of *"ex ante* investment." But see pp.231-2, below.

†The concept corresponds roughly to Ohlin's concept of *"ex ante* saving." But see pp.231-2, below.

whilst a decrease in the rate of consumption is represented by a shift to the right.

The rate of *gross* decumulation is shown to the left of the origin and the rate of net accumulation to the right of the origin. *Net* decumulation is shown when the flow of services into gross accumulation is depicted at a distance to the left of the origin. Thus, when EA represents this flow, OE is net decumulation.

To state some of the implications assumed in the diagram in another way, we can say that, with the saving preference schedule in the position S_1, gross accumulation being OB (i.e., (b)), gross decumulation will be the same. The diagram assumes, that is, that (the demand schedule D, being given) when no savings or dissavings are occurring, the rate of interest will be OH.

In the position S_2, gross accumulation being OC + OF (i.e., (c)), gross decumulation will be OC and net accumulation OF. The diagram assumes, that is, that when realized savings equal to OF are occurring, the rate of interest will be FJ.

In the position S_3, gross accumulation being EA (i.e., (a)), gross decumulation will be OA and net decumulation OE. Thus, if the desire to postpone consumption is negative, not only will there be incomplete replacement, but stocks of assets will be depleted. The diagram assumes, that is, that when dissavings equal to OE are occurring, the rate of interest will be EG.

Starting with the saving preference schedule in the position S_1, a shift to the position S_2, will mean that *the composition* of gross accumulation will change, because it will be profitable, in view of the reduced interest, *to divert services* equal to the real value OF from *"consumption uses"* (i.e., from embodiment into resources of which stocks greater than present stocks cannot be profitably carried through time) to *"net accumulation uses"* (i.e., to embodiment into resources of which it is thought profitable to carry any addition through time). The extent to which this can actually happen will depend upon the versatility of resources as between consumption and accumulation uses.

It has so far been *assumed* that, as the prospective profitableness to entrepreneurs of embodying services into assets rises (a rise in schedule D),* causing the rate of interest to rise, a response occurs in the form of the release of services from providing for "consumption uses" in order to provide for "net accumulation uses." The release is effected through a decline in the rate of decumulation. It *can* take the form simply of a decline in the rate of decumulation of the stocks of those durable con-

---

*The rise in the demand schedule may be due to entrepreneurial forecasts of general prosperity (large future outputs) or to an increasing relative profitableness of capital-intensive methods of production.

sumption goods (in process of replenishment) of which (through the saving induced) it becomes profitable to carry larger inventories through time. In other words, the form of income may change either because the physical nature of output changes or because (for short periods) more of the same physical output is accumulated net in order to acquire time utilities (i.e., the output becomes subject to a different ultimate time use).

The diagram has assumed (for simplicity but unrealistically) a *perfect* response in the composition of output to changes in saving preference. But if we now make the opposite assumption, namely, that there is no response at all of this kind, we can still represent it on a similar sort of diagram, using it to show changes in the *relative* values of different parts of the flow of services. (See diagram in note on p. 231).

Let us assume that the resources devoted to "consumption uses" and those devoted to "net accumulation uses" are absolutely specific to their respective fields, although the former are produced by the latter. In such a situation it will be quite impossible for society to sacrifice current consumption in order to add more rapidly to the stock of assets. Changes in saving preference will then merely affect values—the rate of interest and the relative values of different kinds of services. When the saving preference schedule moves to the right, entrepreneurs will find it possible to borrow at lower interest, but they will be forced to offer more for a rigid flow of services specialized for net accumulation. At the same time, consumers will be able to bid down the value of an undiminished flow of replacement services. In such circumstances, the value of the services making up replacement must fall, whilst that of those making up net accumulation must rise.*

The savings preference schedules which I am using correspond in some respects with Ohlin's notion of *ex ante* saving, just as the demand schedules I use correspond roughly to his conception of *ex ante* investment. But the interest determined (vertical axis), and the values, including real values (of the flow of services and its components) determined (horizontal axis), are *current valuations*. Both types of schedule represent valuations based on forecasts. *The former* envisages (to reiterate a vital contention) the expected relative advantages of consumption in the immediate and distant future in the light of interest, which implies a set

---

*The reader is reminded that gross accumulation is measured on the diagram in abstractly conceived money units of constant "real value." It is a *value* aggregate, not a supposed *physical quantity* aggregate.

Let us begin with the assumption that there is some net accumulation being realized, of the value OC. (There is no *physically identifiable* part of gross accumulation which represents net accumulation; but that part of the flow of services which is devoted to "net accumulation uses" can be assumed to make up, or to be included in, the value "net accumulation," which is still represented to the right of the origin.) Saving preference then shifts from S_1 to S_2, gross accumulation from OA *plus* OC to OB *plus*

of valuations of assets in terms of the flow of services (capital in terms of income). *The latter* envisages the expected relative profitableness of embodying services into assets, which implies another set of valuations of services in terms of assets (income in terms of capital).

It is theoretically possible also that the offer of higher interest, represented by a rise in the demand schedule, may be responded to by an increase in the desire to consume in the immediate future. In that case, fewer resources will be available for expansion. There seems to be some inconsistency in such a situation, however; for the demand schedule will rise because prospective yields are high, and prospective yields will be high only because demands for final products are expected to be high in the future, whilst the situation which we are considering assumes that people are induced to sacrifice consumption (of assets *or their services*) in the future for consumption in the present. It does not seem to be worth while discussing further such highly unlikely preference reactions. But I claim that *all my arguments stand whatever preferences happen to be*. As I have insisted more than once, there is never any obstacle to the self-consistent use of scarce resources in the satisfaction of any set of non-contradictory preferences.* If the supply schedules in the diagram are highly inelastic, i.e., if people cannot be induced to increase their provision for the future by the offer of higher interest, that is all there is to it.

The argument the Keynesians have to answer is not that if the desire

---

OE. Interest falls. The assumption is that the *physical compositions* of OA and OB are identical, as are those of OC and OE. The changes are in relative values. The fact that physical adjustments are ruled out does not mean that value changes are prevented.

It might be thought that the assumed absolute specificity between "consumption uses" and "net accumulation uses" implies vertical supply curves. But induced as well as autonomous changes in saving preference are *theoretically* conceivable (however purposeless under present assumptions) and they would have similar effects upon the relative values of services replacing consumption and entering into net accumulation.

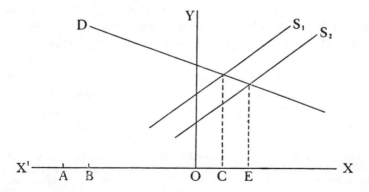

*I regard this as the great praxeological truth, which I often feel is missed by Keynesian economists.

to save increases, the rate of net accumulation of physical productive capacity must necessarily increase. In order to substantiate their contention they must show that the sacrifice of actual consumption *without waste* does not necessarily result in net accumulation. In other words, what they have to deny is that an autonomous increase in that part of the flow of services which is not matched by decumulation (i.e., savings) always means increased net accumulation. Under my definitions, however, this would be denying a truism—a tautology. But this does not imply that a reduced rate of interest due to a shift in the supply schedule *causes* an increased rate of net accumulation, *unless it can be assumed that at the lower interest entrepreneurs, interpreting prospective yields, do in fact compete more successfully against "consumption uses" of the flow of services.*

Such a situation is one which, it is commonly held, cannot exist in the real world. For instance, the Keynesian view is that realized net accumulation cannot be achieved through the reduction of current consumption. But I maintain that it is only through the sacrifice of *possible* present consumption that productive capacity can ever grow, and that there are no important exceptions to this truth.

11.—Let us now drop the assumption that there is no initial growth in utilized productive power and suppose that in fact real income is growing. The same analysis applies, but the extent to which realized net accumulation can occur—through the changes represented—will now depend not only upon the versatility of the services which can be diverted from consumption uses to net accumulation uses, but also upon the extent to which the increasing real income (from the release of withheld capacity or from realized net accumulation in progress) is in the form of services appropriate for net accumulation or consumption purposes. *Saving-consumption preference, however, plays its rôle in exactly the same kind of way.* The greater consumption preference, the smaller will be the rate of realized net accumulation and *vice versa.*

12.—That saving means bidding for assets is least obvious, and may at first seem to be untrue, of assets in the form of inventories of consumers' goods; but it is equally true of such goods *as capital,* i.e., as inventories in process of sale or consumption and replacement.*

---

*Such inventories are normally "unproductive" except for short periods of time, during which they contribute, as inventories, to the sum total of marketing services. The periods are short mainly by reason of perishability, storage costs, or interest costs. The services which have been embodied into assets in this form must be early disembodied into consumption or they will be wasted, i.e., consumed for no-one's benefit.

This may lead to the objection that demand of that nature is "consumption demand."* The consumer, it may be said, expresses his demand by purchasing commodities (i.e., assets) in the market. But the consumer *qua* consumer (i.e., the consumer as I have defined him) does not *demand* assets in the form of consumers' goods. This may well sound like an outrageous and paradoxical verbal quibble. In reality, the distinction (which I stressed in the previous chapter, sections 4 to 7) is vital for clear thinking. The demand for consumers' goods, *from those whom we usually call "consumers"* is a demand for capital of the kind mentioned in the last paragraph. *So-called "consumers"* certainly do hold stocks (in pantries, wardrobes, etc.) for consumption convenience; and they are constantly replacing these stocks as consumption decumulates them. But to the extent to which they do this they are, strictly speaking, (a) performing the entrepreneurial function—choosing assets— (b) performing the productive function of trading on their own account, and (c) *saving*—using their own income for the purpose. When it is perishable goods which are demanded, then saving demand is solely for the necessarily small and rapidly turning over stock which is being maintained by replacement. The fact that this demand is *necessarily accompanied by consumption*, must not cause us to confuse the two. (See previous chapter, section 1).

Consumers as I have defined them, either consume final services or decumulate stocks of assets, just as producers embody services into them. Thus, consumption proper is the opposite of saving demand, the opposite of the demand for assets. It is the opposite even of that part of saving demand which only covers replacement. "Consumption demand" (if we use that term at all) must be regarded as consisting of (i) demand for final services *plus* (ii) demand for services which make up the value of replacement. But (ii) has its origin in a saving decision, whilst the form taken by replacement is an entrepreneurial decision.

Because on the whole people try at least to maintain their capital intact (annuitants and the old generally are the important exceptions), decumulation is usually accompanied by gross accumulation at least to the extent of the replacement of assets in general. But this must not lead us to the quite wrong conclusion that consumption itself *is* demand for (or even *the origin* of demand for) goods which replace what is being decumulated. The exact manner in which the *value* of consumption at any time affects the *composition* of the future flow of services, I shall discuss shortly, but consumption is the *extermination* of power to demand. The failure of the Keynesians to understand this simple truth lies at the root of what I believe to be the most outrageous intellectual error

*See previous chapter, sec. 7.

of this age.* The creation of power to demand, whether for replacement or net accumulation, is production. Certainly production also creates the power ultimately to consume—to decumulate. But with consumption the power to demand (the offer of one thing for something else) is wiped out.

Replacement demand is simply that part of saving demand which is insufficient to bring about net accumulation. It is wrong to think of it as *a response* to consumption. Replacement is a response to saving preference even if this response takes the form of maintaining constant stocks of consumers' goods. *All* demand for assets (including consumers' goods) which is expressed out of income (i.e., out of the flow of services) is a contribution to the process of current saving.

When consumers' goods are accumulated by those who propose to consume them, this act of saving *enables a forecast* (of almost perfect reliability) of their early consumption. Thus, when we re-stock our wardrobes and pantries, we are acquiring things which we predict *we* are going to want to consume in the near or distant future. Although in doing so we are not consuming, *we indicate our preferences as consumers.* Our acts (which are influenced mainly by the fact that the sort of things which we have been consuming we are likely to want to consume again) form the data on which other entrepreneurs—merchants or traders—base their predictions. Similarly, the net decumulation, replacement or net accumulation of traders' inventories create the data to which the producers of physical products react. In that way consumers' sovereignty is exercised, and this ultimately controls the form of replacement *plus* net accumulation and, indeed, the composition of income as a whole. But whilst the current rate of depletion of different kinds of assets is *evidence* on which the entrepreneur can attempt to forecast *the composition* of preferences in the future, and so the *relative* profitabilities of different kinds of accumulation, *it is irrelevant to the amount or rate of net accumulation.*† Indeed, it is not only misleading to think of replacement as *a response to* steady consumption, but equally misleading to think of net accumulation as *a response to* growing consumption. *It is saving preference (induced or autonomous) to which both are a response.*

---

*It is only just to remind the reader that not all of the classical economists had J. B. Say's clear perception that consumption represents extermination of demand. Thus, even Ricardo and J. S. Mill wrote at times as though they were assuming that consumption, and not production, is the source of demands in general. But they were merely led to the fallacious theory that the accumulation of productive power must cause prospective yields and the rate of interest to fall and not to the fear of ultimate ruin by a general surfeit.

†Certain services are enjoyed, certain inventories are decumulated, and certain equipment is used up or otherwise depreciated. From this, entrepreneurs can predict that, *on the whole,* the same sorts of things are going to be consumed in the future, so that there will normally be a demand for the replacement of inventories and the making good of depreciation *in the same form.* Profitable investment in inventories of

Yet the notion has become deeply ingrained in modern teaching that "investment opportunities" are created by consumption. Students in most universities are today taught that an increase in demand for consumers' goods and services will lead in turn to an increase (an accelerated increase) in demand for the producers' goods which make them. If we ignore the acceleration notion (which I propose to criticize in a later chapter), this is undoubtedly true of the predicted demand for any *individual* consumers' good. But this has led some economists to jump to the false conclusion that consumption in general is the source of demand in general, whilst thinking of "demand" as an aggregate magnitude. (See pp. 205-6).

13.—Although saving preference is not a demand for *particular* assets, entrepreneurs must choose between two fields of investment: (a) into inventories of "consumers' goods," which are destined to be relatively rapidly decumulated and (b) into stocks of all other assets, i.e., "producers' goods," which are normally decumulated slowly (through depreciation).* Thus, whilst as entrepreneurs people neither accumulate nor decumulate (being savers or consumers when they do that), in assuming responsibility for *the form* of accumulation or decumulation they interpret *inter alia* the relative weights of the two competing sets of demands which make up consumption-saving preferences.†

It should now be clear that *the extent* to which replacement and/or net accumulation as a whole occur is always determined through the basic choice between current and postponed consumption; and that only if services are released from withholding, or diverted from "consumption uses," or supplied through the form of current replacement and growth, *and directed through consumer-saver preference,* can society *increase* any rate at which the total stock of assets is accumulating. In other words, *there is but one way in which realized net accumulation can increase, namely, through thrift being strong enough to bring it about.*

For the rate of growth to increase without the concurrent release of

---

particular "consumers' goods" (i.e., the rate at which it will pay to embody services in them) depends upon the current rate at which they are being decumulated *and* their price.

Each such entrepreneurial decision influences, of course, other entrepreneurial decisions at different stages of the consumption, marketing and physical production process.

*This is another way of stating what has already been shown, namely, that the greater the magnitude of savings the greater will be the proportion of the flow of services embodied into assets of which it is profitable to carry greater stocks through time, and the smaller the proportion embodied into products of which greater stocks cannot profitably be carried through time.

†In the same sense they are responsible for the proportions in which realized accumulation consists of producers' goods of a lower order and those of a higher order.

capacity, versatility is essential. Savers must place a sufficiently low value on the sort of services which are currently devoted to "consumption uses," in order to divert an increased flow of services to "net accumulation uses." In the absence of such versatility, and of a sufficient decline in such *relative* values, entrepreneurs are powerless to accumulate more rapidly. And as I demonstrated above (p. 217), the case of savings achieved out of income which is in process of inflation constitutes no exception. Net accumulation still requires the exercise of preference against consumption.*

Indeed, there are no real exceptions† to the rule that increased preference for *current consumption in general* tends, in itself, to reduce the rate at which those assets which maintain or increase the flow of output (and ultimately the flow of *consumption goods*) are replaced or accumulated net.

This does not mean that consumption and net accumulation cannot grow together. But this can only happen if real income increases concurrently (from the release of idle capacity, or from a response to past saving decisions, or from current savings facilitated by autonomous growth), i.e., *pari passu* with the rise in consumption. Such is, of course, the usual case; i.e., economic growth normally takes this form. Productive power expands although consumption does not decline or even continues to increase; for the growth of real income can permit realized net accumulation without any fall in the *absolute rate* of realized consumption.

14.—I anticipate the objection that I have given insufficient weight to the possibility of supposed savings increasing through the depreciation of the money unit, which will provide entrepreneurs with more funds (savings) with which to bid for rigidly priced services in the capital goods field. The consequent increase in the money valuation of income, may lead to the release of rigidly priced services in the consumption goods field, with a rise in the marginal efficiency of capital, and multiplied repercussions. Such an explanation is clearly not incompatible with the present analysis.

Alternatively, it may be objected that the mere occurrence of an increase in saving preference may cause real income to decline because, owing to price rigidity, resources will be withheld in the consumers' goods industries. But the thesis which I have stated does not deny (as I

---

*Keynes *appears* to have recognized this point; for his argument that "the savings which result from this decision" (the decision to "invest") "are just as genuine as other savings,"(4) is really suggesting that, if any entrepreneur uses inflationary credit to provide new assets, *society* will have achieved net accumulation through a thrift decision having accompanied the entrepreneurial decision.

†The imaginary case in which all output is perishable (see pp. 224-5) is not a "real exception."

insisted above, Chap. IV) that price rigidity, confronted with a change in saving preference (or any other change in preference) may throw the economic system out of co-ordination. As I must stress almost *ad nauseam*, when the price mechanism is prevented from carrying out its co-ordinative functions, wasteful idleness and a decline in real income must certainly follow, no matter what the original change in economic ends may have been. In such circumstances, it is almost fatuous to say that an increase in savings is responsible for unemployment. If the demand for the services of a specific piece of equipment falls off, so that it is essential for its hire value to fall from £10 to £9 in order that it shall continue to be used, whilst the charge for hire is maintained at £10, we can hardly usefully say that the decline in demand is the cause of the idleness. *For full employment is compatible with the decline in demand whilst it is inconsistent with the maintenance of the charge for hire.*

15.—Is there, then, any possible justification for the view that "consumption demand" in general can be the inducement to accumulation in general. *We can use such a phrase of predicted (not current) "consumption demand" as the inducement to a favorable entrepreneurial offer of interest (which may evoke a response in savings) if we make it clear that it is growth of output in one industry which is providing the source of future "consumption demand" for the product of the increasing capacity of noncompeting industries.* We carry assets through time either because we wish to consume them or use their services ourselves, or because we count on others demanding them in the future for these purposes. What may be called "the demand for savings"—the demand schedule of Diagram II—is derived from prospective yields, which are calculated from (i) the *anticipated flow of products* in the future, and (ii) the belief that these products will be offered for exchange, so that each will give rise to demand for noncompeting things. This view of "demand in general" depends upon a recognition of the essential complementarity of capital resources as a whole. *If a rise in this predicted "consumption demand" induces a rise in saving preference (through a response to a rise in the rate of interest), whilst the required versatilities exist,* it will cause an increase in net accumulation, but not otherwise.* Realized "consumption demand" (which may be the confirmation of the predicted demand which led to the rise in the marginal efficiency of capital) is derived from the complementarity of the accumulation and not from *current* consumption. And (unless the release of capacity can be forecast) the "future consumption demand" predicted is, *as we have seen,* the product of past thrift—decisions against consumption.

---

*The shape of the supply schedule in Diagram II reflects preferences in the light of versatilities.

Hence, when the entrepreneur is trying to predict, not the relative preference of society for the different kinds of goods of which he is contemplating production but, given his predictions on this point, *the general ability* of the community to purchase these goods, he is trying to forecast utilized productive power in the future. He will normally conceive of the degree of prospective utilization of productive power as "the degree of prosperity," or "the amount of purchasing power" to be anticipated, without realizing very clearly the reality that the source of power to demand in general is production.

This brings us to a widely held fallacy which is relevant to the inducement to accumulation. It is assumed that increasing savings *must* force down the long-term rate of interest in the absence of autonomous progress.* The fallacy does not stress the lack of versatility in productive capacity, which we have discussed above (see pp. 223-4), but the decline in prospective yields which is supposed to accompany the growth of productive power.

Now an increased flow of savings need not cause a decline in interest if (a) there is autonomous growth in progress, or (b) withheld capacity is being released, or (c) net accumulation of one kind is creating additional demand for net accumulation of another kind. (a) is universally admitted; (b) is seldom understood; whilst (c) is usually denied, implicitly or explicitly. In so far as the *complementarity* referred to under (c) exists, increased savings are partly or wholly offset by a rise in the demand schedule for savings! In other words, the long-term demand for and supply of savings are not independent, and static analysis can assist very little in explaining the long-term rate of interest.†

This is not to deny of course that, for reasons noticed above, there will be, in the short-run, and beyond a certain point, diminishing predicted and realized returns to an increasing rate of net accumulation. It is legitimate to assume that the schedule of the marginal efficiency of capital will not rise sufficiently, following an increased rate of savings, to prevent some temporary fall in the rate of interest. In explaining the short-run it is permissible to make abstraction of the repercussions of complementarity. But to imagine that growing savings could cause the value of services in relation to the value of assets to fall towards zero, is to imagine an approach towards a Utopian state of satiety, in which productive services (those which are consumed directly, or those which flow into

---

*The works of some of the most careful economists are *misleading* on this point when they use static analysis but fail to point out to the student the possible dynamic repercussions of complementarity.

†As the accumulation of capital resources proceeds it may be possible to use more economic (e.g., more roundabout) methods, so that the demand for savings is actually *enhanced* by savings. But that brings in factors which may be regarded as autonomous. The present argument rests only on the contention that each act of accumulation creates a demand for noncompeting accumulation.

replacement) are tending to become as plentiful and cheap as the atmos-phere. The truth is, of course, that provision for the future has no such tendency. The law of the insatiability of human wants remains without substantial challenge. Indeed, the building up of physical productive power has no greater tendency to force interest towards zero than has the growth of population a tendency to reduce the value of labor to zero.*

16.—I can now state categorically the thesis that consumption does not call forth replacement or net accumulation, and that the growth in the preference, tendency or propensity to consume releases no inducement to real expansion. Indeed, if real income would remain constant in the absence of net accumulation, the reverse is true. Only a decline in the preference for current consumption can then make net accumulation possible. And if real income is increasing in the only way possible, namely, through the release of withheld capacity or continuous realized net accumulation (as influenced by autonomous growth), an increased preference for current consumption will slow down, bring to an end, or reverse the rate of realized accumulation and any rate of growth of real income.

To sum up, an increase in realized net accumulation by society *normally* arises not through a decline in decumulation leaving a net accumula-tion of unconsumed stocks, but (a) through the diversion of the services of some versatile resources from producing "consumers' goods" to pro-ducing "producers' goods," or (b) through additional services, due to an increasing real income, being directed to producers' goods rather than consumers' goods, a process which is influenced by the form in which the flow of services (real income) increases. Such "additional services" can arise from two sources: (i) net realized accumulation in progress (the growth of productive power itself); or (ii) the release from wasteful idleness of services provided by existing resources. A special case of (i) is that in which the "additional services" arise from the growing produc-tive power due to "autonomous developments," i.e., innovations, inven-tions and discoveries.

We reach the following conclusions: (1) Net accumulation, when tech-nically possible (within limits set by the versatility of resources), is caused by saving preference alone; although savings may be *induced or facilitated* by the current form of income, by the release of capacity, by autonomous growth, or by increased interest. (2) The mere wish, or will, or propensity to consume at the current rate, or at a greater rate, must not be viewed as the source of demand for the future services of capital resources and so for their replacement or net accumulation respectively.

---

*See Chap. XVI on "Capital Saturation."

(3) Replacement and net accumulation must be seen as the *source* of maintained and increased consumption demand respectively, and not *vice versa*. (4) The predicted preferences of consumer-savers determine the *form of utilization of productive resources* in the short run, and the *form of these resources themselves* in the long run. (5) Nothing can be more misleading than the contemporary tendency to talk about "the absorption of savings into investment," or similar phrases.

This last conclusion demands special emphasis. There is *always* a "demand for savings." There are *always* "investment outlets" or "investment opportunities." *Such opportunities can be "created," as well as filled, by thrift alone* in the presence of versatility of resources, the release of withheld capacity, or the current growth of productive power due to past thrift.

These conclusions do not imply that discoveries, inventions, innovations and managerial ingenuities which economize resources do not cause prospective yields to rise, or that the resulting high interest (or sometimes prospective yields directly)* may not *call forth* a larger flow of savings (or replacements) and in that sense lead to real expansion. Nor is there any implication that autonomous progress or the release of withheld capacity may not *facilitate* thrift (and hence real expansion) through permitting savings to occur without any sacrifice of the former rate of consumption or even of its former rate of growth. But we cannot escape the basic truth that only decisions against current consumption can permit the emergence of "investment opportunities."

It is in the light of these considerations that all variants of the underconsumption theory of depression or stagnation, as well as all notions which involve the consumption concept (such as the "propensity to consume," the "acceleration theory" and the "multiplier theory") must be considered.

I anticipate the objection that my analysis has overlooked most important issues, particularly those connected with the effects of saving upon the velocity of circulation or the aggregate rate of spending. But these issues have been treated in Chapter V; and the argument presented here cannot, I think, be upset merely by bringing such monetary factors into the reckoning.

---

*While Diagram II with which I have illustrated the above analysis represents the assumed aggregate influence of prospective yields in general upon the incentive of people (as entrepreneurs) *to borrow* for investment (including borrowing from themselves, as savers), it cannot represent the aggregate influence of prospective yields in particular undertakings upon the incentive *to save* (in order to invest in such undertakings) on the part of those who perceive (as entrepreneurs) such yields. But, of course, prospective profits as well as current interest must be assumed to have some influence on the expression of saving preference.

17.—A different objection which may be expected is to the effect that whilst savers may be prepared to offer a flow of loans (e.g., in the form of the purchase of fixed interest securities), entrepreneurs may not think it profitable to use the funds under such conditions, however low the savers bid down the rate of interest. At the same time (to translate the argument into my own terminology) *the managers* would be prepared to advise the flotation of plenty of new ventures, and could do so, if the savers would only supply "risk capital," i.e., if the savers would also be prepared to act as additional entrepreneurs and become residual claimants by investing in equities. The argument amounts to the contention that people as entrepreneurs are insufficiently enterprising,* or that prospects are not favorable enough to evoke the required enterprise.

Now if the value of *assets* in the form of securities is being bid up and entrepreneurial demand for the *services* of nonmoney resources does not increase, the implication is that entrepreneurs are hoarding. But why should they hoard unless they believe that investment in money offers a higher yield than investment in other assets? Such a situation can emerge only if they expect more favorable opportunities to present themselves later than are available at the moment (e.g., a more favorable price-cost ratio or other forecast value relationships). It is quite wrong to assume that unfavorable prospects can deter net accumulation, otherwise than through the discouragement of saving preference, or—indirectly—through the encouragement of the withholding of capacity (although such prospects certainly do influence *the form* taken by accumulation.) We must regard entrepreneurs (as distinct from savers) as interested in *relative* not *absolute* prospective yields.† We can equally appropriately say that their function is to choose the "least unfavorable" as the "most favorable" openings for investment.

I am not suggesting that risk-preference is irrelevant, that the widespread existence of an enterprising temperament may not cause a more productive *form* of accumulation and hence *ultimately* a more rapid rate of net accumulation.‡ In the short run, however, the effect will be merely

---

*Ironically enough, the Keynesian system, in its ultimate effects, works to dampen and discourage enterprise, especially through the inevitable repression of latent inflation. And Keynes himself disparaged the entrepreneurial function as it is performed in practice, implying that supposed enterprise depends upon "animal spirits" more than upon careful prediction and calculation. He was, I think, envisaging then rather the stock-exchange speculator, whom he understood, and not the typical business administrator planning his budgets, whom he certainly did not understand.

†I am here ignoring the argument, which I regard as unimportant, that the cost of investing may exceed interest. (See p. 172).

‡Enterprise, and conditions conducive to the exercise of wise risk-taking are, indirectly, important factors favoring economic expansion—through the reactions of interest upon savings, and the tendency of wise risk-taking to bring about the most productive forms of replacement and net accumulation.

to deepen rather than to broaden the capital structure. And I have already explained why, in the circumstances in which withheld capacity exists, optimism may have considerable expansive effects through inducing the release of that capacity by "producers."*

18.—The failure to recognize thrift as the sole source of expansion has been due, I believe, to two main sources of confusion. (i) The implications of the facilitation of savings by released capacity or current growth have not been understood. (ii) There has been an ages-old misinterpretation of that general disco-ordination which so often breaks the contact between demand and supply (and causes therefore entrepreneurs to wait for readjustments before embarking on the more productive, capital intensive and hazardous undertakings). For in the presence of price rigidities which are regarded as unstable, a tendency for the value of the money unit to rise leads to what is regarded as a decline in the *willingness to spend* (on services of all kinds) accompanied possibly by increased thrift.† Income which was formerly spent on goods for early consumption will then be devoted to savings, whilst entrepreneurs will resort concurrently to hoarding. This condition can easily *appear* as a low "propensity to consume" and a concomitant "absence of investment opportunities." For if there is idle capacity in the consumers' goods industries, it hardly seems rational to add to capacity.‡ The whole deplorable condition then appears superficially to be due to one simple and obvious cause. People are not consuming enough. If they can only be set consuming again, it is thought, there will again be prospects for investment, and expenditure on investment will in turn create purchasing power for still further consumption. But the trouble does not lie in any insufficiency in the desire or propensity to consume, nor in any insufficiency in the incentive to invest. It is to be found in the failure to adjust prices when the underlying values change. And if the changes in these underlying values are due to a deflationary policy, adopted in the interests of distributive justice, or as a matter of honor, then it is obviously a grossly inefficient way of achieving justice and honor to do nothing effective to permit or enforce directly the price co-ordinations which such a policy demands. It is easy to reach the defeatist conclusion that political

---

*See pp. 221-2.

†Until successive breaches in the rigidities have brought the scale of prices down to the height to which it is generally expected to fall, or until the belief in the instability of the rigidities has passed, either of which circumstances will cause the market rate of interest to assume the natural level.

‡If price rigidity did not exist in the producers' goods industries also, it would pay to add to productive capacity with a view to breaking down the price rigidities in the consumers' goods field, and selling at prices (in relation to anticipated prices) at which consumers would be willing to buy.

factors appear to render co-ordination through the price mechanism out of the question in the modern world.* But if that conclusion is reached, the student ought not to be left with the impression that unemployment, depression or stagnation are due, *in any sense,* to too much thrift or insufficient consumption or insufficient investment.

It is true in a sense that the great depression of the 'thirties, in the United States and Western Europe, was due to the failure of society to permit mass consumption. But potential consumption was not frustrated through too little income being left in the hands of those with a high propensity to consume; nor was it due to an excess of thrift of any type; nor was it the consequence of a monetary policy which somehow created *a barrier* to the required consumption. It was wholly attributable to the pricing of output generally, and not specially of consumers' goods and services, beyond the reach of uninflated income and out of consistency with price expectations.

The approach of this and the previous chapter illustrates, incidentally, the folly of the Keynesian notion that there is some "amount" or "level" of *real income* or *employment* corresponding to each level of the rate of interest, or to each "amount" or "level" of net accumulation ("investment"), and so the folly of the remedy implied (and advocated) for unemployment, namely, that the State should determine, by monetary or fiscal policy, a rate of interest which is regarded as consistent with full employment, or alternatively undertake such expenditure (on "investment" or otherwise) as is necessary to achieve full employment.

19.—APPENDIX A

The Relevance of Expenditure by the State and Foreigners

A possible source of confusion needs to be mentioned. It has become usual since Keynes for aggregate income to be regarded as divided into money *expenditures* by consumers, investors, the State and foreigners. But State expenditures, just like private expenditures, are directed either to final services and consumers' goods or to producers' goods. The fact that consumption-saving preference may be expressed collectively as well as individually in no way affects the analysis of this chapter. In the economic field, the State is inevitably a consumer-saver.

Moreover, as far as expenditures by foreigners and payments to foreigners are concerned, *the gain from the trade* must be regarded as a contribution to the flow of services, the product of which is subject either

---

*It would then seem to be the duty of statesmen to point this out, and face the consequences, during the inflations which deliberate deflations are intended, tardily, to rectify.

to consumption or to net accumulation. Hence in the study of any community, its external trade is—in the context of the present argument—best regarded as one form of profitable production.

The export or import of capital can be similarly considered. Capital is exported when the prospective yield from that use (the expected future flow of services from it) is greater than that predicted from any available internal use; and capital is imported when the prospective yield from its employment exceeds the payment for its employment.

It might be thought that so simple an approach hides a fallacy because the balance of expenditures and receipts in foreign trade must influence the real value of money assets, M_r, and hence, if M is constant, the value of the money unit. But in so far as international transactions in goods and money do influence M_r or MV, they have the same effect as all other influences. There appear to be, therefore, no valid reasons for supposing that international economic relations in any way upset our conclusions that net accumulation is a response to thrift and that investment outlets are created by thrift.

20.—APPENDIX B

The Notion of "Failure to Spend" without "Hoarding."

An attempted rationalization of Keynesian teaching which I do not understand is one which is well illustrated in an article by Tobin who holds that "an individual may fail to spend all his income on goods and services currently produced without hoarding—adding to his cash balance—any of the remainder. He may, instead, purchase obligations of indebtedness, real estate, or other existing assets." [5] Let us assume that Tobin is not here thinking of bidding for "hybrid assets"; for that *is,* of course, a particular form of hoarding (see p. 90). When we exercise saving preference we use our income *(a flow* of services) to bid up the value of assets *(a stock),* and (for reasons which we have noticed) this effect may not be wholly offset by concurrent adding to the stock of assets (through the incorporation of services in assets). In consequence, we may bid down the rate of interest, by bidding up of the value of a given *stock of assets* in terms of services. Now this demand for the stock remains the source of a demand for additions to it, and so indirectly a demand for that part of *the flow of services* which can add to the stock. The greater this response in any case, the smaller will be the tendency for the rate of interest to fall. All demand for replacements and additions to the stock of assets (through "goods and services currently produced," as Tobin puts it) proceeds *via* demand for assets as a whole. But changes in this demand affect the *relative money values* of different parts of the flow of services, and not their *aggregate money value* unless hoarding or some other monetary phenomenon is affecting the value of the money unit. And *the whole flow of "goods and services currently produced" will always be demanded at prices consistent with co-ordination.**

If savings are defined as "money income *minus* expenditure on consumption goods," and *"savings"* are supposed to differ from *"investment"* (defined as "expenditure on additional capital goods"), then the only conceivable discrepancy *must* be due to hoarding or dishoarding. In other words, if "savings" in that sense exceed "investment," M_r is being bid up and, M being constant, the *money* value of nonmoney services will be bid down. But that *is* hoarding (an increased demand for money which is not due to an increase in T).

---

*In the case noticed above, in which net accumulation is physically impossible (pp. 222-4), this remains true; for the whole flow of services will be consumed directly or embodied into assets which—because increased stocks cannot be profitably carried through time—are being consumed at an equivalent rate.

REFERENCES

(1) Report of the Radcliffe Committee (Committee on the Working of the Monetary System) par. 42. (2) KEYNES, *Alternative Theories of the Rate of Interest*, E. J., 1937, p.247. (3) Radcliffe Report, *op. cit.*, par. 31. (4) KEYNES, *The General Theory*, p.83. (5) TOBIN, Q. J. E., 1948, *Comment* on Rueff's *The Fallacies of Lord Keynes' General Theory*, p.764.

Chapter XII

THE MARGINAL PROPENSITY
TO CONSUME

SUMMARY

1.—The concept of the "marginal propensity to consume" is the basis of the "multiplier" theory which we are to examine. 2.—Pre-Keynesian teaching recognized the possible dynamic consequences of hoarding and dishoarding, and of credit contraction and expansion. 3.—But the "multiplier" theory alleges that a low propensity to consume, as distinct from a rise in liquidity-preference, causes a slowing down in activity which only further expenditure on investment can rectify, 4.—whilst the propensity tends to be unduly low owing to the "psychological law" that consumption increases less rapidly than income, leaving a "gap" to be filled, 5.—a gap which the Keynesians do not allow to be filled by the assumption of hoarding. 6.—Keynes failed to perceive that the accumulation of productive power is the creation of power to demand; 7.—and he thought also that a rise in interest reduces income and hence saving; but in the absence of deflation, interest can rise relatively to the marginal efficiency of capital only through an increase in the propensity to consume. 8.—The roots of his confusion appear to lie in consumption, instead of production, being regarded as the source of demand, and in the notion of the general satiability of preferences. 9.—Keynes thought fallaciously that a response now to demand for future consumption means an increase in aggregate demand. 10.—The rationalization of the argument along the lines that attempts to save do not mean realized savings assumes that the withholding of capacity is induced. 11.—Thrift is an expansionist, not a contractionist influence.

1.—The concept of the marginal propensity to consume describes the division between "consumption" and "investment" which it is assumed will take place in the expenditure of an additional increment of income. This concept plays a vital rôle in Keynes' theory of the multiplier, a theory which attempts to explain how this division causes a deficiency in aggregate demand, which may be rectified by an addition to aggregate expenditure upon "investment," the effects of which (upon aggregate demand) are supposed to be automatically multiplied.

2.—Before examining this thesis it will be useful to notice, by way of contrast, certain aspects of what orthodox economics in the pre-Keynesian era was teaching about the dynamic relations of monetary policy and employment. The following impressions of that teaching are expressed in a manner which may well have been influenced by Keynes' terminology and post-Keynesian discussions, and they are phrased to some extent in my own terminology which I have already been employing. They state what I believe would have been almost universally accepted before *The General Theory* appeared.

It has always been recognized, I think, that any event which leads to an increase in MV relative to T can induce a further increase in V through the effect upon expectations. Whether the increase in MV arises first through an initial increase in expenditure on consumption goods or investment goods, or *via* private or governmental spending on these things, or through dishoarding or lending (credit expansion) the effect is the same. It has been recognized also that under a monetary system with any degree of flexibility (e.g., as normally under the gold standard) one expansion of real income, financed by noninflationary credit expansion—i.e., an appropriate increase in M—would evoke a further increase in M if T tended to rise in relation to MV. In other words, it has been understood all along that a greater *money income* than that due to any original increase in MV may emerge, owing to the reactions upon V, and that the emerging money income may cause the release of any capacity which may have been previously withheld, and so induce a further noninflationary increase in M.

3.—The theory of the multiplier, based on the concept of the marginal propensity to consume, is an attempt to show that there is something seriously wrong about this view. It alleges that a crucial source of instability is lurking in the fact that saving *per se* (not saving accompanied by hoarding) causes "a gap" in aggregate demand, which only additional expenditure on "investment" can fill. It is held further that the withheld capacity (or other idle capacity) caused by "the gap" in aggregate demand can be coaxed back into use only through additional initial expenditure on "investment." Orthodox theory holds, on the contrary, that additional "demand," induced by inflationary credit, can rectify price-caused unemployment (provided that prices are not raised further in anticipation of this reaction).

Whilst orthodox theory recognizes the possibility of repercussions from the initial demands so caused upon expectations, and hence upon V, or through the reactions upon M (if capacity is released), the multiplier theory confines attention to the repercussions upon those incomes which are affected, in turn, by the money spent initially passing from hand to hand. And whilst orthodox economics lays stress on (i) the flow of products as the source of aggregate demand (in the sense of real income), a demand which increases with every release of withheld capacity or with every growth of capacity (not neutralized by withholding or net decumulation elsewhere); and (ii) the determinants of the value of the money unit (which determine the money valuation of income), the multiplier theory lays stress on the *expenditure* which is set going, an expenditure which is supposed to precede the release or growth of capacity and so to rectify the community's disinclination to *consume*.

In the pre-Keynesian era, the credit system and the demand for monetary services were regarded as working normally under the discipline of the gold standard (or some other appropriate convertibility obligation). It was *believed* that the system would cause money income and real income to vary more or less in proportion. Price adjustments of the kind which affect the value of the money unit,* were recognized as necessary, however, in so far as the nature of convertibility commitments cause the general scale of prices which is compatible with full employment of resources to vary. The multiplier theory, on the other hand, ignores the possibility of continuous co-ordination through those price adjustments which affect the value of the money unit.†

This possibility of adjusting prices, to correspond with changes in free market values, is so fundamental in the orthodox approach that it can-

---

*I.e., as distinct from price adjustments made necessary through changes in the *relative* values of particular services or resources.

†But as we shall see in the following chapter, what I call the "employment" and the "real income" multipliers tacitly assume the release of capacity through inflation-induced price adjustment.

not be fruitfully omitted, as a determining condition, from any situation studied. Yet its exclusion by the Keynesians is not merely an assumption made for the convenience of theoretical simplicity—i.e., as an expositional device. As we have seen, the assumption of price rigidity* is looked upon as a realistic and practically useful premise for the study of the world that we know, and consideration of co-ordinative price adjustments is excluded in the very choice of concepts employed.

4.—The concept of the marginal propensity to consume is used in the discussion of an assumption—a supposed "psychological law"—that, *as real income increases, consumption increases but by not so much as income.* That is, the increment of consumption is assumed to be less than the increment of income. (Even if *the proportion* of the increment of income consumed *exceeds* the proportion which consumption bears to income, the multiplier is supposed to hold).

It should be noticed that the same proposition can be stated the other way round, as follows: *As real income increases, savings and investment increase, but by not so much as income.* Keynes himself stated the law as follows: "if C_w is the amount of consumption and Y_w is income . . . ΔC_w has the same sign as ΔY_w but is smaller in amount, i.e., $\frac{dC_w}{dY_w}$ is positive and less than unity."†(1) But this "law" can be equally well stated as follows: "If S is the amount of savings and Y is income . . . . ΔS has the same sign as ΔY but is smaller in amount, i.e., $\frac{dS}{dY}$ is positive and less than unity." It is, I think, significant that the so-called "law" is never stated in this form.‡ Yet it is an equally valid statement. In short, the "fundamental psychological rule" on which, Keynes argued, the stability of the economic system depends in practice,(2) merely states that the marginal propensity to consume is neither unity nor zero, i.e., that people will neither consume the whole of any increase in income (but save the rest of it) nor save the whole of any increase (but consume the rest of it).

So stated, one would think that the law could hardly be of any importance, even if one could accept the further assumption that the ratio $\frac{dC}{dY}$ is rigid in the short run.** But Keynes deduced from it that, "if employ-

---

*It is wage-rate rigidity which the Keynesians particularly stress. Their thesis that price adjustments are self-frustrating has been dealt with in Chap. IX.

†Keynes regarded these quantities as measured in wage units, and he therefore gave each of the terms the subscript w. But the argument is not affected by the units in which these amounts are measured.

‡It *is* sometimes said that the propensity to consume is merely another term for the propensity to save.

**I.e., in Keynes' words, "unlikely to undergo a material change over a short period of time except in abnormal or revolutionary circumstances."(4)

ment and hence aggregate income increase, *not all* the additional employment will be required to satisfy the needs of additional consumption." [3] Well, this is self-evident if we assume, as he did, that capacity has been released. Some of the "additional employment" will be required to satisfy the needs of additional savings. It did not occur to Keynes that we can equally usefully say: ". . . . Not all the additional employment will be required to satisfy the needs of additional savings, but some will be needed for additional *current* consumption." Nevertheless, he maintained that "this simple principle" leads to the conclusion "that employment *can only* (my italics) increase *pari passu* with an increase in investment; unless, indeed, there is a change in the propensity to consume." [5] He reached this conclusion because, he said, consumers "will *spend less* (my italics) than the increase in aggregate supply price," which will lead (in my terminology)* to the withholding of capacity unless there is additional investment "to fill the gap." [6] I propose to argue that it is solely the assumption (through the phrase "will spend less") that the short-term demand for money somehow increases more than proportionally as income increases (a notion which is due to defective concepts of consumption and savings) which can justify further consideration of the argument.

5.—But Keynes failed completely to perceive the significance of these words "will spend less." Indeed, throughout the whole of his discussion of the propensity to consume, a fundamental confusion is lurking, through a failure to distinguish between (a) "saving" in my sense of savings (the acquisition of additional assets by society) and (b) "saving" in a sense which implies that a rise in saving preference is accompanied by an increased demand for monetary services (a decline in V). From the context in *The General Theory*, (b) might appear to be "saving" in Keynes' sense. But it is not! He regarded saving as the *excess* of the value of current output (income) over consumption, i.e., what I have called "savings."

In other words, at times Keynes appeared to be assuming that when people do not spend the entire increment of income on consumption goods, they accumulate money with the rest. But at other times the context appears to make it obvious that "the gap" which "needs filling" is that caused by *saving* as such. The acquisition of savings, is not the same thing as postponed spending, whereas Keynes wrote as though it is, and used concepts which prevent us from continuously making the distinction.

I have a big expositional difficulty in this chapter and the subsequent

---

*Keynes said that the increased employment "will prove unprofitable." He assumed, of course, a rigid price of labor or other rigid factor prices and hence withheld capacity.

chapter. Most Keynesians deny with vehemence that the theory of the multiplier and the concept of the marginal propensity to consume rely tacitly upon the assumption of liquidity preference, or what I prefer to call hoarding. Moreover, Keynes himself several times expressed himself in a manner which excludes such a suggestion. Yet the assumption that hoarding is implied often seems to make the multiplier argument intelligible (although not acceptable); and some economists, in an attempt to rehabilitate the multiplier theory, have in fact turned to an explanation along these lines.* (See my references to Goodwin, pp. 277-9). I have always had the feeling that, in thinking of the amount by which the value of consumption is supposed to be deficient (when income is increasing), Keynes and his disciples have been, in a muddled sort of way, thinking of this sum as not having been spent at all. Hence, in handling these issues, I have found it to be desirable not only to treat the argument of *The General Theory* in its own terms, but to deal also with the same arguments as rationalized by the assumption that the value of any additional increment of income which is not consumed is hoarded. Unless I do this, I have the feeling that I shall not be answering the real objections which will be in the minds of those modern economists who have been (as it appears to me) endoctrinated by the multiplier teachings.

Consider, for instance, Keynes' discussion of the depreciation of a house, with which he continues the argument referred to in the last paragraph of section 4. He said that if the landlord "neither spends on upkeep nor regards as net income available *for consumption*" (my italics), the provision he makes for depreciation, it "constitutes a drag on employment all through the life of the house" until the fund so accumulated is used for rebuilding the house. Again, one would think that the tacit assumption is that, in the meantime, the landlord invests the whole of the depreciation provision in money, thus tending to bid up the aggregate real value of money assets. Keynes concluded, accordingly, that "sinking funds, etc., are apt to withdraw spending power from the consumer. . . . "[8] But why only from the consumer? If it is "spending power" which is withdrawn, why is it not equally at the expense of those who would otherwise purchase services for embodiment into the sort of resources which make up net accumulation?[†]

---

*It could then be expressed as a high *propensity to hoard* when real income is increasing (due to our not immediately having anything on which to spend the increases). But it is, I am afraid, a pure rationalization of Keynes' case to suppose that he was concerned with hoarding. It is saving, and not hoarding, which he regarded as to blame for "the gap" (discussed on pp. 216-8)—"increased investment" (at the expense of consumption).[7] Yet his remedy is additional expenditure on "investment."

†Actually, it seems to me absurd to suppose that "financial prudence" and "sound finance" (about which Keynes waxed so ironic in the passages in which this argument occurs) lead to sinking funds being hoarded to any extent in normal times. Whilst there may have been a rise in liquidity preference during the great depression, it must

Keynes did not, however, see this as the problem at issue. Thus, the term "liquidity preference" does not appear in Chapter 8, in which he introduced the idea of the marginal propensity to consume. Certainly he talked there of the imperfection with which man adjusts "his *expenditure* to changes in his income" (my italics); and he went on to say: "Thus a rising income will often be accompanied by increased saving, and a falling income by decreased saving. . . . ." But he had defined saving as the excess of the value of current output (income) over consumption. Saving so conceived *is* what I call "savings." Moreover, he followed the passage just quoted by a discussion of the motives toward *net accumulation* "which only acquire effective sway when a margin of comfort has been attained"[9]—again an indication that he was thinking of the devotion of saved income to the acquisition of *nonmoney assets*. This interpretation is strengthened by his argument in Chapter 9, in which he developed further his explanation of the propensity to consume. He discussed the motives which lead to provision for the future, but brought in "the motive of liquidity" merely *as one of many reasons* for the desire to accumulate capital assets.* He did *not* state that, when this reason accounts in part for the saving, there is a special case to be considered. Finally, his attitude on this point is brought out in his discussion of the implications of the fact that "Consumption is satisfied partly by objects produced currently and partly by objects produced previously, i.e., by disinvestment." He contended that "To the extent that consumption is satisfied (out of existing stocks), there is a contraction of current demand, since to that extent a part of current expenditure fails to find its way back as a part of net income."[10] In reality, *all* consumption (except for consumption of "final services," which forms a small proportion of income) is satisfied out of stocks which have been

---

have been due to quite different factors. Sinking funds are in practice invested in securities (unless they can find temporarily profitable employment in the business itself); it is only to the extent to which these securities offer prospective *pecuniary* yields of below the rate of interest that they form (as hybrid money) part of the aggregate stock of money; and only in that case will demand for them tend to raise the aggregate real value of money. But the demand for hybrid money which arises from the investment of sinking funds (e.g., for securities of appropriate maturities) is wholly normal demand for monetary services; and there seems to be no reason why demand for money from this source should not be stable in normal times, and no reason why abnormal changes in it should not be met by noninflationary credit adjustments. There can be no tendency for a decline in V, with a consequent inducement to withhold capacity, unless the aggregate real value of money is in process of being bid up and M remains fixed. Keynes' objection to "financial prudence" was a plea for inflation rather than an objection to deflation.

*This is one of the contexts in which Keynes' failure to distinguish between the saver and the entrepreneur rôles, and his consequent failure to perceive that demand for money is the expression of an entrepreneurial judgment, cause great confusion.

finally produced in a physical sense *over a wide range of points of time.*
The fact that a larger proportion of goods currently decumulated got
their physical form a long time ago (as with the using up of an old loco-
motive or the drinking of an old bottle of wine) does not cause a contraction of "current demand." Only if there is a failure to embody services of a real value equivalent to any current decumulation, will "aggregate demand" decline; and *the demand will decline owing to a failure
of production, not of consumption.*

If we were able, then, to interpret Keynes' phrase about "current expenditure" failing "to find its way back as part of net income" as referring to a rise in liquidity preference, controversy would be shifted to a
different plane. But even if we could assume that he was thinking of
hoarding under monetary and price rigidity, the implications of his argument would be unacceptable. Consumption of previously accumulated
stocks creates no "gap" due to savers being somehow prevented from
"investing" and so forced to hoard. Hence, if Keynes *was* subconsciously
thinking of hoarding when he drew the conclusion that the "problem
of providing that new capital-investment shall always outrun capital-
disinvestment sufficiently to fill the gap between net income and consumption, presents a problem which is increasingly difficult as capital
increases,"[11] he seems to have been confused by a reversal of cause and
effect. To put it in terms of "hoarding," any "gap" is due to the hoarding.
The hoarding is not due to the gap.

There is yet another passage in which Keynes appeared about to recognize that the real problem is that of hoarding, namely, when he referred to the possibility that financial provision for the future might be
separated from physical provision for the future.[12] But financial provision to make good current consumption (replacement) is equally likely
to be separated from physical provision for current consumption! That
is, expenditure may be postponed on services which are normally devoted
to replacing current consumption just as easily as on those which are
normally devoted to current net accumulation. But Keynes did not show
why an increase of income should aggravate the separation (cause hoarding and so "a gap") in either case.

If monetary policy aims at maintaining convertibility, parity, or a tolerable scale of prices, the effect of growing utilized capacity must, *if it is
recognized as such,* bring about an expansion of credit (i.e., an increase
in M). Hence, unless the convertibility obligations, or the parity sought,
or the price index objectives are *in themselves* deflationary, or unless
(through a misunderstanding of the situation) the attempt to administer
an intendedly neutral policy works in a deflationary manner, we have
no grounds for supposing that hoarding, with a consequent stimulus to
the withholding of capacity, will be induced.

6.—Keynes seemed to feel also that the "gap" must be filled in order
to provide *future* consumption demand. Extra *expenditure* on investment, he appeared to suggest, can alone create the purchasing power
necessary. Thus he wrote: "New capital-investment can only take place
in excess of current capital-disinvestment if *future* expenditure on consumption is expected to increase. Each time we secure today's equilibrium by increased investment" (at the expense of consumption) "we are
aggravating the difficulty of securing equilibrium tomorrow. A diminished propensity to consume today can only be accommodated to the
public advantage if an increased propensity to consume is expected to
exist some day."[13]

His reference to "future *expenditure* on consumption" instead of "future *production* to enable future consumption and growth," brings out
the nature of his thinking. *He tended always to think either of consumption or of spending as the source of demand.* Yet the mere fact that
there is a diminished *propensity* to consume now ought, in a rational
society, to be the cause of an expected higher *ability* to consume in the
future. I have shown that if we exclude population growth, then *all* expansion of the ultimate source of demand, i.e., all real accumulation of
productive power, *with no exceptions*, is the result of a consumer-saver
decision against current consumption. And far from "every weakening
of the propensity to consume regarded as a permanent habit" reducing
"the demand for capital as well as the demand for consumption,"[14] it
must always represent a demand for a more rapid piling up of capital
resources, as well as grounds for the prediction of an accelerated growth
of "aggregate demand" in the future. (See pp. 238-240). Of course, if
it happens to be accompanied by the withholding of capacity, a stronger
saving preference will be necessary to achieve this result. And, in the
absence of price co-ordination (i.e., if price rigidity cannot be rectified)
such a withholding may be induced through hoarding, which can in turn
—it might be argued—be caused through pessimistic expectations about
the *immediate* future. It is admittedly *conceivable* that the very phenomenon which ought to cause optimistic expectations concerning prospective future "aggregate demand," in practice causes pessimism. That
is a quite separate point.

7.—We can, I think, get a further insight into Keynes' ideas in his argument that "a rise in the rate of interest will have the effect of reducing
the amount actually saved."[15] He contended that the higher interest
will diminish "investment" and hence reduce income, the rate of saving
falling by the same amount as the decline in income. But the cause of
increased interest is always either a rise in the schedule of the marginal
efficiency of capital (which, he says, will "offset" the rise in interest!) or

a fall in saving preference, *unless monetary policy is deflationary*. In other words, if the marginal efficiency of capital remains unchanged, interest can rise only through an *increased* propensity to consume, or through those influences which Keynes appears anxious to exclude (until they are brought in, *as an independent factor*, in the last paragraph of his Chapter 9), namely, the determinants of M and V.

Saving (as distinct from hoarding) can exert no deflationary influence.* It is unlikely to give rise, therefore, to any *general* tendency to withheld capacity and so to cause a shrinkage of real income.† If the resources devoted to consumption uses are highly specific and the prices of their services rigid, then admittedly an increase in saving-preference may result in withheld capacity in those resources. But on the assumption that there is withheld capacity also in the industries specialized for net accumulation ("investment industries"), an equal release of capacity can be expected there. And as we shall see, the multiplier theory, which builds on the theories which are now under examination, assumes that there *is* withheld capacity in the latter industries; for the initial expenditure on investment is regarded as itself "creating employment."

Hence, Keynes' conclusion that "the more virtuous we are, the more determinedly thrifty . . . , the more our incomes will have to fall when interest rises relatively to the marginal efficiency of capital"[16] is based on a serious fallacy. For in the absence of deflationary policy, interest can rise "relatively to the marginal efficiency of capital" only through an increase, not a decrease, in the propensity to consume. And the rather cryptic qualification at the very end of Keynes' argument (at the end of chapter 9) to the effect that if the rate of interest were always such as to maintain full employment, "Virtue would resume her sway" (i.e., a high rate of net accumulation *would* then be caused by a weak propensity to consume) seems merely to imply once again that all the time, in the course of the argument we have been examining, Keynes was really tacitly assuming what the Keynesians usually emphatically deny,‡ namely, that monetary factors (policy or hoarding) are causing a deflation and withholding.

The truth is that *deflation plus price rigidity would have that effect no matter what consumption-saving preference was expressed*. Obviously, if the market rate of interest is so fixed that, irrespective of the extent to which productive capacity is being withheld, the monetary unit (and so money income) is always depreciated to the extent necessary to induce

---

*Except in the sense that, if it causes the natural rate of interest to fall, any formerly noninflationary market rate will become a deflationary rate.

†It is very difficult to know from the chapter under consideration (Chap. 9) whether Keynes intended "income" to mean money income or real income or whether he expected the reader to assume that income in the two senses varies more or less in proportion.

‡See the remarks of Fritz Machlup on this point.[17]

the release of that capacity,* there can be no decline of real income due to unemployment of resources. But that does not enable us to assume that, when this condition is absent, the failure to spend enough (hoarding) and the withholding of capacity are due to saving.

8.—There is no doubt, I think, that in Chapters 8 and 9 of *The General Theory*, Keynes was assuming that the source of ultimate demand lies in consumption instead of in production. Certainly he wrote as though he held that, because the whole of each increment of a growing real income may not be *consumed*, demand may be insufficient to absorb the growing product. We shall see this sort of conviction reflected in the Keynesians' treatment of invested savings as "leakages" in the multiplier theory. Keynes wrote: "Consumption—to repeat the obvious—is the sole end and object of all economic activity." That is so, but it is certainly not the origin of *demand* in any sense. He continued: "Opportunities for employment are necessarily limited by the extent of aggregate demand. Aggregate demand can be derived only from present consumption or from present provision for future consumption."[18] The wording here is significant. His statement *would* have been more acceptable if he had said "aggregate demand can be derived only from *present provision for both present and future consumption*," i.e., the production of *valuable services*.† Whether the *value* of those services is derived from the expectation that the products into which they flow will be consumed or utilized in the early future or in the distant future is irrelevant.

9.—But it is clear that Keynes would not have accepted this. Thus, he contended that "whenever an object is produced within the period with a view to satisfying consumption subsequently, an expansion of current demand is set up."[19] This is quite wrong in what it apparently implies. It is the *form* of real income (the source of "demands in general") and not its *amount* which is affected. *Aggregate real demands* can expand only through a growth in *utilized* productive capacity, and whether this increase in the flow of services is embodied into goods for early or late consumption or utilization makes no difference.

Similarly, *aggregate money demands* can expand only when M and/or V increases; and the saving-consumption choice concerning the use of the increased money income is equally irrelevant, *unless it can be shown that the manner of spending influences one or both of these terms*, and that

---

*If an increase in M would induce the release of capacity without any depreciation of the money unit, i.e., if the supply of services in general was perfectly elastic, then it could be said that the required depreciation is infinitesimal.

†Actually, expenditure on replacement (which makes up the greater part of all expenditure in practice) must be covered in the term, "future consumption." The true distinction is between the immediate and the distant future.

is just what Keynes fought shy of saying. Hence his thesis that saving as such—thrift—is a contractionist force is untenable. He has *not* shown that a high *propensity to consume* is favorable to employment. He has *not* shown that employment will be more difficult to achieve in an expanding economy (which will be the position when there is a high propensity to save) than it will be in a slowly expanding economy.

Possibly, at the back of Keynes' mind there was lurking the fallacy of the satiability of human preferences or wants. This impression is left by his view that "The greater . . . . the consumption for which we have provided in advance, the more difficult it is to find something further to provide for in advance, and the greater our dependence on present consumption as a source of demand."[20] I shall deal later with the notion of capital saturation. But the only *real* point here is, I suggest, that there are limits to the expression of saving preference, i.e., that there are diminishing returns to provision for the future. The postponement of current consumption is constantly increasing *the ultimate power to consume*; whilst the exercise of that power at any time is purely a matter of choice and freedom.* Was it not due to his failure to understand this that Keynes saw in thrift—in saving—and not in uncompensated hoarding the villain of the piece, whilst constantly writing as though he was identifying or confusing the two concepts?

10.—It may be objected that all these criticisms I have presented ignore the vital contention that a fall in the marginal propensity to consume does not imply the achievement of, but only the attempt to achieve a greater flow of savings. But rationalization of the argument along these lines is equally indefensible; for it cannot be said that the *attempt to save* (through a reduced valuation of consumption) can (a) reduce *money* income, unless it can be assumed that it induces hoarding, or (b) reduce *real* income, unless it can be assumed (through the hoarding or otherwise) to induce the withholding of capacity. In the absence of one or both of these effects, it cannot reduce the source of supposed or realized savings. Samuelson suggests that one of the great contributions of Keynes is his demonstration that "the *attempt* to save may lower income and actually realized saving."[21] Once again, it is only if Keynes meant that saving may be accompanied by hoarding and/or induce the withholding of capacity, that he can be said to have been right. And if Keynes did mean that, then he was merely stating in a tortuous way what I imagine every pre-Keynesian economist would have accepted. In short, arguments to the effect that "attempts" to increase savings may

---

*The withholding of capacity which is capable of providing currently valuable services is always a case of restraint on freedom, even if it is due merely to rigidity; for the rigidity prevents access to demanded services which are running to waste.

fail, i.e., in the words of J. Lintner, that they "do not necessarily or automatically increase new investment expenditures,"[22] can merely mean that saving and hoarding may go together,* or that withheld capacity may emerge and cause *subsequent saving* to fall.

11.—The sound approach to all these problems may be found, I suggest, in a recognition that the rate of growth of real income is always conditioned by the extent to which *the forces making for growth* (namely, thrift, economizing innovations and the release of capacity) in certain parts of the economy are being offset by *the forces making for contraction* (namely, consumption—i.e., decumulation—and the withholding of capacity) in other parts of the economy. If real income is growing, it must be because the forces making for growth are winning. It is, I maintain, impossible to find in the fact of that victory any reasons which might explain why contractionist influences should then tend to exert a relatively greater influence—unless offset by additional expenditure on investment.† Indeed, the contrary is true. The principle that growth and the release of capacity tend to call forth further growth and the release of further capacity, whilst the withholding of capacity tends to induce further withholding and reduce the profitableness of growth (in the absence of inflation), has already been stated. Hence when utilized productive capacity is expanding, only monetary factors *plus* rigidity or such extraneous factors as a wave of trade-union aggression, or monopolistically efficient acquisitiveness in some other form, will be able to account for the withholding. In short, if it is recognized that the source of all real demand is utilized productive capacity, the withholding of which is the withdrawal of real demand, many of the problems appear to solve themselves. And it then becomes clear, in particular, that the conclusion on which Keynes based his Chapter 10 (on the multiplier), namely, that "employment can only increase *pari passu* with investment,"[23] is false. It is *not* true that withheld capacity can be released only in the presence of growth.

---

*It must be remembered that this does not mean that real accumulation is not caused, in the absence of the withholding of capacity.

†I need hardly repeat that if growth due to such factors is not accompanied by an increase in M deflation must follow (unless V is increasing). But that is what Keynes seemed determined not to say in this context.

REFERENCES

(1) KEYNES, *The General Theory*, p.96. (2) *Ibid.*, p.97. (3) *Ibid.*, p.97. (4) *Ibid.*, p.91. (5) *Ibid.*, p.98. (6) *Ibid.*, p.98. (7) *Ibid.*, p.105. (8) *Ibid.*, pp.99-100. (9) *Ibid.*, p.97. (10) *Ibid.*, p.105. (11) *Ibid.*, p.105. (12) *Ibid.*, p.104. (13) *Ibid.*, pp.105-6. (14) *Ibid.*, p.106. (15) *Ibid.*, p.110. (16) *Ibid.*, p.111. (17) MACHLUP, *Period Analysis*

and Multiplier Theory (originally published in *The Quarterly Journal of Economics*, 1939), in *Readings in Business Cycle Theory*). (18) KEYNES, *op. cit.*, p.104. (19) *Ibid.*, p.105. (20) *Ibid.*, p.105. (21) SAMUELSON, *The General Theory* (3), in HARRIS, *The New Economics*, p.159. (22) LINTNER, *The Theory of Money and Prices*, in Harris, *op. cit.*, p.527. (23) KEYNES, *op. cit.*, p.113.

Chapter XIII

THE MULTIPLIER

SUMMARY

1.—The multiplier assumes that an increment of expenditure on investment is multiplied to cause an increased ultimate increment of aggregate demand, the multiplier being unity *when the marginal propensity to consume is* zero *and* infinity *when this propensity is* unity. *2.—But the supposed special stimulus from a particular category of additional expenditure has never been explained, 3.—whilst the notion that expenditure generates income has already been shown to be fallacious. 4.—I distinguish three supposed multipliers: the "money income," the "real income" and the "employment" multipliers, the important distinction being between the first (which is supposed to continue as "true inflation" after "full employment" has been reached) and the second (which ceases at "full employment"). 5.—But most discussions seem to be concerned with the effects upon money income, with an apparent tacit assumption of perfect elasticity of supply of services to the point of "full employment." 6.—In the "serial" interpretations, "newly created money" is supposed to generate further income at each subsequent expenditure on consumption but not on investment. 7.—But no dynamic reactions can be shown to originate in the propensity to consume. 8.—Keynes' apparent conviction that the source of demand is consumption may have led him to the view that a high propensity to consume implies a high multiplier. 9.—The dynamic repercussions upon money income of an initial increase in M or V can be explained solely through an explanation of the reactions upon the determinants of M and V. 10.—Some economists appear to assume tacitly that the so-called "leakages" of any part of the increment of increase not spent on consumption are due to hoarding, 11.—whilst others regard the "leakages" as savings which leave the monetary circulation and are then reinvested; 12.—but if the "leakages" are merely money withdrawn from circulation, the Keynesian multiplier must be discarded. 13.—The suggestion has been made that the multiplier effect is exerted when spending is otherwise than out of income; but this simply implies an increase in M or V, the field of expenditure being irrelevant. 14.—In any case all spending is out of holdings of money, not out of income; and it has not been shown that spendings initially on investments and subsequently on consumption have special effects upon the value of the money unit. 15.—The notion of "leakages" cannot be defended as a mere analytical device for isolating the effects of assumed mechanical relations between income and consumption. 16.—If V is assumed constant, and the marginal propensity to consume is positive, Keynes' multiplier merely represents the purely formal consequences upon the magnitude M of maintaining a given additional rate of expenditure on "investment."*

17.—The possibility that rising real income may be accompanied by a more than proportionate rise in demand for money creates no real difficulty.

18.—Any real income multiplier must depend upon the release or growth of capacity in one field creating demand or an inducement for the release or growth of capacity in noncompeting fields.

1.—Having considered the supposed psychological law of the propensity to consume, we are in a position to consider the theory of the multiplier, of which it is regarded as an integral part.

Stigler has described the "multiplier" as "the fuzziest part of his (Keynes') theory."[1] I believe that the hold which the multiplier theory has obtained is chiefly due to this "fuzziness"; for when we have dispelled it by explaining what might have been meant (or should have been meant) we find that all possible explanations are fallacious. I propose to show that it has been built on (i) the fallacy (which I have already exposed in many different contexts) that only some change in the relationship between prospective yields and the rate of interest, which relationship Keynes assumed would influence expenditure on something called "investment," can cause MV and money income to change,* (ii) the fallacy (which was refuted in Chapter VIII, above) that spending generates income and (iii) the wholly arbitrary tacit assumption that, subsequent to its initial "injection" as expenditure on "investment," "newly created money" is *spent* only if devoted to consumption and not if devoted to "investment."

In its simplest and least unreasonable form, the multiplier thesis can be expressed by saying that the stimulation of industries producing for investment stimulates in turn the industries producing for consumption. At one point, the theory was so expressed by Keynes.

T. Wilson claims this much for the multiplier, that it has attracted attention to the consideration "that, at a time when large numbers are out of work, the beneficial effect on employment of a rise in investment will not be confined to the industries making capital goods; that, if there are idle resources, consumption and investment are likely to move in the same direction instead of being alternatives as the earlier theories, which

---

*That this notion does lie at the root of the multiplier notion is also the interpretation of Hawtrey who writes: "Investment is relevant, because he (Keynes) maintains that only through investment can the flow of money be regulated." Hawtrey refers also to "income being tied down by the multiplier to the limit allowed by the volume of investment."[2]

usually started with the initial assumption of full employment, were wont to suggest."*[3] But if Keynes had said anything like this, no-one would have objected, except to the quite untenable suggestion that earlier theories had implied anything different.

In Keynes' rigorous enunciation, the theory assumes that every additional increment of income is *caused by* an additional increment of expenditure which has been devoted to investment. An increase in "investment" of x will cause an ultimate increase in money income received of Kx.† If the marginal propensity to consume is ⅘ths., so that the multiplier (K) is 5, the increase in income will be $5x$. The multiplier will, then, be greater the greater the marginal propensity to consume, *unity* when the propensity is *zero*, and *infinity* when the propensity is *unity* (an absurdity to which I must later give some attention).

In the usual statement of the theory, it is *tacitly assumed* that an increased rate of "investment" expenditure is *maintained*, in the sense that if for any reason the new level of "investment" due to the initial increase in M declines, M will be further increased to maintain "investment" at its new magnitude. This necessary assumption does not seem to be stated in most of the textbooks. I deal later (a) with the case in which an additional investment expenditure is assumed *not* to be maintained, as a decline in V is assumed gradually to absorb some of the initial addition to M; and (b) with the extreme case in which no part of the additional income which is unconsumed is "invested."

The case chosen by Hague and Stonier to illustrate the principle makes it clear that they are assuming "not a mere once-for-all act of investment, but that the government undertakes to carry out the new, increased volume of investment in each succeeding year—or whatever period of time is most convenient. . . . . Government expenditure . . . . is constant at its new level."[4]

In stating the principle, I used the words "eventually" and "ultimate." But Keynes' multiplier was imagined by him to be *instantaneous*. The consumption goods industries were thought of as advancing *pari passu* with the capital goods industries.[5] Only imperfect foresight, he seemed to think, could account for any time lag; and, after consideration of this possibility, he re-stated his position as follows: ". . . . *in every interval of time* the theory of the multiplier holds good in the sense that the increment of aggregate demand is equal to the increment of aggregate investment multiplied by the marginal propensity to consume."[6] (My italics). (The words "the marginal propensity to consume" here

---

*Surely every pre-Keynesian economist would have agreed that the *most probable* result of changes in income would be that the magnitudes consumption and net accumulation would vary in the same direction, although improbably in the same proportion.

†Keynes' own exposition does not, of course, justify this use of the word "ultimate."

are a slip for "the multiplier"). But as a result of criticisms, subsequent Keynesians have rationalized the theory in what has been termed the "serial interpretation," which I shall in due course examine.

2.—I have a general objection at the outset. Why should the "stimulation" due to the release of capacity devoted to the satisfaction of one set of economic ends (namely, net accumulation) "stimulate" the release of capacity devoted to the satisfaction of all other economic ends (namely, replacement, etc.), in any manner which is not just as possible the other way round? I.e., why should the field in which the initial expenditure is incurred be regarded as having some special significance? And why should the subsequent choice between two kinds of spending (on so-called "consumption" and on net accumulation) have some special significance in respect of the repercussions upon money income? According to Keynes it is the "increment of aggregate investment" which must initiate the first impulse of the multiplier, and hence is the ultimate cause of an increase in money income and real income. But why should not the same *initial* expenditure upon consumption have exactly the same effect?* On this point, Haberler has asked a simple but devastating question. Referring to Keynes' illustration of the increment of investment taking the form of public works, Haberler asks: "But how are we to classify money paid to unemployed workers to perform 'public works' of very doubtful value? Suppose these works consist of digging holes in the ground and filling them up again. Or suppose a road is built at a cost which far exceeds its value to the community."[8] In merely asking this question, I believe that Haberler has exposed the total irrelevance of the broad field in which an initial expenditure is incurred. Only if we distinguish between the degree of withheld capacity in the field of initial expenditure, is the field of spending relevant, and then relevant only to what I shall call (Section 4, below) the *employment and real income multipliers* (unless, as I shall suggest, it affects V or somehow has a further effect on M).†

Curiously enough, Haberler does not seem to perceive just how damaging his question is. He sees the arbitrariness of the distinction between investment and consumption in this special case; he states that in practice the classification of additional expenditure "as consumption or investment is generally of minor importance" and he contends that

---

*Later on, dealing with criticisms which had raised these issues, Keynes said that he chose new "investment" as the multiplicand because it is the "factor which is most prone to sudden and wide fluctuations."[7] I fail to see why that should be a justification.

†On the assumption that "increased expenditure" can induce the release of capacity, the only reason why a release so effected in one large group of industries should not tend to stimulate a similar release in all the rest is that there happens to be no withheld capacity in the latter.

"What matters are the factors stressed by traditional theory; the methods used by the government in raising the money, the rapidity with which the successive recipients spend it, the manner of spending, etc."[9] I agree completely, except that I believe that *the manner of the spending, or where it occurs,* has nothing to do with the position at all, either in respect of initial additions to expenditure or the subsequent additions which are induced. The choice between categories of expenditures which seem to be typical of, on the one hand, *final services plus those needed for replacement (consumption)* and on the other hand, *those needed for net accumulation (investment),* seems to me to be irrelevant to either multiplier effect.

The entrepreneur's incentive to spend on replacement (which class of expenditure virtually makes up the whole value of what can be thought of as consumption expenditure) is identical with his incentive to spend on net accumulation (to "invest"). We can hardly hold therefore that there is some special significance in society's expenditure in buying services for embodiment into assets as soon as this expenditure exceeds the value of replacement. This has never been shown and, I hold, it cannot be shown. Moreover, as in practice some undertakings are always disinvesting—failing to replace—whilst others are expanding, it is impossible to say of any specific item of net accumulation of assets by one firm or person that it represents net accumulation (i.e., "investment") on the part of society. It seems to me that, in the light of this single criticism alone, the whole theory collapses unless it is revised to imply that all *additional* expenditures effect the same kind of stimulus. And the *typical* exposition explicitly denies this.*

3.—But if the argument of my Chapter VIII is accepted, the theory collapses for another simple reason. I have shown that it is fallacious to suppose that *expenditure* either generates real income or the money valuation of income (determined by the value of the money unit) but that, on the contrary, it is the value of the money unit which determines how much expenditure is necessary in order to acquire a given *quantum* of services or assets. Real income may be generated through the release

---

*E.g., Hague and Stonier write: "The multiplier . . . . will not operate at all unless an initial change in *the volume of investment* takes place. In other words, the multiplier cannot operate unless there is something to be multiplied; and that something *must be* a change in investment."[10] (My italics).

Samuelson briefly admitted in 1941,[11] that relief expenditure (i.e., on consumption) could be treated as entering into the multiplicand (the multiplier reaction then being expressed in "investment"); but he did not explicitly answer Dennis Robertson (whose ironic reference to "honorary investment" probably forced the admission); nor did he consider explicitly the implications which Robertson and Haberler had discussed. Subsequent teaching was scarcely affected. (I refer below to Goodwin's treatment of the point, section 13).

of capacity, and inflation may bring this about, but it is still the value of the money unit which makes increased expenditure necessary and not *vice versa.* Every time a money unit passes, the commodity or service which it buys is in turn demanding *it.* The offer of money for nonmoney no more tends to raise prices than the simultaneous offer of nonmoney for money tends to reduce prices. The one cannot occur *more frequently* than the other.

I am not optimistic enough, however, to suppose that I can so simply convince those who have long become habituated to thinking in terms of the generation of income by expenditure, still less those economists who have taken their first steps in the study of economics by mastering the multiplier theory and painfully learning its mechanism from the textbooks. I must therefore examine it in some detail, *assuming for the rest of this chapter that expenditure does generate income!*

4.—We have first to distinguish between three sets of supposed effects of *additional* "investment" expenditure (i.e., expenditure by society in excess of the previous value of the flow of services—final services *plus* replacement *plus* net accumulation*): (a) the effects upon money income, or what I shall call *the money income multiplier*; (b) the effects upon income measured in wage-units, or what Keynes called—most inappropriately—"the investment multiplier," but I shall call *the real income multiplier*; and (c) the effects upon employment, or what Keynes called *the employment multiplier*. All three multiplications start with expenditure on "investment," but the first multiplies the money income which results, the second the real income and the third the employment.

Keynes seemed to think that there are difficulties involved in measuring income in real terms (he said, "in terms of product") which are escaped in the case of wage-units. He said, however, that it is often convenient to regard income expressed in terms of wage-units as "an adequate working index of changes in real income."[12] As his disciples have not followed his use of wage-units as a measure, I propose to dispense with the wage-unit concept and discuss merely the real income multiplier, in the sense in which I have already used the term "real income."†

Because Keynes meant by "employment" the use of only one factor of production, labor, and not the use of all factors, the real income multiplier (his "investment multiplier)" will not be *identical* with the employment multiplier. He discussed the relations between them and explained that, whilst there is no reason in general to suppose that they

---

*This way of putting it gets over, for the time being, the difficulty to which I referred in section 2.

†I.e., the value of the flow of services measured in imaginary money units of "constant value."

will be equal, he found it convenient to deal with the simplified case in which they are assumed to be equal.

But the fundamentally important distinction which is essential for clear thinking is not that between the real income multiplier and the employment multiplier, but that between the money income multiplier and the real income multiplier. For whilst the effects of both the *employment multiplier* and the *real income multiplier* are envisaged as ceasing when a state of "full employment" has been reached (at which stage, additional expenditure on investment is regarded as causing no further increase in real income), the effects on money income (the *money income multiplier*) are supposed to continue and to be expressed in "true inflation,"[13] although the Keynesians do not *explicitly* use the concept of the money income multiplier.

One of the most serious difficulties about Keynes' exposition on this topic arises out of his use of concepts which cause the notions of the real income multiplier and the money income multiplier to be confused.* The clumsy wage-unit expression leads students to inhibit concern with the price consequences of the policies Keynes was envisaging. It obscures the fact that his nostrum was essentially inflationary. The wage-unit formulation facilitates the tacit assumption of perfect elasticity in the release of withheld capacity to increasing expenditure. Only when the "full employment" condition has to be considered does the argument of *The General Theory* face the price consequences, i.e., in the state in which rising prices no longer result in the further release of capacity, the so-called "true inflation."

5.—Now as we have seen, by "true inflation," Keynes meant neither loss of parity in terms of a monetary standard nor a loss of parity in real terms. He argued in effect that, as long as any withheld capacity is being released, any decline in the value of the money unit, i.e., any rise in the scale of prices, is not truly inflationary. Until that point is reached, he admitted that increases in "effective demand" will influence both the cost unit and output. But all this is explained in *The General Theory* very much later than the discussion of the multiplier itself, which leaves the impression with the student that, up to the point of "full employment," there will be perfect elasticity of supply in respect of the whole flow of services (those devoted to consumption and replacement as well as those devoted to net accumulation), whilst suddenly, at the state of full employment, a condition of absolute inelasticity is encountered, when the employment and real income multipliers have exerted their whole effect.

---

*Hazlitt also has made this point. He writes, "Keynes' 'multiplier' jumps without notice from 'real' terms to monetary terms."[14]

If such a condition did exist, then the real income multiplier and the money income multiplier would be equal until no further capacity could be released. But unless they are equal, *the effect of seeking full employment (the release of withheld capacity) through the device of an increase in M (whether spent initially on "investment" or anything else), instead of through price adjustments, must be inflationary in the ordinary sense, as opposed to Keynes' sense.*

Nearly all subsequent discussions of the multiplier and especially those employing "the serial interpretation" (see below) appear to discuss the effects, not upon real income (or income measured in wage-units), but upon money income. Nevertheless, they still treat the subject in such a way as to leave the impression with the student that the elasticity of supply is so perfect that an increase in M (and any consequent increase in V) will induce such a release of capacity that real income increases as rapidly, or almost as rapidly as MV.* The tacit assumption seems to be that deflation has previously caused unemployment without causing prices to fall, i.e., that there has been a purposeless deflation (as distinct from a rectifying deflation).† But if that is the position, if withheld capacity can be coaxed back into use as easily as this, why should not very slight price adjustments be sufficient to secure the same objective? (See pp. 126-7, 286). I must remind the reader that this very reasonable possibility was excluded by Keynes in his assumptions and concepts.

6.—Let us now consider the *money income multiplier*. The case usually chosen to illustrate it in the textbooks is that in which the initial expenditure arises through an increase in M ("newly created" money as distinct from "newly activated" money).‡16 The present discussion will therefore be confined to this case. The additional expenditure on "investment" (public works, for example) is envisaged as being received in due course in the form of wages which go to buy goods in shops, then to buy goods which replace the stocks sold, which means in turn buying the services of producers, and so on. According to this "serial interpretation" of the theory, in each transfer of the money, *part of the sum passed*, being spent on consumption, enters into the income receipts of those who are paid for goods or services; and as

*E.g., Hague and Stonier, whose treatment is quite typical of the textbooks, maintain that, until a condition of full employment is approached, increasing expenditure will mean an increase in employment but no (or little) increase in prices.(15)

†Yet there has never been any political or monetary motive for such a deflation under "sound money"; for credit contraction tends to follow rather than to cause the withholding of capacity. (See pp. 125-6, 150-1). At the same time, *purposeless* deflation may ocassionally have been *inadvertent.*

‡The term "newly *created* money" here means simply an increase in the number of units into which the aggregate real value of money assets is divided.

each unit of money goes on circulating, it goes on entering into the income receipts of later recipients. If the marginal propensity to consume is ½, so that the multiplier is 2, an initial expenditure of 100 is supposed to lead to successive increases of income in each subsequent *income period** of the increments spent on consumption, namely, 50, 25, 12.5, 6.25, etc. That is, as the additional income receipts at each stage of the process are again spent, in part, *on consumers' goods,* each of these expenditures (as distinct from the part spent on goods which add to net "investment") is supposed to set up a further process of "generation" of money income. In this way, we are told (Halm's words), "the money seeps down again through many productive processes and contributes to the income of an ever widening circle of people working in stores, offices and factories,"[17] and *the consumed part* carries on the "income generating" process. In short, each successive act of spending *on consumption* is thought to result in an addition to money income, whilst because some part of each increment of spending is assumed to be on investment, the successive *additions* to money income *from this cause* must, it is thought, dwindle. For in so far as the income of any subsequent recipient is saved, it is regarded as a "leakage" and believed to offset the multiplier effect. *These consequences are supposed to follow whether the "leakage" (the unconsumed part of the increment of income) is spent in the acquisition of nonmoney assets or retained as money.*† But in any case, people in general do not hoard, and must therefore "invest" the balance. Hence it is difficult to conceive of exactly what it is that *leaks away.* I shall, however, shortly show that the assumption *is* sometimes that what is not spent on consumption is not spent at all. Yet the Keynesians always try to maintain at the same time that the failure to spend is not hoarding. That is what is so confusing.

7.—Haberler has argued that the true multiplier will depend upon many other circumstances than the propensity to consume. He mentions, for instance, the marginal efficiency of capital and "the velocity, especially the income velocity of money."[18] It is to be my contention that no dynamic reactions have their origin in the propensity to consume, except in so far as this propensity *happens* to combine with other factors in influencing V (as I have defined it); and I do not think it has been shown that this propensity must have, or that it is likely to have, this effect. Haberler specifically mentions "leakages" in this connection. Only if he is thinking of "leakages" as "hoarding," an interpretation of the

---

*I.e., the period in which each money unit is supposed to become income once.

†I refer to income being *retained* as money, simply because that is the way the Keynesians always look at it. In reality, however, as we have seen, income always accumulates in the form of non-money assets. It is later exchanged for money. See pp. 144-5, 214-5.

multiplier which the Keynesians reject, does it make sense. (See below pp. 275-7).

8.—As I have already insisted, Keynes certainly did *not* have liquidity preference in mind. His thinking on this point, as on others, seems to have been dominated simply by his tendency to think of consumption, and not production, as the source of demands in general. It was this belief which gave rise, I suggest, to his notion that money spent on consumption somehow goes on adding to the effective demand of subsequent recipients, whilst money spent by them on "investment" is treated as responding to, not adding to demand. A similar way of reasoning appears to have caused his successors to think that the latter form of expenditure causes the "leakages" which we have been discussing. Thus, if the additional income resulting from the initial increase in expenditure (due to an increase in M) is in turn spent wholly on "investment," there will be (the Keynesians suppose) a complete "leakage," the multiplier will be unity, and money income will increase only in proportion to the increase in M. Expenditure on consumption alone is thought of as giving any further *stimulus*.

But suppose the income resulting from the initial expenditure on investment is devoted wholly to consumption, i.e., suppose the marginal propensity to consume is unity. Then the money income multiplier is assumed to be *infinite!* In Keynes' words, if people "seek to consume the whole of any increment of income . . . prices will rise without limit."[19] Haberler's explanation of this apparent absurdity is that, "In plain English, there *can be* no increase in I."[20] (My italics). Why *"can be"*? The proposition itself *states* the assumption that there *will be* no voluntary attempt to acquire additional assets out of the resulting money income. But the initial increase in M is tacitly assumed to be spendable in any way which the original recipient of the money "invested" may choose.

I do not see that the absurdity can be explained away on these lines. I shall shortly suggest that the multiplier of infinity has a quite different meaning, and that consideration of this extreme case may serve as a *reductio ad absurdum* of the assumption that the marginal propensity to consume and any multiplier reaction are related, by some stimulus which originates in consumption. (See pp. 280-3).

9.—Surely the truth is that an increase of either M or V, spent initially on *either* "investment" *or* "consumption," will *ceteris paribus* enter into the income receipts of those paid for output and thus cause an increase in money income, whilst there are conditions under which it may be validly supposed that any such initial increase (however caused and wherever spent) will induce (i) a further increase in V or a succession of increases in V, or (ii) (and this is an assumption about the nature of monetary policy) a further increase in M or a succession of increases in M. But the Keynesians refuse to admit this, even when their own attempts to explain what they think Keynes really meant, or ought to have meant, seem to be leading them to the same conclusion. They are at pains to deny, for instance, that the multiplier and "income velocity" are one and the same thing. That is obvious. But is it not equally obvious that the multiplier effect must have time dimensions, and if so and unless we are tacitly assuming a succession of increases in M, that this will be expressible in terms of "income velocity"? (Machlup has made this point).[21] Thus, if an additional expenditure (initiated by an increase of M_1 to M_2) in a particular field results in an ultimate increase of money income by more than $M_2V - M_1V$, it means that V must have increased!*

Keynes himself recognized *other* factors which he thought *did* affect V; but he treated them as quite independent. He explained, for instance, that owing to what he called "the confused psychology which often prevails," expenditure on public works which ought to result in the multiplier effect being experienced is prevented through repercussions upon "confidence" which may "increase liquidity preference." He did not, however, regard this as affecting the multiplier. He classified it as a factor which may have adverse reactions on investment *"in other directions."*[23]

My contention is that these "other factors" are the only factors. The true *money income multiplier* is not explicable through any analysis of the way in which additional money units are passed on through the hands of the successive recipients and the kind of services purchased with them. It is explicable solely through an analysis of the determinants of V and M (in *my* sense of these terms).†

Some Keynesians perceive that we cannot concentrate our attention *solely* on spending by the first and subsequent recipients of the initial addition to money spent. Thus, Benjamin Higgins points out that, for the pump-priming effect of the multiplier to work, *"induced* private spending (*new investment* and consumption by those whose incomes are *not* directly affected by public investment, but whose anticipations are changed) would have to be positive and large."[24] I have not seen this notion related explicitly to the multiplier theory as a whole (although, in italicizing the words *"new investment,"* the passage stresses the similarity to the effects of both kinds of expenditure).

---

*There seems to have been no text-book reaction to Vera Lutz's 1955 challenge on the broad issue discussed here.[22]

†See pp. 90-1.

10.—Haberler, although an acute critic, *seems* not to have thrown off the idea that it is only through *expenditure on consumption,* of the income resulting from an initial investment, that the income velocity of circulation may be multiplied. He retains the Keynesian view that receipts which are re-invested are "leakages," which cause a contraction in the multiplier. As I suggested above, I think this is because he is really regarding the saving of any part of the additional increment of income which is not spent on consumption goods as its hoarding; and this can sometimes be seen to be the *tacit* assumption of many of the Keynesians.

Thus, in Hansen's rationalization of the multiplier, some "leakages" are obviously regarded as due to hoarding, although he does not recognize that *hoarding is implied in each of the five "most important" cases he mentions.*[25] For instance, the purchase of consumers' goods which are not replaced by the seller can cause a "leakage," not because the goods are "excess," as Hansen believes (for the word "excess" has no meaning in his context), but because the money spent and received is tacitly assumed to be hoarded.* Yet the Keynesians are emphatic in their denials that the leakages have anything to do with hoarding. If, however, Haberler had argued that the marginal propensity to hoard of individuals or (the same thing from a different aspect) their marginal propensity to spend (on final services, replacement and net accumulation) will be influenced by additional expenditures incurred under certain defined conditions, and that these propensities will cause subsequent changes in money income and the release of capacity, he would have refashioned the Keynesian multiplier into a more easily intelligible and more acceptable theory. But apparently because of some lingering conviction that the purchase of services flowing into additional assets ("investment") has different effects from the purchase of services flowing into maintenance, repairs, replacement and direct consumption, he appears to have been prevented from seeing and describing the whole problem simply as one of the effects of changes in aggregate expenditures upon "income velocity" or (given a certain monetary policy) upon the number of money units.

11.—Investment in money (hoarding), which may accompany saving,

---

*At one point Keynes came near to admitting that his whole aim was merely to prevent hoarding. He wrote, "The only radical cure for the crises of confidence which afflict the economic life of the modern world would be to allow the individual no choice between consuming his income and ordering the production of the specific capital-asset which, even though it be on precarious evidence, impresses him as the most promising investment available to him."[26] This certainly *implies* that he would wish to prevent the income receiver from preferring to hold money rather than other assets. But inconsistencies elsewhere prevent us from accepting so simple an explanation.

or the settlement of debts without an equal amount of further borrowing on the part of others, *may* perhaps be usefully described as "leakages," in the sense that such a use of income will reduce the multiplicand (the initiating increase in aggregate expenditure).* But Halm argues—with seeming uneasiness—that the practice of treating *nonhoarded savings* as leakages "has its great advantages" (although he does not mention the "advantages"). He says, the effect of such expenditures is not "entirely ignored" because "they are treated under the so-called acceleration principle." It is merely "a terminological decision. . . . . We are driven to the rather artificial construction that invested savings are first considered as leaking out of the monetary circulation and that they are, then, recreated to finance induced investment"[28] This looks like an attempt at justification of a wholly unjustified distinction between expenditure in two fields.

Keynes himself did not perceive that nonhoarded savings have the same effects on money income as consumption; nor did he recognize that recourse to the acceleration principle (to which he attached little importance) might be a way out of the difficulty. Yet it seems almost as though Keynes' successors, having made the multiplier a valued part of their apparatus, have been loth to recognize a weakness which renders it utterly worthless.

12.—Machlup, whose 1939 article has obviously influenced Halm's argument, discusses the unsatisfactory nature of the Keynesians' reply to those critics who have maintained that the "leakages" are nothing more than hoarding (the accumulation of idle cash balances and the cancellation of debts). "This identification of the leakages with hoarding," he says, "is liable to make full-blooded Keynesians furious. They usually react to it with an explanation of the meaninglessness of the concept of hoarding—in the Keynesian language—but they do not tell their misinterpreters 'what happens to the leaked-out funds.' They confine themselves to the contention that all that matters is the fact that these amounts are not spent on consumption. This answer, in turn, is apt to make their opponents furious." [29]

---

*Halm has made the point that "if primary investment (financed by credit creation) is *supplanted by* investment which is financed out of savings, the multiplicand of the multiplier is reduced."[27] (My italics). If all that is meant by the words "supplanted by" is that instead of a particular project (e.g., public works) being financed by inflationary credit expansion it is financed by noninflationary borrowing, then obviously, there will be no multiplier effect on money income from "investment which is financed out of savings," because the inflationary effect on aggregate expenditure is avoided. In other words, the multiplicand is *nil*. "Reduced" is hardly the correct word. I feel that Halm uses the word beause he is still thinking of savings as a *leakage*—as something which permits the beneficent multiplier effects to escape. On the other hand, if "financed out of savings" is supposed to mean dishoarding, then it *is* logically an initiating expenditure in the multiplier sense.

In forcing the discussion to this vital issue, Machlup appears to be maneuvering the Keynesians into a corner. But like Haberler, just as he seems to be ready to knock them out of the ring, he somehow pulls his punches and appears reluctant to carry on the fight. He continues, "As a matter of fact, it *is* irrelevant for the immediate effect what the nature of the leakage really is. It *is* true that it does not make any difference 'what happens to the leaked-out funds.' But the critics have nevertheless a perfect right to know what happens if the funds are not 'hoarded'. . . . ."[30] *Surely the whole question centers around this very issue.* If the leakages *are* merely hoarding, i.e., savings which are "considered as leaking out of the monetary circulation" (Halm), then it can be argued that the *Keynesian* multipliers have to be abandoned on this ground alone. Machlup says that the critics of Keynes are unable to see that if, say, $100 which is "created" as bank deposits, for the purpose of purchasing securities to finance public works, is accompanied by the expenditure of $36 out of savings for the purchase of these securities from the banking system, it will *alleviate* the demands on the bank system, so that "only $64 will flow from new bank credit as a 'contribution to income."[31] The $36 is "invested," he says, but it is still a "leakage." But if there is a "leakage," surely it is due not to saving but to the policy of the monetary authority which, on parting with the securities it had originally purchased, fails to reinvest the money proceeds, $36. Machlup is simply supposing that one increase in M is followed by a subsequent decrease in M.

If Keynes or any of his disciples had meant this, they would have said it and no economist could have misunderstood them. This sort of factor has nothing to do with the multiplier, but merely (as Halm perceives) with the multiplicand. And so, it seems to me, Machlup surprisingly abandons the fight when the multiplier is tottering.

13.—Since Machlup wrote, I have noticed one other attempt worthy of consideration (this time by a would-be Keynesian), to persevere with "the multiplier." In his attempt to refine his theory, R. M. Goodwin[32] seems to have been groping towards the same truth. He reaches the following conclusions (Robertsonian definitions are used in the passage).

> Income increases, decreases or remains stationary, depending on the difference between saving and investment.[33]

This makes the multiplication dependent not on the increases of investment but on the increase, decrease or constancy of MV. The form in which it is expressed seems to imply that, *ceteris paribus,* the money valuation of income increases when uncompensated dishoarding is in progress and decreases when uncompensated hoarding is in progress. If that *is* what. is meant, no-one will dispute it. But if it implies that the money valuation of income cannot increase through an increase in M or V unless investment (in the Robertsonian sense) exceeds saving, it is wrong.

Goodwin explains that whether *subsequent* spending "generates" additional income (i.e., whether the serial multiplier effect is realized) depends in each successive spending upon whether the expenditure is an "injection." It is an "injection," he says, if it is an expenditure otherwise than out of income (i.e., *presumably* out of the dishoarding of money* or credit expansion). Does it not follow, therefore, that, in every case, the multiplier effect must simply be that of an increase in M or in V? All expenditures, says Goodwin, fall "into two classes, those springing from previously received income and all others."[34] But is it not just as easy to spend otherwise than out of "previously received income" on investment as on consumption? And is it not just as likely? Indeed, is it not *more* likely? For are we not all loth to live on capital? Is it not much more probable that we shall deplete our holdings of money to increase our stock of nonmoney resources rather than consume our capital? And if so, must not a low propensity to consume have a greater multiplier effect than a high propensity? But the explanation in the passage just quoted from Goodwin is preceded by another passage of extraordinary obscurity. "To determine in practice what an injection is," says Goodwin, "requires much ingenuity, even though the principle is clear and fairly simple. When once understood, the distinction disposes of the spurious objection that what is done with savings has been ignored. If they lead to injections then it is obviously not so, and if they do not, then they ought properly to be left out of account so far as income is concerned."[35] The only meaning which I can attribute to these sentences amounts to an admission of, rather than the "disposal" of, what he calls "the spurious objection" that Keynes ignores "what is done with savings" (i.e., whether they are hoarded or spent on the acquisition of additional resources). Nevertheless, Goodwin clings to the view that the extent to which successive expenditures are injections depends upon the marginal propensity to consume. He does so quite inconsistently, it seems to me. For once his criterion of an "injection" is accepted, the propensity to consume is admitted to be wholly irrelevant. No reasons remain for regarding successive expenditures on "consumption" as "injections" whilst successive expenditures on "investment" are regarded as "leakages." Yet he stands shoulder to shoulder with Keynes in regarding consumption expenditure as somehow different in kind from investment expenditure. For instance, he describes as "a constant new injection . . . . *that* consumption which people would

---

*Of course, *all* expenditure is out of *holdings* of money!

make if they had no income."[36] (My italics). Admittedly, if people who are receiving no money *buy* things to consume, their expenditure must be an "injection," i.e., dishoarding from their holdings of money. But this does not confer upon *consumption* in general some special attribute which causes expenditure to replace it necessarily to involve dishoarding or even to make dishoarding more likely. If people acquire nonmoney assets by dishoarding without increasing their consumption, the position is just the same. Moreover, there is no reason to suppose that, because there are always some people who will be living on the consumption of capital (e.g., holders of annuities), the demand for money should be less. Thus, the sale of nonmoney assets by those receiving no income in order to spend the proceeds on consumption is *dissaving,* and as such will tend to raise the rate of interest and depress capital values. But dissaving is not dishoarding, and it has no inherent tendency to cause dishoarding.

14.—The initiating expenditure, and each subsequent expenditure which continues the multiplier effect, it is said, must be spending which does not originate out of "current income." But one does not *spend income.* One *consumes income and capital* (income being "final services" *plus* the capital which would have been accumulated (net) over a period if there had been no consumption of assets over that period), and one *saves income. But one spends by changing the form of one's capital,* i.e., by decumulating holdings of money units in exchange for nonmoney assets. One *spends,* not income but money.

All spending is *out of holdings* of money which are normally in process of replenishment and sometimes of depletion or growth. The logical distinction is a two-fold one. We have (a) spending out of *individual holdings of money assets* which (i) people do not wish fully to replenish or (ii) people wish exactly to replenish, or (iii) people wish to hold more of (in short, all the factors which determine V),* and (b) out of *aggregate holdings of money units* which are (i) in process of depletion or (ii) constant or (iii) in process of growth (in short, spending which is possibly accompanied by changes in M). The factors under (a) influence only M_r, the aggregate real value of money, and the factors under (b) influence only M, the number of money units into which that real value is divided.

Keynesian economists as a whole have not, however, progressed even as far as Goodwin. They still generally hold (J. Lintner's words) that, once the schedule relation between consumption and saving is assumed fixed, a "stable relationship between fluctuations in investment and changes in the level of income."[37] has been determined.

---

*T being given.

15.—It has been suggested to me by an able critic (after reading my argument to this stage) that the notion of the "leakage" *can* be defended if it is treated merely as an analytical device for excluding from consideration all repercussions other than those which are implied in *the assumption* of a mechanical relationship between consumption and money income. His argument—put forward, I feel, more or less in the rôle of Devil's advocate—is as follows:

> When money income increases (necessarily—or probably—under the multiplier assumption, through an increase in expenditure on "investment"), consumption will increase at a rate determined by the propensity to consume. Now whilst it is true that further investment spending *might* occur as a consequence, we do not want to consider that, because it must be regarded either as initiating a new multiplier series superimposed, so to speak, on the first, or as introducing an accelerator effect. Hence from the standpoint of an analysis of the direct consequences of the original increase in money income, we must treat not only any hoarding induced, but any expenditure on investment induced, as a "leakage."

In developing this thesis my critic asks us to imagine M to be 100 at the outset, the income of the "income period" being therefore assumed to be 100. (The "income period" is that in which income reproduces itself, each money unit becoming income once).* He assumes then one single increase of expenditure on investment (due to an increase in M) of 10. (We can imagine the monetary authority or Treasury failing to do anything to maintain this additional expenditure on investment after the single initial "injection"). Assuming a multiplier of 2, money income for successive periods will be, according to the theory:

$$100 \quad 110 \quad 105 \quad 102.5 \quad 101.25 \quad 100.625$$
and the saving increments will be
$$0 \quad 0 \quad 5 \quad 2.5 \quad 1.25 \quad 0.625$$

An ultimate addition of 20 will have been contributed over time to money income received, but the rate of receipt of this income (per income period) will gradually have fallen back to its original magnitude of 100.

Now my interpretation of this example is that the increase in money income in the proportion 100 to 110 which, if V (expressed in terms of some fixed time interval) is constant, will remain at 110, is assumed

---

*This is a method of making abstraction of V which has, I am inclined to think, been partly responsible for the Keynesian failure to see that unconsumed income which is not "invested" *must* be hoarded. An assumed decline in V is fallaciously treated as a decline in M.

to be continuously reduced because the so-called "saving increments" are *assumed* (for purely analytical reasons) to be absorbed into hoarding. (This could be expressed as a decline in V, in terms of a fixed time interval). Hoarding remains the only conceivable alternative to the "investment" of the "saved" increment; yet there is never the slightest reason for assuming it!

My critic seems to claim that describing what is assumed to be hoarded by the adjective "saved" is a means of isolating the direct consequences of the initial "investment" increment. But that does not make any clearer what is meant. And as there is no reason why what is saved *should* be hoarded, all that is isolated is what would happen *if* all income saved *were* hoarded. It does not tell us why income does not continue at 110 which, on my critic's argument, is what *would* happen in the absence of hoarding.

Then, to illustrate the effect of *maintaining* a certain increase in the rate of "investment" (M increasing by 10 in each income period) my critic illustrates his position in the following table which shows, he thinks, "the direct consumption effects of each period's investment increment [of 10] superimposed one on the other in the subsequent periods."

MULTIPLIER OF 2

Immediate and subsequent effects of an increment of investment of 10 in period:	Income Period				
	1	2	3	4	5
1	10	5	2.5	1.25	0.625
2		10	5	2.5	1.25
3			10	5	2.5
4				10	5
5					10
Sum total of income increments:	10	15	17.5	18.75	19.375

The assumption is that the aggregate absorption of the successive additions to M (through hoarding) increases continuously until eventually these additions become wholly absorbed. It is a fantastic assumption. M is supposed to grow bigger and bigger whilst money income becomes stabilized at 120!

I am not sure, however, that my critic's example really does illustrate what most of the Keynesians have been imagining. It *is* possible to represent the reactions they claim without the assumption of hoarding. Let us assume that any part of an increment of increase which is not spent on "consumption" is spent on "investment." We do not need to drag in the accelerator to explain what happens. After the first increase in M by 10, the subsequent increases needed to maintain investment at the additional magnitude of 10 in subsequent periods will be (the multiplier being 2) 5, 2.5, 1.25, 0.625. . . . . The reactions may be set out as follows:*

MULTIPLIER OF 2

Immediate and subsequent effects of an increment of investment sufficient *to maintain* an additional annual *"investment"* of 10:

		Income Period					
		0	1	2	3	4	5
	1		*10	10	10	10	10
	2			*5	5	5	5
Income Period	3				*2.5	2.5	2.5
	4					*1.25	1.25
	5						*0.625
			10	15	17.5	18.75	19.375
Increment of Consumption			0	5	7.5	8.75	9.375
Income			110	115	117.5	118.75	119.375

*Successive additions to M assumed.

An ultimate doubling of the initial increase in M has resulted, and so an increase in the money income of 20 per cent. *per income period* (and hence—V being constant—*per annum*) has eventuated through the maintenance of the 10 per cent. increase in "investment." But that is not a *multiplication,* except in the sense that successive (decreasing) additions in M are *assumed* to have raised the original injection from 10 to 20! In this case, the explanation is not that an additional "injection" is needed to offset what is hoarded, but that the maintenance of the initial rate of increase in "investment" requires what is *regarded as* the multiplicand to be raised by successively declining amounts or, in the extreme case in which the marginal propensity to consume is unity, by constant amounts in each period. But if the initial increase in M is regarded as a multiplicand, so should subsequent increases in it. The true multiplier is then always unity! In other words, *the monetary authority, in*

*Our assumptions imply that V is constant. Hence the maintenance of any increased rate of investment per "income period" means the same increased rate per time period.

deciding to maintain a given increase in the rate of 'investment,' com-
mits itself to a series of increases in M; and the greater the marginal
propensity to consume, the larger the successive additions to M which
are required, *via* monetary policy, to achieve this end. Thus if the
marginal propensity to consume is ¾, the *commitment* of the authority
is ultimately to multiply the initial addition to M by 4. Only if the
propensity to consume is zero (the multiplier being unity) so that the
initial increase in "investment" maintains itself, will the monetary authority escape the obligation to increase M in the series I have explained.
And when (owing to the marginal propensity to consume being unity)
the same net addition to M is assumed to be made in each income
period, the ultimate increase in M will be infinite. *This is, I suggest,
the true explanation of what has been thought of as the infinite multiplier.* But there *is* no multiplication of anything.

The propensity to consume notion provides a wholly arbitrary formula for the assumption of a certain degree of inflation—a diminishing
rate of increase of M in each income period, but a steady rate of increase when the marginal propensity to consume is unity, and no subsequent increase when the propensity is zero.

*Exactly the same kind of effects will follow if a given level of addi-
tional expenditure is maintained on consumption,* except that if the
marginal propensity to consume is unity, the so-called multiplier will
then be unity, and if the marginal propensity to consume is zero, the
so-called multiplier will then be infinity. Obviously such effects have
nothing to do with leakages or with hoarding. They represent *the
purely formal consequences upon the magnitude M of a certain monetary policy,* i.e., with Keynes' multiplier, of maintaining a given additional rate of expenditure on "investment" when the marginal propensity to consume is positive. Exactly the same reasoning applies when
the initiating increase in investment (or consumption) expenditure is
supposed to be due to an increase in V ("newly activated money"),
except that there are obvious limits to the extent to which dishoarding
can occur and no limits to the extent to which M may be increased
except under some form of convertibility.

At this stage it is convenient once again to drop the untenable assumption that *spending* generates income. The rate of *spending* is a
consequence not a cause of the factors which determine M_r and M.
Spending does not influence money values. But *demand* (which may be
measured in money terms) does. Thus, an initial increase in M may
have its influence on prices *before* it is spent, i.e., through the negotia-
tions to purchase something on the part of those who have raised credit,
or even the mere knowledge of sellers that prospective purchasers have
raised this credit. The ability to spend influences values because it

confers the power to demand. The actual spending is a consequence,
(See Chap. VIII).

But every act of demand (which, *when it has done its work*, may lead
to the passing of money) has the same relevance to the value of the
money unit, and hence to the money valuation of income, and therefore in turn to the consequences of changes in that valuation upon the
withholding or release of capacity. It follows that, if expenditures on
investment initially and consumption subsequently, do have a different
effect on the money valuation of income from expenditures on consumption initially and investment subsequently, there must be some
reason why they have a different effect upon the demand for monetary
services or upon the number of money units. It is this simple thing
which has never been shown.

Although Keynes' multiplier effect rests on an arbitrary formula for a
certain rate of inflation (or noninflationary credit expansion if the release of withheld capacity is induced), neither Keynes nor his disciples
have perceived this. They have been concerned in a muddled way with
all the factors which determine demand for the services of money. The
phenomena which they have been trying to explain may be clearly
envisaged, I think, through the following very simple and wholly truistical proposition (a proposition which remains true even in the extreme cases in which the marginal propensity to consume is unity or
zero). An increase in M will not cause an increase in money income if
it is accompanied by *an offsetting decrease* in V. Nor will any cumulative monetary effects be experienced (apart from the multiplication of
an increase in M by V, or the multiplication of an increase in V by M!)
unless an increase in V is induced or a further increase in M follows
in consequence of some obligation contained in monetary policy.

17.—Now it is conceivable that, *owing to mere inertia*, a tendency for
money income to grow will be accompanied by a desire to hold *relatively* large cash balances. All sorts of conditions may be responsible
for the changing usefulness (i.e., productiveness) of money over short
periods, and so its aggregate real value. But this possibility (the recognition of which has, I think, prompted the unacceptable multiplier
thesis) seems to be of little practical importance. For such fluctuations
in nonspeculative demand, if identified, can always be met by the issue
or withdrawal of credit. It could be argued for instance that, if people
do find it convenient to hold more cash whilst they are deciding what
they can do with their increasing incomes, credit *can* expand without
any tendency to weaken the ability of the monetary authority to honor
its obligations. Hence, if it can be accepted that growing *real* income
is a cause of a more than proportionate short-term expansion in the

aggregate real value of money,* and that credit policy does not *automatically* cause the number of money units to increase in proportion to this expansion in real value (obviously through some misinterpretation of the situation), then it could be seriously argued that there is a problem to be tackled. The description of this problem in terms of the *marginal propensity to hoard* could then conceivably assist.

I suggest, therefore, that even if we accept the notion that expenditure influences the money valuation of income, it cannot be said that the reactions of "investment" expenditure upon "consumption" expenditure have any special consequences. But all factors which influence the money valuation of income initially may (a) *affect expectations and hence M_r,* and (b) *cause a reaction in monetary policy and hence affect M*; whilst (c) *both reactions may affect the release or withholding of capacity,* in which case the notion of multipliers (the "real income" and "employment" multipliers) might not be inappropriate ways of envisaging Say law reactions.

T. Wilson states that the multiplier (presumably both the "money income" and the "real income" multipliers) assumes "complete elasticity in the supply of funds" and "complete elasticity in the supply of consumers' goods."[38] Yet Keynes himself, and for a long time his disciples, explicitly and emphatically denied the former assumption, whilst Keynes did not explicitly state the second assumption and it is usually glossed over in the literature. If he had made those assumptions clear, most of the controversy could have been avoided. But do the textbooks (elementary or otherwise) which still deal with the multiplier state or place the necessary stress on these assumptions?

Samuelson has claimed that the multiplier explains "why an easy money policy is ineffective at the same time that deficit spending may be effective."[39] It does nothing of the kind. What it has done (intentionally or otherwise) has been to misdirect attention from monetary policy as such (concerned with the value of the money unit) to a politically favoured form of monetary policy—deficit spending.

18.—Finally, as I have already suggested (pp. 126-7, 271), if it can be assumed that there is a high elasticity of supply of services in general (which assumes a society in which there is much easily releasable withheld capacity, and in which, therefore, the money income multiplier is likely to equal the real income multiplier), it must be equally legitimate

---

*Generally speaking (as we have seen, (pp. 93-4) the aggregate real value of money tends to increase, as real income increases, in the same way that the aggregate value of land tends to increase, i.e., more or less *in proportion* but with a long-term tendency towards a more than proportional increase. The theory under examination implies that it expands *initially* more than proportionally to the real value of an expanding income.

to assume that very modest price (and wage-rate) adjustments* will be sufficient to restore full employment. For if, through a slight fall in "aggregate money demand" (the money valuation of income), a great deal of withheld capacity is induced, then there are reasons for assuming that, conversely, a small cut in certain prices is all that will be necessary to ensure the release of idle capacity. This is not, however, a relationship between elasticities which can be represented in demand and supply schedules, because it depends in part upon the release of capacity in one field being the source of demand which induces the release of capacity in noncompeting fields. We are again brought back to the circumstances in which the relevant demand and supply schedules are not independent.

Every increase in utilized capacity induces the release of, or growth in, capacity elsewhere. The value of a *multiplier* in this sense will depend solely (a) upon the degree of withheld capacity or wasteful employment of resources due to price disco-ordinations, or (b) in respect of growth calling forth growth, upon the extent to which the flow of services is versatile (as between consumption uses and net accumulation uses) and the rate at which savings respond to changes in entrepreneurial bidding (i.e., to interest), which means changes in prospective yields.

The *practical* harm wrought by thinking along "investment multiplier" lines has been that it has caused "investment" (expenditure in the process of net accumulation) to be regarded as a causal factor and not, as it ought to be regarded, as the result of the thrift which recovery normally induces.

But the *intellectual* harm has been indirectly even more serious. The conventional multiplier apparatus is rubbish. It should be expunged from the textbooks, its place being taken by an exposition of the dynamic implications of the Say Law.

---

*I do not suggest that modest price adjustments would be sufficient to ensure *optimum* employment as opposed to *full* employment of resources. The worst evils of restrictionism are by no means expressed in withheld capacity alone.

REFERENCES

(1) STIGLER, *Five Lectures on Economic Problems*, p.43. (2) HAWTREY, *Keynes and Supply Functions*, E.J., 1956, pp.483-4. (3) WILSON, *Professor Robertson on Effective Demand*, E.J., 1953, p.564. (4) HAGUE and STONIER, *The Essentials of Economics*, pp.87-8. (5) KEYNES, *The General Theory*, p.122. (6) *Ibid.*, p.123. (7) Keynes, in Q.J.E., 1936-7, reprinted in Harris, *The New Economics*, p.191. (8) HABERLER, Prosperity and Depression, p.230. (9) *Ibid.*, p.230. (10) HAGUE and STONIER, *op. cit.*, p.90. (11) Samuelson, *Period Analysis and Income Distribution*, Q.J.E., 1941-2, pp.577 *et seq.* (12) KEYNES, *The General Theory*, p.114. (13) *Ibid.*, p.119. (14) HAZLITT, *The Failure of the "New Economics,"* p.145. (15) HAGUE and STONIER, *op. cit.*, p.97. (16) E.g., HALM,

Monetary Theory, pp.399 & 402. (17) *Ibid.*, p.400. (18) HABERLER, *Mr. Keynes' Theory of the 'Multiplier': A Methodological Criticism*, in *Readings in Business Cycle Theory*, p.199. (19) KEYNES, *op. cit.*, p.117. (20) HABERLER, *Prosperity and Depression*, p.226. (21) MACHLUP, *Period Analysis and Multiplier Theory*, in *Readings in Business Cycle Theory*, p.220 n. (22) Vera Lutz, *Multiplier and Velocity Analysis, Economica*, 1955. (23) KEYNES, *op. cit.*, pp.119-120. (24) HIGGINS, *Keynesian Economics and Public Investment Policy*, in Harris, *op. cit.*, p.477. (25) HANSEN, *A Guide to Keynes*, pp.89-90. (26) KEYNES, *op. cit.*, p.161. (27) HALM, *op. cit.*, p.404. (28) *Ibid.*, p.404, including footnote. (29) MACHLUP, *op. cit.*, p.223. (30) *Ibid.*, p.223. (31) *Ibid.*, p.225. (32) GOODWIN, *The Multiplier*, in Harris, *op. cit.* (33) *Ibid.*, p.493. (34) *Ibid.*, p.486. (35) *Ibid.*, p.483. (36) *Ibid.*, p.485 n. (37) LINTNER, *The Theory of Money and Prices*, in Harris, *op. cit.*, p.527. (38) WILSON, *op. cit.*, p.564. (39) Samuelson, *op. cit.*, pp.602-3.

Chapter XIV

THE ACCELERATION FALLACY*

SUMMARY

*1.—I propose to show that irregularities of economic growth are not caused
by the acceleration of irregularities in consumption. 2.—Because all growth
in productive capacity is due to the achievement of savings (which may
be induced by the interest offered), 3.—the notion that decreased consumption
can cause a decline in the rate of growth is defensible only on the assumption of disco-ordinative reactions which cause the contraction of income
and savings. 4.—Neither net accumulation nor constructional activity is an
acceleration of an increase in current (or predicted) consumption or in current
(or predicted) output, but a response to saving preference. 5.—One would
expect periods of prosperity to be marked by both high consumption and high
constructional activity; 6.—but J. M. Clark (through unrealistic assumptions
which obscure the determinants of the concentration of construction over
time) enunciated influentially the theory that high constructional activity
is an acceleration of high consumption. 7.—In a* particular industry *in
which consumption is expected to grow, the bidding of services away from
other industries can permit a profitable net accumulation the value of
which must be,* for a short period, *more than proportional to consumption
of the product for the same period. But this is not an acceleration. 8.—In the
case of* all *industries, however, the services needed for net accumulation
must be bid away from consumption uses or released from withholding.
9.—The accelerationists believe that the relation of consumption to growth
can cause instability in an individual industry because they fallaciously compare an annual flow of output with a single addition to the stock of assets.
10.—The absence of anything resembling acceleration in an industry can
be represented diagrammatically. 11.—The rate of concentration over time
of an increase in the capacity of any industry is unrelated to the considerations raised under the acceleration theory. 12.—Current consumption
demands provide data relevant solely to predicted consumption demands,
whilst the latter are* determinants of the form and not of the magnitude of
*general growth. 13.—The invalid transfer of reasoning applicable to a
particular industry to the whole economy can be illustrated by Frisch's
theory of fluctuations. 14.—Hicks' treatment is concerned with changes in
aggregate output (not consumption) but, making arbitrary assumptions, and*

---

*In writing this chapter, I have been greatly assisted by A. D. Knox's article, *The
Acceleration Principle and the Theory of Investment* (Economica, 1952), although I
have not had cause to quote from it.

*ignoring such important factors as saving preference and the costs which
truly determine concentration of* construction *over time, he deduces a theory
of investment humps. 15.—But Timlin appears to have perceived the
real factors which determine such concentration. 16. Although the theory
that stability in the constructional industries depends on continuous growth
is fallacious, 17.—a fall in a former rate of growth* does *require re-allocations
of resources and cognate price adjustments. 18.—The accelerationists fail
to recognize that the release of capacity in the consumers' goods industries
exerts an expansionist, not a contractionist, influence. 19.—Kuznets' treatment, although avoiding the cruder errors, typically jumps from the particular
case to the general and fails to perceive that output grows because the
stock of assets grows (through savings) and not vice versa. 20.—Hayek's
treatment avoids the usual fallacy by stating that capital much larger than
its output is required,* over any short period, *but does not explicitly expose
the truism so stated. 21.—The suggestion that the underlying postulate of
the accelerator is that capital capacity may be excessive or deficient in
relation to output is meaningless. 22.—The accelerationists misinterpret
depression in the constructional industries due to wrong entrepreneurial
predictions aggravated by price rigidity; 23—they fail to see that specificity
of productive capacity under declining demand does not force waste,
24.—but provides correctives and tends rather to mitigate cyclical reactions;
25.—and they do not direct their criticisms of modern institutions against
the disco-ordinations so caused. 26.—Autonomous changes (economizing
discoveries, inventions, etc.) may have been responsible for discontinuities
in growth because, being spasmodic, they have induced and facilitated
irregular bursts of savings. 27.—Hence the achievement of economic stability
lies in the planning of institutions which permit the price adjustments
appropriate for the discontinuity of autonomous factors in progress.*

1.—Although Keynes cannot be held responsible for what is known as the "acceleration principle" or the "principle of accelerated or magnified derived demand" (for it is mentioned almost casually in *The General Theory,* and plays no part on his system), it has become part of the development and rationalization of his theories which I have called "Keynesianism." In particular, the acceleration fallacy (for I propose to show it to be such) has been married to the multiplier and has had an offspring of monstrously erroneous notions. I take this stand in spite of the fact that the acceleration principle itself is at least as old as this century, and in spite of the eminence of many of the economists whose authority has been responsible for the weight given to it in the last twenty-five years.

In its earlier and cruder form, the acceleration principle is based on the notion that the demand for and the rate of flow of services into "constructional activity" during any period is the manifestation of a magnified derived demand for consumption goods over that period. In a slightly less crude form, net accumulation ("investment") rather than "constructional activity" is the magnitude which is supposed to be accelerated. But over the years, economists have been perceiving absurdities in these earlier formulations; some of the more obviously untenable aspects have been tacitly—seldom explicitly—abandoned; and more sophisticated versions have emerged, versions which tend to deal with the relations of output and net accumulation rather than with the relations of consumption and constructional activity. I propose, nevertheless, to spend some time in examining what may be called "the consumption versions." Hence some readers may get the impression that I am criticising an already discarded approach. But I think it important to deal with the fallacy in all the major forms which it has assumed. It is my object in part to expose how seriously the contemporary tendency to concentrate on mechanical, mathematical analysis has been accompanied by a neglect of conceptual clarity, with the result that thinking about the salient problems of economic organization has been sadly vitiated.

Other readers may be easily convinced by the brief preliminary statement (which I begin in the following paragraph) of the case I propose to make against the "sophisticated versions." This short enunciation and refutation of those versions may save them the task of reading this chapter; although even the converted may find that there is something to be gained from the study of a preposterous and most tenaciously held error.

The sophisticated accelerationists contend that net accumulation (S) will tend to vary directly with the rate of growth of output (O), so that

$$S = k\frac{dO}{dt}$$

I contend, on the contrary, (a) that the magnitude *replacement + net accumulation* tends to vary *in direct proportion to* output and not *with the rate of change in* output; (b) that the magnitude *net accumulation* ("investment") is arbitrarily related to output because it is *an overlap*, dependent upon the rate of decumulation (consumption);* and (c) that fallacy lurks in the concept of the time increment, for when output is related to the provision of assets, *the minimum comparable time unit is the economic life of the assets.*† For instance, some accelerationists use the capital output ratio as a constant which describes the relation of net accumulation to output;‡ but because capital (unlike output) has no time dimension, they *assume*—quite arbitrarily—that the provision of additional capital occurs over the space of one year and is therefore comparable with output as a rate *per annum*.

I shall show that, *in particular industries*, the concentration over time of either (i) replacement + net accumulation or (ii) "constructional" activity is determined by factors which have no connection with the acceleration principle; that when we pass to *the co-ordinated economic system as a whole*, the provision of assets may be expected to vary, even in the short run, in direct proportion to output;** and that for such departures from this relationship as do occur, other factors (mainly due to disco-ordination, and unrelated to the accelerator) are responsible, e.g., the particular fields in which withheld capacity capable of release happens to exist.††

I return now to the "consumption version." That economic growth has in practice been more irregular than consumption has never been called into question. That the cause of this irregularity of growth is an acceleration or magnification of the irregularities of consumption is false. The intense use of productive capacity ("full employment" of *all*

---

*See pp. 296-9.
†See pp. 304-11.
‡E.g., Domar, Harrod, Matthews.
**See pp. 302-3. The only reason why output may lag is that additional utilized assets result in additional output and not *vice versa*.
††See pp. 311-14.

resources), although often accompanied by the growth of capacity, is neither the cause of nor dependent upon that growth. Similarly, the under-utilization of capacity, although often accompanied by the cessation of growth, or by a declining rate of growth of capacity, cannot be usefully said to cause or to be caused by the cessation of growth, or by a decline in the rate of growth. But withheld capacity in the constructional industries must develop when a decline in demand for growth is not accompanied by the co-ordinative price adjustments which the situation demands. And the services of highly specialized resources *may* (although rarely in practice) become valueless, and so idle even under price flexibility, when the rate of growth declines (in a particular industry or generally, owing to competing economic objectives being sought—including a decline in savings). Moreover, the productive condition which I have called *"pseudo-*idleness"* may be experienced in durable assets when variations occur in the rate of growth. All these things I propose to demonstrate in proving that that element in trade cycle theory which has become known as the "acceleration principle" is wrong.

In its most common form this principle builds on the theory that the demand for the services of the industries which manufacture assets is *derived from* current "consumption demand," but asserts further that a given increase in demand for consumption goods in the economy generally, results in *an accelerated or magnified demand for capital goods,* the latter bringing a *stimulus* to the whole economy.† Alternatively, the principle is expressed in the form that a given acceleration of the rate of consumption is essential to maintain a given level of demand for capital goods.

There are very good reasons why, in a society which is technically progressive‡ but in which economic institutions have not been moulded and administered so as to bring continuous *efficient* co-ordination through the value system, there should be periods in which productive power is expanding and periods in which it is stagnant or contracting. The theories which I am questioning are those which seek to account for this phenomenon, wholly or in part, by the suggestion that the boom in the constructional industries is due to an acceleration of a relatively small increase in consumption demand, and that the depression in these industries is due to an acceleration of a relatively small contraction in demand for consumers' goods.

---

*See below, pp. 322-3, 335-6 and my *Theory of Idle Resources,* Chap. III.

†Some economists, e.g., Hicks, accept the principle but deliberately avoid the consumption assumption, usually without criticising that assumption.(1) (See below, pp. 319-20).

‡By this, I mean a society in which inventions, discoveries and managerial ingenuities are achieving economies and diversifying economic life.

2.—It follows from my previous argument that all growth in the rate of growth* of real productive capacity is due to one or more of three things: (a) the diversion of the services of versatile resources from "consumption uses" to "net accumulation uses" (see p. 229 for a definition of these terms); (b) the growth of real income through current savings or the release of capacity, some of the additional income being devoted to net accumulation uses rather than to consumption uses; (c) (rigorously considered, a special case of (b)) the autonomous growth of real income, some of the additional income being devoted (in response to saving preference) to net accumulation uses rather than to consumption uses. In each case *the growth is due to saving preference having been sufficient* to cause the flow of services to be devoted in part to uses appropriate for additional accumulation instead of to the former rate of devotion to consumption uses (as in the case (a)), or instead of the devotion to consumption uses of the whole additional flow of real income (as in cases (b) and (c)).

If prospective yields rise for any reason (e.g., from general causes such as growth of utilized productive capacity, or special causes such as a realization that there are prospective economies to be derived from a switch from production methods requiring relatively little capital to those requiring much capital), the increased rate of interest *may* induce an increase in savings and so an increased rate of net accumulation *in general* (as distinct from increased net accumulation in one trade, accompanied by reduced net accumulation elsewhere). In the absence of such a reaction, only *the form* of the response to saving preference will be changed: the magnitudes, consumption and savings, will remain unchanged.

Some authorities have thought that a *transfer* of demand from one consumers' products to another can create a demand for an increased rate of net accumulation, in spite of the community not saving more.† But this is not possible. If consumers, in *spending* less on one product *do not induce withheld capacity*, but merely cause a fall in the prices of the services incorporated in it (or a fall in the value of the resources which provide the services, or a fall in values in that part of the constructional goods field which replaces those resources), whilst in spending more on the other product (to which their preference is directed) they *induce* the release of capacity in that part of the constructional goods field which can add to the capital resources employed, their action *may* be said to have induced a greater rate of net accumulation; *but only because the additional income due to the release of capacity*

---

*This includes a change from no growth to some growth, or from negative growth to no growth.

†Haberler has discussed this point.(2)

*happens to be saved.** Net accumulation is possible without a sacrifice
of consumption, only when real income is growing, whilst as we have
seen, even in that case, saving preference is still the command to which
net accumulation is the response.

In order to see these problems in a clear light it is essential, then, for
us to rid ourselves of the notion that growing consumption (or expenditure with a view to consumption) is the source of *realized demands* for
greater productive capacity as a whole. Such realized demands are, as we
have seen, dependent on (a) means to demand (the consequence of a
greater flow of all outputs, the growing productivity in any one sphere
being the origin of the demand for the growing productivity of all noncompeting spheres) and (b) saving preference. In short, the sources of
maintained and increased demands as a whole are replacement and net
accumulation respectively; and the extent to which growth results, depends upon the response to an expressed preference.

It is true that the value of all individual capital goods and the entrepreneurial inducement for their production is derived from *predicted*
ultimate consumption demand for their services. But just as the value of
a good represents its scarcity relation to (i.e., its rate of exchange with)
all other scarce things, so the crucial prediction is that the services of the
projected capital goods will be *preferred,* to a forecast extent, against all
other economic ends which are achievable through exchange. And if the
entrepreneur is relying, not on *the maintenance* of taste for his product,
or on a *transfer* of preference to it, but on *an increase of demands in
general,* then the phrase, "predicted consumption demand" can only be
taken to mean *a predicted flow of sufficient of those products which are
ultimately to be exchanged for the services of the resources provided and
for their replacement.* It is the expectation of the ability and willingness
of society to make an adequate real offer for future output, *and not the
expectation of consumption,* which is the determining factor in the
entrepreneurs' offer (i.e., interest).†

3.—*The value of the consumption of a period, plus the value of the
net accumulation of that period* has been defined above as *equal* to the
income of the period; and we have seen that there is no *use* of income,
i.e., of the flow of the services, which will make it possible for consumption in the form of decumulation to contract and net accumulation not
to grow, and *vice versa;* but if the co-ordinating machinery of the eco-

*Even so, the assumptions necessary in this example are most far-fetched.

†For instance, durable assets can be produced and their services *fully consumed*
during the physical life of the assets, although to secure this consumption it may be
necessary to price the services so low that the provision of the assets will prove to have
been hopelessly unprofitable. The mere fact that such consumption could have been
forecast would not have induced investment in the assets.

nomic system is working badly, and changes of preference as between consumption and savings are not accompanied by the required price adjustments (and especially if the dislocating rigidities are regarded as unstable),* *withheld capacity* will develop and cause *a shrinkage of real income.* In such circumstances, a decline in consumption may not be accompanied by an increase in net accumulation. On the contrary, savings (and hence net accumulation) may even contract. For the withheld capacity in the consumers' goods industries may give rise to doubts about whether *utilized* productive capacity is going to be maintained in the future, let alone increase; it will therefore tend to weaken entrepreneurs' faith in the power of the community to demand more things in the future, reduce their competition for savings and so, perhaps, reduce the flow of savings; and especially if the services which are devoted to net accumulation uses happen also to be rigidly priced, *withheld capacity will emerge in yet another sphere,* real income will decline still further, and an even greater decline in the rate of savings and net accumulation may be experienced.

Such a decline in net accumulation *is not caused by decreased consumption out of income. It is due to a decline in real income itself*—the consequence of disco-ordination. It is not a question of *savings* not being used—"running to waste instead of being invested"—but a question of *services* running to waste through being priced in a way which prevents their use. Saving-consumption decisions by themselves can affect the magnitude of the real income of society only in the sense that saving contributes to growth and consumption contributes to contraction. If, however, these decisions are *accompanied* by a situation which induces hoarding, or dishoarding, *money income* will tend to be affected,† and if this occurs in a society in which there is both monetary rigidity and price rigidity real income will be affected.

Having reminded the reader of the fallacy in the notion that the demand for replacement and net accumulation as a whole is derived from current or prospective consumption demand, we can consider the acceleration principle itself.

Let us assume initially (i) that all consumers' goods are immediately perishable (so that inventories of such products are negligible); (ii) that all producers' goods are absolutely durable (so that there is no replacement); (iii) that all producers' goods and labor are sufficiently versatile to permit their being diverted from making consumers' goods to making producers' goods; and (iv) that there is no withheld capacity.

As long as people do not on balance demand growth (wish to achieve

---

*For they will then induce speculative hoarding, which (unless offset by monetary policy) may induce a further withholding of capacity.

†It is the Keynesian assumption, of course, that this is always the position.

savings), there will be *no constructional activity* (manufacture of producers' goods) *at all;* but as soon as they do, and savings emerge, constructional activity will begin. This will mean an *infinite increase in
constructional activity* because it had previously been *nil.** It seems
obvious, however, that this is no *acceleration* of anything.†

Let us now drop assumptions (i) and (ii) and assume that consumers'
goods are not immediately perishable and producers' goods not absolutely
durable. There is now replacement not only of consumers' goods inventories decumulated but of producers' goods decumulated (i.e., depreciated). The latter is a form of constructional activity which is present in
the absence of growth.

When savings first emerge, the *composition* of gross accumulation
(i.e., activity in providing assets—inventories of consumers' goods *and*
producers' goods) will change. A smaller replacement of consumers' goods
will accompany a decline in decumulation of their inventories; the replacement of producers' goods will initially remain the same; and *net
accumulation* (equal in value to the decline in consumption of consumers' goods) representing the value of additional producers goods
being provided, *will increase by infinity,* i.e., from *nil* to something.
*Constructional activity will increase considerably, although not by in-
finity* because there was some replacement when savings were *nil;* but
the percentage increase will be greater the smaller replacement in that
form happened to be.

Now *the ratio so established is obviously in no sense an acceleration* of
either the consumption of consumers' goods or of consumption defined
to include depreciation of producers' goods. Yet the essence of the
accelerator is the notion of a *derived* acceleration. The resulting ratio is
simply a response to the community's wish to provide for the future, and
its magnitude (as distinct from its form) merely reflects that wish.

Let us now drop assumption (iv) that there is no withheld capacity,
and assume that there are no *irregularities* in the determinants of saving
propensities (i.e., that all changes in saving propensities are gradual).
The sole cause of irregularities in demand for the services of the *constructional* industries must then be irregularities in the degree of withheld capacity in the other industries. When that is the situation, increasing output (due to the release of capacity) does not at first require the
use of additional *fixed* resources. Thus, if there is much withheld capacity

---

*Baumol has reminded us[3] that dividing by *zero* does not justify the word "infinite." But if constructional activity previously is assumed to be positive but infinitely
small, the phrase "an infinite increase" *is* justified!

†Because the greater part of income is always consumed, with income initially constant a given percentage decline in consumption will always mean a much greater
percentage increase in savings (net accumulation) unless income contracts. But this
is the reverse of the acceleration principle.

in consumers' goods industries generally, the release of that capacity, if accompanied by savings, will lead to gross accumulation (of which net accumulation will make up a larger absolute amount) taking the form at first of net additions to inventories, work in progress, etc. Only later will additional fixed equipment begin to form a considerably larger proportion of gross accumulation.*

We see, then, that a different composition of net accumulation will be appropriate at different stages of the release of capacity in the consumers' goods industries. The additions required to *fixed equipment* (abstraction made of indivisibilities) will tend to be exactly proportional to the contemplated increase in output at the point of full employment, but not until that point has been reached. In respect of *net accumulation in all forms,* however, the additions required will be exactly proportional to the additional prospective output *at all times. The growing aggregate value of assets* (due to net accumulation) *will—the rate of interest being assumed constant—vary in direct proportion to the prospective value of future output.*

A consideration which may well, I think, mislead is the fact that the magnitude *savings* (net accumulation) always constitutes an over-lap of income over consumption, so that the smaller the proportion of income which is made up by current savings, the greater the percentage increase of any *absolute* increase in savings. Thus, if the growth in savings occurs not out of a constant income (in which case, as we have just seen, p. 297, second footnote, it means an acceleration of the amount by which consumption *contracts!*) but out of an expanding income, with consumption also expanding by a smaller *proportion,* it *looks* just as though the increased consumption has been accelerated. For example, if consumption is 1000 and savings are currently 100, and both consumption and savings now increase by 50 (income increasing by 100), consumption increases by 5 per cent, but savings by 50 per cent; if savings are currently 50 and both consumption and savings now increase by 50 (income increasing by 100), consumption increases by 5 per cent, but savings by 100 per cent; and if savings are currently *nil* and now increase by 50 (income increasing by 50) consumption increases by *nil* savings by infinity. This is a staring truism, of course. It is not represented as the acceleration principle itself, but it has, I think, somehow influenced thinking about it.

Simple logic, i.e., common sense, tells us that the *rate of growth of productive capacity* will (on the assumption that there is no withholding of the increasing capacity and no release of existing capacity) be directly

---

*But this point can be greatly exaggerated. If the community is saving steadily, entrepreneurs will demand additional equipment as well as replacement before there is congested use of existing fixed capacity, because they will anticipate future demand. It will pay them to purchase fixed assets whilst they are likely to be relatively cheap. p. 297, second footnote.

related to the *rate of growth in the flow of services provided by that capacity*. The casual significance here is that *a given rate of net accumulation* of capacity to produce causes *an increasing rate of flow of services*, and not *vice versa*. But the expectation of an increasing rate of growth of the flow of services (which is the expectation of a given rate of net accumulation) may, in the light of the Say law, be said to call forth further growth. That is, the expectation may raise the marginal prospective yield to replacement and net accumulation; this in turn may, perhaps, be assumed to induce a greater flow of savings. This is, however, almost the reverse of what has been in the minds of the accelerationists.

5.—In order to examine typical expositions of the accelerator in detail, it is necessary first of all to refer once again to the possibility of making a rigorous distinction between those industries working for consumption and those working for net accumulation. If we define *consumption industries* as those in which resources are devoted to "consumption uses" (i.e., which are used to produce final services consumed directly, or to produce goods of which stocks greater than current stocks cannot be profitably carried through time) we meet the difficulty that these are also the industries which produce for replacement. Most accelerationists talk of "the constructional industries" or some similar phrase. But even so, they envisage industries which work for both replacement *and* growth.

Benoit-Smullyan was, I think, the first accelerationist to ask the question, "Why should new or 'net' investment be supposed to have any different sort of origin or causation from that of replacement investment?" "Net investment is not," he maintains, "qualitatively distinct from other investment but is simply an *amount* of investment larger than necessary for replacement purposes."[5] But I think that neither he nor subsequent accelerationists have adequately faced the issue. In fact there *is* no rigorous line of division. All that we can do is to define *the constructional industries* as those engaged in producing capital resources of a relatively high order or of a relatively high durability. In doing so, it is important that we should not forget that we are rather *arbitrarily* cutting off one part of replacement and net accumulation.

Some economists, possibly because they have perceived the arbitrariness of the concept of the "constructional industries," have stressed rather the relationship of consumption, or sales, or output to "investment," i.e., net accumulation as a whole;* and others have held that the principle applies equally to all forms of *gross accumulation* and that there is to some extent an acceleration of investment in consumers' goods

---

*E.g., Baumol[4] regards "investment" (I) as an acceleration of sales (s). He gives the formula: $I = k \frac{ds}{dt}$

inventories as consumption increases. Moreover, most accelerationists clearly assume that high activity in the constructional industries implies net accumulation. The implication seems always to be therefore that growing rates of consumption, or sales, or output, accelerate net accumulation.

The essential truth is, I suggest, that real income being given, net accumulation must vary *inversely* with consumption, representing as it does a transfer of services from consumption uses to net accumulation uses; and if real income is expanding, it is still true that the greater the flow of services into consumption uses, the smaller the flow into net accumulation uses, unless specialized idle capacity released in producers' goods industries happens to demand no transfer of versatile resources from consumers' goods industries. Net accumulation is *stimulated* through the relative contraction, not the relative expansion of consumption.

6.—We can now turn to the pioneer contribution of J. M. Clark, in 1917, which can be taken as having introduced the fallacy.* The immediate inspiration of Clark's thesis was the publication of Mitchell's synthesis of data and hypotheses in his *Business Cycles*. Mitchell's tables and graphs suggested (i) that periods of prosperity were usually periods of growth of productive capacity, as well as periods of high consumption; and (ii) that during such periods the output of the construction industries tended to increase more than proportionally to the increase in the output of the consumers' goods industries. It was just as everyone would have supposed that periods of prosperity would have been (a) periods of exceptional provision for the future, and (b) periods in which, owing to the growing productive power (and hence growing consumption power), gross accumulation would tend to take the form of goods of a relatively high order (i.e., generally speaking the sort of capital goods suggested by the term "constructional industries").

But such orthodox explanations were not enough for J. M. Clark, who immediately tried to show that the rate of consumption and the rate of activity in the constructional industries (producers' goods in general and raw materials) were causally connected in such a way that any increase in consumption was the cause of an intensified increase in the accumulation of capital goods. This "intensification," he thought, was a cause of disturbance and a strain on the economic system. He described the demand for consumers' goods as being "handed on"[6] in the form of a demand for capital goods and the materials, etc., which make them.

---

*There were earlier articles in which the acceleration notion appeared, by Carver and Bickerdike, to the second of which I shall shortly refer: but these contributions do not appear to have influenced Clark or subsequent writers.

Replacement and *net accumulation** in response to the demand "handed on," he contended, "follow different laws"; [7] for the former varies, he said, "roughly with the speed" at which consumers' goods are taken off the market whilst the latter depends upon "the acceleration." [8] But if we define replacement (including maintenance) rigorously, as that part of gross accumulation which makes good consumption in the form of decumulation, then it is clear that the magnitude, net accumulation, increases relatively to consumption only because it is an overlap!

However, Clark thought that he had found an important "mechanical law." [9] He illustrated it by means of assumptions "on a simplified basis" which included *the ignoring of price,* and imagining that ". . . . finished goods are turned out as fast as wanted, and materials and means of production are instantly supplied as fast as the process of finishing requires them." [10] He thus assumed away what I shall shortly suggest are the crucial determinants of the *concentration* of the production of particular capital goods over time; and in so doing, he set an example which has been followed subsequently by most of the accelerationists.

Clark explained that he assumed this "impossibly fluid condition of industry" [11] . . . . "simply in order to have some figures that would not be too complicated," [12] a method which teems with dangers unless the author refrains scrupulously from drawing conclusions before replacing the simplified assumptions with realistic assumptions. But the only amendment of the assumptions he subsequently brought in was the admission that ". . . . In fact, the supply [of new construction] is almost certain to fall behind the demand, thus lessening the amount of the overrun and of the ultimate revulsion without altering the principle at work." [13] And in his diagram illustrating the demand for durable means of production, [14] he included a curve to represent "the work of supplying the derived demand as lagging somewhat." [15] In these passages he was hinting vaguely at the real factors which determine the concentration of growth over time. But he left the matter here and expected the reader to "supply for himself an allowance for the elements that are not included in the formula." [16] It is a pity that he did not attempt to assist the reader in this vitally relevant task. At the same time, he did not hesitate to draw far-reaching conclusions about the "disturbances" and the "strain" to the economic system he thought his formula disclosed.

Only when he came to the question of what determines the size of stocks (inventories) did he feel that he must consider "what is profitable, rather than merely what is *physically necessary*" [17] (my italics), and

---

*He did not use these terms of course: I am paraphrasing and using what seem to me to be clarifying concepts.

†I think that this was the first use of the term "acceleration" in this connection. The word occurs also, of course, in the title of the article.

very briefly he touched, without gripping, the real issue. That is, he referred to the possibilities of "an extremely sharp rise in supply prices . . . . the inability of manufacturers to make deliveries," together with the quite separate, but relevant consideration, "the fear that the prosperity is temporary."[18] Moreover, in his 1936 reply to the criticisms of Kuznets (discussed below), he agreed that his mechanical formula, ". . . . if taken as a picture of what must happen in real life, ... would involve the absurd condition that . . . . producers of productive equipment have always enough excess capacity to handle instantly any demand which may be put upon them."[19] But in just what manner the scarcity of resources in the constructional industries may influence the degree of *concentration in time* of activity in the supply of particular durable resources, or of durable resources in general, he still failed (like subsequent accelerationists) to discuss.

7.—Let us remind ourselves of the incentives to replacement and net accumulation in the case of *an individual firm*. When specific *replacement* (of inventories of a *particular consumers' good* or of the plant which makes it) accompanies decumulation, it is due to an entrepreneurial prediction (a) that there will be no *transfer* of taste towards other things over the disinvestment period, and (b) that the flow of other services in general (real income) which constitutes the source of demand for that consumers' product (as well as for all other products) will not decline. When *net accumulation* of the same kind occurs, it is due to the prediction that there will be a greater future demand for the product of the resources accumulated, due either (a) to a *transfer* of taste to that product or (b) to an increased supply of other things in general (real income) which is expected to cause an increased demand for it. And the latter may be due to (i) the net accumulation of resources having occurred in noncompeting fields or (ii) the release of withheld capacity in noncompeting fields.

Provided we recognize that there is nothing which could be properly called an acceleration, we may say that current demand for producers' goods *in a particular industry* depends, not upon current demand for the final product, but upon the way that demand is expected to change or fluctuate in the future (the expected changes or fluctuations being strongly influenced, perhaps, by the way in which demand has been changing or fluctuating in the immediate or distant past). But this describes (it does not *explain*) only the relation between prospective demand for the final product and demand for capital resources *in a single industry*; and in such a case the increase in predicted demand for the one final product implies either a decline in predicted demand for some other final product or, in the case in which real income is increasing, a reduction of what the demand for some other product would otherwise have been. (I return to this point below).

We may say also (again provided it is recognized that there is no acceleration) that *ceteris paribus* the amplitude of fluctuations in a *particular* constructional industry will be greater the more durable are the products of that industry. This is less of a truism, but still rather obvious. For the more an industry which can respond to a demand for growth is normally busy with maintenance and replacement of its products,* the narrower will be the range of variations between periods in which future consumption demand is expected to exceed current demand and periods when it is not. For example, in the extreme case of an industry producing an output of capital goods which never depreciate, there will be no demand for its services at all except in periods in which demand for the final product is expected to be the greater in future. The source of the increased output of capital assets when the industry is growing, is a diversion of the flow of services from the other industries from which demand has been transferred. If the flow of services happens to be increasing, the same sort of outbidding of other industries must still occur.

8.—When we are concerned with the demand for *all* final products, however, a predicted increased demand for them implies *not a predicted transfer of demand, but a predicted growth in power to demand,* i.e., in *utilized productive capacity,* or real income; and *the rate of net accumulation which results will be greater, the smaller the proportion of real income which is devoted to consumption uses.* But from the very first major contribution to the accelerationist literature (that of Bickerdike, in 1914)[20] the accelerationists appear to have believed the reverse, through assuming that what applies to the case of a particular industry must apply to the economy in general. How common this sort of blunder has been in the history of economic thought!† In the economy as a whole, the rate of net accumulation can increase solely through the outbidding of "consumption uses" in favor of "net accumulation uses" for the flow of services (the successful offer of interest) unless appropriately specialized withheld capacity can be released.‡

9.—It seems to me that this simple argument refutes the whole acceleration theory. But it might still be contended that the relation between consumption and growth causes serious instabilities in individual industries, or in certain important groups of industries, such as the constructional industries. I propose, therefore, to consider the acceleration alleged in the case of an individual industry in the constructional field.

---

*The products being capital goods.
†J. S. Mill referred to this sort of error as early as 1830.[21]
‡See pp. 232, 300.

Let us consider carefully exactly how the accelerator is supposed to affect the growth of capacity under the following assumptions: (a) in a particular industry, (b) where there are *intensively used and absolutely durable* assets providing "final services" in the industry* (i.e., under the conditions in which the accelerator is usually regarded as having its most powerful effects), and (c) when it is *predicted* and not *current* consumption demand, which is supposed to provide the "stimulus." These assumptions, particularly (c), enable us to consider the principle in its least unreasonable form.

In order to bring about a response in greater output, following a predicted transfer of demand to the product of the industry in question, the output of the constructional trades serving the industry must, for a time, be *something*, in comparison with a previous nothing. Because there has previously been no replacement, any expansion, however small, must involve a proportion of infinity† between replacement and expansion. Thus, an increase of *1 per cent* in predicted consumption demand must result in an *infinite* increase in demand for the capital resources needed, however long the period over which services flow into the additional resources. The acceleration (i.e., the relation to 1 per cent) will be infinity!

This barren truism remains barren even when economists wrap it up in imposing variations and formulae. But it becomes seriously fallacious when finite accelerations are considered.

A predicted demand for a given percentage addition to *the flow* of a particular consumers' product at its current price, leads (given the assumption that resources are fully used and absolutely durable) to a demand for the same percentage addition to *the stock* of producers' goods which make it, at their current price. But the "accelerationists" seem always to compare *a percentage increase in the rate of demand* for a particular consumers' product, with the demand for *a single percentage addition to the stock* of the producers' goods which make the product. That is, an increase in the rate of demand for the consumers' product is customarily expressed as a percentage increase *per annum* (although it is, of course, the same percentage increase per month, or per week, or per day!). The demand for the same percentage addition to the stock of resources, *which is not a rate at all*, is next described as the same percentage increase in demand *per annum*.

Haberler, the most acute and reasonable of those who make use of the acceleration principle,‡ illustrates it, as do most of the accelerationists,

---

*By "absolutely durable" resources, I mean what Kuznets has called "capital goods of eternal life," or "of infinite use in time."

†See first footnote to p. 297.

‡It is with reluctance that I choose Haberler for criticism. I do so because he is my strongest opponent on this issue, which is one of the few issues on which I dis-

by an example which involves replacement. He supposes the demand for shoes to increase by 10 per cent (per week, month, year, etc.!). The capacity of the industry is taken to be 500 machines, and the *annual* replacement 50 machines per annum. The 10 per cent demand increase, he says, "*necessitates* an increase of 10 per cent in the stock of fixed capital—that is, an additional production of machinery of 50, which brings *the total production of machines from 50 to 100*. So an increase of 10 per cent in the demand for, and production of, finished goods necessitates an increase of 100 per cent *in the annual production of equipment*."[22] (My italics). Let us *assume* that what is "necessitated" as demand can in fact occur as production, i.e., that factor prices in the relevant constructional industries do not increase. If we calculate by the week instead of the year, the spread of the *replacement* imagined will be at the rate of about one machine per week. And if we now imagine the whole fifty additional machines being provided in one week, can we say, realistically or usefully, that during that week there has been a magnification of *demand*, in the machine construction industry, of 5000 per cent? Surely *demand* in the constructional industries, conceived of as a *rate of demand*, is just as independent of the time period by which we measure as is the rate of demand for consumers' goods. If we take a longer period than a year for our calculation, say the assumed life of a machine (which is ten years in this example) or any longer period, *then the increase in the rate of demand for the machines is seen to be exactly proportional to the increase in the demand for shoes, i.e., 10 per cent.* Eleven machines will be demanded in the future for every ten which were demanded in the earlier period. I suggest that the economic life-span of the machines is the minimum justifiable period to take.* Any smaller period is hopelessly arbitrary and can lead to absurd results. (See below, pp. 310-11).

Sometimes the word "annual" (meaning for one year) is omitted, thereby enhancing the fallacious implications still further. For instance, Bretherton, Burchardt and Rutherford contend that "a 5 per cent increase in the demand for house-room should mean, if houses last on the average 50 years, an increase of 250 per cent in the activity of builders."[23] The qualification which should have been added to those words is: "in the year following the 5 per cent increase in consumption demand, and *assuming* that the supply of additional houses needed is concentrated at an even rate over that year."

---

agree with him. I have learned so much from his writings, and I have acquired such a respect for his logic, that when I differ from him, my first impulse is to tell myself that I must be wrong.

*I refer here to the *economic* life-span of the plant because its *physical* life-span may be irrelevant. The entrepreneur may expect the demand for the services of the plant he provides to be shortlived, whilst it is technically impossible to provide, more economically, a plant which is cheaper by reason of a lower degree of durability.

The same fallacy (also enhanced by the omission of the word "annual") is found in the example which Samuelson uses. He says, "Sales have gone up by 50 per cent. How much has machine production gone up? By 1000 per cent!"[24] But his 50 per cent and his 1000 per cent (like the 5 per cent and the 250 per cent of the previous example, and Haberler's 10 per cent and 100 per cent) are only comparable ratios when it can be assumed that there will be similar and regular absolute increases in output in subsequent years, in which case both magnitudes are independent of the time unit. Samuelson omits the crucial qualification, namely, "if we compare the regularly recurring replacement of machinery with the single addition to the stock of machines, which is *assumed* to be evenly concentrated over the period of comparison."

Suppose that a small increase in predicted consumption demand leads to an investment in an additional machine, the life of which is x years. If we imagine this predicted consumption demand being projected over the whole future, the constructional industries will be confronted with an additional predicted *and steady* replacement demand of one machine every x years; and the increased future rate of construction *plus* the increase in predicted payment for the services of the machines will be *proportional to* the increase in predicted consumption demand. The additional capital resources are merely, so to speak, the first replacement of the additional capacity demanded.

The assumption (tacit or otherwise) nearly always is that ". . . . both demand for finished goods and demand for capital goods are satisfied within the time unit in which such demand becomes apparent,"[25] which is Kuznets' comment on Clark's 1917 contribution. Moreover, Kuznets reminds us that Clark's assumptions involve "a definite and conscious neglect of some very important factors in determining the demand for capital goods—price changes, the period of production, credit availability, and so forth."[26] These are only some of the factors which determine the spread over time of demand for the embodiment of services into resources. But I cannot see that Kuznets' 1935 criticisms on these points, although never convincingly answered, have affected the form of subsequent expositions of the accelerator, with the exception of Hayek's brief references to the topic.

10.—Let us represent the various possibilities of acceleration in *individual industries* in simple diagrams. For if there *is* anything which, given the ordinary and accepted meaning of words, can be described as an "acceleration" or "magnification," then that is the very thing which diagrammatic treatment ought to bring out. We can best start by returning to the extreme assumption that all assets used to produce a particular consumption good are *absolutely durable* and intensively utilized, the product consisting solely of services, whilst the flow of the product varies directly with the stock of assets.

Consider the case in which there is only one increase in the demand for the flow of services, and that it is expected to be a permanent increase. There will then be only one demand, *at a point of time*, for an addition to the stock of equipment. Assuming that there is a full response (i.e., that an increased supply of services to meet the rise in demand means that the price of services does not increase), the stock of equipment will increase proportionally. That will mean an "acceleration" (of infinity!) in construction activity, like this:

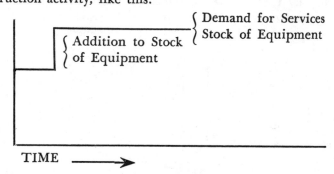

DIAGRAM III

The two curves (one representing a rate and the other a stock) will coincide on a common base line. The demand for equipment over the same time period can be represented only by a vertical line at the point of increased demand, like this:

DIAGRAM IV

Here we have the truism in its most blatant form.

If there is a similar increase in demand after the lapse of a certain period, and then yet another after the same interval, like this:

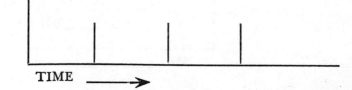

DIAGRAM V

we can begin to think of the *rate of demand* for equipment, (meaning the rate of demand for the flow of services incorporated into equipment), like this:

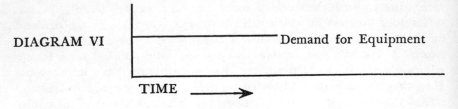

DIAGRAM VI

Let us suppose next that predicted consumption demand is increasing by a given *absolute* amount per annum. The demand for additional capital equipment will *not* then increase more than proportionally to the demand for services (which *would* mean an acceleration*), like this:

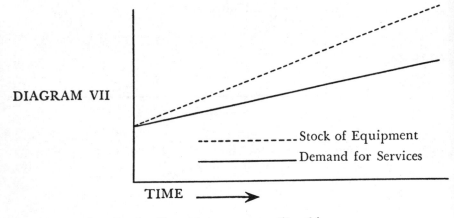

DIAGRAM VII

but proportionally, in discontinuous steps, like this:

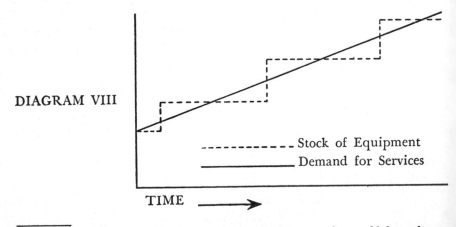

DIAGRAM VIII

---

*I do not suggest of course that any accelerationist economist would have drawn such curves. But many students are under the impression that that is what is implied.

The vertical lines in the curve for "stock of equipment," which are equal to one another, represent the realized demands for additional equipment at different points of time. The larger the economic unit of supply, the larger will be the steps, in both dimensions. The *rate of demand* for equipment over the whole period may be expressed as in Diagrams V and VI. That is, whatever the slope of the curve in Diagram VIII, *even if it is horizontal*, the demand for equipment will be just as steady.

Consider, in the light of these diagrams, the proposition that "slight changes in the demand for consumers' goods produce *much more violent* variations in the demand for producers' goods," or that "changes in demand for consumers' goods are transmitted with increasing intensity to the higher stages of production."[27] These diagrams all represent cases in which the "violence" is at its greatest, namely, when each acceleration is theoretically infinite!

If we imagine instead *a steady percentage increase in demand* for services, we can best represent the same data on a diagram like Diagram VIII, but with a ratio vertical scale. The successive steps in the "stock of equipment curve" will then get smaller in both dimensions (because the economic size of the unit of supply will represent a successively smaller proportion of the whole stock, and because the interval between the supply of each unit will diminish).

The curve of demand for equipment (on an absolute scale) will, however, be like this:

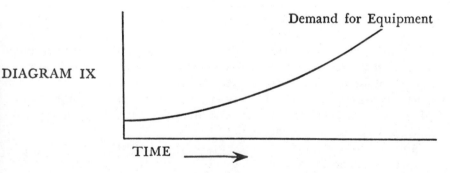

DIAGRAM IX

Demand for Equipment

TIME ⟶

not because of any *acceleration*, but simply because a constant percentage increase to the stock means a rising absolute amount.

And if there is a declining rate of increase in demand for services and capacity, we can expect a proportional decline in the rate of addition to capacity, like this:*

---

*An increasing rate of increase of demand for services can, of course, be similarly represented, the intervals between the acquisition of equipment declining.

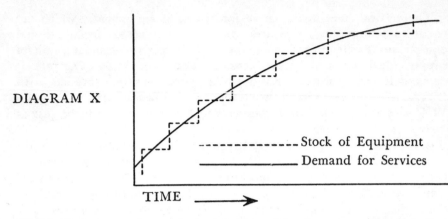

DIAGRAM X

- - - - - - - - - - Stock of Equipment
——————————— Demand for Services

TIME ——————→

The declining rate of growth (or of demand in the constructional industries) is represented in the growing intervals between the acquisition of
units of equipment. But it may be represented, alternatively, like this:

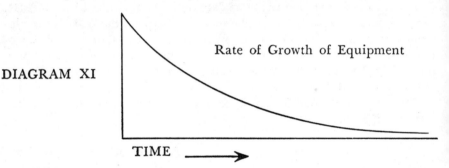

DIAGRAM XI

Rate of Growth of Equipment

TIME ——————→

It is hardly any less of a truism. There is a declining demand for growth
in the industry represented and a response in a declining rate of growth.
And we must not forget that, over the period represented, there is a
slowly increasing demand for the services of the stock of equipment, or
(if we turn for a moment to the case in which there is some depreciation) for services *plus* replacement.

   Must we not conclude that the appropriate comparison of changes in
predicted demand for consumers' goods is not with the amount of equipment which is provided *over a year*, but either (i) with that which is
ordered at a particular moment of time (in which case percentage com-
parisons are invalid, because we cannot then conceive of a *rate* of demand
for equipment) or (ii) with the rate at which any additional equipment
provided will be renewed, or accumulated further, *over a period of time
which is long enough to give the notion of a "rate" some meaning?* The
minimum appropriate period to permit us to conceive of *a rate of supply*
tends to become longer the more durable the resources in question. If
we want a comparable rate, i.e., a rate of flow for additions to or replace-

ments of a stock, then we must take a period sufficiently long to permit each recurrence of the economic life of a piece of plant to be treated as one of the events which are to be counted in relation to time (see above, pp. 305-6). The usual view is that "the degree of magnification of derived demand depends *ceteris paribus* upon the durability of the machines."[28] and that when "there are no durable means of production. . . . . there is no magnification at all."[29] But this is merely another way of stating the platitude that the proportion between *any net accumulation required for a given increase of final output* and *replacement* will be greater, for any period less than the economic life of the plant, the more durable the resources happen to be, and "infinite" when the resources are absolutely durable (simply because replacement is then zero). The truism becomes a fallacy when this comparison with the rate of replacement is regarded as significant. The ratio tells us precisely nothing about the times at which, or the periods into which, the concentration of gross accumulation (or replacement itself) or of the "constructional" part of accumulation, becomes profitable; and that is what we want to know. Moreover, there is *never* any magnification.

11.—It is true that, a demand for an additional stock of certain assets having arisen, and an order for this stock having been placed, we shall get a certain rate of flow of services which are being embodied into the required stock (or a flow out of another kind of stock—materials and parts—from existing inventories). But the determinants of *this* rate can have nothing whatever to do with the accelerator. An eminent critic has asked whether I suggest that it is "absurd to investigate how much investment in, say, power plants and railroads will be in the next three or four years," whilst these assets will last much longer than that. No. But I do suggest that, if the demand for the additional stock is due to an increase in the rate of predicted consumption demand of x per cent, this rate will be completely *unrelated* to the number of years over which it is going to be profitable *to concentrate* the embodiment of services into the additional stock. My critic uses the phrase, "three or four years." But why that degree of concentration? Why not three or four *months*, or *decades*?

Let us take the case of the cable of an aerial railway which, owing to weathering, must by law be renewed every five years. The rate of demand (replacement) will then be one cable per five years, in spite of the fact that the order for a cable having been placed well in advance, the services of necessary equipment and labor will be absorbed into the cables for only a day, or a week, or a month at some point of time which (given other demands for such services) is considered most economic. This kind of *concentration* of production applies, it should be noticed, equally to replacement.

Suppose there are originally 100 such aerial railways in Switzerland,

and that we are considering an increase in predicted consumption demand of 10 per cent. Let us *assume* that the rate at which new cables are demanded also increases by 10 per cent—proportionally and at current costs. The condition "at current costs" may make it essential that the resources which make each cable shall be employed for that purpose only for small periods of time, possibly at random intervals. If, for some reason, the 10 per cent increase in demand for cables is followed by the whole of the increased production being concentrated into a short period, that will be due to the economies of such a concentration of production in time in relation to the rate at which predicted consumption demand has been increasing.

Ceteris paribus, the *less* idle capacity which exists in the aerial railways themselves and the *more* idle capacity there happens to be in the relevant part of the construction industries field, the earlier can we expect an addition to the stock to occur (following a predicted increase in consumption demand) and the greater any resulting *concentration* of production. But there are other factors influencing the economies of concentration in time. Thus, a sudden increase in predicted consumption demand ("burst of optimism") may lead not only to the immediate placing of orders, but also to a willingness to incur the additional costs attendant upon rushed, urgent orders, which cannot "wait their turn." Do any of these factors, which determine the degree of such concentration, have any connection with the accelerator?

The greater the rate of increase in the flow of services into additional stock, the shorter will be the duration of this flow. The diagram below illustrates the complete independence of the determinants of *concentration* from the considerations raised in discussions of the acceleration

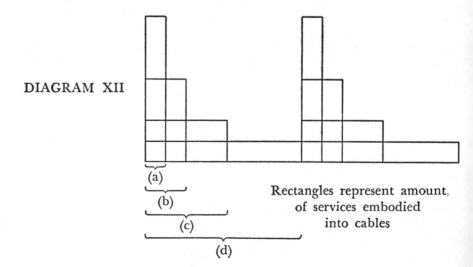

DIAGRAM XII

(a)
(b)
(c)
(d)

Rectangles represent amount,
of services embodied
into cables

principle. It represents different degrees of concentration which are possible *under pure replacement demand,* namely, the replacement of cables of which the legal life is five years.

The rectangles represent the *amount of services* embodied into the whole 110 cables. The horizontal sides represent *the period* over which services actually flow into these cables, and the vertical sides represent *the rate* at which this flow occurs. (d) represents the life of a cable. The equipment necessary *might* be kept going steadily in this use over the whole period, (d).* On the other hand, the production of the cables might be concentrated into periods (a), or (b), or (c), when it pays to specialize. But whatever the spread over time, *the rate of demand for cables* is the same. We get the same number of units provided over time, although the *response* to any increase of demand may be differently concentrated over time. No one would contend that the accelerator has anything to do with *this* concentration. But when the acceleration theorists talk of an accelerated percentage increase in the "annual" rate of provision of equipment for an industry, they are in fact *assuming* such a concentration *into a single year.*

A whole host of factors on the supply side may affect the degree of concentration. Thus, in the case of any particular industry, a large minimum efficient unit of supply of capital equipment will mean that many small increases in consumption demand will be responded to, not by a growth in the stock of equipment but in the more intensive use of existing equipment at higher production costs.† In these circumstances, one small *further* increase in predicted consumption demand, following on a large number of *previous* small increases, will ultimately be sufficient to induce a large investment in equipment, e.g., three months' employment for a small foundry and six men. Obviously, the accelerator has nothing to do with such a concentration in time, or the relation between the small increase in consumption demand and the large unit of equipment which is forthcoming.

Whenever any undertaking or industry grows, it is a response to an increased predicted demand for particular consumers' goods or particular producers' goods; and the value of the equipment supplied will be much greater than the value of its product (which includes the value of replacement) over *any short period.*‡ But I fail to recognize any significance in this self-evident relationship.

12.—The sources of confusion with which I have been dealing are aggravated when simplified but highly misleading assumptions are

*As we are considering the replacement of the whole 110 cables, an even spread over (d) is the more probable.
†The "cushioning effect" so caused is discussed later, pp. 335-6.
‡See below, pp. 329-331.

adopted about the relations of current demand and expectations. Thus, in discussing Samuelson's argument above I assumed that the term "consumption" refers to *predicted consumption*. But the context of the passage I quoted makes it clear that it is *current* consumption which is envisaged; and explicitly or implicitly, most of the accelerationists stress *current* consumption demand.

In reality, however, no rational business man ever treats current demand as more than *evidence* which may be relevant to the intensity of future demand for his product, and he would be foolish if he did. According to the proportion in which the capital resources needed to produce a particular consumers' good are durable or specific (as distinct from rapidly replaced or versatile) *current consumption demand* becomes only indirectly relevant, and *predicted consumption demand* becomes the sole determinant of *the form* of accumulation. Admittedly, the current rate of decumulation of a product, or the current rate of consumption of final services, at current prices, are *data* on which the entrepreneur may forecast by extrapolation. Indeed, as we have seen, it is through "voting," by actual purchases in the market, that "consumers' sovereignty" is normally expressed; and the "consumers' vote" may usually be interpreted in practice as for the continued production of the particular commodity purchased. Yet discussion of the exceptions takes up a large part of the time of every realistic teacher of business administration.

In statements of the acceleration principle, however, neither the words "prospective," nor "predicted," nor other words with a similar meaning, are normally used to qualify "consumption demand" (or equivalent expression), even by those writers who, at some point or other, appear to recognize the point I am making. There seems to be, thus, real confusion about the determinants of the *form*, let alone the *amount* of accumulation. For instance, until recently at any rate the common view, as summarized by Haberler, was that it is only with "adventurous kinds of investments"[30] that *future* demand is the determining factor. He says that "the acceleration principle in its more rigorous form is concerned . . . . [with] . . . . investments, in working and fixed capital, which follow more or less closely the ups and downs of consumers' demand."*[31] Well, we might define "unadventurous investments" as those in which predicted demand for the product may be safely accepted as coincident with current demand. But projects tend to be "adventurous" in proportion to the extent to which the assets needed are durable, whilst it is generally accepted, by Haberler as well as others, that the degree of acceleration is dependent upon the degree of durabil-

---

*By "consumers' demand," here, is meant "current demand."

ity of such assets.[32] There certainly appears to be some contradiction involved.

It seems to me therefore that even the "unadventurous" kinds of investment give rise to no exception to the rule that the form (including durability, specificity, roundaboutness) of accumulation is determined (on the demand side) *solely* by the predicted consumption demand for each kind of good over the whole life of the projected assets, and not at all by the current consumption demand for the different kinds of goods.*

Some of the accelerationists do, it is true, explicitly distinguish between the effects of "current" or "actual" consumption demand and "anticipated" consumption demand, but current demand is then apparently regarded as having almost mechanical or automatic "acceleration" consequences in justifying the provision or nonprovision of additional capital goods. Only anticipated demand is treated as subject to the vaguer factors of gloom or optimism, and it is supposed to be able to cause *an exaggeration* of the acceleration in one or other direction.[33] How wrong the distinction is!

Admittedly, there may be evidence to support the view that entrepreneurs tend in practice to be unduly influenced in their judgment by events of the recent past, including recent prices. This is a highly relevant consideration in the so-called psychological theories of the trade cycle (if it includes the understanding that such cycles of growth must be determined by cycles of interest-induced savings). But it by no means permits us to assume that the representative entrepreneur does not carefully weigh up the future when he plans large investments in specific form.† Such decisions are in fact normally influenced by a whole host of factors. Indeed, Schumpeter has classified the sort of considerations which have been empirically observed to be relevant under 41 headings![35] All such considerations may be regarded as affecting (a) predicted consumption demand (on which predictions of marginal receipts must be based) and (b) predictions of marginal costs; or, more realisti-

---

*Some shrewd entrepreneurs in the field of shipping decided, during 1932, when the demand for the services of shipping was at its lowest ebb, to invest in this field. Those who correctly recognized that this was the proper time to purchase ships (because they correctly predicted that long-term demand for shipping services had little, if any, connection with current demand) were rewarded with lucrative profits. And we had an excellent illustration of the importance of both predicted price, and predicted duration of price in the values of second-hand merchant ships during the lucrative shipping boom of 1951-52. More was then being offered for second-hand tramp vessels than for almost completed new vessels on the stocks. Enterpreneurs wanted to get in before the boom had time to break, although there must have been a wide range of estimated duration probabilities.

†Dennis Robertson has made this point in a criticism of Harrod.[34]

cally, as affecting the typical business man's actual substitutes for these theoretically rigorous concepts with which we economists try to describe rational business behavior.*

I have so far used the simple term "predicted consumption demand," in order to facilitate exposition. But mechanically used, the concept is still a snare. The entrepreneur, as several writers have stressed, is in practice confronted not with one predicted price, but with a range of predicted prices, each of a different degree of probability. And in reality, the position is even more complex than that (a point which I have not seen explicitly made). For corresponding with each of the prices in the probability distribution, there will be another distribution representing the different probabilities of the duration of the predicted price in question. It seems to me to be almost obvious that these complex predictions cannot be successfully related merely to current prices, as seems to have been tacitly assumed by most accelerationists. The relations between current and predicted *prices*, or between actual and expected *price changes*, appear to be far too complex and intricate to be handled as though there were some simple or mechanical relationship between them.† It is not illegitimate for some purposes to assume "a certainty equivalent" for both sets of probabilities, which is what many writers (especially those who have recourse to the acceleration principle) must tacitly do. It *is* illegitimate to assume that current prices, irrespective of their predicted duration or predicted change, are the determinants of the form of accumulation.

13.—Some of the accelerationists, who have explicitly recognized that *current* consumption demand can hardly be a determinant, have nevertheless failed to see that *the individual case cannot be extended to the general*. Thus, Halm says casually that a qualification is to be found in the nature of the *expected* demand for consumers' goods. If the increase is not expected to last, he says, "it will not lead to an increased demand for capital goods."[36] And Benoit-Smullyan has agreed that "investment depends in the first instance not on past consumption, but on anticipated future consumption."[37]

But economists who introduce this qualification do not always perceive that entrepreneurial predictions of yields (derived from predic-

---

*It is because he recognizes this point that Kuznets seems, throughout his criticism of Clark, to be about to reject the acceleration principle in its entirety. I am puzzled at his failure to do so. For when we are concerned with predictions, we are less likely to assume that it can be legitimate to compare short periods of the flow of output with the provision of single units of durable equipment.

†Objections of the same nature render the concept of "elasticity of expectations" of very limited usefulness as a tool of economic analysis. See Lachmann, "A Note on the Elasticity of Expectations" in *Economica*, November, 1945.

tions of future consumption demand) can affect *net accumulation in general* only in so far as these predictions call forth savings by the offer of interest. Indeed, all these considerations of the relations of current and prospective consumption, relevant as they are to *the form* of growth and replacement (and to various aspects of instability) are irrelevant to *the magnitude* of growth except in so far as they influence the flow of output and saving preference.

Whatever conclusions may be reached about the causes of instability from consideration of particular industries (concerning the relations of the consumption of output and additions to capacity), the reasoning cannot be validly transferred to the economic system as a whole. For to reiterate what I explained above, whilst a particular industry must bid against other industries for the services (provided by *unwithheld* or *released* productive capacity) needed for expansion, industries as a whole can bid for such services only against consumption uses. Hence the considerations discussed in sections 9-12 have nothing to do with the rate of net accumulation *by society*. That is what the accelerations have never perceived. They constantly discuss the particular case and jump to the conclusion that it can illustrate the general case.

We have already noticed this unjustifiable jump in the case of J. M. Clark. We meet it also in a well-known contribution of Ragnor Frisch, who may perhaps be regarded as the second of the formal accelerationists. His contribution was published in 1933.[38] He begins, like most writers on the subject, by discussing the case of a particular consumers' product and he then proceeds more or less in the manner which I have illustrated. Thus he imagines that in a certain year there is an increase of 5 units in the *production* of this good. He remarks, "then it is necessary *during that year* to increase the stock of capital goods . . . . in the same proportion. . . . . *During the year in question* it is *therefore* necessary to produce an additional 50 units of capital goods" (the amount necessary to produce the additional 5 "units" of consumption goods per annum).[39] (My italics).* This all represents, of course, nothing more than the usual fallacy which I have been discussing. What is important at the present stage is that Frisch *then proceeds to apply virtually the same reasoning to the economy as a whole* without realizing the necessity for justifying that procedure.

He includes in a formula which expresses the *annual* production of capital goods "necessary" for full replacement (in the whole economy) an additional term to represent the capital stock needed to produce an additional flow of one unit of consumers' goods (multiplied by the

---

*Later passages (cited below) make it clear that by the words "it is necessary," Frisch does not mean, *"it will have been necessary."*

assumed change in the production of consumers' goods). A little later on, he identifies the production of consumers' goods with consumption, by quoting Clark to the effect that the rate of increase in current consumption is a determinant of the rate of production of producers' goods, and says that *that is what he has expressed in his formula.* He goes on to explain that the peak in capital production must therefore coincide, not with maximum current consumption, but with the maximum rate of increase in *current* consumption.*[40]

Very much later in the argument, he refers to the question of the factors which determine the time over which the provision of additional capital goods will be spread. The only factors which he then thinks worth mentioning are the time needed for the completion of large units of fixed plant and the time needed for the planning and organization of the work.[42] But the recognition of these issues does not cause him to abandon the assumption that there will be concentration *into one year.* Hence, handling the assumption mechanically, Frisch sees in the formula a new concept amenable to mathematical treatment; and he goes on to use it in the construction of an explanation of economic fluctuations. That the whole procedure of jumping from the particular to the general might be invalid (quite apart from the other objections I have raised) does not occur to him. And yet Hicks enthusiastically claims for the contribution that Frisch had shown that "the acceleration principle established an analogy between economic fluctuations and the 'waves' which are so elaborately studied in physics; thus a vast amount of knowledge and technique acquired for other purposes . . . . suddenly became relevant to the economic problem."[43] Indeed, the acceleration described by Frisch's formula can, says Hicks, be recognized as "an engine which is capable of inducing general fluctuations."[44] Potentially disastrous fluctuations, suggests Hicks; for if it were not for certain "damping forces," the accelerator would cause a "complete breakdown." As it is, it causes the boat to rock without actually upsetting it.[45]

14.—Hicks' own treatment of the theory, which is the most recent major contribution† is, I feel, more influenced by Frisch than by the many intermediate writers. Hicks considers the effects of *change in output in general* upon accumulation,‡ not because of an express recog-

---

*It is obviously *current* consumption which is intended in the passage. It is identified with the *production* of consumers' goods, the whole annual flow of which is explicitly assumed to be consumed during the year of production.[41]

†I regard Baumol's 1956 article (referred to p. 299 n) as a virtual *abandonment* of the theory.

‡This is similar to Frisch's approach, except that Frisch considers changes in output of consumption goods, and treats such output as consumption. In his *Trade Cycle*, Hicks does not consider the origin of the increase of output which he assumes. He

nition that (as a result of the complementarity we have noticed) growth induces growth, but because one kind of accumulation (new houses) is supposed to induce investment in another kind, capital goods of a higher order (brick works, saw mills, etc.),* which is complementarity of a particular kind. What is unique about Hicks' contribution—what differentiates him from Frisch and most earlier contributors—is that he refrains from claiming that the phenomenon has anything to do with consumption.

But like all the accelerationists, he seems to *assume* that the net accumulation is concentrated into a short period, giving no attention to what seem to me to be the real factors which determine this spread. Is there not a tacit assumption of the release of almost unlimited withheld capacity in the constructional industries?† He contends that the demand for a single increase in the stock of capital goods, due to a growth of output (there is no reference to saving preference here), will cause a "hump of investment" in the construction industries. The *diagram*(47) with which he illustrates this thesis *appears to imply* that all the services needed for embodiment in capital goods, both for the original provision of the assets and their periodical replacement, are available, whenever convenient, and at current prices, in proportion to the demand for growth or replacement. He pictures a series of humps, the first being due to the original demand for growth, followed by cyclically recurring humps of replacement. In the text, however, he has previously said: "It seems reasonable to suppose that the net investment will not take place all at once—it will be spread over a certain length of time, partly because business men will not react at once to the need for new capital goods, partly because the process of making the new capital goods itself takes time."(48) The stress here is on the time it takes to use resources for accumulation. Their *availability* is taken for granted.

Now it certainly does "take time" to make new capital goods, partly for technical reasons (e.g., iron ore has to be smelted, cement has to set, etc.), but mainly because the flow of services out of *utilized capacity* which can be embodied into the assets wanted is a finite flow, so that

---

says, "we need not inquire for what reason." But in his *Social Framework*,(46) he assumes autonomous factors— inventions, population changes, politics, wars, etc., to be responsible for the rise in output, and not net accumulation due to savings, or the release of withheld capacity, or the sacrifice of leisure, which are, for reasons which I have explained, the *crucial* sources of increased output.

*Just like "consumption," however, the provision of certain goods of a lower order affects *the form of accumulation generally,* including the proportion of goods of a higher order.

†With Clark, the same assumption was explicit and admitted to be an "absurd," "impossibly fluid" condition, although conclusions were drawn before the assumption was removed.

all the industries, and all the projects, and all the different parts of the same project, which entrepreneurs would otherwise wish to build up at once, cannot expand at the same time. There is a range of competing possibilities for expansion.

Let us suppose that there *is* a sudden demand for a substantial growth of capacity generally (of which the source must be saving preference) due to the stimulus of an increased real income caused by the release of capacity in the constructional industries. And let us suppose that this is followed by a less intense demand for growth (from the same source, saving preference) which happens to be sufficient to maintain the increased capacity but not to add to it further. In such circumstances, there *will* obviously be an initial "hump" such as Hicks envisages in the constructional industries and, if there is a flexible response to saving preference, a hump in net accumulation as a whole). But this is due wholly to what we have assumed about the release of capacity and saving preference; and *ceteris paribus* this "hump" (in the constructional industries) will be spread over a long or a short period of time, according to whatever factors determine the prospective most economic concentration over time in the provision of capital goods of a high order. That is, in the response to demands for additional fixed assets, and to demands for replacement in the different industries, the price mechanism will (subject to the wisdom and luck of entrepreneurial prediction) tend to distribute the flow of scarce services needed in the optimum manner. If the resources in the constructional trades are fully utilized, then (given our assumption that a sudden, single jump in real income is the initiating cause) accumulation will occur first in those industries in which expansion is judged to be most profitable.

Let us consider the consequences, (a) in a co-ordinated society and (b) in a disco-ordinated society.

In a co-ordinated society, the "hump" in one industry will be followed by the growth of capacity in other industries or projects of a gradually declining order of prospective profitableness, and so on until the constructional industries will no longer be able to bid profitably against "consumption uses" for all the versatile resources they have been employing.

It might be objected that, during this process, the marginal efficiency of capital must be falling, resulting in a declining rate of interest and a falling off in the previously boosted rate of savings. If so, there will have been a *savings hump*. But in so far as the resources in the constructional industries are specific, the fall in the value of the services they provide must, owing to the assumed price flexibility, tend to maintain full employment of resources in general; for at lower costs other projects will become profitable. (See pp. 334-6). Only in so far as those resources which are versatile are attracted away to consumption uses, will the marginal efficiency of capital fall* and cause interest and perhaps (in consequence) the rate of savings and net accumulation to decline.†

Turning now to the opposite case of a *disco-ordinated society* (i.e., one in which the price adjustments required for the full employment of resources are not made), withheld capacity may well arise, or re-emerge, in the constructional trades as the effect of the initial release of withheld capacity wears off. This will occur when consumption industries with an order of prospective profitableness below a certain level begin to provide the greater part of the bidding for the services of the constructional industries. In those circumstances the marginal efficiency of capital *will* fall, causing market interest to fall and possibly the magnitude of net accumulation (i.e., of savings). Hence any initial "acceleration" of activity, or any cyclical "accelerations" in the form of "replacement waves," must be due to some failure on the part of the institutions of the price mechanism,—a failure which causes real income to contract and hence (probably) a contraction in the *savings* available for expansion. It is through the irregular flow of savings (as influenced by the interest inducement, derived from prospective yields) that a disturbance of the steady distribution over time of the flow of (and absorption of) constructional services may be caused.

But if we assume (a) that a rise in the marginal efficiency of capital, and the savings necessary for growth produce a definite "hump" of accumulation initially, (b) that for some reason the physical growth in productive capacity does not mean a further increase of real income (which would probably mean a continued rise in the absolute flow of savings, and so of net accumulation), (c) that all the additional resources supplied have the same economic life, (d) that there is a general failure to provide for depreciation as it occurs, and (e) that the required thrift *is* induced when replacements are under consideration, then Hicks' illustration can be accepted. There will be an initial hump followed by cyclical replacement humps. But what fantastic assumptions these are! The supposed subsequent replacement humps can be expected only if there is a failure to provide for depreciation as it occurs, *and* if sufficient "savings" happen to be forthcoming when "replacement"

---

*I.e., the fall in realized yields in the constructional industries will be minimized under full employment in those industries. It will therefore pay competing entrepreneurs to continue to offer savers as much as before.

†If the rate of savings (the rate of net accumulation) remains constant, the rate of interest must then fall further.

occurs* ("sufficient," that is, to cause the transfer of versatile services from "consumption uses," or to induce the release of withheld capacity in the constructional industries).

The fact that the saving preference intended to maintain capital intact as depreciation occurs *may* be accompanied by a bidding up of the aggregate real value of money† does not, as we have seen, affect the position unless it is accompanied by the withholding of capacity. Provision for depreciation will always mean realized replacement of equal value, in some form, somewhere.‡ When a bigger replacement than normal of *fixed equipment* in general is demanded (through the *assumed* occurrence of replacement humps), it will be purchased, not through increased savings and hence increased net accumulation by society, but through the exchange of one kind of assets for the services which are being embodied into another kind of assets. The rate of gross or net accumulation as a whole will not acquire a hump. In other words, for the time being, services will flow into gross accumulation of a different form, whilst the aggregate demand for services will remain unchanged.**

Under the assumption that all fixed equipment is finally worn out at the same moment, however, it might seem that there *could* be at least waves of replacement of *fixed capital*, if not of 'all accumulation. But even under this preposterous assumption, it is still necessary to explain why the limited resources for meeting this demand (if they are not versatile in respect of different replacement uses), do not force entrepreneurs to a different interpretation of the phrase "finally worn out,"†† and cause them to spread such replacement over time (some firms finding it less unprofitable to work at abnormally high repair or maintenance costs, whilst waiting for the availability of the necessary resources). *** If we imagine that this is physically impossible, then the necessary resources in the constructional industries will not be wastefully idle in the period between replacements but productively idle—in *pseudo*-idleness. They will be waiting for cyclical use—idle in the technical sense, but

---

*I talk of "savings" to cover "replacement" here to conform with Hicks' use of terms. But in view of no provision having been made for depreciation, the savings really represent net accumulation *to cover previous decumulation*. High interest, due to a high marginal efficiency of capital, may call forth the required savings at the expense of current consumption; or inflation may call forth savings out of increased real income caused by the release of capacity.

†This is a most unlikely possibility. See pp. 253-4.

‡See pp. 253-4, second footnote.

**Firms which have provided for depreciation will probably realize securities (which will be purchased by savers) and with the proceeds buy services for embodiment into gross accumulation.

††Such a concept can seldom be validly treated as wholly technical.

***The "cushioning effect" so caused is discussed later, pp. 335-6.

continuously productive in the economic sense*—just like a football ground which is used only once a week. There is nothing in such a phenomenon which tends to cause the whole economy to fluctuate in similar cycles.

15.—The importance of the *spreading over time* of the use of resources for replacement and net accumulation has been fully recognized, however, by at least one of the "rightist" Keynesians. Thus, Timlin has written, although in a different context from that now under discussion: "If existing investment opportunities are husbanded over a longer period of time, the chances for the occurrence of innovations or other autonomous supports to investment will be increased. . . . . Moreover, since elasticity of supply factors will be greater over a longer period, for a number of reasons the *magnitude* of investment, measured in constant dollars, may be greater under such a policy. Since marginal efficiency schedules of capital in particular investment markets will be reckoned on the *excess of returns over costs of production*, the spinning out of existing investment opportunities may actually mean higher marginal efficiency schedules, taken on the average over a period of years. The point is that long-term planning of investment is not only a matter of the level and stability of interest rates to be paid on capital: the level and stability of costs of production and prices of output may be even more important.†(49) She suggests also that, if inflationary forces do happen to be present, "existing inducements to invest" need to be husbanded, and "new investment" restricted "to a level at once consistent with the propensity to consume and with a proper allocation of resources."‡(50) As I prefer to put it, if the State tries to force "invest-

*That resources in *pseudo*-idleness are productive may not be immediately obvious to all readers. My *Theory of Idle Resources,* Chap. III, deals with this question. But such resources will not be in *pseudo*-idleness if their services could be absorbed at lower prices.

†The use of the words "investment opportunities" seem to show the difficulty which Timlin has of breaking away from Keynesian concepts. There are, as I have shown (p. 242), *always* "investment opportunities" for the flow of services *released from consumption uses* or, when income is increasing, *released from withholding* and. if versatile, not bid away to consumption uses. By "investment opportunities" here, Timlin appears to mean the resources (including labor) which can provide services of the kind appropriate for the situation when gross accumulation exceeds replacement. She recognizes not only that the attempt to "stimulate investment," as most Keynesians would put it, must militate against high realized yields and eventually high prospective yields, but also that it is less likely to draw out economizing innovations and autonomous developments generally.

‡This use of the phrase "consistent with the propensity to consume," also suggests that Timlin is hampered by Keynesian shackles. Had she referred to the "propensity to *save*"—the same notion, even under Keynesian definitions—it would have implied better the point I think she is making. I take the passage to mean, "consistent with the expression of saving preference, the greater the rate of savings eventuating, the smaller being the necessity for the husbanding of the inducements to invest."

ment," by itself bidding for the scarce flow of services available, it will merely be diverting the flow from more productive (i.e., more wanted) to less productive channels and aggravating the time concentration of constructional activity (as distinct from replacement and net accumulation in other forms).

16.—I turn now to certain other statements of the principle which seem to me to have been refined to the point at which a mere formal relationship has come to be regarded as of causal significance. (See pp. 298-9, above). Thus Fellner writes: "If, after a period of rapid growth, the economy tends to become temporarily stabilized at a higher level, then the output of the specific industries in question will *fall* to the mere replacement rate. . . . . The most significant proposition involved in the Acceleration Principle is that a decreasing rate of growth during the expansion tends to lead indirectly to an *absolute decline*"(51) in the constructional industries.* Provided this passage means that, if the economy *stops expanding* temporarily, such employment as the "constructional industries" enjoy will be solely for purposes of replacement, then no one would deny it. But if it means that a *decreasing rate of growth* will lead to an "absolute decline" in the industries devoted to replacement and net accumulation, then it is based on unstated assumptions concerning the degree of durability of the resources in the constructional industries and the period over which they will be produced. If the magnitude "replacement" is defined as I have defined it (i.e., as equivalent to "decumulation"), it will normally be increasing as long as real income is increasing. And as long as some net accumulation is in progress, then *ceteris paribus*, real income *will* be increasing.

But when Fellner's sort of enunciation leads to the notion, not that a change in the rate of growth must demand adjustments, but that growing *consumption* is essential for stability in the constructional industries, the error is serious. For instance, Fellner states that ". . . . the durable goods industries . . . . are more nearly geared to some definite rate of growth than to some definite level of output."†(52) But stabil-

---

*I take it that it is the output of consumers' goods which is stabilized at the higher level. The actual quotation continues with the words "of business activity." I take this to be a slip in writing. If it is not, it jumps a big gap in the argument.

†Similarly, Bretherton, Buchardt and Rutherford tell us, in the typical sort of phrase, that "the size of the constructional trades is intimately connected with the *rate of growth of consumption;* and *stability in them* depends rather on the maintenance of a regular rate of growth in consumption than in the maintenance of any given level"(53) (My italics). And Samuelson says that ". . . Consumption has to keep increasing in order for investment to stand still!"(54) Indeed, he says, the economic system "may have to keep running *at an ever-faster pace* just in order to stand still". (My italics).(55)

ity in the durable goods industries as a whole does *not* depend on growth simply because some equipment depreciates slowly, so that replacement and growth *in particular industries* will be spasmodic or intermittent. The maintenance of a given level of predicted consumption demand in an industry means equally that there will be *a steady aggregate demand* for the services of industries which replace its materials and equipment of *all orders of durability*. Steady consumption is not, therefore, as Samuelson implies, "a powerful factor making for economic instability."[56] In itself, it is quite irrelevant to instability. The truth is that all industries, including the "constructional industries," *are equally likely to enjoy constant employment* in the absence of growth, merely by meeting replacement demands.

17.—A fall in the former rate of growth is another question entirely. But growth in consumption demand by a slightly falling absolute amount per unit of time is not incompatible with a steady demand for "replacement *plus* net accumulation."* Samuelson claims, however, from his argument and example (cited above)† that it is "clear that a depression can set in just because *consumption* has stopped growing so rapidly," which must cause a fall in demand for the services of the constructional industries. (My italics).‡[57] If we substitute "savings" for "consumption" (a not unimportant substitution!), the possibility can be admitted, and the situation is obviously one which needs adjustment. During the transition from a period of growth to a period of nongrowth, or to a period of less rapid growth, either price adjustment or the emergence of withheld capacity is inevitable in the constructional industries; whilst to the extent to which the resources employed in construction are specific, *unwasteful idleness*** may be experienced, as I have explained (see pp. 322-3). But a decline in the rate of growth of net accumulation is only one of the many changes which can leave relative prices out of co-ordination and hence valuable resources wastefully idle unless reco-ordination follows. For instance, deflation *caused in any way* will bring about this condition.

---

*As we have seen, replacement must gradually make up a bigger proportion.

†See p. 306.

‡A declining rate of consumption growth is not, however, incompatible with constant employment in the construction industries.

**When, in a co-ordinated economy, specific equipment becomes valueless, this is a result of a change of preference which makes other resources more valuable. If specific equipment has been provided through wrong predictions about the volume or duration of demand for its services, then *the wasteful act occurred at the time of the investment*. The fact that the equipment may have been fully used in the interim does not mean that there is any *waste* when the demand evaporates. In short, *the idleness is not wasteful: the investment was*. If the idle resources still have capital value, although their services are temporarily valueless, the condition is productive. This is the case of *"pseudo-idleness"*. See pp. 323, 334-6.

One cannot object, therefore, to Samuelson's contention that depression (in the sense of some withheld capacity) *can* set in when predicted consumption (or predicted income) begins to grow less rapidly (*and* co-ordinative adjustments of the price system do not follow); but one has to object when it is implied that the cause is the accelerator in reverse. In other words, it cannot be denied that an expanding society which, given a decline in the schedule of the marginal efficiency of capital (because predicted consumption demand has fallen), ceases to want to make the consumption sacrifices needed for expansion which it has formerly been making, must adopt price adjustment or experience wasteful idleness in such resources in the constructional trades as are specific to those trades.

We have exactly the same problem in growth as in contraction. *A society which has not been growing, and then decides to grow* (i.e., starts accumulating savings) must also adopt price adjustments—in the consumers' goods industries in this case—or experience idleness in *them* in so far as the factors employed lack versatility. The fact that it may be more easily and more often *solved* in growth has nothing to do with the acceleration of consumption demand. The relative ease of adjustment during the real growth of productive power is, I suggest, mainly owing to the facts, (a) that normally no absolute sacrifice of the former rate of consumption is called for, and (b) that credit expansion may then occur without tending to threaten convertibility (or cause inflation in some other sense). Price adjustment is relatively easily achieved, as well as less urgently needed, during a noninflationary expansion of real growth than during a period of declining rate of growth (which necessitates a declining rate of monetary expansion if inflation is to be avoided).

This notion that a declining rate of growth necessarily brings unemployment is not an essential part of the acceleration principle, but in practice is nearly always merged with it. The notion suffers not only from the defect of the tacit assumption of price rigidity and the direction of attention away from the most direct remedy (co-ordination through the price mechanism), but enormously exaggerates the degree of adjustment necessary, by tacitly assuming a high degree of specificity in the resources of the constructional industries. The truth seems to be that producers' goods of a very high order tend to be less specialized than producers' goods of a lower order. They usually have a wide range of alternative employments.* The contrary assumption has the effect of aggravating the errors due to habit of discussing *industry in general* as though it were *a particular industry*.

Consider, for instance, Hansen's interpretation of history in his con-

---

*In relation, of course, to the ultimate final products into which their services are embodied.

tention that ". . . . the mere slowing down in the *rate* of growth [in the stock of railway equipment] caused an absolute decline in the volume of new investment required in the plant and equipment of subsidiary industries, such as iron and steel. . . . ."[58] All changes demand adjustments, but the "mere slowing down" in the rate of growth of the railway system meant not only that some of the products of the iron and steel industry were released for other ends which had become *relatively* urgent (and which, we can assume, the development of the railway itself had helped to make profitable) but also the release for *relatively* more urgent needs, of some of the labor and flow of materials which had been devoted to building up the iron and steel industry. Hence, there is no clear reason, apart from the withholding of capacity, why *a cessation of autonomous growth* (such as was reflected in the "mere slowing down" of railway expansion) should be, as Hansen contends, "disastrous,"* or that *a slowing down in the rate of autonomous growth* should, in itself, bring about a contraction in the rate of growth of the constructional industries as a whole and have a "damping effect" upon the economy.†

Growth is a matter of preference. Autonomous *progress* renders growth (the achievement of savings) possible at a reduced sacrifice of current consumption. Autonomous *growth* merely means "autonomous progress (discoveries and economizing inventions) accompanied by increased savings."

18.—The real "damping effect" which is experienced in depression can always be traced, I think, (a) to price rigidity (whether the causes are mere inertia or more deliberate withholdings and restraints) and (b) to the net decumulation of capacity (whatever the causes of the decumulation), just as the "stimulus" experienced in boom is due to the release or growth of capacity (whatever the causes of the release or growth). But the accelerationists appear to be quite blind to this sort of truth. For instance, it is a commonly accepted condition for the operation of the acceleration principle that "full employment" shall exist in the consumers' goods industries. This leads some of the accelerationists to the view that, until intensive use of capital resources in the consumers' goods industries is achieved (i.e., until "excess capacity" is fully employed) the

---

*Hansen says, "It is the *cessation of growth* which is disastrous."[59]

†Hansen says, "Thus, the mere slowing down in the *rate of increase* in new railroad construction was already beginning to have a damping effect on the economy long before there was an actual decline in the volume of new construction."[60] Of course, there may have been over-investment (and so disappointed hopes) in the iron and steel industries through wrong predictions about the growth of demand for other products following the railway boom. If so, this must have robbed other industries of labor and materials (but benefited, temporarily, the suppliers of such labor and materials).

beneficial stimulus of the accelerator is lost. "Sterilized" is a term which has been used.*

What are the implications? Surely, that if producers respond by withholding capacity, in such a manner as to prevent any expansion of outputs from existing assets in the consumers' goods industries, the "sterilization" of the accelerator effect will be avoided, and the full "stimulus to investment" will be won! Indeed, it would seem to follow from the argument that the greater the amount of withheld capacity so brought about, the greater will be the stimulus to new investment and prosperity.

Such is another of the absurdities to which the theory seems ultimately to lead. There is no absurdity of course in the notion that, *in any individual industry*, expansion of capacity will come about only when increased predicted costs (due to congestion, etc.) make the provision of additional capital resources appear the cheaper way of responding to increasing predicted consumption demand. Nor is there anything absurd in the notion that the withholding of capacity in any individual industry may induce investment in that industry (when interlopers can find a way in†) instead of in some other industry which would otherwise have been deemed a more profitable outlet. What *is* absurd, is the notion that *development as a whole* will be rendered more profitable by such withholding, i.e., that accumulation *by society* will somehow be stimulated if existing capacity is not utilized to the full, and that potential growth will be "sterilized" if existing capacity is made use of.

The failure to recognize that the release of capacity in the consumers' goods industries exerts an expansionist and not a contractionist influence leads to an *under-estimation* of the dynamic consequences of growth in real income (under conditions of price rigidity). The accelerationists do not see that increased outputs of consumers' goods and services from *existing resources, the demand schedules for these outputs not having risen initially,* tend to raise the inducement offered to savings (and hence to net accumulation), even though these resources are not yet fully employed. Thus, Halm writes, "Obviously the principle of acceleration does not work when we are able to expand consumers' goods production without producing more investment goods."‡[62] But to the extent to which growing predicted consumption demand in general is the inducement for a particular accumulation, there is no reason why the release of productive capacity in the consumers' goods industries, through in-

---

*E.g., Bretherton, Buchardt and Rutherford say that "the relation" (i.e., the accelerator) "is more or less sterilized in depression by the existence of excess capacity of plant and equipment."[61]

†It will lead to that wasteful form of accumulation which accompanies what I have called "participating idleness." (See my *Theory of Idle Resources*, Chap. VII).

‡See also Haberler, *Prosperity and Depression*,[63] on this point.

creasing real income, should not encourage the belief that a general expansion is likely to follow. Indeed, the release of withheld capacity in the consumers' goods field is normally the first indication observable by entrepreneurs of the factors which cause a rise in the marginal efficiency of capital. And if the marginal efficiency of capital *does* rise, the higher interest may induce a greater flow of savings, over and above that due to the scope for greater savings created by the increased real income. Hence not only may a source be provided for expansion, but a greater inducement to savers is likely to emerge. It follows that a stimulus to net accumulation may occur long *before* all withheld capacity in the consumption industries has been released.

19.—One of the least uncritical expositions of the accelerator is that of Kuznets, who regards the value of the accelerator as a function of the "ratio of the stock of capital goods to volume of current production," and "the time unit of observation."[64] His use of the word "production" here, instead of the word "consumption" is significant. He explains that, given the ratio mentioned in the passage just quoted, the amplitude of fluctuations in demand for capital goods will be greater, in response to changes in the demand for finished products, the shorter the time unit within which the demands for both kinds of goods are *assumed* to be satisfied.*[65] But the very assumption of any such time unit assumes away the very problem which the accelerator purports to explain, namely, the actual period during which the embodiment of additional services into resources will be *concentrated*.

It is self-evident that the assets needed to produce a week's, or a month's, or a year's, or sometimes even a decade's output are usually of a much greater real value than the output of such a period. In other words, the addition of an amount of real value x to the flow of services (i.e., output) *in the course of one of these short periods*, will necessitate a value of services of many times x being embodied into assets over the same period. The flow of services can increase only as that is being done. Obviously, then, the value of additions to the stock of assets, as a proportion of additions to the flow of services will be greater the shorter the period in which the addition to the stock is made. It is through tortuous thinking about this simple, self-evident truth that the acceleration fallacy has arisen.

However, in stressing the importance of the relation of the "stock of capital goods to the volume of current production"[66] Kuznets comes very near to recognizing what, I suggest, is the true principle. For he

---

*"The assumptions . . . . are as follows . . . . both demand for finished goods and demand for capital goods are satisfied within the time unit in which such demand becomes apparent."

states his case in such a way that, wherever he subsequently uses the terms *consumption of*, or *demand for final products*, he could equally well use the terms *production of*, or *supply of final products*. Moreover, he could equally validly go still further, and substitute for the term *final products*, the term *services*, meaning *all* productive services. Had he done so, he would have been forced to ask himself: "Does the fact that there is a certain ratio between the value of the stock of assets and the value of the flow of services they render enable us to say that the rate of change in the stock is determined by the rate of change in the flow?" This has always been assumed (through jumping from the particular case to the general. See pp. 302-3). The truth is, I suggest, the reverse. The reason why the flow of unwithheld services increases is because the stock of assets to produce them is growing.* And such growth is not caused by any magnification or acceleration of either production or consumption: it is caused by saving preference (in which the entrepreneurs' offer—interest—based on prospective yields, may be an inducement).

The rate at which the flow of finished (and unfinished) goods increases, and the rate at which this flow is expressed in demands depend, under price flexibility, upon the rate at which net accumulation is realized. This is the true relation for which the accelerationists have been groping, and it can be stated as follows: *A given rate of growth* in the stock of utilized capital resources results in *an equivalent rate of growth* in the flow of services; and if we reckon over periods of time which are long enough to cover the economic life of the units of resources accumulated, the increased rate of flow of services *into* resources will be proportional to the increased flow of products *from* those resources.† If, however, (i) we reckon by shorter periods, and (ii) it happens that the provision of such resources is (for whatever reasons) concentrated into the shorter periods, then the growth in the value of the stock of resources in any such period will be greater than the growth in the value of the flow of services over that period. It is absurd to describe that relationship as an acceleration.

20.—We can now usefully consider a statement of the acceleration notion which, whilst is tacitly avoids the fallacies with which I have been

---

*Growth in the stock of assets is due to a choice concerning the use of services, which choice ultimately determines the form of the flow. Admittedly, the release of some services not only creates an increased current demand for the rest of the current flow, but serves as a source out of which demand for additions to the stock (savings) may be expected.

†On the assumption that the resources which can provide for growth are specific to that purpose and incapable of use for replacement, the steady employment of those resources will demand continuous growth in capacity (and, *ceteris paribus*, in output). But as we have seen, we can hardly regard that relation as an acceleration.

dealing, does not explicitly reject the conclusions which have been drawn from it. I refer to Hayek's exposition. He states clearly the true relation which it so misleadingly tries to describe. He says: "Since the production of any given amount of final output usually requires an amount of capital several times larger than the output produced with it *during any short period* (say a year), any increase in final demand will give rise to an additional demand for capital goods several times larger than the new final demand."[67] (My italics) But this statement is insufficiently general. All output, and not merely "final output"—that which is consumed directly or decumulated and replaced—*requires* resources of greater value than itself *over any short period*. Hence if the passage from Hayek is extended in this way, it means that *every increase of demand for any product must have any accelerator effect which may be implied!* But the words "in any short period" do *not* imply that effect.

Society's demand for *additional* assets (expressed as saving preference) is a demand for services (not particular services) which can be embodied into assets; and these services are provided in turn by assets the value of which must be several times larger than the value of the output of their services *over any short period*. Assets have to be built up out of services —capital out of income—whilst the process takes time. We can accordingly re-state the supposed principle (as implied by Hayek's formulation of it) as follows: Since the value of capital is several times greater than the value of the product of capital over *any* short period, any increase in output (real income) "will give rise" (Hayek's words) to a much greater increase of capital than the increased output (real income) of a short period.

The essence of the difficulty lies in the words "will give rise." Does the rise in output (real income) *call forth* or *give rise to* the accumulation of capital, or is the rise in output *only achievable as a result of* realized savings—the net accumulation of capital? The answer is, as I have already argued, that only the latter is true. The increased income merely facilitates the necessary savings.

21.—Following earlier criticisms of the acceleration principle, there have been various attempts to cling to its conclusions whilst abandoning the original arguments on which it was based. Thus, R. C. O. Matthews admits that most of the criticism of the principle is deserved, but maintains that "there is wide acceptance of its underlying postulate, that there is a certain level of capital capacity which is 'appropriate' to a given volume of output, and that the trade cycle occurs from the interaction between efforts to achieve this appropriate level of capacity on the one hand and the working of the multiplier on the other."[68] But this so quoted "underlying postulate" appears to me to be nothing more than a scientific-sounding statement of a mere tautology. "Capital capacity" is simply another term for "output capacity." Assets are replaced, or accumulated net, *in particular forms* because certain probable outputs from them are predicted, and because those outputs appear profitable. No acceleration notion is involved in such an idea. Nor has entrepreneurial guidance of the flow of services into particular kinds of assets (e.g., into the *fixed capacity* usually assumed in acceleration discussions, or used for illustration of the principle), through *expenditure* upon such services, any special effect on the magnitudes which are supposed to bring about the multiplier effect.

Without truly bringing in any acceleration notion, Matthews goes on to consider the idea that "capital capacity" (i.e., output capacity!) may at any time be "deficient" or "excessive" in relation to current output. If we state the thesis in its most plausible form, replacing the words "current output" by "anticipated profitable output," we can perhaps interpret the statement to mean that capital capacity is "deficient" when it is deemed profitable to add to it, and "excessive" when it is deemed profitable not to add to it or to allow its net decumulation. But if my earlier argument has been accepted and understood, "excessive capacity" simply means—when the amount of net accumulation and not the form of gross accumulation is under consideration—that savings are not being induced!* It seems to be suggested, however, that "excessive" capacity arises, not because people wish to consume more in the present, but because the flow of services constituting aggregate current demands (which services form the basic data from which *predicted* aggregate demands are derived) appears to *entrepreneurs* to be too small to justify the maintenance or growth of aggregate capacity. But only if the low prospective yields so caused induce a decline in savings will outputs in the industries which serve net accumulation decline. And in these circumstances the deficiency in current demands can be caused solely by withholding, i.e., by pricing the full possible flow of services out of the range of money income or out of consistency with predicted prices. Capital capacity (output capacity) is "excessive" because people refrain from using it!

In this criticism of Matthews, we have a broad answer, I believe, to the formulations of the accelerator by Kalecki, Kaldor and Goodwin, which are restated by Matthews in the following terms: "Investment decisions are a diminishing function of the size of the stock of capital in existence and an increasing function of the national income.[69]

---

*I.e., people do not demand additional assets because they have more than enough!

The first part of this assertion is absolutely wrong.* The net accumulation of capital capacity is the embodiment of services into additional assets; and each element of this accumulation constitutes the source of an additional demand for the services of all other, noncompeting assets. (I shall return to this vital point. (See pp. 362-3).

22.—I sometimes think that the accelerationists have been trying to explain (but have given the wrong explanation) what may be called "unbalanced growth". (See pp. 366-7, 369-371). This situation, which is to be seen (when it occurs) most conspicuously in the constructional industries, arises as a result of a period of generally wrong entrepreneurial forecasting.

Naturally, *wrong predictions* that a given rate of growth (whether autonomous or otherwise in origin is immaterial) will continue may turn out to be "disastrous" for those who have predicted rashly, or with bad luck—as with all cases of incautious, or imprudent, or unlucky planning. But when this sort of error *is general,* is not the immediate cause that a previous trend of increasing savings has not been maintained?† Where savings do not in fact continue to increase (whether due to the withholding or diversion of capacity or otherwise), some part of the equipment provided for the constructional industries will lose value and marginal equipment may even fall to a temporarily valueless condition or to scrap value (because co-operant resources will have more profitable uses).

Some errors of prediction are inevitable; and they are sometimes recognizable in any society in which objectives and achievements are subjected to the test of the market. There is no direct remedy for such errors.‡

But the harmful effects—both in the particular and the general cases—will be at a minimum, the more easily price readjustments can be made

---

*The second part of the statement may merely imply that the more effectively the flow of services is priced to permit its full absorption (i.e., so as to prevent services from running to waste and therefore not forming part of income), the greater will be the demand for additional capital resources (i.e., the saving preference schedule is assumed to rise).

†I stress here the case in which income ceases to rise because of the cessation of savings, and not the case in which there is no further capacity to release. This is the appropriate case to consider because the stimulus to the constructional industries which thrift engenders arises *mainly* when existing capacity begins to be intensively utilized.

‡Wise caution (which means wise enterprise) is not a remedy for past errors of prediction but only a means of minimizing future errors. The spreading of justifiable risks does not prevent the price effects of wrong predictions, but changes the incidence of the distributive effects.

in the new situation. For instance, in the passage I quoted from Hansen (on p. 327), in which *a declining rate of growth* on the part of the railway system is supposed to contribute to the causes of a depression in the iron and steel industries and in the economy as a whole, it may well be that by the time the railway expansion slowed down, it was realized that over-investment in the iron and steel industries had robbed other activities of resources. Our economic system is inevitably subject to the "too much, too little" phenomenon. All stabilizing reactions in the actual world work like the sort of temperature control under which, when the temperature rises above the chosen level (too much heat) cool air is released, and when it falls below this level (too little heat) warm air is released. It may take some considerable time to reach equilibrium. The entrepreneur only knows that there has been over-investment* when it is recognized that it would not pay, at current costs of construction (in the light of prospective revenues and costs), to replace the whole of the existing equipment if it were completely destroyed, whilst the net realized yield since investment on some part of the sum invested, falls below the interest which was obtainable at the time of investment.

23.—There is, however, another aspect of the situation we have been considering. If resources in the constructional industries are highly specific, a decline in saving preference may mean a relatively small decline in the actual rate of *physical* growth,† in spite of a rise in interest and a decline in capital values. The prices of services in these industries will be bid down, but they need not be *wasted*. Under price flexibility, their services are *unlikely* to fall valueless (and even if they do, there will be no waste involved. See above, pp. 325-6). Hence the durability and specificity of the resources needed for growth, although the cause of loss of earnings on the part of their owners (and possibly disappointed entrepreneurial expectations) when saving preference declines, is not *prima facie* a cause of irregular growth. It is rather *a condition which tends to mitigate* irregular cycles in the withholding of capacity or irregular cycles of savings.‡

24.—In considering the consequences of wrong predictions, we must

---

*Such over-investment does not mean that, in a price co-ordinated society, it would not pay to work all the equipment at full capacity, provide for full maintenance, and even invest in expansion. E.g., a railway may have been provided which brings a disappointing return on the original capital invested, whilst abandonment of any part of the track would mean *even smaller* returns. Its shares may have dropped to a fraction of their par value; but the directors could still conceivably think it profitable to provide double tracks on busy sections.

†It would be misleading to use the phrase, "the rate of growth in real terms" here, for reasons explained on pp. 223-4.

‡But if there is general price rigidity and wage-rate rigidity in these industries, any individual industry in which prices *are* adjusted to demand may find that the

not overlook what may be called *the cushioning effects* due to the continuing use of (a) depreciated equipment which requires much costly reconditioning and repair ("replacement" in my terminology) or (b) equipment of normal efficiency worked at abnormal costs owing to congestion or the purchase of the workers' leisure (overtime). These effects are important in practice when there is a shortage of resources in the constructional industries or when short-term demand variations are common. They enable the entrepreneur to exercise caution in responding to predicted increases in consumer demand, and to refuse to bid against others for the supply of services which can provide durable equipment, unless he feels certain of an adequate duration of the increased demand. This will assist in the prevention, *not of excessive net accumulation generally* (which merely means "excessive savings," i.e., saving more at a time when consuming more would turn out to mean a preferred distribution of consumption over time), *but over-investment in particular industries or in particular forms of capital structure.**

Other cushioning effects depend upon the presence of the productive condition of resources which I call *pseudo*-idleness or *pseudo*-idling. When growth is expected, entrepreneurs take the risk of investing in the resources needed for growth.[†] In doing so, they know full well that growth may prove spasmodic, and that the residual claims which they can expect from the employment of the unversatile portion of the resources they provide (or alternatively the most profitable hire value of such resources) may at times fall so low that they will find it unprofitable continuously to outbid others for the co-operant resources needed. Hence resources which are specialized to the provision of additional capital goods *will be provided in response to a prospective irregular demand.* I.e., entrepreneurs will anticipate not only periods in which the earning power of such assets provided will be below the average, but periods in which it may not pay to employ them at all. Idleness in such conditions —*pseudo*-idleness—whether spasmodic or regularly recurrent, is not wasteful. If all capital goods were absolutely durable, the fact that the equipment producing them would be completely idle in the intervals between growth would not deter the provision of that equipment. Periods of *pseudo*-idleness or *pseudo*-idling are an obvious *result* of the trade cycle,

---

prospective yield from investing in the co-operant services needed for the full utilization of its equipment is below interest, so that some part of *its* capacity is temporarily valueless.

*Over-investment here implies that these fields, or forms of investment, bring realized yields less than those which were originally obtainable from other fields or forms of investment. In particular, there may have been too much investment in specific and durable assets, or in the assets appropriate for capital-costly roundabout methods, when resort could have been had to more versatile or less durable assets, or less capital-costly methods.

†Readers who still find a sentence of this kind paradoxical should reconsider it after reading Chapter XVII, on *The Say Law.*

and in no sense a *cause* of it. Whenever, then, resources of some degree
of specificity and durability are provided to satisfy a demand of predicted irregularity or fluctuation, a condition is contemplated, prior to
investment, in which for certain periods the resources will be idle (in
the extreme case) or idling (i.e., being used in ways which are insufficiently profitable *in themselves* to have justified the original investment).
If resources in the constructional industries are in this condition, then
the temporarily lowly valued capacity will act as a continuous inducement to recovery (unless its services are withheld). It seems therefore
that we cannot find in the existence of constructional resources in the
pseudo-idleness or *pseudo*-idling state, an explanation of cyclical growth.

25.—We have seen (in discussing the consumption fallacy and the multiplier) how untenable is the denial that, income being given, saving-
preference alone can result in net accumulation; we have seen that it is
false to suppose that, in the absence of autonomous progress, only inflation can permit net accumulation; and we have seen that it is equally
untrue that only expanding consumption can keep the economy going.

If the argument of the accelerationists had been that, in the displanned,
sectionalist, badly co-ordinated economies typical of the present age,
attempted saving out of a stationary income is nullified by price rigidity
and the withholding of valuable capacity, so that growth of capacity is
possible only as a result of the facilitation of savings by autonomous
progress or by co-ordination through inflation, there would have been
a case to examine. But that is *not* the argument. And even so it would
have to be recognized that the growth of demand for the products of the
constructional industries has its origin, in every case, in decisions against
current consumption and in favor of saving.

26.—Now it *is* plausible, I admit, to suppose that the industries which
supply heavy, durable equipment will boom at times when autonomous
factors are facilitating the achievement of savings (because the growth
of real income then makes it possible for savings to increase without the
sacrifice of customary consumption). Hence, to the extent to which it is
true that the discontinuity of economic progress has been due to the
chance occurrence of great autonomous stimuli, then the phenomenon
must be viewed as caused by large, spasmodic, windfall contributions to
real income from inventions and discoveries which, in an irregular manner, have both facilitated and induced the flow of savings.

One conceivable explanation of the depression periods of economic
history is that, in the situation created when relatively few new inventions or discoveries are being made, the task of economic co-ordination
—i.e., the adjustment of values through the price mechanism—becomes

exceptionally difficult. But if current political and economic institutions allowed this co-ordinative task to be accepted as a principal aim of economic policy, it might be possible to mitigate periods in which the effects of generally wrong predictions of accumulating productive capital and demand were leading to disappointed expectations. However paradoxical the remedy may at first appear to Keynesians and neo-Keynesians, the solution would lie either in great thrift campaigns, or in compulsory saving to accompany action to dissolve such price rigidities as were preventing the recovery of real income.

27.—We must never forget that the effect of the maintenance of a given rate of savings is that the resources which are specialized to growth will be employed if their form is correctly adapted to the form of anticipated consumer preference; and that the decline or cessation of a given flow of savings means that such resources, unless versatile, will be idle—just as changes in all other objectives will have this result if they are confronted with specific resources.

The question at issue is, then, why should *demand* for growth change violently? That is, why should saving preference change violently? We have noticed some possible answers to these questions. But is it not realistic to assume that, generally speaking, the flow of savings would be a steady proportion of income if real income were steady or if it changed steadily?* If so, we are forced to look for the origin of *instability in the rate of growth* in the causes of fluctuations in real income. For when real income is increasing, the proportion of savings can increase without the sacrifice of consumption, and when it is declining, the maintenance of the flow of savings will necessitate the sacrifice of consumption.

The reasons for instability of income lie, I suggest, mainly in the repercussions of withheld capacity in one field upon withheld capacity in other fields, the whole phenomenon being influenced in practice by disco-ordinations of the economic system due to the following of monetary policies which are inconsistent with the pricing policies permitted.

Lack of versatility of resources as between consumption uses and net accumulation uses can be a source of aggravation of the irregularities so caused. But we can easily exaggerate the importance of this factor. I have already argued that the higher the order of capital goods, the less specific their services tend to be, in the sense that their products can usually serve in the lower stages of production of a relatively wide range of final products. Moreover, man-made specificities are of far greater importance in preventing co-ordinative shifts in the use of services *within* the constructional industries themselves than *between* consumption uses

---

*Because both propensities to save and the interest inducement (derived from prospective yields) could be expected to be stable.

and constructional uses. If co-ordination is ruled out, the main practical problem becomes that of "maintaining demand," not for the services of the constructional trades as a whole, but for the services of *particular constructional trades.**

I maintain that we cannot find in the relationship between demand for goods of a lower order and demand for goods of a higher order (and the supposed derivation of the latter from the former), an explanation of cyclical variations in the demand for growth (i.e., in time preference). Nor can we find in those factors the source of great cyclical changes in entrepreneurial optimism affecting prospective yields, the rate of interest offered, and the flow of savings. We cannot even observe those factors to be influences which induce the cyclical withholding and release of capacity.

In the study of all these issues, the relationship which the acceleration principle tries to express is wholly irrelevant. And yet, like the equally worthless multiplier principle, it has had an extraordinary influence.[†] The extent to which it has entangled thought should serve as an awful warning to economists of their susceptibility to mere intellectual fashion. Is it not significant that even that acute and sensible economist, Dennis Robertson, surrendered to the plausibilities of the principle in the 'thirties, when he went so far as to agree (in 1937) that it "deserves pride of place in any analysis of the trade cycle"?[71] By rights, it should accept chief ignominy for having led seriously astray more than two decades of speculation about the nature of economic fluctuations.

---

*But can we, as serious economists, ever rule out the possibility of price adjustment to changing choice and changing means? As soon as economists accept price rigidities as a condition to be assumed as inevitable, they are degrading economic science to a doctrine of casuistry.

†A recent important example is in an article by Dr. Reinhard Kamitz, the Austrian Minister of Finance, in 1959. The principle is stated in its conventional and crudest form.[70]

REFERENCES

(1) HICKS, *A Contribution to the Theory of the Trade Cycle.* (2) HABERLER, *Prosperity and Depression*, pp.99-100. (3) BAUMOL, *Acceleration Without Magnification*, A.E.R., 1956, p.410. (4) *Ibid.*, pp.409-10. (5) BENOIT-SMULLYAN, *Net Investment, Consumption and Full Employment*, A.E.R., 1944, p.874. (6) CLARK, *Business Acceleration and the Law of Demand: A Technical Factor in Economic Cycles*, reprinted in *Readings in Business Cycle Theory*, p.236. (7) *Ibid.*, p.238. (8) *Ibid.*, p.238, footnote. (9) *Ibid.*, p.239. (10) *Ibid.*, p.239. (11) *Ibid.*, p.244. (12) *Ibid.*, p.241n. (13) *Ibid.*, p241n. (14) *Ibid.*, p.243. (15) *Ibid.*, p.244. (16) *Ibid.*, p.241n. (17) *Ibid.*, p.251. (18) *Ibid.*, p.252. (19) *Ibid.*, p.256. (20) BICKERDIKE, *A Non-Monetary Cause of Fluctuations in Employment*, E.J., September, 1914. (21) J. S. MILL, *Unsettled Questions in Political Economy*, p.51. (22) HABERLER, *op. cit.*, p.90. (23) BRETHERTON, BUCHARDT and RUTHERFORD, *Public Investment and the Trade Cycle in Great Britain*, p.10. (24) SAMUELSON, *Economics*, 2nd ed., p.391. (25) KUZNETS, *Relation Between Capital Goods and Finished Products in the Business Cycle*, in *Economic Essays in Honor of Wesley Clair*

Mitchell, 1935, p.213. (26) *Ibid.,* p.213. (27) HABERLER, *op. cit.,* p.86. (28) *Ibid.,* p.98. (29) *Ibid.,* p.98. (30) *Ibid.,* p.98. (31) *Ibid.,* p.98. (32) *Ibid.,* p.91. (33) E.g., BRETHERTON, BUCHARDT and RUTHERFORD, *op. cit.,* p.11. (34) ROBERTSON, Review of Harrod's, *The Trade Cycle, Canadian Journal of Economics and Political Science,* 1937, p.126. (35) SCHUMPETER, *Business Cycles,* Vol. I, pp.15-17. (36) HALM, *Monetary Theory,* p.411. (37) BENOIT-SMULLYAN, *op. cit.,* p.873. (38) FRISCH, *Propagation Problems and Impulse Problems in Dynamic Economics,* in *Economic Essays in Honour of Gustav Cassel.* (39) *Ibid.,* p.177. (40) *Ibid.,* p.178, diagram. (41) *Ibid.,* p.175. (42) *Ibid.,* p.185. (43) HICKS, *The Trade Cycle,* p.4. (44) *Ibid.,* p.6. (45) *Ibid.,* p.37. (46) HICKS, *The Social Framework,* p.76. (47) HICKS, *The Trade Cycle,* p.41. (48) *Ibid.,* p.40. (49) TIMLIN, *Monetary Stabilisation and Keynesian Theory,* in Kurihara, *Post-Keynesian Economics,* p.65. (50) *Ibid.,* p.65. (51) FELLNER, *Employment Theory and Business Cycles,* in *A Survey of Contemporary Economics.* (52) *Ibid.,* p.70. (53) BRETHERTON, BUCHARDT and RUTHERFORD, *op. cit.,* p.9. (54) SAMUELSON, *op. cit.,* p.391. (55) *Ibid.,* p.391. (56) *Ibid.,* p.391. (57) *Ibid.,* p.391. (58) HANSEN, *Fiscal Policy and Business Cycles,* 1941, p.40. (59) *Ibid.,* p.362. (60) *Ibid.,* p.40. (61) BRETHERTON, BUCHARDT and RUTHERFORD, *op. cit.,* p.11. (62) HALM, *op. cit.,* p.410. (63) HABERLER, *op. cit.,* p.94. (64) KUZNETS, *op. cit.,* p.216. (65) *Ibid.,* pp.212-3. (66) *Ibid.,* p.215. (67) HAYEK, *Profits, Interest and Investment,* pp.18-19. (68) MATTHEWS, *Capital Stock Adjustment Theories,* in Kurihara, *op. cit.,* p.171. (69) *Ibid.,* p.171. (70) KAMITZ, *The Maintenance of Full Employment, in Progress* (Unilever Magazine), 1959. (71) ROBERTSON, *op. cit.,* p.126.

Chapter *XV*

DEPRESSION AND BOOM

SUMMARY

1.—Orthodox economics recognizes the phenomena of depression and boom as the common attributes of a price disco-ordinated society, 2.—the disco-ordinations showing themselves in the necessity to rectify unintended inflation or deflation (in the case of cycles in the scale of prices), 3.—and in a cumulative withholding or release of capacity (in the case of cycles in the scale of output), fluctuations which tend to be induced by economic change generally. 4.—Under "sound money," the resulting variations in "expenditure" (money income) are the consequence and not the cause of price disco-ordination. 5.—When disco-ordination has emerged, market pressures tend to force the required adjustments, and hence the more productive use of assets. The State is less likely to assist than restrain this co-ordinative process. 6.—Even in a price co-ordinated society, some assets may fall temporarily valueless or into pseudo-idleness through economic change—conditions which must not be regarded as wasteful. 7—A general reluctance or failure to face these truths seems to have prompted some economists to seek explanations of the trade cycle in mere subsidiary phenomena, 8.—and we shall now consider a group of such theories 9.—which, it is suggested, misuse abstract thinking through the use of models in which the issues we have discussed are ignored (as in the notion of antidamped cycles within the ceiling of full employment and the floor of the necessity to replace). 10.—The assumption that fluctuations in "activity" are caused by fluctuations in "investment" may be due to a misinterpretation of the differential repercussions of withheld capacity upon constructional activities. 11.—Although any serious trade cycle is avoidable if cheap money can be avoided and co-ordination (through price flexibility) achieved, it is impossible to guarantee the absence of all fluctuations in prices and outputs; 12.—but the amplitude of such fluctuations will be least the wiser the anticipations of speculators and the greater the faith in monetary authorities. 13.—Fluctuations of this type are veiled but not avoided under creeping inflation. 14.—The notion that too great or too rapid a growth of productive power precipitates a reaction into depression is a misinterpretation of a distorted production structure.

1.—The multiplier and the accelerator have played an important role in modern discussions of depression and boom—the so-called "trade cycle." If my attempt to expose the fallacies in these notions has been accepted, the theories of which they form the foundation have been refuted. This chapter will suggest briefly an alternative explanation of the trade cycle as it has crystallized in the author's mind after forty years of speculation. It will then go on to examine, in the light of the explanation, a group of theories which, although often enunciated in a manner which makes use of multiplier and accelerator models, do not necessarily stand or fall according to the soundness of this apparatus.

It has been said that every business cycle is unique. Yet any *theory* which purports to explain either unemployment as such or cyclical unemployment must be, in its roots, a universal theory. The form of different "depressions" has certainly been influenced by special factors. I suggest, however, that the causes of *wasteful* idleness have been fundamentally the same during all periods of human history; and that the factors which have resulted in the cyclical idleness of productive power have been similar in all the depressions which have been described since the beginning of the 19th century. The contrary belief has arisen from the fact that every such cycle has occurred under different political conditions, different institutional frameworks, differently distributed withholdings of capacity, different monetary policies and different backgrounds of technological or geographical progress. Such factors appear to have been relevant, in varying degrees of importance, to every cycle.

Yet cyclical fluctuations in the scale of prices and in idleness can still be seen to have had common causes, whilst among the more recent trade cycle theories which have competed for the economists' attention, nearly all seem to skim over what I have diagnosed as the basic causes, if indeed they do not inhibit the consideration of them altogether. They all tend to turn attention instead to particular historical events—events which, to resort to metaphor, resemble the land configuration which determines the course taken by a river, but take for granted or do not examine the force of gravity which is responsible for the movement and the sources which feed the flow.

Because of supposedly inevitable discontinuities in the factors which determine growth, Bowen and Meier say that "a single general theory of the causes of business fluctuations appears to be as infeasible as a general theory of historic causation."[1] But inventions, technological progress, managerial ingenuities, discoveries and so forth cannot be regarded as *explanations* of cycles of prices or cycles of idleness. Even if their alleged inevitable discontinuity is admitted,* they can be regarded merely as explanations of the discontinuity of *growth* (the *propensity* to save—but not realized savings—being assumed constant)† and not of fluctuations in the scale of prices or in the extent to which growing capacity is withheld. And although discontinuous growth must certainly contribute to the overall task for which the co-ordinative institutions of society have been fashioned, it does not explain fluctuations in *wasteful* idleness, or in the scale of prices.

I have already suggested that wasteful idleness of all resources is due to *the withholding* of these resources—directly or through disco-ordinative pricing. I wish now to suggest (i) that depression (in the sense of widespread and growing idleness) is caused by *cumulative withholding* due to the growing disco-ordination of the price system and the consequential destruction of uninflated income and (ii) that the depression of prices generally is due to the need to rectify cheap money episodes (under any non-inflationary monetary standard). The distortions caused by such episodes are, I believe, the root causes of nearly all depression phenomena.‡ And once the causes are perceived, the remedies become obvious (although *the political steps* needed for the application of the remedies have by no means become obvious in the world which has been created).

In the study of economics we have to do with the effectiveness of the choice and use of means to ends, in short, with that prediction and action which is known as *organization*. And organization is continuously necessary (i) because both means and ends are changing and (ii) because the predictions (one's own and those of others) which determine acts of organization are liable to error. Concern with *economy*—the achievement of changing ends with changing means, at least-cost—is postulated as the central object of economics as an applied science. It is not very useful therefore to regard changes in ends and means as *causes* of fluctuations! It is like saying that the cause of a shipwreck is partly due to the ship having sailed from A to B, and partly to faulty navigation on the part

---

*I do not think that such discontinuity can be empirically established as important. Indeed, I think it is unimportant except locally.

†In terms of Diagram II on p. 227, they cause movements in the demand schedule, not the supply schedule.

‡This is, of course, the traditional orthodox view. Keynes typically misrepresented it by suggesting that the supporters of such a thesis wished to check the boom by preventing *employment* from rising about its average level.[2]

of the master having caused the vessel to run on to the rocks! But have the great disasters of economic history been due to uncharted rocks or unpredictable storms? Or have fluctuations in "activity," including cyclical fluctuations, been caused by defects in navigation? I am convinced that the latter is the answer.

In saying this, I am not denying that we may usefully search for empirical sociological laws relevant to this topic. We may attempt to find correlations between certain kinds of changes in ends and means on the one hand, and the motive to withhold capacity or to the motive to cause the value of the money unit to change on the other hand. We may, for instance, find that an increasing rate of growth is conducive to the release of capacity, and a declining rate of growth is conducive to the withholding of capacity. If so, we must reach the conclusion that the existing co-ordinative machinery is for some reason relatively successful during accelerating growth but relatively unsuccessful during decelerating growth or during contraction. But if we do find that this is a valid empirical generalization, it will still be extremely misleading to say that decelerating growth is a *cause* of wasteful idleness (although it might well be a cause of *pseudo*-idleness in some resources).

There are, I suggest, four kinds of economic fluctuations: (a) in the scale (or average) of prices; (b) in relative prices, the scale (or average) perhaps remaining steady; (c) in aggregate output (a value concept*); and (d) in the real or physical magnitude of individual outputs, the aggregate real value of output perhaps remaining steady.

The fluctuations (b) and (d) are seldom discussed under the heading of "economic fluctuations," and I propose to deal only with (a) and (c).

2.—Fluctuations in the scale of prices may be held to be due to the nature of the monetary standard or to monetary policy, in the sense that M is not caused to vary with changes in V and/or T so as to maintain MV in constant relation to T. The time-patterns of boom and depression, as reflected in movements of the scale of prices, can be expected to be quite different when there is a money unit of defined value, from what they are when there is no contractual monetary standard. Under "sound money," within the narrow limits of possible general price fluctuation, any rise is likely to occur fairly rapidly at first, the rate of increase tending to slow down later until a fairly sudden check is brought about by the need to protect reserves. Fluctuations under these conditions are caused through the rectification of unintended inflation or deflation which has occurred. In the absence of contractual convertibility, the desire to protect the relationship with other currencies, or the desire

---

*The value measure of aggregate output may be a money unit of "constant value."

to avoid cost of living grumbles, may work in the same direction; but the disciplines will be much milder. Thus, the world has seldom experienced *a rectifying deflation* (as distinct from a temporary cessation or slowing down of creeping inflation) in the absence of convertibility obligations.*

On the other hand, action to *appreciate* currencies in order to honor contractual obligations which have been suspended in emergencies have occasionally led to *deliberate deflations*.† The return to convertibility has then represented the fulfilment of a collectively sought objective. Hence, in that sort of case, the change in the scale of prices cannot be represented as an instability or fluctuation in the ordinary sense. Similarly, long-term changes in the real value of a monetary standard, e.g., as under the world tendency for prices in terms of gold to fall from 1873-1894 and subsequently to rise until 1914, are not, in my judgment usefully regarded as *fluctuations*. They may be interpreted, perhaps, as a defect in the gold standard, but that is a different question. The *true fluctuations* in prices, I suggest, have been those due to monetary policy. I shall return to this question.

3.—Changes in aggregate output may be held to be due (i) to the factors which influence the withholding and diversion, or release of capacity (and monetary policy must be included among these factors); (ii) saving preference (the rate of growth or contraction of productive power); and (iii) autonomous factors, i.e., (a) population growth‡ and (b) *economizing* inventions, innovations and discoveries, which result in an increased income and (unless offset by a more than proportionate increase in consumption) stimulate saving preference (factor (ii)).

Assuming the absence of withheld capacity, whilst changes in the *form* of activity may be considerable, variations in the aggregate *volume* of activity are likely to be small, and dependent wholly upon the rate of net accumulation (or decumulation). That is, activity will tend to vary solely with changes in the aggregate stock of productive capacity; and although variations due to these causes will be influenced by autonomous factors, we cannot properly regard the latter as contributory causes of any *decline* in activity. In any case those variations in savings which would be experienced in the absence of withheld capacity are not those in which we are interested when we study the trade cycle. We are, then, concerned with *variations in the degree of utilization of resources*, the influence of which upon the magnitude of savings is a secondary consequence.

---

*About *purposeless* deflations, see pp. 104, 125-6, 150-1, 271.

†E.g., the return to gold by the United States after the Civil War and by Britain after World War I are among the rare examples.

‡Strictly speaking, the growth of that part of the population which falls within the productive age group.

As we have seen, unless pricing policies appropriate to monetary measures are adopted, changes in the value of the money unit may induce the
withholding (or, in reverse, the release) of capacity. Hence a rectifying
deflation unaccompanied by co-ordination may set the cumulative reactions going. (See pp. 76-8). But a decline in demand for any kind of
services, *however caused*, i.e., independently of monetary policy, may induce the withholding of capacity (just as a rise in the demand for particular resources may induce the release of capacity). And all sorts of
unpredicted change, including the unpredicted results of entrepreneurial
decisions, may bring about changes in the *forms* in which services are
demanded, and hence cause fluctuations in individual outputs; and these
fluctuations may, in turn, react adversely upon output in general. For
the withholding of capacity in any one field reduces real demands for all
noncompeting services; and this must, in the absence of inflation, cause
some part of the stock of noncompeting assets to lose value and possibly
fall temporarily valueless; and (given rigidities elsewhere) some part of
the flow of noncompeting services may be caused to be withheld and
wasted (although still demanded and valuable). Hence, in the absence
of co-ordinative action to release demanded capacity, noninflationary
credit must contract.

The forms taken by the cumulative withholding phenomenon so induced are many, yet *the causes* seem always to be those which I have just
explained. For instance, during the course of fluctuations, the relative
profitableness of inventories of materials and final products tends to
change, and this is one of the influences which determine the form of
replacement and net accumulation. In practice, although some booms
have been characterized by large accumulations of inventories, in others
we have found attempts to economize in the holding of inventories during the upswing or during periods of inflation, whilst the largest inventories have accrued during the downswing. It seems to me that the
growth of inventories during *depression* can be interpreted as due in
part to the rigidity of selling prices (and so to the withholding of capacity on the part of merchants) and partly to the belief that demand is
likely to recover in the near future (i.e., the accumulations are judged to
be realizable later at better prices, so that it is thought profitable not to
liquidate them by price cuts but to continue to accumulate them even in
face of an increased interest cost of holding). The speculative holding of
inventories in *those* circumstances obviously tends to stabilize prices; yet
such reactions (which are due, it must be remembered, to unstable price
rigidities which are causing the contraction of demands in general) can
obviously set up an infectious general and cumulative withholding of
capacity.

Making abstraction of autonomous factors, it can be said that fluctuations in output as a whole are due to cumulative changes in the degree of success achieved in adjusting values to economic change. And this differential success over time can be seen to be due to various institutional causes. Wrongly conceived or inconsistent value adjustments may be made; or they may be too mild and tentative, setting up false and disequilibrating expectations; or they may be too drastic, setting up a pendulum swing in the opposite direction; or they may be too late, and cause longer and much more involved chains of rectifying action to become necessary for reco-ordination—the longer the lag the greater being the difficulties.

4.—It should be noticed that I have referred to *adjustments* being made too late. I have not referred to *expenditure* being made too late. I.e., I have not spoken of a lag in "consumption expenditure" or in "investment expenditure." For if a money unit of constant value is maintained, a decline in expenditure* as a whole is the result, not the cause of adjustment failures (or other factors leading to a decline in output). The phenomena described as "lags in expenditure" occur only (i) during a rectifying deflation (correcting an inflation), in which case the lags assist policy, or (ii) during an inadvertent or purposeless deflation, or (iii) during the repressed form of latent inflation, when the effects of the lag are stabilizing. Expectations, and the lags they set up (hoarding or dishoarding) are destabilizing only when policy creates false expectations. Their importance as a factor in business cycle causation has therefore probably been greatly exaggerated and certainly misinterpreted. It is when, subsequently to inflationary episodes which have induced a wrong allocation of the community's resources, rectifying deflations can no longer be postponed, that the failure to permit the price mechanism to perform its co-ordinative task transforms a boom into a depression.

5.—The older economists' view was that the best way of dealing with depressions is to prevent their occurrence; and this they thought can be done by avoiding the temptations of cheap money; for cheap money creates situations which can be rectified only by deflations. They understood, at the same time, that if depressions *do* occur, they can always be rectified, although not without pain. They understood also that there is a case for positive governmental action to assist things to right themselves. Their traditional opposition to State intervention was only to such steps as are likely to make things worse; but they thought that the State was more likely to restrain than assist the required adjustments. It was believed (and here I use my own terminology) that the right way

---

*I put it this way because this is the way in which the point is usually expressed. The decline in "expenditure will be the *result* of the decline in the money valuation of income and not its cause.

to work is by way of seeking an increase of real income (i.e., uninflated income), which can be achieved not only through price adjustment as such, but by the transfer of labor and other assets from relatively inefficient firms and relatively unproductive industries to more efficient firms and more productive industries.

The older economists perceived also that thrift means expansion and that depression may quite automatically encourage *this* source of recovery. At the same time, they were not blind to the existence of serious resistances to the required mobilities and the value changes implied. They held that it is these resistances—paradoxically enough, in the form of measures which attempt to maintain demand through sectionalist action—which prevent recovery and cause demand to shrink. It was because of the economists' recognition that the pressures of market forces can ultimately triumph over sectionalist resistances that they felt it to be *inexpedient* for the State to attempt to rectify matters by itself directly taking pricing decisions.*

6.—In arguing that the phenomena of boom and depression are attributes of a disco-ordinated economy, I am implying that, in a co-ordinated (i.e., price flexible) economy, certain aspects of what we have come to regard as a boom situation will become perpetuated. *Apparently* idle resources will persist, but the idleness experienced will be of the same nature as that which can be observed even in booming economies. From time to time, some resources will fall into disuse through changes in ends and means; but those resources will either be *valueless*, owing to their lack of versatility (a possibility which is so rare in practice that it can normally be ignored),† or else the resources released will be eagerly snapped up for use in conjunction with the new means which have become available, or to satisfy the new ends being expressed. *Pseudo*-idleness and the loss of value in specific resources will come to be regarded as everyday, accepted features of a co-ordinated and flexible system. In a price-adjusted economy, however, idleness of this sort will constitute, together with preferred idleness (leisure), virtually the only forms of idleness; and neither can be regarded as wasteful. Of course, as we have seen, the rate of growth in a price co-ordinated economy will not *necessarily* be steady (although there are good grounds for supposing that growth *would* normally be at a steady rate).‡

---

*Moreover, basing their judgment on the extraordinary effectiveness of market pressures, some economists judged that the balance of advantage lies in the State tolerating misconceived hindrances, such as the trade-union organization and other causes of wage-rate rigidity. But the toleration in which they rather hesitatingly believed, was based on pragmatic judgment, not on principle.

†On the rareness of the valueless condition in man-made resources see my *Idle Resources*, pp.50-6. The existence of the condition implies no waste or loss.

‡See pp. 337, above and 353-4, below.

7.—In my diagnosis, almost every case of *general* depression under convertible currencies can be blamed on recourse to cheap money followed by the inevitable deflation; although the temptation to resort to cheap money may well have originated in initial withholdings of capacity which had not themselves been induced by monetary factors. The rectifying deflation seems to set going the cumulative effects of one withholding of capacity upon others. This is the only "inherent" tendency to fluctuations that I have been able to discern.

Now there have always been economists who have avoided this most obvious explanation of the phenomena of boom and depression. Instead of perceiving and explaining in detail how governments are seduced into permitting the early relief of cheap money to drag the community later into depression and (in the absence of courageous price adjustments) unemployment, they misdirect attention (quite unintentionally, of course) to mere subsidiary phenomena.

8.—Keynes himself did not set out in *The General Theory* to provide a theory of depression and boom. He called one of his chapters "Notes on the Trade Cycle," and dealt with the issues (in that chapter and elsewhere) rather casually. There was nothing new in his treatment,* apart from the role which the multiplier plays in it. He left the impression that he regarded the factors which influence entrepreneurial predictions (i.e., the marginal efficiency of capital) as the vital issue. He seemed to suggest that the causes of fluctuations in activity and prices were found when we had determined the causes of fluctuations in entrepreneurial optimism; and to explain the expectations which give rise to optimism or pessimism, he relied principally upon the "investment multiplier." He did not consider the obvious possibility that entrepreneurial confidence is determined by, rather than the determinant of, depression and boom; and the remedy he recommended was simply to keep going a boom which seemed to be petering out, by *reducing* the rate of interest to maintain expenditure. This device, he believed, could maintain the system "permanently in a quasi-boom."[6] I shall give no further attention to this part of his thesis, but direct the reader's attention to certain other ideas on fluctuations in activity—independent, I think, of the multiplier and accelerator—which Keynes' disciples and successors have based on his broad teachings.

---

*E.g., in 1922 Lavington's theory of the trade cycle placed chief stress on "influences which, reacting upon and strengthening one another, cause a *cumulative* increase in business confidence and consequently in business activity . . . This growing activity ultimately destroys the confidence on which it is based, with the result that the influences which work are reversed and there follows a *cumulative* decline in business confidence which leads to a condition of marked business depression."[3] But Lavington, unlike Keynes, tacitly recognizes the importance of the Say Law[4] and perceives that the "originating influence" in recovery is "the growth of production."[5]

9.—Largely, I feel, through the misuse of abstract thinking—particularly in mathematical form—about the economic system, theories have been invented which claim to have exposed other, deep-rooted sources of cyclical instability and inactivity. We have, thus, the doctrines of writers such as Hicks and Kaldor, which suggest that fluctuations in "economic activity" (real income) are subject to cycles of ever-increasing amplitude, held in check only by a *ceiling* due to the full employment of the limited stock of productive capacity in the one direction, and a *floor* due to the "necessity" for replacement in the other direction. It is possible to view such ideas as those in perspective, only if it is understood that income is generated by production and not by spending. But these notions of anti-damped cycles of "activity" appear to have arisen solely through building on the assumption that human society operates mechanically,* and *the use of models in which the issues with which I have been stressing are ignored.*

There is nothing unrealistic about the idea of *a floor to the cumulative withholding of capacity,* if we regard it as set by the unwillingness of people to accept passively a situation in which the wastefulness of the reactions is becoming increasingly burdensome, or in which the social folly of the situation is becoming more and more obvious. In their striving to maintain capital intact, people do tend to smash their way through the barriers which are restricting the use of productive power. That is the only conceivable reason for the "difficulty" or "impossibility" of allowing gross accumulation to fall voluntarily below the "floor" of the full replacement level. But few economists ask why investment "must" be called forth to maintain the "existing volume of output"? What is never explained, as far as I can trace, is why the movement is supposed to stop short of aggregate capital consumption.

The ceiling for the release of capacity is simpler—"full employment." When there are no further resources to release (from idleness or diversion), the growth of "activity" (real income) can result only through successful thrift—net accumulation.† The terms "floor" and "ceiling" are appropriate, provided we recognize that the ceiling may be raised by savings.

But the major weakness of these theories is that they do not assist our understanding of the forces which set going either the cumulative withholding or the cumulative release of capacity, whilst they attract attention merely to expenditure (which they do not explicitly recognize as *co-ordinative* through inflation or *disco-ordinative* through deflation). In any case, the forces which maintain a brake on the cumulative move-

---

*See my criticisms of Frisch on mechanical assumptions, pp. 317-9.

†But if we arbitrarily exclude leisure from the *category of products,* we can treat the substitution of other economic ends for leisure as a particular case of the growth of capacity.

ments do not start operating suddenly near the floor or near the ceiling. They are operative all the time and in both directions. Thus, even in the depths of depression, there will be *some* activities in which the *natural* scarcity (as distinct from a *contrived* scarcity) of at least some of the resources needed, prevents a larger contribution to output; and even near the point of "full employment" there will be some industries in which contrived scarcities—especially those which are reflected not in *idle* resources but in "diverted" capacity—are being broken down. In the sort of world that we know, there is nothing "explosive" in the situation, as some economists, e.g., Hicks,[7] have maintained, through inferences from mathematical analogies or models which make abstraction of praxeological realities (radical or institutional) and the neglect of changes in wage-rates and prices.

Moreover, it is most misleading to regard full employment as a *check* on or an *obstacle* to expansion. Under competitive conditions,* net accumulation of fixed assets will *normally* begin, in any individual field, only when existing fixed assets in that field are fully employed or expected soon to become fully employed. But if withheld capacity exists in capital resources which are specialized for making producers' goods then, until all that capacity has been released, the stock of fixed assets is *capable of being increased* with relatively little burden on the present, and hence in practice relatively rapidly,† whereas after that point the stock can grow only at the expense of a greater sacrifice of the present in respect of any versatile resources needed, and hence in practice *at a relatively stable rate*. The full employment condition constitutes, however, no "obstacle" to further expansion. The only "check" to any expression of saving-preference is the rate at which expansion can occur without sacrifices of current standards of consumption; and this in turn depends upon *the form* in which real income has been increasing as well as its magnitude. Even so, there is a "check" only in the sense that, up to the point at which all withheld capacity has been released, savings need be sufficient only to provide the versatile co-operant resources needed, the relatively fixed or long-life resources being already in existence.

If there is any useful purpose to be served by such concepts, the "investment ceilings" (net accumulation ceilings) should be recognized as determined (1) by the extent to which, saving preference being given, withheld capacity in the "investment goods industries" can be released for net accumulation; and (2) by the extent to which, through the reac-

---

*I say "under competitive conditions," because it is possible for an interloper to contribute an addition to the stock of capital resources in a field in which withheld capacity is being maintained, so that output does not increase.

†This is *not* because savings are then unnecessary but because, owing to the increase in real income, the required savings do not demand a reduction of the absolute rate of consumption.

tion of interest upon the expression of saving preference, versatile services are capable of being attracted from consumption uses.* Similarly, the "consumption ceiling" should be recognized simply as determined by the extent to which withheld capacity in the consumers' goods industries can be released and the extent to which versatile services can be transferred from uses which contribute to the stock of relatively permanent or slowly disinvested resources, to the production of goods which enter into inventories of consumers' goods, or to the production of other assets which may be expected to be decumulated relatively rapidly. But neither "ceiling" imposes a rigid limit. Both represent nothing more than the increasing cost of releasing or transferring capacity; and the term "ceiling" is therefore rather inappropriate.

10.—The relation of fluctuations in "investment" to fluctuations in "activity" needs some discussion. When the Keynesians talk of fluctuations in "investment," they often appear to be meaning something different from what I do when I think of fluctuations in net accumulation. They seem to be thinking not of net accumulation at all, but of *particular forms of gross accumulation,* especially investment in permanent or durable assets. The value of investment in *these particular forms of replacement and net accumulation* is certainly likely to fluctuate more than the value of net accumulation as a whole. It will fluctuate according to the *relative* profit expectations from those kinds of investment. For during a rectifying deflation, the prospects of *rapid* general price adjustment with the recovery of uninflated income may appear so remote that entrepreneurs will not—at current costs—even maintain full replacement of *fixed assets.* And the longer the prospective disinvestment period of any assets, the greater the uncertainty.† Moreover, if the services which enter into such assets have not fallen in price, yet it is thought that they are likely to fall (i.e., if those prices are believed to be *unstably rigid*), a further contraction in the rate of replacement may be expected. Thus, the chain reactions detonated by an initial withholding of capacity, in tending to throw the economy into increasing disorder, are likely to affect differentially the employment, replacement or net accumulation of the more durable types of productive capacity. It is possibly through the misinterpretation of a situation so caused that the Keynesians have come to imagine fluctuations in "investment" as the causes of fluctuations in activity.

But if we regard "investment" as synonymous with net accumulation, the question, "Are fluctuations in investment desirable"? is the same

---

*This depends in part, I must repeat, upon the form of current income.

†This factor is conceptually quite distinct from that dealt with in the sentence which follows.

question as, "Are fluctuations in savings desirable"? And as we have seen, there is no reason to suppose that, in a co-ordinated and price flexible economy, consumption-saving propensities will not be as stable as the preference for beer or cotton. But this does not imply that the *profitableness* of replacing and adding to the stock of assets will be equally stable. Prospective and realized yields might well fluctuate. Thus, an era of innovations may be expected to cause a rise in yields—predicted and achieved —whilst yields are likely to decline during a period of consolidation. It follows that, saving propensities being assumed constant,* there will be fluctuations in the rate of interest, with probable reactions upon the relative value magnitudes of "net accumulation" and "consumption." But in a co-ordinated economy, the magnitudes of these changes will be determined solely by the versatility of the resources which can be shifted from one field of employment to the other.†

11.—Keynes' remedy for fluctuations in activity amounted, as we have seen, to that of perpetuating boom conditions by keeping inflation going. (He would have said, of course, "maintaining a high rate of investment"). I suggest, however, that the trade cycle is avoidable without inflation. Monetary policy can achieve stability in the value of the money unit, and economic policy generally can permit or enforce flexible pricing and thereby prevent the cumulative withholding of capacity. But this does not mean, as I have already emphasized, that all resources released for more urgent uses will be able *immediately* to find co-operant resources which are demanding their services. Still less does it mean that there may be no periods in which such transfers of resources in progress (i.e., resources productively employed in seeking the most profitable employments) will not be exceptionally large; although we are more likely to find this phenomenon during periods of rapid growth or inventiveness than during periods of contraction.

12.—But under any monetary system based on convertibility in some defined sense, the amplitude of *price movements* will be narrower the wiser the anticipations of speculators, and the greater the confidence which exists in the monetary authority. As Cannan put it as early as 1922, "if more people recognized that a boom was a temporary phenomenon, there would be less readiness to buy and more readiness to sell,

---

*That is, the saving preference schedule being regarded as given.

†The relatively large variability of "investment" (net accumulation) over time, contrasted with the relative stability of "consumption," has been dealt with in the previous chapter. If real income is constant, the magnitudes "consumption" and "net accumulation" must vary *inversely by the same absolute amount.* And as we know that in practice only a small proportion of income goes to make up net accumulation, the *proportional* variation of the latter *must* be much greater. Indeed, every fluctuation in net accumulation is a magnification of fluctuations in consumption, *although in the opposite way to what is assumed in the acceleration theory!*

and consequently prices would be lower" and *vice versa*.[8] Moreover, as we have seen (pp. 100-1), if there is faith that a defined value of the money unit is being maintained, the further the real value of the money unit diverges at any moment from a value consistent with long-term convertibility, the greater the probability that it will move towards that value and the smaller the probability that it will diverge still further. But once the lack of confidence in the conversion value of the money unit has arisen, or once this same lack of confidence has caused the future real value of the standard itself to become uncertain, the amplitude of fluctuations can become very much wider.

13.—It has often been supposed that price level fluctuations of the magnitude of those which were experienced during the 19th century have been absent during the creeping inflation era of 1930 to 1962. But this is partly an illusion. These fluctuations have continued in exactly the same superficial form, but have been disguised in a continuous but uneven inflation. Although we have now been experiencing for many years a persistent rise in prices in the major countries, there have been marked fluctuations about the rising trend. Since 1931, there have been intermittent recessions in which national scales of prices have seldom experienced any considerable *absolute* fall. But the interludes of relative price stability have meant a substantial decline in relation to the general upward tendency of prices. The purpose of these interludes appears to have been that of restoring confidence, so that costs may lag in relation to prices and a further round of inflation have some co-ordinative effect. (See Chap. XVIII).

The amplitude of the fluctuations which have marked the post-war creeping inflation may not have been as wide as those which were normally experienced under the gold standard; and it can be claimed that, until very recently, fluctuations in the scale of prices about a rising trend have not been accompanied by fluctuations in employment as large or as frequent as those which are believed to have been typical of the true gold standard days (i.e., before 1914). This is because *serious* recession has not marked the periods in which inflation has suffered a temporary check. But if my diagnosis is correct, the recession which accompanied a still rising scale of prices in the United States in 1958 is a phenomenon which is destined to become increasingly common unless the current policy of engineering creeping inflation is abandoned.

14.—There remains to be considered a notion which has played some considerable part in modern trade cycle theories, namely, that general productive power may grow excessively. This notion has some similarity to all theories of general over-production, or over-stimulation of the economy.

I can find no good reasons for the assumption (which is typical of many treatments of the trade cycle) that it is possible for the productive system to be *excessively* stimulated, whether the stimulus results in expansion taking a form in which net accumulation increases relatively to consumption or *vice versa*. What *may* be called "excessive" is *a particular means* for the stimulation of activity, namely, credit expansion when it is inflationary.* The phrase "excessive stimulation" might be applied to the case of latent inflation which price rigidities upwards have helped to cause. But this is never what is meant. And in so far as inflation induces a more intensive use of resources, *that* result is beneficial and cannot be "excessive." The weakness of co-ordination through inflation does not lie in an unfavorable magnitude of productive capacity achieved. It is found firstly, in a distorted structure of production; secondly (and partly in consequence) in disappointed expectations, with their consequences upon the withholding of capacity,† and thirdly in the distributive injustices caused. But what seems to me to be the extreme form of this idea, the theory of "capital saturation" (too much capital in some sense) demands explicit consideration, and to this subject I devote the next chapter.

This brief treatment of depression and boom may appear to be a very perfunctory way of treating the enormous literature of the subject. But simplicity is not superficiality. I have dealt with the issues which, it seems to me, lie at the root of all cyclical economic phenomena; and these issues seem to me to be tacitly ignored or most superficially treated in the greater part of the *modern* literature.

---

*In the case of a wave of dishoarding, the failure to restrict credit sufficiently may be blamed.

†Disappointed expectations *may* (see pp. 371-2) induce the withholding of capacity in many sectors of the economy, and hence initiate the process of cumulative withholding; and they are especially likely to be a factor under convertibility, or when it becomes politically inexpedient to engineer inflation more rapidly than it is expected to occur; for credit restriction then becomes unavoidable.

REFERENCES

(1) BOWEN and MEIER, *Institutional Aspects of Economic Fluctuations*, in Kurihara, *Post-Keynesian Economics*, p.162. (2) KEYNES, *The General Theory*, pp.327-8. (3) LAVINGTON, *The Trade Cycle*, pp.29-30. (4) *Ibid.*, p.24. (5) *Ibid.*, p.61. (6) KEYNES, *op. cit.*, p.322. (7) HICKS, *A Contribution to the Theory of the Trade Cycle*, p.37. (8) CANNAN, *An Economist's Protest*, pp.315-6.

Chapter XVI

CAPITAL SATURATION

SUMMARY

*1.—The fallacy that productive power may grow to an extent which outstrips
aggregate demand, so that the marginal efficiency of capital falls to zero
2.—seems to be due to reasoning from the particular to the general; 3.—or
to the* unbalanced growth *of productive power being mistaken for over-
growth; 4.—or to a wrong interpretation of the slowing down in the rate
of recovery of activity which is to be expected when little withheld capacity
remains for release, 5.—or to a wrong interpretation of the slowing down
in the rate of growth which is to be expected when an exceptional
period of economizing inventions or discoveries comes to an end; 6.—or
to the failure to perceive that replacement and net accumulation may
properly be said to be "required" only by saving preference, and not by
depreciation, technological progress or population growth. 7.—The
assumptions of diminishing marginal* utility *of capital, or of a "too rapid"
flow of savings are merely assumptions about preference. 8.—But undue
speed of attempted (as distinct from* realized) *growth, due to unfounded
entrepreneurial optimism, may indirectly have adverse repercussions upon
capital structure and income. 9.—The notion that, as non-money assets
accumulate, their yield must fall relatively to that of money, is based on
the unperceived assumption that the process is accompanied by deflation;
10.—whilst the theory that ultimately the full labor force will be required
to maintain capital intact (so that growth must cease and stagnation ensue)
assumes (unrealistically) that it is* impossible to sacrifice consumption without waste, or that current consumption is *preferred to growth, 11.—or that
cheap labor facilitates net accumulation, 12.—or that there is a certain
correct proportion for the combination of labor with capital. 13.—But there
are no limits to the possibility of net accumulation which do not apply
equally to replacement. 14.—The argument that technological progress*
hastens *capital redundancy is due to a failure to perceive that inventions
which cause the abandonment of existing equipment imply a net gain in
productive capacity. 15.—But population growth certainly does tend to
enhance the profitableness of net accumulation in the particular form of
co-operant equipment. 16.—The danger in the capital saturation fallacies
is that they lead to the conclusion that the State can prevent the
"disruptive" growth of productive power by curbing private investment.*

1.—Theories of under-consumption and theories of capital saturation are, logically speaking, virtually the same notions in a different form. For unless we can assume some withholding of capacity (induced by hoarding under price rigidity), "too little consumption" *means* "too much net accumulation" in some sense. But the fallacies to be discussed in this chapter cannot be effectively answered by this simple approach; they appear to emerge out of the ancient conviction which manifests itself in time of depression that there can be a phenomenon of general glut. An intuitive feeling seems to reassert itself in every recession that there must be a surfeit of *things in general*. Thus, in one of the attempted rehabilitations of Keynesian doctrine, this feeling finds explicit expression in the notion that abundance itself may threaten impoverishment. "Abundance of capital," says Dillard, "may interfere with the abundance of output." "Old wealth may be a barrier to new wealth."[1] The suggestion sometimes is that there are diminishing returns to capital growth—a development which is supposed to be aggravated by a diminishing rate of population growth. At other times "investment opportunities" are imagined as limited in some way, and gradually "exhausted" as they are exploited—a fallacious approach with which I have already dealt. But all versions of the theory envisage a superabundance of productive power which is believed to bring about stagnation and depression. Indeed thrift may, it is feared, be so oblivious of declining prospective yields from net accumulation that even inflationary policy *via* operations to influence the market rate of interest may be insufficient to prevent capital redundancy and hence unemployment.

The folly of the notion that productive power may accumulate too rapidly, which had been quite prevalent at the end of the eighteenth century, was explicitly exposed by James Mill, Say, J. S. Mill* and Ricardo. Yet Keynes revived this notion in all its original crudity. I can find no sophistication in his development of the idea, nor in the treatment of Hansen, whose lucid exposition of the fallacy has had much influence. But the Keynes-Hansen version appeared rather in the form

---

*Hazlitt has dealt with J. S. Mill's extraordinarily effective exposure (in his *Unsettled Questions*) of the fallacy.[2]

of *an applied theory*. It was, we understood, supposed to explain a particular institutional framework called *the mature economy*, a socioeconomic order which had evolved in the 'thirties. The special attributes of this system—a low propensity to consume and a chronic dearth of investment outlets—brought about an economic equilibrium, it was thought, under the condition of less than full employment. Of course, subsequent history has made nonsense of such an hypothesis as an applied theory. But refutation by direct appeal to interpretation of the apparent facts is seldom satisfactory in economics; and as the stagnation thesis has by no means been abandoned by all the modern Keynesians, it is essential to give some attention to it.

It is significant that the same sort of notion, unlinked with any particular assumptions about economic maturity, has emerged from time to time, in a host of different forms, since the beginnings of economic science. Thus, Sismondi thought that technical inventions could multiply too rapidly, increase unreasonably the power to produce, and lead societies to ruin. He actually wanted the State to curb inventions. Yet the saturation notion as such had little influence on *serious* economic thought until it received the support of Keynes, since when, some economists (e.g., J. H. Williams) were led to regard it as the "essential content" of Keynesian teaching.[3] Keynes' disciples appear, indeed, to have given even greater weight to the theory of stagnation than their master himself did; and the view was once growing that the threat of capital surfeit had now supplanted the threat of depression as the great economic problem. Certainly this idea has been one of the principal reasons for the influence of Keynesian teachings until, fairly recently, experience of creeping inflation has apparently been destroying some of its plausibility. The theory itself is, however, highly plausible, for it seems to confirm the widely held popular view that recovery from depression must always be delayed until *excess* productive power has been wiped out.*

In some expositions, the fallacy is expressed in the idea that growing productive power becomes superabundant when, together with rising standards of living generally, it reduces the propensity to consume because people become sated.† In this form it is linked to the notion that redistribution of income from the thrifty to the thriftless can increase the propensity to consume and so rectify the tendency to stagnation. But changing distribution and rising standards affect directly the *form* of income, not its *"amount"* in any intelligible sense; and ultimately con-

---

*E.g., Dillard says: "The interval which must elapse before the recovery will set in is conditioned by (1) the time necessary for the wearing out and obsolescence of durable capital and (2) the time that elapses before excess stocks, which accumulate toward the end of the boom, can be absorbed."[4]

†In the least irrational version, there is a tacit assumption that leisure will be demanded instead of other goods. But other passages always seem to contradict this assumption.

sumption means either the achievement of such ends as involve the enjoyment of scarce services, or the decumulation of physical inventories into which services have been embodied. There must always be an unlimited desire to consume in the former sense, and a *power* to consume in the latter, narrower sense which is *naturally* limited only by the aggregate values of the flow of services and the stock of decumulable resources.

The only other conceivable limitations on consumption are manmade, *and equally limitations on production*. Indeed, if the Say Law is understood and accepted, ideas of redundant capital are simply refuted; for the growth of *productive power* is equally the growth of the source of *demand power*, in the sense of the general power to offer output in return for noncompeting output. Utilized productive power is *purchasing power* as distinct from mere *spending power*.

I propose, however, to examine the argument on which these theories of glut are based to see whether they disclose any weaknesses in orthodox teaching which may have been overlooked in previous chapters.

It seems to me that there are two main forms of capital redundancy theory. The first is that which I have been describing. The second rests upon the tacit or explicit assumption that savings are "excessive" when they are accompanied by hoarding. (See sec. 3 below). In practice the two notions seem often to be confused in the same argument. I shall deal later with an example from Dillard. (See sec. 8). But B. M. Anderson has beautifully illustrated the typical confusion in an examination of fallacious arguments which have been used to explain the Wall Street crash of 1929. In this case the over-saving theorists have blamed plowed back profits, firstly on the grounds that (to use Anderson's words) the corporations "withheld dividends from their stock-holders . . . . to build unneeded plant and equipment, which unduly increased the productive power of the country, leading to further unneeded production of goods, which finally broke the markets and brought on the crisis"; and secondly that, "they did not use these surplusses to build additional plant and equipment, but held them in the form of cash which they lent to the stock market . . . . and that their failure to employ these funds in additional plant and equipment led to a falling off in demand for goods from the heavy industries, which brought reaction and depression."[5] Anderson's passage makes the contradiction so clear that it appears to invite the charge of misrepresentation. But the over-saving theorists are seldom explicit in distinguishing the two quite different—and contradictory—arguments.*

---

*In the example taken by Anderson, the facts support neither theory. Corporate savings were tending to fall rather than to rise for some years before the crash, whilst some considerable part of the "profits" which were supposed to have been withheld from shareholders were due to nominal capital gains, their retention being essential merely to maintain real capital intact.

As I have said, Keynes was mainly responsible for reviving and putting into circulation the former theory—the old idea that the world was tending towards capital saturation, a condition which Bronfenbrenner calls capital accumulation "to the point of zero productivity."[6] In the situation envisaged, says R. C. O. Matthews, growth "outstrips requirements."[7] The net accumulation of capital, we are told, must inevitably come to an end through the inherent unprofitableness of adding to it, with the consequent emergence of stagnation. Keynes (who thought that this provided an explanation of the 1929 crash in the United States*), maintained that under conditions of full employment, the marginal efficiency of capital must fall "approximately to zero within a single generation," so that net accumulation will be held to be unprofitable.[9] Unless capital is "kept scarce," in the long period,[10] he suggested, capital goods will become so abundant that the marginal efficiency of capital will vanish.[11] He appears to have been led to these fears through his idea that aggregate effective demand—unless somehow enhanced—will be insufficient to absorb the services of more than a certain aggregate stock of resources. "New capital-investment," he said, "can only take place in excess of current capital-disinvestment if *future* expenditure on consumption is expected to increase. Every time we secure today's equilibrium by increased investment we are aggravating the difficulty of securing equilibrium tomorrow. A diminished propensity to consume today can only be accommodated to the public advantage if an increased propensity to consume is expected to exist some day."[12]

This passage reflects, I suggest, blindness to praxeological realities. Keynes failed to perceive (a) that the prices of services tend, under the institutions which bring about "full employment," always to adjust themselves to whatever *preferences* are being expressed in demand; (b) that the notion of plenty or abundance is as *relative* as that of scarcity and that in so far as the growth of productive capacity and economizing inventions permit the easier achievement of existing ends, it permits the achievement of new and additional ends; and (c) that complementarity (not only in the narrower sense—which has been well discussed in Lachmann's important *Capital and its Structure*—but in the wider sense that the demand for the services of any set of resources has its origin in the supply of services of noncompeting resources) continuously solves the problem of future demand. We shall see that a similar neglect of these issues—the vital issues—is typical of the stagnation thesis in all its forms.

Let us examine the notion that a growing accumulation of capital resources must cause entrepreneurial remuneration (profit) to fall. This idea, for which early classical speculations are partly to blame, arises

---

*He wrote: "New investment during the previous five years had been . . . . on so enormous a scale in the aggregate that the prospective yield of further addition was, coolly considered, falling rapidly."[8]

largely through the failure to understand the nature and universality of the entrepreneurial function. There is no more reason for *profit* to contract and disappear as productive capacity increases than there is for *consumers' surplus* to disappear. Nor is there any good reason to believe that the rate of interest (the value of services in relation to the value of assets) will fall to an extremely low level because the power to produce (the widening of the range of alternatives open to preference) has risen. But it is this fallacy which appears to have led the Keynesians to think that capital redundancy in some sense must lead to disaster (through the consequent disappearance of investment outlets) if it is not offset by (a) population increases, geographical discoveries and technological progress (see sec. 5), or (b) wars or (c) inflation. Yet technological progress, the opening and exploitation of virgin areas, and population increases are only particular kinds of capital accumulation. Logically, they should aggravate the situation! And they do not *destroy* productive capacity as do wars. The fact that they are classed with wars ought to have exposed the fallacy which is lurking in the notion.*

2.—Now the notion of growth outstripping "requirements" is not absurd if applied to *particular kinds* of capital investment. What the Keynesians seem to have done is, quite invalidly, to extend the notion to net accumulation as a whole. We have here once again, I believe, the *main* origin of the fallacy. Resources *in general* cannot be more than are "required" because it is their own services (the incomes they generate) which demand them—in the sense of demanding their product. Moreover, unless my previous reasoning is at fault, the demand for these resources *as capital* is determined solely through the expression of saving preference.

We can examine, in this connection, a recent attempt to explain capital saturation which can be clearly seen (at some points of the exposition) to rest upon this extension of the particular case to the general. Kurihara, developing the theory that only the elimination of the *interest burden* can prevent ultimate stagnation, argues that investment in capital goods is "stimulated" when their "demand price" exceeds their "supply price." Although "stimulated" is the wrong word, the statement is acceptable if what is meant is that when the values (expressed as prices) of the services which can be embodied into *particular* assets fall short of the capital values of existing assets of that kind, the discrepancy will create incentives to bring about equilibrium through the *replacement or net accumulation* of the assets employed, by the incorporation of services into that special type of assets. But Kurihara describes his assertion as "merely another way of saying that investment

---

*But the emergency of war *does* often break through barriers of custom, law and contrivance which have previously prevented the full utilization of resources.

in new capital goods is stimulated by the marginal efficiency of capital which exceeds the rate of interest."*(13) Now as we have seen (Chapters X and XI), this cannot be said of *assets in general*.† For the flow of services which are being embodied into assets can be increased (in the sense of net accumulation increasing or net decumulation decreasing) only (a) through a decline in consumption, or (b) through an increase in the aggregate flow of services accompanied by a less than countervailing increase in consumption.

An apparent failure to reconcile his thesis with this simple truth leads Kurihara to the conclusion that "the rate of interest should be made to fall faster than the marginal efficiency of capital" which, he assumes, must fall when productive capacity increases (presumably beyond a certain limit or beyond a certain rate) to the point at which any addition to the capacity would be unproductive at natural interest. In such a situation, he pleads, "interest as *unearned income* should be made to disappear if capital growth is to be compatible with continuous full employment."(14) Only in that way, he believes, can continuous full employment be obtained through capital growth.‡ But mere inflation —market interest below the natural level—cannot *produce* additional services and so (saving preference schedules remaining constant) capital growth.

Low interest is *the result* of a large proportion of the flow of services being *offered* for provision for the future ("large" in relation to the prospective profitableness of replacement and net accumulation) through a low consumption preference (high saving preference).** *Low interest is not the inducement or cause of the availability of those services.* Indeed, the inducement—saving preference—is *likely* to be enhanced by the opposite, the offer of high interest (through the bidding of entrepreneurs who predict that yields will be high). Kurihara reverses cause and effect.

Keynes believed that "whilst there may be intrinsic reasons for the scarcity of land, there are no intrinsic reasons for the scarcity of capi-

---

*The word "stimulated" is again the wrong word. I take it that Kurihara does not mean *"additional* capital resources" by the term "new capital resources." What is true in the assertion applies equally to replacement of assets of any kind.

†Kurihara obviously *does not mean* that the high marginal efficiency of capital stimulates savings.

‡An *additional* advantage, according to Kurihara, of zero or low interest, is that it may turn out to be "as instrumental in reducing thriftiness as a regime of high wages in promoting a higher level of consumption."(15)

**The lowness of consumption preference here refers to the height of the saving preference schedule. The "amount" of consumption need not change if the specificity of the resources making final products is absolute and prices are flexible. (See pp. 231-2). That is why I have italicized the word *"offered."* I have avoided the word "provided."

tal."[16] This is equivalent to saying that there may be no hire value
for resources in general under conditions of natural scarcity, i.e., that
owners of capital may somehow deliberately contrive a scarcity of it.
Keynes apparently recognized that if all land were State-owned, rent
(i.e., interest on the capital value of land) would still exist. But under
any rational administration of other State-owned resources in the pursuit
of *whatever the community's ends (collective or private) happened to be,*
for exactly the same reasons, the hire value (i.e., the use value or *usury*)
of all assets would be an inescapable element. In any system of self-
consistent economic calculation, it is essential to impute hire values to
all scarce assets. Keynes never stopped to ask himself the obvious question, Why does land differ from resources as a whole?

Kurihara's attempt to interpret Keynes' teachings on this issue,[17]
advocating the euthanasia of the *rentier* (through reducing interest to
zero, in order to increase the stock of capital), merely highlights his
master's shortcomings. Were money interest to be forced to zero, says
Kurihara, the *rentier* "would be unable . . . . to exact from the user of
capital (entrepreneur) an unearned surplus by compelling the latter
to keep capital goods scarce enough to possess a 'scarcity value' that is
in excess of the cost of production."[18] It seems to me that this passage
brings out the absurdity of the idea that the *rentier* can contrive scarcity
in some sense *in order to raise interest* thus forcing the entrepreneur to
contrive scarcity also.* Charging for the hire value of assets, provided
that no part of them is withheld and idle when their services are demanded, does not "compel" entrepreneurs "to keep capital goods scarce,"
as Kurihara contends. The values which result come into being irrespective of whether capacity is being utilized to the full or withheld.
In other words, interest is a reflection of "natural scarcity," not of "contrived scarcity."† *Particular resources may be made scarce to raise their
capital value and the interest value of their services. But that will not*

---

*It would be just as easy to ruin the *rentier* by *taxing away* interest, as by an inflation which forces market interest to zero. But doing that would not eliminate interest as a cost of production. For instance, if the State taxed away the rent of land, the
redistribution of income effected would not cause the hire value of land to fall. All
that would happen would be that the user of the land would have to pay the interest
as a tax. And the rent of land is merely a particular case of interest. It exists because
land supplies us with insufficient services (the advantages of site, etc.) to cause their
value to be zero (like the zero value of the sun's light and warmth, and the air).
And all other productive services which can be embodied in capital goods are scarce
in exactly the same sense, whether the resources which provide them are man-made
or natural. But as I have shown, the withholding of capacity (which I regard as a
producer's and not an entrepreneur's act—see pp. 206-8) raises the interest received
from particular assets *only because it raises their capital value.* It does not raise *the
rate* of interest. I regard the *rentier* as the lender of capital through the initial lending of a money sum.
†See my article, *Natural and Contrived Scarcities,* S.A.J.E., 1935.

cause the rate of interest to rise. The sole reason why the profitable output of *any particular kind of good* is limited by the point at which the marginal prospective yield from the investment of services in it has fallen to the rate of interest, is that *other uses are outbidding the entrepreneur concerned for the services needed at that point.*

Logically, the hire value of assets (interest) can become zero only as a result of the aggregate desire to provide for the future being sufficiently strong whilst the profitableness of embodying services into assets is sufficiently low. And in practice, as I have explained already, long before zero interest could be approached in such circumstances, *the cost of provision for the future* (the sacrifice of the present) would become so exhorbitant that *society,* as distinct from particular individuals, could be realistically expected to make virtually no provision for the future and growth would cease. (See pp. 224-5). Indeed, if we imagine that services cannot be embodied into assets at all, whilst the aggregate desire to consume in the future (under this assumption, of course, the desire to consume services) exceeds the aggregate desire to exercise in the present such rights already acquired, interest will be negative. But when interest is zero or negative, the value of services in terms of services (measured in a money unit appropriate for such a fantastic sort of society)* will not fall to zero or below. The value of services will be zero or negative only in terms of assets, and this merely means that, in order to acquire assets out of income (it being assumed to be impossible to embody services into assets), it will be necessary to exchange services for securities of declining value in terms of services; for the assumptions which are necessary in order to imagine negative interest (as, indeed, zero interest) imply that no-one would be prepared to *exchange* physical assets for services.

3.—The notion of capital saturation sometimes takes the form of a suggestion that, when productive power has multiplied *too rapidly,*† savings (in the Keynesian sense, which implies some hoarding) are likely to exceed "investment" owing to an absence of "investment opportunities." This is likely (it is believed), in turn, to force an instantaneous (or rapid) contraction of income and investment. Such ideas, which emerge in the theories of Kaldor[19] and Kalecki,[20] have been answered above, but they may help us to discern the origin of the fallacy in the stagnation context. What *can* happen is that an unwise *form* of growth may occur, in the sense that the services of the particular assets

---

*Money will have to be of the Silvio Gesell type or it will be hoarded as the most profitable means of providing for the future.

†I know of no attempts to define the criteria by which one judges growth to be "too rapid," or to define ideal or optimal rates of growth.

provided (in replacement and growth) are not in fact demanded to the extent to which investors had predicted, or that for other reasons the resources provided lose value more rapidly than had been anticipated. I.e., *certain kinds* of resources produced may prove not to have been "required" to the extent which was supposed.* But this is essentially a theory of *unbalanced* growth, and seems to be virtually the opposite of the theory which finds the cause of a tendency towards stagnation in *too much* capital having been accumulated. It means that a part of what had been *reckoned as capital resources* is perceived to have ceased to be capital. I refer again to unbalanced growth in sections 6 to 8; but the principle is simple. If every particular growth in productive power is an addition to the source of demand for the services of all noncompeting productive power, there can hardly be such a thing as a *too rapid* expansion.

The fallacy is not diminished if stress is placed on previous "over-saving"—in the sense of too rapid growth—followed by a reversal of saving preference and growth. As we have seen, sudden changes in the valuation of time, like sudden changes in all other preferences, may create circumstances in which countless cost and price adjustments are needed to preserve a co-ordinated and hence fully employed economy. But if there *is* a cessation of growth through the repercussions of disco-ordination upon income and prospects (and hence upon interest offered), it will be a simple response to preference *in the circumstances assumed.* It is impossible to stress too often the relation of preference and growth.

4.—Certain economists who have an apparent hankering for some theory of capital redundancy seem to be comparing the rapid increase in activity which is possible when a great deal of withheld (or diverted) capacity is being released, or reserve capacity (in *pseudo*-idleness) brought into operation, with the relatively slow progress which is possible *after* it has been fully released.† I suggest that writers who regard the development of a state in which there is no further withheld capacity for release as a cause of "depression" (e.g., as in the writings of Hicks[21] and

---

*Nevertheless, even the services of assets which have been provided most unwisely and unprofitably may still be *required* in the sense of being demanded; for at a sufficiently low price there is no reason why their services should not be fully absorbed. It is certainly possible, especially when capacity is being withheld on a large scale, for some part of the stock of assets to be temporarily valueless. But that will be due to *the extermination of demand for its services through the withholding of capacity elsewhere,* or through costs being unduly high owing to the withholding of the capacity which provides co-operant services.

†The reader should be reminded that the existence of *reserve capacity* (i.e., capacity in *pseudo*-idleness) in particular fields contributes to stability. Indeed, its ability to do so may constitute the principal services contributed by such capacity. I do not think the Keynesians have discussed this issue. (See pp. 332-3, 325-6, 335-6).

Goodwin[(22)]) are creating great confusion through turning attention away from an extremely simple reality.

Obviously, the cumulative release of capacity (through direct price adjustment or inflation) *can* bring about rapid *recovery* towards the point of full employment and even towards the point of optimum utilization;* and beyond that point, even although *the form of income* may be that appropriate for growth, the further expansion of income can be achieved only through a more obvious preference for the future as against the present. There is no reason, however, for treating a situation in which the relatively easy progress to the full or optimum use of existing productive power has been completed, as a condition which subsequently "depresses" the economy. The increasing scarcity of factors of production—in the sense of a declining proportion of withheld capacity to be released—merely calls for adjustments in response to the expression of new ends;† and if the recovery of income has been in a form which has left a relative scarcity of services available for growth (in the absence of a compensating growth in thrift), that is merely a particular factor which determines the new choice of ends.

What *can* be said is that, in the process of reaching the situation in which there is no further withheld capacity to be released, and especially when the release of capacity has been effected through inflationary policy instead of through direct price co-ordination, it is possible, or even probable, that false expectations will set up and a consequential misdirection of investment brought about. The structure and composition of the stock of assets may well become distorted, causing a particular form of unbalanced replacement and growth; and when there are objections to *further* inflation, resistance to necessary cost and price adjustment can produce idleness. This is, in fact, the orthodox theory of depression (sometimes called, very inappropriately, the "over-investment" theory) towards which, I think, Hicks and Goodwin have been gropingly retreating.‡

5.—Another theory which is in some resepects similar, is concerned not with the culmination of the rapid growth which is possible during the release of capacity but with the culmination of the rapid growth which is facilitated by autonomous progress. Great bursts of expansion

---

*But optimum utilization requires time for the devising of new production functions to utilize diverted capacity.

†It is equally incorrect to imagine that this increasing scarcity can be "aggravated" by a shortage of *money* capital, unless all that is meant is that deflation would have this effect. What is called "the scarcity of *money* capital" can usually be discerned simply as a representation of the scarcity of *real* capital in a money economy.

‡This has been recognized by Ichimura[(23)] who refers to the similarity of the teachings of Hicks and Goodwin to those of Tugan-Baranowsky, Spiethoff, Wicksell and Hayek, apart from the "unfortunate reliance" [of the latter] "upon the Say Law."

of productive capacity set going by major economizing inventions, discoveries, or the sudden development of formerly underdeveloped territories, may well be of such a nature that *final output* from the accumulating capacity becomes available suddenly, and in a profuse flood, long after the process of rapid net accumulation began. Naturally, formidable repercussions upon preferences and values must be expected in such *fortunate* circumstances, with the necessity for drastic cost adjustments and adaptations in production functions (if wasteful idleness is to be avoided). If we anticipate the emergence of depression through the abundance assumed, it must be solely because we expect that society will be inadequately organized for bringing about the needed adjustments. Even economists of the standing of Pigou, Robertson and Schumpeter have *appeared*, at times, to see in the ultimate productiveness of great accumulations so stimulated, the cause of the final breakdown into depression. But they have not, I think, brought out in the required clarity what seems to me to be the crucial point, namely, that depression in the sense of a contraction in the volume of output is due solely to the failure to permit prices to be determined appropriately to the situation which emerges.

For instance, Schumpeter's assumption that the expansion of activity induced through an innovation *in a particular field* eventually leads to the exhaustion of opportunities in that field, should properly be considered in the light of the fact that it may induce development (or the re-utilization of idle resources) in noncompeting fields.* What I find impossible to grasp is the notion of the exhaustion of possibilities in *all fields*. The effect of economizing innovations is merely to increase full employment income, which effect in turn both *facilitates* the achievement of and raises the yield to savings, and hence *ceteris paribus* induces a more rapid rate of growth. But growth depends on preference and the resources available for growth.

Let us consider the case in which there is a sudden increase in real income over a relatively short period of years due to a series of important economizing inventions or discoveries. A sudden demand for growth (a rise in saving preference and/or a response in savings to higher prospective yields) will then be highly likely, and the first projects to bid successfully for the flow of services available for replacement and growth will be those which seem to offer the highest yields. Now should it happen that the process of growth so initiated does not itself create sufficient additional income (the additional services provided by the assets which are piling up) to raise what were the lower priorities in prospective profitableness to a higher order of profitableness, the marginal efficiency of capital will tend gradually to fall. Yet if there *is* any

---

*At times, Schumpeter clearly recognized this.

contraction in the rate of growth, it will be due solely to a contraction in savings (due to the shape of, or a shift in, the saving preference schedule).

6.—It seems to me that, through a loose use of concepts, the Keynesians fail to realize that any given rate of net accumulation can be said to be *required* at any time only by saving preference. Consider, for instance, R. C. O. Matthew's assertion that "private enterprise might, if left to itself, tend normally to exceed the level *required* to make good depreciation and to provide for such long-term factors as technical progress and population growth."[24] (My italics). But if gross accumulation is sufficient to make good (or more than make good) decumulation (including depreciation), that is only because people do not wish to dissave or do wish to save net. It is not because the making good of depreciation and technical progress *require* the limitation of consumption (i.e., *require* gross accumulation to exceed decumulation) in the sense that they *demand* it. The purpose of achieving savings beyond what are needed to maintain capital intact is not to *respond to* "technical progress and population growth" (except in so far as entrepreneurial predictions affect interest offered and, in turn, affect the response of savers to interest). Saving simply makes available a flow of services for use in whatever kinds of replacement or net accumulation appear to be *relatively* most profitable.* The *purpose* of net accumulation as such is solely to provide for the future. *Its form* is a response to the form of predicted demands.

7.—A more plausible but, I contend, equally wrong proposition is the suggestion that there is a diminishing marginal *utility* of capital† (or savings) in the sense that, the more assets people have, the less are they likely to want additions to the stocks they possess. That would make *saving preference* a negative function of the stock of assets. The implication is that, at any given rate of interest, those people who own large quantities of capital will tend to save a smaller proportion of income than those who own smaller stocks of capital. But this reverses the usual common sense assumption about reality,—an assumption which has never been seriously challenged.‡

When net decumulation occurs, or when no net accumulation is ex-

---

*See pp. 201-3.

†The marginal utility of capital must not be confused with the marginal efficiency of capital.

‡Moreover, as we have seen (pp. 238-9), there is no reason to suppose that the interest *inducement* to saving will fall as capital accumulates. For assets may take *countless complementary forms* and provide an *unlimited variety* of services and products. (See above, pp. 362-3).

perienced, that implies that people feel, in the light of the cost of saving (current consumption postponed) and the prospective return from saving (interest), that they have provided enough for the future and want now rather to enjoy the present. People *prefer* resources to be used in that particular way: that is all there is to it.* And if that *is* their preference, the situation created has an origin which is wholly unconnected with either the quantity of capital or the rate at which it has been recently accumulating. The fact that the relevant saving preference may be expressed largely through the decisions of company directors (see p. 204) must not be allowed to confuse us.

In the opposite situation—under the more usual assumption about saving preference—exactly the same considerations are relevant. If people in general want to use the flow of services to provide for the future to a far greater extent than has ever yet been experienced (say at a rate so high that ten per cent. is added to the flow of services each year) there is not the slightest reason to suppose that unemployment will be threatened, at some time in the near or distant future, through a capital surfeit. It will simply mean a far more rapid expansion of real income and uninflated demand than the world has ever experienced.

I anticipate the objection that I am talking here of net accumulation whereas Keynes was thinking of saving, by which he meant hoarding! But the *stress* in this part of the Keynesian doctrine, is clearly on the growth of production power, although viewed sometimes from the angle of the saver (or *rentier*) and sometimes from the standpoint of the entrepreneur. Thus, the redistribution argument is based on the assumption that the lower income groups will *consume* relatively more of a given income, not that they will hoard less.

8.—In reality, *realized growth* (however rapid) is more likely to lead to a *demand* for the continuance of growth (a rise in saving preference) than for its cessation. Nor does the net accumulation of capital resources *in general*, whatever the speed at which it occurs, imply a fall in the marginal *efficiency* of capital. But "undue" speed of *attempted growth*— unfounded entrepreneurial optimism—may result in the rate of interest being bid up temporarily to an unjustified height; and this is likely to lead not only to disappointed expectations (with possible adverse repercussions in the form of the withholding of capacity by producers), but to the unbalanced form of replacement and growth to which I have referred above.

If we take it, then, that the "excessive" resources intended by the

---

*The pricing of services so as to secure full utilization is just as *possible* (even if much more difficult) in an economy which is not growing, or even in one which is decumulating its capital, as it is in one which is growing.

capital saturation theory are those which are provided through the re-distribution of real income in favor of the entrepreneurs which is caused by inflation, then the theory in question has a superficial resemblance to the Austrian theory of the trade cycle. But the latter is concerned with the *structure* and not the amount of the stock of capital; and the Austrians recognized what the Keynesians fail to recognize, namely, that however seriously cheap money may distort *the composition* of the community's productive capacity, and whatever stresses and strains in the income structure may also thereby be created, it will still always be *possible* to restore the economy to economic health by means of price adjustments and the consequential adaptations of production arrangements.

Under monetary stability, however, individual entrepreneurial misjudgments, whether due to ill-based optimism or pessimism, can be expected to tend to cancel one another out. And if prospective yields generally *are* assessed unduly high in one period, realized yields will disappoint and the prospective yields of the succeeding period will be more soberly assessed. But this has nothing to do with the speed of *realized growth* except to the extent to which (a) the offer of interest and (b) changing income influence the flow of savings.

9.—I have dealt above with the fallacy (in various forms) that the accumulation of productive power in general reduces the rate of return to it (as the accumulation of *a particular kind* of productive power tends, *ceteris paribus*, to cause the prospective yield from further increments of investment in *that* kind of capacity to fall). But some of the Keynesians attempt to base the stagnation theory on an assumed fall in the productivity of nonmoney assets relatively to the productivity of money, although they do not seem to see that such is the implication of their argument. Thus, Dillard explains that wealth means poverty "if the prospective benefit from owning money is more attractive than the prospect of reward from creating new assets"; and this result is likely, he thinks, because "each addition to the stock of real capital assets tends to lower the rate of return and to enhance the preference for liquid rather than illiquid wealth."[25] Accordingly, he reasons, expenditure on "investment" will fall off, the disbursement of income to be spent on consumption will decline also, and there will be insufficient expenditure, therefore, to keep the economic system running. In this way the two kinds of over-saving theory are merged.

This form of the capital saturation theory has content only if it can be shown that, through net accumulation, the marginal prospective yield from nonmoney assets decreases *relatively to that of money*. But *ceteris paribus* the aggregate real value of money increases in direct proportion to the growth in utilized productive power; and only if the number of money units fails to keep pace will there be a rise in the relative prospective yield from money. Such an explanation would, therefore, make the capital saturation theory depend merely upon the assumption of deflationary policy.

There is not the slightest reason why low prospective yields and low rates of interest—however caused—should cause money to be preferred or to become more productive.* When interest is low, it reduces the interest cost of holding *all* assets. Those Keynesians who follow Dillard on this point appear to be assuming that there is an interest cost of holding only in the case of money. Their argument ignores the fact that an element in *all* prospective yields consists of interest; and so they have been drawn into the fallacy that, when interest is low, the attractiveness of money (the return from holding it) must increase. An expected rise in the rate of interest is, of course, a quite different matter. (See p. 99).

10.—The notion that a declining rate of population growth must lead to stagnation through the volume of productive capacity *outstripping the demand for its services* has, of recent years, been supported by what may at first appear to be a quite contradictory notion which I shall examine in this and the four following sections. Stagnation is supposed to be threatened through a decline in *the relative supply of labor.* Keynes himself was originally responsible for this idea in arguing that there must be "a due proportion between the amount of labor employed in making machines and the amount which will be employed in using them."[26] Some of his disciples have subsequently developed from this idea the argument that *it will be impossible for productive capacity to continue to grow* because, in the long run, labor shortage will become increasingly burdensome under *laissez-faire* conditions. Superficially, this thesis seems to resemble the theory of unbalanced growth. (See sections 3, 7 and 8). Actually it turns out not to be this at all. For the "shortage" of labor is regarded as, in itself, unrectifiable.

For some reason it does not occur to those who argue this way to ask: Why should not "shortages," in this or any other form, tend to militate equally against the satisfaction of *all* economic ends? I.e., why should the "shortages" be supposed to be especially serious in respect of the satisfaction of *saving* preference? There is in fact no reason why shortages of labor, or of other nonspecific services, should stand in the way of the satisfaction of any *particular* kind of economic ends, including

*We have already seen (p. 366) that, if interest becomes negative, individual savings will come to be achievable only through the acquisition of securities of declining value in terms of services, whilst the value of any conceivable money unit would have to correspond.

preferences concerning the time of consumption, except in the sense that other ends are assumed to stand higher in people's scales of preference.

In its least unreasonable form, the notion appears to be that, when population begins to increase less rapidly, *constructional* activity loses impetus and capital resources become less urgently needed. But labor scarcity tends to render such equipment as competes with labor of relatively *greater* value. *The form* of gross accumulation is likely to change therefore, but the entrepreneurial offer to savers is more likely to be raised.

A more sophisticated form of the theory, which is even less acceptable, envisages a situation in which the full flow of services is required to maintain capital intact. There are then no services left over for "growth." Now unless we can assume that current consumption *cannot* be sacrificed for the future, this is purely a question of preference, the cost of providing for the future being regarded as *too high* by society (although it may be chosen by individuals). (See sec. 2). But *in practice*, it is virtually impossible to conceive of a state in which people as a whole would like to postpone consumption of the things they can enjoy currently, whilst they are *unable* for physical reasons to sacrifice the present for the future without waste. Such an idea requires far-fetched assumptions like that of Keynes' banana community in the *Treatise*. (See above, pp. 224-5). If we make reasonably realistic assumptions, we must recognize that there are no limits (apart from saving-preference and the versatility of resources) to the extent to which (i) the *form* of gross accumulation and (ii) the *rate* of net accumulation may be changed, especially when replacement follows depreciation. In particular, if there is a high standard of consumption, it will certainly be *possible* to sacrifice current consumption and turn to a form of replacement which has greater durability, or which is subject to a slower rate of disinvestment through use. That is, an increase in net accumulation will always be *possible* in practice. The fact that it may not be chosen is wholly a case of consumption-saving preference exercised somewhere in the economic system, given the versatility of productive capacity.

In some treatments, it appears as though the fallacy can be attributed to the mistake of thinking of net accumulation as a magnitude which is determined independently of consumption-saving preference. This sort of error hinders perception of the fact that, if the whole of the flow of services merely covers replacement, that is because the desire for current consumption is causing a high rate of decumulation. We cannot then say that net accumulation is *impossible* because of the shortage of services for that purpose, whether the services which are short happen to be those of labor or other resources. It is saving preference which insufficiently limits decumulation, insufficiently limits therefore the replacement part of gross accumulation, and hence fails in turn to release services (labor included), for net accumulation.

The scarcity of *some* resources may always be expected to be rising in relation to others; and if it is labor which is becoming relatively scarce, I fail to see why a high natural scarcity price for it can create stagnation any more than a high claim (determined in the free market) from the owners of any other factor of production (including the profits of entrepreneurs). A redistribution of income in favor of labor *may* mean a greater preference for current consumption* and hence a decline in the rate of growth; but solely because that is what people happen to want following the redistribution. It will not be due to the *relative* scarcity of one category of services and the consequent *relative* plenty (or redundancy) of other services. Only on the assumptions (i) that a relative contraction of *services in general* develops, in the sense that real income declines, and (ii) that people then prefer to cut down savings rather than consumption, have we an explanation of how autonomous factors like population decline, increased demand for leisure, union aggression, or the growth of barriers to labor efficiency (demarcations, restrictions on training, restrictions on incentive payments, etc.), may cause net accumulation to slow down or cease. And even so, the explanation lies in the expression of saving preference which may be expected to follow a fall in real income.

Let us examine the idea of an *induced*† scarcity or shortage of labor. It can, I suggest, only arise (a) through increasing efficiency on the part of capital resources other than labor, brought about by inventions, discoveries and managerial ingenuities when these developments are, on the whole, of a capital economizing type or (b) through the net accumulation of the existing kind of capital resources, when they happen to be more co-operant with labor than competing with it. But this should no more cause the profitableness of net accumulation (and hence the entrepreneur's inducement to savers) to decline than the adoption of labor-economizing methods (e.g., effective incentive wage systems) should lead to a *general* decline in the employability of labor.

It is possible, however, that the phrase "labor shortage" may sometimes mean that labor is underpriced. This is particularly likely to be seen in the case of the repressed form of latent inflation which is being kept in check by means of wage-restraint or a wage-rate ceiling. Whilst this situation may have a depressing effect upon real income through the

---

*It *may* also mean an increased preference for leisure. But I have assumed that the saturation case does not envisage this reaction. (See p. 360, footnote).

†I use the term "induced" to distinguish from the autonomous factors mentioned above.

maldistribution of labor which results, it is clearly not the situation which the Keynesians envisage.

I reach the conclusion that it is wrong to suppose that an increase of real wage-rates due to an increase in the natural scarcity value of labor, can have a depressant effect. It is only in the case of *contrived labor scarcity,* when labor is priced too high for its full or optimal utilization, that demand will be restrained owing to a decline in real income.

If, then, there is any sense in assertions like "somewhere a point of diminishing net investment must be reached,"[27] all that can be meant is that a point must be reached at which (the determinants of interest being given) the willingness to save will begin to decline. It has nothing specifically to do with *labor* shortage or any other shortage. For instance, to consider a situation which is commonly misinterpreted, the rate of capital formation *is likely* to decline in formerly undeveloped areas, as virgin resources become more intensively exploited, and in all countries when the rate of technological progress happens to slow down. But this is simply because the sacrifice of current consumption needed for any given rate of growth must increase. People will provide less for the future (a) because, the rate of interest being given, it costs more to do so, and (b) because prospective yields (and hence the rate of interest) decline.

11. It is certainly possible, of course, for a state of underpopulation, or of contrived labor scarcity to exist, in the sense that a greater population or the abandonment of scarcity-creating trade-union practices, etc. would cause the rate of growth of capacity and real income to be greater. And it is true that districts or countries which find it easy to save, or which are thrifty for other reasons, can often invest in resources in other districts or countries which find it difficult to save or prefer not to save, because labor to operate those resources happens to be cheap or plentiful there. But this does not mean, as some have thought, that cheap labor as such facilitates expansion. Thus savings will often be sent to distant or foreign districts or countries, not because *labor* is plentiful there but because, in spite of labor being scarce and expensive, other resources are plentiful. *Economy of labor* (as distinct from *cheapness*), just like economy in the use of all other factors, will facilitate expansion. That is a wholly different point.

Mechanical thinking on simplified assumptions seems to have aggravated the confusion. Thus, through reliance on unrealistic abstract models, Sweezy seems to have been led astray. He adopts, for purposes of simplification, the premise that there are no new inventions, he assumes an expansion brought about through increased expenditure, financed by the State; and he says: "We then run into the following difficulty: as soon as any initial slack in the system had been taken up, the producers' in the consumers' goods industries would find their new investments unprofitable, paradoxically, because of a shortage of labor. The investments would, by assumption, have to be of a duplicative type since we are ruling out new inventions as a source of investment demand."[28] In part, he is concerned with the situation which we considered in section 4, above. But he excludes the problem (and hence the possibility of a solution) in his assumptions, i.e., in his exclusion of inventions and innovations in the form of entrepreneurial effort to create new production functions.* If response to new consumer objectives as productive power accumulates is ruled out, the whole issue of co-ordination to change is ignored, and that is always *the* problem. But of course, without the release of capacity (which is not here to be considered, through the assumption that the "slack" has been taken up), or without new economies (through inventions, managerial ingenuities, etc.), the attempt to finance expansion, through whatever channels, will be unable to "stimulate" the growth of real income (unless it can in some way successfully encourage the achievement of savings). In reality, a changing composition of the flow of services can provide output of different qualities, including better qualities, more attractive designs, etc. To any student of the actual world the fact that the form and content of capital resources is changing continuously (because the content of gross accumulation is under constant adaptation to changing demand and changing supply of co-operant resources) appears as one of the most significant realities. Indeed the whole history of "economic progress" has been that of satisfying elementary wants more easily, so that new and higher wants can be satisfied.

Sweezy has tried to make *arbitrary assumptions which cause the question of growth in general to appear to be similar to the growth of a particular industry or enterprise.* But it is a wholly different question. If growth *is* assumed to take the form only of more of the same things, however, a type of *general* satiability may exist which resembles satiability in respect of particular commodities. It is through that absurd assumption, and not because of the relative dearness of labor, that Sweezy can imagine net accumulation becoming unprofitable.

Admittedly it is difficult to distinguish between those cases in which autonomous technological improvements account for the change of form in gross accumulation and those cases in which managerial ingenuities in adapting production functions to the changing value of labor are responsible. But it is useless to assume away, as writers like Sweezy seem to be unconsciously doing, the co-ordinative activities of forward-

---

*Similar assumptions are included in the usually forgotten basic assumptions of *The General Theory*, which Keynes belatedly listed in Chap. 18.

looking and economizing entrepreneurs. The economic system works because calculations and responsible decisions are constantly being made. Hence it cannot be fruitfully studied if the problems are simplified through the assumption that, when other changes occur, resources continue to be replaced and combined in an unchanged manner.

No-one would deny that *the rate of possible expansion* is limited by the fact that the supply of labor cannot be induced or caused to grow in the way in which the supply of other productive capacity can be caused to grow.* The output of labor using given tools and methods cannot be increased indefinitely. Hence, *ceteris paribus*, in so far as technological conditions do not allow the substitution of machinery for skill and effort, the cost of adding to productive capacity must become greater as the proportion of savings out of a given income increases. But *the form* taken by replacement and net accumulation may still be of such a kind that it facilitates further net accumulation, in spite of the value of labor rising relatively to that of other services; and if mankind continues to want to provide for the future, there is no reason why the rising claim of labor on the value of the product should prevent growing productive power from taking the appropriate form. This possibility or probability does *not* depend upon the occurrence of labor-saving or capital-saving innovations and devices; yet in a society which wants to save, economizing ideas and inventions can reasonably be expected to occur in such a form as will facilitate net accumulation.†

12.—Nevertheless, the conviction is still frequently held that "additional capital cannot yield additional output without the employment of additional labour."[29] This is the way Keynes' thesis is expressed by Murad‡ who, building on Sweezy's notions, has made the most ambitious attempt that I have noticed to supply a rigorous justification for the theory. I propose briefly to examine this attempt.

---

*I hold the view, however, that productive investment in *human capital*—the deliberate fostering of economic skills (such as would, I believe, be greatly encouraged under the incentives of *laissez-faire*) is capable of considerably increasing the supply of valuable effort.

†In practice, the form of gross and net accumulation will be determined (i) in the light of the obstacles imposed by trade unions, the law, custom and prejudice against the optimal use or development of human powers, and (ii) by the predicted rate of growth, age distribution and migration of the population.

‡Murad quotes McC. Wright[30] to the effect that it would be ridiculous to add additional saws to carpenters; but he objects to the latter's suggestion that it would not be ridiculous to add different kinds of saws. The realistic case, however, is that of replacing a hand saw by a mechanical saw; and this is merely a particular illustration of the general truth that the form of gross accumulation will depend upon the current value of labor of different kinds. It may be legitimate to make abstraction of technical progress; but it is definitely not legitimate to rule out changing forms of gross accumulation and the devising of new production functions to meet changing conditions in the light of *existing knowledge and techniques*.

He (Murad) explains that the "operating force" (the resources required to maintain capital intact) grows to such an extent that no "expansion force" is left (i.e., no resources for growth). An attempt to provide additional resources will merely mean that existing resources must depreciate by an equal amount. He talks of a certain operating force being "called for," and says that in consequence of growth, ultimately all workers (all resources) *"must* be included in the operating force, and the expansion force *must* vanish."[31] (My italics). But the words "called for" and "must" beg the whole issue. This division of the "force" is determined solely by preference whereas Murad *assumes* that, in the circumstances he is postulating at any rate, there will be no free will about the extent of saving or dissavings. It seems fantastic to hold that, with a stationary population, no growth in utilized productive capacity will be possible (in the absence of autonomous progress). What would Crusoe and Man Friday have said of such a proposition! But the fallacious conclusion having been stated, it is typically supported by the sheerest dogma. *"Experience forces us,"* we are told, "to reject the assumption that capital can be combined with labor in any desired proportion. . . . . A fairly definite quantity of labor is required at any moment if existing capital is to be fully utilized."[32] (My italics). But as I have already insisted, we cannot draw conclusions relevant to reality by supposing *the form of capital* to be unchanged. Entrepreneurs forecast the availability of labor in exactly the same way as they forecast the availability of all other resources; and the form in which they cause services to be embodied into the assets which make up replacement and net accumulation is determined by such forecasts. Murad says: "It would not make sense for a community to build an automobile plant which, when completed, could be manned only with workers drawn from, let us say, steel plants, thus leaving the latter idle."[33] But entrepreneurs could never contemplate providing such a plant unless they were convinced that their bidding for the scarce factor, labor, would not unduly raise its value or the value of other scarce factors. And of course net accumulation can occur only if saving has left resources, including labor, available for that purpose. It is therefore wholly unjustifiable to assume that there is *some correct proportion* between "the operating force" which is engaged *inter alia* on replacement and "the expansion force" which is engaged in adding to the stock of resources.*

The activities which lead to replacement are treated by Murad as costs of current output, and those which lead to expansion are treated as costs of making net additions to capital.[35] Yet both are equally

---

*Building a plant, says Murad, is work of the one or the other according to whether it is replacing or adding to the capacity. He is thinking specifically of the *labor force* employed and not of the services of all resources.[34]

"current output," and the costs of both are of contributing to what I have called "gross accumulation."

13.—This is what puzzles me most about the confusion on this issue. Why is it believed that replacement can be *maintained yet not exceeded*? Is it due to a failure to realize that replacement involves the same sort of entrepreneurial judgment and motives as net accumulation? Or is it due to a failure to perceive that the magnitude "replacement" is determined by the magnitude "decumulation"? The tacit assumption seems to be that an exact balance of satiety will come to exist at the ruling rate of interest. Yet why should it happen that entrepreneurs, determining profitable forms and combinations in which assets may be arranged and replaced, find that they have in the aggregate acquired assets of a gross value which just covers yet does not exceed current decumulation? Unless it is the absence of either dissavings or savings which is assumed to limit them, I can give no answer. The Keynesians do not, I think, ask themselves such questions; and they do not see, therefore, that there can be no more obstacles to net accumulation than there are to replacement.

If the full flow of unconsumed services is ultimately needed to maintain capital intact, as productive power has grown, that must be because consumption, i.e., decumulation, has grown to exactly that rate which leaves no net accumulation; and no reasons other than consumption-saving preference can explain why that should be. No existing rate of decumulation is a *necessity* (apart from that element of depreciation which is not due to the use of assets*) unless the whole population is on the bread line; and no rate of savings achieved is unprofitable to the *savers* who have satisfied saving preference, although *entrepreneurs* may have given replacement and net accumulation a form which proves to be less profitable than was anticipated.

14.—But Murad goes so far as to hold that even economizing inventions and technological innovations would be unable to overcome the effect of labor shortage and permit real expansion; because for this to be achieved, it would "necessitate the continual undoing of things done. It would be like building a house and immediately demolishing it to build another house of better design, only to discard it for a still better one—while the prospective occupant is camping in a tent, waiting for

---

*Admittedly, a given rate of decumulation having become well established and not expected to change, the composition of the stock of assets will have been determined accordingly, and may well involve a large element of *inevitable* depreciation (i.e., other than that due to use of assets). This is the only element of inevitable consumption. And even so, resources which fall into this category *need* not be replaced. They can be disinvested, and replaced by resources believed to be capable of providing profitable services over time.

his house to be finished."[36] For this reason, he says, "so far from assuring continued investment opportunities, technological advance speeds up the process of industrialization and thus tends to hasten the decline of investment opportunities." Accordingly, "a stage of full industrialization" must eventually be reached, in which "no net investment whatever can take place."[37]

The argument in this form is still more fallacious; for it implies that if an invention economizes so drastically that it forces the abandonment (as distinct from the failure to replace) of existing equipment, no net social gain will have been realized. In truth, the gain is greater in this sort of case than in the more normal case in which an economizing invention forces the utilization of existing equipment at lower charges to co-operant factors until disinvestment has occurred. If we can assume that co-ordination through price adjustment is actually achieved, it will never pay to introduce technical improvements at a rate which involves any *wasteful* scrapping or disinvestment. However unprofitable the provision of the resources scrapped or disinvested may prove to have been to the original investor, there is never any *social* waste in recourse to the least-cost methods.*

15.—Nothing that I have said must be interpreted as a denial that population growth, like all other increases in the stock of resources, is likely to stimulate savings and growth in other forms. For through its potential contribution to output, it contributes to the source of future demand—demand for labor as well as for the services of nonhuman resources. It does so because it brings more hands, not because it brings more mouths. But this creates no justification for the view that population growth "creates investment opportunities" in any other manner, or that its failure to grow withdraws them. Increasing population contributes to the profitability of economic expansion, only in the sense that all growth of productive capacity (if utilized) leads to an increased flow of income, and hence a greater *ability* to save and a greater *incentive* to save. Similarly, a decline in population, unless offset by growing net accumulation in nonhuman resources, or by investment in human capital, or by the sacrifice of leisure, will mean a decline in the source of future demand and *ceteris paribus*, a decreased rate of growth.

A rather blurred view of the truth occasionally shows through Keynesian writings. At any rate, Harrod,[38] Kalecki[39] and Domar[40] recognize that the accumulation of productive capacity is justifiable at all times provided that income grows sufficiently to demand the product of that capacity. I describe this view as "blurred" because they seem to believe

---

*There may be sociological harm through resistance to the co-ordinative adjustments required. But wise policy will anticipate and aim at overcoming such resistance.

that inflationary spending alone can generate the required income. But growing utilized productive capacity *means* rising real and money income, even in the absence of inflationary credit; and hence, it means rising demands as a whole both in real and in money terms.

16.—The dread of "excessive"* or "burdensome"[41] or "disruptive"[42] power to produce income, confronts some of the Keynesians with a dilemma. They teach that full employment is achievable only when "investment" is kept going; but "investment," they fear, may eventually lead to an unwanted growth in the stock of assets. Hence although they advocate the maintenance of investment expenditure in order to preserve a high level of economic activity, they are sometimes led to recommend the withholding the right of private entrepreneurs to add to the stock of assets. They seem to hold that the use of resources in response to consumer-saver preference is somehow inconsistent with stability unless the State intervenes; that cheap money is essential to stave off an ever threatening tendency to capital surfeit, stagnation and depression; that the wisdom of the State can correct this tendency in other ways, through its control of monetary and fiscal arrangements; and that, in particular, the financing of innovations and developments ought not to be permitted unless governmental agencies can perceive that it is desirable. In R. C. O. Matthews words, entrepreneurs should be prohibited from "investment they consider profitable" when that is undesirable, and induced to undertake investment "which they expect to be unprofitable" when, in the opinion of the State, that is desirable.[43] He thinks of this as a means of preventing the "disruptive" growth of productive power; for the growth of capacity may sometimes be "disruptive," he holds, because it can "outstrip requirements" and "become overpowering even in relation to the requirements of a full-employment level of incomes and output."[44] "Investment" is a negative function of the stock of capital resources[45] and, when that stock is too big, "investment" will be insufficient to maintain full employment. Matthews is as unequivocal as this on the point.

The same fallacies have led to the conclusion (as Matthews puts it) that the curbing of private investment by high taxation, together with high government expenditure, "have postponed the prospect of a serious recession"[46] through restraining too great a growth in the power to produce the things consumers are believed to want. Accordingly, he deduces that it will be desirable for the government "itself to be respon-

---

*The adjectives "excessive," "high," "relatively high," etc., which are used to describe the amount of capital resources, I find irritatingly vague. Consider the words "relatively high," for example. Is it in high relation to the capital resources of a previous period, or in relation to income, or in relation to current growth or secular growth?

sible for a large and continuous expenditure,"[47] presumably to protect
the community from the threat of too bountiful a source for satisfying
the community's needs.* Matthews is led therefore to advocate what
he appears to regard as a beneficial compromise—a check which somehow enables just sufficient growth to maintain full employment but not
sufficient growth to cause a "burdensome" power to produce. "The
endeavor must be," he says, ". . . . to render a lower level of private
investment consistent with full-employment income."[48] Government
spending must fill the gap; but government spending must *not* be used
to supply resources which compete with private investment. Presumably, what he envisages is State-provided output which will be valueless;
for if it is not valueless, it must be competing with output supplied in
response to prospective yields. It seems therefore to be a question of
making investments which are not subject to the market test of entrepreneurial wisdom or success. The assets (if, indeed, the word "assets" is
defensible in such a case) into which services are directed must definitely
be such as do not satisfy any preference for which the people would wish
to make a voluntary sacrifice.

Had the argument been that investment in collectively owned assets
(such as the road system, State-owned public utilities, railways and har-
bors, etc.,) tends at times to be unduly low so that aggregate productivity
suffers, the theory would have been at least plausible. It could have
been logically suggested that there was the possibility of over-accumula-
tion of assets in the private sector in the sense that there was an under-
accumulation in the government sector. But this is *not* the suggestion.†
Or had the argument been that, without the guidance of the State, an
unbalanced structure of productive power may emerge, then again the
argument would have been plausible; for entrepreneurs may certainly
forecast wrongly. But why should it be supposed that a group of officials,
removed from the rewards and penalties of the market, and for whose
actions politicians must take responsibility, will be able to make better
or more expert judgments? And is it not naive in the extreme to suppose
that they will make equally disinterested decisions?

The muddled thinking which I allege in this field would have been

---

*This theory of "over-investment" must be distinguished from the theory that cheap
money can result in a misdirection of resources which leads in turn to a distorted
structure of net accumulation. The latter theory has also been called an "over-
investment" theory; but it relates to the *form* taken by the accumulation of resources
and not to its amount.

†In any case, unless the State resorts to boondoggling, the most that it can do is to
discourage investment *in particular forms* at particular times, and to encourage those
forms at other times. If the State wishes to prevent or encourage growth, then it
must prevent or encourage the achievement of savings either directly, or indirectly by
discouraging or encouraging the flow of income (through the withholding or release
of capacity).

avoided, I think, if it had been perceived that *economic growth, in the sense of growing capacity to generate real income, is purely a question of preference.* Admittedly, the preference in this case is *influenced,* as are all other preferences, by autonomous factors. In particular, (a) population growth and (b) discoveries, economizing inventions and the growth of managerial expertness encourage and facilitate decisions to provide for the future. The factors under category (b) all reduce the absolute sacrifice of consumption in the immediate future which is needed to achieve greater consumption in the distant future. On the other hand, population growth is set off, so to speak, by more mouths to feed, more bodies to clothe and house, and more persons to amuse, educate and train.*

But the phenomena of idleness and idling of resources are related to the phenomenon of growth only in the sense that they are related to other phenomena of change. If all discoveries and technological progress came to an end and population growth continued, average standards of living would certainly fall, but it would still be possible for society *to co-ordinate* its activities to the emerging conditions, through the price adjustments needed for the re-allocation of resources. And if discoveries and technological progress continued whilst population ceased to grow, or declined, again co-ordination to meet the new conditions would permit the growth of productive power in response to consumption-saving preference.

The only conceivable stagnation is, therefore, that due to disco-ordination. It cannot be rationally ascribed to deficiency of demand or excess of supply.

---

*The influence of population growth would tend to be neutral (in the sense that a choice between the immediate future and the distant future would be the sole determinant) if it were not affected by age composition (which is influenced by the rate of population growth). For a high proportion of persons below or above working age will, individual saving preference propensities being given, probably reduce the desire for growth.

REFERENCES

(1) DILLARD, *The Theory of a Monetary Economy,* in Kurihara, *Post Keynesian Economics,* p.23. (2) HAZLITT, *The Failure of the "New Economics",* pp.364 *et. seq.* (3) WILLIAMS, A. E. R., *Proceedings,* 1948, p.276. (4) DILLARD, *The Economics of J. M. Keynes,* p.272 (5) ANDERSON, *Economics and the Public Welfare,* pp.384-5. (6) BRONFENBRENNER, *Some Neglected Implications of Secular Inflation,* in Kurihara, *op. cit.,* p.58. (7) MATTHEWS, *Capital Stock Adjustment Theories,* in Kurihara, *op. cit.,* p.173. (8) KEYNES, *The General Theory,* p.323. (9) *Ibid.,* pp.220-1. (10) *Ibid.,* p.217. (11) *Ibid.,* p.221. (12) *Ibid.,* pp.105-6. (13) KURIHARA, *Post Keynesian Economics,* p.269. (14) *Ibid.,* p.269. (15) *Ibid.,* p.271. (16) KEYNES, *op. cit.,* p.376. (17) KURIHARA, *op. cit.,* p.270. (18) *Ibid.,* p.270. (19) KALDOR, *A Model of the Trade Cycle,* E. J., March, 1940. (20) KALECKI, *A Macro-Economic Theory of Business Cycle,* Econometrica, 1935.

(21) HICKS, *A Contribution to the Theory of the Trade Cycle*. (22) GOODWIN, *The Non-Linear Accelerator and the Persistence of Business Cycles, Econometrica*, Jan. 1951. (23) ICHIMURA, *Toward a General Non-Linear Macrodynamic Theory of Economic Fluctuations*, in Kurihara, *op. cit.*, p.216. (24) MATTHEWS, *op. cit.*, p.190. (25) DILLARD, *op. cit.*, p.23. (26) KEYNES, *op. cit.*, p.214. (27) MURAD, *Net Investment and Industrial Progress*, in Kurihara, *op. cit.*, p.236. (28) SWEEZY, A. E. R., Dec. 1944, p.877. (29) MURAD, *op. cit.*, p.232. (30) MURAD, quoting McC. Wright, p. 234n. (31) *Ibid.*, p.229. (32) *Ibid.*, p.235. (33) *Ibid.*, p.235. (34) *Ibid.*, pp.230-31. (35) *Ibid.*, pp. 228 (footnote) and 229-30. (36) *Ibid.*, p.240. (37) *Ibid.*, pp.241-2. (38) HARROD, *Towards a Dynamic Economics*, pp.261-75. (39) KALECKI, *Essays in the Theory of Economic Fluctuations*, pp.148-9. (40) DOMAR, *Expansion and Employment*, p.35. (41) MATTHEWS, *op. cit.*, p.174. (42) *Ibid.*, p.173. (43) *Ibid.*, p.189. (44) *Ibid.*, p.173. (45) *Ibid.*, p.178. (46) *Ibid.*, p.191. (47) *Ibid.*, p.191. (48) *Ibid.*, p.174.

Chapter XVII

THE SAY LAW

SUMMARY

1.—The principal thesis of The General Theory *falls or stands according to the validity or otherwise of the Say Law which, it can be shown, Keynes never understood, 2.—partly because he was misled by the defective macroeconomic method. 3.—The assumption of price rigidity, which can give plausibility to Keynes' suggestion that demand for liquidity may cause income to contract, illustrates and does not refute that law. 4.—Say's explanation that one wanted thing is ultimately bought with another, and that money is not the source of power to buy, did not seek to minimize the importance of demand for money as a determinant of the real value of the money unit. 5.—Say had simply tried to banish the fear of general glut or plenty. Yet that fear still dominates Keynesian thinking, 6.—as can be seen, for instance, in Harrod's defence of Keynes' treatment of the reparations problem 7.—and in Harrod's belief that the temporary elimination of German competition after World War II was advantageous to Britain. 8.—The Keynesians feel that there must be a deficiency of demand in some sense because selling is more difficult than buying; but buying would be just as difficult if buyers were organized as sellers are. 9.—A general understanding of the nature of sellers' resistance to the full expression of demands in the aggregate could have revolutionized policy and brought the great depression rapidly to an end. 10.—Appendix: J. S. Mill on the Say Law.*

1.—If the argument of chapter IX is accepted, not only does it force the abandonment of the theory of unemployment equilibrium but it means that the Say Law stands once again inviolate. I hold accordingly that this law must be reinstated as the basic economic reality in the light of which all economic thinking is illuminated. But I do not think that all the critics of Keynes who have contributed to the refutation of the theory of unemployment equilibrium will immediately accept the inference that the Law has been fully rehabilitated. Indeed, a decade ago, Haberler adhered to a rejection of it at the very stage at which his own reasoning seemed to be prompting him to recognize it.*[1]

Yet even so extreme a Keynesian as Sweezy has been rash enough (and right enough) to admit, in his obituary article on Keynes, that the arguments of *The General Theory* "all fall to the ground if the validity of the Say Law is assumed."[3] And it is not uncommon for Keynesians to admit that their master's contribution to economics consists essentially in a refutation of the Law, and that the validity of his theories can be accepted or rejected according to whether it can be regarded as sound or unsound.

What the Law states is that supply in general constitutes demand in general. More rigorously, it implies that the demand for any valuable thing is a function of the supply of all other valuable things which do not compete with it. The services of money are of course included among the valuable things which people want. I shall suggest therefore that the demand for goods and services in general cannot exceed or fall short of their supply in terms of money, unless (through monetary policy†) the money unit is increasing or decreasing in value. When an inflation

*The acceptance of the Say Law does not imply, as Haberler suggests, the assumption that the phenomena of hoarding or dishoarding cannot exist. It merely accords to money assets and the services which they provide the same economic status and significance as all other assets and the services which they provide. Haberler takes a formulation of the Law by Ricardo as representing its "original meaning." But in that formulation Ricardo was taking for granted the factors which determine the demand for and supply of money. Neither he nor Say denied the existence of these factors, whilst J. S. Mill was as explicit as he could be on the point.[2] See below, pp. 395-6.
†See Chap. V.

or a deflation is in progress the Law is less simple. It holds nevertheless.

As long as this Law was accepted, the problem of unemployment (of men and other assets) was regarded as a question of demand and price. The demands which determine prices* were held to have their source in aggregate output or real income, and the prices of things were thought of as determined (a) in the free market, or (b) in the market through collusion, or (c) by the State. Unemployment (in a wasteful sense) was regarded as possible only when, through collusion or State action, the services of men and other assets had been priced out of reach of existing income, or priced inconsistently with expected prices. But it was recognized that both collusive and State pricing could cause existing income and demands in general to contract,† giving rise therefore to a cumulative aggravation of idle capacity. Here we have the essence of the Law as its implications had been woven, unobtrusively, into the texture of pre-Keynesian teaching.

Keynes' attack on the Law was illustrated by a quotation, not from Say himself, but from J. S. Mill, and it was a quotation which, as B. M. Anderson, Emil Korner and Patinkin have pointed out, was torn from its context. The full passage from J. S. Mill is quoted in the Appendix to this chapter.

J. S. Mill was a poor exponent of Say in his *Principles*. But had Keynes read Mill's treatment of the topic in his *Unsettled Questions in Political Economy* he would, I think, have dropped his attack on the Say Law.‡ Moreover, if the passage from Mill's *Principles* had been continued to include the three sentences which followed, it would have brought into discussion the crucial issues which Keynes ignored. For these three sentences, interpreted in the light of Mill's teaching as a whole, refer, in Anderson's words, "to the conception of balance and proportion and equilibrium which is the heart of the doctrine—a notion which Keynes nowhere considers [in *The General Theory*]. . . . . The doctrine that supply creates its own demand, as presented by John Stuart Mill, assumes a proper equilibrium among the different kinds of production, assumes proper terms of exchange (i.e., price relationships) among different kinds of products, assumes proper relations between prices and costs. . . . ."

---

*As distinct from those demands which determine interest. (See pp. 205-6).

†It is typical of the general misrepresentation of orthodoxy that Scitovsky can still say (in 1956) that, before Keynes, "the business cycle had to be explained within a theoretical framework that made no allowance for the possibility of variations in employment and income."(4) What nonsense this is! It is the very essence of the Say Law that output (i.e., real income or employment) is the source of demands, and that the withdrawal of output is the withdrawal of demands.

‡Becker and Baumol write of J. S. Mill's treatment in *Unsettled Questions:* "In reading it one is led to wonder why so much of the subsequent literature (this paper included) had to be written at all."(5)

But throughout *The General Theory*, Keynes (in Anderson's words) "is working with aggregate, block concepts. . . . . Nowhere is there any discussion of the interrelationships of the elements in these vast aggregates, or of elements in one aggregate with elements in another. Nowhere is there a recognition that different elements in the aggregate supply give rise to the demand for other elements in the aggregate supply. In Keynes' discussion, purchasing power and production are sharply sundered."[6]

Not only was Keynes' illustration of the Law defective, but his enunciation of it was in a form in which the real issue was lost sight of. He described it as the law "that the aggregate demand price of output is equal to its aggregate supply price for all volumes of output." As such, he said, it was "equivalent to the proposition that there is no obstacle to full employment."[7]

Say himself would undoubtedly have rejected both propositions. The first, he would have contended, could be defended only as a tautology, in the sense that aggregate sales and aggregate purchases must be equal.* But, he would have protested, he was obviously not arguing that the value of money had necessarily to be constant! (See pp. 397-8). The second part of Keynes' enunciation would have been equally unacceptable to him; and he would have protested that his Law did not imply that there *is* no obstacle to full employment, but that *if* there is no obstacle to full employment (i.e., to supply), such as can obviously result from wrong pricing, there will be no obstacle to demand. In the Keynesian approach, demand is envisaged as being for some reason *ineffective*, i.e., *prevented* from reaching the market, so that full output is unachievable. The Say Law implies that contractions of output (other than those caused by war, earthquakes, epidemics and similar disasters) are caused by supply *being withheld* from those who would otherwise place a value upon it and demand it. The withdrawal of supply implies a *simultaneous* withdrawal of demand.

There is some doubt whether it was Say's own insight which led to his statement of the Law of Markets. It was enunciated for the first time in the second edition of his *Political Economy;* and similar ideas had been clearly expressed previously by James Mill in his *Commerce Defended.*† Certainly Say lacked the subtlety of James and J. S. Mill and Ricardo. Indeed, at times he wrote with an irritating lack of rigor on important theoretical issues. I think it probable, therefore, that it was a derived inspiration which led to his exposition of the Law which is attributed to him. But he must still be accorded credit for his clear perception of its

---

*Curiously enough, a year after *The General Theory* had appeared, Keynes himself used this phrase in an attempt (inconsistent, I think, with the argument of *The General Theory*) to show the necessary equality of savings and investment.[8]

†But Schumpeter thought that there is no doubt about Say's priority.

implications—the simple truth that the supply of wanted things is the source of demand for wanted things.

2.—The confused notion which Keynes introduced of *ineffective* aggregate demand is traceable, in part, to the inherent dangers of the macroeconomic method—pitfalls which arise when kinds of reasoning which are appropriate to the treatment of the cases of individuals, or of sections of the economy, are extended to the case of the community in general. And this holds even when money is brought into the reckoning.* (See pp. 301-3).

Thus, in respect of a single person or *a group of persons*, we can consider the effect of a change in their holdings of money upon their rate of expenditure. To do so we must, as Patinkin has recently pointed out, assume all other variables to be constant, including the scale of prices and the rate of interest. Quite obviously, we may expect *the individual or the group* to buy more in real terms when his or their holdings of money units increase (at the expense of others, out of a given flow of services) through some injection of new money which they happen to receive. But when we turn to the effects of an increase in *society's* holdings of money units, the same variables cannot be held constant. The whole community will not then be in a position to buy more in real terms. Prices must rise in proportion to the increase in M.† The elasticities of demand in the two cases have no simple relation.

If by "effective aggregate demand" is meant *real* demands in general (i.e., the actual offers of services or of goods for other services or goods), then to say that unemployment is due to an insufficiency of effective demand is like saying that unemployment is caused by insufficient employment. This is not necessarily such nonsense as it sounds, for it may mean that the withdrawal of some part of "real demands in general" through the withholding of services in one field (the pricing of those services too high) is inducing withholding in another field (through the absence of downward price adjustment following a decline in real demand in that field). But seen in this way, "insufficient effective demand" is a phenomenon of contrived scarcity, which may set going a chain reaction of the contrivance of scarcity.

The Keynesian aggregate supply function is essentially an extension of the ordinary supply schedule for a particular commodity, familiar in orthodox theory. It is the same notion applied to the supply of (i.e., the

---

*In his *Unsettled Questions*, J. S. Mill regarded it as a "natural" error that, "in this case as in a hundred others, the analogy of an individual should be unduly applied to a nation."[9] There could not be, he showed, "excessive production of commodities in general"[10] but "merely a temporary fall in their value relatively to money."[11]

†In the absence of the money illusion in the valuation of money.

flow of) *all* scarce and wanted things. Keynes conceived of it in terms of "employment." Now I have always found this notion of a schedule wholly unacceptable.* There is no *physical* unit (i.e., no nonmoney unit) which can be employed for measuring *things in general*. Employment as a measurable quantity is nothing but real income, and that is essentially a *value* concept, not a *physical quantity* concept. As we have seen, real income is merely a particular description of money income, the money unit employed as a measure being abstractly conceived as of "constant value."

The notion of "aggregate demand" is equally misleading unless it is intended to mean all demands expressed, considered as a whole; and in that case it is usually found to be another term for income, just as is the term "aggregate supply." I propose, however, to use these terms in this and the following section as synonyms for income seen from different angles.

When this is understood, the idea that, because the prospective market for a particular kind of final product may be limited, the market for all goods considered together may also be limited, can be seen to be utterly fallacious. The reason why individual commodities have a limited market is that successive increments of any one thing will tend to fall lower on people's scales of preference. In other words, as people obtain more of that thing they will tend to *prefer* relatively more of other things. But the only limit to the market for the flow of all things produced is the power to produce wanted things in exchange. The manner in which the Keynesian propositions have been built up (and that means the manner in which modern economics is widely taught!) has caused this reality to be overlooked. "It is apparent," says Heilbroner (explaining the Keynesian viewpoint), "that the days of great expectation for the radio industry—as contrasted with the television industry—are pretty much a thing of the past. Now if . . . . all industry is in the position of the radio industry, obviously investment will be very small."[12] The fallacy is glaring. *All* industries cannot decline from changes in tastes or preferences!

By "zero elasticity of supply for output as a whole," Keynes meant the position in which "an increase in demand in terms of money will lead to no change in output," but only a rise in prices.† In such a case, however, it is wrong to talk of *an increase* in aggregate demand

---

*I first referred to this in 1939 in my *Theory of Idle Resources*. The argument I used was independently put forward a little later, and developed, by Marget. As far as I am aware, there has been no attempt at an explicit answer from any of the Keynesians.

†The assumption is that credit expansion or dishoarding will not (a) cause the release of withheld capacity or (b) lead to savings which enhance income-producing power.

(measured in terms of money). *The nature* of what is demanded will be changed through the inflation, but it is impossible for society effectively to demand *more* from the flow of services unless the supply of services is increasing, or unless higher interest is being offered (an increase in demand for services in a quite different sense*). Otherwise the effect of inflation can simply be that some demands will rise and others fall. I am assuming that by the term aggregate "money demand" is meant "aggregate real demand measured in money terms." The difficulty about this notion is that an *increase* in such "demand" (as distinct from an inflation of it) would be at one and the same time an increase in both "real output" ("real supply") and "real demand." This would be the position under a system in which the real value of the money unit is maintained constant.

The very unsatisfactory term "aggregate real demand" *could* be used, however, to mean simply aggregate utilized productive power, the demand aspect arising from the fact that the supply of every product enters into the source of "real demand" for all noncompeting products. For instance, an increase in utilized productive power (an increased flow of services in one field, whether due to net accumulation or to the release of withheld capacity, will contribute to an increase in demand for all the services which do not compete with those to which an addition has been made, and perhaps therefore induce a general release of withheld capacity. In other words, the cheapening of one product will release purchasing power for expenditure on other things, and possibly therefore cause a cumulative release of demand. It follows that when the notions of aggregate supply and aggregate demand are clarified, along lines such as these, they turn out to be nothing more than clumsy statements of the Say Law.

3.—In some treatments, it is through the reactions of saving and the demand for liquidity upon income that the Say Law is supposed to be invalidated. But as we have seen, if price flexibility exists, preferences which (under monetary rigidity) affect the value of the money unit do not cause idleness; whilst if price flexibility does not initially exist, any expansion or contraction of "aggregate demand" (other than that due to the growth or decline of productive power) must be due to the release or withholding of *supply*. That is the Say Law in its purest form! And that is what the Keynesians cannot see. Thus, after a brief statement of the Law, Dillard says: "No fault need be found with this type of analysis other than its irrelevance to problems such as crises, business cycles, and unemployment."[13] But it is in the study of these very phenomena that the Law becomes of the greatest practical importance for clarity of

*See pp. 205-6.

thought. If part of the supply of services is held off so that it cannot be expressed as demand for services (which may mean a consequent *cumulative* fall in the aggregate supply of and demand for services), or if an increase of "aggregate demand," expressed as the cheapening of certain products, fails to bring forth a *cumulative* addition to "aggregate supply" in spite of the existence of withheld capacity in the resources producing noncompeting output, the factors which have to be explained are those which operate to prevent this. This is, indeed, the crucial issue in the study of the alternation of boom and depression.

The supply of all valuable output eventually constitutes "aggregate demand" in the sense of the sum of all demands for services (output) from the flow of services (output) (i.e., excluding demand for services from the offer of assets). This is true even if the output is not sold or exchanged. Thus, unsold output "realizes" at least its reserve price, which price is judged to be more than the price at which it can be sold (for consumption or for the next stage of production). Hence all output which has value is "supplied" and "demanded," even although the producer may himself demand it, as when he himself takes the supply (which he does when he invests—i.e., retains—his income in it).* This does not imply, however, that institutions may not be such that the flow of valuable services may be withheld, with a consequent extermination of part of "aggregate demand."

Hence the Law that the supply of goods in general creates demand for goods in general has not been shaken, let alone upset. *Those who have accepted that Law in the past have never believed that all goods produced would always be demanded at prices which roughly fulfilled the expectations of those who invested capital or effort for their production.* They have not regarded the Law as resting on the assumption that things *must* be priced so as to cover their cost, but on the assumption that they *can* be priced so as to enable the utilization of their services or their consumption. Yet economists who have tried to rationalize Keynes' rejection of the Law (e.g., Lange and Neisser) have quite unjustifiably read the former assumption into it.[14] Pre-Keynesian economists merely believed that all output *would* always be demanded *if* it was valued so as to be brought within reach of income and expectations. Nor is there any justification for the view that the Law assumed that a *changing* MV, as distinct from a *changed* MV (in relation to T), was neutral as between costs and final prices (or, more generally, neutral in its relative effects upon different prices or categories of prices). A changed MV was regarded as having had an effect only in the sense that, *to have changed*, it must *have been changing* for a time, unless the change was instantaneous. It is equally unjustified to suggest that adherents of the

---

*We then envisage him as both producer and entrepreneur.

Law believed that, in *the extreme case,* goods produced could never become redundant and thus valueless. If Say had been asked, "Would the Law which has been attributed to you hold if we could assume that prices (including wage-rates) were permanently rigid?," he would surely have replied, "Certainly, in the sense that the law of gravity still works when we send up balloons. If rigid prices and wage-rates cause resources to be unemployed, they are withholding supply and hence withholding demand. Obviously, either monopolies or the State may fix prices at which some goods now being produced will perish or some productive factors now working will be forced out of employment so that their product will cease to enter into demand."* Hence it is not correct, as Neisser contends, that under price rigidity "deflation of any kind . . . . invalidates Say's Law."[15] The unemployment which may accompany deflation *illustrates* it.

What has to be stressed, I think, is the fact that when *other* prices are flexible, a reduction of, say, those wage-rates which have been keeping certain products at prices above the levels at which existing incomes can afford them, must lead to an increase of "aggregate demand"; and in so far as the monetary system has any flexibility at all, an increase of money demand ("money income") also. It would not necessarily mean —indeed, it does not even probably mean—that more will be spent on any particular commodities of which the prices have been reduced. This will undoubtedly mean increased demand for all noncompeting products.

It is significant that the most damaging attempts at clarification of Keynes' doctrine have come through discussion of the implications of price flexibility in his system. These discussions have shattered the arguments which he used in the few brief passages in which he referred specifically to price flexibility.† But in all contexts in which the "income effect" is relevant to his argument, *he assumed (usually tacitly but sometimes explicitly) the presence of price rigidity,* and made no attempt to consider how far such a rigidity could be taken as inevitable.

And yet any study of *economic co-ordination* (i.e., the search for and arrangement of the least-cost solution in the choice and integration of means in the light of given ends), whether it is the study of long-term decisions (planning) or of short-term decisions (administration) must be concerned throughout with changing values; and in a money economy, variations in values are expressed in price changes. The theorems

---

*But Say assumed that the withholding of supply (and hence of demand) could occur, to any serious extent, only through political factors which conferred group privileges.

†Actually, Keynes' own references to this problem are concerned almost wholly with *wage-rate* inflexibility.

of *The General Theory* are therefore wholly unrelated to the economic problems of the real world in just that respect in which the theorems of classical and orthodox theory were deliberately and effectively related. There is, indeed, as Anderson has said, "no more startling instance of deterioration in a great science than the recent trends, largely influenced by Keynes, to turn away from an analysis that takes account of *all* the changing factors in economic life. . . . ."[16]

4.—Let us turn now to some relevant passages in Say's own contribution. "A product is no sooner created," he wrote, "than it, from that instant, affords a market for other products to the full extent of its own value."[17] "Nothing is more favorable to the demand of one product, than the supply of another."[18] "The success of one branch of industry promotes that of the others."[19] Here we have one of the earliest explicit recognitions that the source of demand for services is normally the flow of services,* (i.e., "products"). Now Say was not unaware of the apparent paradox in this thesis. The conclusion that "it is production which opens a demand for products," he said, ". . . . may at first sight appear paradoxical." But contemplating the Keynesians of his day (Sismondi and the like), he denied *explicitly* that demand is moneyed demand.[20] The essential truth was realized, he thought, as soon as it was understood that "one product is always ultimately bought with another, *even when paid for in the first instance in money.*"[21] (My italics).

This did not imply blindness to the phenomenon of refraining from spending, i.e., "hoarding." He recognized quite frankly the wastefulness of the hoarding of *specie*. It brought, he said, only a "precautionary" benefit.[22]

Nor did his denial that money is the source of the power to buy, but merely a technical medium employed in the course of transacting, mean that he neglected the enormous importance of prices—values in terms of money, and the desirability of stability in the value of the money unit.[23] Hence Wicksell's and Haberler's criticisms of the Law appear to me to have been due to a misunderstanding. We can, Wicksell suggested, think of a change in the demand for and supply of all commodities, a change which can only be expressed in their prices.[24] But Say surely never meant to imply that the value of the money unit (and hence the demand for and supply of all commodities measured in money units) could not change. He discussed the possibility categorically, as did J. S. Mill shortly after him.[25]

---

*I say "normally" on the assumption that the forces determining the rate of interest do not cause interest to change. When interest is constant, offers of resources for services exactly offset offers of services for resources, so that the net demand from services is derived wholly from the supply of services.

There is indeed nothing in Say's writings that I have been able to find which justifies the notion that his Law implies (in my terminology) that the prospective yield from money held never changes, or that the demand for money stands in constant relation to income. Yet these are the interpretations on which the more *rigorous* attacks on the Law appear to have been based.* In an economy in which the apparatus we call "money" has been invented to supersede the clumsiness of barter, it is obvious that the aggregate value of the services of this apparatus may change relatively to the aggregate value of other output.† But if we think of demand and supply in terms of the exchange of assets for assets, then money being a form of assets, the value of the things demanded must always equal the value of things supplied. Here we have the meaning of the Say Law in its relation to money; and obviously it involves no assumption that the wantedness or prospective productivity of any type of assets, including money, may not change. Nor is there anything in the Law which justifies the view that there is something which prevents the adoption of a system under which changes in M_r (due to the changing wantedness or prospective productivity of money) may be expected to be accompanied by more or less parallel changes in M, e.g., as under the orthodox gold standard. Indeed, Say dealt very directly with this question, explaining that, under the institutions of his age, the supply of money did, in fact, respond to the demand for it, as the growth of trade caused this growth of demand. The extraordinary thing is that Neisser, in attacking Say for his supposed indifference to "the price level," himself quotes a passage in which that is made clear.[28]

Much of the confusion on this issue is due, I think, to the term "quantity of money" being used in contexts in which it is never really clear whether the magnitude M_r or M is intended. To recognize that M_r may change, with or without proportional changes in M, is not to deny the basic truth which economists have tried to convey by the term "the veil of money." In a vast number of circumstances in which the use of the monetary apparatus is assumed, changes in M_r or in M are irrelevant. But the layman (like some modern economists) usually has difficulty in recognizing this. Becker and Baumol think that when James Mill wrote: "When a man produces a greater quantity of any

---

*Becker and Baumol believe that some of the attacks on the Law (e.g., by Lange, and by Patinkin in his earlier contributions) have been based on the assumption that it implies that the quantity of money demanded, considered either as a stock or as a flow, is independent of the price structure and is always equal to the quantity of money supplied."[26] They call this "the Say Identity." But it appears to attribute to those criticized even more nonsensical ideas of Say's teachings than I do myself.

†Thus, when M_r increases relatively to M, this may be described, in J. S. Mill's words, as "a general anxiety to sell, and general disinclination to buy."[27]

commodity than he desires for himself, it can only be on one account, namely, that he desires some other commodity," he was either assuming money to be a commodity or assuming that the price level is adjusted to the quantity of cash.[29] Surely he was making the former assumption—taking it for granted. I certainly do not think that "the price level" was in James Mill's mind on this occasion at all. He simply perceived the truth that output in excess of the producer's own requirements is produced because it is deemed to have value in exchange for something else, i.e., for other things in general, among which there is no reason to accord money any special importance; for money is merely an item in the aggregate stock of assets, and the seller of nonmoney things may or may not require more monetary services in the future. Hence because James Mill, and other classical economists, insisted that in a money economy one does not produce to acquire money but to acquire other things than those one produces, this does not mean that he did not recognize that money was to be included *among* those other things.

If we make due allowance for a certain lack of verbal rigor in early nineteenth-century enunciations, we can see that money spent was regarded (by James Mill, J. S. Mill and Say) as standing in the same position as the excess of a person's assets above those which he wishes to consume or utilize himself. Although a producer's inventories of such goods are invested in because they are productive, beyond a certain point they are insufficiently productive to be profitably held;* and the same applies to money.†

5.—The interesting thing is that neither Sismondi, nor those subsequent critics of Say who attempted to refute the kernel of his teaching, ever stressed the significance of disco-ordinations, caused (in Say's words) by "the avarice or ignorance of authority,"[31] and expressed in prices, as did Say himself.‡ Their fallacies have usually rested on the idea that the augmentation of the income of an individual or group through scarcity creation is an augmentation of the income of the community, whereas it was one of Say's chief objects to expose this fallacy. And he wanted, also, to banish the general fear of there being too much of wanted things as a whole—the notion of glut and the fear of low prices. Although, as we have seen, he recognized explicitly that there could be a *relative* excess of particular economic goods (in the sense that it would pay to disinvest from certain industries, i.e., not to reinvest in them),

---

*In that their prospective yield on the current capital value falls short of interest.

†This is, I think, a fair interpretation of Say's not every rigorously worded contention that the value of money is "perishable" like that part of a producer's output that he does not wish to consume himself.[30]

‡Attwood recognized the importance of *rigidities*. But Henry Thornton, who also stressed this point, would certainly never have contested the Say Law.

the notion of a *general* excess he dismissed as absurd. He explained that ". . . . the glut of a particular commodity arises from its having outrun the total demand for it in two ways; either because it has been produced in excessive abundance, or because the produce of other commodities has fallen short. It is because the production of some commodities has declined, that other commodities are superabundant."[32] But, he went on to explain, "one kind of production would seldom outstrip the rest, and its products be proportionately cheapened, were production left entirely to itself." If such a lack of balance did come into being it must have been due, he contended, to some political action.[33] It would be a good thing and not a bad thing, he said, if the prices of commodities fell to zero. Should this happen to all economic goods, "every object of human want would stand in the same predicament as the air or water, which are consumed without the necessity of being either produced or purchased. . . . . This would be the very acme of wealth."[34]

Neisser's case against Say is that he admitted the possibility of general overproduction through admitting the possibility of particular overproduction, i.e., the devotion of productive services to output the sale of which does not cover costs. And Neisser goes so far as to suggest that Say tried to deny the possibility of general overproduction by a "meaningless tautology,"[35] namely, the assertion (Say's words) that "in fact, one truly produces only when, productive services having been remunerated, the product is worth its costs of production."* But I interpret this passage as referring to the wastefulness of *particular* overproduction—misdirection of production—the possibility of which, far from attempting to slur over, Say explicitly stressed. Hence, in spite of Say's most unsatisfactory exposition in the context quoted, Neisser's laborious proof that "overproduction" *in the sense of output which cannot be sold at cost* may exist, is a criticism, not of Say's law of markets, but of an imaginary opponent.† Yet Neisser's much quoted article has been treated with respect even by economists of the stature of Haberler. It has, I think,

---

*"Au fait, on ne produit véritablement que lorsque les services productifs étant payés, le produit vaut ses frais de production."[36]

†Neisser's misunderstanding is certainly forgivable; for in the *Cours Complet* Say dealt with this question in one of his weakest pieces of exposition. He introduced a sort of *ex ante* notion of a "product," but he did not adhere rigorously to this *ex ante* concept. "Strictly speaking," he said, "a product is not merely a thing capable of serving the needs of men. It is a thing of which the utility is worth its cost."[37] Obviously, he did not mean to suggest that wastefully produced things have no value. He was rather clumsily trying to show that, production being the creation of value or wealth, one can hardly describe as "production" those operations "of which the result would be the successive annihilation of wealth."[38] Merely to secure physical output (this century, he would have referred to "boondoggling") is not to produce. Unfortunately, he went on to assert that things which have not covered their cost cease "to be able to be sold" and hence lose the power of creating markets for new products,[39] when he should have said, "cease to be worth continued production, and so cease to contribute to demand for other things."

been largely responsible for the idea that the Say Law has received authoritative refutation.

Say's contemporaries and successors were quite clear on the point at issue. Ricardo, for instance, on being asked whether a reduction of demand for commodities would not prevent the owner of capital resources from reaping the advantages of their employment, a situation which an increase in demand might be expected to rectify, answered that an increase in demand could have this effect as far as a particular commodity was concerned. In respect of commodities as a whole, the diminution of demand for one implied the encouragement of the production of another.[40] He was not led by the question, however, to consider the possibility of productive services being priced out of utilization by private collusion. The idea occurred neither to Ricardo nor to his questioner. As K. H. Niebyl has reminded us, "the outstanding characteristic" of "the type of economy in which Ricardo was living . . . . was its money cost flexibility, and this rather fundamental condition distinguishes that society not only from the one with which Jevons and Bohm-Bawerk were concerned but also, above all, from our own."[41]

6.—But it was precisely the fear of plenty—and hence of the supposed difficulty of selling—which Say tried to dispel, that dominated Keynes' thinking and still seems to dominate the minds of his disciples. The nature of this fear is excellently brought out in Harrod's discussion of the German reparations problem after World War I. Having supported Keynes' view that the reparation demands which were originally suggested were absurd and unrealistic—an issue which is irrelevant to the present discussion—he asks what the position would have been if Germany had, in fact, by an heroic effort and acceptance of austerity, actually paid the original sums assessed to France and Britain. He believes that the result would have been an enormous increase in Germany's industrial strength but the ruin of the receiving countries. The people of France and Britain would, for a while, have lived "the life of lotus eaters, with taxation low, hours of work light, their markets gone, enjoying the well-earned fruits of victory for a period of 30 or 40 years." "Was it not obvious," he asks, "that if this were actually to happen, at the end of the period France and Britain would be totally at the mercy of Germany?"*[41]

---

*In this passage, the issue is confused by a red herring. Harrod assumes that the increase in French and British real income (due to the receipt of reparations) would have led not only to a more than proportionate increase in consumption (including leisure) but to a squandering of capital. It is a fantastic and most un-Keynesian assumption. But it is obviously true that any nation *could* ruin itself by failing to replace its assets—by refraining from saving. As there is no good empirical reason, however, for assuming that increased income should discourage the use of resources for replacement or net accumulation, this point need not be pursued.

It is not "obvious." It is wholly wrong. The passage exposes, I believe, the subconscious and wholly fallacious assumption which is responsible for the Keynesian consumption fallacy and the rejection of the Say Law. There are no grounds for assuming that the real gains achieved by France and Britain would have reduced their power to compete (i.e., to supply) in the markets of the world.* The *composition* of productive effort in these countries would certainly have been influenced, in the circumstances, by entrepreneurial judgment about the most profitable form that German effort could take. But if British and French manufacturers lost any markets in consequence, that would have been solely because other markets had become relatively profitable. What so many Keynesians fail to realize is that every particular cheapening of products is releasing income for the acquisition of noncompeting products.

The same blind spots are equally discernible in Harrod's attempt to answer Mantoux's argument that the original demands on Germany were reasonable. (I am not, it should be noted, supporting this contention. I am challenging Harrod's criticism of Mantoux's reasoning). Mantoux referred to the not irrelevant instance of the great sums transferred from the United States and Great Britain to their Allies during the war. Harrod's answer (which turns attention back to the difficulties of the *receiving* countries) is that "in this case demand was ready made." The Allies, he says, "required" munitions and supplies "in amounts altogether far above the ordinary."[43] The crucial concepts here lie in the words "demand" and "required." The word "demand" seems to imply the *willingness and ability* to pay, and suggests that the *necessity to pay* solves the problem of *willingness and ability* for the receiving country. If the word "demand" does *not* imply this, the word "required" suggests that the receipt of gifts is without harm if the goods received are *wanted*. But a country which is receiving *reparations* otherwise than in kind will exercise preference and will *demand* only wanted things. It will be perfectly free to choose how to use its capital and income (including its income from reparations). And free gifts in kind would presumably have *some* value to their recipients; and if they do have any such value, then they must be demanded. There is no conceivable difficulty for the people in the receiving countries but only for those in the supplying countries—their ability to produce and pay the reparations agreed.†

Moreover, Mantoux's argument that if Germany could afford to spend

---

*Unless leisure happened then to stand higher on the scale of preference of people in the countries receiving separations.

†Harrod's confusion can be further observed in his treatment of the similar case of Germany's apparently easy transference of goods from occupied territories during the last war. He mentions as an explanation, "an abnormal demand for goods arising from Germany's war efforts."

15 milliard marks annually on rearmament, she could afford to pay the same sum for reparations, is not upset (as Harrod imagines) because in the case of reparations these proceeds have to be transferred abroad, and foreign buyers have to be found for the exports. Reparations of the value of 15 milliard marks would undoubtedly have demanded the use of German resources in a very different way from armaments; but they would have left an equivalent real value of net income privately disposable at home (although maybe of a greatly different composition). And the factors determining the form of German output would have included demand from abroad of a value equivalent to reparations.

7.—The extent of Keynesian blindness manifested by Harrod is further illustrated in his regarding it as an advantage to Britain, after 1945, "in having one of her principal competitors in foreign markets laid low."[44] It *may* have happened that the elimination of Germany's contribution to world *supply* was more beneficial to Britain than the parallel elimination of Germany's equally valuable contribution to world *demand*. But Harrod does not put the matter in this way. He fails to mention the vital truth that each pair of German hands that was robbed of tools and co-operant resources implied a decreased demand for food, clothing, shelter, amusements and luxuries from the world. Undoubtedly *some* British industries benefited from the slowness of Germany's recovery, but equally others suffered. And from the standpoint of British prosperity, whether these industries were producing for home or foreign markets is immaterial.

8.—Dillard correctly classifies Keynes with writers like John Gray, J. F. Bray, Proudhon and Gesell. For like them, Keynes took a simple view of the "difficulty" of *selling* things, and felt intuitively that some deficiency of demand instead of some defect of pricing was responsible. This led to the belief that, if a seller's market could be achieved, a healthy economy would be created.* Dillard quotes in this connection Gray's suggestion that, under a defensible monetary system, "to sell for money would be as easy as it is to buy for money."[45] The possibility that buying would be just as "difficult" as selling if buyers were organized in the same way as sellers (instead of buyers being almost everywhere engaged in virtually unrestricted competition with one another) never seems to occur to the Keynesians. Yet, properly seen, this is *the* great issue in the consideration of such things as unemployment, the trade cycle, capital formation, the development tempo, and so forth. What the Keynesians seem not to see is that the supposed "difficulty" of selling

---

*This notion became explicit in Beveridge's *Full Employment*.

KEYNESIANISM—RETROSPECT AND PROSPECT

arises solely because people are unwilling to price (in relation to income, and in relation to expected prices) their full potential contribution to output so as to enable the purchase of the whole of that output, i.e., because people are in a position in which they believe it pays them better *not* to sell than to sell the full possible output coming forward.

9.—The harm wrought to mankind through the general failure of their leaders to understand the Say Law over the period of the great depression staggers the imagination. For just one instance of stupidity, out of all the acts of folly which were due to a failure to perceive the implications of Say's fundamental principle, I can refer to the Hawley-Smoot tariff of 1930. Even more disastrous than its passage through Congress was adherence to it in the circumstances which were developing. It was recognition of the international implications of the truth that supply creates demand which led a number of prominent American economists to petition President Roosevelt in 1933, shortly after his election, urging him to lift the United States out of depression and into prosperity by lowering the tariff on manufactured goods. This would, they argued, through facilitating recovery and the restoration of demand in Europe, bring about increased prosperity in American industry generally. "Prompt lowering of the tariffs," wrote B. M. Anderson, ". . . . would have led to a radical revival, an almost explosive revival, of domestic trade. . . . The first effect of reducing the tariffs, well before any goods could have been loaded on ships on the other side . . . ., would have been a great upswing in the prices of farm products and raw materials in the United States. . . . Cables work faster than ships, and speculators work faster than merchants."[46]

Anderson, and those who thought like him, saw to the roots of the situation. An understanding of the Say Law in 1933, expressed in policy generally (as well as in foreign trade relations), could have produced a phenomenal and immediate recovery. There is no exaggeration in the words "an explosive revival." Sellers throughout the world, and governments acting in their interests, were resisting the full expression of uninflated demand by pricing supply (directly or through tariffs and "controls") beyond the reach of uninflated income. Small wonder that superficial thinking should have led to the conclusion that inflation was the remedy.

I have tried to expose the emptiness of attempted refutations of the Say Law. It is difficult to explain the extraordinary influence which such attempts have exerted. I cannot avoid the impression that the explanation lies in their having been sincere efforts, through tortuous formulation of the issues, to rationalize the results of wishful thinking.

10.—APPENDIX

J. S. Mill on the Say Law

J. S. Mill's reference to the Say Law, partially quoted in *The General Theory*, is as follows. The passages in italics are those which Keynes omitted. "What constitutes the means of payment for commodities is simply commodities. Each person's means of paying for the productions of other people consist of those which he himself possesses. All sellers are inevitably, and by the meaning of the word, buyers. Could we suddenly double the productive powers of the country, we should double the supply of commodities in every market; but we should, by the same stroke, double the purchasing power. Everybody would bring a double demand as well as supply: everybody would be able to buy twice as much, because everyone would have twice as much to offer in exchange. *It is probable, indeed, that there would now be a superfluity of certain things. Although the community would willingly double its aggregate consumption, it may already have as much as it desires of some commodities, and it may prefer to do more than double its consumption of others, or to exercise its increased purchasing power on some new thing. If so, the supply will adapt itself accordingly, and the value of things will continue to conform to their cost of production.*"

J. S. Mill provided, however, a very poor exposition of the law of markets in his *Principles*, because he failed to show explicitly the exact significance which the French economist placed upon correct market valuation or pricing. Mill had been much more satisfactory in his *Unsettled Questions*, and was probably taking for granted the argument which he had used in that earlier work. The following sentence (with which he continued a little later, in the *Principles*) could have given Keynes the impression of some confusion: "*But those who have the means may not have the wants, and those who have the wants may be without the means. A portion therefore, of the commodities produced, may be unable to find a market. . . . .*"[47] Say's comment on such a passage, had he been asked to comment, could well have been more or less like this: "If some things produced cannot be sold because those who want them have not the means (given all the other demands on their income), whilst those who have the means do not want these goods (i.e., prefer other things), it implies either that the goods in question are priced too highly (which implies in turn that supply is withdrawn, and hence that demand for the output of others is withdrawn) or that the wrong things are being produced—that the community's resources are being wastefully used (similarly causing the source of demands—the flow of productive services—to contract)." There are many passages in

Say which suggest that he would have given this sort of answer. But there are a few (especially in his *Cours Complet*) which might suggest that he would not, and that he had not fully understood the law to which his name has since become attached.

REFERENCES

(1) HABERLER, *The General Theory* (IV) in Harris, *The New Economics*, pp.173-6. (2) J. S. MILL, *Essays on Some Unsettled Questions in Political Economy*, pp.69-73. (3) SWEEZY, *Keynes the Economist*, in *Science and Society*, 1946, p.400, and in Harris, *op. cit.*, p.105. (4) SCITOVSKY, in discussion on *Keynesian Economics after Twenty Years*, A.E.R., P. and P., 1957, p.93. (5) BECKER and BAUMOL, *The Classical Monetary Theory*, Economica, 1952, p.374. (6) ANDERSON, *Economics and the Public Welfare*, pp.392-4. (7) KEYNES, *The General Theory*, p.26. (8) KEYNES, *Alternative Theories of the Rate of Interest*, E.J., 1937, p.249. (9) J. S. MILL, *op. cit.*, p.51. (10) *Ibid.*, p.73. (11) *Ibid.*, p.72. (12) HEILBRONER, *The Great Economists*, p.218. (13) DILLARD, *Theory of a Monetary Economy*, in Kurihara, *Post Keynesian Economics*, p.21. (14) LANGE, *Studies in Mathematical Economics*, pp.57-61 and NEISSER, *General Overproduction*, in *Readings in Business Cycle Theory*, p.385. (15) NEISSER, *op. cit.*, p.390. (16) ANDERSON, *op. cit.*, p.407. (17) SAY, *Political Economy*, 4th ed., Vol. I, p.167. (18) *Ibid.*, p.170 (continuation of footnote to p.169). (19) *Ibid.*, p.172. (20) *Ibid.*, p.163. (21) *Ibid.*, Vol. II, p.52. (22) *Ibid.*, Vol. I, pp.128-9. (23) *Ibid.*, pp.64-5. (24) WICKSELL, *Lectures*, Vol. II, p.159. (25) MILL, *op. cit.*, pp.69 *et seq.* (26) BECKER and BAUMOL, *op. cit.*, p.357. (27) J. S. MILL, *op. cit.*, p.70. (28) NEISSER, *op. cit.*, p.387 n. (29) JAMES MILL, *Elements of Political Economy*, p.222, quo., BECKER and BAUMOL, *op. cit.*, p.373. (30) SAY, *op. cit.*, Vol. I, p.167. (31) *Ibid.*, p.169. (32) *Ibid.*, p.168. (33) *Ibid.*, p.169. (34) *Ibid.*, Vol. II, pp.46-7. (35) NEISSER, *op. cit.*, p.385. (36) SAY, *Cours Complet d'Economie Politique Pratique*, Vol. I, p.348. (37) *Ibid.*, p.347. (38) *Ibid.*, p.348. (39) *Ibid.*, p.349. (40) RICARDO, CAMB. Edn., Vol. V. p.348. (41) NIEBYL, *Studies in the Classical Theories of Money*, p.123. (42) HARROD, *Life of J. M. Keynes*, p.271. (43) *Ibid.*, p.276. (44) *Ibid.*, p.279. (45) DILLARD, *op. cit.*, p.19. (46) ANDERSON, *op. cit.*, p.304. (47) MILL, *Political Economy*, Book III, chap. 14, par. 2.

Chapter XVIII

ANTICIPATED INFLATION

SUMMARY

1.—In the absence of convertibility, cheap money demands the continuous deception of the public; 2.—and when this fails, great difficulties are encountered, whilst the crude co-ordinate effects of inflation are lost. 3.—Continued inflation as a confessed policy then becomes impossible, except under a totalitarian system. 4.—In "free societies" only intermittent periods of relative stability, which have reassured the public, have permitted creeping inflation to continue. But the conviction has been growing that inflation is now to be a normal phenomenon; 5.—and in the attempt to escape its consequences, recourse to the remnants of the free economy is currently destroying its political usefulness. 6.—Political circles do not yet appear to have perceived, however, the need for an alternative policy aimed at co-ordination through price adjustment. 7.—Appendix: President Kennedy's pledge not to increase the Dollar Price of Gold.

1.—I have already pointed out that, for inflation to succeed it is essential continuously to mislead the public. "The working of inflation," says Mises, "is conditioned by the ignorance of the public. . . . . Inflation ceases to work as soon as the many become aware of its effects upon the monetary unit's purchasing power. . . . . This ignorance of the public is the indispensable basis of the inflationary policy. Inflation works as long as the housewife thinks: 'I need a new frying-pan badly, but prices are too high today; I shall wait until they drop again.' It comes to an abrupt end when people discover that inflation will continue. . . . . The main problem of an inflationary policy is how to stop it before the masses have seen through their rulers' artifices." It is a "system that can work only if its essential features are ignored by the public." Governments are forced "to make the people believe that the inflationary policy is merely a temporary expedient for the duration of a passing emergency, one that will be stopped before long." The effects sought by a policy of inflation "can be attained only if the government succeeds in deceiving the greater part of the people about the consequences of its policy."[1]

M. J. Bailey has pointed out (in the course of a discussion of a model based on the assumption of a deliberate, openly announced inflation) that "governments typically do not admit that they have in any way contributed to an existing inflation . . . . ; in their view they are helpless pawns forced to issue increasing quantities of money in response to price rises generated by forces beyond their control. In practice this has meant . . . . that it was possible for governments to get far more resources . . . . than is implied by our results. . . . ."[2] But governments *dare* not admit their aim.

2.—Since 1931, far from fighting inflation, governments can be seen to have engineered it with great political skill, and this skill has consisted mainly in preventing the speed of inflation from giving rise to a demand for its cessation. *They* have not seen it in this way of course. Yet they have known that the attempt to inflate too rapidly is apt to cause more discontent than it alleviates; they have appreciated the fact that the failure to convince the man in the street that inflation is unlikely to continue indefinitely, will ruin the policy they are pursuing; but they have seldom recognized that the speed of inflation is determined mainly by the adroitness with which the changing climate of expectations is handled. The authorities simply know that they must take account of psychological factors and the general state of economic enlightenment.* Indeed, the community's economic shrewdness is probably the ultimate limiting factor. Treasuries perceive that *the public must be persuaded at all costs that an intended depreciation is not intended,* otherwise a chaotic rush is likely, (a) to force up the prices of services in advance of inflation and (b) to realize fixed interest securities.†

If we imagine the extreme and hardly realistic case of a fully enlightened society, no inflation will be possible at all. For *as soon as the community begins to understand the aim, expectations cause movement towards the objective to occur much too quickly, without the "lags" which are the real inspiration of the policy, and so without any coordinating effects.* That is, the changes in *relative* prices (the relation between "costs" and "final prices") which induce the release of capacity, are then likely to be missed. When this is the situation, it often seems that the danger is an acceleration of private spending instead of a gradual increase in government spending.

Thus, trade associations agree to raise prices because, as they put it, "costs are rising," although what they ought to mean is *"because demand in terms of money is rising and it pays us to get in first."* Similarly, the trade unions, as soon as they come to realize that an inflation is in progress, raise wage demands because they say "the cost of living is increasing," although what they ought to mean is, *"because of perpetual inflation, the acceptance of our demands will not cause unemployment and we have to get in first."* And when they come increasingly to insist upon contracts in terms of escalator clauses, Keynes' simple assumption

---

*It is for reasons of this kind that the Keynesians, although they reject the "tyranny" of the international gold standard, feel forced to acquiesce in the not dissimilar discipline of fixed exchange rates. The inherent contradiction in their policies would be exposed too rapidly (as "fundamental disequilibria") if the free market were allowed to determine the relative value of currencies, with no supports other than rediscount and open market operations; and the co-ordinative effects of inflation (during periods of competitive depreciation or during the intervals between devaluations) would consequently be lost.

†Whilst such expectations last they will have caused a cessation of that extraordinarily fertile division of labor in which many savers accept a contractual market value for the hire of their savings, thereby sacrificing entrepreneurial remuneration. Savers in general cannot be experts in those particular branches of economic activity which most urgently need savings. (See p. 417).

that "when money-wages are rising . . . . it will be found that real wages are falling"[3] begins to appear as an absurdity.

Mises maintains that Keynes' contention that the reduction of money wage-rates is much more strongly resisted than the reduction of real wage-rates as a result of prices rising "had already been outdated and refuted by the march of events," when *The General Theory* was written. "The masses had already begun to see through the artifices of inflation. Problems of purchasing power and index numbers became an important issue in the union's dealings with wage-rates."[4] Since that time there has been a sort of race between inflation and the unions, the former being persistently co-ordinative in a crude sort of way, and the latter continuously throwing the system out of co-ordination. (See below, pp. 415-6). Moreover, the man in the street is now gradually coming to learn that he must avoid gilt-edged investments, and even the life insurance companies are beginning to see that they also must abandon the Bailey canons and choose portfolios which will enable them to some extent to insure insurance. Is it not obvious that an openly planned, continuous and regular inflation would be wholly self-defeating and have no co-ordinative effects?

As we have seen, at the root of Keynes' convictions lies the notion that prospective yields (the marginal efficiency of capital) in relation to current interest determine "activity." But he did not perceive that (unless the community is deceived) current interest will be similarly determined by what is in prospect, i.e., by expectations. At one point only did he refer to the issue explicitly, and he then began as though he was going to face it. He admitted that "*if* the rate of interest were to rise *pari passu* with the marginal efficiency of capital, there would be *no* stimulating effect. . . . . For the stimulus to output depends on the marginal efficiency of a given stock of capital rising *relatively* to the rate of interest." But he dismissed the possibility with the questionable and unexamined assertions that expectations will only be "partially reflected" in current interest,[5] and that "the rate of interest is, virtually, a *current* phenomenon."[6] And in the obscure sections from which I am quoting, he made no attempt to explain why expectations of higher or lower interest yields should not raise or lower current interest; nor did he come to grips with the obvious question of why, if the value of the money unit is expected to depreciate, lenders should not demand and borrowers be prepared to pay interest rates which make due allowance for the prospective depreciation of contracts defined in money terms.

Keynesians like Hicks have extravagantly praised their master for his having supposedly brought expectations into economics. The supposition is absurd; but the irony of it is that Keynes failed to grasp the rôle of expectations at just this crucial point.

3.—Once there no longer exists any defined monetary standard, it becomes the over-riding requirement of monetary policy that the community shall be misdirected. And a particular form of the control of opinion comes, thus, to be an inevitable adjunct of control of the monetary system. E.g., as E. Nevin has put it. in his advocacy of cheap money, "given a favorable disposition of expectations, monetary authorities can achieve a very great deal by measures carefully adjusted to stimulate and channel the tide of opinion amongst investing circles, relying on the characteristic self-propelling tendency of that tide to secure the aims which they have in mind."[7]

This is very mildly expressed. I wish the reader to consider that, unless Ministers of Finance and Chancellors of the Exchequer have full recourse to what may be called the technique of "necessary untruths," every inflation must soon become a runaway inflation and defeat the purpose.

The phrase, "necessary untruth" was used by *The Manchester Guardian* in an attempted justification of the action of Sir Stafford Cripps who, just before the British devaluation of 1949, and after it had been finally planned, had several times categorically denied that devaluation was intended.* The British government had secretly discussed and contemplated devaluation for some time, almost inevitably setting into circulation rumors of what was being contemplated, and the speculative consequences which were to be expected.† They finally decided to take the step. They did so, it seems, at least three weeks before they were ready to put their decision into effect. They had to discuss it first with the United States, Canada and the I.M.F. In the meantime, it was essential to mislead the trustful for the benefit of the mistrustful.

But it had for some time past been the technique used by governments to pretend, in order to dissuade rational reactions, that suspensions of convertibility were merely temporary breaches of obligations. For instance, in 1931 there occurred one of the most disturbing examples of the necessity to mislead in order successfully to reduce the value of a nation's currency. It has been described by B. M. Anderson (referring to Britain's departure from gold in 1931) in the following passage: "On Friday, September 18, Dr. Vissering, Head of the Netherlands Bank, 'phoned Governor Montagu Norman of the Bank of England to enquire if it were safe for him to continue to hold sterling, and received unqualified assurance that England would remain on the gold standard.

Manchester Guardian, Sept., 21, 1949. "Necessary Untruth" was the title of a leading article in defence of Cripps' nine explicit denials.

†If, when the difficulties first presented themselves, the Chancellor of the Exchequer had immediately denied unequivocally the intention to devalue *and stated the case against such action,* the rumors could have been killed and the direction of speculation reversed.

He held his sterling."*(8) In consequence, his bank lost the whole of its capital.† Through the same act, the Bank of France lost seven times its capital.

Two years later, using the argument that he wanted "to control inflation," Roosevelt persuaded Congress to give him extraordinary discretionary powers in the monetary field. Then, in April of that year, he decided to call in all privately owned gold "as a temporary measure," there being no hint that his real purpose was the forced depreciation of the dollar in terms of gold, the issue of an enormous number of notes, with open market operations by the Treasury and Federal Reserve banks to acquire government securities.

The fact that the Bank of France was forced by the government to falsify its balance-sheet in 1925 in order to maintain an unjustified confidence, had been regarded as a shocking incident by those who understood what had happened. But exactly the same *kind* of deception as was then practiced, even if it is seldom *intended* to be deception, is inevitable if inflation is ever to be continuously successful.

It is the moral factor on which I am now again placing emphasis. A system which must rely upon persistent deception is obvious evidence of the corruption of government and of the disintegration of trustworthy relations between governments. In 1922, in negotiating a settlement with the American Debt Funding Commission, Britain confined herself, on the whole, merely to asking that the rate of interest should be 3½ per cent. in accordance with her credit standing. "The British were superb in this. They were proud . . . . magnificently proud . . . ." commented B. M. Anderson. "They asked little consideration."(10) The benefits which Britain obtained from the possession of this fine character are difficult to estimate, but they were substantial. Am I irresponsible if I shout, What a deterioration—over a quarter of a century—to the era of "necessary untruths"! What a deterioration since the pre-1914 era! *Simply because no-one ever doubted then that governments would honour convertibility obligations* there were no balance of payments difficulties, no hot money flights, no devaluation scares, no complaints of world liquidity shortage, no restraints on international settlements, no blocking of foreign balances and no quantitative trade restrictions for payment-balancing purposes. World disco-ordination is the product of the continuous misdirection of expectations which the Keynesian technique necessitates.

Apart from the moral issue, there is this inescapable reality, which needs constant stressing, that *the stronger the belief that inflation is in progress, the greater will be the degree of inflation needed to achieve co-*

---

*Anderson heard of these conversations shortly after they occurred. He refers to another account of the incident in W. A. Morton's *British Finance, 1930-1940*.(9)

†Half of this was made good by the Dutch government.

ordination. And as people are now learning to expect inflation, the burden and injustice of this method are likely to become increasingly heavy.

The quotation from Mises with which I began this chapter draws attention, in my opinion, to the most significant aspect of cheap money policy since 1931. If the value of the money unit falls in spite of the wish of the monetary authority to prevent this, i.e., in spite of ministers of finance conducting a vain "fight against inflation," then the monetary authority must be regarded as hopelessly incompetent. But generally speaking, what is meant when it is claimed that "inflation is being fought" is not this at all. What is meant in practice (when the claim is not merely humbug) is usually that conduct which is incompatible with full employment under monetary stability is being fought.

Those economists who, like Vickery, Slichter and H. G. Johnson, have discussed the possibility of continued and open inflation at a given rate have certainly not given sufficient attention to the operation of expectations.* To make a confessed inflation possible, controls so numerous and so drastic that they amount to a complete suppression of economic democracy and its replacement by an authoritarian system are needed.† Only a totalitarian government could curb the powerful forces which are set up, and so prevent the tendency for the scale of prices to jump to its expected destination. I have found it impossible not to wonder, at times, whether some Keynesians do not recognize that the system they advocate is, as Bronfenbrenner has shown, a useful means of destroying the institutions of the free economy, and hence a method of building up a totalitarian, Marxist State. That may of course be the ulterior reason for much of the support of continued inflation. But many, if not most Keynesians, reject the totalitarian ideal. Yet when they advocate deliberate inflation (i.e., without deception), they somehow fail to perceive that it must have an effect which they would deplore.

4.—If Keynesianism is widely abandoned, it is unlikely to be due to any ability to learn from *past* experience or to changes in theoretical convictions due to *a priori* speculation. Only current realities—serious realities—may be expected to force an adjustment of ideas. As I write, there are still plenty of people who are prepared to say: "The raising of prices has meant prosperity; so let us keep the inflation going." But I believe that people generally, and entrepreneurs in particular, are coming at last to realize that a creeping or spasmodic inflation has become chronic. They are beginning to adjust their own individual policies to it. Sooner or later, none will be content to be left in the race. Infla-

---

*See W. A. Morton, *Trade Unionism and Inflation*, A.E.R., 1950, pp.33-4.
†Slichter did, indeed, advocate such controls.(11)

tion will at once cease to be workable, however skilfully the technique
of inflation is wielded by treasuries and cabinets.

I am not convinced that my interpretation of current events can be
accepted. But it certainly appears to have been necessary, for perseverance with cheap money since 1931, that there should have been periods
of relatively stable prices in order continuously to restore, from time to
time, expectations that inflation is at last ending. I do not suggest that
monetary authorities have deliberately planned these interludes of
relative stability with that objective clearly in mind. They have, I think,
simply felt the need, at times, to restore confidence and discourage collusive price raising.* But the effect has been to win a longer life for the
epoch of creeping inflation.†

People are now tending to believe that inflation is certain to recur;
they are beginning to expect that apparent price stability over any
period is merely the prelude to the taking of steps calculated to set prices
still higher; and they will, I think, increasingly require something much
stronger than the pie-crust pledges of governments to reassure them. It
is a not unnatural reaction of the trade-unions, in these circumstances,
to resist co-ordinative wage-rate adjustments far more powerfully than
previously, even during recessions, and for employers of labor to be
much less willing to fight to achieve such wage-rate adjustments or
prevent disco-ordinative increases. Business men acquire the firm belief
that the State will get them out of their difficulties by means of a further
burst of inflation.

For such reasons as these, the operation of the so-called "money illusion" as a factor determining the behavior of the trade-unions has been
rapidly changing. Both the rank and file and their leaders are to-day
only too well aware that the maintenance of money wage-rates does not
mean the maintenance of standards. The tendency is, rather, more and
more to attempt to push up money wage-rates *in advance* of the continuing rise in the prices of final products. Annual increases of wage-
rates come to be looked upon as normal. Union leaders are encouraged
to claim the credit and even to compete against one another in securing
sensational increases. They soon emerge as the most powerful vested
interest against any policy which might aim at bringing inflation to an
end. And is it surprising that eventually they come to insist upon wage
contracts being concluded in terms of escalator clauses?

A. F. Burns who, a few years ago, was Chairman of the Council of

---

*See Appendix to this chapter on President Kennedy's pledge, of February, 1961,
not to increase the dollar price of gold.

†It is sometimes suggested that the interludes of apparent stability are periods in
which, after a round of wage-rate increases, labor is temporarily satisfied and the
political necessity for further inflation therefore temporarily reduced. But relative
price stability tends to moderate the tendency to trade union aggression and to stiffen
marginal resistance.

Economic Advisers, says that he has faith that "an acceptable solution of the problem of creeping inflation" will be worked out in the United States. He believes that "economic literacy is spreading among the American people." People are beginning to understand "that inflation creates difficulties for many salaried workers as well as for those living on pensions or on income from fixed-interest securities. They know that inflation may reduce our nation's ability to sell in foreign markets. They know even that a gradual inflation distorts the calculation of profits and therefore can impair the growth of business on which they depend for their livelihood or advancement. . . . . Most important of all, they know that inflation is not an act of God, and they believe that a mature people should be able to conduct their private and public affairs so as to avoid both depression and inflation."[12]

Perhaps enlightenment of this kind *is* spreading. But the really significant enlightenment which is spreading is a wider recognition that, the political factor being what it is, inflation must be continuous unless some most radical change is brought about. People *are* very slowly awaking to the truth that *inflation is an act of government, and that it is almost always (in these days) the consequence of calculated, even if reluctant action.* However well-meaning the motive, and however ingenious the verbal formulae by means of which Finance Ministers and central bank officials disguise the reality, that is the truth; and the man in the street is catching on.

5.—It is, however, only since the last war, and particularly since the beginning of the Korean troubles, that we have witnessed in several countries, the first clear effects of *widely anticipated* creeping inflation. For the first time in economic history, I believe, *we have encountered on a large scale, and simultaneously in many countries, the phenomenon of rising prices together with rising interest rates and budget surpluses, and in some parts even recession with unemployment.* We have seen such apparent absurdities as widespread complaints of credit shortage in the United States from 1954 to 1958 although the scale of prices was then tending continuously to rise. It has *appeared* as though the traditional weapons against inflation—such as high market interest rates—have lost their effectiveness.* But the high rates of interest have been needed in order to offset the expectations of lenders that their money claims are going to be worth very much less on the maturity of loans. Thus, whereas it has always been possible in the past to avoid unemployment by allowing the scale of prices to creep up more rapidly than costs, *in the future, governments are likely to be confronted with the alternatives of exorbitant interest or gradually accelerating inflations.*

---

*This appearance is an illusion.

The British *Council on Prices, Productivity and Incomes* have observed this ominous development. They warn the government that "once . . . . a steady upward trend of prices came to be generally accepted and anticipated, something would have to be done to mitigate the rentier's losses—otherwise the government would cease to be able to borrow any money on fixed interest terms. In the summer of 1957 there were, indeed, signs that such a development was far from being merely an academic possibility."[13] Moreover, "it seems, indeed, highly probable that if the rise in prices is not successfully checked, sliding scale adjustments . . . . will naturally develop under the pressure of the groups who suffer most from the present regime."[14] The Council say that they do not regard sliding scales as a satisfactory alternative to the policy of arresting inflation, because they think it would merely accelerate the inflation. It might lead, they say, to "a situation so disastrous that a remedy would have to be found at all costs, including perhaps heavy unemployment and distress."[15] That it would destroy the political usefulness of inflation, they do not make sufficiently clear.*

In the United States "concern over inflation has been increasing," says A. F. Burns, although it "has not yet become articulate enough to wring from Congress a declaration of policy that would have a moral force such as the Employment Act exercises with regard to unemployment."[17] But *I do not think it will ever be representations to Congress which will bring inflation to an end. It will be the people's recourse to the remnants of the free economy which will have this effect*—their insistence upon escalator clauses; their refusal to invest in gilt-edged securities except at enormously high rates of interest; their flight into nonmoney assets or at least into hybrid money (by which I mean liquid assets which bring some pecuniary yield†); their gradual abandonment of that useful division of labor under which savers do not take the risk of determining (or delegating to others the right to determine) the form of the assets which their savings provide.

6.—So far does the reaction seem to have gone (in the United States) that Burns can claim that "the classical remedies for inflation . . . . are again in good repute and have of late been diligently applied" (in fact, since 1954).[18] But the F.R.B. have been trying to use the classical remedies without the classical penalties and, being subordinate to government, have lacked the incentive to use effectively the remedies at their command. As a politically influenced institution, the F.R.B. could hardly

---

*The Radcliffe Report also admits (in 1959) that "the expectation of a continuing decline [in the value of money] has become stronger than it has been, in time of peace, for several centuries."[16]

†See pp. 90, 92.

be expected to hinder the necessary vote-buying by the ruling party. How unrealistic, then, to expect great expenditures like price supports for agriculture, increases in old-age pensions, etc., to be met out of overt taxation! And how hopeless to think of any other effective check on nongovernmental expenditure! Thus, if the United States government is to retain the support of those classes for whom minimum wage-rates have been fixed, and if it is politically essential continuously to increase these minima, it seems quite out of the question to burden commerce and industry with credit restraint. Burns suggested a few years ago that "governmental resistance to inflation has significantly stiffened of late." But so far the government has increasingly exhorted and warned. It has hardly dared to use significant force in the labor field. And to the extent to which its attitude *has* stiffened, it has been due to inflation slowly coming to be regarded, as someone has put it, as a built-in institution, with entrepreneurial, consumption and saving decisions being adjusted to its continuance.

Is it wishful thinking when I suggest that the American and British governments are being forced once again to consider means of permitting price and wage-rate adjustment to bring disordered economies into co-ordinated activity? Perhaps so. But even if my suggestion *is* correct, it still does not mean that the required reforms for the achievement of noninflationary full employment appear imminent in any country.

The great inflations of history were the product of a primitive past or the aftermath of the anarchy of war. That they have become endemic in the modern age has been due, I think, mainly or largely to the fact that the transfer of the kingly power to elected governments has not yet led people to limit the power of their rulers to debase the currency. The power of the princes to do so was long ago eliminated. As representative democracy was allowed to develop into what Mises terms "omnipotent government," no limits were placed on the power of the group of men who form governments to compete with their rivals in the purchase of office from the politically dominant sections. Inflation has continued because it has facilitated that process; because Keynes' teachings made it respectable; because the people who suffer have so far been successfully fed with the notion that governments conduct an unavailing fight against inflation; because electorates have failed to realize that modern inflations are, in practice, *engineered* with reluctance, but nevertheless with skill and with careful calculation of the rate at which the parties who suffer will not squeal too loudly.*

But more and more people are now beginning to understand. If this

---

*A friendly critic thinks that I am here attributing greater intelligence to those responsible for the policies of treasuries than can in fact be claimed for them.

enlightenment spreads, as I think it will spread (I hope, again, this is not wishful thinking), they will sooner or later call upon governments to renounce the right to debase the community's money. They will insist that governments take responsibility for maintaining the flow of *uninflated* purchasing power and hence full employment. And that will mean that the operation of the monetary system will be removed from the function of vote-buying; or, as the Keynesians euphemistically put it, from the use of the monetary system as an instrument of "national policy."

7.—APPENDIX

President Kennedy's Pledge not to Increase the Dollar Price of Gold

The real purpose of President Kennedy's pledge, in February, 1961,[*] not to devalue the dollar, seems to have been the immediate necessity to restore confidence in order to check the outflow of gold. Through this explicit assurance, he managed to convince the world that previous official assertions to the same effect were not "necessary untruths." Accordingly, the dollar price of gold fell at once almost to parity. It is, of course, true that the creation of confidence lowers the natural level of interest and cheapens noninflationary credit; but in the United States the confidence created may equally well facilitate further temporary recourse to the inflationary credit which had been causing all the difficulties. Hence, unless other countries step up their inflations in harmony, or unless technological progress happens to validate monetary policy and high production costs, or unless a wave of successful lock-outs protects the flow of uninflated wages and income from labor union aggression, the confidence created is likely to peter out to a sudden crisis within a few years, successive Presidential re-assurances commanding diminishing trust. Either deflation or a dishonoring of the President's pledge will then become necessary; and deflation will force the United States policy makers to choose between unemployment and the politically even more difficult decision to permit the economy to rely upon the co-ordinative mechanism of the price system.

[*]The President's statement was made during the final revision of this book.

REFERENCES

(1) MISES, *Theory of Money and Credit*, 1953 ed., pp.418-420. (2) BAILEY, *The Welfare Cost of Inflationary Finance*, J.P.E., 1956, p.110. (3) KEYNES, *The General Theory*, p.10. (4) MISES, *op. cit.*, p.425-6. (5) KEYNES, *op. cit.*, p.143. (6) *Ibid.*, pp.145-6. (7) NEVIN, *The Mechanism of Cheap Money*, p.108. (8) ANDERSON, *Economics and the Public Welfare*, p.246. (9) MORTON, *British Finance*, 1930-1940, p.46, quo. *Ibid.*,

(10) ANDERSON, *op. cit.*, p.293.   (11) SLICHTER, *How Bad is Inflation? Harper's Magazine*, Aug. 1952.   (12) BURNS, *Prosperity Without Inflation*, pp.21-22.   (13) Report of Council on *Prices, Productivity and Incomes*, No. 1, par. 96.   (14) *Ibid.*, par. 98. (15) *Ibid.*, par. 98.   (16) Report of Radcliffe Committee (Committee on *the Working of the Monetary System*), par. 23.   (17) BURNS, *op. cit.*, p.35.   (18) *Ibid.*, pp.36-7.

Chapter XIX

THE RETREAT

SUMMARY

1.—Although their position is obscured by an attempt to persevere with the remnants of Keynes' apparatus, the "Keynesians of the Right" have been groping their way back to orthodoxy. 2.—But their attempt to rehabilitate The General Theory *as a "special theory," applicable to recession conditions, breaks down; 3.—whilst the notion of "excessive demand," introduced by the modern "Rightist" Keynesians to explain boom conditions, is as useless as the concept of lack of effective demand. 4.—Keynes himself regarded his analysis as having universal validity, 5.—and although his misgivings became obvious shortly before his death, he never more than hinted at his dissatisfaction with his former teachings. 6.—The subsequent retreat of his "Rightist" disciples has not yet led to the eradication of his fallacies from the conventional textbooks. 7.—Bitter experience—especially of anticipated inflation—has recently been spreading doubts, but it is not yet certain how far governments have been learning the lessons. 8.—Appendix: The Retreat as Recorded in D. Mc.C. Wright's* The Keynesian System.

1.—According to Bronfenbrenner, the term "Keynesian" has now largely lost its meaning as a result of the splitting of the school into two camps, on the Right and on the Left. "The Keynesian Right," he says, "have taken policy positions on inflation control not greatly dissimilar from those of monetary theorists who have never seen the Keynesian light." "They rely mainly on tight money," he continues, "tax increases, and reduced public spending to curb inflation, look with equanimity on whatever unemployment may result from a 'stabilization crisis,' and distrust direct controls over individual prices." [1] This can hardly be said to be "not greatly dissimilar" to the orthodox position in respect of the situation which has existed since 1945. It is identical with it. The truth is, I shall maintain, that the Keynesians of this "Right" group have, in fact, been forced to retreat towards the orthodox position. But their thinking and exposition is still encumbered by all the confusing apparatus which Keynes introduced.

Bronfenbrenner suggests that, had Keynes been living, he would have identified himself with the "Right." If so, he would have had to renounce his teachings of the middle 'thirties. For his teachings *did* imply the policies to which the Keynesians of the Left are now obstinately clinging.

It is true that the "Leftist" Keynesians have tended to some extent to replace their master's own theories with new and perhaps even more subtle ones; but this does not mean that their doctrines are essentially different. And they have this merit as against the Keynesians of the "Right," that the policy implications of *their* teachings are unmistakeably clear. "If the choice must be made," says Bronfenbrenner, "they prefer inflation to underemployment," and instead of relying upon interest and the price mechanism to curb the rate of inflation, they believe in the use of controls such as price fixing, official allocation of resources, rationing, exchange control, etc. [2]

We know where we stand with these Keynesians. But where do we stand in relation to the Keynesian "Right"? How much inflation would *they* permit in order to prevent a little unemployment? What criteria have they on this obviously vital point? They have no criteria at all. And what criteria have they for the degree to which the interest and price

423

mechanism should be superseded by "conscious controls"? The answer, again, is none whatsoever. Is not the absence of any such criterion proof of some inherent defect?

Timlin, who is one of the leading members of the "Right" group (I hope I do not do her an injustice by including her in Keynesian company) tries to develop Keynesianism by suggesting that the *"monetary parallel to the classical and neoclassical problem of the allocation of resources is the problem of the structure of prices."*[3] This may suggest —quite wrongly—that teaching in the classical tradition has not always seen the problem in just that way. But Timlin goes further. She recognizes that, once the relevance of the structure of prices has been perceived, "policy considerations no longer involve simple aggregates such as consumption, investment, saving, and 'the' interest rate but rather rates of consumption of particular types of goods and services, investment in particular markets, and the *asset* structure as well as the *time* structure of market rates of interest."[4] In this passage, she is developing, or rather refining, Keynesian teaching back to the purest orthodoxy. Moreover, largely because she has again brought into consideration the issues which the Keynesian approach had excluded or obscured, we find that, in respect of actual recommended policy *for the postwar world* she takes unequivocally the orthodox line. Not only does she contemplate the deliberate use of interest as the means to monetary stability, but she says that, "perhaps the logical time for the use of the interest rate as a regulator is *before* an inflationary rise in costs takes place."[5] She says that "attempts to hold to policies of artificially low rates of yield on securities traded in by central banks could be expected to increase existing disequilibria in these markets."[6] There is a "theoretical flaw," she contends, in the policy of encouraging, "through low interest rates, the investment of funds in productive capital contributing to employment."[7] "The *minimum* sound objective" in a post-war period "would seem to be to prevent any extension of accumulations of currency and bank deposits; this would involve yields on securities entering into the portfolio of the central bank high enough to deter any flow of these securities toward the bank. Those who wished to liquidate their holdings would be compelled to offer them at prices that would be acceptable to other potential holders. . . ."[8] "There is no real substitute for adequate control over the quantity of currency and bank deposits, exercised through flexibility of yields."*[9] "It is precisely because investment opportunities may be limited that this policy is urged."[10] In other words, avoiding the misleading Keynesian terminology to which Timlin clings, it is precisely because the resources which can be employed for the process of

---

*Timlin explains the inflationary consequences of maintaining security prices.

replacement and growth are limited, that attempts to "stimulate" this process by interest below the natural may be purely inflationary.

2.—As I have stressed, Timlin is assuming the conditions which existed after World War II—conditions which she contrasts with those existing when Keynes wrote *The General Theory*. And as we have seen, there is a general tendency today to say that Keynes really meant his teachings to apply only to a state of unemployment or under-employment; and that it ought to have been realized that, under full employment, his *General Theory* becomes irrelevant. The suggestion is that the various special forms of cheap money which he advocated were intended, ultimately, merely to bring unutilized capacity into operation. We are told that it is true, as Keynes contended, that savings do not determine "investment" (net accumulation) but that "investment" determines savings *up to the point at which unutilized capacity no longer exists*. Beyond that point, savings *do* determine "investment." As soon as the last little bit of idle capacity has been brought into operation, orthodox teachings become unassailable. As Timlin puts it, in the middle 'thirties, demand for liquidity "constituted the neglected margin."[11] ". . . . The post-war situation differed vitally from the pre-war situation."[12] Before the war there had been idle labor and equipment in existence. After the war it no longer existed.

What this suggestion of Timlin amounts to is that the so-called "general theory" was a "special theory"—an analysis based upon assumptions which were realistic at a particular period only. Similarly, Patinkin (who seems to have studied economics wholly during the Keynesian era, but who has also read the classical economists) argues that "the propositions of Keynesian monetary theory are much less general than *The General Theory* would lead us to believe"; but, he adds, "this in no way diminishes the relevance of Keynesian unemployment theory for the formulation of a practicable full employment policy."[13]

Now we have seen that orthodox teaching has always recognized that credit expansion can, in certain circumstances, bring idle resources into utilization (a) to an extent which *is not* inflationary and (b) to a further extent which *is* inflationary; and that in so far as the expansion is noninflationary, decisions which result in savings out of increasing *money* income imply decisions to acquire savings out of increasing *real* income (and hence real net accumulation).*

My argument in Chapters X and XI has shown that this does not justify the conclusion that, even in the presence of withheld capacity, the expression of saving preference (influenced by interest offered and *the form*

---

*As full employment is approached, however, the repercussions upon real income (out of which real savings are made) gradually cease.

of current income) ceases to be the *sole* determinant of the rate of net accumulation. Indeed, the conclusion stands that the achievement of savings *by individuals* is alway contributing to net accumulation by the community unless it is being offset by dissavings made by others. In other words, unless net accumulation (supposed or realized) is occurring, the community cannot be achieving savings (supposed or realized) and *vice versa*. Hence, far from Keynes' "special theory" assisting in "the formulation of a practicable full employment policy," it obscures the crucial distinction between inflationary and noninflationary co-ordination, and between inflationary and noninflationary credit expansion.

If Keynes had *really* intended his *General Theory* to be a special theory, he would certainly have brought in the notion of a gradual rise in the ability of savings to determine "investment" as fuller employment is attained. Of course, the attempt to do so would have produced absurd results. Imagine having to contend, for instance, that if "employment" is 4/5ths. of full, savings will determine 4/5ths. of "investment" and "investment" 1/5th. of savings! Hence the thesis is just as *untenable* as a special theory. What can be claimed is that it is more *plausible* when withheld capacity is serious, but simply because inflation *is* one way of inducing the release of that capacity.

3.—The switch from condemnation of insufficient "effective demand" to condemnation of "excessive demand," which characterizes the new doctrine of the "Rightist" Keynesians, has merely confounded the confusion.* For the latter concept is no more satisfactory than the former. The term "excessive demand" *could* be used to mean over-consumption (in the sense that, in the light of the collective objectives of a community engaged in the effort of war, for instance, resources *ought* to be released to a greater extent from "excessive" normal uses for the pursuit of war objectives). But if it does not mean this, it can only mean "inflation." Yet when Keynes talked of an *insufficiency* of effective demand, he certainly did not mean deflationary *demand*. If he had, he would have said so, and where we were all puzzled by *The General Theory* we should have understood.

Since his death, we have seen the Keynesians—even those of the "Left" —occasionally demanding that inflation shall be kept in check by the curtailment of "nonessential investment." But they never seem to ask that the persistent increase in the number of money units in relation to the flow of real income shall be curbed. They think always in terms of "controls" to prevent entrepreneurs from reacting rationally to the situation which monetary policy creates. Their complaint against "nonessen-

---

*It has vitiated also many non-Keynesian contributions when the writers have attempted to use Keynesian concepts.

tial investment" has not, as far as I am aware, been explained by any rigorous consideration of the criteria of "nonessentiality." Few "Keynesians of the Left" would doubt that State expenditure is always essential; hence the tendency is usually to suggest that private investment is non-essenial or less essential.

4.—But neither in title nor explicit claim did Keynes present his contribution as a special theory. Nor did he himself *explicitly* retract, or rebuke his many influential followers who, throughout the war years, continued to argue (as many still do) for the continuance of low interest throughout the post-war period in order to stimulate investment, maintain employment, etc. Statesmen, governors of central banks, ministers of finance, demagogues and others were all arguing, up to the time of Keynes' death, for the very policies the disastrous flaw in which Timlin exposes. But Keynes was silent. True, he occasionally seemed to hedge by broad references to the virtues of orthodoxy, a point with which I shall shortly deal. Unfortunately, he was never explicit. He did not force the bulk of his loyal followers into an opposing camp. To have confessed that *The General Theory* ought to have been named "a special theory"—a theory which provided a justification for what may have been *politically expedient* in the 'thirties—would certainly have seriously deflated the unprecedented power and influence (for an economist) which he had attained. But in my judgment he had failed to think himself out of the confusions into which a clumsy method had led him.

Timlin appears to think Keynes would have approved of her recent refutation of what the majority of Keynesians have believed him to have taught. She quotes in this connection the passage in *The General Theory* in which he said: "If our central controls succeed in establishing an aggregate volume of output corresponding to full employment as nearly as practicable, the classical theory comes into its own again from this point onwards."[14] She maintains that, when unemployed resources exist, interest below the natural level—what she calls "an artificaly low" interest rate—is the appropriate remedy, but it is no longer to be recommended when resources are fully employed.

Yet the vital point of controversy is on this very issue. The trouble about using "artificially low" interest to achieve re-employment is that there is never any moment at which it can be legitimately contended that the abandonment of inflation will not mean *some* unemployment, in the absence of the price and cost adjustments which Keynesianism excludes from consideration. This means that, in practice, the classical theory can never be justified!

There is nothing to be gained by blinking the fact that Keynes gave the green light to governments who preferred to inflate rather than take steps to permit or directly to bring about the co-ordination of prices. Governments preferred to inflate for exactly the same reasons that have always actuated them, when they have not been restrained by constitutional or legal enactments. As Timlin herself so strikingly puts it: "Debasement of the currency in the face of difficulties is a very old resort of princes. Modern methods through depreciation are more subtle. . . . Temptations to use these methods to meet contemporary fiscal or political problems may be relatively continuous. Governments may resort to them as drunkards may take to drink, little by little, under the plea of imperative necessity."[15] The post-war inflations have been in no way different except that the Keynesian philosophy has been available to clothe them with respectability. And this philosophy was announced in "white papers" and other official documents during Keynes' lifetime, with direct quotations from his writings and in his own terminology. He lived long enough to have been able to inaugurate the plowing under of what he had sown. He failed to do so and the modern Western world has reaped the harvest.

It looks as though Timlin is trying, with consummate tact, to lead the Keynesians back to orthodoxy. But she will never do that by suggesting that *The General Theory* was orthodox. It can be done only by showing, as she has in fact shown, that Keynes was causing confusion both in thought and action, through diverting attention from co-ordination through price adjustment.

In the middle 'forties, the Keynesians felt superior and triumphant. During the 'fifties they were mostly losing their confidence. Their loss of confidence was manifest, I suggest, in Hicks' attempt (in 1957) to meet Patinkin's criticisms, and especially in the former's assertion that a "properly equipped 'classic' . . . " would agree with Keynes. Hicks' hypothetical "classic" would argue, we are told, that an "increase in saving would *directly* reduce the rate of interest, so that employment would increase in the investment-goods trades as it diminished in the consumption-goods trades; but he could (or should) go on to admit that the increase in saving would carry with it a diminution in the velocity of circulation (some of the savings would be hoarded), so that, with an inelastic monetary system, and the fixed money wages that are being assumed, there would still be a net decline in employment."[16]

Well, if Keynes had said anything like this, there would have been little controversy. The answer to him would have been simply that the proposition was stated in an unnecessarily clumsy way. Using the terminology which I have here introduced, the reply would have been:

"What you are saying is that an increase in saving preference will, *ceteris paribus,* reduce the natural level of interest. On the (absurd) assumption that monetary policy is inflexible (so that the market rate of interest does not fall in harmony) there will be a deflationary reaction. Similarly, if we make the further (doubtfully justifiable) assumption that an increase in saving preference implies (for some *other* reason) an increase in demand for the services of money, monetary policy being assumed to be inflexible, there will be a further reason for deflation. If therefore deflation is not a deliberate objective (to correct a previous inflation, so as to keep faith with those who had trusted convertibility obligations) it must be regarded as a purposeless deflation due to a defect in monetary organization.* And if at the same time the trade unions are allowed to reduce the flow of wages by refusing to permit the product of labor to be priced so as to permit the sale of the full valuable output, serious sociological consequences will follow; and this will be attributable, not so much to the failure to adjust to changes in consumption-saving preference, but to a wholly unintended monetary situation."

The only reason why this sort of rejoinder was not made to Keynes in 1936 was that he did *not* say what Hicks now claims that he *should* have said.

5.—There are plenty of signs that Keynes occasionally felt misgivings. Already, in the last chapter of *The General Theory*, he was paying tributes to the working of a competitive society, and indirectly praising institutions which were completely incompatible with the remedies implied by his analysis. And during the war years, we can discern his reaction against his own teaching. It may well be that, had he lived, he would have become the leading anti-Keynesian. In his *How to Pay for the War*, he appeared to be concerned with the dangers of inflation. But I do not think that, when he wrote that contribution, he was already beginning to see the disastrous consequences which could flow from his own teachings. Had he merely argued that the aim should have been to prevent the necessity of a rationing system which would place an undue strain on administration, or had he urged the necessity of preventing the prices of consumers' goods from rising to an extent which would have caused a demand for increased money income, his argument would have been perfectly *understandable*. But his case had not been thought through. It remained woolly. He *may* have been recognizing at last that the speed of inflation must never be allowed to be so rapid that the people are led to expect it and fully to allow for it in concluding current contracts. He *may* also have felt that, if an inflation is allowed to progress too rapidly, the people are likely to demand its cessation. Then suddenly, shortly before his death, he showed much more definite signs of being in retreat. There

---

*Several non-Keynesians would have regarded with sympathy such a criticism applied to the Federal Reserve System in the early 'thirties.

is a story that, in a conversation with a number of economists towards the end of the war, he showed impatience with what was being said and told one of his best known supporters not to be silly. But reliable evidence of his wavering is to be found in his last *Economic Journal* article, which appeared just before he died.[17] The word "wavering" is not unjust. How else can we regard his assertion that "the classical teaching embodied some permanent truths of great significance," and his reference to "deep undercurrents at work, natural forces, one can call them, or even the invisible hand, which are operating towards equilibrium"?[18] How else can we treat his contrast of "much modernist stuff turned sour and silly" and "the wholesome long-run doctrine"?[19] He used the term, "classical medicine" four times in this article. Yet he had been the one who had prescribed champagne for the patient and popularized this pleasant remedy when the castor oil of "classical medicine" had been called for.

But in that article he was hinting at the truth, not proclaiming it. J. H. Williams told us that "Keynes changed his mind, and almost the last time I saw him was complaining that the easy money policy had been greatly overdone and interest rates were too low both in England and here;*[20] and we know that he expected the great post-war problem to be inflation rather than unemployment.

Had Keynes lived, he *might* have led the retreat from his own doctrines.

It is sometimes claimed that even if Keynes' main theories must now be admitted to be fallacious, his contribution at least introduced new and useful tools like liquidity preference, the propensity to consume, the marginal efficiency of capital, etc. But these are all ancient *concepts.*† Only the names and uses to which they have been put are new. Fellner thinks that "fundamental-theoretical Keynesianism" and "stagnationist Keynesianism . . . . might not survive, or at least not in much strength," but that "cyclical Keynesianism" will continue to be influential doctrine in the predictable future.[21] But if my argument in chapter XV is accepted, it is precisely in attempts to understand the nature of cyclical fluctuations that Keynesian teaching and concepts are most seriously defective.

6.—There are some signs, then, that Keynesianism is now being refined back to pure orthodoxy by the "Keynesians of the Right." Indeed, they seem tacitly to have abandoned the notion of unemployment equilibrium, which was the crucial originality of the "new economics" and the "Keynesian revolution". Modigliani, Timlin, Mc.C. Wright and Patinkin have, I think, led the reaction.

---

*Hayek has told me that he had a similar experience.

†The most original and useful concept which Keynes introduced, in my opinion, was the notion of user cost. But his discussion of it constitutes one of the most confusing parts of *The General Theory*. It *could* have been used to mean that part of depreciation which is due solely to the use of assets and not the passage of time.

So far has the retreat gone that Dillard (who has been the most consistently uncritical disciple of Keynes) could remark (in 1956), quite without justification, that "one should bear in mind that Keynes was careful not to say that classical economics is wrong."[22] But *the Keynesian fallacies remain deeply rooted, and the lag is likely to be long before they are eradicated. In spite of the retreat, there have so far been practically no changes in the textbooks or in undergraduate teaching. Students of this generation are still, on the whole, being trained in defective methods. A minority of them manage ultimately to think their way through. The majority are unable to. The confused thinking on which Keynes' case was framed remains the conventional foundation of the modern teaching of economics.* It is too early to expect that progress in economics will resume perceptibly from its pre-Keynesian achievements, i.e., from the stage to which Wicksell, Cannan and Mises had led it in the field of money.

7.—The academic retreat from Keynesianism has been accompanied, of recent years, by a retreat in policy. The connection between academic thought and political action is difficult to discern with any certainty. Statesmen and laymen generally who had supported the policy at one time through an "instinctive" or "common sense" feeling about the appropriateness of the remedies implied, have been shaken by the actual course of events. It is no longer doubted that, in the long run, repressed inflation breaks down. Expenditure intended to maintain investment and hence employment, in a regime in which prices are no longer powerfully influenced by market forces, is recognized as being incompatible with the hoped for stability of prices. Moreover, it has become obvious that Keynesianism, especially when it is combined with the policy of the welfare State, is destructive of labor incentives to productivity; and other disastrous sociological results of the Keynesian experiment are being perceived. In some parts of the world at any rate the lay public are resisting, particularly the middle classes. Thus, Bowen and Meier deplore the fact that despite all the persuasion of economists and the experience of recent decades, the public and their representatives in the United States cling to belief in the soundness of budget balancing and in the evil of debt. The arguments "that 'we owe it to ourselves' or 'that for every liability there is a corresponding asset' have," they regret, "fallen on sceptical and unwilling ears." Such resistance, they continue, "places grave obstacles in the way of compensatory fiscal policies such as deficit spending."*[23] It will, I think, be fortunate for the United States that the

---

*It *is* true of all borrowing that society owes the debts to itself, and that for every liability there is a corresponding asset—the debt. But this does not imply, as they appear to infer, that the multiplication of liabilities and debt through credit expansion must not be checked if inflation is to be avoided!

instincts or common sense of the public on the issue, happen to have
been shrewdly or intuitively intelligent.

Recently—the most disturbing experience of all—*anticipated inflation*
has been creating insoluble problems. This phenomenon has arisen, as
I have explained, through the reluctance of governments to move rapidly
towards complete totalitarianism. The fact that some parts of the economy have been left free for rational entrepreneurial action by the
people has been weakening the political motive for recourse to cheap
money; for it has robbed inflation of its crude co-ordinative power; and
when this happens the absurdity of the whole business begins to become
obvious to a widening circle. Per Jacobsson of the I.M.F. expressed the
opinion a few years ago that "world forces" seem to be bringing world
inflation to an end. The world forces are simply *anticipation.**

Through the lessons of sour reality, then, we have seen the gradual
spread of doubts about the soundness of Keynesian doctrines: we have
seen the intelligentsia beginning to wonder whether, after all, the price
mechanism did not do things better in the days when it was permitted
at least some freedom. But although doubts springing from all these
issues have modified public discussion and although there has been some
effect upon influential opinion, it is still not certain how far *governments* have learned the lesson from bitter experience. Of recent years it
has often occurred to me that the politicians *have* seen the light but too
late—too late because it now appears to them impossible to turn back.
They would like to return to the security of sound finance, but they are
now afraid of taking the unpopular steps needed to maintain or enhance
the flow of wages and income. Those of their official advisors who have
authority to speak publicly are increasingly hinting at, or exposing with
tactful frankness, the folly of creeping inflation. But they seem not to
do so in language sufficiently unequivocal to make the avoidance of anti-
flationary action difficult.

Thus, although the clarity of the message contained in the First Report
of the Cohen Council (the British Council on *Prices, Productivity and
Incomes*) is clouded by its being expressed in the fashionable Keynesian
language, the gist of that message is wholly anti-Keynesian, and contains
advice which is as old-fashioned as the maxim: "Exhortations to business
men to reduce prices, if indulged in, should, we think, be coupled with
exhortations to work-people and other consumers to increase savings."[24]
And the Radcliffe Committee (although their Report is couched—even
more misleadingly—in the equivocal terms of Keynesian dialectics) are
forced to confess that the consistency of the objectives of full employ-

---

*But the problems created thereby are now leading to the complaint of a world
shortage of liquidity, and ultimate recourse to a wholly purposeless inflation cannot be
ruled out.

ment, the avoidance of inflation and the maintenance of stable exchange rates is "no longer regarded as self-evident;"[25] and that for many years the gilt-edged market has been realizing that inflation has been "gradually eroding all fixed money values." The authorities have believed, they say, that the "chronically weak market" has been "resistant to substantial sales not merely at current prices but at any prices."[26] Anticipated inflation is forcing them reluctantly to a vague recognition of orthodox teaching. The recourse to a 7 per cent. Bank Rate in 1957 may have marked the turning point.

But although resort to short-term borrowing (Treasury Bills and the like) has been postponing the day of reckoning, and whilst a further bout of inflation will greatly aggravate the Treasury's quandary, the British government have certainly not yet abandoned the view that the maintenance of full employment and the avoidance of depression is a matter of monetary policy. Occasional references to the desirability of "reasonable stability" in the value of the pound (with a studious unwillingness to define "reasonable") are by no means convincing evidences of the growth of genuine governmental enlightment.

In the United States the position is not greatly dissimilar. But A. F. Burns suggested a few years ago that the Keynesian belief that orthodox credit methods can "check a boom with dangerous ease" but "do little to speed recovery once a depression developed," had been abandoned officially in the United States; for he referred to this belief as having actuated "earlier policy."[27] What is more, he stated that "the heavy emphasis that the government has recently placed on a restrictive credit policy has served to bring us back to the best thought that ruled on the subject during the 1920's."[28] How far the Kennedy régime have re-embraced "earlier policy" is not clear (in early 1962).

A formidable barrier to the return to sound policy (not only in Britain and the United States but in all other countries) remains, I believe, in the general failure to perceive that the flow of wages and income can be maintained or increased through downward wage-rate and price adjustment. What governments, or those who influence electorates, have not learned is that competitive cost and price reductions cause the release of idle or wastefully used resources for forms of production (and hence of income) which have been starved of resources.

It has, I hold, been tragic for the world that Keynes' ideas should have had so large an influence in the 'twenties and 'thirties; for not only did the political attractiveness of his sort of convictions contribute first to unparalleled depression and then to an era of debilitating inflation but even worse, it discouraged thought about fundamental reform. Yet perhaps, in deploring Keynes' influence in economics, one should really be deploring the degeneration of politics. For his teachings gave apparent respectability to policies which earlier generations would have regarded as reprehensible.

It can well be argued, against the stand which I am taking, that in the circumstances which have existed, uniformity among economists could have had no influence. Mere academic teachings would have remained inert unless they were based on hidden assumptions of a politically acceptable kind. Nothing, apart from inflation, could have prevented the trade unions and price rings of Western Europe and the United States from repressing the flow of wages and income, creating unemployment and precipitating the dilemma of depression or inflation. But those who believe this ought always to express their views in these unequivocal terms. Had Keynes himself so expressed his case, his influence on the world would undoubtedly have been much less. But it might not have been inconsiderable and it would have been exerted in exactly the opposite direction.

If perseverance with Keynesianism has, indeed, been due to a failure to understand and not to lack of courage, my contribution may have some influence. As I see things, the apparent revolution wrought by Keynes after 1936 is being reversed by a counterrevolution, largely waged unwittingly by higher critics who tried very hard to be faithful. Whether some permanent indirect benefit to economic science will eventually have made up for the destruction and intellectual disorder which the revolution has left in its train, is a question which the future historian of ideas will have to answer.

8.—APPENDIX

*The Retreat as Recorded in D.McC.Wright's, "The Keynesian System."**

Although McCord Wright has been largely responsible for forcing the Keynesian retreat, his exposition in *The Keynesian System* takes the form, superficially viewed, of a defence of Keynes against his extreme followers and some of his critics.

Discussing *The General Theory*, he tells us that "the continual switching of assumptions, which goes on through the book, forms a continual trap for the *careless or biased* reader."[29] (My italics). But has it not been equally a continual trap for the most careful and detached reader? Is it bias or carelessness to proceed in the belief that an assumption which is stated on one page must hold on the next page unless it has been explicitly changed? Wright refers to the "caricature of Keynes which is generally preached by his more dogmatic disciples and attacked by his

---

*This important contribution was published whilst the present book was in the hands of the printers.

enemies;"*[30] and he seems to rebuke Keynes' most enthusiastic followers for misunderstanding their master. Yet Keynes lived long enough to renounce the earlier "dogmatic" interpretations, and he did not do so in published writings. Naturally the critics—like policy-makers—accepted as the new gospel the uncontradicted interpretations of the "dogmatic disciples"; for the latter had, at any rate, translated the untidy jumble of theorems which makes up *The General Theory* into a more or less intelligible system. Had the sceptics (Keynes' "enemies") any alternative to attacking the *Keynesianism* which had evolved?

In my judgment (as I explained in Chapters I and II), *the enormous appeal of Keynes' thesis originated precisely in doctrines which were rendered plausible through the obscuring of unrealistic assumptions,* the tacit changing of which Wright has tracked down (obviously with the patience of years of sympathetic re-reading). In particular, *the unemployment equilibrium thesis—which he admits must be abandoned—was the main source of the political attractiveness of Keynes' contribution.* If Keynes had presented *The General Theory,* as Wright implies that he did, "not as a 'new economics' but as a convenient new method of analysis, and a shift in policy *emphasis,*"†[31] he would not have weakened the authority of orthodox economists at the very epoch when reliance upon their authority could have saved the western world from disastrous blunders.

Yet Wright is really now attempting to restore respect for teachings which Keynes effectively ridiculed. He tries to do this by rationalising *The General Theory,* i.e., by showing what Keynes *ought to have meant.* His rationalisation is supported by those few odd passages (most of which I have quoted also) which puzzled and exasperated the persevering and careful reader because of their *unresolved inconsistency* with the main body of the argument.‡ He uses these passages as a justification for a construction which he calls Keynes' "model of a dynamic world."[33] The truth is rather, as I have claimed (p. 23), that *The General Theory* models are "almost wholly static and blatantly mechanical. Only occasionally do dynamic insights and realistic assumptions seem to intrude, and then nebulously and inconsistently."

I fear also that Wright tends to accept at their face value Keynes' reck-

---

*It would have helped if Wright had mentioned a few *undogmatic* disciples, i.e., Keynesians who interpret Keynes more or less as he does. I do not know of any other Keynesian who has done so *in writing.* But Lerner (whose 1938 and 1939 articles in the *Q.J.E.* would undoubtedly have to be classed as "dogmatic" interpretations) now seems to stand fairly close to Wright. (Address at the University of Chicago, May 14, 1962).

†Wright's italics.

‡Wright talks of "the two Keyneses."[32] If there *were* two, it was the one whom Wright refutes so relentlessly who achieved fame, title and unparalleled academic influence.

lessly unjustified assertions about the teachings of the pre-Keynesians. For instance, which economists believed, as he suggests they did, that "the rate of interest would *always,* or necessarily move with profit expectations, and . . . . that the desire to save would *always* and necessarily move with changes in the rate of interest"?[34] I cannot recall any example. And far from disturbing any "pleasant illusions" of orthodox economists on the subject, which Wright believes was Keynes' accomplishment,[35] the true influence of *The General Theory* was (as I have shown) the initiation of a tradition which obstructed the refinement of a perfectly valid general insight into the nature and causes of interest. Nor can I accept the suggestion[36] that pre-Keynesian economists were unaware of that element in the demand for money (a determinant—unless offset—of the relation of *market* interest to the *natural* level) which is due to fear of capital loss from a subsequent rise in interest. I have suggested that it was Keynes' treatment of this possibility which was fallacious.* Again, as far as my reading goes, neither pre-Keynesian nor subsequent non-Keynesian economists have attempted to deny that "savings plans and investment decisions are very different things", as Wright suggests they have done;[37] and it is not a "logical quibble" when economists like myself insist, for reasons quite different from those advanced by Keynes, that *the magnitudes* realized "savings" and realized "investment" are identical notions. (See Chapters X and XI).

The pro-Keynes slant of Wright's essay may well secure for his contribution a more tolerant or sympathetic hearing than my own book is likely to receive. But a large part of the argument which I have submitted amounts to *a plea for the rejection of much of the rationalized version of Keynesianism which Wright now offers.* For instance, whereas he tries to persevere with the Keynesian tools, I have urged that the whole of that apparatus should be abandoned; and whereas he claims that Keynes' models "were merely convenient headings under which to group the important forces shaping the economy,"[38] I have maintained throughout that they are *models which tacitly assume away the important forces shaping the economy.* Curiously enough, Wright himself presents ample evidence to justify this view. The Keynesian tools remain crude, clumsy and inappropriate. Indeed, the clarity of Wright's own exposition is vitiated whenever he attempts to persevere with Keynesian concepts.† But his penetrating contribution will, nevertheless, have assisted

---

*See pp. 106, 241, 373.

†Thus, his phrase (intended to summarize pre-Keynesian theory), "people will stop saving *and start spending*"[39] (Wright's italics), instead of "start consuming" or "start dishoarding and consuming", leaves the very impression which he is trying to dispel. As I have shown, the convention of considering "saving" and "spending" as alternatives has had seriously adverse consequences upon the thinking both of economists and policy-makers.

my own aim—that of breaking through a formidable barrier to fruitful thought and action.

REFERENCES

(1) BRONFENBRENNER, *Some Neglected Implications of Secular Inflation*, in Kurihara, *Post-Keynesian Economics*, p.34n. (2) *Ibid.*, p.34n. (3) TIMLIN, *Monetary Stabilization Policies and Keynesian Theories*, in Kurihara, *op. cit.*, p.59. (4) *Ibid.*, pp.59-60. (5) *Ibid.*, p.80. (6) *Ibid.*, p.60. (7) *Ibid.*, p.62. (8) *Ibid.*, p.64. (9) *Ibid.*, p.86. (10) *Ibid.*, p.65. (11) *Ibid.*, p.60. (12) *Ibid.*, p.62. (13) PATINKIN, *Money, Interest and Prices*, p.3. (14) KEYNES, *The General Theory*, p.378, quo. Timlin, *op. cit.*, p.87. (15) TIMLIN, *op. cit.*, p.87. (16) HICKS, *A Rehabilitation of "Classical" Economics*, E.J., 1957, p.279. (17) KEYNES, *The Balance of Payments of the United States*, E.J., June, 1946, p.172. (18) *Ibid.*, p.185. (19) *Ibid.*, p.186. (20) WILLIAMS, *An Economist's Confessions*, A.E.R., March 1952, p.14. (21) FELLNER, *What is Surviving?* A.E.R., P. & P., 1957, p.67. (22) DILLARD, *The Influence of Keynesian Economics on Contemporary Thought*, A.E.R., P. and P., 1957, p.77. (23) BOWEN and MEIER, *Institutional Aspects of Economic Fluctuations*, in Kurihara, *op. cit.*, p.164. (24) First Report of Cohen Council *(Council on Prices, Productivity and Incomes)*, par. 158. (25) Radcliffe Report *(Committee on the Working of the Monetary System)*, par. 55. (26) *Ibid.*, par. 68. (27) BURNS, *Prosperity Without Inflation*, pp.55-6. (28) *Ibid.*, pp.43-4. (29) McC.Wright, *The Keynesian System*, p.47. (30) *Ibid.*, p.71. (31) *Ibid.*, p.67. (32) *Ibid.*, p.75. (33) *Ibid.*, pp.66-7. (34) *Ibid.*, p.9. (35) *Ibid.*, p.10. (36) *Ibid.*, p.34. (37) *Ibid.*, p.42. (38) *Ibid.*, p.66. (39) *Ibid.*, p.8.

INDEX

Note. *Subsidiary topics are indexed under appropriate main headings. For example, "Latent inflation" is to be found under "Inflation" and "Hybrid money" under "Money." The initials of well-known economists and others are omitted except where this might cause confusion.*

Abstract theory: *see* Mathematical exposition

Academic appeal: of Keynesian doctrine, viii, I, *passim,* 49, 435

Acceleration principle: 6, 13, 233-5, 240, 276, 280, 282, XIV *passim,* 343, 350

Acquisitiveness: unrelated to profit, 57

"Administered prices": 59n

"Aggregate demand" (demands): 22, 25-30, 195, 205-6, 221, 249-50, 254-60, 266, 273, 277-9, 392-4. *See also* Effective demand.

Aggregate real value of money: *See* Money, real value of

Anderson, B. M.: X, 54, 126n, 159, 361, 390-1, 397, 404, 412-3

Angell: 87

Attwood: 60n, 399n

Austrian economics, economists: 64, 372

Authority of economists: xi, 4-5

"Automatic" adjustments — "stabilizers": concept of, 53, 57, 63, 65, 95, 101, 175-6

Autonomous growth: 20-1, 183, 236-40, 294, 327, 336, 346, 377-8, 383-4

Bailey, M. J.: 409

Ballvé: 12

Bank-rate action: alleged ineffectiveness of, 100

Banks: do not "manufacture" money, 94. *See also* Credit

Barter: 137, 138n

Baumol: 297n, 299, 319n, 390n, 398

Becker and Baumol: 319n, 390n, 398

Beckhart: 42

Benoit-Smullyan: 299, 317

Beveridge: 129, 403

Bickerdike: 300n, 303

Bohm-Bawerk: 401

"Boondoggling": 217, 267, 383n

Boulding: viii, 4-5, 10, 167n

Bowen and Meier: 344, 431

Bray: 403

Bretherton, Burchardt, and Rutherford: 305, 325n, 328n

Bronfenbrenner: 48-9, 64, 414, 423

Burns, A. F.: 415-8, 433

Cannan: x, 87, 119n, 178n, 354, 431

Capital: appreciation, is income when interest is constant, 190, 202n, 215n; depreciation, is consumption when interest is constant: 190; consumption, *See* Decumulation; formation, *see* Net accumulation; saturation, redundancy, stagnation, 238-9, XVI, *passim;* shortage, 217; import and export of, 242; issues, restriction of, 96, 100

Carver: 300n

Casuistry in Keynesian Doctrine: 5, 65, 119-20, 338n.

"Ceiling" to boom: notion of, 351

Chain reactions: *See* Dynamic factors

Champernowne: 12, 14n

Changing and changed number of money units (changing and changed value of the money unit): importance of distinction, 22, 29, 103-4, 106n, 226n

Chicago school: 90

Claims: as assets, 197, 215

Clark, J. M.: 300-2, 306, 317-8, 319n

Cohen Council: 81-3, 152-4, 417, 432-3

Collective bargaining: *See* Trade-unions.

Collusion in fixing output or prices: IV *passim*, 128

Competition: nature of, 20, 22, 28, 56-8

Complementarity of resources in general: 65-70, 75-7, 237-8. *See also* Say Law

Composition of income, of replacement, and of net accumulation: *See* Income, importance of form

Concentration of capital goods production over time: 301-2, 306, 311-4, 318-24, 329

Conceptual defects of Keynesianism: xi, I *passim*, 23, 34, 59, 70-1, 89-90, 129, 183-5, 252, 351-2, 376-8, 396-7, 425, 434

Consumer, concept of: 186-7, 194, 196, 233-5

Consumer-saver, concept of: 187, 196, 228. See also (i) Saver, (ii) Pure saver

Consumers' sovereignty: 31, 57, 192, 235

Consumers' surplus: 57n, 203

Consumption: in the "broad sense," 192; in the "restricted sense," (i) the process, 192-5, 236-7, 278-9, 283-4 (*see also* Decumulation); neither demand nor the source of demand, 195, 233-40, 250-1, 256-9, 272, 295-6, 361; demand, 195, 232-4, 237-9, 293-6; uses, 229, 232, 255-7, 294, 299-300; preference, 194-5; fallacy, X-XII *passim;* (ii) the magnitude: 183-4, 188, 192-4, 249-50, 267-8, 273-4, 294-7, 299-300

Consumption-saving preference: *See* Saving preference

Contractual prices: distinguished from rigidities, 60-1, 175n

Contrived scarcities: *See* Withheld capacity

"Controls": a necessary adjunct of technique of inflation, 10, 48-9, 120, 128-9, 413, 423, 426

Co-ordination: of economic system, (i) the process: *See* Price-adjustment process; (ii) the motives: *See* Loss-avoidance, profit-seeking incentives; (iii) the definition: 54

Corporation: possesses delegated entrepreneurial and saving powers, 204, 207

Costs and pains of noninflationary co-ordination: 62 *et seq.*

Cost reduction: as expansive innovation, 66-7

Cost of Living Index: defects as measure of real value, 111-2

Council of Economic Advisers (President's, U.S.A.): 82-3

Council on Prices, Productivity, and Incomes: *See* Cohen Council

"Cranks": monetary, 128-30

Credit: expansion and contraction, 93 *et seq.*, 249-50, 255, 284-5, 398, 431; rationing, 96

Cripps, Sir Stafford: 412

Croce: 12n

Crusoe economy: 213-4, 379

Cumulative withholding or release of capacity: *See* Dynamic factors; Complementarity; Say Law

Cushioning effects of working at high maintenance costs: 313, 335-6, 367n

Deception: needed for sucessful inflation. *See* Inflation, technique of

Decumulation: X-XI *passim*, 254. *See also* Consumption, in "restricted sense"

Deflation: concept of, 111; alternative to devaluation, 98; "burden" of, 63 *et seq.*, 419; possibility of monetary standard implying, 255; purposeless, 54n, 104, 125-6, 151, 271, 345, 429; "rectifying", 44, 63, 101, 122, 150-1, 171, 242, 271, 345-50; as cause of unemployment, 125-6, 257, 260, 350

Demand (demands, aggregate, "in general"): (i) the source of, VIII *passim*, 205-6; (ii) the concept of, *see* Aggregate demand; Effective demand; confused with inflation, 81-2; "deficient," *see* Gap; "excessive," *see* Inflation

Depreciation: business, 253-5

Development tempo: *See* Net accumulation

Dillard: 30n, 31-2, 70, 359, 360n, 372-3, 394, 403, 431

Directors: *See* Manager

Disinvestment: 196, 204, 254

Dis-saving: 196

Diverted capacity: *See* Withheld capacity

"Dogmatic" Keynesians: 434-5

Domar: 281

Douglas, C. H.: 129

Douglas, Paul: 165n

Durability of assets: relevance to acceleration principle, 77, 299, 304 *et seq.*

Dynamic factors: inactivity and growth, 23, 66-70, 75-7, 115, 154, 350-1, 435. *See also* Say Law

Economic Consequences of the Peace, Keynes': 119

Economic theory; nature of, I *passim*, 34

"Economically durable or perishable" goods: notion of, 223-4, 227, 229, 232n

"Effective demand": 4, 22, 25-30, 42-3, 46, 72, 89, 102, 105, 184, 249-50, 270, 391-2, 426. *See also* Aggregate demand

Effective price flexibility: 63-5

Elasticity of release of capacity: 54n, 123-6, 149-51, 270-1, 285-6, 319, 393-4

Employment: concept of magnitude of, 25

Employment Act (U.S.A.): 417

Entrepreneur: his function, 26-7, 68, 186-7, 190, 201-6, 211-2, 215-22, 226-38, 240n, 241-2, 254n, 315-6, 383; his errors of interpretation (optimism, pessimism, etc.), 60-1, 67-8, 220-1, 241-2, 333-4, 337, 344, 350, 371-2, 383; his offer of interest, *see* Prospective yields; his remuneration, *see* Profit; not a contriver of scarcity, 206-7, 365-6

Escalator clauses: 410, 415, 417

"Excessive demand": *See* Inflation

Expectations: as assisting the aims of monetary policy, *see* Monetary policy; and values, 44, 54-6, 69, 100, 106, 138, 354

Expenditure: confused with demand, 30, 102, VIII *passim*, 252, 256; confused with consumption, 252, 436n; always out of capital, not income, 143-4, 279; in relation to the money valuation of income, ix, 22, 134 *et seq.*

Fashion of Keynesianism: 10

Federal Reserve System: 120, 417, 429n, 432

Fellner: 74, 324-5, 430

"Fight against inflation": *See* Inflation, technique of

Fiscal policies: compensatory, *see* Money units, determinants of number of

Fisher, Irving: 87, 88n, 186

Fixed costs: *See* Overhead costs, Contractual prices

"Floor" to depression: notion of, 351

Fluctuations: in "activity", 20-4, 36, 39, 42, 44-5, 53, 62, XII, XIII, XIV, XV *passim*, 433; in the scale of prices, 35-6, 39-40, XII, XIII, XV *passim*; valid theory of its necessarily universal, 343-5

Fordney-McCumber tariff: 76

Form of income, of replacement, and of net accumulation: *See* Income, importance of form

Foster and Catchings: 129

Foundation for Economic Education: ix-x

Fraser, Lindley: 185n

Friedman: 90n, 126n, 171

Frisch: 13, 317-9

Gap in aggregate demand: alleged to be caused by saving, 249, 252-6, 277-9

General Theory: Keynes', *passim*

Gesell: 128, 366n, 403

Gilbert, M.: 71n

Glut: notion of, 359, 399

Gold Standard: 10, 111, 249, 355

Goodwin, R. M.: 253, 268n, 277-9, 333, 368

Gordon, R. A.: 166n

Graham, F. D.: 49, 104

Gray, John: 403

Gregory: 87

Greidanus: 106

Gross accumulation: 189-92, 197-200, 212, 215, 222, 226-33

Gross decumulation: 192

Gross investment: 200

Growth: economic, *see* Net accumulation

Gurzynski: x

Haberler: 134n, 168, 171-3, 186, 267-8, 272-3, 275, 294n, 304-6, 309, 311, 315, 329n, 389, 397

Hague and Stonier: 266, 268n, 271n

Halm: 272, 276, 317, 329

Hampton, J. D.: x

Hansen, A.: 275, 327, 359

Harris, S.: 10n, 104

Harrod: 12, 33, 88, 119n, 121, 123-4, 162, 316n, 381, 401-3

Harwood: 13

Hawley-Smoot Tariff: 76, 404

Hawtrey: 154-6, 265n, 368n

Hayek: ixn, 331, 430n

Hazlitt: x, 11n, 121n, 157n, 185, 270n, 359n

Heilbroner: 145-6, 393

Heilperin: 189

Hicks: 12, 172, 175, 293n, 318-23, 351-2, 367-8, 412, 428

Higgins, B.: 274

Hobson, J. A.: 128

Hume: 39, 87, 106, 149

Ichimura: 9, 368n

Income: concept of, 25, 134-44, 187-92, 269; "uninflated," use of concept of, 35, 59, 71, 82, 128, VIII *passim*, 165-6, 169-70, 243, 271, 296, 349, 404, 419; importance of form of, 183, 201-4, 220-3, 232, 353n, 361, 368, 378, 402-3; confusion between determinants of magnitude and form of, 27, 220-1, 360-1; generation of, 5, 22, 31, VIII *passim*, 200, 268-9, 271 *et seq.*; money valuation of, VIII *passim*, 249-50 (*see also* Credit, Money unit, and Money Units); "analysis," defects in approach to, 134 *et seq.*; effect, 169; velocity, *see* Velocity

Inflation: concept of, VI *passim*; anticipated, 40-1, 44, 47n, 73, 122, 127-30, XVIII *passim*, 429, 432; "true," Keynes' notion of, 105, VII *passim*, 270; "Cost-induced," "wage-induced," "price-in-duced," "cost-push," "demand-pull," "im-ported"-fallacy in notions of, 114-5; creeping, 9, 39, 65, 74, 98-100, 105, 112, 123, 127n, 128, 355, 360, 414-6; "moder-ate," 43, 74, 126-7; hyper (runaway), 112, 114, 243-4; latent (including repressed), 39, 45, 66, 80n, 97, 100, 106, 112-3, 119n, 123n, 140, 356, 375; described as "exces-sive demand," 81-2, 218, 426; causes in-justice, 43, 46-8, 54, 120; causes insecurity, 44-5; self-perpetuating nature of, 41; destroys efficiency incentives, 46; discour-ages basic reform, 41-2, 70, 81-2, 433; en-courages disco-ordinative pressures, 45-6, 73; causes distortion of capital structure, marketing structure and resource alloca-tion, 42; crudeness of its co-ordinative effects, 9-10, 39, 42-7, 54, 73, 81, 101, 105, 150-1, 257-8, 270-1, 351-2; "achievements" or "successes" of, 9-10, 72-4; nature of its "stimulus," 9-10, 73, 105, 257-8, 270-1; alternative to unemployment as expres-sion of a disco-ordinated system, 3, 43, 61, 100, 179, 390; fallacy that it can finance "investment" without the occurrence of savings, 216-7; notion that it is always deliberate policy, 43-5, 96-100, 114-5, 122, 127-8, XVIII *passim;* right to cause con-ferred on elected governments although removed from princes, 418, 428; tech-nique of, 40-1, 44, 75, 99, XVIII *passim;* as a "built-in institution," 418; as taxa-tion, 46

"Injection": expenditure otherwise than out of income, 277-9

Input-output analysis: 189-90

Insatiability of human wants: 240, 259, 360-3, 377. *See also* Says Law

Interest: nature of, 211 *et seq.;* determi-nants of, 29-30, 102-4, 155, 195n, 197, 205-6, 211-3, 221-32, 238-9, 257, 295, 354; Keynes' theory of, 29-30, 102-6, 243, 256-7; legitimacy of, as a share in income, 46, 48, 364-6; expectations of changes in, 99, 106, 241, 373, 436; relation of planned output magnitudes to, 57, 77-8, 203, 212-3, 365-6; as a form of rent, 364-5; as an inducement to saving (the entrepreneur's demand for savings), 211-2, 221-32, 240-1, 257, 294-5, 337n, 364, 436; zero or nega-tive, 171-3, 213n, 224-6, 238-9, 365-6; in relation to "cost of investment," 171-3; absolute level does not influence demand for money, 106; "burden" of, as cause of

"stagnation," 363-4; noninflationary level of, 103-4; natural level, its relation to market level, 29-38, 89-90, 96, 102-6, 212, 226, 257, 364, 436; receiver of (rentier), as "pure saver," 214n

International Monetary Fund: 45n, 47, 412

Investment: in sense of choice of form of replacement and net accumulation, 185, 201-5, 235, 240; "nonessential," 426-7; Keynes' concept of, 122, 183, 185, 200, 203, 249, 255, 260, XIII *passim*, 425-6; outlets or opportunities, *see* Outlets for investment; demand, *see* Prospective yields

Jacobsson, Per: 432
Jevons: 401
Johnson, H. G.: 128n, 414
Johnson, Dr. Samuel: 29

Kaldor: 333, 351, 366
Kalecki: 333, 366, 381
Kamitz, R.: 338
Kennedy, John F.: 419, 433
Keynes: *passim*
Keyserling, Leon: 162n
Kirzner: 12n
Klein, L. R.: 13
Knight: 165n, 171n
Knox, A. D.: x, 289
Korner, Emil: 390
Kurihara: 363-5
Kuznets: 135n, 302, 304n, 316n, 329-31

Labor shortage: as supposed cause of "capi-tal saturation," 373-81
Labor unions: *See* Trade-unions
Lachmann: x, 316n, 362
Lange: 159, 171, 395, 398n
Lavington: 66, 350n
"Leftist" (and "Rightist") Keynesians: 323, 434-5
Leisure preference: 59, 177, 192, 360n, 375, 375n
Lenin: 119n
Lerner: 121n, 139n, 159, 160n, 435n
Lindahl: 189
Lintner: 279
Liquidity preference: *See* Money, demand for
Locke: 87
London School of Economics: ix-x
Loss-avoidance, profit-seeking incentives: 32, 55-9, 63
Loveday: 71
Lutz, F. A.: 171n
Lutz, Vera: 274n

Machlup: 123n, 171n, 257n, 274, 277

Macmillan Committee and Report: 80, 162

Macro-economic concepts and methods: 6-7, 25-9, 89, 165-7, 183, 390-3

"Manager": possesses delegated entrepreneurial and saving powers, 203, 207n

Manchester Guardian: 412

Mantoux: 402

Marget: x, 88n, 89, 171n, 393n

Marginal efficiency of capital: *See* Prospective yield

Marginal utility of capital: 370

Marshall, Marshallian economics: 26n, 87-9, 189

Marx, Marxism: 48, 414

Mathematical exposition: pitfalls in, 6-14, 301, 318, 351-2

Matthews, R.C.O.: 331-3, 362, 370, 382-3

"Mature economy": *See* Capital saturation

Maximum price fixation: as means of co-ordination, 62

Meade: 121n, 129

Mill, James: 87, 88n, 359, 391, 398-9

Mill, J. S.: 19n, 87, 234n, 359, 389n, 390, 397, 404-5

Mints: 87

Mises: x, 48, 87, 88n, 136, 186, 409, 411, 414, 418, 431

Misrepresentations of classical teachings: xi, 19, 36, 344n

Mitchell: 300-1

Modigliani: 179n, 171-2, 430

Monetary authority: concept of, 96-7, 100; services, *see* Money, productiveness of; standard, *see* Money units, importance of defined value; theory, as an integral part of economic theory, 34, 87 *et seq.*

Monetary policy: definition, 95, 98; role of confidence-creation in, 44, 101, 419; always assisted by justified expectations, 40, 100-1, 106, 169-70, 419; if wise, demands nonmonetary co-ordination, 66, 80-1, 242-3, 346-7; to serve the State or society?, 22, 99-100, 104, 119-20; as instrument of "national policy," 46, 48n, 99, 418; flexible, or rigid?, 24, 96, 103, 249, 255, 296, 396; "neutral" or "noninflationary," 105, 156, 255; solely responsible for value of money unit, 43-4, 95, 97-100, 114-5, 121, 123-5, 153-6, 256-7, XVIII *passim;* influence on the form of assets held, 215-6

Money: definition of, 91; "pure," 90, 92, 96; "hybrid" (substitutes), 90, 92, 96, 254n, 417; homogeneity of, 92-3; aggregate real value or "quantity" of, x, 11, 92-3, 106-7, 136, 141, 176, 218-9, 249, 279,

284-5, 372, 398; functions of, 91 *et seq.;* services of (productiveness of), 32, 88, 91, 93, 106, 147-9, 190-1, 215-9, 222, 284; demand for, 41, 79-90, 93, 102, 196, 136-7, 147, 184-5, 192, 215-9, 244, 252, 273-9, 283-5; speculative demand for, 41, 95, 99-101, 106, 170, 218, 285-6, 373, 412; supposed infinitely elastic demand for, 171-2; the "veil" of, 88, 397-9; not manufactured, 94; "illusion," 47, 61, 128-9, 149, 161, 199, 392n, 415

Money unit: (i) actual, (ii) abstract-of constant real value, 53, 91 *et seq.,* 111-2, 194; as a container of money, 91-5; value of, *see* (i) Money units, concept of number of, (ii) Money real value or "quantity" of; importance of defined value of, 22, 31, 35, 44, 47-9, 68, 95-105, 111, 120-1, 412; stability of value in short-run and in long-run, 100

Money units: concept of number of, 91-6; General Theory's assumption of constant number of, 89, 103, 169; number of solely a question of policy, 39, 43-4, 93 *et seq.,* 114-5, 121, 124-5, VIII *passim,* 249-50, 257, 274, 284, XVIII *passim;* inappropriateness of concept of "velocity of circulation" of, 90, 95, VIII *passim*

Mont Pelerin Society: ix

Morton, W. A.: 115, 413n, 414n

Multiplier: 6, 133, 148-50, 240, 249-53, 257, 260, XIII *passim,* 291, 343, 350; "true," 285-6; "real income," 250n, 267, 285-6; "employment" (Keynes' "investment"), 250n, 267, XIII *passim;* infinite, 266, 273, 283; instantaneous case of, 266-7; serial interpretation of, 267, 270 *et seq.;* "leakages," 258, 272-84

Murad: 378-81

Myrdal: 185n, 199-200

N.R.A. policy: 76n, 163-4

"Near money": *See* Money, "hybrid"

"Necessary untruths": 412-3, 419

Neisser: 395-6, 398, 400

Net accumulation: the process and the magnitude, 24, 75, 133-4, 185-205, XI *passim,* 267-8, 286, XIV *passim;* diminishing return to, 238; not a response to growing consumption, 232-40, XIV *passim;* "uses," 229-30, 232, 235-6, 257, 294

Neutral monetary policy: 105, 156, 255

"Neutral money": Hayekian concept of, ixn

Nevin: 128, 412

Newcomb: viin

Niebyl: 401

"Nonessential" investment: 426-7

Norman, Sir Montagu: 412
Novick, D.: 12-13

Ohlin, 217n, 228n
"Outlets for investment": absence of, fallacy in concept of, 77, 211, 217-21, 233-40, 244, 359, 366 *et seq.*
Overhead costs: 60-1, 76
Overinvestment (overproduction): 69
Ozga: x

Paish: x, 112-3, 151-2
"Participating idleness": 177, 328n
Patinkin: x-xi, 106, 147-8, 171-6, 390, 392, 398n, 425, 428, 430
Phillips, A. W.: x
Pigou, Pigovian economics: 134, 167n, 172-3, 369
Placement: *See* Investment, in sense of choice of form
Polyani: viii, 4-5, 54n, 121, 126-30
Population growth: in relation to capital saturation, 373-9
Praxeology: 11, 88, 136, 231n, 352, 362
Preferred idleness: 177. *See also* Leisure preference
Price adjustment (i) the process: IV *passim;* (ii) the social purpose of: IV *passim*
Price flexibility: concept of, 61-4; supposed difficulty of achievement, 61-4; conducive to stability of the scale of prices, 67-8; relation to the dynamics of expansion, x-xi, 75-8, IX *passim;* secures consistency of values over time and space, 79, 174-7; "effective," 63-5; "perfect," 61-4
Price mechanism (price system): definition of, 53n
Price rigidity: nature and causes of, 22, 168-71, 174-6. *See also* Unstable price rigidity
Price rings: *See* Colusion
Prices: the scale or level of, 90, 95; "administered," 59n
Procrastination in reform, permitted by inflation: 42-3
Producer: 186-7, 190, 206-8
Profit: 55, 187, 202-5, 207, 212-3; expectations, motive, incentive, *see* Prospective yield, Loss-avoidance
Propensity to consume: 24, 53, 78-9, 239, 242, XII-XIII *passim*
Prospective yield: 26n, 55, 68, 195n, 201-3, 211-3, 221-2, 227-32, 294
Proudhon: 403
Psuedo-idleness: 293, 323, 325, 326n, 335-6, 349, 367

Public works: 122, 129, 274, 382-3
Pure Money: 90, 92, 96
Pure Saver: 201-3, 214n, 219-20

Quantity theory identity: 90-1, 93, 140n

Radcliffe Committee: 35, 137n, 216-7, 417n, 432
Real value: concept of, 91-3, 111-2, 188-9, 223-4, 269
"Real balance effect": *See* Money, aggregate real value
"Realized" (and "supposed") magnitudes: 188, 194, 198-9, 203
Reder, M. W.: 133
"Reflation": 121
Rentier: his reaction to anticipated inflation, 417; Keynesian attitude towards, 46, 48, 120, 365
Replacement demand: not a response to consumption, 233-4
Repressed inflation: 45, 112. *See also* Inflation, latent
Resale price maintenance: 61, 82
Restriction of output: *See* Collusion in fixing output and prices
Retreat from Keynesianism: xi, 5, 10, 74, 90, XIX *passim*
Ricardo: 19-20, 87, 234n, 359, 389n
"Rightest" and "Leftist" Keynesians: 323, 434-5
"Risk Capital": 241
Risk preference: 194, 241
Robertson, Sir Dennis: 87, 88n, 90, 152, 184, 268n, 316n, 338, 369
Robertson, H. M.: x
Robinson, Mrs. J.: 58n, 59-60n
Roosevelt, Franklin D.: 120, 404, 413
Röpke: 8, 13
Rothbard: 203

Saturation thesis: *See* Capital saturation
Samuelson: viii, 171, 259, 268n, 285, 306, 314, 325-6
Satiability of wants: *See* Insatiability, Says Law
Saver: 186, 196, 201-3, 214-5, 219-21, 225-6, 254n. *See also* Pure Saver
Saving: the process-acquisition of assets with services, 184-6, 195-203, XI *passim,* 249, 254-5; fallaciously conceived of as "not spending," 104, 184, 218-9, 252-3, 436n; not deflationary, 184-5, 218, 252-4, 257-60; saving money, fallacious notion of, 216
Saving Preference: homogeneity of, 212-3; as "demand," 24, 29, 183, 192, 195-8, XI-

XII *passim,* 294-5; autonomous and induced, 211, 222, 224, 226-7

Savings (Net Accumulation): the magnitude, 24, 183-5, 188-205, XI *passim,* 252, 259-60, XIV *passim;* absorption in investment, fallacy in concept of, 77, 201, 211, 216-28, 233-40, 359, 366 *et seq.;* "forced," 73n; divergence from, or equality or identity with "investment," 36, 104, 184-5, 201, 215-6, 436

Say: 87, 88n, 146-7, 191n, 193, 234n, 359, XVII *passim*

Says Law: 7, 69-70, 147, 205-6, 237-9, 260, 286, 299, 335n, 350, 361-2, XVII *passim*

Sayers: 94n

Scarcity creation: *See* Withheld capacity

Schultze: 61n, 65n, 128n

Schumpeter: 67n, 161, 171, 316, 369, 391n

Scitovsky: 390n

"Secondary liquidities": *See* Money, hybrid

Sectionalist pricing: *See* Price Adjustment, the process

Security: economics, 21-2, 44-5

Self-frustrating nature of price adjustment: Keynes' theory of, 33, 65, 133, IX *passim,* 389

Simons, H. C.: x, 171n

Sismondi: 359-60, 397, 399

Sinking funds: 253-4

Slichter: 128n, 414

Sliding scale contracts: 410, 415, 417

Smith, Adam: 5, 26n, 87

Smithies: 160n

Social control through the market (or value) mechanism: IV *passim*

"Socialization" of investment: consequences of, 45-9

Soper: x

"Special theory": Keynes', 80-1, 172, 425-7

Specificity of resources: 77, 222-4, 231-2, 257; is most serious when man-made, 337-8; tends at times to mitigate fluctuations, 321, 334-7

Spending: *See* Expenditure

Spiethoff: 368n

Stagnation thesis: *See* Capital saturation

State: role of, in co-ordination of the economy, 53, 65, 77, 81-3, 348-9; as consumer-saver, 196, 243; as entrepreneur, 187, 243

Stigler: 11n, 14n, 87, 200, 265

Substitution of least-cost method: *See* Competition

"Supposed" (and "realized") magnitudes: 188, 194, 198-9, 203

Sweezy: 12, 376-8, 389

Synchronization of economic processes: 54-7, 63, 68

Thornton, Henry: 60n, 87, 399n

Thrift: *See* Saving, Saving preference

Time prefrence, time utilities: *See* Saving preference

Timlin: 323-4, 424-8, 430

Tinbergen: 13

Tobin: 171, 220n, 244

Torrens: 87

Tract on Monetary Reform, Keynes': 87, 119-20

Trade-unions: practices of, 48-9, 61, 72-3, 81-2, 126-8, 160-1, 177, 260, 349, 375-6, 378n, 415, 419, 429, 434

Treatise on Money, Keynes': 9, 87, 89, 120, 122, 224n, 374

Tugan-Baranowsky: 368n

Turn-over: p a r t i c u l a r decumulation matched by replacement, 192, 198

Turroni: 45-6, 48

Unbalanced growth: 333, 367, 371-3, 383

Under-consumption: XI *passim,* 258

Unemployment: as a monetary phenomenon, 80-1; sense in which created by every economy achieved, 20-1, 159; alternative to inflation as expression of a disco-ordinated system, *see* Inflation; unemployment disequilibrium, 173-8; unemployment equilibrium, 33, 65, IX *passim,* 389, 435

Unstable price rigidity: 25, 44, 64, 106, 170-1, 174-6, 242, 296, 347, 353

"Unwillingness" to buy or sell: *See* Willingness to buy or sell

Valueless capacity: resources, 190-1, 293, 344-5n, 396, 400

"Velocity of circulation": inappropriateness of term, V *passim,* 272

Versatility: of resources, 64, 176-7, 222-4, 229, 232, 237, 239, 294, 296, 337, 352-3; natural attribute of labor and skill, 64, 177, 337-8

Vickery: 128n, 414

Viner: 87, 160n, 166n, 171n

Vissering: 412

Von Wieser: 87

"Wage level": the general—"the price of labor," 74, 167

Wage-price spiral: 115, XVIII *passim*

846446 INDEX

Wage-units: 269
Walras: 9, 87
Warburton: x, 126n, 171
Waste, of assets or services: conceived of as consumption or as reduction of income, 191, 193-6
"Welfare State": 48-9, 431
Wicksell, Wicksellian economics: 30, 87, 88n, 101m, 104, 106-7, 120, 178, 184, 185n, 198, 368n, 397, 431
Wicksteed: 88n, 102n, 186
Williams: J. H.: 19, 360, 430

Willingness to buy or sell: 55, 68-70, 78, 170, 216-7
Wilson, T.: 178, 265, 285
Withheld and diverted capacity (explanatory passages): 7, 21, 24, 30, 33-4, 40, 41-3, 59-60, 63, 75-8
Wright, D. McC.: xi, 10n, 165n, 378n, 430, 434-7

Yeager: x
Yield, on money held: *See* Money, productiveness of

THE AUTHOR

W. H. Hutt was born in 1899, educated in London and served in the R.F.C. and R.A.F. from 1917-1919. After the war he studied at the London School of Economics. He served for a few years in a publishing business before entering academic life in Cape Town, in 1928. He was appointed Professor of Commerce and Dean of the Faculty of Commerce in 1931, which post he still holds.

His article, *The Factory System of the Nineteenth Century* (1926) was republished in 1954 in Hayek's *Capitalism and the Historians,* and his *Theory of Collective Bargaining* (1930) was republished in 1954. His 1954 article, *The Significance of Price Flexibility,* was reprinted in Hazlitt's, *The Critics of Keynesian Economics* (1960) and he contributed an article, *The Yield from Money Held,* to the symposium in honour of economist Ludwig von Mises: *Freedom and Free Enterprise* (Ed. Sennholz) **in** 1955. Other major contributions of his have been *The Theory of Idle Resources* (1939) and *Plan for Reconstruction* (1943).